Lecture Notes in Artificial Intelligence 2564

Edited by J. G. Carbonell and J. Siekmann

Subseries of Lecture Notes in Computer Science

Springer
Berlin
Heidelberg
New York
Hong Kong
London
Milan
Paris
Tokyo

Walt Truszkowski   Chris Rouff
Mike Hinchey (Eds.)

Innovative Concepts for Agent-Based Systems

First International Workshop on Radical Agent Concepts
WRAC 2002
McLean, VA, USA, January 16-18, 2002
Revised Papers

Springer

Series Editors

Jaime G. Carbonell, Carnegie Mellon University, Pittsburgh, PA, USA
Jörg Siekmann, University of Saarland, Saarbrücken, Germany

Volume Editors

Walt Truszkowski
Mike Hinchey
Goddard Space Flight Center, Code 588 and 581
Greenbelt, MD 20771, USA
E-mail: {walt.truszkowski,michael.g.hinchey}@nasa.gov

Chris Rouff
SAIC, 1710 SAIC Drive
McLean, VA 22102, USA
E-mail: rouff@saic.com

Cataloging-in-Publication Data applied for

A catalog record for this book is available from the Library of Congress

Bibliographic information published by Die Deutsche Bibliothek
Die Deutsche Bibliothek lists this publication in the Deutsche Nationalbibliographie;
detailed bibliographic data is available in the Internet at <http://dnd.ddb.de>.

CR Subject Classification (1998): I.2.11, I.2, D.2, C.2.4, H.5.2-3

ISSN 0302-9743
ISBN 3-540-40725-1 Springer-Verlag Berlin Heidelberg New York

Springer-Verlag Berlin Heidelberg New York,
a member of BertelsmannSpringer Science+Business Media GmbH

http://www.springer.de

© Springer-Verlag Berlin Heidelberg 2003
Printed in Germany

Typesetting: Camera-ready by author, data conversion by Da-TeX Gerd Blumenstein
Printed on acid-free paper   SPIN: 10871843   06/3142   5 4 3 2 1 0

Preface

This collection represents the proceedings of the 1st GSFC/JPL Workshop on Radical Agent Concepts (WRAC), which was held on 16–18 January, 2002 at the Science Applications International Corporation (SAIC) Conference Center in McLean, VA, USA.

Over the past few years, agent technology has emerged as a powerful force in computing. Agent technology may well form the foundation for the next generation of computing systems. New and innovative agent concepts and techniques may bring further developments to this exploding area of research. Such work is often strongly inspired by theoretical or empirical studies of human behavior, social intelligence, psychology, arts, biology, computer science and philosophy.

This workshop aimed at bringing together, in an interdisciplinary event, original thinkers, practitioners and academics with an interest in radical (very innovative) concepts for agent-based systems. The workshop provided a forum to present the latest research findings in many aspects of agent technology. The organizers welcomed participation by those working in agent architectures, agent communities, agent communications, agent modeling, agent applications and other agent-related areas. We were particularly seeking papers on novel and innovative ideas, pushing the envelope of current agent technology. Contributions without a prototype or working system, i.e., purely conceptual contributions, were welcomed, and "out-of-the-box" thinkers were especially encouraged to participate.

The workshop was structured so as to allow the participants adequate time for discussion and interaction, to exchange ideas and reflect on the motivations, scientific grounds and practical consequences of the concepts presented.

We would like to extend our thanks to NASA Goddard Code 588, JPL and SAIC for the support they provided to this endeavor.

We hope you enjoy the fruits of the first WRAC.

April 2003

Walt Truszkowski

Table of Contents

IV   Agent Architectures

V   Communication and Coordination

VI   Innovative Applications

VII   Poster Presentations

VIII Panel Reports

Part I

Invited Presentation

A Personalizable Agent for
Semantic Taxonomy-Based Web Search

Larry Kerschberg[1], Wooju Kim[2], and Anthony Scime[3]

[1] E-Center for E-Business
George Mason University, 4400 University Drive, Fairfax, VA 22030, USA
kersch@gmu.edu
http://eceb.gmu.edu/
[2] Department of Industrial Engineering
Chunbuk National University, Korea
wjkim@chonbuk.ac.kr
[3] Department of Computer Science
SUNY-Brockport, USA
ascime@brockport.edu

Abstract. This paper addresses the problem of specifying Web searches and retrieving, filtering, and rating Web pages so as to improve the relevance and quality of hits, based on the user's search intent and preferences. We present a methodology and architecture for an agent-based system, called WebSifter II, that captures the semantics of a user's decision-oriented search intent, transforms the semantic query into target queries for existing search engines, and then ranks the resulting page hits according to a user-specified weighted-rating scheme. Users create personalized search taxonomies via our Weighted Semantic-Taxonomy Tree. Consulting a Web taxonomy agent such as WordNet helps refine the terms in the tree. The concepts represented in the tree are then transformed into a collection of queries processed by existing search engines. Each returned page is rated according to user-specified preferences such as semantic relevance, syntactic relevance, categorical match, page popularity and authority/hub rating.

1   Introduction

With the advent of Internet and WWW, the amount of information available on the Web grows daily. However, having too much information at one's fingertips does not always mean good quality information, in fact, it may often prevent a decision maker from making sound decisions, by degrading the quality of the decision. Helping decision makers to locate relevant information in an efficient manner is very important both to the person and to an organization in terms of time, cost, data quality and risk management.

W. Truszkowski, C. Rouff, M. Hinchey (Eds.): WRAC 2002, LNAI 2564, pp. 3-31, 2003.
© Springer-Verlag Berlin Heidelberg 2003

Although search engines assist users in finding information, many of the results are irrelevant to the decision problem. This is due in part, to the keyword search approach, which does not capture the user's intent, what we call meta-knowledge. Another reason for irrelevant results from search engines is a "semantic gap" between the meanings of terms used by the user and those recognized by the search engines. In addition, each search engine has its own uncustomizable ranking system, where users cannot "tell" the search engine what preferences to use for search criteria. For example, a shopping agent may go for the lowest price, while the user might want the "most flexible return policy."

To overcome these three problems, we propose a semantic taxonomy-based personalizable meta-search agent approach. We build upon the ideas presented by Scime and Kerschberg [1,2]. We develop a tree-structured representation scheme with which users specify their search intent. We call this representation scheme the "Weighted Semantic Taxonomy Tree (WSTT)", in which each node denotes a concept that pertains to the user's problem-domain. To address the second weakness, we present an elaborate user preference representation scheme based on various components, each of which represents a specific decision-criterion. Users can easily and precisely express their preference for a search using this representation scheme.

In order to rate the relevance of a page hit, we use a rating mechanism combining the WSTT and the component-based preference representation. Since Web page rating can itself be viewed as a decision-making problem, where a decision maker (a user) must evaluate various alternatives (Web pages) for his/her problem (user's Web search intention), we use decision-analytic methods in the design of our rating mechanism.

Finally, we have designed and implemented a meta-search agent called WebSifter II that cooperates with WordNet for concept retrieval, and consults well-known search engines. For the empirical validation of our approach, we also present some real world examples of our system.

The remainder of the paper is organized as follows. Section 2 presents related research. Section 3 presents the major aspects of our semantic-based personalizable approach to represent user intention, and the multi-component rating of search hits. In Section 4, we discuss the system architecture of WebSifter II, the search agent that implements our methodology. We also deal with some collaboration issues too in this section. The results of empirical studies are presented in Section 5.

2   Related Work

Most of current Internet search engines such as Yahoo, Excite, Altavista, WebCrawler, Lycos, Google, etc. suffer from *Recall* and *Precision* problems [3]. The relatively low coverage of individual search engines leads to using meta-search engines to improve the recall of a query. Examples are MetaCrawler [4], SavvySearch [5], NECI Metasearch Engine [6], and Copernic (http://www.copernic.com). This meta-search engine approach partly addresses the recall problem but still suffers from the precision problem.

We can categorize research regarding the precision problem into three major themes: content-based, collaborative, and domain-knowledge approaches.

The content-based approach first represents a user's explicit preferences and then evaluates Web page relevance in terms of its content and user preferences. Syskill & Webert [7], WebWatcher [8], WAWA [9], and WebSail [10] fall into this category. Further, some research takes into account not only Web page content but also its structure (e.g. hyperlinks) to evaluate relevance [11, 12].

The collaborative approach determines information relevancy based on similarity among users rather than similarity of the information itself. Example systems are Firefly and Ringo [13], Phoaks [14], and Siteseer [15]. In addition, some hybrid approaches incorporate both approaches for example Fab [16], Lifestyle Finder [17], WebCobra [18].

The third category is the domain knowledge approach that uses user and organizational domain knowledge to improve the relevancy of search results. Yahoo! uses domain knowledge and provides a pre-defined taxonomy path. So, classifying Web pages automatically into a pre-defined, or a dynamically created taxonomy [19] is a related issue to this approach. NorthernLight (www.northernlight.com) is a search engine that supports this kind of dynamic taxonomy service. Using NorthernLight's *Custom Search Folder* service, users can refine their search query to a specific domain, when the search engine presents too much information.

Some research incorporates user domain knowledge in a more explicit way. For example, Aridor et al. [20] represent user domain knowledge as a small set of example Web pages provided by users. Chakrabarti et al. adopted both a pre-defined (but modifiable) taxonomy and a set of example user-provided Web pages as domain knowledge [21].

From this survey of related research, we have identified several aspects that merit further consideration. First, most approaches force users to use a search engine in a passive rather than active manner. Often, the user cannot understand why extraneous and irrelevant results are retrieved. There is a pressing need for users to be able to express their query intent in a more natural and structured manner. Second, current approaches lack sufficient expressive power to capture a users' search intent and preferences, because most of the representation schemes are based on a vector space model [22] or its variants. Third, most approaches do not take full advantage of domain-specific knowledge with which to scope the search, filter the hits, and classify the query result.

Regarding the first limitation, there is another related research category, the ontology-based approach by which users can express their search intent in a more semantic fashion. Domain-specific ontologies are being developed for commercial and public purposes [23] and OntoSeek [24], On2Broker [25], GETESS [26], and WebKB [27] are example systems.

Although the ontology-based approach is a promising way to solve some aspects of the precision problem, it still requires two major pre-requisites. First, the entire collection of Web pages must be transformed into ontological form. Second, there is as yet no common agreement on the representation of the ontology, nor the query or reasoning mechanisms. Even if these two prerequisites were satisfied, the precision problem in Web search would remain due to the huge amount of the information on the web. A user-centric information relevancy evaluation scheme will complement the above approaches.

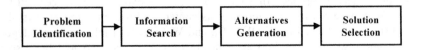

Fig. 1. Four Phases of Decision Making Process

3   Semantic Taxonomy-Tree-Based Approach for Personalized Information Retrieval

3.1   Weighted Semantic Taxonomy Tree

Usually a keyword-based search representation is insufficient to express a user's search intent. By postulating a user's decision-making process as depicted in Figure 1, we can support readily query formulation and search.

This process starts with a problem identification phase and then a user seeks relevant information to solve the identified problem. Based on the collected information, listing alternatives, evaluating them, and selecting a solution are the subsequent steps. One implication of the decision-making process is that the more we understand a user's problems, the better we can support a user's information search. In our approach, we represent a user's search intent by a hierarchical concept tree with weights associated with each concept, thereby reflecting user-perceived relevance of concepts to the search.

Let's assume that a person has started a new business and is looking for office equipment. He wants to search for information about office equipment on the Web. Suppose he wants information about chairs, so he might build a query using a single term, "chair". If he is a more skilled user of Internet search engines, he might build a query using two terms, "office" and "chair" to obtain more precise results. He may also use the 'AND' or 'OR' operator between them. In this case, the term "office" provides added context for the search. However, this formulation is still very implicit and passive. As we mentioned earlier, one way to express this kind of context information is by using a taxonomy tree as shown in Figure 2. Figure 2(a) shows a simple taxonomy tree that represents a search intention to find a chair in the context of office, while a search for finding an office in the context of chair is expressed by Figure 2(b). The taxonomy tree provides more expressive semantics than simple keyword-based representations used by most current search engines.

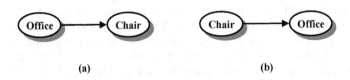

(a)   (b)

Fig. 2. A simple example of a taxonomy tree

The taxonomy tree approach is already used in many search engines such as Yahoo! We have devised a tree-based search representation model that allows users to present their search intention by defining their own taxonomy topology. We call this the *Weighted Semantic Taxonomy Tree* (WSTT) model. Now, let us formally define this model. The WSTT consists of a set of nodes that is denoted as N in the sequel. Because it is a tree, all nodes, except the root node, must have one parent node. Every node should have one representative term and a weight that represents the importance of this node for a search. For a node $n \in N$, we denote a representative term, or label, and its weight as $rt(n)$ and $w(n)$, respectively. We restrict the feasible range of the value of $w(n)$ from 0 to 10. Figure 3 shows a realistic example of the businessman's search intention using our WSTT scheme. Users can build their own hierarchical taxonomy tree, and assign importance levels to each term within the context of their antecedent terms. For example, we can translate the upper sub-tree as that a businessman wants to find information about chairs, desks, and phones within the context of office furniture and office equipment where the numbers that appear to the left to each term, 10, 9, and 6 denote the respective importance levels of chairs, desks, and phones.

One drawback is that the terms may have multiple meanings, and this is one of the major reasons that search engines return irrelevant search results. To address this limitation, we introduce the notion of "word senses" from WordNet [28] into our WSTT scheme to allow users to refine their search intention. WordNet is a linguistic database that uses sets of terms that have similar semantics (*synsets*) to represent word senses. Each synset corresponds to terms with synonymous meaning in English and so each word may be associated with multiple synsets. In this paper, we rename this synset as *Concept* for our own use and the user can choose one of the concepts available from WordNet for the term of a specific node in WSTT. We denote an available concept, that is, a set of terms for a node n as $c(n)$. For example, the "chair" term has the following four possible concepts from WordNet.

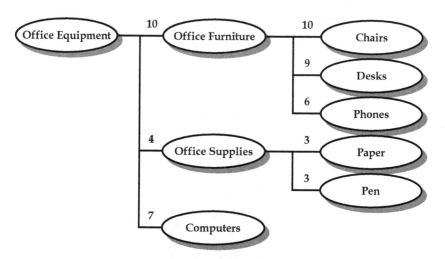

Fig. 3. An example of a WSTT representing a businessman's search intention

1. {chair, seat} // a seat for one person, with a support for the back,
2. {professorship, chair} // the position of professor, or a chaired professorship,
3. {president, chairman, chairwoman, chair, chairperson} // the officer who presides at the meetings of an organization, and
4. {electric chair, chair, death chair, hot seat} // an instrument of death by electrocution that resembles a chair.

If the user wants to search for a chair to sit on, he would choose the first concept. If the user selects the first concept, then without loss of generality, we can assume that the remaining concepts are not of interest, thereby obtaining both positive and negative indicators of his intent. Now, let's distinguish the set of terms of selected concept from the set of terms of the unselected concepts as *Positive Concept Terms* and *Negative Concept Terms*, and denote them as $pct(n)$ and $nct(n)$ for a node n, respectively. If we denote a term as t and assume that a user selects the k-th concept, then we can formalize the definitions of them for a given node n as follows:

$$pct(n) = \left\{ t \mid t \in c_k(n) \right\} \tag{1}$$

$$nct(n) = \left\{ t \mid t \in \bigcup_{i \neq k} c_i(n) \right\} - \left\{ rt(n) \right\} \tag{2}$$

where $c_i(n)$ denotes the i-th concept available from WordNet for a node n and $rt(n)$ denotes the representative term of n.

If a user selects the second concept from our example, according to the definitions from (1) and (2), $pct(n)$ and $nct(n)$ are as follows: $pct(n) = $ {professorship, chair} and $nct(n) = $ {seat, president, chairman, chairwoman, chairperson, electric chair, death chair, hot seat}.

Figure 4 shows an internal representation of the user's intention via the WSTT schema, after the concept selection process has finished; the user however sees the tree of Figure 3. Another advantage using the tree structure is that it is possible to represent many concepts at the same time. This allows the user to specify a broad range of interests simultaneously.

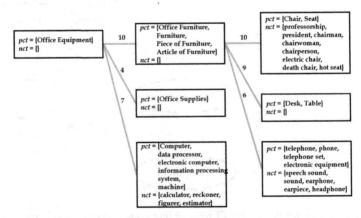

Fig. 4. An example of the internal representation of the user's search intention

3.2   Multi-Attribute-Based Search Preference Representation

The ranking of Web search hits by users involves the evaluation of multiple attributes, which reflect user preferences and their conception of the decision problem. In our approach, we pose the ranking problem as a multi-attribute decision problem. Thus, we examine the search results provided by multiple search engines, and rank the pages, according to multiple decision criteria. Both Multi-Attribute Utility Technology (MAUT) [29] and Repertory Grid [30] are two major approaches that address our information evaluation problem. Our ranking approach combines MAUT and the Repertory Grid. We define six search evaluation components as follows:

1. *Semantic* component: represents a Web page's relevance with respect to its content.
2. *Syntactic* component: represents the syntactic relevance with respect to its URL. This considers URL structure, the location of the document, the type of information provider, and the page type (e.g., home, directory, and content).
3. *Categorical Match* component: represents the similarity measure between the structure of the user-created taxonomy and the category information provided by search engines for the retrieved Web pages.
4. *Search Engine* component: represents the user's biases toward and confidence in search engine's results.
5. *Authority/Hub* component: represents the level of user preference for *Authority* or *Hub* sites and pages. Authority sites usually have larger in-degree from Hub sites and Hub sites usually have larger out-degree to Authority sites [31].
6. *Popularity* component: represents the user's preference for popular sites. The number of visitors or the number of requests for the specific page or site can measure popularity.

Further, in this multi-component-based preference representation scheme, the user can assign a preference level to each of these components, and also to each available search engine within the search engine component. Then, these components and the assigned preference level are eventually synthesized into a single unified value resulting in the relevance measure for a specific Web page. Figure 5 conceptually depicts our scheme. In this figure, each number assigned to an edge denotes the user's preference level for that component. This multi-component preference scheme allows users more control over their searches and the determination of a page's relevance.

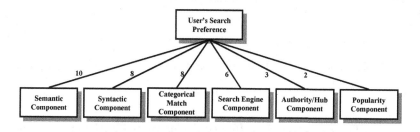

Fig. 5. A conceptual model of user's preference representation scheme

Thus far, we have discussed how to capture and represent semantically the user's search intention and search preferences. Now, we turn our attention to deriving a good estimate of the relevancy of a Web page based on these semantics. In the following sections, we will discuss how to obtain Web information using existing search engines and then address the derivation of relevance estimates.

3.3   Gathering Web Information Based on Search Intention

Since we adopt a meta-search approach to Web information gathering to preserve the benefits of meta-search engines discussed in [4,5,20], we neither create nor maintain our own index database of Web information. At present, there is no search engine that accepts a search request based on the WSTT. We have developed a translation mechanism from our WSTT-based query, to Boolean queries that most of current search engines can process.

As already mentioned, we represent a user's search intention as a tree, as shown in Figure 4. The leaf nodes denote the terms of interest to the user, and the antecedent nodes for each node form a search context. We transform the entire tree into a set of separate queries where each is acceptable to existing search engines. To do this, first we decompose the tree into a set of paths from the root to each leaf node. Then for each path, we generate all possible combinations of terms, by selecting one term from the positive concept terms of each node in the path from a root node to a leaf node. Finally, we pose each query to search engines to obtain query results.

We now provide definitions to formalize the above discussion. Let's first define a *Leaf Path* as an ordered set of nodes, $\{n_0, n_1, n_2, ..., n_{l-1}, n_l\}$, where n_0 is a root node, n_l is a leaf node, and $n_1, n_2, ..., n_{l-1}$ are consecutive intermediate nodes on the path from n_0 to n_l in the WSTT. We denote a leaf path as *lp*. We also define a set of all distinct leaf paths available from the WSTT as *lpset*. For example, we have six leaf paths from the example WSTT as in the Figure 3 and its *lpset* becomes {{Office Equipment, Office Furniture, Chairs}, {Office Equipment, Office Furniture, Desks}, {Office Equipment, Office Furniture, Phones}, {Office Equipment, Office Supplies, Paper}, {Office Equipment, Office Supplies, Pen}, {Office Equipment, Computers}}. Now, let's define a *Term Combination Set* for a *Leaf Path lp*, as a set of all possible combinations of terms by selecting one term from each *pct(n)*, where $n \in lp$ and denote it as *tcslp(lp)*. We also denote a set of all term combinations available from a given WSTT and each of its elements as *tcs* and *tc*, respectively. Then, using the above definitions, a *tcslp(lp)* and *tcs* can be formally represented respectively as follows:

$$tcslp(lp) = pct(n_0) \times pct(n_1) \times pct(n_2) \times ... \times pct(n_l) \qquad (3)$$

where symbol × denotes the Cartesian product of sets.

$$tcs = \bigcup_{lp \in lpset} tcslp(lp) \qquad (4)$$

If *lp* is the first element, that is, {Office Equipment, Office Furniture, Chairs} of the *lpset* in the case of Figure 3 and Figure 4, then according to equation (3), *tcslp(lp)* = {{Office Equipment, Office Furniture, Chair}, {Office Equipment, Office

Furniture, Seat}, {Office Equipment, Furniture, Chair}, {Office Equipment, Furniture, Seat}, {Office Equipment, Piece of Furniture, Chair}, {Office Equipment, Piece of Furniture, Seat}, {Office Equipment, Article of Furniture, Chair}, {Office Equipment, Article of Furniture, Seat}}.

Once we get *tcs*, then we make each term combination, *tc* ∈ *tcs* as a separate request and pose them to each search engine for Web information gathering. Now, the problem is how to generate actual query statements to each query engine based on each *tc*. We have trade-offs between *Precision* and *Coverage* depending on which logical operators we impose between terms. Actually, each *tc* is a set of terms and so, it can be represented as $\{t_1, t_2, ..., t_n\}$ where $t_1, t_2, ..., t_n \in tc$. To generate an actual query statement from a *tc*, we can have two different alternative choices, "$t_1 \wedge t_2 \wedge ... \wedge t_n$" and "$t_1 \vee t_2 \vee ... \vee t_n$" where $\wedge$ denotes AND and $\vee$ denotes OR. The first one provides more precise search results, while the second allows greater coverage.

Based on the fact that a general user tends to use the AND operator between terms when considering additional terms for the context of a search, we adopt the AND operator in generating actual query statements. We leave the more general scheme for future research. For the illustration of our query generation method, let's use the case depicted in Figure 4 again. According to the procedures mentioned thus far, the upper-most leaf path of the WSTT in Figure 4 is translated into eight separate query statements as follow. (1) "Office Equipment" AND "Office Furniture" AND "Chair", (2) "Office Equipment" AND "Office Furniture" AND "Seat", (3) "Office Equipment" AND "Furniture" AND "Chair", (4) "Office Equipment" AND "Furniture" AND "Seat", (5) "Office Equipment" AND "Piece of Furniture" AND "Chair", (6) "Office Equipment" AND "Piece of Furniture" AND "Seat", (7) "Office Equipment" AND "Article of Furniture" AND "Chair", and (8) "Office Equipment" AND "Article of Furniture" AND "Seat".

These queries can now be submitted to each target search engine, and the query results are stored for further processing, as discussed in the next section.

3.4   Unified Web Information Rating Mechanism

In this section, we discuss a rating mechanism to evaluate each resulting page hit from the target search engines for the generated query statements. Through this mechanism, each Web page will have its own value representing the relevance level from the user's viewpoint. To accomplish this goal, six relevance values of a Web page are computed, corresponding to each of the six components. Then a composite value of these six relevance values is computed based on a function of the multi-attribute-based search preference representation scheme. In the following sub-sections, we will first discuss how this composite relevance value is computed, and then a set of methods to compute each of component's relevance values.

3.4.1   Composite Relevance Value Computation

Let's first assume we have evaluated the six components' relevance values for a Web page retrieved from search engines. Then we need to synthesize these six values into one single composite relevance value to compare Web pages to each other and to list them to the user in an order of relevance. This problem can be viewed as a multi-attribute decision-making problem.

One of the popularly accepted approaches in decision science community is AHP (Analytic Hierarchy Process) [32]. It converts user's subjective assessments of relative importance between preference components into a linear set of weights, which is further used to rank alternatives. Although we adopt AHP approach as a basis of our synthesizing mechanism, we have modified the original AHP to fit to our weight acquisition scheme, because it requires pair-wise comparisons between all components to obtain importance ratios between each pair of them. Actually in our approach, a user assigns an absolute importance weight on each component rather than relative ratios between components. However, since we still need those relative ratios, we first approximate them by dividing absolute importance weights of components by each other. Then, we follow the same remaining steps of AHP to compute the composite relevance value for each Web page.

We now provide notations to formalize the above discussion as follows.

compset: denotes a set of preference components to be considered in our scheme.

$cw^U(x)$: denotes a weight provided by the user to represent the importance of a component x.

$rvc(x, pg)$: denotes a relevance value of a Web page pg with respect to a component x.

$lr(x, y)$: denotes a relative importance ratio of component x compared to component y.

$ns(z)$: denotes a function that returns the number of elements in a set z.

We first approximate $lr(x, y)$ by (5) based on the user-provided importance weights for each pair of components:

$$lr(x, y) = cw^U(x) / cw^U(y) \qquad (5)$$

where $x \in compset$ and $y \in compset$.

Then, the AHP computes normalized importance weights for each component based on these relative ratios. We denote the normalized importance weight for a component *com* and the composite relevance value of a Web page *pg* as $cw^N(com)$ and $rv(pg)$, respectively. According to AHP, these two values can be calculated respectively as follows:

$$cw^N(com) = \left[\sum_x \left(\frac{lr(com, x)}{\sum_y lr(x, y)} \right) \right] \Big/ ns(compset) \qquad (6)$$

where $x \in compset$ and $y \in compset$.

$$rv(pg) = \sum_x cw^N(com) \cdot rvc(com, pg) \qquad (7)$$

where $com \in compset$.

Finally, Web pages are presented to users in descending order of rv. This, together with the page relevancy value indicates the relative importance of that page to the user.

Thus far, we have discussed how to synthesize the relevance values of a user's preference components into a single composite value, under the assumption that these relevance values of the components have already been computed. Now, we show how to compute relevance values of each of the six preference components based on the user's preference, as well as the user's search intent as represented by the WSTT.

3.4.2 Semantic Component Relevancy Computation

The semantic component represents relevancy of a Web page to a user's search intent represented by the WSTT with respect to its content. To compute this relevance, we conceptually follow the reverse steps that we performed in the section 3.3 to generate separate queries from the WSTT.

First, we evaluate the semantic relevancies of a retrieved Web page for each of the term combinations. We then combine the semantic measures for each leaf path and bind each of these semantic measures to the corresponding leaf node. Finally we compute a semantic component relevancy of the Web page using an AHP-based WSTT relevance value composition mechanism. This mechanism propagates the bound values on the leaf nodes toward the root node, thereby providing a single combined relevance value at the root node.

Now, let's explain the details of this procedure in a formal manner. We first define $rvtc^{SM}(tc, pg)$ as a semantic relevance value of a Web page pg to a term combination tc and it is computed by a simple counting method as follows:

$$rvtc^{SM}(tc, pg) = \frac{\sum_{t \in tc} appear(t, pg)}{ns(tc)} \tag{8}$$

where t is a term and the function $appear(t, pg)$ returns 1 if t appears in pg and 0, otherwise.

Based on these $rvtc^{SM}$ values, we define $rvlp^{SM}(lp, pg)$ as a semantic relevance value of a Web page pg to a leaf path lp. When we compute this $rvlp^{SM}$, we have to consider two aspects. First, we have to synthesize multiple $rvtc^{SM}$ values obtained from equation (8) for a leaf path into a single measure and we adopt a max function for this. Second, we have to consider negative concepts related to a leaf path. To incorporate these negative concepts into computing $rvlp^{SM}$, we first develop a measure to evaluate irrelevancy of a Web page pg in terms of negative concept terms related to a leaf path lp and we denote it as $irv(lp, pg)$. The following equation (9) shows its mathematical definition.

$$irv(lp, pg) = \sum_{t} appear(t, pg) \tag{9}$$

where t is a term and also $t \in \bigcup_{n \in lp} nct(n)$.

Now, we can compute $rvlp^{SM}$ using the following equation (10).

$$rvlp^{SM}(lp, pg) = \left(\frac{\sum_{tc} rvtc^{SM}(tc, pg)}{ns(tcslp(lp))} \right) \cdot (1 - \theta)^{irv(lp, pg)} \tag{10}$$

where $tc \in tcslp(lp)$ and θ is a given [0, 1] scale degradation rate.

In equation (10), θ denotes the level of degradation with respect to the irrelevance caused by negative concepts. So if θ is close to 1, then a little irrelevancy results in a big impact on $rvlp^{SM}$. On the other hand, if it is close to 0, the irrelevancy does not have any impact on the rvp value. The user can control this rate and we set it to a default of 0.1.

Now, we synthesize a single semantic relevancy value of a Web page according to the WSTT. Since AHP was originally developed to derive a unified measure to evaluate decision alternatives based on a tree like the WSTT, we apply this approach to our WSTT scheme by combining our $rvlp^{SM}$ values for each leaf path into a single semantic relevance value of a Web page. However, we need to normalize the user-provided weights for the nodes of WSTT, for reasons similar to those discussed in the previous section. For this normalization, we apply equation (5) to each hierarchical branch of the WSTT, and we obtain a set of normalized weights for each node within the scope of the branch to which the nodes belong. We denote this normalized weight for a node n, $w^N(n)$. With the normalized weights, let's formalize the AHP-based WSTT relevance value composition mechanism.

Equation (11) shows a relevance value determination rule on each node of WSTT for a Web page pg and we denote a relevance value of a Web page pg on a node n as $rvn(n, pg)$.

$$rvn(n, pg) = \begin{cases} bndfn(lp, pg) & \text{if } n \text{ is a leaf node} \\ & \text{of a leaf path } lp. \\ \sum_{x \in children(n)} w^N(x) \cdot rvn(x, pg) & \text{otherwise.} \end{cases} \qquad (11)$$

where $children(n)$ is a set of nodes that is a child of n and $bndfn(lp, pg)$ is an arbitrary value binding function to leaf nodes.

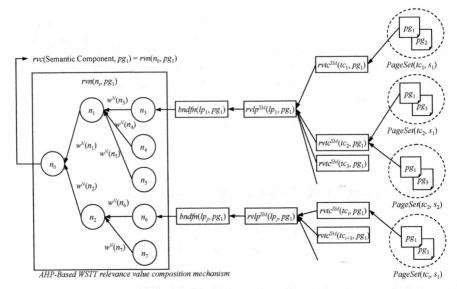

Fig. 6. Conceptual flow of computation of semantic component relevancy

To perform this mechanism, we first bind relevance values from $bndfn()$ to all corresponding leaf nodes and then these values are propagated from leaf nodes to the root node, finally obtaining a single composite relevance value of a Web page for the WSTT. In this semantic component case, by setting $bndfn(lp, pg)$ as $rvlp^{SM}(lp, pg)$ in the equation (10), we can obtain a single composite semantic relevance value of a Web page pg as $rvn(n_0, pg)$, where n_0 is the root node of the WSTT. This obtained value is then assigned to rvc(Semantic Component, pg) for further computing of composite relevance value with other preference components, discussed in the previous section.

Figure 6 shows conceptually the entire flow of computation from relevancy computing for a term combination to relevancy computing across the WSTT, which is required to compute a semantic relevance value of a Web page. In this figure, $PageSet(tc_i, s_j)$ denotes a set of resulting pages from a search engine s_j for a term combination tc_i. Actually, we will use a similar method when computing categorical match and search engine components' relevancies in the following sections.

3.4.3 Syntactic Component Relevancy Computation

The syntactic component of Web document measures the structural aspects of the page as a function of the role of that page within the structure of a Web site. Our approach takes into account the location of the document, its role (e.g., home, directory, and content), and the well formedness of its URL.

We define three types of Web pages:

1. *Direct-Hit* – the page may be a home page or a page with significant content within its domain.
2. *Directory-Hit* – this page has links to other pages in the domain of the Web site.
3. *Page-Hit* – Web pages that are subordinate to direct-hit and directory-hit pages fall into this category. These pages contain partial information about the Web site domain.

Scime and Kerschberg [1,2] define a set of heuristics to classify a Web page returned from a search engine as either a direct, directory, or page hit. Further, a page may have more than one classification. In order to manipulate syntactic relevancy, we assign a numeric value to each type as a real number in the interval [0,1]. Default values for direct, directory, and page hits are 1.0, 0.6, and 0.4 respectively. The assumption is that users would prefer to view direct hits over the other two.

Since a Web page might be classified into more than one class, we need to synthesize those multiple matches into one measure. To do this, we introduce an averaging mechanism and define some necessary notations and a formula to compute the syntactic relevance value of a Web page pg, rvc(Syntactic Component, pg) as follows:

- $rset(cl)$: denotes a set of rules to classify a Web page into the class cl.
- $rsc(r)$: denotes a score of a rule r and it returns 1.0 if $r \in rset$(Direct Hit), 0.6 if $r \in rset$(Directory Hit), and 0.4 if $r \in rset$(Page Hit).

- *mat(r, pg)*: denotes a function that returns 1 if a rule *r* is matched to a Web page *pg* and 0, otherwise.

$$rvc(\text{Syntactic Component}, pg) = \left(\sum_r rsc(r) \cdot mat(r, pg) \right) \bigg/ \sum_r mat(r, pg) \qquad (12)$$

3.4.4 Categorical Match Component Relevancy Computation

Categorical Match component represents the similarity measure between the structure of user-created taxonomy and the category information provided by search engines for the retrieved Web pages. Nowadays, many popular search engines respond to the users query not only with a list of URLs for Web pages but also with their own categorical information for each Web page. For example, the following is an extract of search results provided by Lycos for the query "chair".

(1)   Donald B. Brown Research Chair on Obesity
       Health > Mental Health > Disorders
       > Eating Disorders > Obesity
(2)   Steel Chair Wrestling
       Sports > Fantasy > Pro Wrestling
       ...
(3)   Chair Technologies
       Business > Industries > Manufacturing
       > Consumer Products > Furniture
       > Seating > Office Chairs
       ...

In the search results, the numbers on the left hand side denote the ranks of the corresponding Web pages and the associated lines below each title show the related category information for those Web pages. Although different search engines associate different category information to the same Web page, such categorical information helps users filter out some of the returned search results without actually visiting the URL. Actually, the categorical match component is designed to provide the benefits of manual filtering by automatic means; this is accomplished by comparing the WWST terms with the categorical information provided by search engines. This is one of the major contributions of this paper.

Now, let's discuss how to measure the relevancy between the WSTT and the categorical information in more detail. We first represent the category information for a Web page *pg* from a search engine *s*, as an ordered set of category terms in a form such as $\{cat_1, cat_2, ..., cat_m\}$, where cat_i is the *i*-th category term and *m* is total number of category terms in the set and we denote it *catinfo(pg, s)*. For example, *catinfo*(Chair Technologies, Lycos) in the above case, can be represented as the ordered set of category terms, {Business, Industries, Manufacturing, Consumer Products, Furniture, Seating, Office Chairs}. However, since it is hard to directly compare such *catinfo* to the entire WSTT, here we adopt an approach similar to that applied to the Semantic Component case, where we first measure the relevance of a *catinfo* to a single term combination, and then, combine them up to a single composite measure with respect to the entire WSTT.

So now, the relevance between a *catinfo* and a term combination *tc* can be measured from two different aspects, co-occurrence of terms and order consistency of terms. To measure the co-occurrence, we use the following formula (13).

$$\text{coccur(tc, catinfo)} = \left(\frac{\sum_{t} member(t, catinfo)}{ns(tc)} \right) \cdot \left(\frac{\sum_{cat} member(cat, tc)}{ns(catinfo)} \right) \qquad (13)$$

where $t \in tc$ is a term, $cat \in catinfo$ is a category term, and $member(x, y)$ is a function that returns 1 if x is a member of y and 0, otherwise.

To consider the order consistency, let's first denote the precedence relationship of two arbitrary terms, t_l and t_r as (t_l, t_r), and that means t_l precedes t_r in an ordered terms set. We also define a set of all available precedence relationships from an ordered set of terms x, as *prelset(x)*. Then we measure the consistency of *catinfo* with respect to a precedence relationship, (t_l, t_r) as follows:

$$\text{cons}((t_l, t_r), \text{catinfo}) = \begin{cases} 1 & \text{if } t_l, t_r \in catinfo \text{ and } t_l \text{ precedes } t_r \text{ in } catinfo. \\ 0 & \text{otherwise} \end{cases} \qquad (14)$$

Now, let's define a consistency of a category information *catinfo* to a term combination *tc* as *constc(tc, catinfo)* and the equation (15) shows how to compute it. Because we want to focus only on order consistency between *catinfo* and *tc* not depending on co-occurrence between them, we additionally define an ordered intersection set of *tc* and *catinfo*, where order of its element terms follows *tc*, as *isset(tc, catinfo)* and then we can remove co-occurrence effect by only considering the precedence relationships in that set.

$$\text{constc(tc, catinfo)} = \sum_{pr} cons(pr, catinfo) \left/ \left(\frac{ns(isset(tc, catinfo))}{2} \right) \right. \qquad (15)$$

where $pr \in prelset(isset(tc, catinfo))$, is a precedence relationship.

For example, let a term combination *tc* be $\{a, b, c, d, e\}$ and a category information *catinfo* be $\{a, e, c, f\}$. Then *isset(tc, catinfo)* becomes $\{a, c, e\}$ and also *prelset(isset(tc, catinfo))* becomes $\{(a, c), (a, e), (c, e)\}$. According to the formula (14), *cons((a, c), catinfo)*, *cons((a, e), catinfo)*, and *cons((c, e), catinfo)* have their value as 1, 1, and 0, respectively. Since *ns(isset(tc, catinfo))* is 3 in this case, the denominator of the equation (15) becomes 3, and finally *constc(tc, catinfo)* becomes $(1+1+0)/3 = 2/3$. Also in this case, *coccur(tc, catinfo)* becomes $3/5 \times 3/4 = 9/20$, because 3 of 5 terms of *tc* appear in *catinfo* and 3 of 4 terms of *catinfo* appear in *tc*.

To synthesize both the above aspects of categorical match between a term combination and a category information, we define the following measure, *rvtcc(tc, catinfo)*.

$$\text{rvtcc(tc, catinfo)} = \alpha \cdot coccur(tc, catinfo) + (1 - \alpha) \cdot constc(tc, catinfo) \qquad (16)$$

where α is a [0, 1] scale factor to represent the relative importance of co-occurrence to order consistency and it is set to 0.5 by default.

Actually since a Web page can have several category labels from different search engines for a given term combination, we need to further synthesize to obtain a single categorical match relevance value of a Web page pg for a term combination tc, $rvtc^{CM}(tc, pg)$ and it is formalized in (17).

$$rvtc^{CM}(tc, pg) = \frac{\sum_{s \in SC} rvtcc(tc, catinfo(pg, s))}{ns(SC)} \tag{17}$$

where s is a search engine and SC is a set of search engines that have categorical information for the page pg.

As in the case of Semantic Component, we adopt the max function to synthesize $rvtc^{CM}$s to obtain a categorical match relevance value of a Web page pg for a leaf path lp, $rvlp^{CM}(lp, pg)$ as follows:

$$rvlp^{CM}(lp, pg) = \max_{tc \in tcslp(lp)} rvtc^{CM}(tc, pg) \tag{18}$$

We also can obtain a single composite categorical match relevance value of a Web page pg, rvc(Categorical Match Component, pg) using the AHP-based WSTT relevance value composition mechanism that is formalized in (11). To do this, we first set $bndfn(lp, pg)$ in the equation (11) as $rvlp^{CM}(lp, pg)$, then we propagate values from leaf nodes to the root node. At the root node n_0, we obtain a single composite categorical match relevance value of a Web page pg as $rvn(n_0, pg)$ and we finally assign this value to rvc(Categorical Match Component, pg), which will be used to obtain a composite relevance value with other preference components.

3.4.5 Search Engine Component Relevancy Computation

The Search Engine component represents the user's biases toward and confidence in a search engine's results. To measure this search engine component, let's first define a basic unit information, that is, rank of a Web page pg by search engine s for the request from term combination tc as $rank(tc, pg, s)$ and also define the number of resulting Web pages from search engine s for term combination tc as $npg(tc, s)$. In order to synthesize the search engine component with other components, we transform the rank information to a [0, 1] scale normalized rank, $rank^N(tc, pg, s)$ according to the following equation.

$$rank^N(tc, pg, s) = 1 - \frac{(rank(tc, pg, s) - 1)}{npg(tc, s)} \tag{19}$$

The above normalization implies our intention to further discriminate the similarly ranked pages depending on the size of populations of those pages. For example, it transforms the second ranked page of ten result pages to a larger value than the same second of five results. Now, to obtain a composite search engine relevance value of a Web page pg for a term combination tc, $rvtc^{SE}(tc, pg)$, we adopt a weighted average method based on user's search engine preference as follows:

$$rvtc^{SE}(tc, pg) = \sum_s sw(s) \cdot rank^N(tc, pg, s) \tag{20}$$

To synthesize this in terms of a leaf path, we also define a search engine relevance measure of a Web page pg for a leaf path lp as $rvlp^{SE}(lp, pg)$ and formalize it as the equation (21).

$$rvlp^{SE}(lp, pg) = \frac{\sum\limits_{tc \in tcslp(lp)} rvtc^{SE}(tc, pg)}{ns(tcslp(lp))} \qquad (21)$$

Finally to obtain a search engine relevance value of a Web page with respect to WSTT, we also adopt AHP-based WSTT relevance value composition mechanism and so, we set $bndfn(lp, pg)$ in the equation (11) as $rvlp^{SE}(lp, pg)$. After value propagation process, we obtain a single synthesized search engine relevance value at the root node n_0 and assign its value, $rvn(n_0, pg)$ to rvc(Search Engine Component, pg).

3.4.6 Authority/Hub Component Relevancy Computation

Authority/Hub component: represents the level of user preference for *Authority* or *Hub* sites and pages [31]. At present, no such authority or hub ranking service exists on the Web. Therefore, we have not incorporated this component into our proof-of-concept prototype.

3.4.7 Popularity Component Relevancy Computation

Our final component to be considered is the Popularity component and it represents the user's preference for popular sites. Popularity can be measured by the number of visitors or the number of requests for the specific page or site and there exist some publicly available services for this popularity information like www.yep.com. To compute the relevance value of a Web page pg in terms of the popularity component, let's introduce some definitions as follows.

$pop(pg)$: denotes the average number of daily visitors to the Web page pg.

$pgset$: denotes the set of whole Web pages retrieved.

Based on the definitions, we formalize the popularity relevance measure of a Web page pg as follows:

$$rvc(\text{Popularity Component}, pg) = \frac{pop(pg)}{\max\limits_{x \in pgset} pop(x)} \qquad (22)$$

So far, we have presented our approach for users to express their search intent, their search preference in terms of six preference components, have proposed a series of rating methods to compute for each a relevance value of the component, and provided a mechanism to combine them into a single measure of relevance. Finally we use this single measure to provide the users more relevant information with a list of resulting Web pages in a descending order of relevance value.

4   WebSifter II System Architecture

In this section we present the architecture of WebSifter II. Figure 7 shows the overall architecture of WebSifter II and its components. Major information flows are also depicted. WebSifter II consists of eight subsystems and four major information stores.

Now let's briefly introduce each of the components, their roles, and related architectural issues.

1) WSTT Elicitor

The WSTT elicitor supports the entire process (see section 3.1) of specifying a WSTT in a GUI environment. A user can express his search intent as a WSTT through interactions with the WSTT elicitor. This includes building a taxonomy tree, assigning weights to each node, and choosing a concept from an available list of WordNet concepts. To achieve this goal, the WSTT elicitor also cooperates with an Ontology agent, a Stemming agent, and a Spell Check agent. Once a user finishes building a WSTT, then the WSTT elicitor stores the WSTT information into the WSTT base in XML format.

2) Ontology Agent

The ontology agent is responsible for requesting available concepts of a given term via a Web version of WordNet (http://www.cogsci.princeton.edu/cgi-bin/webwn/) and also for interpreting the corresponding HTTP-based results. The agent receives requests for the concepts from WSTT elicitor and returns available concepts in an understandable form. Although WebSifter presently supports cooperation only with WordNet, its design can be easily extended to cooperate with other ontology servers such as CYC [33] and EDR [34].

3) Stemming Agent

Our stemming agent is based on Porter's algorithm [35]. It has two major roles: 1) to cooperate with the WSTT elicitor in transforming the terms in a concept to stemmed terms, and 2) to transform the content of Web pages into the stemmed terms internally through cooperation with a page request broker. As a result, the terms in concepts and the terms in Web pages can be compared to each other via their stemmed versions.

4) Spell Check Agent

The spell check agent monitors user's text input to the WSTT elicitor and checks and suggests correct words to the user in real time.

5) Search Preference Elicitor

The search preference elicitor, via a GUI, supports the process (cf. section 3.2) to capture the user's search preferences. A user can express his search preference by assigning their preference weights to each of the preference components and also to their favorite search engines. Moreover, it allows the user to modify the default values assigned to each syntactic URL class such as Direct Hit, Directory Hit and Page Hit. Whenever the user modifies them, it updates the related information stored in the Personalized Evaluation Rule Base, the Search Engine Preference Base, and the Component Preference Base.

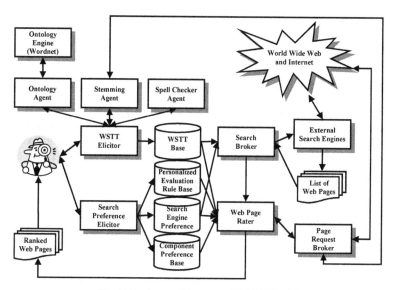

Fig. 7. System architecture of WebSifter II

6) Search Broker

The search broker performs the processes specified in section 3.3. It first interprets the XML-based WSTT and then generates all corresponding query statements. Using this set of queries, it requests information from a set of popular search engines simultaneously. Finally, it interprets the results returned from the search engines and then stores parsed information in a temporary data store. When it finishes its work, it activates the Web page rater to begin the rating process.

7) Page Request Broker

Page request broker is responsible for requesting the content of a specific URL and it cooperates with both the stemming agent and the Web page rater.

8) Web Page Rater

Web page rater supports the entire Web page evaluation process specified in section 3.4 and also is responsible for displaying the results to users. This subsystem is the most complex and computationally intensive module of WebSifter II, and it uses all four major information stores and also communicates with search broker and page request broker.

5   Empirical Results

5.1   Implementation

We have implemented the semantic taxonomy-based personalizable meta-search agent in a working prototype using Java, with the exception of the spell check agent. Now, we plan to incorporate a commercial spell check agent into this system.

Figure 8 shows an illustrative screen where the user builds a WSTT using the WSTT elicitor. Figure 9 shows another screen of the WSTT elicitor supporting the selection of an intended concept from available concepts for a given term, obtained through cooperation between the ontology agent and WordNet.

Figure 10 shows a panel by which a user specifies his search preference using the search preference elicitor. The four tab windows in Figure 10 accept user preference for the relevance components, search engines, advanced parameters, and classification rules for Web pages, respectively. However, only the tab window for preference components is shown in Figure 10.

Finally, Figure 11 is a main screen of our WebSifter II system and it shows illustrative results for a given search query generated through the above steps.

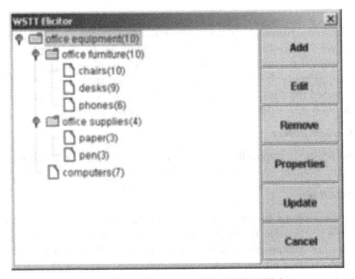

Fig. 8. An illustrative screen of the WSTT Elicitor

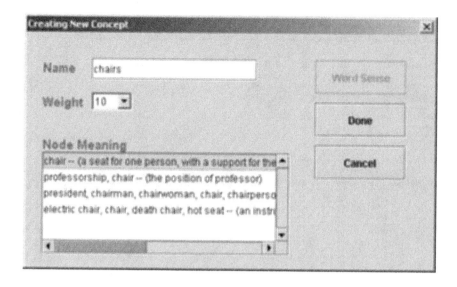

Fig. 9. An illustrative screen for concept selection

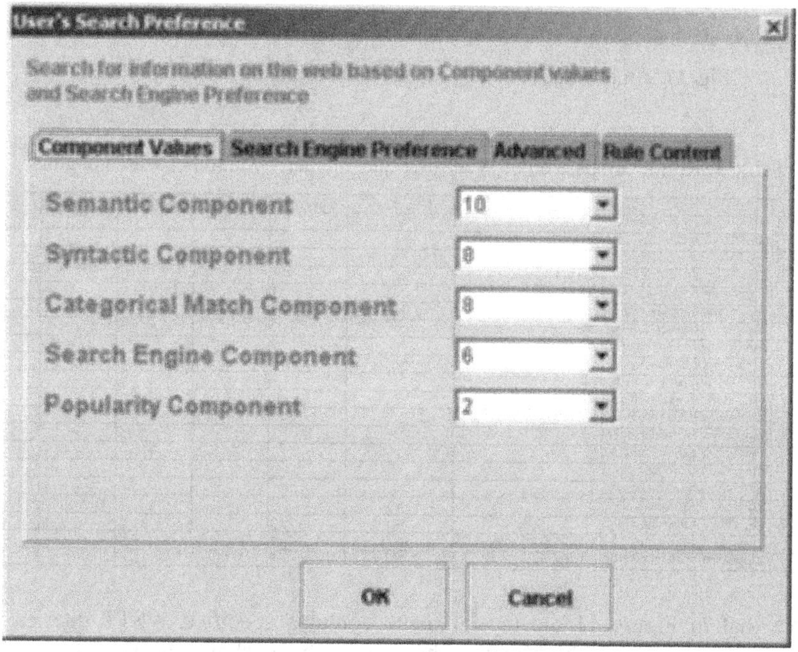

Fig. 10. A tab window of the Search Preference Elicitor

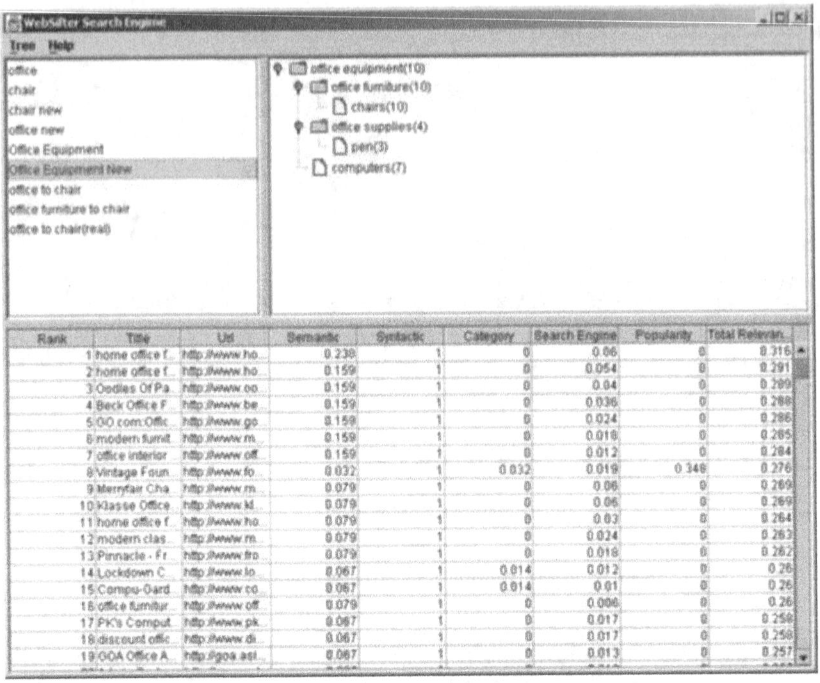

Fig. 11. An illustrative screen of the results from the Web Page Rater

Table 1. Result comparison of WebSifter query "chair" with other search engines

Rank	URL	Relevancy	Copernic	Altavista	Google	Yahoo	Excite
1	http://www.countryseat.com	Y	-	-	-	-	-
2	http://www.infant-car-seat.com/	N	-	-	-	-	-
3	http://www.chairmaker.co.uk/	Y	-	-	-	19	-
4	http://www.convertible-car-seat.com/	N	-	-	-	-	-
5	http://www.booster-car-seats.com/	N	-	-	-	-	-
6	http://www.booster-seats-online.com/	N	-	-	-	-	-
7	http://www.booster-car-seat.com/	N	-	-	-	-	-
8	http://www.podiatrychair.com/	N	-	-	-	-	9
9	http://www.carolinachair.com/	Y	-	-	-	9	-
10	http://www.chairdancing.com/	N	-	-	-	-	-
11	http://www.massage-chairs-online.com/	N	-	-	-	-	13
12	http://www.panasonic-massage-loungers.com/	N	-	-	-	-	14
13	http://www.fairfieldchair.com/	Y	-	-	15	-	-
14	http://www.gasserchair.com/	Y	-	16	-	-	-
15	http://www.chairtech.com/	Y	-	18	-	-	-
16	http://www.snugseat.com/	N	-	-	-	-	-
17	http://www.seat.com/	N	-	-	-	-	-
18	http://www.fifthchair.org/	N	3	2	5	8	3
19	house.com/mainframes/About_each_show/show_list/	N	19	-	9	-	-
20	http://www.jeanmonnetprogram.org/	N	5	1	1	-	5

Note that in Figure 11 the top-left pane contains specified WSTT queries with "Office Equipment New" highlighted, the top-right pane shows the WSTT of "Office Equipment New" and the bottom pane shows the search results ranked by the Total Relevance component.

5.2   Experimental Results

We are currently doing empirical experiments on our approach and some of them are presented. We first show results from the experiments related to the relevancy enhancement in the page hits by considering both positive and negative concepts obtained through user's concept selection as shown in Figure 9.

Table 1 shows the page hits retrieved by WebSifter II for the search of a just a single term, "chair", associated with the selected concept as a seat for one person, which appears as the first concept in Figure 9. In this table, the ranks of web pages provided by WebSifter appear in the first left column and the next column shows their corresponding URLs.

The right five columns show a comparison of our result to the results by the search engines, Copernic, Altavista, Google, Yahoo, and Excite. The number in each cell of those columns indicates the rank assigned by the corresponding search engine (column) for the given page-hit (row). Especially, the '-' sign in the table indicates the corresponding Web page was not retrieved, or was ranked lower than 20th by the corresponding search engine. Actually, most of the page-hits, which do not have any corresponding ranks from other search engines, are due to WebSifter's use of *semantic concepts* rather than *terms*. A concept usually consists of multiple terms as mentioned in Section 3.1, and so, our approach generates multiple queries based on such multiple terms. For this "chair" case, not only "chair" but also "seat" is used in the search. But when we just use the search engines, "chair" is the only term posed to them because they do not support query extensions using concepts.

Relevancy column shows the relevancies of the corresponding page-hits, where 'Y' means the page is relevant to the query, while 'N' means it is irrelevant. The decisions are based on our subjective but clear evaluation criterion as to whether the corresponding Web page is relevant to a real chair or seat. As shown in Table 1, we found six relevant Web pages in our page-hit result based on this criterion and most of them are also relatively high-ranked. The results also show most of high-ranked pages in the search engines appeared to be irrelevant and were low-ranked in our page-hits list.

In Table 2, we also compare our results with Copernic, which is one of the leading commercial meta-search engines. Copernic retrieved only one relevant Web page and the reader can easily find its rank information is strongly related to the ranks from the search engines in this table. Evidence for this is the fact that the first-ranked Web page is "www.theelectricchair.com" and has strong support from Google and Yahoo, where its ranks are 2 and 1, respectively. However, it is about the real electric chair and totally irrelevant to the chair that we are looking for. Our approach ranked it as lower than 20th and so, it does not appear on our list. Even though our approach also considers the rank information from the search engines, WebSifter ranks that electric chair page lower using negative concept.

Overall search performance comparison between WebSifter and other competing search engines are summarized in Table 3. In this table, hit ratio means the percentage of the relevant page-hits to 20 high ranked pages and average rank of relevant pages partially measures the quality of ranking. That is, as far as the hit ratios are same or similar, the search method that produces the smallest average rank of relevant pages is the best ranked.

Table 2. Comparison of Copernic with WebSifter and other search engines

RANK	URL	Relevancy	WebSifter	Altavista	Google	Yahoo	Excite
1	http://www.theelectricchair.com/	N	-	-	2	1	-
2	http://www.chair-sales.com/	N	-	-	-	-	1
3	http://www.fifthchair.org/	N	18	2	5	8	3
4	http://www.urbanlegends.com/death/electric_chair/electric_chair	N	-	-	-	15	-
5	http://www.jeanmonnetprogram.org/	N	20	1	1	-	5
6	http://www.the-perfect-chair.com/	N	-	-	-	-	2
7	http://www.widc.org	N	-	3	4	2	4
8	http://www.law.harvard.edu/programs/JeanMonnet/	N	-	-	3	-	-
9	http://www.chairpage.com/	N	-	-	-	-	6
10	http://www.obesity.chair.ulaval.ca/	N	-	-	7	12	-
11	http://www.tdcrc.com	N	-	-	-	3	-
12	http://www.titanicdeckchair.com	N	-	-	-	6	-
13	http://www.electricchair.com/	N	-	-	8	-	11
14	http://www.gsb.stthomas.edu/ethics/	N	-	-	-	4,5	-
15	http://www.producerschair.com/	N	-	-	6	-	-
16	http://www.nantucketbeachchair.com	N	-	-	17	20	-
17	http://www.emf.net/~troop24/scouting/scouter.html	N	-	-	-	-	7
18	http://www.examchair.com/	N	-	-	-	-	8
19	http://www.painted-house.com/mainframes/About_each_show/sh	N	19	-	9	-	-
20	http://www.windsorchairresources.com/	Y	-	-	10	-	-

Table 3. Overall search performance for the query *chair*

Search Engine	Hit Ratio
WebSifter	95%
WebSifter (w/o Categorical Match)	80%
Corpenic	75%
Altavista	65%
Google	60%
Yahoo	85%
Excite	65%

Table 4. WebSifter results for the query *office* and *chair*

Rank	URL	Relevancy	w/o Categ
1	http://www.seatingvfm.com/	Y	1
2	http://www.officechair.co.uk/	Y	2
3	http://www.AmericanErgonomics.com/	Y	9
4	http://www.ompchairs.com/	Y	22
5	http://www.klasse.com.au/	Y	4
6	http://www.cyberchair.com/	Y	46
7	http://www.leap-chair.com	Y	47
8	http://www.seizaseat.com/	Y	50
9	http://www.zackback.com	Y	49
10	http://www.fairfieldchair.com	Y	2
11	http://www.chair-ergonomics.com/	Y	5
12	http://www.buy-ergonomic-chairs.com/	Y	6
13	http://www.jfainc.com/	Y	7
14	http://www.chairtech.com/	Y	8
15	http://www.plasticfoldingchairs.com/	Y	13
16	http://www.kneelsit.com/	Y	10
17	http://www.home-office-furniture-store.com/	Y	11
18	http://www.home-office-furniture-site.com/	Y	12
19	http://www.amadio.it/uk/	Y	19
20	http://www.newtrim.co.uk/	N	15

As shown in the table, the WebSifter approach outperforms other approaches in both measures. By the way, Copernic shows the poorest performance and this seems to be caused because most of relevant page hits were low-ranked by the search engines in this case, but meta-search engine like Copernic, tends to consider high-ranked page hits, first.

The above results show that consideration of the positive and negative concepts can contribute greatly to the precision of the ranking. To further validate the effect of the hierarchical concept tree in search, we extend the test query to a chair for office use. This query is represented as the case (a) in Figure 2 in our approach and we use "office" and "chair" terms for other search engines.

Table 4 shows the retrieved page-hits by WebSifter II for this query and their ranks. WebSifter shows 95%-hit ratio in this case and the only irrelevant page-hit is ranked as 20th. In this experiment, we also tested the WebSifter approach for the case where we suppress the effect of the categorical match component mentioned in 3.4.4, by setting its weight to zero. Through this additional test, we can evaluate the contribution of both the hierarchical concept tree and the categorical match component to relevancy precision by comparing the normal case with the suppressed one. The corresponding ranks generated by the suppressed case for each page-hit are shown in the right most column in Table 4.

Table 5 also shows the retrieved page-hits and their ranks from the case where we turn off the categorical match component. In this table, the column labelled by 'with Categ' also shows the corresponding ranks of the page-hits from the case when we include the categorical match component into the WebSifter II rating mechanism. By comparing both Tables 4 and 5, we can find that the consideration of concept hierarchy and the categorical match component affects greatly the resulting rankings. As shown in the results, three of four irrelevant page-hits were ranked lower than 20th, and were replaced with relevant page hits. One remaining irrelevant page hit is also downgraded from 15th rank to 20th rank. In summary, the hit ratio from Table 5 (80%) is enhanced to 95% in Table 6. This implies consideration of concept hierarchy and categorical match component contributes a 15% performance enhancement in this case and they are very important factors to be considered in retrieving the relevant page-hits.

Overall search performance comparison results for the query, "office" and "chair" are shown in Table 6. WebSifter II approach also outperforms the other approaches and even our approach without consideration of the categorical match component is still better or quite competitive to other approaches.

These results from the experiments so far show most promising evidence to validate our approach. We are still performing additional experiments to validate the performance of our approach in more broad cases.

Table 5. WebSifter result for query *office* and *chair* without category match component

Rank	URL	Relevancy	with Categ
1	http://www.seatingvfm.com/	Y	1
2	http://www.fairfieldchair.com	Y	10
3	http://www.officechair.co.uk/	Y	2
4	http://www.klasse.com.au/	Y	5
5	http://www.chair-ergonomics.com/	Y	11
6	http://www.buy-ergonomic-	Y	15
7	http://www.jfainc.com/	Y	13
8	http://www.chairtech.com/	Y	14
9	http://www.AmericanErgonomics.c	Y	3
10	http://www.kneelsit.com/	Y	16
11	http://www.home-office-furniture-	Y	17
12	http://www.home-office-furniture-	Y	18
13	http://www.plasticfoldingchairs.co	Y	15
14	http://www.office-interior-	N	21
15	http://www.newtrim.co.uk/	N	20
16	http://www.oa-chair.com/	N	23
17	http://www.buy-ergonomic-	Y	24
18	http://www.countryseat.com/	Y	26
19	http://www.amadio.it/uk/	Y	19
20	http://www.mobile-office-desk.com/	N	28

Table 6. Overall search performance comparisons for the query *office* and *chair*

Search Engine	Hit Ratio
WebSifter	95%
WebSifter (w/o Categorical Match)	80%
Corpenic	75%
Altavista	65%
Google	60%
Yahoo	85%
Excite	65%

6   Conclusions

We have proposed a semantic taxonomy-based personalizable meta-search agent approach to achieve two important and complementary goals: 1) allowing users more expressive power in formulating their Web searches, and 2) improving the relevancy of search results based on the user's real intent. In contrast to the previous research, we have focused not only on the search problem itself, but also on the decision-making problem that motivates users to search the Web.

Now, let's briefly summarize our contributions as follows. We have proposed a search-intention representation scheme, the Weighted Semantic-Taxonomy Tree, through which users express their real search intentions by specifying domain-specific concepts, assigning appropriate weights to each concept, and expressing their decision problem as a structured tree of concepts. We also allow users to express their search result evaluation preferences as a function of six preference components.

Second, to enhance the *precision* of the retrieved information, we present a hybrid rating mechanism which considers both the user's search intent represented by the WSTT and user's search preference represented by multi-preference components such as semantic relevance, syntactic relevance, categorical match, page popularity, and authority/hub rating.

Third, we have designed and have implemented a meta-search agent system called WebSifter II that cooperates with WordNet for concept retrieval, and most well known search engines for Web page retrieval. Our open and extensible architecture allows new services to be incorporated in WebSifter II, as they become available. For the empirical validation of our approach, we empirically validate our approach already for some limited cases and we are also doing some real world experiments of our system.

References

[1]   Scime, A. and L. Kerschberg, "WebSifter: An Ontology-Based Personalizable Search Agent for the Web," *International Conference on Digital Libraries: Research and Practice*, Kyoto Japan, 2000, pp. 493-446.

[2]   Scime, A. and L. Kerschberg, "Web Sifter: An Ontological Web-Mining Agent for E-Business," Proceedings of the 9th IFIP 2.6 Working Conference on Database Semantics (DS-9): Semantic Issues in E-Commerce Systems, Hong Kong, 2001.

[3]   Lawrence, S. and C. L. Giles, "Accessibility of Information on the Web," *Nature*, vol. 400, 1999, pp. 107-109.

[4]   Selberg, E. and O. Etzioni, "The MetaCrawler Architecture for Resource Aggregation on the Web," *IEEE Expert*, vol. 12, no. 1, 1997, pp. 11-14.

[5]   Howe, A. E. and D. Dreilinger, "Savvy Search: A Metasearch Engine that Learns which Search Engines to Query," *AI Magazine*, vol. 18, no. 2, 1997, pp. 19-25.

[6]   Lawrence, S. and C. L. Giles, "Context and Page Analysis for Improved Web Search," *IEEE Internet Computing*, vol. 2, no. 4, 1998, pp. 38-46.

[7]   Ackerman, M., et al., "Learning Probabilistic User Profiles - Applications for Finding Interesting Web Sites, Notifying Users of Relevant Changes to Web Pages, and Locating Grant Opportunities," *AI Magazine*, vol. 18, no. 2, 1997, pp. 47-56.

[8]   Armstrong, R., et al., "WebWatcher: A Learning Apprentice for the World Wide Web," Proceedings of the 1995 AAAI Spring Symposium on Information Gathering from Heterogeneous, Distributed Environments, 1995.

[9]   Shavlik, J. and T. Eliassi-Rad, "Building Intelligent Agents for Web-based Tasks: A Theory-Refinement Approach," *Proceedings of the Conference on Automated Learning and Discovery: Workshop on Learning from Text and the Web*, Pittsburgh, PA, 1998.

[10]   Chen, Z., et al., "WebSail: from On-line Learning to Web Search," *Proceedings of the First International Conference on Web Information Systems Engineering*, vol. 1, 2000, pp. 206-213.

[11]   Chakrabarti, S., et al., "Enhanced Hypertext Categorization using Hyperlinks," *Proceedings of ACM SIGMOD International Conference on Management of Data*, Seattle, Washington, 1998, pp. 307-318.

[12]   Li, Y., "Toward a Qualitative Search Engine," *IEEE Internet Computing*, vol. 2, no. 4, 1998, pp. 24-29.

[13]   Maes, P., "Agents that reduce work and information overload," *Communications of the ACM*, vol. 37, no. 7, 1994, pp. 30-40.

[14]   Terveen, L., et al., "PHOAKS: a System for Sharing Recommendations," *Communications of the ACM*, vol. 40, no. 3, 1997, pp. 59-62.

[15]   Bollacker, K. D., et al., "Discovering Relevant Scientific Literature on the Web," *IEEE Intelligent Systems*, vol. 15, no. 2, 2000, pp. 42-47.

[16]   Balabanovic, M. and Y. Shoham, "Content-Based, Collaborative Recommendation," *Communications of the ACM*, vol. 40, no. 3, 1997, pp. 66-72.

[17]   Krulwich, B., "Lifestyle Finder," *AI Magazine*, vol. 18, no. 2, 1997, pp. 37-46.

[18]   de Vel, O. and S. Nesbitt, "A Collaborative Filtering Agent System for Dynamic Virtual Communities on the Web," *Working notes of Learning from Text and the Web, Conference on Automated Learning and Discovery CONALD-98*, Carnegie Mellon University, Pittsburgh, 1998.

[19]   Chen, H. and S. Dumais, "Bringing Order to the Web: Automatically Categorizing Search Results," *Proceedings of the CHI 2000 conference on Human factors in computing systems*, The Hague Netherlands, 2000, pp. 145-152.

[20]   Aridor, Y., et al., "Knowledge Agent on the Web," Proceedings of the 4th International Workshop on Cooperative Information Agents IV, 2000, pp. 15-26.

[21]   Chakrabarti, S., et al., "Focused Crawling: A New Approach to Topic-Specific Web Resource Discovery," *Proceedings of the Eighth International WWW Conference*, 1999, pp. 545-562.

[22]   Salton, G., et al., "A Vector Space Model for Automatic Indexing," *Communications of the ACM*, vol. 18, no. 11, 1975, pp. 613-620.

[23]   Clark, D., "Mad Cows, Metathesauri, and Meaning," *IEEE Intelligent Systems*, vol. 14, no. 1, 1999, pp. 75-77.

[24]   Guarino, N., et al., "OntoSeek: Content-based Access to the Web," *IEEE Intelligent Systems*, vol. 14, no. 3, 1999, pp. 70-80.

[25]   Fensel, D., et al., "On2broker: Semantic-Based Access to Information Sources at the WWW," *Proceedings of the World Conference on the WWW and Internet (WebNet 99)*, Honolulu, Hawaii, USA, 1999, pp. 25-30.

[26]   Staab, S., et al., "A System for Facilitating and Enhancing Web Search," *Proceedings of IWANN '99 - International Working Conference on Artificial and Natural Neural Networks*, Berlin, Heidelberg, 1999.

[27]   Martin, P. and P. W. Eklund, "Knowledge Retrieval and the World Wide Web," *IEEE Intelligent Systems*, vol. 15, no. 3, 2000, pp. 18-25.

[28]   Miller, G. A., "WordNet a Lexical Database for English," *Communications of the ACM*, vol. 38, no. 11, 1995, pp. 39-41.

[29]   Klein, D. A., Decision-Analytic Intelligent Systems: Automated Explanation and Knowledge Acquisition, Lawrence Erlbaum Associates, 1994.

[30]   Boose, J. H. and J. M. Bradshaw, "Expertise Transfer and Complex Problems: Using AQUINAS as a Knowledge-acquisition Workbench for Knowledge-Based Systems," *Int. J. Man-Machine Studies*, vol. 26, 1987, pp. 3-28.

[31]   Kleinberg, J. M., "Authoritative Sources in a Hyperlinked Environment," *Journal of the ACM*, vol. 46, no. 5, 1999, pp. 604-632.

[32]   Saaty, T. L., *The Analytic Hierarchy Process*, New York, McGraw-Hill, 1980.

[33]   Lenat, D. B., "Cyc: A Large-Scale Investment in Knowledge Infrastructure," *Communications of the ACM*, vol. 38, no. 11, 1995, pp. 33-38.

[34]   Yokoi, T., "The EDR Electronic Dictionary," *Communications of the ACM*, vol. 38, no. 11, 1995, pp. 45-48.

[35]   Porter, M., "An Algorithm for Suffix Stripping," available at http://www.muscat.co.uk/~martin/def.txt.

Part II

Adaptation and Learning

AlphaWolf: Social Learning, Emotion and Development in Autonomous Virtual Agents

Bill Tomlinson and Bruce Blumberg

Synthetic Characters Group, The Media Lab, MIT
77 Massachusetts Avenue, NE18-5FL, Cambridge, MA 02139 USA
{badger,bruce}@media.mit.edu

Abstract. We present research in synthetic social behavior for interactive virtual characters. We describe a model from the natural world, the gray wolf (*Canis lupus*), and the social behavior exhibited by packs of wolves, to use as the target for an interactive installation entitled *AlphaWolf*, which was shown at SIGGRAPH 2001. We offer a computational model that captures a subset of the social behavior of wild wolves, involving models of learning, emotion and development. There is a range of real-world applications of synthetic social behavior, from short-term possibilities such as autonomous characters for computer games, to long-term applications such as computer interfaces that can interact more appropriately with humans by utilizing human social abilities. Our research offers initial steps toward computational systems with social behavior, in hope of making interactions with them more functional and more inherently rewarding.

1   Introduction

This paper presents research in social learning currently under way in the Synthetic Characters Group at the MIT Media Lab, headed by Professor Bruce Blumberg. The goal of our group is to understand the nature of intelligent behavior by creating computational entities that are inspired by animals. Over the last several years, we have developed a synthetic-character-building toolkit with which we create our virtual entities. By drawing lessons from nature, we hope to shed some light on certain hard problems in artificial intelligence, including action selection, machine learning, motor control and multi-agent coordination. The focus of one of our current projects, entitled *AlphaWolf*, is social learning in a virtual 3D-animated wolf pack (see Fig. 1). *AlphaWolf* is an interactive installation in which people play the role of wolf pups in a pack of autonomous and semi-autonomous virtual wolves. By howling, growling, whining or barking into a microphone, each participant is able to influence how his or her pup interacts with the other members of the pack. The pups, in turn, form emotional memories that color how they will interact with their packmates in future encounters. *AlphaWolf* premiered in the Emerging Technologies section of SIGGRAPH 2001.

W. Truszkowski, C. Rouff, M. Hinchey (Eds.): WRAC 2002, LNAI 2564, pp. 35–45, 2003.
© Springer-Verlag Berlin Heidelberg 2003

Fig. 1. A wolf pup and his father howl together

Various other researchers have studied synthetic social systems from natural models, including flocking in birds [29], schooling in fish [37], virtual gorillas [1], chimpanzees [35] and primate-like artificial agents [19]. Our research differs from these efforts in our focus on learning as a key component of social competence. Social learning allows creatures to benefit from context-preservation [9] – in each successive inter-character interaction, individuals can bring their interaction history to bear on their decision-making process. In the process of building this installation, we have augmented our character-building toolkit (described elsewhere – [3], [6], [13], [20]) with a variety of computational representations that are necessary to enable social learning in our virtual wolves. By taking an animal model and trying to replicate the social phenomena found in that species, we seek to create computational mechanisms that will enable social competence, learning and development in a wider range of socially intelligent agents and other computational systems.

We are pursuing two main areas of research that pertain to social learning. The first is the relationship between social learning and emotion. Our wolves feature a model of emotion and a dynamic range of behavior that is influenced by their emotional state. Wolves' emotions also play into their formation of context-specific emotional memories, which affect how they will interact in the future. Our research group has completed simple implementations of these representations, featured in the virtual wolves we showed at SIGGRAPH 2001.

The second area of research involves development as it relates to social learning. Animals are born with certain innate behaviors; suckling, for example, is too crucial a behavior to be left to learning. Simulating the timing of innate behaviors (i.e., when they become active or inactive) in the context of our learning system will allow virtual creatures to be created who are more similar to real animals. A blend of hard coded behaviors and learned behaviors will create virtual creatures with predispositions to behave in certain fashions, but the ability to adapt to the vagaries of their local environment. This is the main area of future work for our project, which we hope to implement in the coming months. Each of our wolves will play different roles as it grows up, depending on the composition of its pack, its built-in developmentally-timed behavioral predispositions and the learning it has undergone during its life.

There are a variety of real-world applications of our research. Any population of virtual or physical agents, from crowd scenes in animated movies to autonomous robots collecting samples on Mars, could benefit from computational models of social learning. Just as individual animals provide good models for creating individual agents, populations of animals may inspire mechanisms by which those individual agents will interact. Because the environments inhabited by many populations of artificial entities are variable and uncertain, it is important to have creatures who are predisposed toward certain behaviors but can learn and adapt to meet the constraints imposed by their environment.

2   The Gray Wolf

In their natural environment, gray wolves form complex social groups called packs. The core of most packs is a family – a breeding pair of adults, their puppies, and sometimes a few adult offspring of the breeding pair. [26], [23] The average pack size is approximately 7-9 individuals, but some packs may contain more than 25 wolves. Large packs may contain more than one breeding pair. Most young wolves disperse from their natal pack in their second or third year to find a mate and begin their own pack. [23]

Wolves communicate with each other in a variety of ways. They have a wide array of vocalizations, including "whimpering, wuffing, snarling, squealing and howling". [40, p. 68] They express their intentions and motivational and emotional states through body posture as well – a mother wolf assumes different postures with her pups than she does with her mate. The sense of smell is also integral to wolf social behavior (e.g., scent marking). In wolves, as in most social creatures, communication is central to the social relationships that are formed.

When the pack has young pups, the adult wolves travel away from the den to hunt, and carry back meat in their stomachs to feed the pups. Upon their return, the pups perform stereotypical food-begging behavior, in which they crouch in front of an adult and lick or peck at the adult's muzzle. This pup behavior incites the adult to regurgitate the meat, which the pups excitedly consume. [32]

Wolf social behaviors appear to be derived from other behavioral patterns exhibited by wolves. [32] For example, there are two main types of submission that wolves exhibit – passive submission and active submission. Passive submission involves a wolf lying on his side or back, exposing the ventral side of his chest. The ears are held close to the head, and the tail is tucked between the legs. These behavioral patterns bear a resemblance to infantile behaviors involved in reflex urination (in which a pup urinates when his mother licks his belly). [14] Active submission involves a crouched posture with backward directed ears, and licking or pecking the mouth of the dominant wolf. This behavior is very similar to the food-begging behavior of pups described above. Similarly, dominant behaviors appear to be a form of "ritualized fighting". [17]

We chose the gray wolf as the model for our simulation for several reasons. First, they manifest distinct social phenomena that are complex enough to be interesting, yet clear enough to provide direction for our simulation. Second, wolves are closely related to the domestic dog, for which we have a strong conceptual and technical base as a result of previous installations that we have done featuring virtual dogs. Finally, the social behaviors of wolves are similar enough to those of humans that some of the lessons we learn from wolves might be relevant to human social behavior and simulation.

3   Computational Representations: Social Learning and Emotion

There are a variety of computational elements that must be in place for virtual wolves to interact socially in a way resembling real wolves. Our virtual wolves must be able to choose different behaviors; to move around their world; to learn that certain interactions lead to positive results while others lead to negative repercussions. These components are already functional parts of our character-building toolkit, and have been described elsewhere. [20], [13], [6], [3]

The fundamental representation of an action in our system is the ActionTuple. Each ActionTuple consists of four components: the action itself; a TriggerContext, which determines when the action will take place; a DoUntilContext that determines when the action will cease; and an object to which the action will happen. ActionTuples are arranged into ActionGroups that determine which actions are mutually exclusive and which can be run simultaneously. In accord with Thorndike's Law of Effect [36], ActionTuples that are correlated with positive results will be chosen more frequently in the future. Each action is executed in an emotional style, which we discuss below.

Social learning is intimately linked with the ability to have emotions, to express those emotional states, and to remember an association between environmental stimuli and emotional states. The main extensions to our system that have already been implemented for this project are: the ability to have and express emotional states, and the ability to form context-specific emotional memories. We will describe each of these elements in greater depth below.

3.1   Having Emotions

In order to simulate emotional virtual characters, it is necessary to choose a computational representation that captures the range of emotional phenomena we wish our characters to exhibit. Much research has already been done both in understanding emotions and in simulating them computationally. Darwin's ideas about emotions [11] form the basis for much of modern research into understanding emotions scientifically.

For the *AlphaWolf* project, we have considered two main emotional paradigms – a dimensional approach and a categorical approach. The dimensional approach (e.g., [33], [28], [31], [34]) maps a range of emotional phenomena onto explicitly dimensioned space. Various researchers have implemented versions of the dimensional approach; for example, Breazeal [4] maps a 3-dimensional space

(Arousal, Valence, Stance) onto a set of emotions that influence both the behavior system and the motor system.

The categorical approach separates emotional phenomena into a set of basic emotions – for example, fear, anger, sadness, happiness, disgust and surprise. [14] Ekman's model provided the basis for an implementation by Velasquez [38]; others (e.g., [16]) have also implemented categorical models. For a far more comprehensive discussion of emotional models in computational systems, the reader is directed to Rosalind Picard's book, *Affective Computing* [27].

A dimensional approach better captured the range of emotional phenomena that we wanted our wolves to display. Our emotion model is based most directly on the Pleasure-Arousal-Dominance model presented by Mehrabian and Russell [24]. At each moment, a wolf has three continuous variables describing a 3-dimensional emotional space. Emotional categories may also be mapped onto these axes; for example, anger is equivalent to low Pleasure, high Arousal and high Dominance. The value for each variable is affected by the wolf's previous emotional state, by some drift that each emotional axis undergoes, and by attributes of his surrounding environment. Currently our Dominance axis is most thoroughly fleshed out; we hope to elaborate on the other two axes in the coming months.

3.2   Expressing Emotional States

The emotional state of our virtual wolves affect the action selection mechanism by feeding into the TriggerContexts. For example, a wolf's dominance value (D, where 0 < D < 1) will factor into a trigger that causes growling to occur, and (1 - D) will factor into the trigger that makes the wolf submit.

In addition, the emotional states of our wolves feed into our motor control system [13] and affect the style in which they take their actions. This system is based on the "verbs and adverbs" system of Rose [30], in which an action (a "verb") is taken in a certain style (an "adverb"). Because of our motor control system, which can blend between example animations, our animators need only create a few extreme emotional styles of each action (for example, one high Arousal walk and one low Arousal walk) to get the full dynamic expressive range between those examples. Finally, emotion is central to our creatures' social interactions.

Fig. 2. The wolf pup play-bows at his father

3.3   Context-Specific Emotional Memories

A component of real wolf social behavior is that submissive wolves know to submit *before* the dominant wolf even reaches them, and thus avoid a potentially harmful interaction. [32] Similarly, our virtual wolves need some way of triggering submissive behaviors before they are actually pinned to the ground by a dominant individual. How can our wolves remember previous interactions that they have had? In our simulation, we utilize *context-specific emotional memories* (CSEMs) for this purpose. CSEMs cause a wolf who is experiencing a suite of environmental stimuli (for example, a dominant wolf) to return to an emotional state similar to the one he experienced on previous encounters with those stimuli. In addition to storing the values of Pleasure, Arousal and Dominance that the wolf was feeling when he last experienced the relevant stimuli, the CSEM also features a Confidence value that reflects how reliable he believes the CSEM's values to be. Each continuously changing CSEM effectively reflects the interaction history between the wolf and some bit of his context, without the need for specific memories of past interactions.

Our CSEMs are based on the "somatic marker hypothesis" presented by Damasio [10], in which he proposes that people attach emotional significance to stimuli that they encounter in their environment, and then re-experience that emotion when they encounter those stimuli on future occasions. Other researchers have implemented models of emotional learning or memory, for example "affective tags" [39], "emotional memories" [38], and others (e.g., [21], [16], [2]).

An important extension to our system would be to allow our wolves to form multiple CSEMs for one object, depending on the context in which the wolf has encountered that object. For example, a wolf pup might form one CSEM about his father when the father smells of meat (i.e., "He'll probably regurgitate food for me if I harass him!"), and a very different one when he doesn't smell of meat (i.e., "He'll probably pin me to the ground if I harass him!") Both of these CSEMs would have high values for Arousal, but very different values for Pleasure.

4   Future Work: Social Learning and Development

A primary area of research that we hope to pursue in the near future involves giving our wolves the ability to learn to use behaviors in novel social contexts. We mentioned above that wolf submission behaviors are similar to infantile behaviors. How do wolves learn to use these behaviors to negotiate their social relationships? Over the next few paragraphs, we will describe some of the elements of our learning system that pertain to this co-opting of one behavior for another purpose.

In our previous project, entitled "Clicker by Eire", our virtual terrier Duncan had the ability to learn to exhibit a behavior in response to an appropriate context. [3] A human participant could train Duncan to do a variety of tricks in response to voice commands. Duncan's learning system back-propagated the value of a food treat to reinforce actions that he had been taking during a certain time window that preceded the treat. In addition, Duncan was able to distinguish between contexts in which he was rewarded and those in which he was not rewarded, and only propagated the value of the treat to those contexts in which a reward occurred. This is the essence of the mechanism by which our wolves will learn to perform certain behaviors in the correct context.

Here is an example of how this learning might proceed in our wolves. Imagine a pup and a father wolf who habitually eat from the same carcass. As the pup gets older, the father will become less tolerant of the pup grabbing food away from him. At a certain point, the father may discipline the pup for eating too close to him, by growling and dominating the pup. The act of disciplining will continue until the pup submits or escapes. If submission behavior tends to cause the father wolf to relent, the pup should rapidly learn to submit in the context of being disciplined. Fleeing will also separate the pup from the noxious stimulus that is an annoyed father wolf. By this mechanism, the pup will learn to submit or flee in the presence of a growling adult.

A related behavioral component of our virtual wolves is that dominant individuals need to be willing to relent once the submissive individual actually submits. Possibilities include a hard-coded "evolutionary taboo" against hurting things that act like pups or a learned association that a submitting individual will no longer perform whatever action caused the dominant's distress.

The *AlphaWolf* project is changing the way we build characters – rather than assembling finished adults, we are creating young pups with certain built-in behaviors and allowing them to grow up in a social context where they can re-use and modify these behaviors for other purposes. Additional suites of behaviors may be scheduled to "come online" at certain points in development. For example, at sexual maturity, a whole new group of behaviors become eligible for expression. In addition to changing behaviorally as they age, the wolves also change anatomically, their physical forms growing and morphing from pup to adult.

Change on developmental time scale is finding its way into both academic research and commercial products. For example, the computer game "Creatures" [18] and other virtual pets grow up as you interact with them. Cañamero's Abbotts project [7] also features a developmental perspective.

5   Applications

While our group's research is not explicitly directed toward any specific application, we often discuss our work with people who have some interest in commercial, industrial or academic applications. Through these discussions, we have considered a variety of applications for socially competent computational systems. While our group does not work on implementing these ideas, we present them here as potential reasons why socially intelligent agents might be useful research.

The entertainment industry might have a use for socially competent agents. Computer games would be more fun to play if the "good guys" and "bad guys" were able to form relationships with each other and with the players. Animated agents could help make movies by interacting socially to create more realistic crowd scenes and background action. Toys that could learn about the kids who play with them might be more engaging to those kids.

Socially competent agents could serve as an instructional tool for teaching social skills to a variety of age groups, from children to corporate managers. For example, the *AlphaWolf* installation makes social relationships explicit. When a participant growls, his pup growls. When he growls *at* another wolf, that wolf becomes more submissive. In addition, the wolf he growled at will be more likely to submit to him in the future. By making a clear connection between social action and social effect, the *AlphaWolf* project or some other experience involving social synthetic characters could make it easier for people at all stages to become aware of their own social behavior.

Any complex ecology of entities must have some mechanism for introducing new members, allocating resources, and resolving conflicts. Wild wolf populations do this, with new pups integrating into the pack each season, dominance relationships aiding in resource allocation, and status signals helping to prevent conflicts by mutual consent. Perhaps there are lessons to be learned from natural social organizations of heterogeneous (e.g., different ages) entities, which can be applied to systems created by humans.

Finally, since humans are such social creatures, there might be some use for computational models of social behavior in human-computer interfaces. Building interfaces that are able to take advantage of humans' natural social abilities will make the systems behind those interfaces both more functional and more inherently rewarding.

6   Conclusion

Social behavior is often evolutionarily advantageous in the natural world. Research in synthetic social agents allows us to harness the benefits of natural social behavior for use in computational systems. Taking one species, in this case the gray wolf, and using it as a model for our simulation allows us to have a yardstick by which to measure our success.

The essential mechanism by which our wolves form social relationships is this: each wolf has an emotional state at every moment; the wolf is able to recognize all of the other wolves; he is able to form an association between each other wolf and the emotional state that he tended to experience during previous interactions; finally, that emotional association influences his current emotional state when he again encounters a wolf for whom he has formed an emotional memory. This simple mechanism allows our wolves to remember each other and pick up where they left off in their social interactions.

Potential real world applications of synthetic social behavior are as diverse as the applications of real social entities. From characters in computer games, to educational aids for social skill development, to mechanisms for conflict negotiation in virtual or robotic entities, social awareness and interactions may play a significant role in a range of industries.

We have just exhibited the *AlphaWolf* installation at SIGGRAPH 2001, where more than a thousand people interacted with our virtual wolves. While we did not collect user data at SIGGRAPH, most participants appeared to enjoy playing with socially competent virtual wolves. People frequently brought their friends back to see the wolves, describing to them the behavior that their pups exhibited. Participants were very willing to become engaged with our wolf pups, immersing themselves in the interactive experience.

Humans are social animals; our computational systems should be able to engage our social abilities. The research described in this paper helps address how we can make computational entities who can learn to have social relationships with each other. This is a small step toward making systems that can take advantage of the natural benefits of social organization, and an even smaller step toward introducing computers to the complex world of human social interactions.

Acknowledgements

We would like to thank all the members and friends of the Synthetic Characters Group who have helped make our wolves possible: Marc Downie, Matt Berlin, Jesse Gray, Adolph Wong, Robert Burke, Scott Eaton, Damian Isla, Yuri Ivanov, Michael Patrick Johnson, Spencer Lynn, Ben Resner, Derek Lyons, Jennie Cochran, Bryan Yong, Steve Curcuru, Geoffrey Beatty, Jed Wahl, Dan Stiehl, Rusmin Soetjipto, Dan Zaharopol, Aileen Kawabe, Madaline Tomlinson and Professor Irene Pepperberg. In addition, many of the ideas in this paper were fleshed out through discussions with Professors Rosalind Picard and Richard Wrangham, and with the participants in SIGGRAPH 2001 who interacted with the *AlphaWolf* installation and with us.

References

[1]   Allison, D., Wills, B., Hodges, L., and Wineman, J.: Gorillas in the Bits, Technical Report, GIT-GVU-96-16, Georgia Institute of Technology. (1996)

[2]   Balkenius, C. and Moren, J.: A Computational Model of Context Processing, in SAB '00, (2000) 256-265

[3]   Blumberg, B.: Building characters that learn what they ought to learn. International Workshop on Story Telling. Avignon, France. (2001)

[4]   Breazeal, C.: Sociable Machines: Expressive Social Exchange Between Robot and Human. Ph.D. Thesis, Artificial Intelligence Laboratory, MIT.(2000)

[5]   Buck, R.: The Communication of Emotion. New York, NY: Guilford Press. (1984)

[6]   Burke, R., Isla, D., Downie, M., Ivanov, Y. and Blumberg, B.: CreatureSmarts: The Art and Architecture of a Virtual Brain, in Proceedings of the Game Developers Conference, (2001) 147-166

[7]   Cañamero, D.: Modeling Motivations and Emotions as a Basis for Intelligent Behavior. In Proceedings of 1st Int'l. Conf. on Autonomous Agents (1997)

[8]   Cañamero, D.: Issues in the Design of Emotional Agents. In Emotional and Intelligent: The Tangled Knot of Cognition. Papers from the 1998 AAAI Fall Symposium. Menlo Park, CA: AAAI Press.(1998) 49-54

[9]   Cohen, M.D., Riolo, R.L., and Axelrod, R.: The Emergence of Social Organization in the Prisoner's Dilemma: How Context-Preservation and Other Factors Promote Cooperation. Santa Fe Institute Working Paper 99-01-002. (1999)

[10]   Damasio, A.: Descartes' Error: Emotion, Reason, and the Human Brain. New York, NY: G.P.Putnam's Sons. (1994)

[11]   Darwin, C.: *The Expression of the Emotions in Man and Animals*. Chicago: The University of Chicago Press. Originally published in 1872. (1965)

[12]   Dautenhahn, K.: Socially Intelligent Agents and The Primate Social Brain – Towards a Science of Social Minds. In Socially Intelligent Agents: The Human in the Loop. Papers from the 2000 AAAI Fall Symposium. Menlo Park, CA: AAAI Press. (2000) 35-51

[13]   Downie, M.: Behavior, Animation and Music: The Music and Movement of Synthetic Characters. M.S. Thesis, Media Lab, MIT. (2001)

[14]   Ekman, P.: An Argument for Basic Emotions. Stein, N. and Oatley, K. eds. Basic Emotions. Hove, UK: Lawrence Erlbaum. (1992) 169-200

[15]   Fox., M.: The Wild Canids. Van Nostrand Reinold. (1975)

[16]   Gadhano, S. and Hallam, J.: Emotion-triggered Learning for Autonomous Robots. in SAB '98 Workshop on Grounding Emotions in Adaptive Systems. (1998)

[17]   Golani, I. and Moran, G. A motility-immobility gradient in the behavior of the "inferior" wolf during "ritualized fighting". in Eisenberg, J. F. and D. G. Kleiman, ed. *Advances in the study of mammalian behavior*. The American Society of Mammalogists, Special Publication No.7. (1983) 65-94

[18]   Grand, S., Cliff, D., and Malhotra, A. Creatures: Artificial Life Autonomous Software Agents for Home Entertainment. in In Proceedings of 1st Int'l. Conf. on Autonomous Agents (1997)

[19]   Hemelrijk, C.: An individual-orientated model of the emergence of despotic and egalitarian societies. Proc. R. Soc. Lond. B 266 (1999) 361-369

[20]   Isla, D., Burke, R.,   Downie, M. and Blumberg, B.: A Layered Brain Architecture for Synthetic Characters. IJCAI (2001)

[21]   Kitano, H.: A Model for Hormonal Modulation of Learning. in IJCAI (1995) 532-538

[22]   Mech, L.: Alpha status, dominance, and division of labor in wolf packs. Canadian Journal of Zoology 77 (1999) 1196-1203

[23]   Mech, L D., Adams, L. G., Meier, T. J., Burch, J. W., and Dale, B. W.: The Wolves of Denali. Minneapolis, MN: University of Minnesota Press. (1998)

[24]   Mehrabian, A. and Russell, J.: An Approach to Environmental Psychology. Cambridge, MA: MIT Press. (1974)

[25]   Morss, C.: Seminar on wolf behavior. Wolf Hollow Ipswich, Ipswich, MA. (Fall 2000)

[26]   Murie, A.: The Wolves of Mount McKinley. Fauna of the National Parks Series, No. 5. Washington, DC.: U.S. National Park Service. (1944)

[27]   Picard, R.: Affective Computing. Cambridge, MA: MIT Press. (1998)

[28]   Plutchik, R.: The Emotions. Lanham, MD: University Press of America. (1991)

[29]   Reynolds, C.: Flocks, Herds and Schools: A Distributed Behavioral Model. Computer Graphics, 21(4). In Proceedings of the SIGGRAPH '87 Conference (1987) 25 - 34

[30] Rose, C.: Verbs and Adverbs: Multidimensional Motion Interpolation Using Radial Basis Functions. Ph.D. Dissertation, Department of Computer Science, Princeton University. (1999)

[31] Russell, J.: Reading emotions from and into faces: resurrecting a dimensional-contextual perspective. in Russell, J. and Fernandez-Dols, J. (eds.) The Psychology of Facial Expression. Cambridge: Cambridge University Press. (1997)

[32] Schenkel, R.: Submission: its features and function in the wolf and dog. American. Zoologist. 7 (1967) 319-329

[33] Schlosberg, H.: Three dimensions of emotions. Psychological Review, 61(2) (1954) 81-88

[34] Smith, C.: Dimensions of appraisal and physiological response in emotion. Journal of personality and social psychology, 56 (1989) 339-353

[35] teBoekhorst, I. and Hogeweg, P.: Self-structuring in artificial 'CHIMPS' offers new hypothesis for male grouping in chimpanzees. Behaviour 130 1994) 229-52

[36] Thorndike, E.: Animal Intelligence. Darien, CT: Hafner. (1911)

[37] Tu, X. and Terzopoulos, D.: Artificial Fishes: Physics, Locomotion, Perception, Behavior. In Proceedings of ACM Computer Graphics, SIGGRAPH'94. (1994) 43-50

[38] Velasquez, J.: When Robots Weep: Emotional Memories and Decision-Making. In Proceedings of the Fifteenth National Conference on Artificial Intelligence. Madison, Wisconsin: AAAI Press. (1998)

[39] Yoon, S., Blumberg, B. and Schneider, G.: Motivation Driven Learning for Interactive Synthetic Characters. In Proceedings of 4th Int'l. Conf. on Autonomous Agents (2000)

[40] Zimen, E.: The Wolf. New York, NY: Delacorte Press. (1981)

Control and Behavior of a Massive Multi-agent System

Alain Cardon

LIP6, Laboratoire d'informatique de Paris VI
UPMC Case 169, 4 Place Jussieu, 75252 Paris Cedex 05 France. LIH
Faculté des SciencesUniversité du Havre, 76057 Le Havre Cedex France
Alain.Cardon@lip6.fr

Abstract. Massive multi-agent systems are systems built with several thousands of agents. We characterize these systems as unsteady, evolutionary and adaptive. We show that their design is made while using an incremental agentification method, using functionalities distributed in the behavior of the agent organization. But modifications of the number of agents, modification of their structures and of their capacities of communication during the running is no compatible with an a priori complete specification nor with a fine prediction of the behavior. The control of this system achieves itself while endowing agents in their running with characters of self-assessment of their organization. We claim that we can control such a system while defining a new organization of agents observing the initial in real time, valuing modifications of its morphological characters and using this assessment to modify the initial organization, in a systemic loop of self-control.

Keywords: massive multi-agent systems, self-adaptability, behavior, self-organization, morphology, design of complex systems

1   Introduction

The researches in the domain of multi-agent systems (MAS) have currently a very important development. The plastic, dynamic and distributed characters of the these systems give several advantages: in simulation, they can easily express the behavior of real systems for which equational models are insufficient and, in effective working, they allow to produce some typically adaptive behaviors for mobile systems. MAS are used in varied domains where they present an interesting alternative to the classical approaches, and especially to the object approach. But there exists a limitation to their utilization: one doesn't know how easily conceive or cleverly control the behavior of multi-agent systems of very large size.

Massive multi-agent systems (MMAS) are system composed of weak agents where the number passes thousand. We think that they are especially adequate to represent very complex phenomena, like autonomous behavior of robots with sensations and social intentions, or ecosystem simulators of large size developing scalability, or again

W. Truszkowski, C. Rouff, M. Hinchey (Eds.): WRAC 2002, LNAI 2564, pp. 46-60, 2003.
© Springer-Verlag Berlin Heidelberg 2003

systems generating sense as an artificial consciousness. Agents, in these systems, are components at the conception level, that have a simple structure, in order to be constructed easily and generated by automatic reproduction in running [Cardon - Vacher 2000]. They have, structurally, a limited knowledge, a rational behavior and they can reconsider their goals according to the knowledge they manipulate with their communications.

In MMAS, agents have been created while using a specific method of agentification that permitted to reify the multiple functionalities of which we wanted to initially endow the system. Agents endeavor to reach their goals while organizing themselves at the best, while using their capacities of communication via their acquaintance networks, to form some multiple groups: they exchange messages between them according to the language of which they are endowed. They achieve, by their actions and their pro-actions, the activation of the organization in the whole. The system has a general behavior determined, on one hand, by the action of interface agents dedicated to the action on the system environment and, on the other hand, by the activity of the strictly internal agents in the system.

The question is then to define, to conceive and to control the behavioral characters of the organization of agents, and this during its working. We are going to present two examples before presenting a solution for massive multi-agent systems. But a multi-agent system has the particularity to unify in its architecture the knowledge and the processing of the knowledge. The processing of this distributed knowledge will be expressed as the state of a morphological space, depicting actions of agents in a geometrical way. This expression of re-organization of MAS will be computed using a specific organization of agents, the morphological organization. Then, we could use the analysis of this morphology to modify in real-time the actions in MAS, realizing the self-adaptativity of the system on a systemic loop.

There is a rupture between the classical mechanics of the steady systems and the one of systems evolving far of the equilibrium. There is also a rupture between the classical software systems foreseen entirely and constructed to achieve some precise tasks, like with UML, and the unsteady software systems, adjusting to their environment and even to their own inner characters of working. There is a rupture between the ideal mechanics that produces things of use entirely mastered and the living systems, natural or artificial, that evolve in their length and for their account.

We present the general characters of the unsteady particulate systems, and massive multi-agent systems. We propose an incremental agentification method with self-learning, and we develop a means to have control of the system, but by itself, in the behavior of its internal organization of agents, by the definition of a morphological space of which we specify characters and the agent interpretation at a time.

2   Particulate Systems and No-Predictability of the Behavior

The first example of a system with a complex behavior will be chosen in physics. Let's consider an enclosed system formed of a large number of particles. Every particle is a certain ideal elementary material entity. It is, in the setting of the classic mechanics, entirely definite by its position p and its moment q = mV product of its mass by its speed. The knowledge of the particle comes down to those of position and moment therefore. Equations of the movement, that are the equations of Newton, give as solution the position and the moment of a particle from its initial conditions, taking into account force to which is submitted the particle. The core notion, in classic mechanics, is the one of trajectory that defines the exact situation of all material particles during all the time.

In the equations of calculation of the trajectory, the variable expressing time plays a reversible role. We can foresee the position and the moment of the particle thus to all ulterior and previous instants of the time, while changing t into - t. We can determine the state and the place where are the particles at each instant of the future or of the past therefore. We characterize a particulate system in which the behavior of its particles is given by equations in which the time is reversible, a *deterministic* system.

With this approach of particulate systems based on the determination of trajectories, one goes in fact to interest to states that will be especially steady: the so-called *equilibrium* states where characters of the system don't change even though some particles are in movement. For such a system, an equilibrium state is a state that is necessarily reached while leaving from initial conditions valued in a certain domain: if the initial conditions change a little in this domain, it is always this same equilibrium state that will be reached. This equilibrium state will be therefore meaningful of the system. This case is in fact ideal and doesn't seem to correspond to the situation of the living systems and not for all of the particulate ones.

In fact, when the system is composed of particles in permanent interactions, it is impossible to determine its global behavior from the only trajectories of the particles. In this case, that to be-to-say whose movements are correlated, H. Poincaré showed [Poincaré 1893] that the equations of the movement are not anymore integrable, that they cannot produce any solution. This result, clearly negative, was a long time ignored because it puts out a fundamental problem: it is impossible to based on the individual trajectory particle notion to describe the behavior of a system composed of numerous particles in permanent interactions (in fact more than two).

The systems composed of particles in permanent interactions are categorized as *unsteady* systems [Prigogine 1996]. It will remain then, to define and to predict the states of the system, a probabilistic description of the position of the particle in the space of phases, while using models with suitable operators. But the distinction between the deterministic behavior provided at the level of individual trajectories of particles and the global probabilistic behavior goes farther. Ilya Prigogine [Prigogine ref. mentioned] showed that for systems constituted of numerous particles in interaction, the probabilistic description produces states that the individual trajectory notion cannot provide. The probabilistic description, by its global character, contains additional information that the individual trajectory notion doesn't have. He has shown in fact that there is not anymore, for the unsteady systems, equivalence between the two descriptions, the individual based on trajectories and the global based on probabilities. Only the probabilistic description permits to represent the non-deterministic characters of the behavior of such an unsteady system.

In the object systems, any object can be discerned like a multi-facet particle whose trajectory is completely defined: its behavior is fixed once and for all the time. The behavior of the system is then easily expressible: it is given by the whole of behaviors of all the objects that we can consider one by one. And we clarify this behavior in advance, in the famous diagrams of classes, of spreading and of dynamic of the UML method [Muller 1997].

3   Design of Massive Multi-agent Systems, No-Determinism and Control Problem

Nowadays one takes an interest for systems that have not a strictly regular behavior, that must develop original actions or even creative' ones. The perspectives asked by the Situated Artificial Intelligence [Steels & al. 1995] and the New Artificial Intelligence [Meyer 1996] are not anymore those definite for the regular and steady systems, whose behavior is specified in a definitive manner into the step of design. Such systems are not some clever solvers for a well-set problem class: they are systems that must adjust to very varied environments, thanks to their capacities of structural modifications and theirs multiple actions. These capacities of modifications and actions will result from the self-promoter faculty of their plastic internal structure.

This means that the organization of their components is competent of deep enough re-structuring and that the system works like rather an operational closure of autopoïetic system [Varela 1989]. Indeed, the organization of the system components cannot be steady or regular and the research of permanent links definitely fixed will be only very local and temporary. The structure of components will be only generative for the behavior of the system and, besides, the system will be a few more that the sum of its definite components stated in the step of construction.

We will set up the architecture of these systems with the agent's paradigm and this in a strictly multi-agent point of view. There is, in Computer Science, one way to define weak agents [Wooldridge & Jennings 1994]. That is the case where agents are like software or material entities that are:

- autonomous,
- with some social faculties,
- reactive and pro-active, to be-to-say that is capable to redefine its goals and to take initiatives without any external solicitation.

The general agent's structure will be expressed with four parts more or less developed according to the specificity of the agent [C.f. Fig. 1]:

- a module for knowledge,
- a module for communication,
- a module for behavior,
- a module for action.

A multi-agent system (MAS) is constituted of a set of agent organizations and is situated in an environment composed of many objects that are not agents that are essentially reactive in a permanent way. This system communicates with its environment by the action of specific agents so-called the interfacing agents. The agents of the

MAS use objects of their world as well as actions of the other agents achieve some various actions and unite their actions to define some collective behaviors.

We have specified an incremental method of construction for a massive multi-agent organization [Cardon - Vacher 2001]. Every agent will be considered like a simple enough software entity, that to be-to-say it will be a weak agent that communicates with others and whose behavior takes into account the result of these communications. It is therefore a system whose behavior is based on the variable interactions between its agents.

We will choose granularity at a time finer with regard to functionalities, and typically plurivoc, that to be-to-say based on the redundancy and the plurality of characters. We set that the system will have its functionalities distributed in no steady and no consistent agents: at every precise functionality we will associate groups of agents whose cooperative actions should permit to achieve the concerned function, but also its opposite, inverse, contrary, near and similar functions.... This agentification process leads to a certain redundancy and large diversity with regard to faculties of agents. That will be necessary to permit a complex behavior in an organizational way and also to make operate the system strictly by emergence. Groups of agents won't be in anything functional but rather versatile, ambiguous and they will be able to make groups emerging using communications between them, in reifying certain functions rather than others.

Such a multi-agent system is seen therefore like a collective of agents that has social characters of aggregation and regrouping, and a very strong restructuring capability. One will be able to distinguish two parts in the system:

1. one part composed of interfacing agents, communicating with the environment, taking in charge the information coming from the outside and also managing actions on the environment,
2. another internal part with agents taking information from objects of their world and of the interfacing agents, acting and exchanging messages between them.

These two organizations are necessarily strongly interactive and the global organization, by communication between agents, have integrating processes permitting the cooperation and the meaningful emergence of groups.

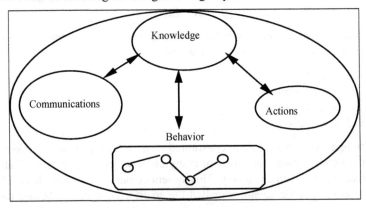

Fig. 1. The general structure of an agent

We claim that a MMAS won't have a deterministic behavior. For each stimulus coming from the environment, agents will be activated while filtering it. Because the agents are constructed using a plurivoc manner, similar, nearly similar and opposite agents ... will be activated for this input. And these agents transitively will activate some others, by their communications according to the acquaintances.

Each of these agents is pro-active, it is a process or at least a thread. All these processes will have the same priority to be processed or a priority distributing in few groups of priorities. The scheduler of the system won't be able to sort these processes and should choose randomly one that will be activated (in the case of a mono-processor computer). The access to the shared variables, in the case of competitor's process on a distributed system, will undergo the exclusion in critical section, what will lead to satisfy some process randomly taken rather than others, that finally goes to activate some agents before some others.

However, the activations of the agents are not commutative. These activations are contextual and, for each agent, the activation depends of previous activation of its acquaintance agents. We will obtain a running of the system, steps by steps of execution of processes that won't be reversible to the computing sense of the term. The functioning pulls at random for certain options of treatment, like the choice of processes or accesses to the shared variables, that will generate the global state of the system undergo with bifurcations. Some states of the agent organization, and while solving the problem of the dead-lock of activations and communications, will be very different and depend on whether a sequence of action between agents will be operated before or after the activity of a some agent.

One will also note that for certain *stimuli* very close by at the signification of information they express, the behaviors of the system, after a certain number of steps of work, will be very different: some close by inputs produce distant states therefore. The working of such a system is then no deterministic and sensitive to the initial conditions: it is therefore about an unsteady system. We will propose a means to reduce this instability, while produce the system as self-adaptive, by analogy with the living systems.

4   Self-Control on a Massive Multi-agent System: Notion of Morphology

We now need to determine the behavioral characters of a massive agent organization. The problem will be solvable at the computable level because weak agents are simple active software entities. It will be possible, at the conceptual level and at the implementing level, to follow-up agent's organizations in progress by means of evaluation of the meaning of the activations. Let's note that it is impossible to achieve such an observation for particulate systems without change them.

We are going to represent the behavior of a set of agents, in a way independent of the problems the organization solves and therefore without usage of the semantic of the system. This semantic will be added to this representation, to increase it thereafter.

We consider a form as an element of R^n provided of a metric. A dynamic space is the product of a topological metric space by the time, supplying transitions between current state and the next states. Let's notice that weak agents are considered like some simple rational entities: it is possible to associate at each of them a precise notion of state.

4.1   The Morphological Space, the Correspondent of the Space of Phase in MMAS

We can define first the concept of state of any agent:

Definition of the State of a Weak Agent

- *A weak agent's state is the meaningful characters that permit to entirely describe its current situation in its organization at every instant, this state being an element of R^n.*

We wish to express each of these characters with an element of R. That is possible because a weak agent is rational and deterministic. Thus, an agent's state will be expressed as a point of R^n if there are n characters that define it. The problem is to determine these characters independently of its semantics.

Definition of an Activity Map [Lesage 2000]

- *The activity map of an agent organization is a representation of the temporal evolution of the significant characters of every agent's state.*

If we want to represent an activity map by geometric forms evolving in the time, we need to represent every agent by a vector. Let's look for what are the meaningful characters of every agent's behavior. Let's notice that an object doesn't have such characters, because it is permanent and doesn't undergo some structural evolution: at most we can define for it the number of time each of its methods has been triggered.

The agent's intrinsic characters will be defined from the three following categories:

- the appearance of the agent from its outside, that is for the other agents. This category characterizes the agent's situation in relation to its environment,
- the agent's internal appearance facing of the reach of its goals. It is about its state in relation to goals it must reach again, the relation to functions that it must necessarily assure,
- the agent's state at the level of its own working, that is its internal dynamic. This is the measure of the quality of its organization and the variation of this one along the time.

We go, while taking account of these three categories, to propose ten dimensions for the agent space of representation.

1 - The agent's first category is its ***external appearance*** for its immediate environment, that to be-to-say its actor's own situation in relation to its acquaintances and its environment. One keeps notions of:

- **Supremacy**: it is the measure of the fact the agent is either located in position by force for agents recognized by its acquaintances, that it has or no many allies and that its enemies are or no powerful,
- **Independence**: it is the measure of the agent's autonomy in its actions, specifying if it is necessary or not to find allies to reach its goals, if its actions are submitted in relation to actions of other agents, if its knowledge structure is included or not in those of some other agents,
- **Persistence**: it is the measure of the agent's longevity, of its life that can be possibly very brief or strong long.

2 - The second category is its **internal aspect** that is its structural state in relation to its assigned functions. One keeps notions of:

- **Easiness**: it is the measure of the fact the agent reached its current state with difficulties, with more or less resistances. For example, if its behavior is represented by an ATN, this character measures the easiness of transition clearing, the rear returns. This indication specifies also the support, or the resistance, met by agent from other agents to reach its goals,
- **Speed**: it is the speed taken by the agent to reach its goals that it fixes itself either that are given at construction. It is for example the speed of get over the states of its behavioral automaton when the agent possesses one.

3 - The third character concerns its organizational internal states, that is its own functioning understood like a process of information exchange between its modules and that forms its structure. One keeps the following notions:

- **Intensity of the Internal Activation Flux**: it is the measure of the quantity of information exchanged between its intern components permitting it to lead to a visible activation from the outside in groups to which it belongs,
- **Complexification**: it is the measure of its structural transformation generated by certain dysfunction or certain difficult situations, and having required to transform some elements of its structure. This measure determines its structural evolution, so is a simplification or a complexification,
- **Communicating Frequency**: it is the measure, out of the semantic, of communicational relations between the agent and the others, representative in fact of a measure of its linkage in the organization,
- **Organizational Gap**: it is an assessment taking in account the operationality of the agent's structure that permitted it to achieve some social actions leading to put itself an appreciation of the distance between its own state and the global state of the environment (there is not a supervisor in the system!). It is the appreciation of the adequacy of its "put in situation" in its world. This character is fundamental and precise the relation between the agent, understood like an autonomous entity, and the organization, composed of all agents, that is between each part of the organization and the whole.

External aspect	Supremacy
of the agent	Independence
	Persistence
Internal aspect	Easiness
of the agent	Velocity
Organizational	Intensity of the internal flux
State of the agent	Complexification
	Communicating frequency
	Organizational gap
Opening of the system	Transport of information

Fig. 2. The ten characters of behavioral aspect of an agent

Each of these nine characters can be represented by a measure in R, or by a suitable function. It is necessary to consider that the multi-agent system, as we already noted it, is immersed in its environment: it is in continuous communication with its environment. It exchanges information therefore with this one and interface agents achieve this action. We must have to add a typical character therefore because the system is **opened** in its environment, while importing and exporting information. We will define a character measuring the intensity of this transport of information, that represents the quantity and the ***transport of information*** exchanged with the environment thus. Note that agents of interfacings assure this measure that appears situated at the level of the system itself, normally, but these agents evidently communicate with the others about this external information. The measure specifies all agents' implications therefore in the environment of the system.

These ten characters, grouped in three general categories, can be represented in R^{10} and permit to associate to every agent what one will call its ***aspect vector*** thus. The agent's structure will be increased, merely, to be able to produce, at each moment, these ten indications, which are only numerical.

Definition of a Morphological Space

- *It is the sub-space of R^{10} presenting in a vector the characters of activity of each agent, according to notions of supremacy, independence, persistence, easiness, velocity, intensity of the internal flux, complexification, communicational frequency, organizational gap and transport of information.*

This means that an agent for whom these ten fundamental characters are given has behavior perfectly defined in its environment, in the organization, that to be-to-say in the domain of application where it is operational. We will interest to the form of the cloud of points representing behavioral state of agents thus, as well as to the distortion of this form. On the other hand, the number of agents varies during the working and it is desirable to preserve a permanent dimension in the space of representation.

It is now possible to specify the notion of representation of an agent organization: the notion of landscape of agents.

Definition of the Landscape of Agents

- *A landscape of agents is a geometric expression of an activity map.*

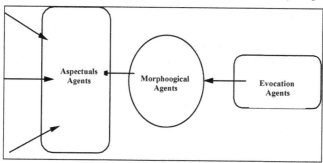

Fig. 3. The three agent organizations

This representation leans on the essentially geometric characters of the cloud of points. It will be in fact achieved by a specific agent organization. The geometric elements that we are going to consider are elements of the dynamic system $R^{10} \times T$ [Thom 1972] that measure the behaviors of agents and groups of agent, for a while. The conformation of a form of this space can be represented by a polyhedron. We can express the fact that this form has, for example, prominent parts, ravines or trays, lengthening or dense parts, discontinuities that permits to represent the behaviors, the manner of which the agent activities have produced the behavior of the system, enough faithfully. We go to use, to describe these concepts, some particular agents we call the ***morphological agents***.

4.2   The Organization of Morphological Agents Assuring the Representation of the Aspectual Organization

We are going to manipulate two organizations of agents therefore: one organization of agents that defines, by their actions in group, the functionalities of the system and another representing the activation of this organization in terms of the morphological space. We will call the first organization the ***aspectual organization,*** with aspectual agents that give the aspects of functionalities and operationality of the system, and the second the ***morphological organization*** with morphological agents that expresses the behavior of the first organization in a geometrical way [C.f. Fig 3].

Definition of the Reified Morphological Space

- *The reification of the morphological space corresponds to the definition of a specific agent organization that dynamically expresses with agents the characters of the morphological space: that is the reified morphological space.*

We need to represent the characters of the aspectual agents activation with an organization of agents rather than operate with the set of points of the morphological space, for the two following reasons:

1. the notion of point, or of pinpoint particle, in the morphological space is not adapted to the characters of our survey. It is another category than agent's concept that stands typically in an equation setting. We don't try here to produce an operator for the change of state of the agent organization but we want follow in real time the changes of this organization, and at the computable level. We prefer therefore the notion of dynamic attraction basins, changing in the time, in which the same attraction basin absorbs close by agents like groups absorb lonesome agents, and this while the system is running. Thus, the morphological space will be formed of organizations of agents reifying basins of attraction and expressing, according to their depth and to the variation of this depth, the aspectual agent density in the considered region of the morphological space.

2. the geometric indications appearing in the morphological space will have to be used immediately, to react with the aspectual agents, and only an organization of agents can interact well with another. We wish in fact to strongly link the aspectual agents and those representing theirs characters, the morphological agents, to give the system as a self-controllable one.

A morphological agent will have for function to represent, according to its type and role, the local activations and the modification of activations of the aspectual agents, according to the ten characters of the morphological space [C.f. Fig 4].

Morphological agents, whose structure is simple [Cardon - Durand 1997], are going to achieve "in-line" a behavioral analysis of the aspectual agent organization. They operate according to theirs strictly rational goals, tempt to clear typical forms from the set of characters expressed by the aspectual agent landscape, while assembling in groups that is while constituting *chreods* [Cardon 2000]. A chreod is a structured and meaningful aggregation of morphological agents. This is a heap made of close by morphological agents, for a certain metrics on the morphological agent space, valued by an internal measure to the agent while appraising proximity with its acquaintances.

Chreod is a reified emergence in the set of morphological agents (that is a set of groups of potential wells each holding aspectual agents). These sets endowed of geometric signification (density, form, development) on morphological agents. They are represented by particular polyhedrons of which topological forms have an applicable significance to represent the way whose aspectual agents group themselves, according to their behavior. The landscape of morphological agents (a landscape on a landscape!) admits different readings that will be done by a third agent organization: the evocation agents.

4.3   Evocation Agents and Self-Adaptativity of the System

The system in its whole, in the communicational movement of its agents, is going to draw, in the morphological organization, some chreods from the aspectual activations. The analysis of the morphology of the aspectual agent landscape, and particularly of the chreods, produces an active picture of the organization to every instant providing its organizational state. It is well about producing characters precisely defining the state of the system, like an operator as the one of Liouville provides the state of a particulate system at every instant of the time. The knowledge of this state permits to say for what way the system goes, what is effectively its global evolutionary action.

But this knowledge is not direct; agents can't be analyzed one by one. It is no more statistical but, in our way, it is a geometric and global analyze, done in real time, during the working of the aspectual organization.

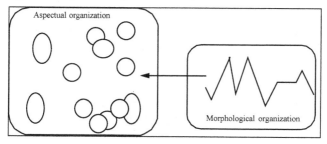

Fig. 4. Morphological agents producing a representation of the aspectual organization

A third agent organization, after aspectual and morphological ones, is going to take in consideration the state of the landscape of morphological agents, to achieve an analysis of the morphology of the system, interpreting chreods [C.f. Fig. 3]. It is about representing the meaning of the activation of the aspectual organization, from its characters of aspect expressed by morphological agents into chreods. This organization of agents, the *evocation agents*, is going to provide an interpretation of that has been expressed by the geometric and semantics information coming from the landscape of morphological agents. This organization operates above the aspectual agent landscape that detains the semantics of the actions.

Evocation agents have a similar structure to the aspectual ones but while being very cognitive. They are going to represent the significance of the activation of agent organizations, interpreting the activity of the aspectual agents of interfacing, the aspectual agent behavior and its analysis with the morphological agents.

And the organization of evocation agents is going to permit to make a lot more that this analysis, because the system is a computable one. It is going to permit to achieve a control of the aspectual agent organization, by the action of the evocation agents while using the morphological analysis. The system is going to be able to take account of the significance of its morphology in progress, to memorize it organizationally, that is to take account implicitly of it in its future activations, in its future commitments. The system can function like a *self-organizational memory.*

Evocation agents will be able to act thus on the global aspectual activation consistency. They will be able to make choices and to take decisions for the global behavior of the aspectual and morphological organizations. They will be able to take account of past actions, of the tendencies of aspectual agents, while keeping strategies of inhibition of action for certain aspectual or morphological agents of interfacing, controlling so the general line of organizational emergence achieved in the system. Let's notice that these strategic actions will be indirect in relation to every agent's behavior, permitting to constitute a system with emergence of organizational meaning, with intrinsic characters of no-stability and learning by regular structural distortion [Cardon 2000]. The systemic loop is now curled and the system controls itself by self-adaptativity.

Definition of a Self-Adaptive System

- *A self-adaptive system is a system composed of three organizations of elements: a first plastic organization of pro-active elements that generates the elementary functionalities, a second organization that expresses the geometric characters of the re-organizational actions of the previous one, and a third organization that values the behavior and semantics of the first one using the second and that can, from this analysis, influences the behavior of the first organization continuously.*

It is clear that all the living organisms can be represented according to this characterization, the last two organizations doing the self-control and the regulation of behaviors done in the first. It is also well obvious that only some massive agent organizations are adequate to the computable representation of such systems.

Finally, the action of evocation agents, by the fact that they tamper the active aspectual agents, achieve to each instant in a continuous way, some control and a kind of memorization of the behavior of the system. This looped action permits to control of the stability of the system, to advise it in a loop without end for production of states compliant to its capacities of reorganization and adequate to its "setting in situation" in its environment. The running of the system amounts to a continuous succession of self-controlled emergent states. For the system, the complexity of the interfacing and aspectual agents drags the complexity of all other organizations of agents. The system can generate an elementary organizational emergence thus: the organizational significance of the prominent form exhibited. It can also generate a very fine emergence: for example the emergence of sentences from intentions expressing linguistic tendencies [Lesage 2000].

5   Realizations

We have developed a system involving MMAS in the domain of Crisis Management, in two Ph.D. thesis [Durand 1999], [Lesage 2000]. The system allows the communications between actors and realizes the interpretation of the messages. It is coded in Distributed Smalltalk^{TM}. In this system, each actor has a message window with a communicating box. The actors may send or receive different kinds of messages. When an actor communicates he or she may express his or her different opinions on the message to other actors. The opinions encompass the message and are represented by several agents in a MMAS of so-called aspectual agents linked to the site of the local actor and expressing the semantic traits of the messages. The same operation of generation of aspectual agents is realized on the receiver but under the local conditions. A morphological MMAS expresses the significant traits of the messages and a MAS of evocation agents finally determines the interpretation of the messages.

6   Conclusion

The massive multi-agent systems are presented like unsteady software systems whose behavior develops some emergent characters. These systems have evolution; they are made to learn and to adjust themselves to the situation on the environment. Their design is not an usual way producing all the specifications and a strong a priori validation. They are systems functioning with a behavior oriented in the time and following their continuous development.

Reasons of the reorganization, in such systems, use laws of the non-equilibrium of aspectual agent organizations and are achieved by the habits acquired by the system to function as it ordinarily functions. The same working tampers agents, creates some of new by cloning or by reproduction. But tendencies draw themselves that are lines of habit of the behavior of agent organizations, according to the control operated by evocation agents on the aspectual organization and all that lead the system to generate such a peculiar state rather than another one. Thus, the system has implicit intentions to enter into certain ways of emergence. Such a system is an organizational memory that operates by continuous implicit learning while self-controlling its re-organizations. It is self-adaptive by nature, not being able to be otherwise.

The number of agents is not stationary, agents are not steady, communications between them are variable, the working is at a time appreciable to the initial conditions and no deterministic. Such a system, of which the behavior is oriented in the time, learns and evolves by the fact of its self re-organization. This is not anymore a system understood and conceived in a finish fashion and delivered for a technical use at the benefit of the users: it is, in the software domain, an artifact of a real living system. It is now applied for the representation of artificial sensations in autonomous robots.

References

[Cardon - Durand 1997] Cardon A., Durand S., *A Model of Crisis Management System Including Mental Representations*, AAAI Spring Symposium, Stanford University, California, USA, march 23-26, 1997.

[Cardon - Lesage 1998] Cardon, A., Lesage F.,Toward adaptive information systems: considering concern and intentionality, Procc; KAW'98, Banff, Canada.

[Cardon - Vacher 2000] Cardon A. , Vacher J.P., Galinho T., *Genetic Algorithm using Multi-Objective in a Multi-Agent System*, Robotic and Autonomous Systems, 33 (2-3) (2000) p. 179 - 190, Elsevier, 2000.

[Cardon 1999]   Cardon A., *Conscience artificielle et systèmes adaptatifs*, Eyrolles, Paris, 1999.

[Durand 1999]   Durand S., Représentation de points de vue multiples dans la couche communicationnelle d'un Système d'Information et de Communication, Thèse d'Université, Université du Havre, décembre 1999.

[Kieras - Polson 1985] Kieras, D., Polson P.G., *An approach to the formal analysis of user complexity*, 22, p. 365-394, Int. J. of Man-Machine Studies.

[Lenat & al. 1990]   Lenat D., Guha R.V., Building Large Knowledge-Based Systems, Representation and Inference in the Cyc Project. Addison Wesley Publishing Co. , 1990.

[Lesage 2000]   Lesage F., Interprétation adaptative du discours dans une situation multiparticipants : modélisation par agents. Thèse de l'Université du Havre, Décembre 2000.

[Meyer 1996]   Meyer J.-A., *Artificial Life and the Animat Approach to Artificial Intelligence*, in Boden (Ed.), Artificial Intelligence, Academic Press, 1996.

[Muller 1997]   Muller P.A., *Modélisation objet avec UML*, Eyrolles Paris, 1997.

[Poincaré 1893]   Poincaré H., *Les méthodes nouvelles de la mécanique céleste*, Gauthier Villars Paris, 1893.

[Prigogine 19996]   Prigogine I., *La fin des certitudes*, Ed. Odile Jacob Paris, 1996.

[Steels & al. 1995]   Steels L., Brooks R., The Artificial Life Route to Artificial Intelligence, Building Embodied Situated Agents, Lawrence Arlbaum Associates, 1995.

[Thom 1972]   Thom R., *Stabilité structurelle et morphogénèse*, W. A. Benjamin, INC, Reading, Massachusetts, USA, 1972.

[Varela 1989]   Varela F., *Autonomie et connaissance, Essai sur le vivant*, Seuil, Paris, 1989.

[Wooldridge - Jennings 1994] Wooldridge M., Jennings N.R., *Agent Theories, Architectures and Languages: a Survey*; Lectures Notes in A.I., 890, Springer Verlag.

Developing Agents Populations
with Ethogenetics

Samuel Landau and Sébastien Picault

LIP6, Université Pierre & Marie Curie
4 place Jussieu, 75252 Paris Cedex 05, FRANCE
{Samuel.Landau,Sebastien.Picault}@lip6.fr
http://miriad.lip6.fr/atnosferes

Abstract. This paper proposes the use of developmental and evolutionary metaphors to automatically design organization in adaptive multi-agent systems. We propose therefore a novel evolutionary approach to design agent behaviors in situated MAS, called "Ethogenetics". We also describe ATNoSFERES, a framework implementing the concepts of Ethogenetics and discuss its specific properties.

Keywords: Adaptive multi-agent systems, Ethogenetics, Development, Evolution, Artificial life.

1 Introduction

The design of a Multi-Agent System (MAS) is often driven by specifications regarding both the collective task the agents have to achieve (i.e. the *function* of the system) and their social organization (i.e. constraints and dependencies among the behaviors and abilities of the agents).

In some applications of MAS (such as social simulation [18, 17, 5, 8]), the simulation or reproduction of a given organization pattern is a finality of the system. But, in other cases, the relevance of explicitly designing organization in MAS might be more controversial. To be fully adaptive, a MAS has indeed to deal with physical or social environmental changes that can force it to modify its own organization. The corresponding process in human cognition is known as "epigenesis" (Piaget, Vygotsky).

Thus a prior design of the organization of a system should take into account all possible reorganizations due to adaptations to the environment – which becomes quite impossible in massive MAS [3] or "real-world" applications (e.g. collective robotics in open environments [19]).

The use of multi-agent machine learning (ML) techniques [24] is not always of a sufficient help in that way, since most of them are concerned in setting parameters in *fixed* agent behaviors. The complexity of these behaviors is a constitutive part of the model: the behaviors can be *fine-tuned* through more or less sophisticated techniques, but they cannot *change* during the system lifecycle. Furthermore, multi-agent ML techniques raise difficult issues related to the very

W. Truszkowski, C. Rouff, M. Hinchey (Eds.): WRAC 2002, LNAI 2564, pp. 61-70, 2003.

distribution of the collective tasks in MAS (e.g. problems linked with credit assignment).

In addition to this, there is no indication that prior organizational features would produce adequate behaviors (in terms of functionalities) in a given situation. There is no necessary relationship between specified collective functions and a prior designed organization assumed to produce them.

Therefore, we propose in section 2 to address the issue of organization in MAS through developmental and evolutionary metaphors. We then propose (§ 3) a set of principles that are required to make agents behavior really evolve in a situated system (called "Ethogenetics"). As an illustration of that, we describe in section 4 a model that implements those principles. We finally discuss the properties of such a model and its possible applications, and sum up its results.

2   Development as a Support for MAS Adaptivity

To our point of view, the explicit design of an organization introduces a strong bias between the collective behavior of the system and its adequation to a given environment. It is all the more the case since the system might have to re-organize itself in order to maintain its adaptation towards the collective task or an environment. In such a situation the organization cannot be addressed as a preexistent feature of the system, but rather as a permanent process [2]. Thus, we prefer to consider organization as an emergent property, that reflects *the equilibrium in an ecosystem* (coordination, cooperation between behaviors, competition for resources...).

Thus we emphasize the double metaphor underlying an adapative MAS:

- As a whole, the system can be described as a single *organism* (an entity with an internal organization) that exhibits a *behavior*. The progressive and permanent adaptation of such an organism to its environment is the result of and ontogenetic (developmental) process.
- As an *ecosystem*, the MAS relies on the behaviors of its agents. These agents have to adapt to their environment but also one to each other. This can be seen as the result of a phylogenetic (evolutionary) process.

The issue of obtaining a given collective behavior in a MAS mainly relies upon the first metaphor. But, due to the difficulties raised by the distribution among agents, it seems easier to work on the second metaphor.

According to that perspective, the natural selection paradigm might provide a convenient approach, provided that agent behaviors are able to *evolve*. The general principle of Evolutionary Algorithms involves the following steps:

1. *individuals* representing potential solutions for the problem are built *from a hereditary substratum* (the *genotype*)
2. these individuals belong to a population
3. their adequation to the problem is evaluated (either explicitly through a fitness function, or implicitly through survival criteria for instance)

4. some of them (mainly the most adapted) are selected to produce offspring (by mixing their genotypes) ; others are removed from the population
5. the process cycles with the new population.

The approach we propose consists in adapting this general paradigm to the evolution of multi-agent systems in place of individuals. A MAS exhibits indeed a collective behavior that is usually considered as the solution to a given problem.

Unfortunately, the existing evolutionary computing paradigms are inadequate for the evolution of true agents behaviors (a more detailed discussion will be found in [14]):

- On the one hand, Genetic Algorithms [9, 4, 6] and Evolutionary Strategies [21, 23] have a very poor expressive power, since their purpose is the optimization of a set of parameters [1] in behaviors which *have to be given a priori*. However, they allow fine-grain encoding, so that small variation in the *genotype* (the genetic substratum) generally induce small variations in the *phenotype* (the resulting behavior).
- On the other hand, the Genetic Programming paradigm [10], which is based on the evolution of *programs* (i.e. instruction trees), has a much higher expressive power. But in such a tree structure, genetic variations most of the time have a strong impact on behaviors (not only parameters, but also instructions are subject to modification), all of the more since the impact of variations tightly depends on the location in the tree hierarchy.

The "Ethogenetics" approach we propose tries to conciliate advantages of both paradigms.

3   The Ethogenetics Approach

In previous papers [20, 13], we have introduced the Ethogenetics approach. Ethogenetics is an attempt to combine the advantages of Genetic Algorithms and Genetic Programming (continuity and expressive behavioral power [20]). The Ethogenetics principles have been implemented in the ATNoSFERES model [15] (cf. § 4), and are under experimentation.

The purpose of "Ethogenetics" is to provide general principles for the design of evolutive agent behaviors – the ability to *build* agent behaviors (with a large expressive power) from a meaningless genetic substratum. Since Darwinian evolution is a blind process, its use to produce collective behaviors in MAS implies several properties, mainly consequences of two principles: continuity and expressive behavioral power.

3.1   Continuity

The environmental selection pressure acts on the whole system, on its ability to react, to perform a task, to reach collective goals and so on. Adapted individuals are selected to produce "offspring": other individuals, the genotype of which is a mixture of those of their "parents". The adaptation degree of the offspring systems should be close to their parents ones (if not, the adaptive effect of natural selection gets lost). Thus, the behavior building process has to be:

- *robust towards mutations*: small variations in the genotype should induce in most cases only small variations in the phenotype;
- *independent from the structure of the genetic substratum*: unlike Genetic Programming (where the hierarchical tree structure has heavy consequences), distant parts of the genotype should have few effects on each other. Thus it is useful to dissociate the semantic structure (that produces the behavior) from the "syntactic" one (the genetic substratum). When this requirement is not fulfilled, semantics tightly constrains syntax, so that syntactic manipulations (resulting from "blind" genetic operations) often destroys the semantic structure.

3.2   Expressive behavioral power

The second major requirement in order to produce *agent behaviors* is the ability to design *complex* behaviors. Thus the semantic structure used for that goal should have at least the expressive power of a program tree (a tree provides more interesting features as a semantic structure rather than as a syntactic structure). But these behaviors, even if complex, should meet some requirements:

- *Behaviors should be understandable.* It may be useful to provide the agents with *understandable behaviors*: some control architectures such as artificial neural networks might be very efficient, but the resulting behavior cannot be clearly described. The ability to easily interpret the behaviors would allow on the one hand to understand *what* has been selected, and on the other hand, to explicitly specify some of the behaviors using this same structure, allowing to set *a priori* the behaviors of some agents.
- *Behaviors should be able to adapt.* Since the system will have to operate in a given environment, it should be able to adapt itself, to reconfigure according to environmental constraints. Thus the semantic structure representing behaviors should avoid using explicit parameters: parameters are a kind of shortcut, they reflect prior knowledge about the environment. The building of *situated behaviors* has to be independent from any parameters, in order to keep more flexibility.

In the next section, we present ATNoSFERES, a framework aimed at implementing a concrete agent model featuring the properties required by Ethogenetics.

4   The ATNoSFERES model

4.1   General principles

The principles of Ethogenetics are currently implemented in a multi-agent framework, ATNoSFERES [15, 20, 13]. It is part of the SFERES framework [11] which provides tools for modelling the agents classes, integrating them to the system, designing an environmental simulator and providing classical evolutionary techniques.

The main feature of the ATNoSFERES model consists in using an ATN[1] [25]. ATN have already been used for designing agent behaviors [7]. In an ATN, edges linking the states or nodes can be labelled with a set of *conditions* and a sequence of *actions*. Thus it is particularly adequate to describe the behavior of an agent.

ATNoSFERES provides a general class, the ATNAgent, which is intended to behave according to an ATN graph. Each subclass of ATNAgent is associated with two collections of tokens: condition ones and action ones. The actions are behavioral "primitives" that can be performed by the agent, the conditions are perceptions or stimuli that induce action selection. Those action and condition tokens are used to label the edges of the graph (see figure 1).

A structure such as an ATN graph would not fulfil the *continuity* requirement if it had to evolve through a blind, darwinian, process. Thus, it has to be *built* from a finer-grain substratum, e.g. a bitstring. Therefore, we use the following steps:

1. The population (initial population or offspring of adapted individuals), is composed of agents having their own bitstring (the genotype or hereditary substratum).
2. For each agent:
   (a) a *translator* produces *tokens* from the bitstring,
   (b) an *interpreter* uses these tokens as instructions and data to *build a graph* (the ATN),
   (c) finally, the graph is used as a state machine to produce the behavior of the agent.
3. The agents behave in their environment, according to their own ATN.
4. The agents are selected and reproduced according to their capabilities in surviving in their environment or performing a specified task. They produce offspring and the process cycles with the new population.

The translator and the interpreter themselves are agents; in the following lines, we will consider that their behavior is given and will not change in time, but it could evolve as well to provide the system with higher autonomy.

We will now detail the above steps, starting with the behavior of the agent and going back to the translation process.

4.2 The ATN Graph and the ATNAgent

The ATN is built by an interpreter (see § 4.3) by adding nodes and edges to a basic structure containing two nodes: a "Start" node and an "End" node. Once the ATN has been built, it can be used *as an automaton* to produce the behavior of the agent during its life cycle. At each time step, the agent (initially in the "Start" state) randomly chooses an edge among those having either *no*

---

[1] ATN stands for "Augmented Transition Network".

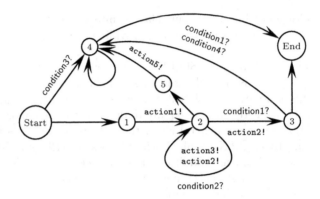

Fig. 1. An example of ATN

condition in their label, or *all conditions simultaneously true*. It performs the actions associated with this edge and jumps to the destination node. At the following time step, the process iterates from the new state. The agent stops working when its state is "End".

We emphasize that this approach is different from classical evolutionary methods for producing adaptive behavior (Genetic Programming for instance) since in the latter, the structure used to determine the behavior is used *as a whole* at each timestep (for instance, the tree is executed again at each time step to select actions).

4.3   The Interpreter

The purpose of the interpreter is to build an ATN from tokens. Some of these tokens will be action or condition ones that are used to label edges between nodes in the ATN. The other ones are interpreted as instructions, either to create nodes or connect them, or to manipulate the structure under construction.

As we mentioned in section 3, the structure built by the tokens sequence has to be robust towards mutations. For instance, the replacement of one token by another, or its deletion, should have only a *local impact*, rather than transforming the whole graph. Therefore, we use a "stack-based" programming language, the specific properties of which are discussed in detail in [14] (see table 1).

If an instruction cannot execute successfully, it is simply ignored, except instructions operating on nodes (i.e. *connect* and *dupObject*) which are "pushed" in the list until new nodes are produced; then they try to execute again with the new data. Finally, when the interpreter does not receive tokens any more, it terminates the ATN: actions and conditions tokens still present between nodes are treated as *implicit connections* (so that new edges are created) and the consistency of the ATN is checked ("Start" is linked to nodes having no incoming edges, except from themselves; in the same way, nodes having no outgoing edges are linked to "End").

token	(initial list state)	$\longrightarrow$	(resulting list)
dup	$(x\ y\ ...)$	$\longrightarrow$	$(x\ x\ y\ ...)$
del	$(x\ y\ ...)$	$\longrightarrow$	$(y\ ...)$
dupNode	$(x\ y\ N_i\ z\ ...)$	$\longrightarrow$	$(N_i\ x\ y\ N_i\ z\ ...)$
delNode	$(x\ N_i\ y\ N_i\ z\ ...)$	$\longrightarrow$	$(x\ y\ N_i\ z\ ...)$
popRoll	$(x\ y\ ...\ z)$	$\longrightarrow$	$(y\ ...\ z\ x)$
pushRoll	$(x\ ...\ y\ z)$	$\longrightarrow$	$(z\ x\ ...\ y)$
swap	$(x\ y\ ...)$	$\longrightarrow$	$(y\ x\ ...)$
node	$(x\ ...)$	$\longrightarrow$	$(N_i\ x\ ...)^a$
startNode	$(x\ ...)$	$\longrightarrow$	$(N_i\ x\ ...)^b$
endNode	$(x\ ...)$	$\longrightarrow$	$(N_i\ x\ ...)^c$
connect (c1? c2? $x\ N_i\ y$ c1? z a2! a1! $t\ N_j\ u\ ...$)		$\longrightarrow$	$(x\ N_i\ y\ z\ t\ N_j\ u\ ...)^d$
condition?	$(x\ ...)$	$\longrightarrow$	(condition? $x\ ...$)
action!	$(x\ ...)$	$\longrightarrow$	(action! $x\ ...$)

Table 1. The ATN-building language.

---

[a] creates a node N_i

[b] creates a node N_i and connects "Start" to it

[c] creates a node N_i and connects it to "End"

[d] creates an edge between N_j and N_i, with (c1?& c2?) as condition label and the list {a1!,a2!} as action label

4.4   The Translator

The translator has a very simple behavior. It reads the genotype (a string of bits) and decodes it into a sequence of tokens. It uses a *genetic code*, i.e. a function

$$\mathcal{G} : \{0,1\}^n \longrightarrow \mathcal{T} \quad (|\mathcal{T}| \leq 2^n)$$

where $\mathcal{T}$ is a set of tokens, which includes both action and condition ones (specific to the agent to build) and those understood by the interpreter (see table 1).

Depending on the number of tokens available, the genetic code might be more or less redundant. If necessary, it can be designed in order to resist mutations, but we will not discuss this issue in this paper.

4.5   Features of the **ATNoSFERES** Model

Evolutionary computation considerations. As an evolutive approach, the ATNoSFERES model provides three main features.

First, it separates the genetic information structure (plain bit string, the lexical structure) from its interpretation (ATN, the semantic structure). Thus, thanks to the interpreter language, the semantic structure that is built is *always correct*. The behavior described by the ATN always has a meaning – even if it is not adequate.

The second main evolutive feature is related to the genetic operators. The level of influence of the classical genetic operators – mutation and crossover –

does not depend on the parts of the bitstring they involve (neither on their location in the bitstring nor on their size). This is also a main advantage over many evolutive approaches. As a matter of fact, mutations only have a local impact in the expression of the genetic information, and crossovers involve bit substrings which carry locally functional genetic code. We might also consider more exotic genetic operators, such as deletions/insertions in the bitstring. These operators in particular permit to smoothly manage string resizing, since they only have a local impact in the ATNoSFERES model.

The third feature is that the model does not use any parameter to build behaviors. The behaviors execution only depends on environmental conditions, thus hard-coded genetic parameters are not even needed. Apart from behaviors design, parameters encoding is a problem in many evolutive approaches, (see for example discussion on epistasis in [22]), but as long as building behaviors is concerned, we think it should be considered not to rely on fixed parameters in order to produce situated, adaptive behaviors.

MAS design considerations. As a model for designing multi-agent systems, the ATNoSFERES model does not set any restriction neither on the agent level specification nor on the choice of the agents. The granularity of the system modelisation is free ; furthermore, agents can be introduced later on at a lower organization level (for instance inside an agent), keeping the latter structure, if a finer-grain agent specification is needed.

In order to cope with these different levels of specification, we are now introducing a CompositeAgent in the framework, in order to allow encapsulation of agents at one level by other agents at a higher level.

If the designer has prior knowledge about the system structure, he can specify and fix some agents behaviors, and use them as a constraint to drive the evolution of the system organization. On the other hand, the only specification that must be given for the evolving agents of the system is their sets of actions and perceptions, and consequently the micro-environment in which they operate. Not only can this micro-environment be a part of the system environment, but it can also for instance be the inside of an upper-level agent.

Agents behaviors design considerations. As a model for automatic behavior design, the ATN structure used in ATNoSFERES provides a simplified tool, since only the conditions and actions of each agent class have to be specified.

The ATN structure for behavior production allows to directly describe the behavior of any agent: this is an interesting perspective for explaining *how* the behavior operates or *why* it has been selected, for bootstraping the system, for re-using parts of existing behaviors, for applying "high-level" operations such as learning techniques, etc.

The ATNoSFERES model with regard to Ethogenetics. The ATNoSFERES model fulfills the Ethogenetics requirements expressed in section 3. Preliminary experiments [15, 20] have validated the use of ATNoSFERES regarding the following aspects:

- the ability to evolve *adequate* agents behaviors in a simple situation, from *random graphs*;
- the consistency of the ATN-building evolutionary language.

The experimental results have also confirmed that the generation of behaviors do not rely on a precise structure in the genotype: various adequate solutions have been found, based either on different graph-building strategies, or on the use of properties of the graphs (more details can be found in [15], and genetic-related issues are discussed in [20]).

5   Conclusion

We have presented Ethogenetics, an approach for the design of evolutive agents behaviors, and discussed its specific features. To summarize, interesting agents behaviors can be built through an evolutionary approach that is able to ensure *continuity* between the genetic substratum and the phenotypic behavior, and a *high expressive power* in the behavior produced. We propose therefore a two-step building that leads to graph-based behaviors (the ATNoSFERES model).

This model has been tested on simple agents behaviors [15, 20], and recently on the more complex maze problem [12]; we are currently experimenting collective strategies on the one hand, especially predator-prey simulations in order to study multi-agent ecological equilibrium and developmental dynamics; and on the other hand, real-robots applications[2]).

We assume that a multi-agent system, in which agents behaviors have been evolved that way, exhibit organizational features as a consequence of the selection pressure that shaped individual behaviors. This hypothesis will be investigated in the next months.

References

[1] T. BÄCK AND H.-P. SCHWEFEL, *An overview of evolutionary algorithms for parameter optimization*, Evolutionary Computation, 1 (1993), pp. 1–23.

[2] A. CARDON, *Conscience artificielle & systèmes adaptatifs*, Eyrolles, Paris, 1999.

[3] ——, *The Approaches of the Concept of Embodiment for an Autonomous Robot. Towards Consciousness of its Body*, in Mařík et al. [16], pp. 218–229.

[4] K. A. DE JONG, *An analysis of the behavior of a class of genetic adaptive systems*, PhD thesis, Dept. of Computer and Communication Sciences, University of Michigan, 1975.

[5] A. DROGOUL AND J. FERBER, *Multi-Agent Simulation as a Tool for Modeling Societies: Application to Social Differentiation in Ant Colonies*, Proceedings of the MAAMAW'92 Workshop, (1992).

---

[2] As part of the MICRobES Project: see http://miriad.lip6.fr/microbes.

[6] D. E. GOLDBERG, *Genetic algorithms in search, optimization, and machine learning*, Addison-Wesley, 1989.

[7] Z. GUESSOUM, *Un environnement opérationnel de conception et de réalisation de systèmes multi-agents*, thèse de doctorat, Université Paris VI, 1996.

[8] P. HOGEWEG AND B. HESPER, *The Ontogeny of the Interaction Structure in Bumble Bee Colonies: a MIRROR Model*, Behavioural Ecology and Sociobiology, 12 (1983), pp. 271–283.

[9] J. H. HOLLAND, *Adaptation in natural and artificial systems: an introductory analysis with applications to biology, control, and artificial intelligence*, Ann Arbor: University of Michigan Press, 1975.

[10] J. R. KOZA, *Genetic Programming: On the Programming of Computers by Means of Natural Selection*, MIT Press, Cambridge, Massachusetts, 1992.

[11] S. LANDAU, S. DONCIEUX, A. DROGOUL, AND J.-A. MEYER, *SFERES, a Framework for Designing Adaptive Multi-Agent Systems*, technical report, LIP6, Paris, 2001.

[12] S. LANDAU AND S. PICAULT, *Mazes and ethogenetics.* (in prep.), 2001.

[13] ———, *Modeling Adaptive Multi-Agent Systems Inspired by Developmental Biology*, in Mařík et al. [16], pp. 238–246.

[14] ———, *Stack-Based Gene Expression. An Approach Based on Ethogenetics Principles*, Journal of Genetic Programming and Evolvable Machines, (2001). Submission.

[15] S. LANDAU, S. PICAULT, AND A. DROGOUL, *ATNoSFERES: a Model for Evolutive Agent Behaviors*, in Proceedings of the AISB'01 Symposium on Adaptive Agents and Multi-Agent Systems, 2001.

[16] V. MAŘÍK, O. ŠTĚPÁNKOVÁ, H. KRAUTWURMOVÁ, AND J.-P. BRIOT, eds., *Proceedings of the Workshop on Adaptability and Embodiment Using Multi-Agent Systems (AEMAS'2001)*, Prague, 2001, Czech Technical University.

[17] S. PICAULT, *A Multi-Agent Simulation of Primate Social Concepts*, Brighton, 1998, John Wiley & Sons, Ltd.

[18] S. PICAULT AND A. COLLINOT, *Designing Social Cognition Models for Multi-Agent Systems through Simulating Primate Societies*, IEEE Press, 1998.

[19] S. PICAULT AND A. DROGOUL, *The MICRobES Project, an Experimental Approach towards "Open Collective Robotics"*, in Proceedings of DARS'2000, 2000.

[20] S. PICAULT AND S. LANDAU, *Ethogenetics and the Evolutionary Design of Agent Behaviors*, in Proceedings of the 5th World Multi-Conference on Systemics, Cybernetics and Informatics (SCI'01), vol. III, 2001, pp. 528–533. ISBN: 980–07–7543–9.

[21] I. RECHENBERG, *Evolutionsstrategie: Optimierung technischer Systeme nach Prinzipien der biologischen Evolution*, Frommann–Holzboog, Stuttgart, 1973.

[22] R. SALOMON, *Increasing Adaptivity through Evolution Strategies*, in From Animals to Animats 4. Proceedings of the 4th International Conference on Simulation of Adaptive Behaviour, P. Maes, M. J. Mataric, J.-A. Meyer, J. Pollack, and S. W. Wilson, eds., Cambridge, Massachusetts, 1996, MIT Press, pp. 411–420.

[23] H.-P. SCHWEFEL, *Evolutionsstrategie und numerische Optimierung*, Dr.-Ing. Thesis, Technical University of Berlin, Department of Process Engineering, 1975.

[24] P. STONE AND M. VELOSO, *Multiagent systems: A survey from machine learning perspective*, Autonomous Robots, 8 (2000).

[25] W. A. WOODS, *Transition networks grammars for natural language analysis*, Communications of the Association for the Computational Machinery, 13 (1970), pp. 591–606.

Distributed Coordination of Resources via Wasp-Like Agents

Vincent A. Cicirello and Stephen F. Smith

The Robotics Institute
Carnegie Mellon University, 5000 Forbes Avenue, Pittsburgh, PA 15213
{cicirello,sfs}@cs.cmu.edu

Abstract. Agent-based approaches to scheduling have gained increasing attention in recent years. One inherent advantage of agent-based approaches is their tendency for robust behavior; since activity is coordinated via local interaction protocols and decision policies, the system is insensitive to unpredictability in the executing environment. At the same time, such "self-scheduling" systems presume that a coherent global behavior will emerge from the local interactions of individual agents, and realizing this behavior remains a difficult problem. We draw on the adaptive behavior of the natural multi-agent system of the wasp colony as inspiration for decentralized mechanisms for coordinating factory operations. We compare the resulting systems to the state-of-the-art for the problems examined.

1 Introduction

Distributed, agent-based approaches to scheduling have gained increasing attention in recent years. One inherent advantage of agent-based approaches is their tendency for robust behavior; since activity is coordinated via local interaction protocols and decision policies, the system is insensitive to unpredictability in the executing environment. At the same time, such "self-scheduling" systems presume that a coherent global behavior will emerge from the local interactions of individual agents, and realizing this behavior remains a difficult problem.

To address this problem, we have taken a view of multi-agent resource coordination as an adaptive process, and have been investigating adaptive mechanisms inspired by natural multi-agent systems. Theraulaz et al. (see [13], [2], [12], [1], [11]) have developed a computational model of the adaptive behavior of a colony of wasps. They model two aspects of wasp behavior: 1) self-coordinated task allocation and 2) self-organized social hierarchies. Both of these have proved to provide useful bases upon which to build multi-agent coordination mechanisms.

The first aspect of wasp behavior that we have utilized is the stimulus-response mechanism which they use to perform task allocation. Wasps have response thresholds for the various tasks required of the colony such as foraging and brood care. The magnitude of a particular wasp's response thresholds to these

W. Truszkowski, C. Rouff, M. Hinchey (Eds.): WRAC 2002, LNAI 2564, pp. 71–80, 2003.

tasks determines the likelihood of that wasp's engagement in a task given environmental stimuli for the task. We have applied this model in a dynamic factory setting for the assignment of jobs to machines (see [6], [3]). The machines in our model are multi-purpose and we consider the constraint of sequence-dependent setup (i.e., our machines may be capable of performing more than one task but there is a cost associated with reconfiguration). As a new job arrives at the factory, it emits a stimulus and continues to do so at increasing magnitudes. Each machine is represented by a wasp-like agent which we call a *routing wasp*. Such a routing wasp maintains response thresholds for the various tasks its machine is able to perform and responds to job stimuli stochastically according to the magnitude of these thresholds as well as the magnitude of the stimuli. Response thresholds adapt to account for the current product demand.

The second aspect of wasp behavior of interest to us is their self-organizing social hierarchy. When two wasps encounter each other in the nest, they may with some probability engage in a dominance interaction. The wasp with the higher "force variable" wins the contest with a higher probability. Its force variable is then increased and the force variable of the loser is similarly decreased. A dominance hierarchy emerges from such interactions. We have shown this model of dominance contests to provide an effective basis for randomizing dispatch scheduling policies (see [6], [4]). In this work, we associate an agent which we call a *scheduling wasp* with each job in the queue of a given resource. The force variable of the scheduling wasp is defined by a dispatch heuristic (and hence can be chosen to match the characteristics of the problem at hand). Scheduling wasps engage in tournaments of dominance contests to stochastically prioritize the jobs in the queue. When the resource becomes available, the job represented by the current most dominant wasp is processed.

In this paper, we summarize initial results obtained with both the routing wasp and scheduling wasp coordination models. Section 2 details our routing wasp formulation. In Section 2.2 we benchmark our routing wasps on the real-world problem of scheduling a paintshop. Section 3 details our scheduling wasp framework. In Section 3.2 we compare our scheduling wasp framework to a state-of-the-art deterministic dispatch policy for the problem of weighted tardiness scheduling under a sequence dependent setup constraint. Finally, in Section 4 we conclude.

2 Routing Wasps

2.1 Formulation

Our routing wasp model is concerned most generally with the configuration of product flows. In the simplest case the problem involves a set of multi-purpose machines, each capable of processing multiple types of jobs but with a setup cost for reconfiguring from one type to another. Each machine in the system has an associated routing wasp (see Figure 1 for illustration). Each routing wasp is in charge of assigning jobs to the queue of its associated machine. Each routing

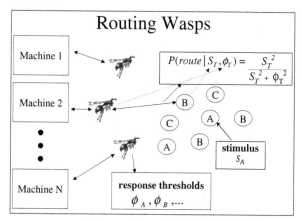

Fig. 1. Routing wasps

wasp has a set of response thresholds:

$$\Theta_w = \{\theta_{w,0}, \ldots, \theta_{w,J}\} \tag{1}$$

where $\theta_{w,j}$ is the response threshold of wasp w to jobs of type j. Each wasp only has response thresholds for job types that its associated machine can process.

Jobs in the system that are awaiting machine assignment broadcast to all of the routing wasps a stimulus S_j which is equal to the length of time the job has been waiting to be routed and where j is the type of job. So the longer the job remains unrouted, the stronger the stimulus it emits. Provided that its associated machine is able to process job type j, a routing wasp w will pick up a job emitting a stimulus S_j with probability:

$$P(\theta_{w,j}, S_j) = \frac{S_j^2}{S_j^2 + \theta_{w,j}^2} \tag{2}$$

This is the rule used for task allocation in the wasp behavioral model as described in [12]. In this way, wasps will tend to pick up jobs of the type for which its response threshold is lowest. But it will pick up jobs of other types if a high enough stimulus is emitted.

The threshold values $\theta_{w,j}$ may vary in the range $[\theta_{min}, \theta_{max}]$. Each routing wasp, at all times, knows what its machine is doing, including: the status of the queue, whether or not the machine is performing a setup, the type of job being processed, and whether or not the machine is idle. This knowledge is used to adjust the response thresholds for the various job types. This updating of the response thresholds occurs at each time step. If the machine is currently processing job type j or is in the process of setting up to process job type j, then $\theta_{w,j}$ is updated according to:

$$\theta_{w,j} = \theta_{w,j} - \delta_1 \tag{3}$$

If the machine is either processing or setting up to process a job type other than j, then $\theta_{w,j}$ is updated according to:

$$\theta_{w,j} = \theta_{w,j} + \delta_2 \tag{4}$$

And if the machine is currently idle and has an empty queue, then for all job types j that the machine can process the wasp adjusts the response thresholds $\theta_{w,j}$ according to (t is the length of time the machine has been idle):

$$\theta_{w,j} = \theta_{w,j} - \delta_3^t \tag{5}$$

In this way, the response thresholds for the job type currently being processed are reinforced as to encourage the routing wasp to pick up jobs of the same type; while the response thresholds of other types not currently being worked on are adapted to discourage the routing wasp from taking these jobs. This specialization of routing wasps (i.e., machines) helps to minimize setup time. The first two ways in which the response thresholds are updated (equations 3 and 4) are analogous to that of the model described in [1, 12]. The third (equation 5) is included to encourage a wasp associated with an idle machine to take whatever jobs it can get. This last update rule acknowledges that although specialization can reduce setup time, over-specialization to a job type with low demand may result in lower system throughput.

We now need a method to reconcile a competition between two or more routing wasps that are interested in routing a single job to their respective machines. The method we employ is based on the self-organized social hierarchies of real wasps. First define the force F_w of a routing wasp w as:

$$F_w = 1.0 + T_p + T_s \tag{6}$$

where T_p and T_s are the sum of the processing times and setup times of all jobs currently in the queue of the associated machine, respectively[1]. Now consider a dominance struggle between two competing routing wasps. This contest determines which routing wasp gets the job. Let F_1 and F_2 be the force variables of routing wasps 1 and 2, respectively. Routing wasp 1 will get the job with probability:

$$P(F_1, F_2) = \frac{F_2^2}{F_1^2 + F_2^2} \tag{7}$$

In this way, routing wasps associated with machines of equivalent queue lengths will have equal probabilities of getting the job. If the queue lengths differ, then the routing wasp with the smaller queue has a better chance of taking on the new job. In the event that more than two routing wasps compete for a given job, a single elimination tournament of dominance contests is used to decide the winner.

---

[1] In this definition of force, the "stronger" wasp is the wasp with the smaller force. This may seem counter-intuitive with the usual connotation of the word "force", but defining force in this way is cleaner mathematically. Perhaps "weakness" may have been a more accurate term to use rather than "force", but we chose the latter to correspond more closely to the terminology of the model of real wasp behavior.

Table 1. Comparison of average number of setups of R-Wasps (routing wasps) and Morley's system. Smaller numbers are better. 95% confidence intervals and two-tailed p-values from a paired T-test is shown. Result is average of 100 runs.

Morley	R-Wasps	p-value
438.22±3.70	**287.61±2.15**	<0.0001

2.2   Paintshop Problem

To benchmark the performance of our routing wasp framework, we conducted experiments comparing it to Morley's GM Paintshop system (see [8], [7]). Morley devised a simple bidding mechanism in which booth agents submit bids for trucks as they arrive according to their current queue length and the required color of the last truck in the queue. This simple multi-agent bidding system was shown in simulation to be more effective than the previously used centralized scheduler, and was subsequently put into use at a General Motors truck painting facility. When put into practice in the GM facility, Morley's system was found to be 10% more efficient (in terms of number of paint color changes) than the previously used centralized scheduler [8] and resulted in savings of nearly a million dollars in the first nine months of use [7]. Due to its effectiveness and real-world implementation, we feel that Morley's system is an excellent choice to use as a benchmark for our system and is indicative of the state-of-the-art in agent-based systems for this class of problem.

In Morley's problem, trucks rolled off the assembly line at a rate of one per minute. The system was faced with the problem of assigning each truck to a paint booth as it emerged from the end of the assembly line. There were seven paint booths in Morley's problem and it took three minutes to paint a truck. Each truck could possibly require any of fourteen paint colors and the trucks arrived in no particular order. Approximately 50% of the trucks required a single color. The other 50% required colors drawn uniformly at random from among the other 13 colors. A paint booth could only be set for one color at a time and there was a cost to reconfigure the booth for another color in terms of both the time it required to perform this color change as well as a monetary cost associated with paint usage. They gave no details regarding the monetary cost of such a change so we do not consider that objective here. There was a further constraint that the queue of a paint booth could have at most 3 trucks. Presumably, this constraint was due to physical space limitations in the factory. In any case, it is a very realistic constraint and characteristic of real-world problems.

Table 1 shows how the routing wasps compare to Morley's system on this problem[2]. Shown in the table is the average number of setups performed during the course of a simulation over 100 runs. Every setup (switching of paint color) requires some amount of time. Also, there is some chance that the system will fail to flush all of the previous paint color from the system during setup. This can

---

[2] More detailed results can be found in [5].

result in an incorrect coat of paint applied to the next truck after the setup. This increases paintcosts, requiring a rework of the truck. It also affects cycle time. To this end, minimizing the number of setups should be our objective in this problem and as can be clearly seen, the routing wasps is significantly superior to Morley's system in this regard.

3 Scheduling Wasps

3.1 Formulation

Our scheduling wasp model is the result of recognition of the fallibility of dispatch scheduling policies. If dispatch policies are viewed as good rules of thumb and if the deterministic use of such a policy leads to a schedule that lies in close proximity to many good schedules, then perhaps a better solution can be obtained by randomizing the decision-making process in some way biased by the heuristic. Our approach to randomization derives from a naturally-inspired computational model of the self-organization that takes place within a colony of wasps (see [13], [11], [1]). In nature, a hierarchical social order among the wasps of the colony is formed through interactions among individual wasps of the colony. This emergent social order is a succession of wasps from the most dominant to the least dominant (analogous to a prioritization of jobs on a set of machines). In the model of Theraulaz et al., the results of these interactions are determined stochastically based on the "force" variables of the wasps involved. The probability of wasp 1 winning a dominance contest against wasp 2 is defined based on the force variables, F_1 and F_2, of the wasps as:

$$P(F_1, F_2) = \frac{F_1^2}{F_1^2 + F_2^2} \tag{8}$$

This model can be directly mapped to the problem of prioritizing jobs in a queue, and as such provides a natural basis for the randomization of dispatch policies. In our "scheduling wasp" formulation, each job is represented by a wasp and the concept of a force variable is used to define job priority (i.e., the value that the dispatch policy in use assigns). The scheduling wasps then interact with each other to prioritize the jobs in the queue. This framework for dynamic scheduling was first introduced in [6], where we considered the problem of sequencing jobs to maximize throughput under different and dynamically changing job mixes. Here, as in [4], we explore the use of this wasp model on due date problems, where dispatch-based solutions are more commonly employed.

To fully specify our scheduling wasp model for minimizing weighted tardiness with sequence dependent setups, we need to provide a definition of force. We will define force with the dispatch policy known as R&M [9]. This dispatch policy was not originally designed with sequence-dependent setups in mind. We have here modified it to account for setup time. This modification of R&M was made originally in [10].

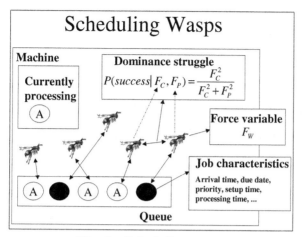

Fig. 2. Scheduling wasps

Noting this, force is defined as:

$$F_w = \frac{W_w}{T_w^p + T_w^s} \exp(\frac{-(D_w - T_w^p - T_w^s - T_{\text{now}})^+}{h\,\overline{T^p}})$$ (9)

where T_w^p and T_w^s are the processing time and setup time of wasp w's job, D_w is the duedate, W_w is the weight, T_{now} is the current time, $\overline{T^p}$ is the average processing time, and $(A)^+ = \max\{A, 0\}$. The winner of a dominance contest in this context is determined stochastically in the same manner as in the model of real wasp behavior.

In the typical dispatch scheduling approach, the job in the queue with the highest value of the dispatch heuristic is chosen next. Given the scheduling wasp formulation of the previous section, our system instead chooses the next job based on a tournament of dominance contests. In this tournament, the scheduling wasps are seeded based on their current position in the queue. The last two wasps in the queue engage in a dominance contest. The winner then engages in a dominance contest with the next wasp and so forth along the length of the queue. As this occurs, the jobs associated with the winning wasps move closer to the front of the queue. Whatever job is at the front of the queue when this process completes is chosen next by the machine.

3.2   Weighted Tardiness Problem

To analyze our scheduling wasp framework for randomizing dispatch policies, we have examined its performance on weighted tardiness problems under sequence dependent setup constraints. As stated earlier, there are only a few dispatch policies in the literature for this problem, all of which are modifications of policies that do not consider setups. We have taken R&M as defined earlier as the

Table 2. Average weighted tardiness comparison between S-Wasps (scheduling wasp stochastic framework) and deterministic dispatch scheduling (R&M). The problem has 1 machine and either 2 or 3 job types for various job mixes. 95% confidence intervals and two-tailed p-values from paired T-tests are shown.

Mix	S-Wasps	R&M	P-value
50/50	**2081.4±219.9**	2637.8±288.9	<0.0001
85/15	699.2±108.7	**660.7±115.1**	0.1713
100/0	214.3±31.0	**172.5±23.8**	<0.0001
33/33 /33	**2834.5±217.1**	3307.4±274.8	<0.0001
50/25 /25	**2582.4±226.1**	2912.6±299.3	0.0021

definition of the force variable for our scheduling wasps and have compared the stochastic policy that results to the deterministic policy.

Table 2 shows the results of this comparison[3]. The problem in question consists of a single machine and either two or three types of jobs with unknown arrival times. We consider 5 different job mixes as seen in the table. Processing time is chosen randomly for each job from a Gaussian centered at 15 time units. Setup time to switch a machine from one type to another is 30 time units. A job's weight is drawn uniformly from the interval $[1, 20]$, and its duedate is drawn uniformly from one of the following intervals (where P is process time, W is weight, and T is current time):

- $[T, T + 4P]$ if $W > 16$
- $[T, T + 6P]$ if $12 < W \leq 16$
- $[T, T + 6.5P]$ if $8 < W \leq 12$
- $[T, T + 8P]$ if $W \leq 8$

Simulations are 1000 time units in length and results shown in the table are averages of 100 runs.

What can be seen in Table 2 is that problems of a single job type or very nearly a single job type problem are best solved with the deterministic policy (the 100/0 job mix and the 85/15 job mix problems). A single job type problem is what the dispatch policy in question was originally designed for. However, you can also see in the table that the "harder" problems with more diverse mixes of jobs are best solved with the stochastic policy of the scheduling wasps.

4   Conclusion

In this paper, we have presented mechanisms for coordinating factory operations in a decentralized manner inspired by the natural self-organization that takes place within a colony of wasps. The routing wasp framework provides superior

---

[3] More detailed results can be found in [4].

performance to a real-world proven system for sequence-dependent setup problems. The scheduling wasp framework proves an effective stochastic framework for randomizing dispatch scheduling policies in instances where they are less informed.

We believe the computational mechanisms underlying these wasp behavioral models have broader applicability to task allocation and resource coordination in other multi-agent domains. We are currently pursuing application of these models to two distinct types of problems. First, we are exploring generalization from the dynamic factory routing and scheduling problem to the broader-scoped problem of supply chain management. Just as factories must reconfigure product flows as the mix of jobs changes over time, supply chains must realign material flow to capitalize on new market opportunities, and current trends toward specialization and increased partnering increase the need for good distributed solutions. Second, we are also considering applicability of our "self-scheduling" models to the somewhat different problem of multi-robot coordination. We are interested in domains such as space exploration and hazardous waste cleanup, where multiple robots with differential capabilities must dynamically configure themselves into teams and cooperate in the performance of complex tasks over time.

Acknowledgments

This work has been funded in part by the Department of Defense Advanced Research Projects Agency and the U.S. Air Force Rome Research Laboratory under contracts F30602-97-2-0066 and F30602-00-2-0503 and by the CMU Robotics Institute. The views and conclusions contained in this document are those of the authors and should not be interpreted as necessarily representing the official policies or endorsements, either expressed or implied, of the Air Force or U.S. Government.

References

[1] E. Bonabeau, A. Sobkowski, G. Theraulaz, and J. L. Deneubourg. Adaptive task allocation inspired by a model of division of labor in social insects. In D. Lundh and B. Olsson, editors, *Bio Computation and Emergent Computing*, pages 36–45. World Scientific, 1997. **71, 74, 76**

[2] E. Bonabeau, G. Theraulaz, and J. L. Deneubourg. Fixed response thresholds and the regulation of division of labor in insect societies. *Bulletin of Mathematical Biology*, 60:753–807, 1998. **71**

[3] Vincent A. Cicirello and Stephen F. Smith. Improved routing wasps for distributed factory control. In *The IJCAI-01 Workshop on Artificial Intelligence and Manufacturing, Working Notes*, pages 26–32. AAAI SIGMAN, 4-9 August 2001. Seattle, WA. **72**

[4] Vincent A. Cicirello and Stephen F. Smith. Randomizing dispatch scheduling policies. In *Using Uncertainty Within Computation: Papers from the 2001 AAAI Fall Symposium, Technical Report FS-01-04*, pages 30–37. AAAI Press, 2-4 November 2001. North Falmouth, Massachusetts. **72, 76, 78**

[5] Vincent A. Cicirello and Stephen F. Smith. Wasp-like agents for distributed factory coordination. Technical Report CMU-RI-TR-01-39, Robotics Institute, Carnegie Mellon University, Pittsburgh, PA, December 2001. **75**

[6] Vincent A. Cicirello and Stephen F. Smith. Wasp nests for self-configurable factories. In J. P. Müller, E. Andre, S. Sen, and C. Frasson, editors, *Proceedings of the Fifth International Conference on Autonomous Agents*, pages 473–480. ACM SIGART, ACM/SIGGRAPH, ACM/SIGCHI, ACM Press, May-June 2001. Montreal, Quebec, Canada. **72, 76**

[7] D. Morley. Painting trucks at general motors: The effectiveness of a complexity-based approach. In *Embracing Complexity: Exploring the Application of Complex Adaptive Systems to Business*, pages 53–58. The Ernst and Young Center for Business Innovation, 1996. **75**

[8] D. Morley and C. Schelberg. An analysis of a plant-specific dynamic scheduler. In *Final Report, Intelligent Dynamic Scheduling for Manufacturing Systems*, pages 115–122, June 1993. **75**

[9] R. V. Rachamadugu and T. E. Morton. Myopic heuristics for the single machine weighted tardiness problem. Working Paper 30-82-83, GSIA, Carnegie Mellon University, Pittsburgh, PA, 1982. **76**

[10] N. Raman, R. V. Rachamadugu, and F. B. Talbot. Real time scheduling of an automated manufacturing center. *European Journal of Operational Research*, 40:222–242, 1989. **76**

[11] G. Theraulaz, E. Bonabeau, and J. L. Deneubourg. Self-organization of hierarchies in animal societies: The case of the primitively eusocial wasp polistes dominulus christ. *Journal of Theoretical Biology*, 174:313–323, 1995. **71, 76**

[12] G. Theraulaz, E. Bonabeau, and J. L. Deneubourg. Response threshold reinforcement and division of labour in insect societies. *Proceedings of the Royal Society of London B*, 265(1393):327–335, February 1998. **71, 73, 74**

[13] G. Theraulaz, S. Goss, J. Gervet, and J. L. Deneubourg. Task differentiation in polistes wasp colonies: A model for self-organizing groups of robots. In *From Animals to Animats: Proceedings of the First International Conference on Simulation of Adaptive Behavior*, pages 346–355. MIT Press, 1991. **71, 76**

Homo Egualis Reinforcement Learning Agents for Load Balancing

Katja Verbeeck, Johan Parent, and Ann Nowé

Computational Modeling Lab (COMO)
Vrije Universiteit Brussel, Belgium
kaverbee@vub.ac.be
jparent,asnowe@info.vub.ac.be
http://como.vub.ac.be

Abstract. Periodical policies were recently introduced as a solution for the coordination problem in games which assume competition between the players, and where the overall performance can only be as good as the performance of the poorest player. Instead of converging to just one Nash equilibrium, which may favor just one of the players, a periodical policy switches between periods in which all interesting Nash equilibria are played. As a result the players are able to equalize their pay-offs and a fair solution is build. Moreover players can learn this policy with a minimum on communication; now and then they send each other their performance. In this paper, periodical policies are investigated for use in real-life asynchronous games. More precisely we look at the problem of load balancing in a simple job scheduling game. The asynchronism of the problem is reflected in delayed pay-offs or reinforcements, probabilistic job creation and processor rates which follow an exponential distribution. We show that a group of homo egualis reinforcement learning agents can still find a periodical policy. When the jobs are small, homo egualis reinforcement learning agents find a good probability distribution over their action space to play the game without any communication.

1 Introduction: Periodical Policies and Load Balancing

When an agent is learning in a dynamical distributed multi-agent system, some form of communication is generally required between the agents. This is due to the fact that the quality of a policy used by a single agent is dependent on the policies adopted by the other agents. Agents very often have to work together toward achieving a common global goal. However each agent also wants to fulfill its own task as well as possible and because resources are generally limited, agents experience conflicting objectives. When the overall performance of the system can only be as good as that of the poorest performing agent, some agreements have to be made between the agents and information needs to be exchanged. Since communication has its price in distributed systems, the communication required has to be limited, however without preventing coordination.

In [5] the notion of a periodical policy has been introduced. A periodical policy can be learned by a group of fair homo egualis reinforcement learning

---

W. Truszkowski, C. Rouff, M. Hinchey (Eds.): WRAC 2002, LNAI 2564, pp. 81–91, 2003.

agents, [2]. It means that the group periodically alternates between policies that are good for some agents but not for all. It is assumed that there is no policy which is the best for all and so it is better to alternate between the best policies of the individuals rather than settling for some less rewarding compromise. Thanks to the homo egualis characteristic of the agents in [5] communication can be kept minimal. Only after a fixed period of time the agents communicate their pay-off to compare their respective performance.

A homo egualis agent has an inequality aversion, [2]. In [5] agents use this to change their action space. When performing well, a good action is excluded for play in the next period, so as to give others the benefit of converging to their best strategy. During each period the agents are self interested reinforcement learners, during communication agents are homo egualis individuals who can change the action space. As a result the agents are able to equalize their pay-off optimally.

In [5] the above approach is illustrated on statical one-step games with synchronous action-selection. In this paper we investigate whether periodical policies can also work for real-life situations. The kind of applications we have in mind is for example routing in telecommunication networks [6]. A natural multiagent approach to this problem is to put an agent at each router. An agent is responsible for sending the packets to the destination specified by selecting an appropriate neighboring router which in turn becomes responsible for getting the packet to the destination. Clearly, agents have to collaborate to perform the global task of routing, in the sense that a sequence of actions by different agents has to be optimized. This can be achieved by a classical reinforcement learning approach, provided resource availability, i.e. bandwidth, is plentiful. If on the other hand resources are scarce, competition arises between the agents and collaboration becomes necessary in order to perform the global task as well as possible.

In a first attempt to address this problem with homo egualis reinforcement learners and periodical policies, we neglect the sequential character of the routing problem and concentrate on a less complex one-step load balancing problem with asynchronous action selection and delayed reinforcement. More precisely this paper concentrates on homo egualis reinforcement learning agents who are involved in a job scheduling game of the common pool resource type [2]. The game is asynchronous in that jobs are created according to an exponential law and processors handle jobs with a time consumption taken from an exponential distribution. This game with two players was already briefly touched upon in [5]. In this paper we continue the experiments and adapt the algorithm of [5] for use in this kind of asynchronous, real-life games. We are especially interested in the added difficulties arising from the asynchronism. Our experiments show that a group of homo egualis reinforcement learning agents are still able to find a periodical policy. They even find a good probability distribution on their action space, which can be used to play the game without any communication.

This paper will be organized as follows: in the next section a more game theoretic definition of periodical policies is given. This section also quickly reviews how homo egualis reinforcement learners are able to learn periodical policies in synchronous games. Section 3 reports on load balancing and gives the setup for the experiments. In section 4 some adaptations to the algorithm are suggested to cope with the asynchronism. Section 5 reports on the experiments, while section 6 discusses related and future work. The last section gives some conclusions.

2 Periodical Policies and the Homo Egualis Society

2.1 Periodical Policies

A non-sequential multi-agent problem can be straightforwardly modeled as a game. Just as in an MAS, a game consists of more than one player and results in an outcome for every player depending on the overall behavior of all the players. Formally it can be described by a tuple $(n, A_1 \ldots A_n, R_1 \ldots R_n)$ where n is the number of players, A_i the set of actions available to player i and $R_i : A_1 \times \ldots \times A_n \to \Re$ the pay-off function of player i. This can be visualized as an n-dimensional matrix of instantaneous rewards, see for example the game in figure (1). The information available to each player, the extend to which they can communicate and the different performance criteria of the players all characterize the game. Solutions are formulated in terms of equilibrium situations for the players. The concept which attracts the most attention these days in the MAS community is that of a Nash equilibrium and even more precisely that of a mixed Nash equilibrium. In an n person game a set of n strategies or policies $\alpha^1 \ldots \alpha^n$ (one for each player) is said to be an equilibrium point if no player has a positive reason for changing his strategy assuming the other players continue to play their given strategy α^i. In a mixed equilibrium the participants' strategy α^i is not deterministic but a probability distribution on the action set of the player. Nash proved that there exists at least one pure or mixed strategy equilibrium for all n-player games with finite strategy sets. The problem however is that equilibrium points should not be unique nor give the same outcomes for the different players.

The Bach/Stravinsky game of figure (1) captures the problem we are interested in very well. There are two pure Nash equilibria $(2, 1)$ and $(1, 2)$ which represent conflicting objectives for the two agents. There is also a unique mixed Nash equilibrium, which is, agent 1 playing Bach with probability 2/3 and Stravinsky with probability 1/3, and agent 2 playing Bach with probability 1/3 and Stravinsky with probability 2/3. None of these equilibria seem interesting to converge to. If the strategy to which the agents converge is the pure equilibrium (2,1)

$$\begin{pmatrix} (2,1) & (0,0) \\ (0,0) & (1,2) \end{pmatrix}$$

Fig. 1. The Bach/Stravinsky game

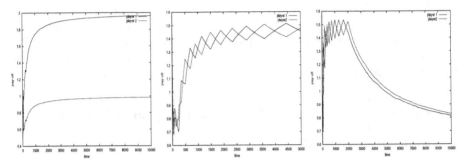

Fig. 2. Bach/Stravinsky game. Left: the average payoff for 2 Q-learners converging to one of the Nash equilibria, Middle: the average payoff for 2 Homo egualis Q-learners playing a periodical policy, Right: the average payoff for 2 players playing the mixed Nash equilibrium

then agent 1 has a maximal possible payoff, and agent 2 is left with a suboptimal payoff, and visa versa for the other pure Nash equilibrium. The expected payoffs both agents receive for the mixed equilibrium is 2/3, which is less than what they could get in the pure Nash equilibria. The solution proposed by periodical policies introduced in [5] is to alternate between periods of time during which each Nash equilibrium is played. The average pay-off for the agents is now equalized optimally, see figure (2).

2.2 Homo Egualis Reinforcement Learning Agents

In [5] the algorithm for learning a periodical policy is fully described, however we repeat the main characteristics here. First of all the agents do not only care about their own pay-off, but also how it compares to the pay-off of others, i.e. they belong to a homo egualis society, [2]. A homo egualis agent is willing to reduce his own pay-off to increase the degree of equality in the group. This characteristics is reflected in the communication part of the algorithm, which is given in figure (3). The algorithm has two parts. The first part is executed for a constant period of time. During this period the agents behave as selfish utility optimizing reinforcement learners trying to reach a Nash equilibrium without communication. Results from Learning Automata theory assures that this convergence will take place[1], [4]. The second part is the communication part in which they synchronously send each other their performance. When an agents feels he is on *top*, he will exclude his best action from his action set. Agents who perform under the average will reset their full action space. As a result, another part of the joint action space will be explored in the next period and another

---

[1] Players in an n-person non-zero sum game who use a reward-inaction update scheme with an arbitrarily small step size will always converge to one of the equilibrium points. Which equilibrium point is reached depends on the initial conditions.

```
## COMMUNICATION PHASE
if (time_to_communicate) {
communicate_to_all ( cumulative_payoff , last_payoff );
payoff_all := receive_from_all ( cumulative_payoff );
last_period_payoff_all := receive_from_all ( last_period_payoff );
if (not_equal_payoffs ( payoff_all ) ) {
   if (and (has_best_payoff ( payoff_all ))
       (has_best_payoff ( last_period_payoff_all)))
     actionSet := actionSet - best_action;
   else
     if ( not (has_best_payoff ( payoff_all )))
       actionSet := original_actionSet;

   INITIALIZATION ;
   }
}
```

Fig. 3. Pseudo code of the communication part of the algorithm executed by each Homo egualis Q-learner

agent will become the best, i.e. another Nash equilibrium will be found. Even when some players have better best Nash equilibria than others, the algorithm is able to equalize pay-off by learning different period lengths in which these Nash equilibria can be played, [5].

3 Load Balancing: The Setup

The problem of adaptive load balancing has already been studied extensively even in the framework of multi agent learning, [7, 1, 3, 4]. The general problem for a group of individual agents is to adaptively distribute and share (work)load between some private or common passive/active resources, so as to ensure overall system efficiency or minimize time consumption of the global work. Many load balancing tasks exist in real life, cfr the routing example mentioned in the introduction. Depending on the view and settings of the problem different solution scenario's are proposed, going from purely negotiating agents to agents who can only use local information without any explicit communication, [7].

An important aspect of load balancing in view of our work is fairness concerning the use of common resources. Our setting consist of a group of autonomous agents who generate jobs and have to learn to select passive processors who will execute them, so that the load is nicely distributed and the overall job around time of all the jobs generated in the system is minimized. In fact in our setting an agent has only two choices. Or he uses a private resource which no one else can use but which has a cost associated to it (i.e. it is slower). Or he chooses a public resource which is free. Therefore the agents have to develop their resource selection behavior relative to the behavior of others and to changing variables such as load and resource capacities.

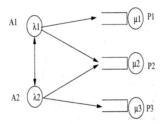

Fig. 4. A simple job scheduling game. Two agents can use either their private processor or a common processor. The agents generate jobs according to an exponential law with a mean value of 1.5 time units. The private processors handle the jobs with a time consumption chosen from an exponential distribution with mean value of 1 time units, while the common processor works with a mean of 0.5 time units

The exact setup for a two agent setting is depicted in figure (4). It is a slightly different version of the experiment found in [3]. This setup can straightforwardly be extended to more than 2 agents, each agent having a private and a common (shared) processor to send jobs to. The experiment can be viewed as a game and described in terms of equilibria. With the current settings of load and processor rate, the above job scheduling game has two pure Nash equilibria: one agent always chooses the common resource and the other one uses the private resource and vice versa. Note that the payoff should be minimized here. Although the common resource looks more interesting to use from an individual agents' point of view (because it can handle the jobs more quickly on the average), the benefit disappears when there is an overconsumption of the common good by the agents. With these settings the game belongs to what is called common pool resource game, [2] and reflects the situation we are interested in. However this game is not statical anymore. Reinforcement or pay-offs are delayed, jobs are created probabilistically and processor rates follow an exponential distribution[2].

In the rest of the paper we try to answer the following questions: Are periodical policies still useful in this more real-life situation? And are homo egualis agents still able to learn them? All experiments reported are simulated with the QNAP2 modeling language, [9].

4   Periodic Policies and Asynchronous Games

How robust is the above algorithm when reinforcement or pay-off is delayed? We first tested the original algorithm on an instance of the job game experiment of figure (4) with 3 agents. The results can be found in figure (5) (middle). The problem with this run was that although the agents communicated synchronously and changed their action space and thus also their policy synchronously, they were still getting reinforcement of the previous policy because of the inherent

---

[2] All jobs are considered to have the same size.

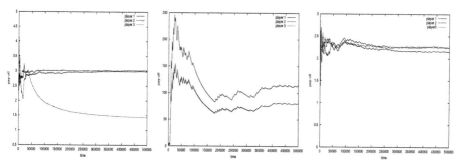

Fig. 5. Average job turnaround time for the job scheduling game with 3 agents. Left: 3 agents using Q-learning, middle: 3 agents using the algorithm for synchronous games, right: 3 agents using the adapted algorithm

delay. So at the beginning of a new period, just after the communication phase, agents were confused with reinforcements from the previous period. Therefore we added two stabilizing features to the algorithm. First processors were prohibited to give information about jobs they handled if these jobs arrived in the queue during the previous period. So just after communication, delayed information should not be sent. Delivering reinforcement restarts for every new policy. Second, we smoothed out the reinforcement send back. In the current algorithm, reinforcement is sent every 10 time units. Averages are now calculated with a low discount factor. The results of this adaptation can be seen in (5) (right). In (5)(left) the averages for 3 Q-learners are shown. Here the agents converge to the Nash equilibrium in which one agent selects the common queue and the others use their private queue. Note that pay-offs have to be minimized.

This and the following experiments show that with some stabilizing features a group of homo egualis learners still finds a fair periodic policy.

5   Further Experiments

5.1   Adding More Players

We extended the game to more players. Figure (6) show the results for the game of figure (4) extended to 5, respectively 9 players. Pay-offs are still equalized and the obtained average is better than when playing the private queue.

5.2   Comparison with Probabilistic Play

In synchronous games, periodical policies were motivated by the fact that mixed policies are fair, however they do not guarantee optimal play, see for instance figure (2) (right). There is a real chance of not coordinating (which is 5/9 for the Bach/Stravinsky game). This explains why periodical policies perform better in

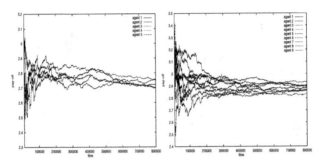

Fig. 6. Average job turnaround time for the job scheduling game with 5 (left) and 9 players (right)

this case, they only play coordinated actions, exploration not included. However does this argument still works in asynchronous games? Because the above calculation can only be made when the action selection is synchronous.

In fact, for some 2 player instances of the job scheduling game[3] performances are better when the agents just play the mixed Nash equilibrium without communication. For a 2-player game the mixed Nash equilibrium is easily calculated, however the problem is that these equilibria are not easily found in games with more than two players. However it turns out that periodical playing agents find a good probability distribution over their action space offline[4]. They keep track of the Q-values of every action while playing periodically and after a while these values can be normalized to a probability measure. These action probabilities can then be used to play the game without any communication.

In figure (7) (left) you find the global average pay-off for players playing periodically and players playing probabilistically with the offline learned probability distribution. The latter ones perform better in all experiments, ranging from 2 to 9 players. In figure (7) (right) the standard deviation of the individual agents' pay-offs is given. It shows that with the offline learned probabilities, the individual pay-offs are less deviated. We also compared these results with results from agents playing with a uniform probability. However the latter agents performed very poor compared to both periodical playing agents and the agents playing the learned probability.

The experiments we did used small job sizes. We believe that for larger jobs the game is becoming less asynchronous and playing periodically may become more interesting than playing probabilistically. However we did not test this yet. What we can conclude however is that a periodical policy can find good action

---

[3] We made the jobs a little larger: jobs are created according to an exponential law with a mean value of 10 time units. The private processors handles the jobs with a time consumption chosen from an exponential distribution with mean value of 5 time units, while the common processor works with a mean of 3.5 time units.

[4] In the 2-agent case, this matches with the probability distribution of the mixed Nash equilibrium. We did not check this however for the more agent cases.

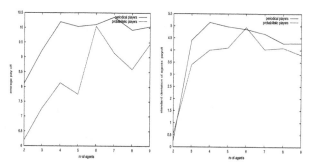

Fig. 7. Comparison of the global average pay-offs (left) and the standard deviations of the individuals pay-offs (right) for homo egualis players and probabilistic players in the job scheduling game. The probabilistic players play with the probabilities learned during periodical play

probabilities to play the game without communication and without the need to compute a mixed Nash equilibrium.

5.3   Load Differences

In a last experiment we let one of the agents handle more jobs than the others. All parameter settings of figure (4) are used, except for the first agent, his jobs are created with a mean value of 1 time unit. The algorithm now must be able to give the busiest agent more opportunity to send to the common queue, so that pay-offs are still equalized. Figure (8) (left) gives the averages for 2 homo egualis players and Figure (8) (middle) and (right) gives the number of jobs in the common queue for player 1 and player 2 respectively. As Figure (8) shows, the algorithm forces the least overloaded agent to use his private processor more.

6   Related & Future Work

An important issue which still has to be investigated is how the length of the non-communication period influences the results. In [7] it is shown that naive use of communication may not improve and might even harm the system. In [1] it is proved that there exists a maximum communication delay before decision quality begins to suffer. An important difference with these systems and ours is that in the other mentioned systems agents communicate their local state so that the other agents are able to model their environment. In our case only performances are communicated.

Another interesting path to explore is how periodical policies can help to find mixed Nash equilibria. The results from section 5.2 suggest a link between the two, which should be further investigated.

Finally the algorithm in general should be extended so that other type of games are also recognized. Games in which the are good Pareto optimal policies, or games which can never be fair, etc.

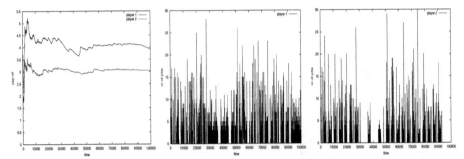

Fig. 8. Left: Average job turnaround time for the job scheduling game with 2 agents with different load, middle: number of jobs in public queue send by player 1, right: number of jobs in public queue send by agent 2

7 Conclusion

In this paper we investigated the use of periodical policies in asynchronous games. We showed that a group of homo egualis learning agents is able to find a periodical policy, when they ignore delayed information just after communication or policy change. We also questioned the usefulness of periodical policies in asynchronous games. We showed that when a good probability distribution over the action set exists, a periodical policy can still be useful for learning this distribution.

References

[1] Billard E. A., Pasquale J. C.,: Adaptive Coordination in Distributed Systems with Delayed Communication. IEEE Transaction on Systems, Man and Cybernetics, **25 - 4** (1995) 546 - 554   85, 89

[2] Gintis H.,: Game Theory Evolving: A Problem-Centered Introduction to Modeling Strategic Behavior. Princeton University Press, (2000)   82, 84, 86

[3] Glockner A., Pasquale J.,: Coadaptive Behavior in a Simple Distributed Job Scheduling System IEEE Transactions on Systems, Man and Cybernetics, **23 - 3** (1993) 902 - 907   85, 86

[4] Narendra K., Thathachar M., : Learning Automata: An Introduction. Prentice-Hall (1989)   84, 85

[5] Nowé, A., Parent, J., Verbeeck, K., : Social Agents Playing a Periodical Policy. Proceedings of the 12th European Conference on Machine Learning, Freiburg Germany (2001) to appear   81, 82, 84, 85

[6] Nowé, A., Verbeeck, K.,: Distributed Reinforcement learning, Loadbased Routing a case study. Proceedings of the Neural, Symbolic and Reinforcement Methods for sequence Learning Workshop at ijcai99 (1999)   82

[7] Schaerf A., Shoham Y., Tennenholtz M.,: Adaptive Load Balancing: A Study in Multi-Agent Learning Journal of Artificial Intelligence Research **2** (1995) 475 - 500   85, 89

[8] Sutton, R.S., Barto, A.G. : Reinforcement Learning: An introduction. Cambridge, MA: MIT Press (1998)
[9] QNAP2 reference manual, SIMULOG (1996) 86

Experimental Swarm Design

Alfred D.M. Wan

Vrije Universiteit, Department of Artificial Intelligence
De Boelelaan 1081, 1081 HV Amsterdam, The Netherlands
wan@cs.vu.nl
http://www.cs.vu.nl/~wan

Abstract. The emphasis in swarm intelligence research is on the division of tasks needed to keep the swarm functioning. The topic of this paper is on macroscopical patterns emerging from interacting swarm members and the environment. It is argued that these patterns are invaluable for maintaining the integrity of the swarm. A preliminary catalogue of macroscopical patterns and an experimental method are proposed to engineer the patterns in the swarm, test them and redesign the agents to achieve the desired patterns.

1   Introduction

Swarm behavior is an area in artificial intelligence (AI) and artificial life (ALife) that has been receiving increased research effort over the last couple of years. Although the fields of AI and ALife remained rather separate for some time, recent developments show a merger. This has resulted in attention from AI in the principles of life as a source of intelligence, and the role of architecture in the thinking about the principles of life. This cross-pollination has resulted in the study of intelligent swarms that consist of agents with a limited action repertoire exhibiting intelligence as a whole.

Where in AI the emphasis is on the architecture of the agents - the intelligent entities - in ALife the emphasis is more on the interaction between the agents and the behavioral patterns that emerge from the society of agents. Also in the very area where AI and ALife converge - the area of *swarm intelligence* - this distinction can clearly be observed. Where AI emphasizes task division, the division of all the tasks needed to have a swarm functioning such as guarding the nest or collecting food, ALife emphasizes the macroscopical patterns that *emerge* from the interaction between the agents among themselves and their environment. The most notable of the macroscopical patterns is *flocking*. In Flocking agents behave in a coordinated, simultaneous and synchronous way. We call these emergent behavioral patterns *Macroscopical Dynamical Synchronous* (MDS) behavior.

MDS patterns abound in natural swarms such as bee colonies, penguin colonies, flocks of birds and schools of fish. MDS patterns increase the chances of survival of both the individuals as the group, e.g., to deter predators, to spread adversary environmental conditions over the individuals, or to attack prey more

W. Truszkowski, C. Rouff, M. Hinchey (Eds.): WRAC 2002, LNAI 2564, pp. 92–105, 2003.

effectively. In artificial swarms such as microrobots performing surveillance missions, synchronized coordinated behavior may be required to maintain, e.g., an optimal overall scanning resolution, i.e., preventing robots from scanning the same area while omitting other areas.

MDS patterns receive far less attention than task division in the area of swarm intelligence research, mainly because there is currently a lack of a catalog of MDS patterns and that MDS patterns are emergent phenomena [1, p. 7]. The problem we address in this paper is how to design swarms with MDS patterns. MDS patterns can not be directly engineered into the swarm because the required MDS patterns are *emergent*, i.e., the patterns can not be deduced from the properties of the individual agents, they arise through interaction of the agents with themselves and the environment. [1, p. 7]. Because the properties of artificial swarms that should exhibit MDS patterns can only be designed in an indirect way, doing so requires a special methodology that we call *experimental swarm design*. Central to this methodology is, that it contains a trial-and-error component through which the desired properties are achieved.

In section 2, the area of swarm intelligence is placed in perspective; in section 3 the nature of the MDS patterns and the difference between MDS behavior and task division are discussed; in section 4 MDS patterns are characterized as morphological dynamics of swarms, a preliminary catalogue is drawn up and attention is given to how morphological dynamics of swarms can be modelled and formally described; in section 5 the design methodology for swarms exhibiting MDS behavior is disccussed; in section 6 some concluding remarks are made.

2   Swarm Intelligence

Research into ALife usually takes on one of two forms, viz., studying complex networks of interacting elements, such as autocatalytic networks, or models of collectives of artificial animals such as bee colonies or flocks of birds. Research into swarm intelligence (SI) [1], usually concerns the latter.

Examples of complexity studies in ALife are cellular automata (due to Langton [2]), chemical reaction networks and boolean networks (due to Kauffman [3]), and complex adaptive systems (due to Holland [4]). Typical of this research is that the elements in the model are usually simple, such as reacting molecules. Connectivity and interaction rates are the main parameters through which different emerging (complex) patterns are studied. The best known example of such a pattern is the Belousov-Zhabotinsky (BZ) reaction (cf. [5]). In this reaction, chemicals in a petri-dish exhibit concentric waves through local interactions of the chemicals (cf. fig. 1).

The Belousov-Zhabotinsky reaction are now often classified as *excitable media*: periodic wave dynamics that arise in many areas of science [6, p. 184]. Excitable media can typically be modelled by one out of a family of systems of cellular automata, cf. [7, 6]. In the same vein as Kauffman [3] describes autocatalytic networks, the dynamics of the familiy of systems of cellular automata can described, viz., the (number of) attractors, the regimes of order and general

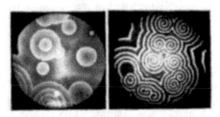 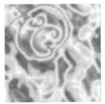 

Fig. 1. The left two figures depict the waves produced by the Belousov-Zhabotinski reaction in a petri-dish. The left two pictures are snapshots of a system of cellular automata modelling the Belousov-Zhabotinski reaction

types of patterns, such as number of origins where the waves originate from, type of generator, etc. Our contention is, that these notions also play an important role in the description of MDS patterns of swarms, i.e., in the case elements have certain cognitive or intelligent capacities [1].

In distinguishing swarm intelligence (SI) from complexity studies (CS) an artificial ingelligence (AI), the issue of intelligent capacities of the individuals *and that of the swarm as a whole* play an important role. In general, cognitive processes produce intentional states [8] and the presence of intentional states marks the division between CS where the intentional states are absent, and SI, where they are present. Where for instance, in chemical reactions only physical process can be observed, in swarms the interactions leading to flocking or other MDS patterns have a purpose that can be described and explained (e.g., in terms of increases in survival chances). Swarms are autonomous in the sense that they are directed to maintain their integrity and adaptive in the sense that they respond to environmental changes to do that (cf. [9]).

The distinction between SI and AI can best be made by referring to the locus of the cognitive process. Where in AI cognitive processes are traditionally seen as located within individuals, in SI the cognitive processes arise out of interaction between the individuals and their environment. There has been a growing acknowledgement in AI over the last decade of the role of interaction, which has created a duality in the view on the locus of the cognitive processes in intelligent agents. Cognitive processes may originate fully from within an agent, partially from within it and from interaction, and fully from the interaction. We call this issue the *completeness of coding* issue, because the behavioral rules (the coding) may lie fully or partially in the individual and in the swarm together with the environment. We will discuss this issue in more depth in section 3.2.

The duality in the completeness of coding issue causes a duality in modelling swarm behavior. For instance, in bee colonies it is quite clear that besides the behavior the insects exhibit in their roles, such as workers or drones, they possess no other or not much more cognitive capacities. Human behavior, on the other

---

[1] We use the term 'cognitive', in a specific way, as explained later. Also, with regard to this special meaning, we use 'cognitive' and 'intelligent' processes as synonyms.

Table 1. Three levels of agency in swarms. The higher the agency, the more elaborate their cognitive capacities and/or richness of their behavioral repertoire. When human behavior is restricted (e.g., in traffic situations) they also categorize under 'lower animals'

level of agency	nature	type of agency	emergence
low	complexity studies	reactive chemicals	patterns in chemical interaction networks
middle	swarm	insects, lower (artificial) animals	colony organization flocking
high	intelligent agents	autonomous, intentional cognitive, rational	distributed problem solving cognitive emergence

hand, can in some situations be modelled by simple behavioral rules, while capable of executing uncountably more and qualitatively different types of cognitive processes at the same time or in different situations. Modelling swarm behavior can thus be gradually more complete for different kinds of swarms.

An example of the case where the swarm model describes the MDS behavioral pattern accurately, but the cognitive processes of the elements poorly, is human group behavior. In certain circumstances, such as panic situations [10] and behavior (queuing) in traffic [11] human group behavior can be modelled by simple rules acting on the individuals. However, the MDS patterns that emerge, hold only for specific situations, and the individuals (the elements) may at the same time or later carry out other cognitive processes that have no relation to the processes that give rise to the MDS patterns. In general, SI concerns itself with behavior that can be *modelled* by simple rules where the MDS patterns emerge from the interaction between the elements and the environment, while these rules may model the actual cognitive processes of the elements (the individuals) veridically or less veridically. In table 1 the three different types of agency that are the subject matter of CS, SI and AI are summarized by their properties, examples and phenomena that are under study.

The implication for swarm design of this duality, is that there is an aspect of design that concerns only the agent's capacity and that there are other aspects that concern the functioning of the swarm. For instance, microrobots that survey a territory or a part of space, the agents may have both properties that are relevant to the swarm's behavior, such as keeping a certain distance from others and aligning with others, and properties that are not, such as collecting samples or processing sensory data from the surface. The former constitute the MDS behavioral patterns that need a special design methodology because they can not be engineered directly into the swarm.

Within SI, an additional distinction between flocking behavior and task division in a swarm is usually made. Bonabeau et al. [1] refer to the former as *social insect* behavior, which we call *task division*, and to the latter as *coordi-*

nated behavior (pp. 1-7; we have called this flocking and MDS behavior). In the next section we point out why task division receives much more attention in SI research and swarm design than MDS behavior.

3   Emergence, Task Division and MDS Behavior

MDS patterns are *emergent* phenomena. We use the concept of emergence in the sense that patterns in a dynamical system can be described at a higher level than that of the behavior of the individual elements, and that these phenomena occur spontaneously, i.e., through *self-organization* (cf. [12, p. 816]). Processes of Self-organization (SO) result in a spontaneous increase in order in the system, i.e., there is no central directing agent, authority or otherwise externally imposed restriction that achieves order in the system. Emergent properties of swarm behavior can not be inferred from the properties of the elements of the swarm for two reasons, viz., 1) macroscopic properties of the swarm arise through the interaction between the elements and are typically non-linear and 2) the agents are adaptive, which means that their behavior may change under influence of the environment. It is recognized that this is these are the main difficulties in designing swarms [1, p. 7].

Some of the complex behavior and organization that natural swarms exhibit *as a whole* are genetically determined, such as the roles in a colony and how to perform them, while other phenomena are due to SO. For instance, the behavior of following a pheromone trail is largely genetically determined, while the prevalence over time of a few trails and the diminishing of the rest is due to SO. The emergence of a few trails out of the initially many, is an emergent phenomenon because it emerges from simple rules and the interactions the agents have with each other and the environment. If a swarm exhibits a shift from one type of organization (or complete disorganization) to another, this is called *multi-level behavior*. We discuss multi-level behavior in the next section.

Although some processes in natural swarms are due to SO, colony organization as a whole isn't. The genetic endowment of the animals includes the roles that have to be fulfilled in a colony, and sometimes predestines individuals to fulfill particular roles exclusively. Agents in natural swarms may switch roles, depending on demand, but the structure as defined by the roles is fixed. Colony organization divides tasks in manageable parts and enables the colony as a whole to exhibit complex behavior. There is a kind of SO involved in this behavior because there is no central agent directing the activities. However, because the behavior is coded into the individuals, the behavioral patterns do not arise spontaneously and not through the interaction of individuals and their environment, while this *is* the case in MDS behavior. The distinction between task division and MDS behavior is discussed further in section 3.2.

3.1   Multi-level Behavior

Multi-level behavior is a term that is derived from dynamical systems theory, in which it is usually called a *bifurcation* [13]. Bifurcations happen when the track through the state space of a system suddenly changes to move to another attractor. When an agent changes its course of action such that it exhibits a qualitatively different type of behavior, the same happens. If for instance, an ant encounters a hot object on the pheromone trail it is currently following, it may change the state transitions of its motor apparatus in such a way not to follow the trail, but to get away from the object. Such changes are discontinuous, and comprise a change in the attractor(s) of the state space of the ant's 'system'. In other words, the agent goes through a *bifurcation in behavior* [13, pp. 272-273].

Bifurcations of behavior play an important role in adaptation because it enables agents to respond with qualitatively different behavior when current (adapted) behavior is no longer adequate [14, p. 4], [1, p. 13]. This may be due to the environment, e.g., the appearance of a hot object, or due to internal conditions of the agent, e.g., energy depletion. However multi-level behavior in swarms has received little attention as yet. In section 4.2 we discuss how multi-level behavior can be formally described as a design requirement.

3.2   Task Division and MDS Behavior

Task division sometimes involves multi-level behavior of individuals, i.e., individuals sometimes switch from roles, but the colony as a whole doesn't exhibit multi-level behavior when it is functioning. Insect colonies often do go through different structural stages, e.g., during initial formation, fertilization of the queen by the drones and migration. However, this is a self-regulatory cycle and not an adaptation to a specific environment.

AI has adopted swarm models as a way of Distributed Problem Solving [1, p. 6-7], and improved on them. However, as said before, MDS behavior has received much less attention. MDS behavior involves the same behavior or a substantial amount of agents simultaneously or *synchronously*, that form a macroscopic pattern, (hence the term MDS). Natural swarms exhibit at least two modes of behavior. Usually a disorganized mode in which the animals are e.g., foraging, and on the approach of a predator, they all lump together and fly or swim in a coordinated way to confuse the predator.

A paradigmatical example of how MDS patterns can be realized through SO *by design*, is provided by Reynold's BOIDS [15]. BOIDS move in a two or three dimensional space, and the BOIDS follow only local rules in which they align with each other and keep a certain distance from their neighbors. In BOIDS flocking behavior can be observed that is similar to flocking in natural swarms.

The reason MDS behavior plays a subsidiary role in swarm design, is that design of behavior of the individuals does not directly relate to MDS patterns. However, the benefits of MDS behavior are of major importance when designing swarms that can not be controlled by an agent (human or artificial) that has global information. Again, the typical example here is that of (micro)robots surveying a remote terrain and have to exhibit coordinated and adaptive behavior.

Task division is a way to optimize efficiency of (necessary) tasks within the collective. A number of individuals are devoted to special tasks, such as guarding the nest, or caring for the brood, and this division of labor may depend on the needs of the collective. MDS behavior can best be seen as a way to maintain the collective's integrity. Attacking predators may be confused by the simultaneous movements of the swarm, and predators may hunt more effectively if they are in formation. The distinction between task division and MDS behavior is a gliding scale. There may be specific tasks in the collective that consist of defending the collective (as in ant colonies), and some tasks may involve the coordination of multiple individuals at the same time. However, the action patterns for task division behaviors are usually coded *in* the individual completely and do not emerge as a consequence of *interactions* between the members of the colony and the environment. For instance, the behavior that constitutes guarding the colony is completely present in the individual carrying it out, while the pattern that emerges when a school of fish swim synchronously in the same direction is coded in partially in every individual fish. One fish can not exhibit synchronous behavior because it simply needs others that behave the same at the same time to do that.

Richness of behavioral patterns, thus can consist of several *complete* patterns, and several *partial* patterns. In fig. 2, the two dimensions of richness and completeness of coding are depicted with typical species indicated as examples. We roughly divide the space spanned by richness and completeness in four areas, viz., 1) agents that have a small behavioral repertoire, both as complete action sequences in themselves as distributed over the group (chemical reaction networks), 2) agents that can complete tasks prescribed by a role, i.e., some degree of completeness but a lower degree of richness (ants in ant colonies), 3) agents that exhibit collective behavior or MDS patters, but have a lower degree of completess (flocks of birds), and 4) agents that have both a rich behavioral pattern but can also involve in task division and exhibit MDS patterns.

If the richness of coding increases, the agent or collective of agent is able to perform more different kinds of behavior, e.g., searching for food or defending the nest. If the agents exhibit a rich pattern of behaviors but the variety is in the different roles of the collective, as is the case in ant colonies (exploring the surroundings and defending the nest), the behavioral richness of the *collective* is high, but not that of the individuals. Also, this type of collective may be adapted, but the adaptations have been achieved by evolution and are not extended in one and the same colony or generation. The adaptations have come about *phylogenetically*. In MDS, a change in behavioral pattern of the whole collective can be observed, as in flocking on arrival of a predator. This ability to shift to another *type* of behavior, or presence of multi-level order in the colony [14, p. 4], is a mark of richness of coding in the individual as well as in the collective.

In general, the greater the variety of behaviors a group can exhibit, the more adaptive it is as a group, but not necessarily as individuals because they require others to fulfill parts of the tasks needed to survive. The more completely behavioral patterns are present in the individuals, the greater the independence or autonomy of the individuals, because they are less dependent on others. Hence,

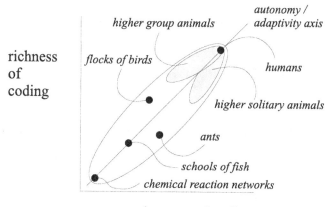

Fig. 2. The space spanned up by completenss of coding and richness of coding. Richness of coding increases the adaptivity of groups of agents or individuals, while completeness of coding increases the autonomy

to optimize swarm functionality, both completeness and richness should be high, and both MDS behavior and task division capabilities should be present. In swarm design, there is always a trade-off between the richness in behavioral capacities and the cost and the practical feasibility of the design of the individuals. However, the duality in the locus of the intelligent processes (cf. section 2) allows designers to spread the intelligence over the swarm so as to keep the weight of the design of the individuals light.

In the next section we discuss *how* to describe MDS patterns, how to formulate them as design requirements for artificial swarms and how to test if they have really been achieved.

4   Morphological Dynamics of Swarms

In the discipline of *spatial ecology* it has occasionally been attempted to "describe the diverse roles that organisms' exploitation of space play in ecology" [16, p. 119]. In this work, one step further than classification is taken: first a spatial pattern is identified (usually a cluster, or a patch) and after this the development of the cluster is described. In [16] patches are identified by means of spatial covariance which indicates spatial continuity of a or patchiness of spatially indexed variables. With the same objective, Balch [17] developed a method of classifying (spatial) agent distribution on the basis of hierarchical social entropy, i.e., in the way they differ. If the MAS consists of different[2] agents the entropy is high, but

---

[2] Different or similarity means some measure over the properties of the agents. This may include inherent properties of the agents such as color or size, but also spatial properties, such as physical distance.

if similar agents are located near to each other, a clustering can be made so that the entropy in subclusters is low (dispersed homogeneous clusters). Dynamics in the MAS may be such that the hierarchical entropy decreases over time because similar agents attract each other (a selforganizing process). In Sumpter and Broomhead [18] cluster formation is also seen as the decrease of entropy. They determine with a χ^2 test whether the bees they study are still uniformly distributed or lumped together.

Measures like spatial covariance, patchiness and social entropy are more fine-grained than the predominant measure in population dynamics, i.e., population size, but they are still too crude to describe actual MDS patterns. Also the way to model the dynamics, traditionally in terms of massive interaction modelled by simple differential equations such as the Lotka-Volterra model of predator-prey interactions (cf. [19]), rely on assumptions such as homogeneity of the population and their interactions, i.e., similar interactions producing the same effect. Keitt and Johnson [19] observe that due to either environmental or interactional inhomogeneity, the latter caused by agent differences, emergent phenomena appear. Highly symmetrical wave fronts of prey and predators appear that are similar to those observed in the Belousov-Zhabotinski reactions [19, p. 132], cf. fig. 1. However, they do not attempt to describe the characteristics of the phenomena themselves other than providing a graphical snapshot of them. In the same vein as Dalthorp, Nyrop and Villani [16] propose, to have a better way of describing morphological dynamics of ecosystems and in our case that of swarms, some primitives need to be defined and how they can be combined. Below a tentative catalogue is given.

Static Properties of Non-homogeneous Systems

Patchiness: By means of a cluster-analysis of some kind (e.g., cf. [17]), a number of patches or clusters may be identified. Clusters may take on any shape, e.g., from a sphere to a line (see below). The first step towards a description of (dynamical) structures in the system is identifying *subsystems*. The overall structure of the whole system is described by the structural properties mentioned below.

Size: physical volume of the subsystem, as measured in two- or three-dimensional units. Form: form may be characterized by primitives such as triangles, squares, circles, spheres, etc.

Structure: the structure of the subsystem; it's homogeneity, density, variety, dottedness, patchiness, stratification, etc. Subsystems may in this way be divided into new subsystems.

Dynamic Properties of Non-homogeneous Systems

Patch Dynamics: This indicates change in patch identity, i.e., dissolution, division and amalgamation. Clustering depends on the choice of criteria for determining the identity of a cluster. Similarity of members is an obvious one, similarity measures may be weighted, cluster identity may depend on the amount and the identity of (some of) its members, etc.

Size Dynamics: Patches may shrink or grow and change position relative to each other.

Structural Dynamics: Structural characteristics may change over time. This may result in complex patterns to occur. Patches may be stretched, stratify, contract, members and layers may rotate relative to each other, patches may exhibit spirals and swirls, etc.

Because there has been little attention in Biology, ALife and AI for the description of behavior at this level, it is a matter of exploration to discover some more primitives and combinations in the first place and the usefulness of them in the second place.

4.1   Modelling Morphological Dynamics in Swarms

BOIDS (as discussed in section 3.2) are a good example of how clustering and alignment within clusters happen on the basis of simple interactive behavioral rules of individuals. However, the morphological dynamics *inside* the clusters are minimal due to the alignment behavior. When swarms are confronted with a dynamical external environment the behavior of the swarm may need adaptations to maintain an adequate fitness. For instance, when a swarm consists of hunters that try to achieve a maximum yield from their hunt, under some conditions hunters and prey may form waves that propagate from an origin in concentric rings around it, similar to the waves emerging from the Belousov-Zhabotinsky reaction (cf. [19]). The wavefronts that emerge from this behavior may be described by a set of multiple spirals. The endogenous MDS pattern of the swarm thus can be modelled by the equations of the archimedean spirals, their origin and their periodicity, cf. fig. 3.

Another example is the behavior of Emperor Penguins hibernating on the Antarctic. To spread the exposure to the cold, the penguins huddle together in a dense group in which warmth in the center is highest, and on the outside the lowest. To achieve a maximum spread over the individuals in the colony, the penguins exhibit individual behavior that may consist of a spiral-like movement

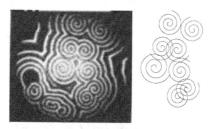

Fig. 3.   A snapshot of the Belousov-Zhabotinsky reaction with the model of multiple spirals next to it

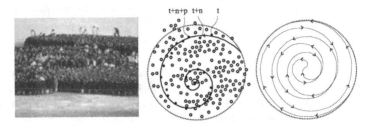

Fig. 4. In a colony of penguins spiral-like behavior of the individuals can be observed. In the middle the behavior is modelled as a hyperbolic spiral, and on the left as an archimedean spiral

towards the center, and after reaching the center, a spiral like-movement to the outside. Again, this behavior may be modelled by overlaying a spiral-like pattern on the track of the individuals, as is depicted in fig. 4.

4.2   Formally Describing and Checking MDS Patterns

In order to specify and check whether the design goals with regard to the MDS patterns are met, we need to describe the patterns and indicate when and for how long they occur. This can be done in a standard temporal logic [20] such as the computational tree logic (CTL) [21, p. 150]. Here we give an indication of how this can be done.

Usually in temporal logics there is a set of points in time $t \in T$, where a valuation function V maps proposition letters to the sets $V(p)$ of those points in time where they hold [22, p. 247]. Triples $\mathbb{M} = (T, <, V)$, in which $<$ is a binary precedence order on T are called temporal models that may be thought of as a flow of time decorated with a history over it. The truth of a formula ϕ at a moment t in a model $\mathbb{M}$ is given by: $\mathbb{M}, t \models \phi$ iff $t \in V(\phi)$. Distinct sets of formulas describe the state of the world at various time points, without any a priori restrictions. This makes temporal logic suitable to describe systems in which emergent phenomena occur, because typically, a new way of describing the system is necessary to recognize the emergent phenomenon after a phase transition (or bifurcation) has occurred.

To illustrate this, let p indicate a low value for entropy (as discussed in the previous section). We can express the phase transition from a state of high entropy to low entropy at time t' by: if $\mathbb{M}, t \models \neg p$, then for $t < t'$: $\mathbb{M}, t' \models p$. In fig. 5 this is depicted.

Emergent properties can be described formally, and with a temporal logic, it can be indicated when, and under what conditions they should occur. Designers can make use of the formal specifications of the emergent properties, by designing their systems and check whether the properties of the system match the design specifications, the *requirements*. Checking whether the requirements hold, is a *model-based approach*, in contrast to semantic entailment, or proof theory [21, p. 150]. Model checking is done solely with the notion of satisfaction,

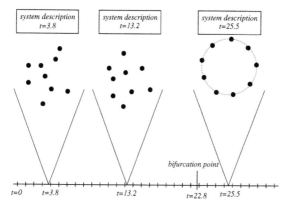

Fig. 5. A bifurcation occurring in the spatial organization of the elements. Afther the bifurcation, a greater amount of order is visible, and a spatial relation can be defined that is true after the transition, but not before

i.e., the satisfaction relation between a model and a formula ($\mathbb{M} \models \phi$, in which ϕ is the desired property). Although model checking is not new, it is new to the design of systems with emergent properties. Model checking is appropriate because it doesn't check requirements by inferring them from the elements and their logical structure, but just by observing the development of the dynamical system and checking for the properties as they occur. In the next section the design method for swarms is presented.

5   A Design Methodology for Swarms

Because MDS behavior is *emergent*, as discussed in section 3, there is no one-to-one correspondence between the design of the agents and the MDS patterns. This requires that design parameters of the agents need to be changed and the effects be *experimentally* determined. This process is described below.

1. Identify the goal of the swarm. This can be a terrain survey, collection of samples or even attacking a target.
2. Identify the atomic properties of the agents. This can be movement, sensing, communicating and all kinds of behavior affecting the environment, and incorporate them in the design (these are the design parameters).
3. Identify possible perturbations on both the individual agents and the swarm as a whole. Formulate the behavior of the swarm as requirements in a temporal logic. Design a simulation environment, and observe the behavior of the swarm.
4. If the swarm exhibits goal-directed behavior and is stable, and if the swarm jump-changes (through multi-level behavior) to another appropriate kind of behavior, i.e., it meets the swarm-behavior requirements identified above,

finish. Otherwise hypothesize about the cause of the persistent instability, change the design parameters of the agents and start from 3.

Effectively, the designers create a world, which, although they have designed it themselves, they do not and can not know it completely because of the emergent phenomena that occur. In fact, they are proceeding through the empirical cycle laid down by De Groot [23] in order to understand and manipulate this world. They have to build an 'evaluation chamber', that consists of the world and the requirements on swarm behavior, test the actual behavior and evaluate it. Because we are designing, we are not adapting the theory, but the design of the agents so that they meet the requirements. This is the only modification, and this modification always applies in engineering, that has to be made on the empirical cycle of De Groot.

6   Conclusions

Designed swarms will undoubtedly play a large role in the future of AI, ALife and robotics, because, among other reasons, their higher level of adaptivity as compared to monolithic agents. However, the design and verification of swarms is still a largely unexplored field, especially concerning MDS behavior. Because of the emergent properties swarms exhibit, this behavior is not completely predictable, which has to be the case to some extent to benefit from it. We proposed an experimental design method through which swarm behavior can be determined and modified until the desired properties are achieved. We propose to use a temporal logic to capture the swarm dynamics and the required emergent phenomena.

In the future this method has to be tested on a wide variety of swarms and environment in order to assess the full extent of its benefits. To do this, it is necessary to extend the tentative list of primitives we have provided for describing the morphological dynamics of swarms. Together with the experimental design method we have presented, it is then possible to engineer MDS behavior into the swarm, test and fine tune the design parameters until the swarm exhibits the desired properties.

References

[1] Bonabeau, E., Dorigo, M., Theraulaz, G.: Swarm Intelligence: from Natural to Artificial Intelligence. Oxford University Press, New York (1999) 93, 95, 96, 97

[2] Langton, C. G.: Self-reproduction in cellular automata. Physica D 10 (1984) 135-44 93

[3] Kauffman, S. A.: The Origins of Order: Self-organization and selection in evolution. Oxford University Press (1993) 93

[4] Holland, J. H.: Hidden Order: how Adaptation Builds Complexity. Addison-Wesley, Readin, MA (1995) 93

[5] Zhabotinsky, A. M., Zaikin, A. N.: Autowave processes in a distributed chemical system. J. Theor. Biol. 40 (1973) 45-61 93

[6] Durrett, R., Griffeath, D.: Asymptotic behavior of excitable cellular automata. Experimental Mathematics 2 (1993) 183-208 93

[7] Dewndney, A.: Computer recreations: The hodgepodge machine makes waves. Scientific American (1988) 86-89 93

[8] Dennett, D. C.: Intentional systems. Bradford Books, Montgomery, VT (1978) 3-22 94

[9] Wan, A. D. M., Braspenning, P. J., Vreeswijk, G. A. W.: Limits to ground control in autonomous spacecraft. Telematics & Informatics 12 (1996) 247-259 94

[10] Helbing, D., Farkas, I., Vicsek, T.: Simulating dynamical features of escape panic. Nature 407 (2000) 487-490 95

[11] Treiber, M., Hennecke, A., Helbling, D.: Congested traffic states in empirical observations and microscopic simulations. Phys. Rev. E 62 (2000) 1805-1824 95

[12] Damper, R. I.: Editorial for the special issue on emergent properties of complex systems. Int. J. Systems Science 31 (2000) 811-818 96

[13] Hirsch, M. W., Smale, S.: Differential Equations, Dynamical Systems and Linear Algebra. Academic Press, New York (1974) 96, 97

[14] Boden, M. A.: Introduction: The intellectual context of artificial life. In Boden, M. A., ed.: The Philosophy of Artificial Life. Oxford University Press (1996) 1-35 97, 98

[15] Reynolds, C.: Flocks, herds and schools: A distributed behavioral model. Computer graphics 21 (1987) 25-34 97

[16] Dalthorp, D., Nyrop, J., Villani, M. G.: Foundations of spatial ecology: The reification of patches through quantiative descriptions of patterns and pattern repitition. Entomologica Experimentalis et Applicata 96 (2000) 119-127 99, 100

[17] Balch, T.: Hierarchic social entropy: An information theoretic measure of robot group diversity. Autonomous Robots 8 (2000) 209-238 99, 100

[18] Sumpter, D. J., Broomhead, D.: Shape and dynamics of themoregulating honey bee clusters. J. Th. Biology 204 (2000) 1-14 100

[19] Keitt, T. H., Johnson, A. R.: Spatial heterogeneity and anomolous kinetics: Emergent patterns in diffusion-limited predator-prey interaction. J. Theor. Bio. 172 (1995) 124-139 100, 101

[20] Schlinhoff, B. H.: Verification of finite state systems with temporal logic model checking. South African Computer Journal 19 (1997) 70-89 102

[21] Huth, M., Ryann, M.: Logic in Computer Science: Modelling and Reasoning about Systems. Cambridge University Press, Cambridge, UK (2000) 102

[22] Van Benthem, J.: Temporal logic. In Gabbay, D. M., Hogger, C., Robinson, J. A., eds.: Handbook of Logic in AI and Logic Programming. Clarendon Press, Oxford, UK (1995) 102

[23] Groot, A. D. D.: Methodology: Foundations of Inference and Research in the Behavioral Sciences. Mouton, Den Haag, The Netherlands (1969) First published in Dutch, 1961 104

Learning in the Broker Agent

Xiaocheng Luan[1], Yun Peng[2], and Timothy Finin[2]

[1] Aquilent Inc. 22215 Overview Lane
Boyds, MD 20841, USA
xluan1@cs.umbc.edu
[2] Department of Computer Science and Electrical Engineering
University of Maryland Baltimore County
1000 Hilltop Circle, Baltimore, MD 21250, USA
{ypeng,finin}@cs.umbc.edu

Abstract. Service matching is one of the crucial elements in the success of large, open agent systems. While finding "perfect" matches is always desirable, it is not always possible. The capabilities of an agent may change over time; some agents may be unwilling to, or unable to communicate their capabilities at the right level of details. The solution we propose is to have the broker agent dynamically refine the agent's capability model and to conduct performance rating. The agent capability model will be updated using the information from the consumer agent feedback, capability querying, etc. The update process is based on a concept of "dynamic weight sum system", as well as based on the local distribution of the agent services. We assume that the agents in the system share a common domain ontology that will be represented in DAML+OIL, and the agent capabilities will be described using DAML-S.

1 Introduction

Finding the right agent(s) for the right task is critical in achieving agent cooperation in large, open agent systems. A popular approach to this problem is to use a broker agent (or in general, the middle agents) to connect the service provider agents and the service consumer agents, via service matching. Typically a broker agent recommends service providers based on the capabilities/services advertised by the service provider agents themselves. The matching scheme has evolved from the early age, simple KQML performative based matching [17], to syntax and semantic based matching [27]; from returning yes/no exact matches to returning matches with probabilities [32]. However, there are still issues that need to be addressed. The ability to learn is one of the key properties of the agents, therefore, the capabilities of an agent, both in terms of what it can do and how well it can do it, will likely to change over time. Moreover, the advertised capability information may not be always accurate - some agents may be unwilling or unable to advertise their capability information at sufficient level of details, some might unknowingly advertise inaccurate information,

W. Truszkowski, C. Rouff, M. Hinchey (Eds.): WRAC 2002, LNAI 2564, pp. 106–121, 2003.

while others might even purposefully provide misleading information of their capabilities. Even when the capability information is "accurate", the agent selected may not be able to provide quality service(s).

We have similar problems in the real world: we don't know whether the colorful, fancy, and even convincing commercials are true or not. There is no perfect solution to this real world problem - people have to learn their lessons. People can learn from their own experience - if you bought a bottle of milk from a super market, but the milk was sour, you will be less likely to buy milk from that store again. People can also learn from their friends' experience. While this kind of learning is very helpful, it's usually insufficient, because an individual usually has a limited social circle and therefore, the experience is limited, both in terms of the variety of experience and the number of occurrences. That is why there are the consumer reports. Consumer reports are created using the information from the manufacture's specification, the consumer's feedback, and their test results on the products. It provides guidance for consumers to choose the right products. We believe that this consumer reports approach should work in the agent world, too.

A particular agent can certainly try to learn which agents can provide good services for it. However, its contact with other agents is usually limited, not to mention that it usually has its own specialized work to perform. Therefore, to have each agent to perform the learning would create a huge burden both for the agent itself and for the agent developer(s). The broker agent, however, typically interacts with many (if not all) of the agents in the system, and therefore is the ideal candidate for collecting and summarizing the agents' experience and composing the "consumer reports" for the other agents. This new task is consistent with its ultimate goal, that is, to provide the best recommendations to the service consumer agents. By following a brokering protocol, the broker agent will not only collect the information advertised by the service provider agents, but will also learn from the experience the consumer agents have about their service providers. It can also interrogate (query) a service provider agent to get more detailed information on the services it can provide. Moreover, the broker agent can dynamically capture the local probabilistic distribution of the agent services and use this information to assess the probability of a service match.

For the same reason that an agent's capability (description) may change over time (e.g., through learning), the significance of a piece of feedback data may also change over time. For example, recent feedback data might be considered "more important" than the earlier feedback data. To address this problem, we model the system as a dynamic, weighted sum system. When new data come in, new weights are generated for them and the weights for the data obtained earlier will be recomputed based on a pre-specified pattern or trend, so that the total weights still sum to 1. There is a family of weight sequence functions that is of special interest - the sequence functions that have the "incremental property". When a new weight sequence is generated due to the increase in the number of data samples, the new "total result" can be computed based on the previous total result and the new data (and of course, the new weights), without re-computing the whole thing.

Finally, our approach goes beyond the simple notion of a "reputation server" in that it discovers and refines a complex, symbolic model of a service provider's capability and performance.

The rest of this article is organized into three sections. In Section 2, we briefly introduce the related work in the area, as well as the technologies that will be used in this work, such as DAML+OIL and DAML-S. In Section 3 we discuss the refinement of an agent's capability model as well as the performance rating on the agents. We conclude the paper with the discussions on some related issues in Section 4.

2   Related Work and a Background

The area of agent service matching has been intensively researched in the past years because of its significance to the success of an agent system. In the early time, Agent Based Software Interoperation (ABSI) architecture [17]), a special kind of agent in the system, called the facilitator, is responsible for content-based message routing (basically based on the KQML performative in a message). This is essentially a KQML performative-based service matching, that is, the capability of an agent is described by what KQML performatives it can handle. More recent brokers usually support semantic based service matching, like the broker agent in the InfoSleuth Agent Architecture [27]. The SIMS information mediator [1] does more than simple service matching, it provides access and integration of multiple sources of information. When no direct mapping can be found, it can extend the search through concept generalization and specialization.

An interesting work on service matching is the LARKS (Language for Advertisement and Request for Knowledge Sharing) [32]. LARKS is an agent capability description language developed at CMU. It describes an agent's service by specifying the context, the data types, the input and output variables, and the input and output constraints. It also has a slot for the definition of the concepts used in the description. The matchmaking scheme in LARKS is fairly flexible. There are five filters, each of which addresses the matching process from a different perspective. "Context matching" determines if two descriptions are in the same or similar context; "profile comparison", "similarity matching", and "signature matching" are used to check if two descriptions syntactically match; while the "semantic matching" checks if the input/output constraints of a pair of descriptions are logically matched. Based on the need of a specific application domain, these filters can be combined to achieve different types/levels of matching.

The work in [33] compares concepts in differentiated ontologies. Differentiated ontologies are (different) ontologies evolved from a common base ontology. The concepts to be compared are represented in description logic. The paper describes roughly a dozen different measures that can be used to compute the compatibility of two concept descriptions. These measures fall into 3 main categories: the filter measures, the matching-based measures, and the probabilistic measures. The filter measures are basically based on how "close" the two concepts are in the concept hierarchy, and are inexpensive. The matching-based measures build and evaluate one-to-one correspondences between elements of concept definitions represented as graphs. The probabilistic functions require domain-specific knowledge of the joint distribution of primitives.

Most of the research/work on reputation management is in the context of electronic marketplaces. In [37], the author described two reputation mechanisms. Sporas is a simple reputation mechanism that provides a global reputation value for each user. After each rating, the reputation value is updated based on a formula. The second mechanism described in the paper is more interesting. It models the pair-wise ratings (between two users) using a directed graph, in which the nodes represent the users and the weighted edges represent the most recent reputation rating given by one user to the other. With this graph, a more "personalized" reputation value of B (in the eye of A) can be computed from the ratings on the paths from A to B, based on certain criteria (e.g., the length of a path must be less than a given number N). The idea is that "social beings tend to trust a friend of a friend more than a total stranger". The collaborative sanctioning model used in [25] is based on a concept called "encounter". "An encounter is an event between 2 agents (a_i, a_j) such that the query agent (a_i) asks the response agent (a_j) for a_j's rating of an object". "The reputation of a_j in a_i's mind is defined here as the probability that in the next encounter, a_j's rating about a new object will be the same as a_i's rating".

In comparison to the existing researches, our proposed approach allows the broker agent to refine the capability model of an individual agent, and to provide performance rating. Moreover, the performance ratings of an agent are considered an integral part of an agent's capability model. This is consistent with the DAML-S service ontology, in which a qualityRating attribute is defined in the service profile. The broker agent also approximates the probabilistic distribution of the agent services by capturing the local distribution. In this work, the ontology and the service description will be represented with DAML+OIL and DAML-S, respectively.

DAML+OIL is the result of the joint effort by the US DARPA Agent Markup Language project and the EU Information Society Technologies Program (IST). It is a semantic markup language for Web resources. It builds on earlier W3C standards such as RDF and RDF Schema, and extends these languages with richer modeling primitives. DAML+OIL provides modeling primitives commonly found in frame-based languages [7]. Therefore, we think it is suitable for use in ontology definition, manipulation, and reasoning. With DAML+OIL, one can define classes and properties, specify property restrictions, etc.

DAML-S is a web service ontology built on top of DAML+OIL. It is still an ongoing work at the DAML program. It supplies Web service providers with a core set of markup language constructs for describing the properties and capabilities of their services in unambiguous, computer-interpretable form [8]. It describes a service in terms of "service profile", "service model", and "service grounding". The service profile tells what the service does; the service model tells "how the service works"; the service grounding specifies how the service can be accessed. DAML-S could facilitate the automation of Web service tasks including automated Web service discovery, execution, interoperation, composition and execution monitoring.

3   Capability Model Refinement and Performance Rating

As mentioned earlier, finding the right agent(s) for a given task is critical in achieving agent cooperation in large, open agent systems. Typically a broker agent recommends service providers based on the capabilities or services advertised by the service providers themselves. But there are issues yet need to be addressed. For example, given the adaptive nature of the agents, the capabilities of an agent are likely to change over time; the advertised capability may not be always accurate, and that an agent with the right capability description may not provide quality services. In this work, we propose to extend the capability of the broker agent, i.e., to assign broker agent with new responsibilities of refining the capability description of individual agents, and conducting performance rating, based on the feedback and other collected information.

To simplify the problem, but without lose of generality, we make the following assumptions:

- All the agents (including the broker agent) in the system share a common domain ontology. Agents with different ontologies could work together through ontology translation and/or semantic resolution (For example, [29]).
- We assume a cooperative environment, in which all of the agents are cooperative.
- We consider security and privacy issues orthogonal to what we discuss here.

3.1   Basic Model of a Multi-agent System (MAS)

In our model of agent system, there are three types of agents: service provider agent, service consumer agent, and broker agent.

Service provider agent, or *service provider*, in short, is an agent that has certain capabilities of providing certain services, such as some piece of information or computing power. See also *service consumer*.

Service consumer agent, or *service consumer*, in short, is an agent that consumes the service(s) provided by other (service provider) agents. An agent can be a consumer of one service, and a provider of another service at the same time.

A broker agent, or *broker*, in short, is a middle agent that can recommend service providers (to the service consumers) based on the information it has. Generally service providers advertise their services to the broker agent, and service consumers can ask the broker agent what service providers can provide the services they need. In this work, broker agent has two more tasks to do: to refine the capability model of individual service providers, and to conduct performance rating based on the information it collects. However, an agent is not required to go through a broker agent to find a service provider.

Advertise refers to the process that an agent voluntarily tells other agents, e.g., the broker agent, about its capability information. It is similar to the "advertise" performative in KQML.

Recommend refers to the process that an agent (typically a broker agent) tells another agent what agents can perform certain tasks, usually in response to such a request.

Matching or *Matchmaking* refers to the process that the broker agent tries to match a recommendation request against its knowledge about the capabilities of the agents to find some agent(s) that can provide the service requested.

The term *recommendation request* and the term *matching request* are sometimes used interchangeably to refer to a request for recommendation of agents that can provide certain services.

3.2   The (Advisory) Brokering Protocol

To enable the broker with its new capabilities, the other agents as well as the broker agent itself need to follow an advisory brokering protocol, so that the individual agents can provide, and the broker agent can collect, useful information for refining the capability description and for conducting performance rating. The protocol is advisory because an agent without the knowledge about the protocol should at least be able to work with other agents in the system. However, it may not be able to take the full advantage of the broker's capability, as well as to contribute to the success of the broker agent. Note that the protocol described here is conceptual, in the sense that it may be implemented in various ways, e.g., as KQML performatives, or at service ontology level.

The protocol has the following (communicative) acts:

1. <advertise> If an agent wants other agents to know about its capabilities or services it can provide, it can send an <advertise> message (with its capability description) to the broker agent.
2. <request-for-recommendation> If an agent needs some services and wants to know who (what agents) can provide such services, it can send a <request-for-recommendation> message (with the service description) to the broker. The broker agent can respond with <recommend> if it can find some suitable service providers, or <sorry>, if it can't make an appropriate recommendation.
3. <recommend> The communicative act that the broker agent will use to recommend service providers (if any) in response to a <request-for-recommendation>
4. <follow-on-recommend> The broker agent (if it chooses to) may notify an agent about the availability of a new (better) service provider for a service that was previously requested.
5. <feedback> An agent can voluntarily, or in response to a request, send <feedback> to the broker agent about some previously recommended service providers.
6. <request-for-feedback> The broker agent can ask an agent how well a previously recommended agent works. The agents asked are encouraged to give a timely response.
7. <capability-query> An individual agent is expected to be able to answer queries such as "Can you do...?", "what are your capabilities", etc. The response to such a query can be a <advertise>, <confirm> or <disconfirm>.
8. <confirm> and <disconfirm> An individual agent can confirm or disconfirm about a capability query.

If an individual agent does not comply with the brokering protocol, it does not affect the others. As long as an agent observes the first three items, i.e., <advertise>, <request-for-recommendation>, and <recommend>, it can work with the broker, although it might not be able to take the full advantage of the broker's learning capability.

3.3   An Illustration

The refinement of an agent's capability model and the agent performance rating are based on the information the broker collected from the agents. The information may come from various channels, such as:

-   The information voluntarily advertised by a service provider agent
-   The feedback from a service consumer agent about some service providers
-   The result of a capability query
-   The local distribution of the agent services (will be explained later)
-   Feedback/ratings (if any) provided by the human users
-   The domain knowledge (e.g., the domain ontology)
-   If the broker also performs task brokering[1], then the requests and the results are useful, too (there are some privacy/security issues, which are outside the scope of this work).

Now we use an example to illustrate the process. Consider selling televisions as a service with three sub-service classes: selling traditional TV, selling HD-ready TV, and selling HDTV. Suppose that agent A advertised that one of the services it can provide is selling TV. Then agent B requests the broker to recommend some agent that sells HDTV and agent C asks for a traditional TV seller. But unfortunately, nobody has advertised for HDTV or traditional TV so far. Suppose the best the broker can do is to recommend agent A to both B and C. Moment later, agent B came back said "No, I'm disappointed with A" (Feedback on HDTV, not TV). But C came back and said, "The service provided by A is great!". Given all that information, the broker figured that although agent A advertised for selling (all kinds of, by default) TVs, it looks like its strength is in selling traditional TV service, and its selling HDTV service may not be that good. To take advantage of the brokering protocol, the broker agent can ask A if it really sells HDTVs. If A confirms, it won't help much to raise its reputation, but if A disconfirms, the broker agent can then just disqualify it for any future HDTV requests. Why agent A wants to reply, then? There could be two reasons: one is to be cooperative, the other is to avoid bad reputations - claiming that you can do something you can't do would adversely affect your reputation. The broker agent can prove, disprove, or refine its belief about an agent through more feedback from other agents, and make use of this knowledge in the future matching processes.

From this example, we can see that the refinement is based on the advertised capability description, guided by the domain knowledge (e.g., selling HDTV is a sub-class of selling TV service), using the information collected from various channels. At the same time as the capability description is refined, the broker agent will also assign ratings on the various aspects (or properties) of the service provided by certain agents. Therefore, capability description refinement and performance rating are really two results of the same process, or alternatively, one may view the performance rating as part of the capability description model.

---

[1] Task brokering refers to the process that the broker receives a query, finds an appropriate agent, and forwards the query to that agent. When finished, the result is sent to the broker, and the broker forwards the result to the requested agent.

Now we use a similar example to illustrate how the information on local service distribution can help in achieving better matching results. It's certainly the best if we know the exact probabilistic distribution of the various agent services, but that is not something always available. By local service distribution, we mean the distribution of the services seen so far. Suppose that through the course of matchmaking service, the broker discovers the following: 85% of the advertisements/requests are about traditional TV, 8% are about HD-ready TV, and the rest (7%) are about HDTV. Suppose that the only advertisements on selling TVs are the one from agent B, which advertised "selling traditional TVs", and the one from agent C, which advertised "selling HDTVs". If agent A requests a recommendation on "selling TV" service, then with the knowledge of the local service distribution, the broker would be able to recommend the traditional TV seller (agent B) over the HDTV seller (agent C), assuming all the other factors equal. Five years later, the distribution of the three sub service classes might change to 30%, 20%, and 50% respectively. The broker agent will then be able to dynamically capture the changes in the probabilistic distribution of services, and makes appropriate recommendations accordingly.

On the other hand, while most of the TV sellers (those who advertise that they sell TVs) sell traditional TVs, not that many TV sellers sell HDTVs. So based on the probabilistic distribution, the broker agent would be more confident to recommend a TV seller if the request is about traditional TV, while it would be less confident (to recommend a TV seller) if the request is about HDTV. When computing the probabilistic distribution, we consider both how many sub classes a service class has, and the frequency of a service being referenced (requested/advertised).

In large, heterogeneous agent systems, while exact service matches are always desirable, it's not always possible to find exact matches. The approach introduced here should help achieve more accurate partial matching.

3.4   Agent Capability Refinement Model

Now, let's take a closer look at the agent capability refinement model. A service has a set of direct super (parent) services (empty if top-level service) and a set of direct sub (child) services (empty if leaf level service). Among other information in an agent's capability description, there is a set of ratable features or properties (when no ratable features are specified, then there is one default ratable feature, which is the capability description itself). An importance vector can optionally be defined to specify the (relative) importance of each ratable feature.

The refinement is performed along three lines: service specialization, service generalization, and service performance rating. Specialization and/or generalization will be performed in situations when no (exact) match could be found for a requested service, or some (exact) matches could be found but the ratings on these services are not good. If some parent service p of the requested service can be found, and the rating r of p is good, we may assume that the agent could perform the requested service with similar ratings as r - basically we specialize the service that the agent can perform. Or on the other hand, if an agent can be found that can perform most (if not all) of the direct sub services of the requested service, we could estimate how well the agent can perform the requested service based on ratings on the sub services. The assumption or estimation (or belief, in one word) that the agent can perform the requested service with a certain rating can be further refined based on future feedback or capability queries. Specialization and generalization, together with performance rating, give the broker agent deeper insight in what an agent can do, and how well it can do it.

Performance rating is orthogonal to specialization and generalization. In order to discuss how the performance rating will be conducted and updated, we first need to introduce our abstraction of the problem and the concept of weight function.

The Dynamic Weighted Sum System. Our abstraction of the problem is to compute the weighted-sum of a set of dynamically obtained data samples. "Weighted" because the capability of an agent may change over time (e.g., through learning) and therefore, data samples obtained at different times usually carry different significance. The number of data samples may increase as new samples are obtained. The weights for these data samples are modeled as a weight sequence, whose length increases as new data samples are obtained. The data samples can be of any type (scalar, vector, matrix, or whatever) as long as it meets certain requirements as discussed below. The goal here is to dynamically and systematically assign a weight for each new data sample, adjust the weight for the existing data samples (implicitly or explicitly), and then compute the new weighted-sum, preferably in an incremental way.

A **weight sequence** is a sequence W_n $\{w_1, w_2, w_3, w_4 \ldots w_n\}$ of n (n>0) real numbers w_i such that $0 <= w_i \leq 1$ for all $1 \leq i \leq n$ and that $\sum_{<i=1, n>} \{w_i\} = 1$ (the sum of w_1 to w_n)

In this context, a **weight function** is a function f that, given a natural number n, can generate a weight sequence $\{f(n, 1), f(n, 2) \ldots f(n, n)\}$ of length n. Note that a weight sequence or a weight function is independent of any data sets, although it could be associated with a data set. A weight function is said to be **incremental** if, when a new data sample is obtained and a new weight sequence is generated for the increased data set, the new weighted sum can be computed incrementally based on the current weighted sum.

Why is this property of incrementality so important? First, you don't have to keep all the data samples around. Second, in contexts like broker learning, information about individual agents is obtained dynamically, and that information should be taken into account as soon as possible. If everything is recalculated from all the data obtained since the very start, the cost may be prohibitively high.

In order to study the dynamic properties of some weight functions, we need to define the concept of a dynamic weighted sum system.

Definition 1:
A 4-tuple $(f, X, +, *)$ is said to be a **DWS (Dynamic Weighted Sum) System** if:

➤ f is a weight function with range $d \subset R$ and $d = [0, 1]$. (R is the set of real numbers)
➤ X is a set of sample data (whose size may increase over time)
➤ + is the addition operator
➤ is the multiplication operator

Such that, with x, y, z ∈ X, and a, b, c ∈ d, the following hold:

> ➤ + and * on d are just the same as what/how they are defined on R.
> ➤ Closure: $x + y \in X$
> ➤ Associative law: $(x + y) + z = x + (y + z) = x + y + z$
> ➤ Distributive law: $a * (x + y) = a * x + a * y$, $(a + b) * x = a * x + b * x$.
> ➤ Commutative law: $a * x = x * a$

Theorem 1:
Suppose f is the weight function of a DWS system $(f, X, +, *)$. If for any given n (n>0) and i $(1 < i <= n)$,

$$f(n+1, i)/f(n, i) = c(n)$$

holds, where $c(n)$ is a function of n, $f(m, j)$ is the jth element in the (generated) weight sequence of length m, then f is incremental in the framework of the DWS system.

Proof:
Suppose the current size of X is n. Let $\{w_1, w_2, w_3, ..., w_n\}$ be the weight sequence generated by $f(n, i)$, and $\{w'_1, w'_2, w'_3, ..., w'_n, w'_{n+1}\}$ be the new weight sequence generated by $f(n+1, i)$ when the new data sample x_{n+1} is acquired. Let S_n be the weighted sum, we have:

$$S_n = \sum_{<i=1, n>}\{x_i * w_i\}.$$

With the latest acquired data sample x_{n+1}, let S_{n+1} be the new weighted sum, we have:

$$\begin{aligned}
S_{n+1} &= \sum_{<i=1, n+1>}\{x_i * w'_i\} \\
&= \sum_{<i=1, n>}\{x_i * w'_i\} + x_{n+1} * w'_{n+1} \\
&= \sum_{<i=1, n>}\{x_i * w_i * c(n)\} + x_{n+1} * w'_{n+1} \\
&= c(n) * \sum_{<i=1, n>}\{x_i * w_i*\} + x_{n+1} * w'_{n+1} \\
&= c(n) * S_n + x_{n+1} * w'_{n+1}
\end{aligned}$$

Therefore, the result S_{n+1} can be computed from S_n, so f is incremental.

End of proof.

Corollary 1:
Suppose $f(n, i)$ is the weight function of a DWS system $(f, X, +, *)$. For any given $n = N$, and any $1 < i <= N$, if $f(N+1, 1)/f(N, i) = c$ holds, where c is a constant, then f is incremental.

Proof:
It follows directly from theorem 1.

So, how to create/find a weight function that is incremental? As a first step, let's find out how we can find weight functions that can generate weight sequences of any given length. One solution is to construct weight functions from other mathematical sequence functions, e.g., the natural sequence function (a function that generates the natural sequence $\{1, 2, 3...\}$). Let $b(n, i)$ be a positive sequence function for sequence $\{b(n,1), b(n,2) ... b(n,n)\}$ of length n, where $1 <= i <= n$, and $b(n, i) >= 0$. Let $T(n) =$

$\sum_{<i=1, n>}\{b(n, i)\}$ be the sum of the sequence b(n, i). Now we construct a new sequence function f(n, i) of length n as follow:

$$f(n, i) = b(n, i)/T(n), 1 <= i <= n, \text{ and } x/0 = 0 \text{ for any number x.}$$

It's not difficult to show that $0 <= f$(n, i) $<= 1$, and that $\sum_{<i=1, n>}\{f(n, i)\} = 1$. Therefore, f(n, i) is a weight function. In this context, b is called the **base function**; T is called the **sum function** of b; and f is the **constructed weight function** with base function b.

Theorem 2:
For a positive sequence function b(x, i), if b(n+1, i) = b(n, i) holds for any given n (n>0) and any i (1<=i<=n), then the constructed weight function f(x, i) with base function b is incremental in any DWS system (f, X, +, *).

Proof:

$$f(n+1, i)/f(n, i) = (b(n+1, i)/T(n+1)) / (b(n, i)/T(n))$$
$$= (b(n+1, i)/ (b(n, i)) * (T(n) /T(n+1))$$
$$= T(n) /T(n+1)$$

The last step above is because b(n+1, i) = b(n, i). From theorem 1 we know that the weight function f(n, i) is incremental.

End of proof.

An Example Weight Function. Evidently, theorem 2 can lead to the discovery of some weight functions that are incremental in the framework of a DWS system. As an example, let's look at the weight function constructed from the geometric sequence function. The geometric sequence function (of length n) can be written as follow:

$$b(n, i) = r^{i-1}, \text{ where } 1 <= i <= n, \text{ and r is called the "ratio term".}$$

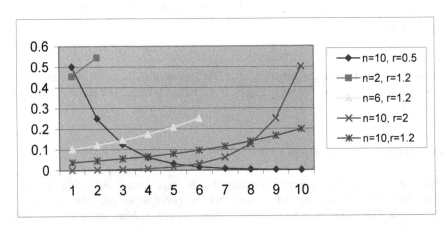

Fig. 1. Geometric Sequence Based Sequence Functions

When $|r| \neq 1$, the sum function is:

$$T(n) = (1 - r^n)/(1 - r)$$

Therefore, the weight function with base function b is:

$$f(n, i) = b(n, i)/T(n) = r^{i-1}/((1 - r^n)/(1 - r)) = (r^i - r^{i-1})/(r^n - 1)$$

Since $b(n+1, i) = b(n, i) = r^{i-1}$, it follows from theorem 2 that this geometric sequence based weight function is incremental. Figure 1 shows a family of weight functions with different length "n" and ratio "r". Here are some more observations:

1) For two geometric sequences with ratio r1 and r2. If $r1 = 1/r2$, their corresponding weight functions are symmetric along $x = n/2$, that is, $f_{r1}(n, i) = f_{r2}(n, n-i+1)$.
2) The sum function T(n) converges to $1/(1-r)$ when $0 <= r < 1$. Therefore, the minimum possible value for $f(n, 1)$ is $1-r$, and is therefore independent of n.
3) When $0 <= r < 1$, the weights decrease monotonically. When r is small, the weights of the first few examples decrease sharply and then turn almost flat. Moreover, the first few weights totaled almost to 1.0. But when r is closer to 1.0, the curve becomes quite flat.
4) Given (1), the conclusions in (2) and (3) are also applicable to the case of $r > 1$, but need to be mirrored along n/2.

Rating Computation. Finally, we can discuss the computing of the performance ratings. A ratable feature of a service is the smallest unit for rating. The rating of a service is therefore a vector of ratings for its ratable features.

Suppose the current rating on some service (of some agent) x is R(n), which is the combined effect from the previous n ratings. We just received a rating p on x and we want to compute the new rating R(n+1) as the combined result of the n+1 ratings received so far. If the weight function f is incremental, we can compute R(n+1) as follow:

$$R(n+1) = c(n)*R(n) + p*f(n+1, n+1),$$

where c(n) is some function of n, and is decided by f. On the other hand, if f is not incremental, we need to re-compute the whole thing:

$$R(n+1) = \sum_{<i=1, n>}\{p_i*f(n+1, i)\} + p*f(n+1, n+1),$$

where p_i is the ith rating received. If the overall rating on a service is needed, it can be computed from the feature ratings, optionally weighted by an importance vector (for features), that is,

$$r = R' * I,$$

where R' is the transposed rating vector, and I is the importance vector.

Rating Propagation. But things won't stop there. When the rating(s) on a service is updated, the changes propagate up as well as down the service hierarchy. The degree of effect on the services up and/or down the hierarchy is governed by the local service distribution, which is captured dynamically. If the service whose rating is to be updated through propagation (the target service) has common ratable features with the propagation origin service, then the set of common features will be updated. Otherwise, the target service itself is considered to be the only feature. Here we only discuss the case of tree-shaped hierarchy. In more general hierarchies like the DAG hierarchy, propagation can performed in a similar fashion.

Upward propagation refers to the process that when the rating on a service x is updated, the rating on its parent service p will also be updated. This update propagates upward along the service hierarchy, to the most general service a specific agent has to offer. Suppose x accounts for α percent of p. Let R_p and R'_p be the ratings of p before and after the update, respectively; let R'_x be the rating of x after the update. We have the upward propagation rule:

$$R'_p = (R_p + \alpha * R'_x)/(1 + \alpha)$$

Therefore, the more percentage x is of p, the more p will be affected.

Downward propagation refers to the process that when the rating on a service x is updated, the ratings on its child services will be updated accordingly. The update propagates along the service hierarchy all the way down to the most specific service the agent has to offer. Suppose c is one of the child services of x and accounts for β percent of x. Let R_c and R'_c be the ratings of c before and after the update, respectively. Then we have the downward propagation rule:

$$R'_c = (R_c + \beta * R'_x)/(1 + \beta)$$

Therefore, the more percentage c is of x, the more c will be affected.

In general (for both downward and upward propagation), the further a propagation target is from the origin, the less it will be affected by the propagation. How much a propagation target will be affected depends on the local distribution of the services.

4   Discussions

This paper presents a framework for an adaptive service broker that learns and refines a model of a service provider's performance. The system design and implementation are on the way. However, significant additional issues still remain. One issue that will need to be addressed is the situation when the child services of a service do not strictly disjoint with one another. This might be addressed using the local service distribution information. Next is the fairness issue. Although we believe that in general the broker agent can improve the quality of service matching through learning, the ratings on specific services may not always be "accurate". Over or under estimate the capability of any agent is unfair to that agent, and is unfair to the other agents as well. The problem might be lessened if the "bad" agents were given some chances - but that might compromise the quality of the matching service. We will also explore other formal methods for rating update and propagation. We believe that the security issue and the privacy issue are orthogonal to what we've discussed here.

One of the ideas behind this work is the law of locality. The more frequently a subset of the agents' capability is referenced (e.g., asked for recommendation), the more likely this sub-set will be referenced again later. The good news is, the more frequently the subset is referenced, the more likely the detailed information on this subset will be obtained through learning. Therefore, the approach captures the temporal locality. Moreover, the (spatial) distribution of the agent services is dynamically captured and used in computing agent service ratings.

Although we choose the DAML framework, we think the approach proposed here should work with other languages/frameworks, too. For example, LARKS can be extended with a set of (domain-dependent) rating slots and a new type of filer(s) that can be used to handle the new slots. Then what we discussed here should apply.

References

[1]   Arens, Y., Chee, C., Hsu, C., In, H. and Knoblock, C. A., Query Processing in an Information Mediator.

[2]   Tim Berners-Lee, James Hendler and Ora Lassila, *The Semantic Web*, Scientific American, May 2001.

[3]   Byrne, C. and Edwards, P., Refinement in Agent Groups, in Weiss, G., Sen, S. editors, (LNAI 1042), *Adaptation and Learning in Multi-Agent Systems*, Pages 22-39. 1995.

[4]   Harry Chen, Anupam Joshi, Tim Finin. Dynamic Service Discovery for Mobile Computing: Intelligent Agents Meet Jini in the Aether. *The Baltzer Science Journal on Cluster Computing*. March 2001 (Volume 3, No. 2).

[5]   Cohen, W., Borgida, A. and Hirsh, H. Computing Least Common Subsumers in Description Logics. *Proceedings of the National Conference on Artificial Intelligence* - AAAI 92, pp 754-760, 1992.

[6]   DAML specification, http://www.daml.org/, October 2000.

[7]   http://www.daml.org/2001/03/reference.html.

[8]   http://www.daml.org/services/.

[9]   DAML-S: A DAML for Web Services, White paper, SRI, http://www.ai.sri.com/daml/services/daml-s.pdf.

[10]   Decker, K, and Sycara, K and Williamson, M, Modeling Information Agents: Advertisements, Organizational Roles, and Dynamic Behavior. Working Notes of the *AAAI-96 workshop on Agent Modeling*, AAAI Report WS-96-02. 1996.

[11]   Decker, K, Williamson, M and Sycara, K, Matchmaking and Brokering, 1996. Downloaded from the site of cs.cmu.edu.

[12]   Dellarocas C, , Immunizing online reputation reporting systems against unfair ratings and discriminatory behavior. *Proceedings of the 2nd ACM Conference on Electronic Commerce*, Minneapolis, MN, October 17-20, 2000.

[13]   Dennis D. Berkey, Paul Blanchard. Calculus, Third edition, (Instructor's Preliminary Edition) Saunders College Publishing, 1992.

[14]   FIPA 97 Specification Part 1, Agent Management.

[15]   FIPA 97 Specification Part 2, Agent Communication Language.

[16]   Friedrich, H., Kaiser, M., Rogalla, O. and Dillmann, R., Learning and Communication in Multi Agent Systems, In Weiss, G., editor, (LNAI 1221), *Distributed Artificial Intelligence Meets Machine Learning*, pages 259-275. Springer Verlag, 1997.

[17]   Genesereth, M. R. and Singh, N. P., A Knowledge Sharing Approach to Software Interoperation. Stanford Logic Group Report Logic-93-12.

[18]   Gruber, T. R., The Role of Common Ontology in Achieving Sharable, Reusable Knowledge Bases, in Allen, J. A., Fikes, R., and Sandewall, E. (Eds), Principles of Knowledge Representation and Reasoning: *Proceedings of the Second International Conference.* San Mateo, CA: Morgan KaufMann, 1991.

[19]   Gruber, T. R., A Translation Approach to Portable Ontologies. *Knowledge Acquisition,* 5(2):199-220, 1993.

[20]   Yannis Labrou, Tim Finin, Benjamin Grosof and Yun Peng, Agent Communication Languages, in *Handbook of Agent Technology,* Jeff Bradshaw, ed., MIT/AAAI Press, 2001.

[21]   P. Lambrix and J. Maleki. Learning Composite Concepts in Description Logics: A First Step. *Proceedings of the 9th International Symposium on Methodologies for Intelligent Systems* - ISMIS 96, LNAI 1079, pp68-77, 1996.

[22]   McIlraith, S., Son, T.C. and Zeng, H. `Semantic Web Services, *IEEE Intelligent Systems.* Special Issue on the Semantic Web. To appear, 2001.

[23]   Michalski, R. S., Carbonell, J. G., Mitchell, T. M., *Machine Learning, An Artificial Intelligence Approach,* Tioga Publishing Company.

[24]   Mui, Lik, Szolovitz, P, and Wang, C., Sanctioning: Applications in Restaurant Recommendations based on Reputation, *Proceedings of the Fifth International Conference on Autonomous Agents,* Montreal, May 2001.

[25]   Lik Mui, Mojdeh Mohtashemi, Cheewee Ang. A probabilistic Rating Framework for Pervasive Computing Environments. The Oxygen Workshop, 2001.

[26]   Collaborative Brokering. Technical report, MCC, INSL-093-97. Abstract.

[27]   Nodine, M. & Perry, B., Experience with the InfoSleuth Agent Architecture, To appear in *Proceedings of AAAI-98 Workshop on Software Tools for Developing Agents,* 1998.

[28]   Nwana, Hyacinth S., Software Agents: An Overview. *Knowledge Engineering Review,* Vol. 11, No 3, pp.1-40, Sept 1996, Cambridge University Press, 1996.

[29]   Yun Peng, Nenad Ivezic, Youyong Zou, and Xiaocheng Luan. Semantic Resolution for E-Commerce. To appear in the *Proceedings of the First Workshop on Radical Agent Concepts.* Greenbelt, Maryland. September 2001.

[30]   Smith, Reid G., The Contract Net Protocol: High-Level Communication and Control in a Distributed Problem Solver, *IEEE Transactions on Computers,* Vol. C-29, Pages 1104-1113, 1980.

[31]   Singh, N. P., A Common Lisp API and Facilitator for ABSI, version 2.0.3 Stanford Logic Group Report Logic-93-4.

[32]   Sycara, K., Lu, J. and Klusch. M. Interoperability among Heterogeneous Software Agents on the Internet. CMU-RI-TR-98-22.

[33]   Weinstein, P. and Birmingham, W.P., Comparing concepts in differentiated ontologies. *Proceedings of the Twelfth Workshop on Knowledge Acquisition, Modeling and Management* (KAW'99).

[34]   Wickler, G. CDL: An Expressive and Flexible Capability Representation for Brokering. gw@itc.it.

[35]   Michael Wooldridge and Nicholas R. Jennings, Intelligent Agents: Theory and Practice, *The Knowledge Engineering Review* 10 (2), 115 – 152, 1995.

[36]   Web Services Description Language (WSDL) 1.1, January 23, 2001, Microsoft Corporation, http://msdn.microsoft.com/xml/general/wsdl.asp.

[37]   Giorgos Zacharia, Alexandros Moukas and Pattie Maes, Collaborative Reputation Mechanisms in Electronic Marketplaces. *Proceedings of the 32nd Hawaii International Conference on System Sciences*, 1999.

Part III

Agent-Based Software Engineering

The CoABS Grid

Martha L. Kahn[1] and Cynthia Della Torre Cicalese[1,2]

[1] Global InfoTek, Inc
1920 Association Drive, Suite 200, Reston, VA 20191, USA
[2] Marymount University
2807 North Glebe Road, Arlington, VA 22207, USA
{mkahn,cindy}@globalinfotek.com

Abstract. The CoABS Grid integrates heterogeneous agent-based systems, object-based applications, and legacy systems. The CoABS Grid does not mandate the network protocol used to deliver messages to an agent or the agent communication language. A CoABS Grid agent registers a proxy object supporting a well-known message-delivery interface in a lookup service. Default proxy implementations are provided that use Java Remote Method Invocation (RMI) and RMI over Secure Socket Layer as the network protocol. Lookup of agents based on agent type and agent capability advertisements is supported. The CoABS Grid provides a simple, agent-specific application programming interface, layered over the Jini™ Network Technology developed by Sun Microsystems. However, it also exposes the underlying Jini™ application programming interface for the advanced developer. The CoABS Grid provides support for mobile agent systems by allowing the creation of CoABS Grid agents that may be transported across the network, resuming operation in a new location.

1 Introduction

Control of Agent-Based Systems (CoABS) is a research program of the US Defense Advanced Research Projects Agency and the US Air Force Rome Labs. The aim of the program is to investigate the use of agent technology to improve military command, control, communication, and intelligence gathering. The CoABS Grid is middleware that integrates heterogeneous agent-based systems, object-based applications, and legacy systems. The CoABS Grid is only one part of the overall CoABS program – the plumbing that connects the components developed by all of the CoABS researchers to solve real-world problems.[1]

Over twenty universities and companies have participated in the CoABS research effort. Each participating organization brings to the program its own agent

---

[1] More information on the program is available from the website http://coabs.globalinfotek.com. The CoABS Grid software may be obtained from this site as well.

W. Truszkowski, C. Rouff, M. Hinchey (Eds.): WRAC 2002, LNAI 2564, pp. 125-134, 2003.
© Springer-Verlag Berlin Heidelberg 2003

architecture, with different agent communication languages, ontologies, and agent-based services. The CoABS Grid is being used to integrate RETSINA agents from Carnegie Mellon University, TEAMCORE agents from the University of Southern California Information Sciences Institute, and AAA agents from the Oregon Graduate Institute, to name just a few. Mobile agent systems being integrated include D'Agents from Dartmouth College, EMAA from Lockheed Martin Company, and Nomads from the University of West Florida.

The CoABS Grid includes a method-based application programming interface to register agents, advertise their capabilities, discover agents based on their capabilities, and send messages between agents. Agents can be added and upgraded without reconfiguring the network. Failed or unavailable agents are automatically purged from the registry.

The CoABS Grid has some unique characteristics that distinguish it from other agent infrastructures. The CoABS Grid is transport neutral in terms of agent communication. The CoABS Grid defines a well-known message-delivery interface. CoABS Grid agents must have a proxy that supports the message-delivery interface, but the agent is free to use any transport to communicate with that proxy. In order to send a message to an agent, the sender makes a local method call to an agent proxy. The proxy transfers the message to the actual agent using a protocol private to the agent and proxy. If the transport mechanism is changed, the sender code is not affected. The CoABS Grid provides a means of obtaining agent proxies based on agent characteristics and types.

CoABS Grid communication is fully distributed, in that each agent sending a message communicates directly with the receiver, using the proxy registered by the receiver. That is, all agent-to-agent communication is point-to-point. Thus, as the number of agents on the Grid increases, agent communication performance is only affected by the distribution of the agents in the network, the network bandwidth, and the details of the particular proxy implementation.

2   Jini™ Layer

The CoABS Grid is built using the Jini™ Network Technology developed by Sun Microsystems. The CoABS Grid software is written in Java and also uses Java Remote Method Invocation (RMI) for default inter-agent communication. Members of the CoABS research community have created proxies that integrate the CoABS Grid with agent systems written in C++ and Lisp and for the Palm Pilot KVM.

The CoABS Grid takes advantage of three important components of Jini™:

1. the Jini™ concept of a service, which is used to represent an agent,
2. the Jini™ Lookup Service (LUS), which is used to register and discover agents and other services, and
3. Jini™ Entries, which are used to advertise an agent's capabilities.

Jini™ provides helper classes that use a multicast protocol to find any LUSs that are running within a local area network. No prior knowledge of the machine name or port that the LUS is running on is required. Jini™ provides a unicast protocol to find

LUSs outside the local area network. Service registration is maintained in all local and distant LUSs. The registration is automatically propagated to any new LUS processes that are started. LUSs grant leases to registered services. If a service dies, or if the network connection between the service and the LUS fails, the lease expires, and the service is removed from the LUS. The LUS is thus able to maintain a current directory of available services. The LUS also assigns globally unique identifiers to services, and supports wildcard and exact match search based on service type, attributes, and unique identifier. LUSs can be associated with group names. A service registers with LUSs that support a specified group name. A sample LUS is provided in the Jini™ Development Kit and is currently used by the CoABS Grid.

A Jini™ service is a Java object that is serializable, implements some well-known interface, and is stored in a LUS. When a Jini™ client looks up a service, a service object is returned to the client. The returned service object may be a proxy to a remote service, or may be completely self-contained. The CoABS Grid defines two well-known Jini™ service interfaces, AgentRep and ServiceRep. These interfaces and default proxies that implement them are shown in Figure 1.

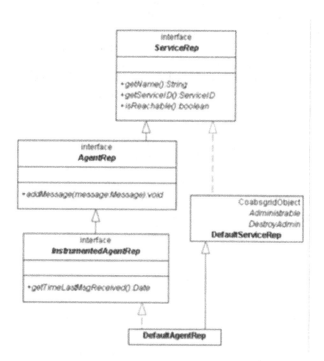

Fig. 1. CoABS Grid Proxy Classes and Interfaces

The Grid design makes a distinction between a Grid agent, represented by an AgentRep, and a Grid service, represented by a ServiceRep or any other Jini™ service. A Grid agent uses a message-passing mechanism for communication, while a Grid service uses a method-based mechanism. Although this is not a universal distinction within the agent community, it assists in the organization of Grid functionality. Since a primary goal of the Grid is to integrate agent, object, and legacy systems, support for both communication styles is provided. Many of the Grid agent classes subclass a Grid service class that provides basic functionality. A common practice is for the Grid service classes, such as the ServiceRep, to be subclassed by developers to easily integrate legacy systems.

A Grid agent provides a Jini™ service that implements the AgentRep interface when it registers with a LUS. AgentRep defines a method addMessage(). When a client looks up a Grid agent and calls the addMessage() method on the AgentRep that is returned, a message is delivered to the remote agent. The client can also include its own AgentRep in the message sender field, so two-way communication can be established with no further lookup. Grid services act similarly, except that the client will call service-specific methods on the returned Jini™ service rather than calling an addMessage() method. Grid developers must agree on well-known Grid service interfaces containing these service-specific methods.

Jini™ services are described in the form of Jini™ Entries, which are stored in the LUS along with the service. Many Entries can be stored for a single service. An Entry is an object with public fields. Entry templates are used in Jini™ and Grid lookup methods to match registered services. A null Entry field in an Entry template is a wildcard. Non-null fields are used for exact matching.

The CoABS Grid uses Jini™ Entries for agent capability advertisements. The CoABSAgentDescription Entry includes fields for agent name, description, organization, architecture, display icon URL, documentation URL, and unique ID. Other Grid Entries are provided for ontology, content language, location, signature, and agent status.

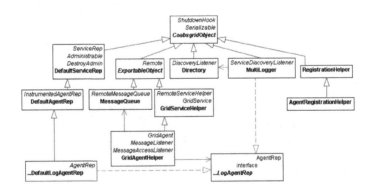

Fig. 2. Local CoABS Grid Classes and Interfaces

The Jini™ ServiceUI specification defines a standard means of providing user interfaces. The CoABS Grid provides a simple user interface for communicating with an agent.

The CoABS Grid provides an agent middleware layer built on top of Jini™. The Grid was designed to meet several goals. We tried to make the Grid simple to use for the average user, yet still provide full flexibility for those that needed to use the Grid in less common ways. We attempted to make our design efficient, with classes shared where possible to minimize both instance creation and Jini™ processing. In addition, we sought to create easily extendable Grid classes, to simplify wrapping of legacy systems.

3   CoABS Grid Implementation

The CoABS Grid classes and interfaces can be divided into two broad categories. The first category consists of those classes and interfaces that reside local to an agent, shown in Figure 2. They hide the complexity of Jini™ and provide an infrastructure for agent registration, communication, search, and serialization. This category of Grid elements can be further divided into those that have a one-to-one correspondence with an individual agent, such as the AgentRegistrationHelper and MessageQueue classes, and those that can be shared by multiple agents, such as the Directory class.

Most of the local Grid classes have simple constructors that will instantiate or reuse default instances of other classes on which they depend. This allows instances to be shared wherever possible to minimize processing and instance creation. These simple constructors are sufficient for most users' needs. For example, the AgentRegistrationHelper is the top-level class used for registering an agent. This class provides access to all other core Grid classes that might be needed by the agent. For instance, a Directory class is accessible, to support search for other agents and services. The Directory used by default is shared with all other agents created within the same Java virtual machine to minimize multicasting and instance creation. The AgentRegistrationHelper needs the Directory to support automatic logging of Grid messages. These top-level Grid classes also have constructors that take more parameters, allowing the user to pass in the other core classes that are needed. This allows more flexibility in customizing the Grid behavior. In the case of the AgentRegistrationHelper, other constructors are available that take underlying Jini™ helper classes as parameters.

The other broad category of Grid classes and interfaces consists of those that are highly distributed. These include AgentRep implementations and associated agent capability advertisements, as well as various message classes. Typically, many copies of the AgentReps and capability advertisements exist throughout the network. Copies are stored locally to the agent, in any LUS that may be running, and in any processes that have retrieved them from a LUS through a search method call. Messages are passed from agent to agent across the network by calling the addMessage() method on the distributed AgentReps. In the following subsections more detail on CoABS Grid functionality is provided.

3.1   Initialization, Termination, and Support for Mobile Code

The CoABS Grid provides a GridManager graphical user interface to start and monitor underlying processes used by Jini™, set default parameters, and display currently registered services.

The local Grid classes all inherit from a class named CoabsgridObject, as shown in Figure 2. This class takes care of initialization tasks such as setting the RMI security manager and the codebase, if this has not already been done. It also takes care of termination, stopping all Jini™ processing and canceling leases if the Jini™ service is killed. This is important, because it would otherwise take some time for the leases to expire.

Instances of the Grid classes may be serialized and written to a file or sent as marshaled objects in Message data attachments. This allows an entire agent either to be saved to a file for later reactivation or to be moved to a remote host. When an agent arrives at a remote host, it can resume processing with its message queue intact, its registration state maintained, and all shared components and groups restored. This provides a foundation for integration efforts between mobile agent frameworks that are being conducted within the CoABS program.

By default, when a Java RMI server object is serialized, a remote reference to the object, rather than the object itself, is actually serialized. In order to serialize the object itself, it must be unexported, making the object unavailable to receive remote method calls, prior to serialization, and then reexported when it needs to be able to receive remote method calls again. The Grid classes that are RMI servers extend a class named ExportableObject shown in Figure 2, which correctly handles unexportation and reexportation.

3.2   Registration, Directory, Event Notification, and Logging Functions

The RegistrationHelper class is used to register any Jini™ services, and its subclass the AgentRegistrationHelper is used to register Grid agents. Agent registration involves the registration of the agent's AgentRep proxy with Jini™ LUSs along with the appropriate agent capability advertisements. It is not necessary for an agent to register in order for it to use the Grid. The purpose of registering an agent is to make its services available to other agents, which can look it up based on its characteristics. An agent that is not registered can search for other agents and send them messages and get replies without registering.

The Directory class provides service and agent lookup and message forward methods. Lookup can be based on types, advertised capabilities, and predicates. Predicate-based search happens locally to the agent, so it should be combined with an initial filter based on service type and exact-match and wildcard matching of attribute values to limit the amount of data downloaded over the network. The Jini™ ServiceDiscoveryManager class is used to implement lookup. The Directory exposes the ServiceDiscoveryManager, as well as related Jini™ classes. The Directory constructors block until at least one LUS is found.

Directory lookup methods all return arrays of ServiceItems. A ServiceItem is a Jini™ class that has a field for the globally unique identifier, service object, and attribute sets. The service can be cast to the interface or class to which it corresponds. For instance, CoABS Grid ServiceItems can usually be cast to AgentReps. The attribute set contains the advertised capabilities of the service returned.

The Directory also exposes the ServiceDiscoveryManager's LookupCache mechanism, which is used for event notification. This allows notifications when agents or services register, deregister, or modify their advertised capabilities. Users can subscribe to notifications for only those agents or services that match a given template or predicate. The criteria of interest are expressed in the same manner as those used for search methods.

LogAgentRep is an extension of the AgentRep interface that is used to capture Grid activity in an XML-based log, using the Grid Log Markup Language. Results can be browsed using XML parsers or using ISX's Grid Agent Sequence Visualizer or Carnegie Mellon University's Retsina Visualization Tool. A LogAgentRep instance can be used to make a log entry, set or remove triggers on the log, or query the log for entries matching a pattern. A trigger is a pattern that is matched against incoming messages. The trigger setter is informed through a message when a match is found. By default all Grid messages are logged if a LogAgentRep agent is running. Each agent can turn automatic logging off, however. A MultiLogger class allows logging to multiple loggers.

3.3   Security Functions

The CoABS Grid provides security functions based on the Java Developers Kit Security application programming interface and the reference security provider implementation provided by Sun. However, the Grid security classes are not dependent upon Sun's implementation and will work with any properly installed service provider. The SecureMessageQueue supports message encryption over the network using RMI over SSL. In addition, the Grid supports encryption of arbitrary objects. A secure logger, which uses the SecureMessageQueue and encrypts the log entries before they are stored to file, is provided with the Grid.

Agent or service authentication is provided through a SignatureEntry class, which is registered in the LUS with an agent's other advertised capabilities. The SignatureEntry contains a signature field, which contains the agent or service signature, and a trust chain that contains an array of certificate objects. The Grid security utility uses the Signature Entry to validate that the agent or service is from a trusted source and that it has not been tampered with.

A public key infrastructure graphical user interface is also provided to generate public/private key pairs and sign certificates. A CoABS Grid certificate with public and private keys is provided for research purposes and can be replaced by a certificate from a real certificate authority.

Researchers at the Institute for Human Machine Cognition (IHMC) at the University of West Florida and Boeing have extended the Grid core classes to integrate their Knowledgeable Agent-oriented System (KAoS) policy-based domain management extensions. Simply by substituting the KAoSAgentRegistrationHelper for the default AgentRegistrationHelper, any group of Grid agents can be structured into agent domains and subdomains for easier administration. Through the use of policy-based mechanisms, dynamic constraints on Grid agent behavior can be defined and enforced without modification to agent code. Policies can be scoped to an arbitrary group of agents across multiple hosts, to all agents on a single host, or to an individual agent instance. These policies not only address typical security concerns such as authentication, encryption, and access control, but also agent conversation, mobility, domain registration, resource control, and obligation policies.

3.4   Agent Communication

The Grid proxy classes and interfaces are shown in Figure 1. The AgentRep addMessage() method, which is part of the AgentRep interface used for message delivery, throws a RemoteException if there is a network problem during message delivery. Thus, if no RemoteException is thrown, one can be sure that the message sent to an agent was delivered successfully. If a RemoteException is thrown, the message may not have gotten through. All users of the AgentRep must be able to take appropriate action when faced with network failure. A common strategy is to try to lookup a fresh AgentRep from the LUS, in case the failure was caused by a stale reference.

An agent provides its own proxy for communication. Thus, the receiver of a message is in control of communication, rather than the sender. For instance, a CoABS Grid agent that uses the DefaultAgentRep provided with the Grid can use either a MessageQueue or a SecureMessageQueue for communication from the proxy local to the sender to the receiver agent's queue. A MessageQueue uses RMI, but a SecureMessageQueue uses RMI over SSL, which assures that messages are encrypted over the wire.

Although the Grid provides a default AgentRep implementation that uses RMI, the Grid user is free to provide alternative implementations. An agent implementer may create a new proxy implementation that uses a completely different transport mechanism, as long as the proxy supports the AgentRep interface. For instance, researchers at IHMC have developed a custom AgentRep for their Nomads mobile agent system. If an agent has moved locations, the standard DefaultAgentRep proxies downloaded previously from the LUS will be stale, and RemoteExceptions will be thrown if message senders try to use the old proxies. The Nomads custom AgentRep will fetch the new AgentRep in a manner transparent to the sender, so that messages can still be received after a move. Other transport mechanisms such as CORBA, or even email, are also possible.

The Message classes provided by the CoABS Grid, shown in Figure 3, are an important part of the communication infrastructure. Since the sender field of a message can contain an AgentRep, two-way communication can be established between Grid members without both being registered with the Grid. A message sender can look up a registered Grid member and send a message with its own AgentRep in the sender field. The receiver can respond using the sender's AgentRep without any further lookup. DataMessages allow arbitrary serializable attachments and are a useful way of moving data and even code between applications. Even agents can be sent in data attachments. AutoReplyMessages support message receipt feedback. The sender receives a message when the receiver accesses the message, not when it is received. Agents can disable AutoReplyMessages if they don't wish to respond to an AutoReplyMessage.

Fig. 3. CoABS Grid Message Classes

Another important component of the communication infrastructure is the MessageListener interface. Agents that implement this interface can be notified automatically of incoming messages and, therefore, do not need to poll their message queues.

The CoABS Grid is Agent Communication Language (ACL) neutral. A field of a message contains the name of the ACL used in the message, but no specific ACL is dictated. This property of the Grid derives from its original purpose of integrating existing Multi-agent systems. Since there are a variety of ACLs used by individual multi-agent systems, standardizing on one language would have been detrimental to integration. It was left to the participants in agent conversations to make sure that they can communicate. It is hoped that in the future ACL and ontology translation agents will be developed to provide translation services to Grid agents.

4   Conclusion

The CoABS Grid provides an infrastructure to integrate multi-agent systems, individual agents, and objects. Its use of an agent proxy to support agent-to-agent communication is key to its flexibility. Grid classes and interfaces are easily extensible in order to wrap legacy systems or provide additional functionality.

Acknowledgements

The development of the CoABS Grid was funded by DARPA under its Control of Agent-Based Systems program through Air Force Research Laboratory Contract No. F30602-98-C00267. We thank our sponsors Jim Hendler and LCDR Dylan Schmorrow of DARPA and Dan Daskiewich of AFRL for supporting our research. We also thank the other members of the CoABS Grid development team. Team members from Global InfoTek, Inc. include Dennis Brake, Aaron Glahe, Philip Sage, Todd Suralik, and Doyle Weishar. Team members from ISX Corp. include David Brill and Brian Kettler. We are also grateful for the help provided by Jeff Bradshaw, Renia Jeffers and Niranjan Suri of IHMC for their explanations of Nomads and KAoS domain management.

References

[1]   Hendler, J. and Metzeger, R., "Putting it all together – The Control of Agent-Based Systems and Their Applications," *IEEE Intelligent Systems*, March 1999, p.37.

[2]   Bradshaw, J., Suri, N., Canas, A., Davis, R., Ford, K., Hoffman, R., Jeffers, R., Reichherzer, T., "Terraforming Cyberspace," *Computer*, July 2001, p.48.

[3]   Kahn, M. and Cicalese, C., "CoABS Grid Scalability Experiments," *Proceedings of Second International Workshop on Infrastructure for Agents, MAS, and Scalable MAS*, (Ed. Tom Wagner and Omer F. Rana), Montreal, Canada, May 28, 2001.

Agent Based Approach to Service Description and Composition *

Stanislaw Ambroszkiewicz

Institute of Computer Science, Polish Academy of Sciences,
al. Ordona 21, PL-01-237 Warsaw, Poland
and Institute of Informatics, University of Podlasie,
al. Sienkiewicza 51, PL-08-110 Siedlce, sambrosz@ipipan.waw.pl;
www.ipipan.waw.pl/mas/

Abstract. An approach to service description and composition is presented. It is based on agent technology, and on the idea of separating description and composition language from biding, i.e., from specification of data format (exchanged by applications) and transport protocol. Usually, the biding is an integral part of description language, e.g., WSDL, and DAML-S. Starting with this idea, a simple service description language is constructed as well as a composition protocol is specified. Agents play crucial role in our approach; they are responsible for service composition.

1 What are Web services?

Perhaps the most popular definition can be found in IBM's tutorial [8]:
Web services are self-contained, self - describing, modular applications that can be published, located, and invoked across the Web. Web services perform functions that can be anything from simple requests to complicated business processes ... Once a Web service is deployed, other applications (and other Web services) can discover and invoke the deployed service.

In order to realize this vision simple and ubiquitous protocols are needed. From service providers' point of view, if they can setup a web site they could join global community. From a client's point of view, if you can click, you could access services.

What are the solutions proposed by the prominent vendors? Web services are getting to mean just UDDI, WSDL, and SOAP. SOAP (Simple Object Access Protocol) is a standard for applications to exchange XML - formatted messages over HTTP. WSDL (Web Service Description Language) describes what a web service does, where it resides, and how to invoke it, i.e., the interface, protocol bindings and the deployment details of the service. UDDI (Universal Description, Discovery and Integration) is a standard for publishing information about web services in a global registry as well as for web service discovery. Does the stack of standards mentioned above provide sufficient means for automatic service invocation, composition, and integration? The problem is hard. UDDI provides a mechanism for automatic service discovery of potential business partners. At the moment, it is supposed that after discovery, programmers affiliated with the

---

* The work was done within the framework of KBN project No. 7 T11C 040 20. The assistance of Dariusz Mikulowski and Leszek Rozwadowski is acknowledged.

W. Truszkowski, C. Rouff, M. Hinchey (Eds.): WRAC 2002, LNAI 2564, pp. 135–149, 2003.

business partners program their own systems to interact with the services discovered. Automatic Web service integration requires more complex functionality than SOAP, WSDL, and UDDI can provide. The functionality includes transactions, workflow, negotiation, management, and security. There are several efforts that aim at providing such functionality, e.g., WSCL, WSFL, XLANG, BTP, and XAML. All these languages are based on SOAP+WSDL+UDDI basic stack, and are complex procedural languages very hard to implement and deploy.

On the other hand there is DAML-S. It is a part of DARPA Agent Markup Language project that aims at realizing the Semantic Web concept. DAML-S is also a complex procedural language for web service composition.

The basic question is whether the proposed technologies are simple and ubiquitous, and which one is the right one. As we see above, the landscape of solutions for the new emerging technology is rich and complex so that it is not easy to find a clear and straightforward path to the one common standard. It seems that the path starts with the basic stack SOAP+WSDL+UDDI, however, it is not clear how to go further. Perhaps the basic stack is not appropriate, i.e., it is too complex so that the next protocols (based on the initial stack) accumulate the initial complexity. There is a consensus that SOAP is the right protocol for the message exchange. However, there is a growing criticism of WSDL and UDDI, e.g., [4, 5]. As a response to that criticism, a new Web Service Activity of W3C was created [14].

2   Our approach

We are going to propose an alternative solution to service description and composition. Our approach is based on agent technology. Perhaps the most related work is LARKS [6] that now has evolved and became a part of DAML-S.

Before we introduce our idea, let us present some details of WSDL and DAML-S. According to the Web Service Activity (see [14]) the basic definitions of WSDL are as follows.

A Web Service is a software application identified by a URI [IETF RFC 2396], whose interfaces and binding are capable of being defined, described and discovered by XML artifacts and supports direct interactions with other software applications using XML based messages via internet-based protocols.

A Client is a software that makes use of a Web Service, acting as its 'user' or 'customer'.

A Message is the basic unit of communication between a Web Service and a Client; data to be communicated to or from a Web Service as a single logical transmission.

A set of Messages related to a single Web Service action is called Operation.

Interface is a logical grouping of operations. An Interface represents an abstract Web Service type, independent of transmission protocol and data format.

An InterfaceBinding specifies the protocol and/or data format to be used in transmitting Messages. EndPoint (Port) is an association between a fully-specified InterfaceBinding and a network address, specified by a URI, that may be used to communicate with an instance of a Web Service. An EndPoint indicates a specific location for accessing a Web Service using a specific protocol and data format. A collection of EndPoints is called Service.

As we see above, WSDL is strongly related to the concept of binding. Also DAML-S concept of grounding is consistent with WSDL's concept of binding. The biding is a specification of data format (exchanged by applications) and transport protocol.

Our idea is to separate biding from service description language as well as from service composition protocol. To realize our idea we must give a different meaning to the notion of message. This meaning is based on the following assumptions:

- Message contents is not a data exchanged by communicating applications.
- Message contents describes how to arrange and synchronize the data exchange between the applications. Transmission of the data is realized in the layer below, where the biding is implemented.

Hence, we have two layers: The first one is for arranging and synchronizing data passing between applications; it is called *service description and composition layer*. The second one is for message and data transmission; it is called *binding layer*. We claim that the binding layer can be arbitrary, for example, SOAP is an excellent candidate here, so that service description and composition layer can be specified independently from the biding layer.

One of the important consequences of our assumptions is that we must have one universal message format for communication between services, and the message contents is a formula of some fixed language rather than data to be processed by an application. The second consequence is that, in our approach, service is composed of an application and universal interface for communication in the language.

The language of message contents is called service description and composition language. We are going to construct one specific language called *Entish*.

General overview of the environment, the language is supposed to describe, is the following. Services perform some operations, that is, process data (called e-documents or resources). The processing consists in the following: Given input resources, operation produces an output resource. Client (user or an application) wants to realize a task. Task specifies the properties of a final resource to be produced and delivered to a fixed place by a timeout. Task should be realized by a composition of a number of operations performed by services. Agent is a process dedicated for a single task realization. The agent is obliged to discover, arrange, and synchronize appropriate services (whose operations are in the composition) into a workflow. Then, the workflow is executed and controlled by the agent. It is supposed that there are registries (called infoServices) for publication of operation tytpes performed by services on the one hand, and for service discovery by agents on the other hand. There are four types of actions that can be executed in our environment: *send/receive message* executed by agent or service; *perform operation* executed by service; *get resource* executed by service; *change state* executed by agent or service.

The tasks are expressed as formulas in our description language. The language describes situations between agents, services, and resources before and after action executions. However, actions and causal relations are not described explicitly in our language. Agents and services have several mental attitudes (e.g., intentions, commitments, goals, knowledge) that describe the workflow formation process in our language.

More detailed description of our approach is presented in the next Section. The description language is presented in Section 4. Formal XML syntax of the language as well as XML format of message, and agent / service state are defined in the documents: message.xsd, state.xsd, formula.xsd, definitions.xsd, and properEntish.xml that are available on request (mailto: sambrosz@ipipan.waw.pl) and will be available shortly on our web site: www.ipipan.waw.pl/mas/

A protocol for service publication, discovery as well for as workflow formation, execution and control is specified in the Section 5. It is called *entish v. 1.0*. Although the protocol should be considered as a simple example, it is quite powerful; it implements two-phase commit (2PC) transactions.

The description language, the universal format of message and state as well as the proposal of a composition protocol constitute together the service description and composition layer. The problem is how this layer is implemented in the biding layer, i.e., how the message and resource transport is realized. The solution we have adopted to solve the problem is natural and extremely simple. The sender as well as the recipient name is a URI, i.e., it contains the absolute address of the sender (or the recipient) and the name of a transport protocol for communication (e.g., SOAP is the protocol of choice). As to the resource passing between services, we have chosen the "pull" method, that is, the service (say, service1) that wants to pass a resource to the another service (say, service0) sends the following information to the service0: "The resource you are supposed to receive has the name *url0*". Once the service0 got to know the name of the resource (i.e., *url0*), it can download the resource by HTTP, i.e., the resource names are supposed to be URLs.

The present work is based on our earlier work published in [1, 2, 3], where the basic ideas of our approach were introduced. In the paper we present a concrete realization of these ideas in the form of formal specification of description language and composition protocol. The space limit does not allow to present details of the ongoing implementation of our composition protocol.

3   General view of description language and composition protocol

Two basic components are necessary to realize our vision of service integration: description language, and composition protocol.

Description language should allow to describe not only the type of operation performed by a particular service, but also relations between agents (responsible for task realizations) and services engaged in these task realizations. Agent intentions, and service commitments are examples of these relations. The language must be open. It means that any user / programmer can add to the language new primitive concepts, i.e., new types of resources (e-documents), new relations, as well as new functions. However, this must be done according to the fixed rules (see definitions.xsd), so that the integrity of language syntax is preserved.

The composition protocol is a conversation protocol between agents, services, and infoServices. During a conversation (i.e., a protocol session) messages are exchanges that may effect the state of sender / recipient. The language of message contents is supposed to be our description language, i.e., the contents is an evaluated formula of our language describing a situation between an agent, services and e-documents.

Hence, the *Message* format is extremely simple (see message.xsd) and consists of the following items:

- *Header;*
  - *From;* sender address.
  - *To;* recipient address.
  - *Protocol;* name of protocol.
  - *Version;* version of protocol.
  - *Session;* session identifier.
  - *Order;* type (order) of the message in the protocol.
- *Body;* contents of the message.

Body contains facts, i.e., evaluated formulas. A fact is called *Info* (an element defined in message.xsd) and is composed of the following items: *formula, time, place, signature*. The meaning of *Info* is that *formula* was true at *time*, in *place*, and this was stated by the one who *signed* it.

We propose one universal state format for agents as well as for services (see state.xsd). The *State* format consists of the following items:

- *Owner;* the name of the owner (i.e., an agent or a service) of the state.
- *Goal;* agent's task (or the type of operation performed by a service if the *State* belongs to the service).
- *Intentions;* lists of agent's intentions.
- *Commitments;* a set of service's commitments.
- *Knowledge;* the container for agent's/service's knowledge; it is a collection of *Info* elements.

Note that in our framework, agent has no commitments, and service has no intentions. However, it is also reasonable to consider agents that make commitments, as well as services having intentions.

Goal consists of two elements: *formIn* and *formOut*. Each of them contains a formula of our description language. If the state belongs to a service, the *Goal* represents the type of operation performed by the service, so that *formIn* describes precondition of service invocation, whereas *formOut* describes the post condition (effect) of performing the operation by the service. If the state belongs to an agent, then *formIn* is either empty or contains a formula that describes precondition for realizing the agent's task, whereas *formOut* formula describes the agent's task.

Commitments is a set of service's commitments. A *commitment* consists of two elements: *formIn* and *formOut*. Each of them contains a formula of our description language. *formIn* describes precondition of the commitment, whereas *formOut* describes the post condition, i.e., effect the service has committed to realize. Once a commitment is realized, it is removed from *Commitments*, however the information about the realization is stored in *Knowledge*.

Intentions is the element composed of the following three parts:

- *Plan* is a sequence (list) of formulas (called intentions) describing agent's plan.

- *Workflow* is a set of intentions moved from *Plan* for which agent has already arranged commitments with services. They are supposed to form a workflow for realizing agent's task.
- *Realized* it is w set of intentions moved from *Workflow* that have been already satisfied by realization of the associated commitments.

An intention is moved from *Plan* to *Workflow* if agent has found a service that has committed to realize this intention. An intention is moved from *Workflow* to *Realized* if this intention has been already realized.

An algorithm of agent functioning can be sketched as follows.

1. Agent's task is set as its first intention and put into *Plan*.
2. The first intention is decomposed into a sequence of intentions on the basis of an *Info* received from an infoService.
3. Agent is looking for a service that can realize the first intention from its *Plan*.
4. Once the agent has found a service that has committed to realize its current intention, the intention is moved from *Plan* to *Workflow* whereas the precondition of the service commitment is set as a new intention and is put as the last element of the agent's *Plan*.
5. If *Plan* is an empty sequence, a workflow for task realization is completed and may be executed.
6. Once the agent gets confirmation that an intention from *Workflow* is realized, it is moved to *Realized*.
7. If *Workflow* is empty, then the workflow has been already executed successfully, so that the task is realized, and the agent can send the final confirmation approving the transaction performed by the workflow.

4   Description language

Formula of our description language is the basic component of all the data structure defined in the previous section. In order to specify the formula formally, we must define the syntax of our description language.

The description language is a simple version of the language of first order logic with types, and without negation and quantifiers. The syntax of our language is specified in formula.xsd, where a XML syntax of the language is defined. Specific primitive concepts, i.e., types, relations, and functions are introduced in properEntish.xml that defines the standard part of the language Entish. It is worth to note that these specific concepts are introduced in the same way (using the schema definitions.xsd) as another concepts can be introduced, i.e., properEntish.xml is an instance of the schema definitions.xsd.

Since XML syntax is hard to read, we also introduce more readable syntax for presentation. So that, if ψ and ϕ are formulas, then *(ψ or ϕ), (ψ and ϕ), (ψ implies ϕ)* are formulas. Terms and atomic formulas are defined in the usual way however, quantifiers and negation are not used. Predefined types, relations and functions (defined formally in properEntish.xml) are listed below:

Types:

- *Agent* is a primitive type; agent (i.e., element of type *Agent*) is a process equipped with its own state (i.e., element *State* defined in state.xsd). It is supposed that all essential data of the agent is stored in its state. Agent is dedicated for a single task realization. It is created when there is a task to be realized, and is terminated after the task realization or if the task can not be realized.

- *Service* is a primitive type; service (i.e., element of type *Service*) is a process having its own state (i.e., element State defined in state.xsd). The main service's component is an application that processes data (e-documents). Processing e-documents may result in effecting the real world, e.g., purchasing a commodity or withdraw of some amount of money from a bank account, or just taking some physical actions like switching off/on a washing machine.

- *Time*; element of this type is a time written according to xsd:time format.

- *Token*; token (i.e., element of type *Token*) is an arbitrary string. It is used as value of function *token(?resource)*, (the question mark ? before a string indicates that this string is a variable). Tokens are a general way to identify resources (e-docs) at the language level. Note that our language is independent from data format of resources; the format may be arbitrary, e.g., XML, MS Word, txt, binary, and so on.

Relations:

- *timeout(?t)* can be evaluated at any host. It is true if the time *?t* is less or equal to the current GMT time at the host.

- *(?x=?y)* is a polymorphic equality relation. It can be evaluated if *?x* and *?y* are of the same type.

- *isIn(?resource, ?service)* states that *?resource* is in *?service*. It can be evaluated locally only by *?service*.

- *intentions(?agent)* is an atomic formula. It is evaluated only locally by *?agent*. During an evaluation it is replaced with the disjunction of all formulas from the element *Plan* of the *State* of the *?agent*.

- *formInOperationType(?service)* is an atomic formula to be evaluated only by *?service*. During an evaluation it is replaced with the formula from the *formIn* element of *Goal* of the *State* of *?service*. The formula describes the precondition necessary for *?service* invocation.

- *formOutOperationType(?service)* is an atomic formula to be evaluated only by *?service*. During an evaluation it is replaced with the formula from the *formOut* element of *Goal* of the *State* of *?service*. The formula describes the post condition of *?service* invocation, i.e., the result of performing the operation by *?service*.

- *formInCommitment(?service)* is an atomic formula evaluated only by *?service*. During an evaluation it is replaced with the disjunction of formulas from *formIn* elements of all *commitment* elements of *Commitments* of the *State* of *?service*. It describes the preconditions of the commitments made by the *?service*.

- *formOutCommitment(?service)* is an atomic formula evaluated only by *?service*. During an evaluation it is replaced with the conjunction of formulas from *formOut* elements of all *commitment* elements of *Commitments* of the *State* of *?service*. It describes the post conditions of the commitments made by the *?service*.

There is only one predefined function: *token(?resource)* that returns token (an element of type *Token*) determined for *?resource* by the service that expects it to be delivered as its input resource.

A formula is syntactically valid (well constructed) if it is constructed according to the syntax specified in formula.xsd, and properEntish.xml, and if the names of types, relations, and functions occurring in the formula have been already defined in XML documents (instances of definitions.xsd), and the documents are available by HTTP. And the names are used according to their specifications in the documents.

5   Composition protocol

Now, we are ready to specify our protocol for service composition. Generally, protocol is a specification of message exchange between parties, and how sending / receiving a specific message type changes the state of sender / recipient. The parties that participate in conversation (protocol session) are: agent, service, and infoService.

The format of agent / service state was specified in the previous section. The state format of infoService is extremely simple; it consists of a collection of facts, i.e., of elements of type Info. The protocol is divided into three main parts: publication, discovery, and workflow formation and execution. The publication part is a conversation between service and infoServices, the discovery part is between agent and infoServices, whereas the workflow formation and execution part is between agent and services.

Once implemented, the protocol serves for the following purpose: 1. Applications could be joined to our infrastructure as services. 2. Tasks, issued by the clients, could be realized.

Although tasks and intentions could be defined as arbitrary formulas of the description language, we define the canonical format of task formula, and intention formula that will be used in our composition protocol. The canonical format of intention formula is the following.
(isIn(?finRes, service0) and ?finRes = fun(?input1, ?input2, ... , ?inputN) and token(?finRes) = tok0 and prop(?finRes) and timeout(date0))
The meaning is that *tok1* is the identifier of the final resource *?finRes* that must be delivered to the *service0* by the time *data0*, and the final resource is the output of some operation that implements the abstract function *fun*. And the final resource has the properties expressed in *prop(?finRes)* . The canonical format of *prop(?finRes)* is the following: *(prop1(?finRes) or prop2(?finRes) or ... propK(?finRes))* . It is disjunction of K subformulas. Each of the subformulas is conjunction of atomic formulas describing the resource *?finRes*. The formula is satisfied if one (or more) of its subformulas is satisfied. Hence, the subformulas may be viewed as offers, from which one should be chosen.

However, sometimes the formula *prop(?finRes)* may be reduced to the following:
(?finRes = fun(?input1, ... , ?inputN) and ?input1 = res1 and ... ?inputN = resN)
where *res1, ... resN* are names (URIs) of concrete resources. It means that the final resource is the result of processing the concrete resources in the way denoted by the abstract function *fun*.

The canonical format of task is similar to the format of intention. Only the second component of the conjunction (i.e., *?finRes = fun(?input1, ?input2, ... , ?inputN)* is changed to the formula of the following format: *?finRes = fun(fun1(...), ... , funN(...))* . The meaning is that the final resource *?finRes* is the result of a function composition. The function composition represents the abstract production process that must be performed for the task realization. The types of variables (represented as "..." and occurring on the right side of the equality) are the types of the initial resources necessary to realize the task.

Operation type of service is described in our language by the following pair of atomic formulas: *formInOperationType(service)* and *formOutOperationType(service)* . When evaluated they are replaced with the formulas in *formIn* (resp. *formOut*) elements of *Goal* of the service's *State*. We fix the format of the formulas in *formIn* and *formOut* elements in the following way. Suppose that the operation (the service performs) implements an abstract function *fun* already introduced to our language. The function has *N* arguments of some types (say, *?x1, ?x2, ... , ?xN*) and returns the value *?y = fun(?x1, ?x2, ... , ?xN)* of some type. Then, the precondition of operation type (i.e., the formula in *formIn*) has the following format:
(isIn(?input1, service) and isIn(?input2, service) and ... (isIn(?inputN, service)
Whereas the post condition, i.e., the formula in *formOut*) has the following format:
(isIn(?output, ?anyService) and ?output = fun(?input1, ?input2, ... , ?inputN)

The commitments of service are described in our language by the following pair of atomic formulas: *formInCommitments(service)* and *formOutCommitments(service)*. The first formula describes the precondition of a commitment whereas the second formula describes the effect (post condition) the service has committed to realize. It is worth to note that the syntactic form of commitment corresponds to the form of operation type. When evaluated, *formInCommitments(service)* is substituted by disjunction of the formulas from all *formIn* of *commitment* elements of *Commitments* of the service's *State*, whereas *formOutCommitments(service)* is substituted by conjunction of the formulas from all *formOut* of *commitment* elements of *Commitments*.

The format of post condition of commitment, i.e., the formula in *formOut*, is the same as the format of intention. The format of the precondition of commitment, i.e., the formula in *formIn* is the following: *(φ1 and timeout(t1)* where the format of *(φ1)* is:
(isIn(?input1, service) and token(?input1)=tok1 and prop1(?input1))
and
(isIn(?input2, service) and token(?input2)=tok2 and prop2(?input2))
and ...
(isIn(?inputN, service) and token(?inputN)=tokN and propN(?inputN))

Let us present here a sketch of two integration protocols: service invocation, and service composition. Service invocation protocol is composed of the following five steps:

1. Agent sends to the service0 the message: "my intention is (*ψ0*)" , formally it is the following formula (*ψ0 implies intentions(agent)*)
2. *The service0 responds with the following commitment: "I commit to realize (ψ0) if (ψ1) is satisfied", formally:*
   ((ψ1 implies formInCommitments(service0)) and (formOutCommitments(ser-

vice0) implies $\psi 0$))

It is supposed implicitly that the commitment can be realized, i.e., it is consistent with the operation type performed by the service0. It means that once ($\psi 1$) is satisfied, it follows that the precondition for the service0 invocation is satisfied, and the operation can be performed by the service0. Once the operation is performed (i.e., the post condition of the operation type is satisfied), it follows that the formula ($\psi 0$) is satisfied.

3. Suppose that the formula ($\psi 1$) is satisfied by another service1.
4. Then, the formula ($\psi 0$) is satisfied, and the agent intention is realized.
5. Finally, the service0 sends a confirmation to the agent.

Composition of two services (service0 and service1) is arranged by the agent in the following way. The agent arranges the realization of its first intention ($\psi 0$), with the service0. Service agrees to realize this intention conditionally, i.e., if the formula ($\psi 1$) is satisfied. Then, the agent puts the formula ($\psi 1$) as its current intention, and looks for another service that could realize this intention. Suppose that the agent got to know that it follows from the operation type of the service1 that the service could realize its current intention. The agent starts conversation with the service1 by sending the message: "my intention is ($\psi 1$)" . Once the service1 agrees to realize this intention, the operations of the service0 and the service1 are composed, and form a part of a workflow the agent must construct in order to realize its task.

5.1   Specification of entish v. 1.00

We specify the following message elements.

- *Protocol* (i.e., the protocol name) is set as "entish".
- *Version* is set as "1.00".
- *Session* is set as the name (URI) of the process (agent or service) that has initialized the conversation session. There are two cases. A newly created agent can initialize a session dedicated to its task realization; the session last as long as the agent exists. Or a newly created service initializes a session for publishing the type of operation it performs; the session lasts as long as the service exists.
- *Order* denotes the message type, or message order in the protocol.

We distinguish the following message types:

- Order="000" - service sends *Info* containing its operation type to infoServices. The *Info* can be forwarded in a message having the same order and session.
- Order="111" - infoService sends *Info* to a service confirming the publication of the service's operation type, and setting a timeout for its validity.
- Order="001" - agent sends *Info* with its current intention to an infoService or a service. The contents, i.e., the *Info*, may be forwarded in a messages having the same order and session.
- Order="021" - a service sends *Info* about its commitment to realize the agent's intention sent in a message of order 001.

- Order="222" - agent sends (synchronously) confirmation to the all services, arranged into workflow, informing them that the workflow is completed and rady to start, i.e., there are no elements in the agent's *Plan*. The contents of the message is *Info* with the formula *(true)*. After successful sending, the workflow is executed.
- Order="321" - service sends *Info* about the resource (it has already produced) to the next service in workflow. The next service is supposed to download the resource.
- Order="333" - the next service in the workflow (after successful resource downloading) sends *Info* that confirms the downloading to the service (that has produced this resource) which in turn forwards the confirmation to the agent in a message having the same order and session.
- Order="999" - agent sends (synchronously) confirmation, to all participants of the workflow, informing that the workflow has been successfully executed. The message may be sent if *Plan* and *Workflow* in agent's state are empty. The contents of the message is *Info* with the formula *(true)*. This message type implements two-phase commit (2PC) transaction.
- Order="020" - agent sends *Info* to a service that its commitment should be canceled. The message contents (i.e., *Info*) is the same as the contents of the message of order 021 that was sent by the service to inform the agent about the commitment made by the service.

In order to complete specification of our composition protocol, the following items must be specified for each of the message types presented above.

1. Session name.
2. What is sender? What is recipient?
3. Precondition needed to send a message of this type.
4. The name of agent/service that has created the *Info* in the message body. Format of the formula in the *Info*.
5. How the sender's state is changed and/or what action should be executed: send message, perform operation, or get resource.
6. How the recipient's state is changed and/or which action should be executed.

The specifications for particular message orders are listed below.
Message of Order="000".

1. Session is the name of service.
2. Sender is a service. Recipient is an infoService or an agent.
3. The precondition: the formula $(\phi1)$ is in *formIn* of *Goal* of the *State* of the service, whereas the formula $(\phi0)$ is in *formOut* of *Goal* of the *State* of the service.
4. *Info* is created by the service. Formula format:
   $(\phi1$ implies *formInOperationType(service)* $)$
   and
   $($ *formOutOperationType(service)* implies $\phi0)$
5. No state change and no action execution by the sender.
6. The recipient may put the message contents into its *Knowledge*.

A message of order 000 may be also sent by infoService to an agent as the reply to its message of order 001. Then, the *Info* of the message of order 000 is an *Info* from

Knowledge of the infoService.
Message of Order="111".

1. Session is the name of service.
2. Sender is an infoService. Recipient is a service that sent message of order 000.
3. Precondition: the contents of message of order 000 (sent by the service) is in *Knowledge* of the sender.
4. *Info* is created by the infoService. Formula format: (*timeout(t)*)
5. No state change and no action execution by the sender.
6. The recipient may put the message contents into its *Knowledge*.

Message of Order="001".

1. Session is the name of agent.
2. Sender is an agent. Recipient is a service or infoService.
3. Precondition: The formula *($\phi 0$ and timeout(t0))* is the first formula in *Plan* of the agent's *State*.
4. *Info* is created by the agent. Formula format: ((*$\phi 0$ and timeout(t0)*) *implies intentions(agent)*)
5. No state change and no action execution by the sender.
6. The recipient may put the message contents into its *Knowledge*.

Message of Order="021".

1. Session is the name of agent.
2. Sender is a service, say service0. Recipient is the agent.
3. Precondition: The service0 has received message of order 001 from the agent; the message contents was *Info* with the formula: (*($\phi 0$ and timeout(t0)) implies intentions(agent)*) . Service0 can realize the formula *($\phi 0$ and timeout(t0))* , i.e., it follows from the post condition of its operation type.
4. *Info* is created by the service. Formula format:
   ((*$\phi 1$ and timeout(t1)*)) *implies formInCommitment(service0)*)
   and
   (*formOutCommitment(service0) implies* (*$\phi 0$ and timeout(t0)*))
   the time t1 must be less than t0.
5. The sender commits to realize the agent intention (i.e., the formula (*$\phi 0$ and time-out(t0)*) however under the condition that some other formula, i.e., (*$\phi 1$ and timeout(t1)*) , determined by the service, is satisfied. This results in the following change of *State* of the sender. New *commitment* element is created, and the formula (*$\phi 1$ and timeout(t1)*) is put into the *formIn* element of *commitment*, whereas the formula (*$\phi 0$ and timeout(t0)*) is put into the *formOut* element of the *commitment*. The formula *($\phi 1$ and timeout(t1))* is the precondition for performing operation by the sender. Generally, the formula *($\phi 1$)* states that input resources, say
   ?res1, ?res2, ... , ?resN, have certain properties, i.e.,
   prop1(?res1), prop2(?res2), ... , propN(?resN);
   for each of these resources a token has determined, i.e.,
   token(?res1)=tok1, token(?res2)=tok2, ... , token(?resN)=tokN,
   and these resources are delivered to the sender (*service0*), i.e.,

isIn(?res1, service0), isIn(?res2,service0), ... , isIn(?resN, service0).
Hence, *(φ1)* is conjunction of the following elementary formulas:
(*isIn(?res1, service0) and token(?res1)=tok1 and prop1(?res1)*)
and
(*isIn(?res2, service0) and token(?res2)=tok2 and prop2(?res2)*)
and ...
(*isIn(?resN, service0) and token(?resN)=tokN and propN(?resN)*)
Each of the formulas *prop1(?res1), prop2(?res2), ... , propN(?resN)*, is disjunction
of subformulas. Each of the subformulas of the formula (say *prop2(?res2)*) is conjunction of atomic formulas describing the resource *?res2* . Formula *prop2(?res2)*
is satisfied is one (or more) of its subformulas is satisfied. Hence, the subformulas
may be viewed as offers, from which one should be chosen.

6. The recipient changes its *State* in the following way: puts the message contents (i.e.,
   the *Info* into its *Knowledge*, moves the formula *(φ0 and timeout(t0))* from *Plan* to
   Workflow. Then, it decomposes the formula (*φ1 and timeout(t1)*) into the following
   elementary formulas:

   *φ01 = isIn(?res1, service0) and token(?res1)=tok1 and prop1(?res1) and time-
   out(t1);*

   *φ02 = isIn(?res2, service0) and token(?res2)=tok2 and prop2(?res2) and time-
   out(t1);*

   ...

   *φ0N = isIn(?resN, service0) and token(?resN)=tokN and propN(?resN) and time-
   out(t1)*

   Then, the agents creates intentions from these elementary formulas by adding, for
   example to the first one, a formula of the form *?res1 = fun1(?res11, ... ?res1K)* .
   It is supposed that the agent already knows the abstract production process needed
   to produce the final resource. The abstract process is a function composition that
   occurs in the task formula, i.e., the formula in *formOut* element of *Goal* of the
   agent's *State*. The process is expressed as function composition, e.g.,
   ?finalRes = fun(fun1(...), ... funN(...))

Let's assume that for all of these new intentions the agent has arranged services that
has committed to realize them, i.e., the *service01* committed to realize the intention
corresponding to the formula *(φ01)*, the *service02* committed to realize the intention
corresponding to the formula *(φ02)*, ... the *serviceON* committed to realize the intention
corresponding to the formula *(φ0N)*.

This means, that each of these services has sent to the agent the appropriate message
of order 021 containing the *Info* about its commitment to realize the corresponding
agent's intention.

Message of Order="222".

1. Session is the name of agent.
2. Sender is the agent. Recipient is any service that has sent to the agent a message of
   order 021 with *Info* about its commitment to realize an intention of the agent, and
   the agent has not canceled this commitment, i.e., has not replied with the message
   of order 020.

3. Precondition: the list *Plan* of *Intentions* of the agent's *State* is empty.
4. *Info* is created by the agent. Formula format: (*true*)
5. No state change and no action execution by the sender.
6. Any of the recipients executes its operation if the precondition is satisfied.

Message of Order="321".

1. Session is the name of agent.
2. Sender is service01. Recipient is service0.
3. Precondition: Service01 has committed to realize the intention (corresponding to $\phi 01$). Service01 has received the message of order 222 from the agent. The precondition of the commitment was satisfied. Operation was performed successfully by the service01, and as the result the resource *url-res1* was produced by the service01. The name of the resource is an URL, which means that it can be downloaded by HTTP.
4. *Info* is created by the sevice01. Formula format: (*token(url-res1)=tok1*)
5. The sender's state is not changed.
6. The recipient puts the message contents (i.e., an *Info*) into its *Knowledge*, and downloads the resource. After the successful downloading, the recipient is obliged to send confirmation, i.e., the following message of order 333. If a precondition of a commitment made by the service0 is satisfied, then the service0 performs its operation.

Message of Order="333".

1. Session is the name of agent.
2. Sender is the service0. Recipient is the service01.
3. Precondition: sender (i.e. service0) received the above message of order 321 from service01.
4. *Info* is created by the service0. Formula format: the intention corresponding to ($\phi 01$)
5. No state change and no action execution by the sender.
6. The recipient (service01) puts the message contents into its *Knowledge*, and then forwards the message contents with the same session and order to the agent. The agent moves the intention corresponding to the formula ($\phi 01$) from *Workflow* to *Realized*. The service01 removes the *commitment* corresponding to the realization of the intention.

Message of Order="999".

1. Session is the name of agent.
2. Sender is the agent. Recipients are all services arranged into workflow.
3. Precondition: the lists *Workflow* and *Plan* of the agent's *State* are empty.
4. *Info* is created by the agent. Formula format: (*true*)
5. After successful message sending, the agent process is terminated.
6. The recipients finish successfully their transactions.

Message of Order="020".

1. Session is the name of agent.

2. Sender is the agent. Recipient is a service that has sent appropriate message of Order="021" to the agent.
3. There is no precondition.
4. Formula format: the same *Info* is returned as in the message of order 021.
5. The corresponding intention formula is moved back from *Workflow* to *Plan* by the agent. The corresponding *Info* is removed from agent's *Knowledge*.
6. The corresponding *commitment* is removed by the recipient.

5.2   Abstract architecture and implementation details

Actually, the paper describes the work in progress. Although the description language and composition protocol have already been specified formally, they must be verified by several independent implementations. Once it is shown that different and independent implementations interoperate, the language and the protocol may be considered as a proposal of some interest.

The first prototype implementations are in progress. More details will be published progressively on our web site.

References

1. S. Ambroszkiewicz and T. Nowak. Entish: Agent Based Language for Web Service Integration. In *Cybernetics and Systems 2002*, Proc. of the Sixteenth European Meeting on Cybernetics and System Research (AT2AI-3 Workshop). Vienna, Austria, 2 - 5 April, 2002, pp. 701 - 706. ISBN 3 85206 160 1
2. S. Ambroszkiewicz and T. Nowak. Agentspace as a Middleware for Service Integration. In Proc. ESAW'2001. Springer-Verlag LNAI, vol. 2203 , pp. 134 - 159
3. S. Ambroszkiewicz, W. Penczek, and T. Nowak. Towards Formal Specification and Verification in Cyberspace. In Proc. of Goddard Workshop on Formal Approaches to Agent-Based Systems, 5 - 7 April 2000, NASA Goddard Space Flight Center, Greenbelt, Maryland, USA. Published in Springer LNAI 1871, pp. 16-32
4. M. Gudgin and T. Ewald. All we want for Christmas is a WSDL Working Group. www.xml.com/pub/a/2001/12/19/wsdlwg.html
5. M. Gudgin and T. Ewald. The IDL That Isn't. www.xml.com/pub/a/2002/01/16/endpoints.html
6. K. Sycara, S. Widoff, M. Klusch, and J. Lu. LARKS: Dynamic Matchmaking Among Heterogeneous Software Agents in Cyberspace. In *Autonomous Agents and MultiAgent Systems*, 5, 173 - 203, 2002. Kluwer Academic Publishers
7. L. Wittgenstein. Philosophical Investigations
8. IBM's tutorial and WSFL www-4.ibm.com/software/solutions/webservices/
9. DAML-S www.daml.org/services
10. OASIS BTP www.oasis-open.org/committees/business-transactions/
11. UDDI www.uddi.org
12. SOAP SOAP www.w3.org/2000/xp/
13. XLANG www.gotdotnet.com/team/xml_wsspecs/xlang-c/default.htm
14. Web Service Activity of W3C www.w3c.org/2002/ws/

Intelligent Software Agents Technology
at the Air Force Research Laboratory

James Lawton, Daniel Daskiewich, Mark Gorniak, and Dale Richards

Air Force Research Laboratory, Information Directorate
525 Brooks Rd, Rome NY 13441, USA
{lawtonj,daskiewichd,gorniakm,richardsd}@rl.af.mil

Abstract. Intelligent software agents are a key technology needed to achieve the capabilities required of future military information systems. The Information Technology Division of the Air Force Research Laboratory's (AFRL) Information Directorate has partnered with the Defense Advanced Research Projects Agency (DARPA) to develop a broad-spectrum of agent technologies through a collection of research programs. These programs, funded by the Information Technology Office (ITO) at DARPA, are collectively researching nearly all areas of software agents technology: from fundamental modeling of agent-based systems to the application of mature agents technology in military information systems. This article presents the scope of these programs and their state of progress.

1   Introduction

The information requirements of military operations are expected to continue their current, increasing rate of growth. To meet this need, future information systems will have to differ radically from today's client/server-based approaches. Military information systems must provide commanders with the capability to request information through an easy-to-use, high-level interface, gather the appropriate information from a variety of distributed sources, and present a dynamically tailored view of that information in response to the request.

Intelligent software agents are expected, indeed counted upon, to play a key role in achieving this vision for future information systems. The collective research program in agent-based systems run by AFRL's Information Directorate and the ITO office at DARPA addresses a broad-spectrum of intelligent software agent technology needs and capabilities. This includes research and development in areas as diverse as agent infrastructure, ontological languages, fundamental modeling of agent-based systems, and resource negotiation strategies.

This article discusses the progress being realized in the software-agent revolution through these programs, which will ultimately enable the creation of distributed heterogeneous information systems operating in highly dynamic environments. Much of the research making up these programs is described in more detail in the many

W. Truszkowski, C. Rouff, M. Hinchey (Eds.): WRAC 2002, LNAI 2564, pp. 150-154, 2003.

papers and presentations by the individual investigators - including some participating in this same workshop - which are too numerous to list. Thus only a summary of the programs is presented, including links to the program's respective webpages.

2   Control of Agent-Based Systems (CoABS)

 The objective of the CoABS program is to develop and evaluate a wide variety of alternative agent control and coordination strategies to determine the most effective strategies for achieving the benefits of agent-based systems, while assuring that self-organizing agent systems will maintain acceptable performance and security protections. Through the effective control of agent systems, the intelligent agents will work in harmony to significantly strengthen military capability by reducing planning time, automating and protecting Command and Control (C2) functions, and enhancing decision making. Unlike much of current agent-based research, CoABS has focused on heterogeneous agent systems. CoABS has pushed the envelope in the design of agent-based systems in areas such as communication languages, construction tools, mobility, scaling, and team coordination and cooperation. The *CoABS Grid* provides a common infrastructure for integrating these capabilities. The *Grid* facilitates communication across agent communities, provides security functions and logging of agent activity, and enables heterogeneous agent systems to: register, advertise their capabilities/needs, find available resources, form task-based teams and utilize event notification. The current focus of the CoABS program is on transitioning agent tools and the *Grid* to military systems.

The *CoABS Grid* has been successfully demonstrated in several application domains: (1) A prototype was developed for Air Mobility Command (AMC) to show the benefits that agent-based systems could provide for integrating a range of information systems. Interface agents were connected to the *Grid* to allow operators to monitor and query various existing/legacy systems. "Mocked up" versions of the Global Decision Support System (GDSS), Prior Permission Request (PPR) and Notice To Airman (NOTAMs) systems were also connected to the *Grid*. Agents were used to monitor relevant changes to the mission and send reports to the operator. (2) The *CoABS Grid* was used to successfully integrate numerous C2 components of the Defense Automated Addressing System (DAAS). The CoABS Grid was used to provide connectivity between the legacy systems and to allow monitoring of the various logistics transactions. (3) The CAST/MACOE agent system was used in conjunction with the *Grid* to integrate C2 applications for Navy Fleet Battle Experiments. The resulting information agent application provided targeteers and Intel analysts with the ability to crosscheck multiple information sources within the tight timelines of Time Critical Targeting (TCT). (4) An initial Coalition Technology Integration Experiment (CoAX TIE) was developed to address numerous issues involved with rapidly forming C2 systems in a coalition force environment. The prototype was demonstrated at the Defense Evaluation Research Agency (DERA) in the United Kingdom. (5) The *CoABS GRID* will also be used in initial spiral developments of the Joint Battlespace Infosphere.

More information about the CoABS program can be found at http://coabs.globalinfotek.com. The AFRL/Rome POC for CoABS is Dan Daskiewich, 315 330-7731.

3   DARPA Agent Markup Language (DAML)

Today's web users are frequently overwhelmed with volumes of irrelevant search results. To address this human information overload, the DAML Program has as its goal to facilitate conversion of the web from a human-readable information medium into a machine-readable medium. The DAML program has brought together university, industry, and World Wide Web (WWW) Consortium researchers (including WWW creator Tim Berners-Lee) with expertise in artificial intelligence, knowledge representation, logic, and web technologies to help realize the "Semantic Web" - where machines are able to *reason* over the information space of the web.

Web search engines must advance beyond simple keyword searches before software agents are truly able to understand and utilize the information available on the web. The DAML Program is addressing this need by developing ontology modeling formats, ontology-based content mark-up tools, and ontology inferencing strategies.

The DAML approach for realizing semantic interoperability on the web is to build on existing standards work, e.g., XML (Extensible Markup Language), RDF (Resource Description Framework), and RDF-Schema standards. Drawing on these standards, DAML researchers are developing an ontology modeling format and tools that will allow web-site creators to readily generate domain ontologies. These ontologies will define the web-creator's domain terms, relations, operations, rules and constraints in a DAML-compliant manner. The web-site creators will then use the ontology vocabulary to mark-up the content of their web-site including web-objects such as data, computing functions, sensor capabilities, or appliances. DAML search engines, agents, and other DAML enabled programs will then be able to use this mark-up, in conjunction with inferencing techniques, over these marked-up pages to decipher the **meaning** of the web contents. Ontology translation techniques are also being explored in the DAML Program to allow mapping of independently developed domain ontologies.

A promising example of a military application within the DAML program is the HORUS effort, which is exploring new methods for marking-up, linking, annotating and retrieving documents, in particular those of interest to or generated by the intelligence community. Other applications being considered include: imagery analysis, logistics and simulation applications, along with commercial information retrieval, and transportation and financial applications.

More information about the DAML program can be found at www.daml.org The AFRL/Rome POC for DAML is Mark Gorniak, 315 330-7724.

4   Taskable Agent Software Kit (TASK)

Agent development is often characterized as a "black art" – an arbitrarily complex software development process. Part of the problem is that while there are many *ad hoc* agent creation methodologies, and many partial modeling solutions, there is very little agreed upon formalism for the analysis and modeling of complex, large scale agent systems supporting interaction between large numbers of diverse and distributed heterogeneous information systems.

The Taskable Agent Software Kit program focuses on analyzing agent behaviors by exploring both mathematical modeling and empirical analyses of agent behaviors. In addition, TASK is striving to get participants to compare agent-creation approaches using these models, and to perform qualitative and meaningful quantitative comparisons of agent behaviors with respect to domain and problem features. The goals of this work include a better understanding of what agent-oriented programming really is, formal methods for the description and analysis of the behaviors of multi-agent systems, and methodologies for predicting and/or analyzing the behaviors of large-scale systems.

The TASK program seeks, through interdisciplinary efforts, to examine the understanding of computation via the techniques of other fields, i.e., models inspired by biological systems; the application of mathematics not traditionally used for computer modeling, e.g., the use of statistical physics for large scale modeling; and the integration of techniques from differing computing traditions (such as hybrids of discrete and continuous analyses). Also of interest are approaches that may prove successful for the analysis of data sets collected during the solving of complex problems by multi-agent systems.

A final goal of TASK is to explain and formalize the notion of an "emergent behavior." Although this term is often used in an almost semi-mystical way to explain the performance of a complex task by a set of simple entities (such as the building of a complex termite hill by simple termite behaviors), there is little mathematical or other formal analysis of the meaning of the term. Additionally, how to computationally recognize that a specific goal has been reached by a system "emergently" is still an open problem that TASK seeks to solve. The results will be applied to the verification and validation of agent-based code.

More information about the TASK program can be found at http://www.task-program.org. The AFRL/Rome TASK POC is James Lawton, 315-330--4476, lawtonj@rl.af.mil.

5   Autonomous Negotiating Teams (ANTs)

The objective of the ANTs program is to provide technology that enables the development of information systems that autonomously negotiate the allocation of resources to tasks in real-time, distributed systems. The expected benefits of ANTs are: (1) flexible, self-organizing systems, based on negotiation, that are capable of handling dynamic environments (2) faster distributed computation, through bottom-up agent team formation and (3) "hard" real-time solutions for agent-based systems. The ANTs approach to this problem utilizes highly decentralized and autonomous negotiation of tasks, roles and resources, to provide solutions that are both "good enough" and "soon enough."

Efforts within the ANTs program are divided into two categories: demonstration (efforts with direct transition links) and technology (efforts which further the ANTs technology development and are assessed via a common challenge problem).

Demonstration projects include automation of flight scheduling (Harrier aircraft), autonomic logistics (targeting the Joint Strike Fighter), a Unmanned Combat Air Vehicle (UCAV) simulator, and an adaptive scan scheduler (targeting an Electronic Counter Measures (ECM) system within the Joint Strike Fighter.

ANTs technology efforts primarily focus on development of negotiation protocols and their supporting architecture. A common challenge problem was formulated to provide a demonstration testbed. The challenge problem has two aspects, a physical testbed and a simulation environment. The problem domain for the challenge problem is a distributed sensor testbed. There is a fixed region containing a collection of sensors with varying capabilities and parameters, with "target" objects moving through the environment. Targets need to be detected, tracked, jammed, and/or eliminated. The simulator is intended to correlate directly to the physical testbed. The simulator (RADSIM) was developed internally by AFRL/IFT. Resources for the problem include sensor sector, sensor mode (detect, track, on/off), communication channels, and power consumption. The simulator allows for scalability testing of the negotiation methodologies, as the physical testbed will not allow for testing large numbers of agents

The AFRL/Rome ANTs POC is Dan Daskiewich, DSN 315-330-7731, daskiewichd@rl.af.mil.

6   Summary

The primary focus of intelligent agents research at AFRL is geared toward developing science and technology to facilitate the creation of software agents and the infrastructures on which they will exist and operate. Only when software (agents) can be shown to be autonomous, collaborative and adaptive will the promises of agent intelligent agent technology bear fruit. And only when agents can be easily created, efficiently deployed and securely managed will the goal of distributed, heterogeneous information systems operating in highly dynamic environments become a reality.

Testing and Monitoring Intelligent Agents

Christopher Rouff

SAIC
1710 SAIC Drive, McLean, VA 22102
rouffc@saic.com

Abstract. Current research and development of agent-based systems has focused primarily on architectures, protocols, frameworks, messaging infrastructure and community interactions. As intelligent agent-based systems take over operations in the financial community, transportation, manufacturing, utilities, aerospace, and the military, assurances will need to be given to the owners and operators of these systems that these non-deterministic, learning systems operate correctly. In many of these environments errors in software can result in large financial losses or bodily harm. To build confidence in the owners and users of agent-based systems, testing and monitoring will need to be done that will instill confidence that these systems work correctly and that errors can be quickly found.

1   Introduction

Monolithic and networked deterministic systems can be rigorously tested to determine proper operations. Monitoring of these systems often consists of watching processes or data values the system generates, either historically or in real time, to determine proper functioning of the system. When errors occur, the errors can usually be repeated or found by back tracking through the code or examining runtime stack dumps. Testing and monitoring the functionality of multiple, intelligent, asynchronous agents in a system is a much more difficult task. Agent test and monitoring systems are needed that will allow developers to systematically and automatically test agent and agent community functionality, and to monitor the agents after they are deployed to ensure that they continue to operate correctly.

This paper describes some of the challenges in developing single and communities of agents. It also describes a system under development that will assist developers in testing agent-based systems and to monitor the activity, learning and functionality of intelligent agents after they are deployed.

W. Truszkowski, C. Rouff, M. Hinchey (Eds.): WRAC 2002, LNAI 2564, pp. 155-164, 2003.
© Springer-Verlag Berlin Heidelberg 2003

2   Challenges in Testing Agent-Based Systems

By nature, agent-based systems tend to be asynchronous, parallel entities. These are some of the most difficult systems to develop and debug. Because of their asynchronous and parallel nature, there are several challenges in developing them. Some of these challenges include:

- Agents communicate through message passing instead of function or method calls, so traditional component testing techniques are not applicable,
- Agents are autonomous and operate in parallel, so they may run correctly by themselves, but incorrectly in a community,
- Message specifications are often changing as the system matures so they can sometimes be incorrect, incomplete or out of date,
- Agents may use learning techniques, causing successive tests with the same test data to give different results.

The process of testing agents is different when testing a single agent and when testing a community of agents. When testing a single agent a developer is more interested in the functionality of one agent and whether that agent operates correctly for a set of message inputs, environmental inputs and error conditions. When testing a community of agents the tester is interested in whether the agents operate together, are coordinated and if the messages passing between the agents are correct. The following section discusses these challenges and differences in testing single and communities of agents.

2.1   Testing Single Agents

When developing a single agent, testing is usually done incrementally while the software is being developed. Developers tend to test agents as they progress, testing functionality as it is added. Much of this testing requires another agent to send messages to the agent being tested, which trigger events inside the one being tested, and events from the environment to test the proper handling of those events (Figure 1). Additional testing is also required to test proper agent learning when it is used.

From experience, testing functionality with other agents is the most time consuming part of agent development. When developing a single agent for inclusion into a community, developers want to make sure that the agent responds correctly to given inputs from other agents. To accomplish this, a developer will often end up developing a dummy agent (or use one supplied by the framework, such as with JADE [1]) to send specific messages to the agent under development to tests its functionality and response to the message.

This was the case for the Lights Out Ground Operations System (LOGOS) agent community that was developed at NASA Goddard [7, 8]. A Catch-22 situation arose when developers wanted to test their agents before making them available to other developers. Developers were waiting for someone else to provide the first agent so they could test their own agent. Also, having one other agent usually did not help since that agent also needed other agents to send it messages to trigger the messages it sent out. Therefore, a sizeable set of agents, none of which had been tested, was needed to test a single agent. To get around this, developers wrote dummy agents that did not take any inputs and just sent out hard-coded messages to a specific agent (the one being tested). Eventually an agent was developed that had a user interface that allowed a specific message to be inputted and sent to another agent. This allowed developers to do initial testing without having to have access to the other agents.

Making sure that an agent responds correctly to inputs from its environment must also be taken into account. When testing an agent for proper functioning with the environment, either the environment must be available or it must be simulated. This is the same case as in most software development. Either a simulator needs to be developed if it is a complex environment, or if the environment is simple or easily obtained (e.g., a database system), then testing with the environment can be accomplished with some degree of independence from the rest of the community.

Testing agents for proper learning can be difficult and is something that needs to be monitored during the agent's operation until confidence in the system is gained (and perhaps even after that). Representative samples of learning can be tested deterministically. In this case, since an agent is designed to learn certain properties, predetermined data can be fed into the agent to see if the expected results are actually learned. If there is learning, then given the set of inputs, a new learned behavior should result. More rigorous testing or analysis may need to be done using formal methods [5, 6] or other formal techniques in mission critical situations or where the agent cannot be easily monitored after it is deployed.

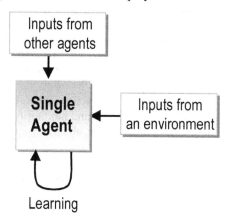

Fig. 1. Testing a single agent – checking inputs from other agents, the environment and learning

2.2   Testing Communities of Agents

Testing communities of agents involves making sure the agents in the community work together as designed. This involves checking that each agent receives the correct messages from the correct agent, provides the correct responses, and interacts with the environment correctly as a whole (Figure 2). Testing this functionality can be complex due to having to monitor a large number of agent and environment interactions.

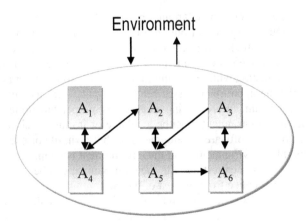

Fig. 2. Testing a community of agents – checking flow of messages and actions as a whole

One of the biggest problems when developing interacting concurrent systems, such as agent communities, is the potential for race conditions. These types of errors can be difficult to find and reproduce. With the development of more agent communities, these types of errors will become more common. To make development of communities more cost effective, new tools and techniques (preferably automated) will be needed to address race conditions.

Visualization of the message passing at runtime also needs to be available and be re-playable so that developers can watch the agent interactions in a visual manner and then playback parts of the interaction when needed. To help with this, a centralized control needs to be available to start, pause and control the speed of execution of agents during testing.

Models or rule-bases that describe the interactions between agents and the environment would help to automate the debugging and monitoring of agents. Patterns of message passing could be monitored and when abnormal interactions occurred, the proper person could be notified. Building up of these models or expert systems could be done during testing or through the message specifications. This would provide a means to detect when messages are not flowing properly and should be investigated for bugs or race conditions.

3   A Test Agent

Testing the functionality of multiple asynchronous autonomous systems is a much more difficult task than testing traditional single threaded systems. A test agent that can interact with the developer and an agent community would speed development, testing and debugging by giving the developer an insight into the interaction within and between agents. A test agent could also read in a specification of each of the agents and automatically produce test cases to run against the agents individually and together as a community.

There are several ways a test agent could be used to test other agents. Some of these include:

- Asking questions, much like a teacher giving a test or oral exam. Not all an agent's knowledge would necessarily need to be tested, but a representative amount to gain a high degree of confidence.
- Testing an agent's learning mechanism by giving the agent several pieces of information and checking to see if it makes the proper conclusion. This would be similar to a geometry or algebra exam where theorems are given along with a question.
- Asking the agent how it would solve a problem and how it came up with the solution. The agent should be able to provide the rules, cases or models that it used to compute its answer.
- Testing that an agent will say it is not capable of answering a problem if it is not able or if the problem is outside of its scope.
- Testing an agent's ability to recognize and handle trick questions.
- Testing an agent's knowledge of its community and how it would utilize members of the community in answering a question or performing a service.
- Testing an agent's ability to say its role in the community.
- Asking an agent to provide a model of the community and environment in which it belongs.
- Asking an agent to answer a query about its abilities, what type of reasoning it uses (if any) and checking if the answer is incomplete or overstated.
- Stimulating the learning component of an agent to see how it learns and validate the learning mechanism and method.

In addition to the above, a test agent could also act as a teaching aid by correcting wrong answers or helping an agent come up with an answer to a question that it does not know how to solve (a person could also be behind such an agent). Agents could also have a fitness function or self-test that would allow them to automatically evaluate themselves and report the result to a test or monitoring agent.

Once an agent or agent community has been deployed, monitoring of the community is also needed to watch for errors and to give the users or administrators a tool to visualize and query the agent's operations. To provide these services, a test and monitoring agent could be inserted or plugged into the agent community and be deployed along with the community. It would be part of the community and would exercise each of the agents in the community as well as the community as a whole during testing and lulls in operation and watch the community for undesirable behaviors and potential errors. Things that may need to be monitored may include the modifications an agent makes to its knowledge base, what it would do in a particular situation given its current knowledge, why it performed a particular action, as well as monitoring the message content and flow between agents against a model or expert system, as discussed earlier.

3.1   Overview of the SAIC Test and Monitoring Agent

A test and monitoring agent is under development at SAIC that addresses many of the above issues. It will be able to be inserted or plugged into a community of agents to exercise each of the agents in the community as well as the community as a whole. The test agent will support both regression and progression testing of agents. The regression testing is used to insure that agents perform to their stated specifications and that modifications to these systems do not affect existing message handling capabilities, while the progression testing is used to support agent developers as they add new messaging capabilities to their software.

Some of the test agent's capabilities will be:

1. Test a single agent's ability to react to a specific set of messages,
2. Test a single agent's ability to handle all messages the system can send and receive as well as invalid messages,
3. Test a collection of cooperating or coordinating agents' ability to handle all defined messages and a representative number of invalid messages,
4. Maintain the official message specifications for a collection of agents,
5. Maintain message specifications in the design and other documents,
6. Collect metrics on network usage, communications, and other specified metrics for scalability issues, and
7. Monitor a system for potential errors and performance problems.

3.2   Architecture of the Test Agent

Figure 3 shows the architecture and data flow for the test agent in its completed form. The test agent receives message specifications either interactively from the user or from a formal specification and stores it in a message specification file (as XML, which allows for easy reuse). From this information test scripts can be generated to test each of the defined agents.

Testing individual agents are done by sending specific messages from the test agent to the target agent and examining the messages returned (if any). The test agent acts just like another agent in the community, but sends out an entire range of valid and invalid messages to an agent or community that are generated from the message specification file. The specification file contains the valid messages that each agent can send and receive as well as any constraints between the messages. From this definition, the test agent is able to generate a set of test messages and interpret the responses as valid or invalid. Rules to apply to the test messages are stored in a rule base and are generated from user inputs and the agent specification. In the future, case-based and model-based reasoning will also be used to direct the testing as well as test agent learning and for monitoring purposes.

Developers can test their agent-based systems either interactive or in a batch mode. Interactive testing can be used to test the operation of new messages, debugging existing messages, or checking a particular nuance of an agent or community. To test a system interactively, the developer first defines the parameters of the specific messages to test, then starts up the target agent(s) and any other appropriate systems that act as the environment and are needed to run the test. The developer then enters the name of the agent that the test agent will simulate (messages are sent out using the simulated agent name so the receiving agent will respond as if it is the real agent), enters messages for the receiving agents, sends them, then views any resulting messages sent back from the target agents.

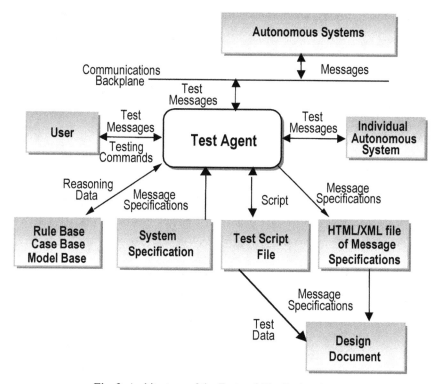

Fig. 3. Architecture of the Test and Monitoring Agent

Once test messages have been defined for an agent, they can be stored in a script file for later use. In the future, developers will also be able to fold progression tests into the regression test script to form a new regression test script. Batch testing simply executes a predefined set of regression tests and has the results saved to a file. Batch testing will also be expanded so it can be done automatically on a periodic basis (e.g., nightly) or when it detects a change in the message specification file or agent code.

The developer currently has the capability to either completely test a system or execute a portion of the test script to only test specific capabilities. A future feature will make use of the message specifications to automatically generate a test script to exercise and check the message handling of an agent or community. In either case, the tests can be run interactively or in a batch mode. Errors are displayed to the user interface if performed interactively or saved to a file if performed in batch mode.

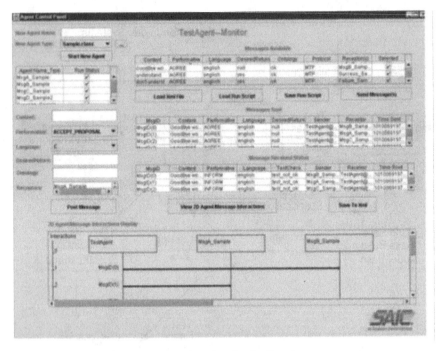

Fig. 4. User interface for the Test Agent

Since a complete specification of communications are stored in the message specification file, it will be fairly trivial to output the contents of the file into HTML, XML or other format that can then be used in a design or other document. Each time the specification file is changed, it will be possible for the documents to be automatically updated. This will allow the desired documents to always reflect the current implementation.

Testing communities of cooperating agents will also be based on the message specification file. From the specification a test script for the entire community will be able to be generated. Testing the proper operation of a community of agents requires several techniques. One will be similar to the testing of individual agents. The test agent will masquerade as another agent in the community and will send valid and invalid messages to the other agents to determine the reaction of each and the community as a whole. The test agent will then be successively substituted for each agent in the community.

An additional feature being considered will be for messages to be specified in a formal language, such as Communicating Sequential Processes (CSP) [2, 3]. This will allow the message specification to be generated directly from the formal specification, which in turn will ensure that the content is always correct and reflects the current message specification. In addition, various properties of the messages can be proven to be correct and errors (such as possible deadlock conditions) can be found before implementation or testing by converting the specification into a model checking language and run through a model checker [4].

3.3   Test Agent User Interface

Figure 4 shows the user interface of the test agent. The upper left corner is where the user can type in the name of an agent they want to test as well as select the main class library of the agent. Below the agent name and agent type is a list of the current agents that will be executed (or currently executing) along with their status. Below the agent status is a message template where the user can type in the contents of a test message to send another agent.

The right side of Figure 4 shows the list of messages that can be sent. Under that are some execution buttons for loading messages from an XML file, running a script, saving a script and sending selected messages. Under the execution buttons is a list of messages sent, and the third list is the messages received by the test agent indicating whether they are correct or not. At the bottom, a timeline is shown showing the flow of messages between the agents. All of the features shown in the user interface have been implemented.

4   Conclusion

Testing agent-based systems can be a difficult and time intensive task. Using traditional testing techniques for monolithic systems will not work for asynchronous, parallel, and intelligent systems like agents.

As agent systems become more prevalent and agent communities become larger, it will become increasingly difficult to test these systems. Automated techniques need to be used to test the large number of interactions between agents as well as the correctness of any learning done.

A test agent is being developed at SAIC to help with the stated challenges. The test agent will allow developers to more quickly and thoroughly test and debug their systems allowing them to deliver higher quality autonomous systems in less time. This test agent can be used to test a single agent or inserted into a community of agents to test the community as a whole. In addition, a subset of the test agent will be able to be deployed with an agent community that will provide data on how well the community is performing and to give feedback on their correct operation.

References

[1]   Bellifemine, F., Caire, G., Trucco, T., Rimassa, G.: JADE Programmer's Guide. CSELT S.p.A. (2000)
[2]   Hinchey, M.G., Jarvis, S.A.: Concurrent Systems: Formal Development in CSP, McGraw-Hill International Series in Software Engineering, London and New York (1995)
[3]   Hoare, C.A.R.: Communicating Sequential Processes, Prentice Hall International Series in Computer Science, Hemel Hempstead (1985)
[4]   Holzmann, H. J.: Design and Validation of Computer Protocols, Prentice Hall Software Series, Englewood Cliffs, NJ (1991)

[5] Rouff, C., Hinchey, M., Rash, J.: Verification and Validation of Autonomous Systems. IEEE/NASA Software Engineering Workshop, Greenbelt, MD (2001)

[6] Rouff, C., Rash, J., Hinchey, M.: Experience Using Formal Methods for Specifying a Multi-Agent System. Sixth IEEE International Conference on Engineering of Complex Computer Systems (2000)

[7] Truszkowski, W., Hallock, H.: Agent Technology from a NASA Perspective. CIA-99, Third International Workshop on Cooperative Information Agents, Uppsala, Sweden. Springer-Verlag (1999)

[8] Truszkowski, W., Rouff, C.: An Overview of the NASA LOGOS and ACT Agent Communities. World Multiconference on Systemics, Cybernetics and Informatics, Orlando, Florida (2001)

Wireless Agents in Ad Hoc Networks

Stephen Quirolgico[1], L. Jay Wantz[1], Michael Miller[1], Naveen Srinivasan[2], Vlad Korolev[1], and Michael Fay[1]

[1] Applied Research Group
Aether Systems, Inc.
Owings Mills, MD 21117
{squirolgico, jwantz, mmiller, vkorolev, mofay}@aethersystems.com
[2] Department of Computer Science and Electrical Engineering
University of Maryland, Baltimore County
Baltimore, MD 21205
nsrini1@cs.umbc.edu

Abstract. With the current trend toward ubiquitous computing comes wireless devices capable of direct, peer-to-peer communication. Such devices will be capable of forming the nodes of ad hoc networks. In the near future, it is expected that ad hoc networks will be saturated with heterogeneous hardware and software requiring mechanisms to facilitate interoperability. At the application layer, such interoperability may be facilitated using software agents. Unfortunately, it is currently impractical to design, implement, and study device-based software agents within ad hoc networks as the required hardware and software configurations do not yet exist. In this paper, we present a software framework for developing and studying device-based software agents in the context of ad hoc networks. We refer to this framework as the Wireless Agent Simulator.

1 Introduction

Using current wireless technologies, devices including laptops, PDAs and mobile phones can be equipped to communicate with each other directly and form the nodes of *ad hoc networks*. Ad hoc networks are local-area networks that are dynamically created through the connections between two or more nodes. Unlike other networks, ad hoc networks are formed and maintained in a decentralized fashion; that is, each node in the network is responsible for handling network management functions including establishing connections and maintaining routing protocols without a centralized controller. In addition, the topology of an ad hoc network continually changes based on the physical location of its nodes. Ad hoc networks may be used for a number of applications including file exchange and games, and may be especially useful in disaster relief situations or military theater operations where spontaneous network formations are necessary. In the near future, the continued proliferation of Bluetooth-, IrDA- and 802.11-equipped wireless devices is expected to result in ad hoc networks saturated with heterogeneous systems (i.e., heterogeneous devices, applications and

W. Truszkowski, C. Rouff, M. Hinchey (Eds.): WRAC 2002, LNAI 2564, pp. 165–174, 2003.

configurations) requiring technology that can support interoperability between these systems.

In an ad hoc network, interoperability between wireless devices is required at both the network and application layers. Regarding the network layer, wireless technologies including IrDA and Bluetooth may be used to establish the low-level interoperability between devices. At the application layer, protocols including FTP, HTTP, and WAP may be used to facilitate interoperability between homogeneous applications. However, no such protocols exist to facilitate interoperability between heterogeneous wireless applications and services. This is problematic in an ad hoc network where such applications may need to interact. One way to facilitate interoperability between both homogeneous and heterogeneous wireless applications and services is to use software agents. We refer to such agents as *wireless agents*.

We envisage wireless agents playing an increasing role in facilitating interoperability at the application-layer in ad hoc network environments. Unfortunately, it is difficult to study wireless agents in the context of ad hoc networks as most OEM vendors do not yet fully support the required hardware and software configurations [8]. Even if such devices and applications were fully supported, it may be impractical to analyze the behavior of wireless agents between possibly numerous heterogeneous hardware and software configurations. To adequately design, implement, and test wireless agents, it is useful to have a framework to simulate the execution of such agents in an ad hoc network environment. In this paper, we present the *Wireless Agent Simulator* (WAS) system for simulating the execution of wireless agents. WAS facilitates the development of wireless agents by providing a framework within which developers may design, implement, and test wireless agents (e.g., their behaviors, services, GUI designs, and interaction with other agents) within virtual ad hoc network environments.

2   Wireless Agents

We define a wireless agent as a software agent that resides on a wireless device and directly communicates with agents on other devices. A wireless agent may be an application or service, or may provide a wrapper around, or interface to, an existing wireless application. We distinguish between wireless agents and *mobile agents* by noting that the latter migrate between hosts [10]. A wireless agent may be a mobile agent if it migrates between wireless devices, but this property is neither a requirement nor a focus of this work.

Like other types of agents, wireless agents embody a number of general properties including autonomy (i.e., control over their own actions and internal state), reactivity (i.e., responsiveness to the environment) and pro-activity (i.e., initiation of behavior to achieve their goals) [19]. Thus, wireless agents may function on their own with little or no user interaction and may also act as both a client and server simultaneously to facilitate peer-to-peer communication. Wireless agents exhibit additional properties to (1) facilitate interoperability at the application layer, (2) function on small-footprint wireless devices, and (3) operate in an ad hoc network.

2.1 Application-Layer Interoperability

Because the primary goal of wireless agents is to facilitate interoperability between heterogeneous applications and services, such agents may be required to conduct some form of reasoning to infer the beliefs, desires, and intentions of other agents. In a multiagent system where agents influence the behavior of one another through direct communication, an agent may use an agent communication language (ACL) to help communicate such mental states. One ACL that has recently gained attention within the agent research community is being specified by the *Foundation for Intelligent Physical Agents* (FIPA). This ACL, known as *FIPA ACL*, is a high-level, message-oriented communication language and protocol for supporting run-time knowledge sharing among agents. Like other ACLs, FIPA ACL is distinguished by its objects of discourse and semantic complexity [11].

Agents use FIPA ACL by passing FIPA messages that contain a *communicative act* [9]. A communicative act is a language primitive that identifies the message type (e.g., assertion, query, or command). Each communicative act has well-defined semantics that may be used by a receiving agent to help infer the intention of the sender. A FIPA message also contains a set of message elements that may be used by a receiving agent to further refine the context surrounding a received message. There are a number of reserved FIPA message elements including `content` (i.e., the content of the message), `ontology` (i.e., the ontology that describes the content), and `language` (i.e., the language used to encode the content).

Even using a standardized communication language, a wireless agent may be unable to exploit the knowledge encapsulated by a received FIPA ACL message. This is because FIPA ACL does not mandate specific reasoning methodologies to be used by agents. Ultimately, application-layer interoperability will entail additional mechanisms that must be defined by the agent developer. Such mechanisms may involve the use of representation schemes to structure knowledge as well as the use of ontologies to provide adequate semantics for reasoning about knowledge. An agent will also need to employ a suitable reasoning mechanism. Although knowledge representation, ontologies and reasoning mechanisms are beyond the scope of this paper, we briefly discuss how these may be used to facilitate application-layer interoperability in Section 3.3.

2.2 Platform Considerations

Although this paper focuses on wireless agents in a simulated environment, platform considerations must be taken into account in order to yield a valid simulation of the system as well as to assess potential portability of simulated wireless agents to actual devices.

One issue related to platform portability concerns the agent-based platform to be used for the simulation. Here, the goal is to identify a platform that supports the porting of simulated wireless agents to actual devices. Since virtually all FIPA-based platforms are implemented in Java, a platform is needed that allows agent-based components written in J2SE/EE to port to small-footprint devices that support KVM, PersonalJava, and J2ME [12]. In addition, a suitable layer of abstraction between simulated wireless agents and lower-level components is required to further support portability to actual devices.

Unlike *infrastructured* networks that utilize fixed and wired gateways, ad hoc networks are *infrastructureless*; that is, they are formed by mobile devices that can be connected dynamically in an arbitrary manner [16]. In an ad hoc network, the devices on which wireless agents reside must support a wireless, device-to-device communication technology such as IrDA or Bluetooth rather than technologies associated with infrastructured networks like wireless WANs (e.g., GSM, CDMA, and GPRS) and wireless LANs (e.g., HomeRF). In a simulated ad hoc network environment, care must be taken to ensure that the simulated behavior of wireless technologies is valid.

2.3   Ad Hoc Network Considerations

In addition to interoperability and platform issues, any framework for the development of wireless agents must take into consideration issues related to the nature of ad hoc networks. Such issues are typically concerned with the mobility of nodes within the network.[3] Because nodes are always moving in an ad hoc network, the topology of the network is continually changing.

One issue related to the movement of nodes within an ad hoc network concerns the maintenance of sessions between wireless agents. When two wireless agents reside on devices that move in and out of *connectivity* (i.e., the ability to communicate directly) with one another, mechanisms are needed in order to both quickly establish dialog as well as gracefully terminate interaction. In addition, wireless agents may need to be able to re-establish sessions in an appropriate manner if a connection is re-established.

A related issue to session maintenance is system performance. Because nodes may move quickly and unpredictably in an ad hoc environment, performance of wireless agents is crucial in order to complete interactions before the devices on which they reside move out of proximity. Often, performance will be restricted by a number of factors associated with wireless and mobile computing in general including platform constraints and limited bandwidth[18]. Thus, care should be taken to ensure that wireless agents utilize efficient mechanisms to carry out their functionality.

Another issue of ad hoc networks is how to route messages through a set of intermediate devices. Recently, a number of research efforts have proposed

---

[3] Here, the term 'mobility' refers to the movement of wireless devices in physical space and *not* the migration of agents between hosts (as is the case when we talk about mobile agents).

the use of *ad hoc network routing protocols.* Ad hoc network routing protocols are concerned with discovering and establishing multi-hop paths through the network to other nodes. Such protocols may allow communication between two wireless agents using intermediate agents as routers.

Though ad hoc networks require consideration of network security issues [20], the topic of security in ad hoc networks is beyond the scope of this paper.

3   Wireless Agent Simulator

The Wireless Agent Simulator (WAS) is a framework for building and simulating wireless agents in virtual ad hoc network environments. WAS is implemented on top of the FIPA-based *Java Agent DEvelopment Framework* (JADE) platform [4]. The motivation for the use of JADE over other FIPA-based platforms stems primarily from its potential for portability to wireless devices [1].

The WAS architecture is comprised of a *Simulator for Wireless Ad hoc Networks* (SWAN) and a set of agent-enabled, virtual devices. Figure 1 shows the general WAS architecture with SWAN and two agent-enabled virtual devices.

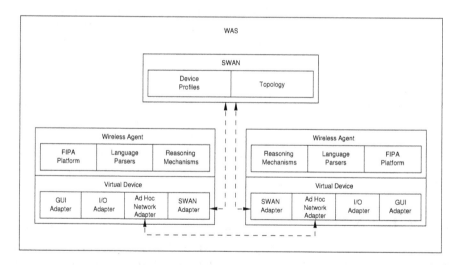

Fig. 1. General WAS architecture with SWAN and two agent-enabled virtual devices.

3.1   Simulator for Wireless Ad hoc Networks (SWAN)

In an ad hoc network, the ability of a wireless agent to initiate and maintain a conversation with another wireless agent is dependent upon a number of factors including the wireless hardware, protocols, and physical proximity of the devices on which the agents reside. In WAS, SWAN simulates these characteristics of an ad hoc network. SWAN is comprised of a *device profiles* component and a *topology* component.

The device profiles component receives and maintains information on wireless technologies and profiles used by virtual devices within the simulated ad hoc network. It also provides a set of services to virtual devices including notification services for alerting virtual devices of other devices with which they may communicate. Information about a virtual device is sent to the device profiles component when a virtual device is initialized. During initialization, a virtual device subscribes to the services of the device profiles component by sending it a device ID as well as information about its wireless technology.

The topology component maintains information about the topology of a virtual ad hoc network. The topology component is used to (1) initialize and modify the geospatial locations of virtual devices, (2) manipulate the physical orientation of virtual devices, and (3) graphically display the virtual ad hoc network. When a virtual device registers with SWAN, the topology component generates an initial geospatial location for the device and displays the device's location graphically within a GUI that represents a bounded virtual geospatial region. Once a virtual device is registered, the GUI may be used to alter the location of the device by dragging an icon of the device within the bounded region.

In addition to simulating movement and physical orientation, SWAN assesses the potential for connectivity between virtual devices. Connectivity is dependent upon factors including: (1) the wireless technologies used by the devices, (2) the physical orientation of the devices, and (3) the physical proximity between the devices. For example, connectivity between two IrDA-enabled virtual devices may occur when both are in physical proximity and each is within line-of-sight of one another. In a simulated Bluetooth environment, however, establishing connectivity is more complex. Here, connectivity between two Bluetooth-enabled virtual devices is determined by factors including (1) maximum RF range allowed by the simulated Bluetooth receivers, (2) the number of virtual devices in the associated piconet, and (3) whether the simulated Bluetooth technology supports point-to-point or point-to-multipoint communication.

3.2   Virtual Devices

In WAS, wireless agents are deployed on virtual devices. Like device emulators that provide PC-based versions of a device for testing application-layer software, WAS virtual devices provide an environment for testing wireless agents prior to deploying on (JADE-enabled) devices. However, WAS virtual devices differ from device emulators in that the former implements an architecture that is not specific to any particular device manufacturer. A WAS virtual device is further distinguished from current device emulators as the latter do not typically emulate wireless transmissions nor embody the notion of movement in physical space. A WAS virtual device is comprised of a number of components including a SWAN adapter, ad hoc network adapter, GUI adapter, and I/O adapter.

A virtual device may join a simulated ad hoc network using a *SWAN adapter*. A SWAN adapter is used by a virtual device to subscribe to SWAN notification services and to receive updates on other virtual devices with which connections may be established. When a virtual device receives notification that a connection may be established with another device, it makes this information available to its *ad hoc network adapter*.

An ad hoc network adapter is an interchangeable component comprised of a set of APIs, protocol stacks, and hardware simulators that mimics the properties of a specific infrastructureless, wireless technology like Bluetooth, IrDA, or 802.11. Although an ad hoc network adapter may reflect a vendor-specific implementation of a wireless technology, custom adapters may be used to simplify or enhance the simulation environment. Virtual devices may use one of possibly several different ad hoc network adapters and thus may simulate a variety of wireless hardware and software configurations. To ease portability from the simulated environment to actual devices, however, virtual devices should use standardized APIs and protocol stacks whenever possible.

When a virtual device is initialized, it is configured to use a specific ad hoc network adapter. During subscription to SWAN notification services, a virtual device sends information to SWAN about its ad hoc network adapter. This information may include the class of wireless technology (e.g. Bluetooth, IrDA, or 802.11), the vendor of the implementation, and properties of the simulated hardware components. When a virtual device receives notification that a connection may be established with another device, it makes this information available to its ad hoc network adapter which, in turn, uses this information to provide a connection for wireless agents at the application-layer. Using protocols embodied by an ad hoc network adapter, a communication channel between two virtual devices may be established. Note that in addition to providing a communication channel between virtual devices, an ad hoc network adapter may also provide additional services. For example, an ad hoc network adapter for Bluetooth may also provide service discovery through the Bluetooth Service Discovery Protocol (SDP) or the Salutation service discovery and session management protocol.

In order to provide a simulation environment that resembles a typical handheld device, WAS virtual devices include GUI and I/O adapters. A GUI adapter provides access to the GUI of the virtual device. This access is provided by a set of APIs. By using the GUI component of a virtual device, developers may design, implement and test the behavior of GUIs for their wireless agent. An I/O adapter allows for the reading and writing of files by a wireless agent. Like an ad hoc network adapter, both GUI and I/O adapters are components that may be interchanged with other adapters to reflect different GUI and I/O environments.

3.3   Wireless Agent

In WAS, a wireless agent is a user-defined agent that provides peer-to-peer functionality between it and other wireless agents. A wireless agent resides on top of a WAS virtual device and utilizes APIs from that device in order to access GUI, I/O and wireless technology components. Although WAS provides a framework for building wireless agents, it does not mandate the use of any particular application-layer functionality. Some particularly important applications of wireless agents may include service discovery and ad hoc routing.

Using FIPA ACL, wireless agents may communicate in a standardized fashion, thereby facilitating interoperability. However, since neither WAS nor FIPA ACL dictate a specific reasoning methodology, agent developers may need to extend their agents in order to support the level of interoperability that they require. Although various methods may be used to support enhanced interoperability, we have implemented some proof-of-concept wireless agents that utilize standardized knowledge representation schemes, ontologies and reasoning mechanisms.

One emerging standard for representing knowledge is the Resource Description Framework Schema (RDFS). RDFS is an XML-based language that provides a means to define vocabulary, structure and constraints for expressing metadata about Web resources. Although RDFS is sufficient for structuring knowledge, it does not embody the formal semantics and expressivity required to support ontological modeling and reasoning. However, an extension to RDFS to allow for the proper representation of ontologies has been specified in the Ontology Inference Layer (OIL) [7]. By using FIPA ACL in conjunction with OIL, wireless agents may exchange semantically richer knowledge and improve the potential for heterogeneous interoperability. Inferencing on such knowledge requires an appropriate parser and reasoning mechanism (e.g., Prolog or the Java Expert System Shell (JESS)).

4   Related Work

Recently, a number of research efforts have looked at using agents in ad hoc networks. Most of these efforts have been focused on using mobile agents to facilitate ad hoc routing protocols [14, 2, 13, 17]. Some efforts have also used agents for service discovery in ad hoc networks [3]. The work described in this paper is distinguished from these other efforts by its use of agents that utilize FIPA ACL to promote interoperability between agents in ad hoc network environments.

A few research efforts are also using FIPA ACL in wireless environments. Two specific efforts include the Lightweight Extensible Agent Platform (LEAP) project [5] and the CRUMPET project [12]. The former is concerned with porting JADE to wireless devices while the latter involves porting the FIPA-OS framework [15] to wireless devices. Although these projects entail the use of FIPA-based agents on wireless devices, they are currently designed for use in wireless, infrastructured networks with fixed gateways. The work described in this paper is distinguished from these efforts through its focus on FIPA-based agents in wireless, infrastructureless networks (i.e., ad hoc networks).

There are also a number of research efforts looking into the development of simulators for ad hoc networks. One such effort concerns an extension to the *ns* discrete event simulator for providing multi-hop ad hoc network simulation [6]. Although such simulators provide very detailed implementations of low-level networking components, they do not target issues at the application-layer. The work presented in this paper is distinguished from these other efforts primarily by its focus on interoperability between wireless agents at the application layer.

5 Conclusions and Future Work

In this paper, we presented WAS, a framework for developing wireless agents in a simulated ad hoc network environment. The motivations for developing WAS stems from a lack of suitable wireless hardware and software configurations for deploying wireless agents, and the lack of a framework for studying the behavior between wireless agents on possibly numerous hardware and software configurations.

Currently, the implementation of WAS is undergoing refinement and the addition of new features. Refinements to WAS will include the integration of more standardized APIs for ad hoc network adapters to further facilitate portability to wireless devices. New features of WAS may include support for GPS and mapping functionality to facilitate the development of wireless agents for location-based services. Refinements to SWAN will include support for additional ad hoc network characteristics. In addition, we intend to verify the portability of wireless agents to appropriate wireless devices as such devices become available.

We believe WAS will provide an important framework for studying software agents within the context of ad hoc networks. Some areas of research that may be furthered using WAS include negotiation of ad hoc routing protocols among FIPA-based wireless agents, modeling ad hoc services, wireless agents for m-commerce, and interoperability assessment between heterogeneous wireless agents.

References

1. Adorni, G., Bergenti, F., Poggi, A., Rimassa, G.: Enabling FIPA Agents on Small Devices. Fifth International Workshop on Cooperative Information Agents. Modena, Italy, 2001
2. Bandyopadhyay, S., Paul, K.: Evaluating the Performance of Mobile Agent-Based Message Communication among Mobile Hosts in Large Ad Hoc Wireless Network. Proceedings of the 2nd ACM International Workshop on Modeling, Analysis and Simulation of Wireless and Mobile Systems. Seattle, WA, 1999
3. Barbeau, M.: Service Discovery Protocols for Ad Hoc Networking. CASCON 2000 Workshop on Ad Hoc Communications. Toronto, Canada, 2000
4. Bellifemine, F., Poggi, A., Rimassa, G.: Developing Multi-Agent Systems with a FIPA-compliant Agent Framework. Software - Practice and Experience, 13, 2001
5. Bergenti, F., Poggi, A.: A FIPA Platform for Handheld and Mobile Devices. Eighth International Workshop on Agent Theories, Architectures, and Languages. Seattle, Washington, 2001
6. Broch, J., Maltz, D.A., Johnson, D.B., Hu, Y., Jetcheva, J.: A Performance Comparison of Multi-Hop Wireless Ad Hoc Network Routing Protocols. Fourth ACM/IEEE International Conference on Mobile Computing and Networking. Dallas, TX, 1998

7. Broekstra, J., Klein, M., Decker, S., Fensel, D., van Harmelen, F., Horrocks, I.: Enabling Knowledge Representation on the Web by Extending RDF Schema. Proceedings of the 10th World Wide Web conference. Hong Kong, China, 2001

8. Finin, T., Joshi, A., Kagal, L., Ratsimore, O., Korolev, V., Chen, H.: Information Agents for Mobile and Embedded Devices. First International Workshop on Cooperative Information Agents. Modena, Italy, 2001

9. Foundation for Intelligent Physical Agents: FIPA Communicative Act Library Specification, 2000

10. Gray, R.S., Cybenko, G., Kotz, D., Rus, D.: Mobile agents: Motivations and State of the Art. In: Bradshaw, J. (ed), Handbook of Agent Technology. AAAI/MIT Press, 2001

11. Labrou, Y., Finin, T., Peng, Y.: Agent Communication Languages: The Current Landscape. IEEE Intelligent Systems, 14(2), 1999

12. Laukkanen, M., Tarkoma, S., Leinonen, J.: FIPA-OS Agent Platform for Small-footprint Devices. Eigth International Workshop on Agent Theories, Architectures, and Languages. Seattle, Washington 2001

13. Li, Q., Rus, D.: Sending Messages to Mobile Users in Disconnected Ad-Hoc Wireless Networks. Proceedings of the Sixth International Conference on Mobile Computing and Networking. Boston, MA, 2000

14. Minar, N., Hultman Kramer, K., Maes, P.: Cooperating Mobile Agents for Dynamic Network Routing. In: Hayzelden, A. (ed), Software Agents for Future Communications Systems. Springer-Verlag, 1999

15. Poslad, S., Buckle, P, Hadingham, R.: The FIPA-OS Agent Platform: Open Source for Open Standards. Fifth Internation Conference and Exhibition on The Practical Application of Intelligent Agents and Multi-Agents. Manchester, UK, 2000

16. Royer, E., Toh, C-K.: A Review of Current Routing Protocols for Ad Hoc Mobile Wireless Networks. IEEE Personal Communications, 1999

17. Rus, D., Gray, R.S., Kotz, D.: Transportable Information Agents. Journal of Intelligent Information Systems, 22(3), 1997

18. Satyanarayanan, M.: Fundamental Challenges in Mobile Computing. Fifteenth Symposium on Principles of Distributed Computing. Philadelphia, PA, 1996

19. Woolridge, M., Jennings, N.: Intelligent Agents: Theory and Practice. Knowledge Engineering Review, 10(2), 1995

20. Zhou, L, Haas, Z.J.: Securing Ad Hoc Networks. IEEE Network, 13(6), 1999

Towards Complex Team Behavior in Multi-agent Systems Using a Commercial Agent Platform

J. Vaughan[1], R. Connell[1], A. Lucas[2] and R. Rönnquist[2]

[1] Land Operations Division, Defence Science and Technology Organisation
Department of Defence
PO Box 1500, Salisbury, SA 5108, Australia
http://www.dsto.defence.gov.au
[2] Agent Oriented Software Pty. Ltd.
156-64 Pelham St., Carlton, Victoria 3053, Australia
http://www.agent-software.com

Abstract. This paper describes the results of a joint Defence Science and Technology Organisation (DSTO), Agent Oriented Software Pty. Ltd. (AOS Australia) technology development project, known as TeBAT. Team Based Agent Technology (TeBAT) is a programming framework supporting specification of coordinated activity among software agents.

TeBAT is based upon the BDI (Belief, Desire, Intention) paradigm, which evolved from early work by Bratman on rational agency. Key to this approach is an emphasis on intentionality, with teams of agents possessing collaborative intentions. In TeBAT, team movement is characterized as structured flocking behaviors with formation control. Conceptually, each team entity is aware of its place in the formation, and it is aware of any entities around it as well as the terrain and environment in which it operates. TeBAT further enables dynamic formation and re-formation of teams, reasoning over team goal failures at the team level, as well as automatic sharing and aggregation of beliefs betweens teams and sub-teams.

Applied to land combat simulation, TeBAT allows team-based tactical operations of military doctrine to be captured and played out in simulation scenarios with minimal effort, in contrast to the previous laborious construction of complex, scenario-specific scripts involving multiple interdependencies between entities.

1   Introduction

The field of intelligent agent technology, particularly that of BDI (Belief, Desire and Intention) agents, has lead from early theoretical work by Bratman [Bratman, 1987] in the mid 1980's. Bratman proposed that an agent's *intentions* play a crucial role, and that the agent and its behavior cannot be simply described in terms of its beliefs and

W. Truszkowski, C. Rouff, M. Hinchey (Eds.): WRAC 2002, LNAI 2564, pp. 175-185, 2003.
© Springer-Verlag Berlin Heidelberg 2003

desires, or goals. Cohen and Levesque [Cohen and Levesque, 1990] provided one of the early formalisation of intentions. Early work on BDI agents [Rao and Georgeff, 1991] resulted in experimental practical implementations, notably PRS (Procedural Reasoning System) developed at SRI International.

PRS was applied to a number of practical applications at the Australian Artificial Intelligence Institute (AAII), notably the OASIS air traffic management system [Ljungberg and Lucas, 1992], [Lucas et al., 1995] and the SWARMM air mission modelling simulation system [Rao, Lucas, Morley, Selvestral and Murray, 1993], [McIlroy, Smith, Heinze and Turner, 1997]. OASIS is a decision support system developed in conjunction with Airservices Australia, the country's air traffic organization. OASIS was designed as an "intelligent assistant" to the Flow Director; the person responsible for tactical air traffic management, to reduce the Flow Director's workload and allow more efficient management of arrivals. It was developed as a proof of concept prototype and successfully trialed by controllers in parallel with the existing manual approach at the Area Control Center for Sydney Airport in 1995. These trials demonstrated that a multi-agent system could work effectively in a real-time operational environment, performing many of the low-level reasoning and computational tasks previously performed manually by the Flow Director.

The OASIS system interfaced with the key air traffic systems, receiving: real-time radar data from four secondary surveillance radars; flight plan data from the Flight Data Processing System; as well as information on actual atmospheric conditions via digital data link from aircraft. In addition, the system held a database of airline-specific aircraft performance and Standard Approach Routes to determine Estimated Times of Arrival for aircraft. The OASIS software architecture comprised an agent created for every aircraft approaching Sydney, as well as agents for each of the runways, a user interface agent and a global coordination agent. In operational trials up to 85 agents were concurrently active in the system, managing the inbound sequence of aircraft to the airport. However, while a multi-agent system, OASIS did not use explicit team concepts.

SWARMM is a defence air mission simulation system, designed as a tool for operational analysis in support of defence procurement and tactics development. SWARMM integrated an existing legacy Fortran simulation system with dMARS, a second-generation, multi-agent system developed from PRS. SWARMM extended the concept of a multi-agent system to one where the agents became part of a team formation of aircraft performing air intercepts using the military doctrine of the Royal Australian Air Force. The Defence Science and Technology Organisation (DSTO) of the Australian Department of Defence successfully used SWARMM over a number of years for defence studies.

The development of SWARMM represented two milestones: the enhancement of a legacy simulation system to provide an advanced pilot reasoning capability; and the introduction of team tactics to a simulation system for defence operational analysis.

More recently the success of SWARMM has led to the development of Battlemodel by DSTO's Air Operations Division [Heinze et al., 2001]. Battlemodel, a flexible simulation architecture for defence simulation, was initially integrated with dMARS. In the current version of Battlemodel, DSTO is replacing dMARS with

Agent Oriented Software's JACK Intelligent Agents. Recent operational studies by DSTO, using Battlemodel, have extended team modelling to include:

- on the "Blue" side, a team of eight on board an airborne early warning and control aircraft, eight friendly fighters in two sections of four, ground-based sector air defence and two strike aircraft; and
- on the "Orange" side, eight intruders, in two sections of four, in addition to Orange ground-based command and control.

Battlemodel, represents the "state of the art" in deployed multi-agent systems, using the concepts of teams and sub-teams of agents. The teams used in Battlemodel and SWARMM, being based on BDI agents, are teams incorporating intentional behavior.

The concepts of teamwork, and team behavior, are well introduced by Cohen and Levesque's landmark paper [Cohen and Levesque, 1991], which explored the way that teamwork can be seen as a joint activity by individuals that share joint commitments and intentions. Grosz [Grosz and Kraus, 1993] made a valuable contribution to the development of formalisms for team behavior. Grosz highlighted that team behavior cannot be simply "bolted on" to a multi-agent system; instead it must be included from the beginning.

The application of teamwork to defence simulation, and to computer generated forces, by Laird and others in TacAir-Soar, [Laird et al., 1994] was based upon the Soar architecture [Laird et al., 1987]. Tambe has made a substantial contribution to the area, including the STEAM re-usable teamwork module [Tambe, 1997].

Recent development by DSTO and Agent Oriented Software Pty. Ltd. (AOS Australia) has focussed on building team-oriented infrastructure with BDI agents. This work, over the period 1999-2001, lead to the development of JACK SimpleTeam [Busetta et al, 1999], [Hodgson et al., 2000], [Hodgson et al., 1999], an extension to JACK that allows for the specification of simple teams and the coordination of joint activities among the team members. This includes the centralised specification of coordinated behavior, and its realisation through actual coordinated activity.

In parallel with the work on SimpleTeam, work proceeded on introducing intentional agents into land-based simulation [Rönnquist et al., 1999]. SAI (Simulation Agent Infrastructure), the integration of JACK with the UK-developed CAEN (Close Action EnviroNment) simulation system, replaces the scripted actions with intentional agents [Rönnquist et al., 2000]. The most recent work, encompassed in TeBAT II_[Lucas et al., 2001], provides the foundation for the work described in this paper. The range of recent defence applications based upon JACK is shown on the right of Figure 1.

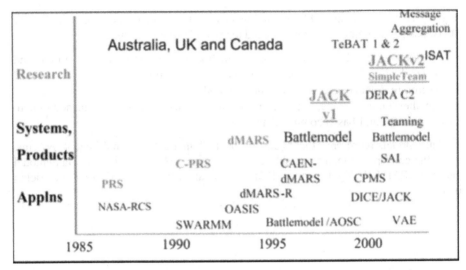

Fig. 1. Agent-based aerospace and defence applications based upon PRS, dMARS and JACK

2   Commercial Agent Platforms

Widespread use of intentional agent technology necessitates the availability of platforms upon which such technology can be deployed. The earliest implementation of the BDI paradigm was the experimental PRS, developed in Lisp by SRI International in the late 1980's. This was followed by derivations: the C-based C-PRS in France; dMARS in C++ by AAII in Australia; the University of Michigan's UM-PRS; and JAM, in Java, by Intelligent Reasoning Systems. Soar has also been utilised as a platform for team-based reasoning, but as a public domain development. Soar Technology, Inc. provides services to develop applications on top of the public domain core.

JACK Intelligent Agents, developed by AOS Australia, was first released in 1997 with the team-based capability JACK SimpleTeam. JACK, now released in Version 3.2 and now supported in the USA by Agent Oriented Software, Inc., was built with a number of objectives in mind:

- To bring agent-oriented software into the mainstream of software engineering.
- To provide a fully commercially supported platform for a wide range of commercial and defence applications.
- Using a component-based approach, allow system developers the option to use other agent models other than BDI, or to use their own communications infrastructure, rather than the default JACK broadcast facility.
- To provide a lightweight kernel, which will run on a wide range of hardware platforms, from personal assistants through to mainframe servers, and to allow hundreds of agents to run on one hardware platform. JACK agents may be within one process on one computer or distributed across a network.

The JACK architecture is shown in Figure 2 below.

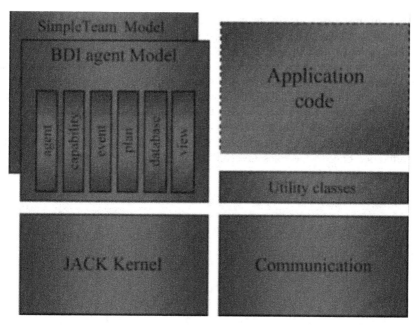

Fig. 2. JACK component-based architecture

The JACK Agent Language has been designed to be straightforward to learn and use, for programmers with an object oriented and Java background. Incorporating sound software engineering, the language is type safe. The knowledge representation includes the concept of Capabilities, which is a modular representation of agent behavior, allowing simpler re-use and re-engineering. JACK provides safe multi-threading, and is blended in with Java, allowing easy integration with existing Java code.

3 TeBAT Modelling Concepts

The TeBAT modelling framework is an extension to JACK targeted the modelling of 'systems with internal organisation'. To this end, the TeBAT modelling language includes the concept of *teams* as reasoning entities that form organisational structures by taking on *roles* within enclosing teams. This organisational modelling includes the means to capture both static and long-term obligation structures, such as those that compose the military command and control hierarchy, and the transient skills-based groupings that are formed to perform individual missions. An obligation structure is then firstly defined as a type, with each team type including the definition of its inner structure in terms of the roles it requires. An actual obligation structure is established by instantiating individual teams and sub-teams, and then linking them to each other in accordance with the roles taken on by the sub-teams.

In addition to the modelling of team structure, the TeBAT modelling framework includes statements for expressing how a team operates by way of the concerted activities of its sub-teams. A team reasons about the coordination between its members, and ultimately decides upon appropriate team plans by which the members in concert achieve the required missions. The expression of team activity, and its coordination, includes all the performance primitives of JACK agents. In addition, it offers statements for parallel activity and issuing directives or sub-goals to sub-teams. Notably, rather than combining the activities of cooperating agents into emergent teamwork, the activity of a team is directly attributed to it. Also, it is modelled as team activity separately from the sub-teams (performing their individual roles). The consequential benefit is that coordinated activity can be programmed and explored with reference only to the roles involved, independent of the sub-teams eventually performing the activities.

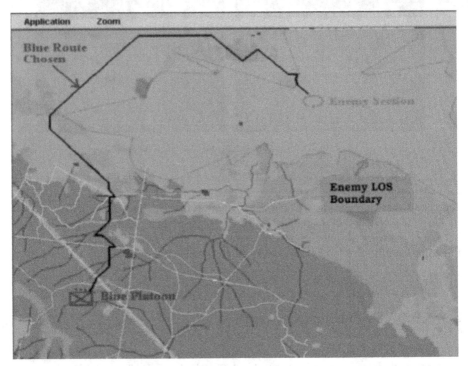

Fig. 3. Blue platoon team agent approaches Red position, negotiating terrain and avoiding enemy line of sight

4   Applications and Benefits of the TeBAT Infrastructure

The initial aim for TeBAT was to support the modelling of tactics in computer simulations of military operations. These tactics are typically team tactics that involve coordination of sub team activity, and in general, TeBAT was developed to support the modelling of coordinated activity.

5   Agents in Land Terrain Navigation

Land military applications require agents with the ability to traverse terrain, according to the gradient and nature of the terrain, and the capability of the vehicle or formation being simulated. Agents do not simply move between pre-programmed waypoints. They work to achieve goal, e.g., "capture the red force on hill to the north, approach as close as possible before exposing the platoon to the opposition" (Figure 3). The agents do not simply follow scripted way points programmed by the user prior to execution.

This approach cannot be achieved with scripted entities, as the scripts cannot accommodate changes in circumstance (e.g., a route blocked by an enemy section, or destroyed after the command was given). This land-based agent technology, based upon the JACK platform, is in operation at DSTO's Land Operations Division.

5.1   Coordinated Movement

One of the initial applications to which TeBAT has been applied was in generation of coordinated movement of army units. The army uses many tactical formations when moving. These formations change based on the physical environment and the tactical environment. Formation movement is also an example of team tactics that should be simple to express in a team-modelling framework. TeBAT's support for movement in concert could equally be applied to control of autonomous vehicles. It could be used to manage coordination of several vehicles, or for synchronising multiple actuators within a single vehicle – for example, where different configurations are required for different environments.

Within the team-modelling framework, making each entity aware of its place in the formation relative to other entities ensures formation rigidity. The entity is then responsible for keeping its position within the formation as well as the maintaining an overall direction and speed.

The entity moves in a formation by means of changing its direction and speed in accordance with a set of fuzzy rules. These rules take into account the required speed and direction as well as the distance and bearing to the entities that this entity is maintaining station on. The super team provides the information on required heading and speed as well as the formation to the sub-teams. Each sub-team then maintains its position in the formation by using the fuzzy rules.

5.2   Command Agents

A command agent is defined to be an intelligent agent capable of receiving situational awareness from a war game or simulation and to use this information to carry out some planning and then interact back into the simulation environment to effect some change in an individual simulation entity or unit, this relationship is illustrated in Figure 4. Their role is to replace the crude, in-built, behavioral mechanism within a war game or simulation with a more flexible, doctrine-based reasoning agent that can autonomously plan and control interactions.

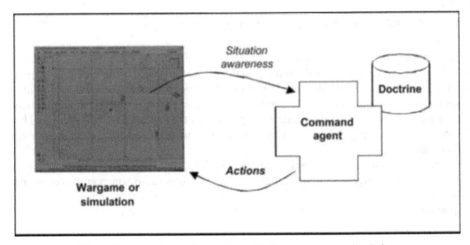

Fig. 4. Command agent interacting with the war game or simulation

Current work with command agents is intended to reduce the workload of the human war game operator by allowing the agent to autonomously plan and execute a high-level instruction passed to a war game unit. The unit is typically composed of a number of individual entities with a command component and hence we are employing TeBAT to handle the team interaction and coordination, which is required to carry out the order.

As an example, consider a command to a mounted infantry company to attack a specific enemy position. The command agent dealing with this instruction must follow doctrine in order to plan a basic concept for the execution. It might then pass on sub-goals for this concept to its sub-team members (who are themselves command agents) who can then plan their components of the attack. One unit may be assigned the role of providing covering fire, whilst another may flank the third unit who will carry out the actual assault. This model aligns well with the concept of directive command, employed by most military forces, where a commander directs his intention to his subordinate commanders, leaving them to work out their own plans and not giving them direct instructions on what to actually do to execute the mission. By using a hierarchy of command agents, linked through the TeBAT framework, it is practicable to break down the actual planning and problem solving into smaller chunks, and focus on each military aggregated unit in turn, rather than try and map the whole command process into one agent representation.

TeBAT's ability to handle sub-goal failure makes it highly suitable for modelling command and control through command agents, as it can deal with unexpected situations where a given sub-team is unable to carry out its initial mission. If the command agent tasks three subordinates to execute the company attack, and the unit assigned with providing covering fire is ambushed en-route to its battle position, the agent receives notification of this goal failure, with a reason, and can re-plan accordingly. Additionally TeBAT's ability to allow team reformation may allow a reserve unit to be re-assigned the task, or allow the original unit to reconstitute using elements of other reserve forces.

Another benefit of TeBAT for use in simulation is the ability to run each team member as a separate process, either on the same machine, or distributed across the network. This is a key requirement in order to allow simulations to scale-up smoothly as the number of entities increases. It also makes is possible to locate the agent code for a given command node on a specific workstation which may permit monitoring by a human expert, to give visibility of the decision processes being performed by that agent.

6   Further Applications and Future Work

TeBAT technology has now found its way into two further novel applications – in robotics. The first is in mobile robotics, via the international robotic soccer competition, Robocup. In the current competition, recently completed in Seattle, the Melbourne University team, the "Roobots", competed in the small league with a team of five mobile robots, each managed by a JACK agent [Thomas, Yoshimura and Peel, 2001]. The robots were programmed to play using team tactics based upon JACK SimpleTeam, which facilitated rapid development of playing tactics, and modification of tactics during a game (e.g., in 3 minutes). Although the team tactics utilised were limited, a substantial enrichment of the tactics library is planned for the 2002 competition in Fukuoka, Japan.

The second application is in Holonic Manufacturing Systems. Agent Oriented Software Limited (AOS UK) in conjunction with Cambridge University's Institute of Manufacturing, has implemented a team-based controller using JACK combined with TeBAT technology [Rönnquist *et al.*, 2002], to control the Institute's Robotic Assembly Cell for the purpose of assembling a water meter. This is the first time that a resource-bounded manufacturing assembly process has been controlled using agent-based control.

These applications have provided the following information:

- Confirmation that multiple agents, acting as a team, can interact with real-time robotic control systems in a timely manner.
- The power of team-based control in real-time control and monitoring operations.
- The ease of integrating a multi-agent platform (in this case JACK) within a distributed real-time system.
- Those agent implementations are portable, and can be run in a PC environment controlling a distributed system.

Future developments include integration of the upstream and downstream logistics chains into the assembly environment, and demonstrating that a team-based controller can efficiently implement multiple, context-dependent, manufacturing strategies in real-time.

References

[Bratman, 1987]   M. E. Bratman. *Intentions, Plans and Practical Reason*. Harvard University Press, Cambridge, MA, 1987.

[Busetta *et al*, 1999] Paolo Busetta, Nicholas Howden, Ralph Rönnquist, Andrew Hodgson, Structuring BDI Agents in Functional Clusters, *Proceedings of the Sixth International Workshop on Agent Theories, Architectures, and Languages (ATAL-99)*, held in cooperation with AAAI, Orlando, Florida, USA, July 1999.

[Cohen and Levesque, 1990] P. R. Cohen and H. J. Levesque. Intention is choice with commitment. *Artificial Intelligence*, 42(3), 1990.

[Cohen and Levesque, 1991] P. R. Cohen and H. J. Levesque. Teamwork. *Nous*, Special Issue on Cognitive Science and Artificial Intelligence, 25(4):487-512, 1991.

[Grosz and Kraus, 1993] B.Grosz and S.Kraus. Collaborative Plans for Group Activities. In *Proceedings of the 13th International Joint Conference on Artificial Intelligence*, pages 367-373, Chambry, France, 1993. Morgan Kauffman Publishers.

[Heinze *et al.*, 2001] Clinton Heinze, Simon Goss, Torgny Josefsson, Kerry Bennett, Sam Waugh, Ian Lloyd, Graeme Murray & John Oldfield, Interchanging Agents and Humans in Military Simulation, In *Proceedings of the AAAI Workshop on the Innovative Applications of Artificial Intelligence (IAAI)*, Seattle, August 1-3, 2001.

[Hodgson *et al.*, 1999] Andrew Hodgson, Ralph Rönnquist, Paolo Busetta, of Specification Coordinated Agent Behaviour (The SimpleTeam Approach), *Proceedings of IJCAI-99 Workshop on Team Behaviour and Plan Recognition*, Stockholm, 1999.

[Hodgson *et al.*, 2000] Andrew Hodgson, Ralph Rönnquist, Paolo Busetta, Nicholas Howden, Team Oriented Programming with SimpleTeam, *Proceedings of SimTecT 2000*, Sydney, Australia, Feb 2000.

[Laird *et al.*, 1987]   J. E. Laird, A. Newell and P. S. Rosenbloom. Soar: An architecture for general intelligence. Artificial Intelligence, 33(3), 1987.

[Laird *et al.*, 1994]   J. E. Laird, R. E. Jones and P. E. Nielson. Coordinated behavior of computer generated forces in TacAir-Soar. In *Proceedings of the Fourth Conference on Computer Generated Forces Behavioral Representation*, Orlando, FLA, May 1994.

[Lucas *et al.*, 1995]   Andrew Lucas, Rick Evertsz, Paul Maisano, David Morley, Jamie Curmi and Rick Scott. New Techniques for Tactical Air Traffic Management for Single and Multiple Airports. In *Airport Engineering and Innovation, Best Practice and the Environment*, IE Aust, 1995.

[Lucas *et al.*, 2001] Andrew Lucas, Ralph Rönnquist, Nick Howden, Andrew Hodgson, Russell Connell, Geoffrey White, Dr Jonathan Vaughan, Towards Complex Team Behaviour in Multi-Agent Systems, *Proceedings of SimTecT 2001*, Canberra, Australia, May 2001.

[Ljungberg and Lucas, 1992] Magnus Ljungberg and Andrew Lucas. The OASIS air traffic management system. *Proceedings of the Second Pacific Rim International Conference on Artificial Intelligence*, PRICAI '92, Seoul, Korea, 1992.

[McIlroy, Smith, Heinze and Turner, 1997] D. McIlroy, B. Smith, C. Heinze, and M. Turner. Air Defence Operational Analysis - Using the SWARMM Model. In *Proceedings of Asia Pacific Operations Research Symposium*, 1997.

[Rao and Georgeff, 1991] A. S. Rao and M.P. Georgeff. Modeling rational agents within a BDI-architecture. In J. Allen, R. Fikes and E. Sandwell, editors, *Proceedings of the Second International Conference on Principles of Knowledge Representation and Reasoning.* Morgan Kauffman Publishers, San Mateo, CA, 1992.

[Rao, Lucas, Morley, Selvestral and Murray, 1993] Anand Rao, Andrew Lucas, David Morley, Mario Selvestrel and Graeme Murray. Agent-Oriented Architecture for Air Combat Simulation, AAII Technical Note 42, April 1993.

[Rönnquist *et al.*, 1999] Ralph Rönnquist, Nick Howden, Andrew Lucas, Jon Vaughan, Russell Connell, Justin Millikan, Intelligent Agents in Ground Simulation, *Proceedings of the 2nd International Synthetic Environment Symposium ISES 1999*, Shrivenham, UK, October 1999.

[Rönnquist *et al.*, 2000] Ralph Rönnquist, Andrew Lucas, Nick Howden, The Simulation Agent Infrastructure (SAI) - Incorporating Intelligent Agents into the CAEN Close Action Simulator, *Proceedings of SimTecT 2000*, Sydney, Australia, Feb 2000.

[Rönnquist *et al.*, 2002] Ralph Rönnquist, Dennis Jarvis, Jacquie Jarvis, Andrew Lucas and Duncan McFarlane. A Teams Based Approach to Manufacturing Task Execution. IEEE Aerospace, 2002.

[Tambe, 1997]   M. Tambe. Towards flexible Teamwork. *Journal of Artificial Intelligence Research (JAIR)*, 7:83-124, 1997.

[Thomas, Yoshimura and Peel, 2001] Jason Thomas, Kenichi Yoshimura and Andrew Peel Roobots, in *RoboCup-2000: Robot Soccer World Cup IV*, Lecture Notes in Computer Science, Springer (to be published).

Creating Context-Aware Software Agents

Harry Chen[1], Sovrin Tolia[1], Craig Sayers[2], Tim Finin[1], and Anupam Joshi[1]

[1] eBiquity Research Group
University of Maryland Baltimore County
1000 Hilltop Circle, Baltimore, MD 21250, USA
{hchen4,stolia1,finin,joshi}@cs.umbc.edu
[2] Software Technology Laboratory
Hewlett-Packard Laboratories
1501 Page Mill Road, Palo Alto, CA 94340, USA
craig_sayers@hpl.hp.com

Abstract. Sharing ontology, sensing context and reasoning are crucial to the realization of context-aware software agents. This document describes our effort on using Resource Description Framework (RDF) and the Prolog Forward Chaining (P_{fc}) system to provide support for ontology sharing and reasoning in the CoolAgent Recommendation System (CoolAgent RS), a context-aware multi-agent system. This document also describes the implementation of the CoolAgent RS document and cuisine recommendation services that provide tailored services by exploiting user's context.

1 Introduction

We humans are context-aware. We are able to use implicit situational information, or context, to increase our conversational bandwidth [2]. This ability allows us to act in advance and anticipate other's needs.

For example, when two people are in the same room, Person A asks Person B, "close the door please." Naturally, Person B would reason that Person A is requesting the door in the same room to be closed, not the door in any other room.

This simple example demonstrates context-awareness in human beings. The fact that Person B is able to take the right action is due to the following three valuable capabilities of humans:

1. Ontology sharing – humans are able to share communication languages and vocabularies
2. Sensing – humans are able to perceive their environment through sensory organs
3. Reasoning – humans are able to make sense out of what they have perceived based on what they already know

If Person B is unable to share ontology with Person A or unable to sense from Person A or unable to make sense out of what he/she has perceived, then

W. Truszkowski, C. Rouff, M. Hinchey (Eds.): WRAC 2002, LNAI 2564, pp. 186–197, 2003.

Person B would not be able to close the door that Person A desires. In other words, Person B becomes context-aware only when he/she possesses all of the three capabilities described above.

We believe ontology sharing, sensing and reasoning are not only crucial to human context-awareness, but also significant to the realization of context-aware applications.

1.1   Context-Aware Applications

The construction of context-aware applications is cumbersome and challenging [15]. Exploiting context in applications requires sensing infrastructures to capture contextual information in the physical environment, and reasoning infrastructures to support inferencing in distributed applications.

After reviewing existing context-aware systems [7, 11, 17], we find that much of the current effort has been focused on the creation of reusable infrastructures for sensing contextual information. Futhermore, from a survey of context-aware research [3], we learn that context modeling and reasoning have not been seriously considered in the existing context-aware systems.

The Mobisaic Web Browser [18] is one of the early context-aware application that exploits location-related, and time-related, contextual information. Mobisaic extends standard client browsers to allow authors to reference dynamic contextual information in dynamic URLs containing environment variables. The dynamic URL is interpreted using current values of the environment variables, and an appropriate page is returned. Mobisaic neither includes any context modeling framework nor does it provide a domain-independent sensing infrastructure.

The Conference Assistant [6] assists attendees by exploiting context from their location, the current time, and the schedules of presentations. After a mobile user enters a conference room, it automatically displays the name of the presenter, the title of the presentation and related information.

Available audio and video equipment automatically record the current presentation, comments, and questions for later retrieval. The core of the Conference Assistant is the Context Toolkit [15], which has limited expressive power to support context modelling and reasoning.

Other systems [19, 13] that we have reviewed also possess similar weaknesses in providing support for ontology sharing and reasoning. In particular, generic contextual information is often directly programmed as part each domain-specific implementation. Such design forces the overall systems to be tightly coupled, and the system behavior becomes highly dependent on the structural representation of the contextual information.

In this document, we describe our efforts on using RDF and P_{fc} to provide support for sharing ontology and reasoning in CoolAgent RS, a context-aware multi-agent system. We also describe the implementation of the CoolAgent RS document and cuisine recommendation services that provide tailored services by exploiting user's context.

Section 2 discusses the use of contextual information in the CoolAgent RS recommendation services. Section 3 provides a design overview of the CoolAgent

RS and reviews some of the related work. Section 4 describes the implementation details of the CoolAgent ontology, reasoning and agents. Conclusion and acknowledgement are given in Sect. 5 and Sect. 5.1, respectively.

2   Context-Aware Services in CoolAgent RS

Our context-aware multi-agent system is designed around the three important factors that contribute to human context-awareness: ontology sharing, sensing, and reasoning. In this section, we describe two context-aware recommendation services that exploit those three factors.

2.1   CoolAgent RS Document Recommendation Service

Similar to many of the existing document recommendation services, this recommendation service is designed to recommend relevant documents to meeting participants. Nevertheless, unlike most of the existing services that often make recommendations based on the relevance rankings between the document contents and user requests, the CoolAgent RS Document Recommendation Service makes recommendations based on the dynamic contextual information of the users.

The recommendation service exploits the following contextual information:

- *the presence of a meeting participant*: a person is a meeting participant if and only if that person is present in a location during the time when that location is anticipated to have a scheduled meeting
- *the profile of a meeting participant*: this includes the personal and professional background information of the participant (e.g. what is job title of the participant? what are the research interests of the participant? what is the placement of the participant in the company's organization chart?)
- *the planned meeting context*: this includes the subject of the meeting, research work and projects that are related to the meeting, the schedule of the meeting and the anticipated participants etc.
- *organizational information*: this includes the employment relationships among the participants (e.g. is person A the supervior of person B? is person A working with person B on the same project?) and the company internal policies (e.g. what kind of documents would a department manager be interested in?)

It is easy to see how some of the described contextual information can be used in a document recommendation process. For example, the presence of a participant can be used to pinpoint the recommenation candidates, and the research interests of the participant can be used to limit the search space of finding relevant documents.

On the other hand, some others (e.g. the schedule of a meeting) cannot be used independently to support recommendations. Nevertheless, this information, as a piece of integrated knowledge, can be used to deduce new contextual information to allow more sophisticated reasoning that would otherwise not be possible. For example, by knowning Person A is supervising Person B, and Person B is working on project CoolTown, then it is appropriate to recommend CoolTown documents to Person A.

2.2   CoolAgent RS Food Recommendation Service

Similar to the CoolAgent RS Document Recommendation Service, this recommendation service recommends customized lunch specials to the people in a cafeteria during lunch hours. This service exploits the following contextual information:

- *the presence of a diner*: a person is a diner if and only if that person is in a dining venue during the lunch hours
- *the profile of a diner*: similar to the profile information that is used in the document recommendation service
- *the daily lunch special menu*: the description of the lunch specials, including the ingredients and cuisine information

2.3   The Need to Share Ontology

One interesting observation from the services described above is that the same contextual information is exploited by two different services in very distinct application domains. For example, the presence of people, the profile of people etc..

This observation leads us to conclude that ontology sharing is important to our context-aware system. If services can share a common representation and context semantics, then overlapping information can be easily shared and exchanged, thereby increasing the interoperability and flexiblity of the overall system.

3   Designing CoolAgent RS

The CoolAgent RS was started in the summer of 2001 as a Summer Intern project at Hewlett-Packard Laboratories. The goal was to develop a context-aware extension to a prototype multi-agent Meeting Management system termed CoolAgent[16].

CoolAgent RS is a multi-agent system that can automatically recommend different types of tailored information to users by reasoning from their context without any explicit manual input. The goal is to develop a proof-of-concept agent system that demonstrates the significance of logical reasoning and ontology sharing in a context-aware distributed computing environment.

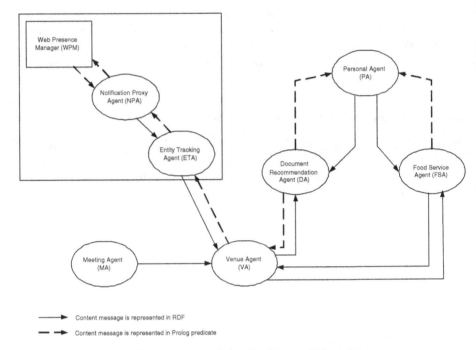

Fig. 1. An overview of the CoolAgent RS architecture

3.1 Design Goals

To support the context-aware services that we have described in Sect. 2, the design goals of our system are the following:

- separate the representation and interpretation of the contextual information from the system's operating implementation
- provide a knowledge representation infrastructure to allow contextual information to be represented, shared and manipulated
- provide a reasoning mechanism that supports cooperative reasoning

4   Implementing CoolAgent RS

The core of CoolAgent RS is a collection of agents, all of which are FIPA-compliant JADE agents [1]. The following is an overview of the agents in CoolAgent RS (also see Figure 1):

Notification Agent Proxy (NAP) This agent is responsible for polling the CoolTown Web Presence Manager (WPM) [5] to determine the presences of physical objects in a particular location. NAP acts a proxy to WPM for agents that do not have direct access to WPM. In particular, NAP provides an ontology mapping service, translating contextual information from the

CoolTown WPM ontology to the CoolAgent RS ontology, for agents subscribing to it.

Entity Tracking Agent (ETA) This agent is responsible for tracking entity presences in a particular location. ETA subscribes to NAP. ETA requests to be notified when any physical objects are present in a particular location.

Venue Agent (VA) This agent is responsible for mediating contextual information among the agents. VA collects contextual information of a particular location, including people presences, anticipated meeting information and relationship among various types of entities, by receiving entity presence notification from ETA and communicating with the Meeting Agent.

Personal Agent (PA) This agent is responsible for providing personal and professional profiles of human users. PA shares common ontology with other agents, and it does not have any built-in reasoning capability.

Meeting Agent (MA) This agent is part of the existing CoolAgent Meeting Management prototype. It creates an RDF-encoded web page to describe each new meeting. The VA extracts details for upcoming meetings by examining those published pages.

Document Recommendation Agent (DA) This agent is responsible for providing document recommendations to the meeting participants based on their context.

Food Service Agent (FA) This agent is responsible for providing cuisine recommendations to the diners in a cafeteria based on their context.

In the following subsections we describe the ontology sharing and the logical reasoning aspects of the CoolAgent RS implementation.

4.1   CoolAgent RS Ontology

The CoolAgent RS ontology consists of 231 classes and 179 properties. Classes describe the concepts in the CoolAgent RS application domains. Properties describe various features and attributes of the classes.

The CoolAgent RS ontology is constructed using Protege-2000, a frame-based ontology authoring tool [14]. Using Protege-2000, classes are modulated into 12 RDF Schema files constituting different namespaces.

These RDF Schema files contains ontologies that capture a wide range of domain concepts that describe software agents, documents, meetings, organizations, people, places, times, FIPA device ontology, HP CoolTown ontology and HP CoolAgent meeting ontology.

4.2   Reasoning

Reasoning takes place when an agent needs to make sense out of the contextual information that is captured from the sensing infrastructure, and when an agent needs to determine its subsequent behavior.

When a piece of contextual information is captured from the physical environment, the raw contextual information is mapped into the corresponding

RDF data model based on the CoolAgent RS ontology. For example, when the presence of a RFID (Radio Frequency Identification) badge is detected in the HPL Cafeteria, the corresponding RDF data model can be constructed as the following:

```
<dev:RDF_Badge rdf:about='urn:badge_001'
    dev:badge_id='000565319'
    badge_label='Harry Chen'/>
<plc:Cafeteria rdf:about='urn:cafeteria_001'
    plc:name='HPL Cafeteria'/>
<plc:Is_In rdf:about='urn:is_in_001'>
    <plc:entity rdf:resource='urn:badge_001'/>
    <plc:location rdf:resource='urn:cafeteria_001'/>
</plc:Is_In>
```

To make sense out of the contextual information in RDF, the agents rely on the support from P_{fc} and reasoning rules. The same approach applies when an agent needs to determine its subsequent behavior.

Reasoning over RDF RDF is a foundation for processing meta-data. RDF itself is not a language; it is data model for representing meta-data [12]. At present, RDF data model is commonly represented in XML statements, RDF graphs, and triple statements.

Different RDF representations are suitable for different processing needs. The RDF XML representation is suitable for machine processing (parsing in particular) and for information exchange. RDF graphs provides a diagrammatic representation of the RDF data model, which is suitable for human visualization. On the other hand, the triple representation provides the means for logical reasoning.

To support reasoning over RDF, we developed our infrastructure based on the P_{fc} [8] package and the SICStus Prolog system. We first constructed a set of Prolog rules that express the standard RDF model in first-order logic [4]. We called them *the basic RDF rules*.

For example, the `rdfs:subClassOf` property, which specifies a subset/superset relation between classes, can be interpreted by the P_{fc} rules as

```
triple(A, subClassOf, B) => subClassOf(A,B).
triple(A, subClassOf, B), subClassOf(B,C) => subClassOf(A,C).
```

And the `rdf:type` property, which indicates a resource is a member of a class, can be interpreted by the P_{fc} rules as

```
triple(I, type, C) => instanceOf(I,C).
subClassOf(B,C), instanceOf(I,B) => instanceOf(I,C).
```

Domain specific rules, that allow agents to provide their own interpretation of the contextual information and to determine their subsequent behaviors, are constructed from the basic RDF rules. For example, domain specific reasoning that infers the ownership of a badge can be constructed using the following rules:

```
instanceOf(P,personClass) => person(P).
instanceOf(B,badgeClass) => badge(B).
instanceOf(R,ownsClass), triple(R,owner,P),
   triple(R,thing,T) => owns(P,T).

person(P), badge(B),owns(P,B) => badgeOwner(P,B).
```

Implementing the Rule Shipping Technique The FIPA Agent Communicative Acts and Interaction Protocols specifications [9] have defined the communication language and policy for agent communications. There are also FIPA specifications for different content languages. However, it is up to the implementation to provide an ontology, and the interpretation of messages using that ontology.

In the CoolAgent RS, the communication is mainly based on the FIPA Subscribe Interaction Protocol [10]. For example, the Venue Agent sends a `subscribe` message to the Entity Tracking Agent requesting to be notified when a person is present in a particular location. When a person is present, the Entity Tracking Agent notifies the Venue Agent by replying with an `inform` message. In both messages, the content messages, the request for notification and the reply to subscription, are to be defined by the CoolAgent RS.

To provide a flexible implementation for the Subscribe Interaction Protocol, we have developed a rule-based content message representation technique. This Rule Shipping technique allows an agent to send Prolog rules as the content of a `subscribe` message. The content rules are evaluated by the receiver to deduce new facts. Deduced facts are replied back to the sender as the content of a `inform` message. The following example illustrates the Rule Shipping Technique:

The Entity Tracking Agent has the following contextual information expressed in RDF triples:

```
K1:  triple('urn:loc1',rdf_type,place_Cafeteria)
K2:  triple('urn:loc1',place_name,'HP Cafeteria')
K3:  triple('urn:person1',rdf_type,people_Person)
K4:  triple('urn:person1',people_fname,'Harry')
K5:  triple('urn:person1',people_lname,'Chen')
K6:  triple('urn:utc1',rdf_type,times_UTC),
K7:  triple('urn:utc1',times_utc_value,'2001-03-27:T13:26:00Z')
K8:  triple('urn:isin1',rdf_type, place_Is_In)
K9:  triple('urn:isin1',place_entity','urn:person1')
K10: triple('urn:isin1',place_location','urn:loc1')
K11: triple('urn:isin1',times_start_time','urn:utc1')
```

The Venue Agent is interested in the people presences in a particular location. It subscribes the following forward-chaining rules as the content of its `subscribe` message:

```
R1: instanceOf(CafeteriaInst,place_Cafeteria),
    triple(CafeteriaInst,place_name,PlaceName)
      => cafeteria(CafeteriaInst,PlaceName).
```

```
R2: instanceOf(PersonInst,people_Person),
    triple(PersonInst,people_name,FName,LName)
      => person(PersonInst,FName,LName).
R3: instanceOf(UTCInst,times_UTC),
    triple(UTCInst,utc_value,UTCTime)
      => utc(UTCInst, UTCTime).
R4: instanceOf(IsInInst,place_Is_In),
    triple(IsInInst,place_entity,EntityInst),
    triple(IsInInst,place_location,LocationInst),
    triple(IsInInst,times_start_time,UTCInst)
      => isIn(IsInInst, EntityInst, LocationInst, UTCInst).
R5: isIn(IsInInst,PersonInst,LocationInst,UTCInst),
    utc(UTCInst,Time), cafeteria(LocationInst,LocName),
    person(PersonInst,FName,LName)
      => {add(shouldInform('com.hp.agent.palo-alto.va',
                           'com.hp.agent.palo-alto.eta',
                           'va.ruleid.131'
              msg(IsInInst, LocationInst, LocName, UTCInst, Time,
                  PersonInst, FName, LName)))}.
```

Upon receiving the subscribe message, the Entity Tracking Agent asserts these rules into it Knowledge Base (KB). The forward-chaining system in the Entity Tracking Agent automatically adds new facts that can be deduced. Based on the triple statements K1–K11, the following facts can be deduced and are added to the KB:

```
N1: utc('urn:time1', '2001-03-27:T13:26:00Z')
N2: cafeteria('urn:loc1', 'HP Cafeteria')
N3: person('urn:person1', 'Harry', 'Chen')
N4: isIn('urn:isin1', 'urn:person1', 'urn:loc1', 'urn:time1')
N5: shouldInform('com.hp.agent.palo-alto.va',
                 'com.hp.agent.palo-alto.eta',
                 'va.ruleid.131',
                 msg('urn:isin1','urn:loc1','HP Cafeteria',
                     'urn:time1','2001-03-27:T13:26:00Z',
                     'urn:person1','Harry','Chen'))
```

N1 says there is a *UTC* time instance referenced by the Unique Resource Identifier (URI) 'urn:time1' with the UTC value '2001-03-27:T13:26:00Z'. N2 says there is a *cafeteria* instance referenced by the URI 'urn:loc1' with the venue name 'HP Cafeteria'. N3 says there is a *person* instance referenced by the URI 'urn:person1' and with the first-name value 'Harry' and the last-name value 'Chen'. N4 says a person referenced by URI 'urn:person1' is in a location referenced by URI 'urn:loc1' at UTC time referenced by URI 'urn:time1'. N5 says the Entity Tracking Agent should inform the Venue Agent, in reply to the message ID va.ruleid.131, the fact

```
msg('urn:isin1','urn:loc1','HP Cafeteria',
    'urn:time1','2001-03-27:T13:26:00Z',
    'urn:person1','Harry','Chen')
```

The Entity Tracking Agent queries for `shouldInform/4` whenever new facts are asserted to its KB. In the example above, as soon as the rules from the Venue Agent are asserted, the Entity Tracking Agent queries its KB for `shouldInform/4` and returns N5.

The above example shows how the Rule Shipping Technique exploits the triple representation of the RDF data model to enable reasoning. This technique allows the Venue Agent to construct customized reasoning rules to infer about people presences with the only requirement being that both the Venue Agent and Entity Tracking Agent share a common ontology.

5 Conclusion

Enabling context-awareness is one step closer to the realization of computing systems that can act in advance and anticipate users' needs. Ontology sharing, reasoning and sensing are the three important properties that the context-aware systems need to possess.

In this document we have described a context-aware multi-agent system, CoolAgent RS. We have demonstrate the feasibility of using RDF data model and P_{fc} to support ontology sharing and reasoning in a context-aware system. We have presented the reasoning infrastructure in the CoolAgent RS, which enables distributed reasoning and knowledge sharing among agents.

5.1 Future Work

The Rule Shipping Technique provides the foundation for building distributed cooperative reasoning and knowledge sharing. In the current implementation, the sender is required to provide a complete set of reasoning rules to be evaluated by the receiver.

We believe such requirements impose potential scalability issues on the communication message size and the rule construction overhead. One of our immediate objectives is to develop a more effective and scalable distributed cooperative reasoning and knowledge sharing infrastructure to support context-aware systems. Moreover, it provides scope for doing research on security considerations under this scheme.

Acknowledgment

The research work described in this document was conducted by Harry Chen and Sovrin Tolia as part of their research internships at Hewlett-Packard Laboratories. The active support from all the members of the Agents for Mobility Group and Cooltown Group at HPL is gratefully acknowledged.

Harry Chen would like to thank HPL for the fellowship support that helps him to begin his initial research work on developing context-aware software agents.

References

[1] F. Bellifemine. Jade: what it is and what it is next. In *Workshop on Models and Methods of Analysis for Agent Based Systems (MMAABS)*, Genova, April 2001. 190

[2] P. J. Brown, N. Davies, M. Smith, and P. Steggles. Towards a better understanding of context and context-awareness. In H.-W. Gellerson, editor, *Handheld and ubiqitous computing*, number 1707 in Lecture Notes in Computer Science, pages 304–7. Springer, September 1999. 186

[3] G. Chen and D. Kotz. A survey of context-aware mobile computing research. Technical Report TR2000-381, Dept. of Computer Science, Dartmouth College, November 2000. 187

[4] W. Conen and R. Klapsing. A logical interpretation of rdf. In *Linköping Electronic Articles in Computer and Information Science*, volume 5 (2000):nr 013 of *ISSN 1401-9841*. Linköping University Electronic Press, 2000. 192

[5] P. Debaty. *web presence manager documentation*. Hewlett-Packard Laboratories. http://cooltown.hp.com/dev/reference/coolbase/wpm/wpm_user_guide.asp. 190

[6] A. K. Dey, M. Futakawa, D. Salber, and G. D. Abowd. The conference assistant: Combining context-awareness with wearable computing. In *Proceedings of the 3rd International Symposium on Wearable Computers*, pages 21–28, San Francisco, CA, October 1999. 187

[7] A. K. Dey, J. Mankoff, and G. D. Abowd. Distributed mediation of imperfectly sensed context in aware environments. Technical Report GIT-GVU-00-14, Georgia Institute of Technology, September 2000. 187

[8] T. Finin, R. Fritzson, and D. Matuszek. Adding forward chaining and thruth maintenance to prolog. In *Proc. of the Fifth Conference on Artificial Intelligence Applications CAIA-89*, pages 123–130, Miami, FL, 1989. 192

[9] FIPA. *FIPA Communicative Act Library Specificaiton*, pc00037h edition. http://www.fipa.org/specs/fipa00037/. 193

[10] FIPA. *FIPA Subscribe Interaction Protocol Specificaiton*, pc00035d edition. http://www.fipa.org/specs/fipa00035/PC00035D.pdf. 193

[11] K. Hinckley, J. Pierce, M. Sinclair, and E. Horvitz. Sensing techniques for mobile interaction. In *Proceedings of the 13th annual ACM symposium on User interface software and technology*, pages 91–100, San Diego, CA USA, November 2000. 187

[12] O. Lassila and R. R. Swick. *Resource Description Framework (RDF) Model and Syntax Specification*. W3C, February 1999. 192

[13] N. Marmasse and C. Schmandt. Location-aware information delivery with commotion. In *Proceedings of Second International Symposium on Handheld and Ubiquitous Computing, HUC 2000*, pages 157–171, Bristol, UK, Spetember 2000. Springer Verlag. 187

[14] N. F. Noy, R. W. Fergerson, and M. A. Musen. The knowledge model of protege-2000: Combining interoperability and flexibility. In *2th International Conference on Knowledge Engineering and Knowledge Management (EKAW'2000)*, Juan-les-Pins, France, 2000. 191

[15] D. Salber, A. K. Dey, and G. D. Abowd. The context toolkit: Aiding the development of context-enabled applications. In *Proceedings of the 1999 Conference on Human Factors in Computing Systems (CHI '99)*, pages 434–441, 1999. 187

[16] C. Sayers and R. Letsinger. The coolagent ontology: A language for publishing and scheduling events. Technical Report HPL-2001-194, Software Technology

Laboratory, Hewlett-Packard Laboratories, 1501 Page Mill Road, Palo Alto, CA 94340, USA, 2001. **189**

[17] B. Schiele, T. Starner, B. Rhodes, B. Clarkson, and A. Pentland. Situation aware computing with wearable computers. `citeseer.nj.nec.com/ schiele99situation.html`. **187**

[18] G. M. Voelker and B. N. Bershad. Mobisaic: An information system for a mobile wireless computing environment. In *Proceedings of IEEE Workshop on Mobile Computing Systems and Applications*, pages 185–190, Santa Cruz, California, December 1994. IEEE Computer Society Press. **187**

[19] H. Yan and T. Selker. Context-aware office assistant. In *Intelligent User Interfaces*, pages 276–279, 2000. **187**

Part IV

Agent Architectures

An Evaluation of Philosophical Agent Architectures for Mission Robustness

John R. Rose, William H. Turkett, Michael N. Huhns, and Soumik Sinha Roy

Department of Computer Science and Engineering
University of South Carolina
Columbia, SC 29208 USA
{rose,turkett,huhns,rssinha0}@cse.sc.edu
http://www.engr.sc.edu/research/CIT

Abstract. This paper reports on initial investigations of an agent architecture that embodies philosophical and social layers. A key feature of the architecture is that agent behavior is constrained by sets of agent societal laws similar to Asimov's laws of robotics. In accordance with embedded philosophical principles, agents use decision theory in their negotiations to evaluate the expected utility of proposed actions and use of resources. This enables more robust decision-making and task execution. To evaluate the robustness, our investigations have included the effect of misinformation among cooperative agents in worth-oriented domains, and active countermeasures for dealing with the misinformation. We demonstrate that propagating misinformation is against the principles of ethical agents. Moreover, such agents are obligated to report on misbehavior, which minimizes its effects and furthers the progress of the agents and their society towards their goals. We also show how dedicating some agents to specialized tasks can improve the performance of a society

1 Introduction

The improvements in Internet-based software agents that are underway at many laboratories and corporations are fulfilling the promise of personalized, friendly Web services. The improvements come at a cost, however, of greater implementation complexity. Thus, as we gradually rely more on the improved capabilities of these agents to assist us in networked activities, such as e-commerce and information retrieval, we also understand less about how they operate.

For example, consider future NASA missions. As they involve longer durations, more remote locations, and more complex goals, the software systems controlling them will of necessity become larger, more intricate, and increasingly autonomous. Moreover, the missions must succeed in the face of uncertainties, errors, failures, and serendipitous opportunities. While small, well-specified systems with limited types of known external interactions can be proved correct, consistent, and deadlock-free via formal verification, such conditions do not hold for concurrent network-based systems, and constructing large error-free software

W. Truszkowski, C. Rouff, M. Hinchey (Eds.): WRAC 2002, LNAI 2564, pp. 201–214, 2003.

systems appears not to be achievable by current means. Additionally, the large size of the systems and the unknowns to which they will be subjected cause them to be untestable to even find out if, when, or where they might fail. We will have no choice but to trust these crucial but complex software systems, so there should be a principled basis for our trust.

Abstraction is one technique we use to deal with complexity. What is the proper kind and level of abstraction for dealing with complex agent-based software? We think it will be reasonable to endow agents with a philosophy, and then describe their expected behavior in terms of their philosophy. By understanding their philosophies, we can use and interact with the agents more effectively. We can trust the agents to act autonomously if they embrace ethical standards that we understand and with which we agree. We expect that this will lead to fault tolerance, graceful degradation, recovery, and, ultimately, trust in our systems. Also, an explicit philosophy might help the agents understand and anticipate each other's behavior.

2   Philosophical Agents

To endow agents with ethical principles, we as developers need an architecture that supports explicit goals, principles, and capabilities (such as how to negotiate), as well as laws and ways to sanction miscreants [16]. Figure 1 illustrates such an agent architecture that can support both trust and coherence, where coherence is the absence of wasted effort and progress toward chosen goals [8]. An agent-based approach is inherently distributed and autonomous, but when the communication channels that link the agents are bandwidth-constrained or noisy, the agents will have to make decisions locally, which we hope will be coherent globally, as well as worthy of trust. For agents to interact effectively, they will have to communicate their own principles and model the principles of others.

Awareness of other agents and of one's own role in a society, which are implicit at the social commitment level and above, can enable agents to behave coherently [9]. Tambe et al. [18] have shown how a team of agents flying helicopters will continue to function as a coherent team after their leader has crashed, because another agent will assume the leadership role. More precisely, the agents will adjust their individual intentions in order to fulfill the commitments made by the team.

If the agents have sufficient time, they can negotiate about or vote on which agent should become the new leader. When time is short or communication is not allowed, the agents can follow mutually understood social conventions, such as *the agent with the most seniority becomes the new leader.*

The lowest level of the architecture in Fig. 1 enables an agent to react to immediate events [12]. The middle layers are concerned with an agent's interactions with others [5] [6] [7] [13], while the highest level enables the agent to consider the long-term effects of its behavior on the rest of its society [11]. Agents are typically constructed starting at the bottom of this architecture, with increasingly more abstract reasoning abilities layered on top.

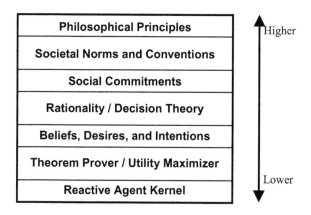

Fig. 1. An architecture for a philosophical agent. The architecture defines layers of deliberation for enabling an agent to behave appropriately in society

2.1   Ethical Abstractions

Ethics is concerned with codes and principles of moral behavior [4]. Most ethical theories distinguish between the concepts of right and good:

- Right is that which is right in itself
- Good is that which is good or valuable for someone or for some end.

Should software agents favor right or good? Deontological theories emphasize right before good. They oppose the idea that the ends can justify the means, and they place the locus of right and wrong in autonomous adherence to moral laws or duties. A proponent of these, the German philosopher Immanuel Kant (1724-1804), defined his *categorical imperative* as an absolute and universal moral law based entirely on reason. For right action by an agent, the categorical imperative would be: *Agents should act as they think all other agents should act.* For example, breaking a promise would not be right, because if all agents did it, the system they supported would not function.

Kant's categorical imperative does not contain a way to resolve conflicts of duty. Also, an action is not wrong unless the agent explicitly intends for it to do wrong. For example, an agent on a NASA deep space probe who is responsible for managing communications with ground control would not be wrong to shut down the communications link for diagnostics, even if that might leave other agents on the probe unable to communicate, because the agent did not intend to disrupt communications. Deontological theories can also legitimize inaction, even when inaction has predictably bad effects, if the agent did not intend those effects. For example, an agent could morally justify not turning off an overheating component, if it did not intend for the component to overheat.

In contrast, teleological theories choose good before right: something is right only if it maximizes the good; in this case, the ends can justify the means.

In teleological theories, the correctness of actions is based on how the actions satisfy various goals, not the intrinsic rightness of the actions. Choices of actions can maximize either individual or societal good, where good may be pleasure, preference satisfaction, interest satisfaction, or aesthetic ideals.

What agents need to decide actions are not just universal principles (each can be stretched) and not just consequences, but also a regard for their promises and duties. Agents have prima facie duties to keep promises, help others, repay kindness, etc. [11]. In the context of a NASA mission, an agent could repay a kindness to another agent by offering, without being asked, to donate a resource such as excess battery power. While agents have such duties, there is no ranking among the duties, which are instead defeasible. For example, an agent on a NASA deep space probe might find it acceptable to monopolize a communication channel to ground control to the detriment of other agents, because it overvalues the success of its own task without regard to the consequences for other agents.

2.2 Machine Ethics

Isaac Asimov proposed a moral philosophy for intelligent machines in a Handbook of Robotics [1] that defined three Laws of Robotics. These were subsequently augmented by the *Zeroth Law* [2]. An adaptation of these laws for a collection of agents sent on a NASA mission might be:

Principle 1: An agent shall not harm the mission through its actions or inactions.

Principle 2: Except where it conflicts with Principle 1, an agent shall not harm the participants in the mission.

Principle 3: Except where it conflicts with the previous principles, an agent shall not harm itself.

Principle 4: Except where it conflicts with the previous principles, an agent shall make rational progress toward mission goals.

Principle 5: Except where it conflicts with the previous principles, an agent shall follow established conventions.

Principle 6: Except where it conflicts with the previous principles, an agent shall make rational progress toward its own goals.

Principle 7: Except where it conflicts with the previous principles, an agent shall operate efficiently.

As a simple example of how such principles might apply, distributed systems, *which most Internet applications are,* are susceptible to deadlocks and livelocks. However, if the components of the distributed system obey these seven philosophical principles, then the susceptibilities would disappear, because deadlock and livelock would violate Principle 6.

2.3 Applying Ethics

A philosophical approach to distributed system design presupposes that the components, or agents, can

- enter into social commitments to collaborate with others,
- change their mind about their results, and
- negotiate with others.

However, the ethical theories above are theories of justification, not of deliberation. An agent still has to decide what basic *value system* to use under any ethical theory it might adopt.

The deontological theories are narrower and ignore practical considerations, but they are only meant as incomplete constraints = that is, the agent can choose any of the right actions to perform. The teleological theories are broader and include practical considerations, but they leave the agent fewer options for choosing the best available alternative. All of these ethical theories are single-agent in orientation and encode other agents implicitly. An explicitly multiagent ethics would be an interesting topic for study.

3   Methodology

The goal of our research is to evaluate the utility of different combinations and precedence orderings of behavior-guiding principles. To make the most progress toward our goal, we chose to use an agent-development toolkit (ZEUS) to provide most of the low-level functionality we need. We also selected the FIPA ACL, because it is the closest to a standard agent communication language that is available. We then chose an exploration type of scenario, in which a group of agents move through a two-dimensional domain trying to find and retrieve mineral samples.

We developed an initial set of four agent architectures. All agent architectures use the same two algorithms for checking memory for previous mineral samples and controlling the actual movement of the agents. The decision of which mineral sample to move towards is defined separately for each agent.

Checking Memory
1. Check to see if there are mineral samples the agent remembers and has not picked up that are currently out of the viewing area.
2. If there are mineral samples in memory,
   - determine the closest mineral sample to the agent from memory.
   - make a move of one space towards that mineral sample.
3. Else if there are no mineral samples in memory, then make a random move of one space along the current path.

Movement
1. The agent moves one position either in a random direction, if it has chosen to move randomly, or in the direction of its chosen mineral sample.
2. If the agent reaches the same position as the mineral sample it is searching for, it picks up the mineral sample and then senses again.
3. If the agent reaches an empty spot, it senses again.
4. If the agent cannot move into a spot because there is another agent already there, the agent attempts to make a random move of one space along its current path.

Our baseline agent, termed *self-interested,* is purely self-interested and unaware of other agents. Conflicts and inefficiencies arise as agents of this type attempt to pick up the same samples.

A more capable agent, termed *cooperative,* is aware of other agents and, by estimating their behavior, attempts to avoid conflicts. It communicates its true intentions to other agents, thereby reducing conflicts even further. It also communicates opportunities by which other agents might benefit, thereby improving the overall societal performance towards a global mission.

A *prevaricating* agent pretends to be cooperative and instead provides misleading information to other agents. By this behavior it hopes to make more resources available for itself, but possibly at the expense of the other agents in its society.

A specialized *scout* agent can travel faster and farther because it does not gather any mineral samples, so its purpose is to aid the other agents in its society by searching for and reporting on the locations of mineral samples. The next section describes our experiments with these agents in different scenarios.

4   Evaluation

4.1   Scenario Considerations

We require a test scenario that will allow us to make clear comparisons between the performances of agent architectures with different combinations and precedence orderings of philosophical principles. There are several features that we considered in selecting a scenario:

1. The scenario must justify multiple simultaneous tasks.
2. The tasks must be uniform to simplify performance evaluation.
3. It should be possible to carry out the tasks without explicit cooperation.
   - Communication between agents should not be required.
   - Global knowledge of the task scenario should not be required.

Based on these features, we considered abstract tasks such as:

1. Exploring (rover-type exploration)
2. Inspecting (inspecting a space station for damage from space debris)
3. Gathering (collecting mineral specimens on a Mars)
4. Building (space station construction)
5. Delivering (transporting supplies to appropriate destinations)

We then considered these abstract tasks in the context of future NASA scenarios involving unmanned probes, such as sample collection on Mars, evaluation of asteroids, and exploration of the hypothesized liquid ocean beneath the icy crust of Europa. This analysis indicated a large overlap between abstract gathering and inspecting tasks and moderate overlap with exploring and delivering tasks.

Next, we considered a matrix of types of test cases. Essentially, the test matrix is an enumeration of goal types, i.e., independent or shared, and combinations of philosophical principles. The combinations are:

1. Independent agents; independent goals; various combinations of philosophical principles
2. Independent agents, shared goals; various combinations of philosophical principles
3. Flat agent confederations; shared goals; various combinations of philosophical principles
4. Hierarchically organized agents; shared goals; various combinations of philosophical principles

Metrics that we considered for evaluating performance include:

1. Measure of independent goals accomplished
2. Measure of shared goals accomplished
3. Time required for goal accomplishment
4. Communication cost
5. Resource usage
6. Number of collaborative actions pursued

4.2   Initial Agent Test Scenarios

We developed several test scenarios for our agent architectures based on a simulated mineral specimen collection task on an unspecified planet. The test area is a 60x45 rectangular area. The tests were run with n= 50, 100, 150, 200 mineral samples with varying degrees of clustering. The degree of clustering ranged from a random distribution of mineral samples at one end of the spectrum to a single cluster of all n samples (the mother lode) at the other end. We did not allow more than one mineral sample to occupy any given position.

Tests were run with m= 6, 12, 24 randomly distributed agents, each sharing the same architecture. We also varied the size of the agent's field of view, defined as a v-by-v rectangle. All agents share the same size field of view in a given test run. The value of v was varied in the range (v= 7, 9, 11). Each simulation lasted for 100 time steps. At each step, each agent chose and executed one action from its repertoire of capabilities.

We collected statistics for the total number of samples collected, the number of samples collected per agent, and the number of cooperative actions taken per agent, as well as averages and standard deviations. The results produced by these experiments are documented [14] and include:

– **Worth-Oriented Evaluation of Mission Success**. On long-term missions, overall success will depend on the ability to conserve resources in order to meet long-term objectives. In this study, we examined an agent architecture that seeks to minimize the expenditure of resources in a distributed gathering task (the mineral sample collection scenario described above). We used two types of cooperating agents: an early finishing agent that terminates its activity after collecting its limit (8) of mineral samples, and a continuing cooperative agent that continues to cooperate with other agents after having collected its limit of samples by communicating to other agents the existence of samples that it finds or relaying messages that it receives.

- **Detecting Misinformation from Agents.** In order to achieve mission robustness, the agent architecture must be able to handle misinformation. We considered three different agent architectures for addressing misinformation. In all three of these, agents keep track of the information they receive from other agents and which agent they receive the information from, as well as the originator of the information if it has been relayed.

  1. The gullible agent architecture is an extension of the cooperative architecture in which agents assume that all agents provide correct information. When an agent determines that information it receives does not match its own direct observations, it classifies the agent from which it received the information as malicious and ignores future information provided by that agent.

  2. The gullible-original agent architecture is a refinement of the gullible agent architecture. The difference is that while the gullible agent disbelieves all agents that it perceives to have proffered misinformation, the gullible-original agent only discredits the agents from which it gets information directly and not those from which it receives information indirectly by relay through other agents.

  3. The skeptical agent architecture, in contrast to the gullible and gullible-original architectures, disbelieves all agents until it is able to verify through observation that the information it receives is correct. In other respects it conforms to the cooperative agent architecture.

- **Passive Response to Misinformation.** Once an agent determines that another agent is responsible for misinformation, the passive response taken is simply to ignore the agent that is perceived to be malfunctioning or malicious.

- **Active Response to Misinformation.** Agents concluding that some agent is malfunctioning or malicious report that agent to a coordinating agent. Once the coordinating agent has received bad conduct reports from n distinct agents, it *terminates* the malicious agent.

4.3   Agent Test Scenarios for a Large World

Our investigations next focused on the impact of role-division. To this end we developed a scouting-agent architecture. The purpose of a scouting agent is to scout for mineral samples and pass this information on to collection agents, which then collect the samples. The collection agents are the same cooperative agents described above. The scouting agent architecture differs from the cooperative agent architecture in two principle areas. First, its mission only involves scouting for mineral samples and communicating its finding to other agents. It does not collect any samples. Second, it moves twice as fast as collection agents and is able to communicate its findings over a much greater distance.

In order to evaluate a society comprised of scouting and collection agents and make comparisons with self-interested agent societies and homogeneous cooperative agent societies, we had to employ a larger simulation world than that described in the previous section. The test scenarios for our agent architectures are based on a simulated mineral specimen collection task on an unspecified planet. The test area is a 180x135 rectangular area. This was constructed by creating a 3x3 tiling of the 60x45 rectangular area world described in the previous section. The tests were run with n= 1800 total mineral samples. The samples were grouped in randomly placed clusters of size s=1800, 450, 200, 100, 50. We did not allow more than one mineral sample to occupy any given position.

All tests were run with m= 200 agents. The 200 agents were randomly distributed as 10 groups of 20 agents in the 9 tiles (recall the world is a 3x3 tiling of rectangles of size 60x45). An agent's field of view is defined as a v-by-v rectangle. All agents collecting mineral samples share the same size field of view, 11x11. Scout agents have a larger field of view of size 41x41. Scout agents are also able to communicate their findings to agents within their 41x41 field of view. Each simulation lasts for 300 time steps. At each step, an agent may take one action from its repertoire of capabilities.

The simulations involved a comparison of three types of agent societies: homogeneous self-interested agents, homogenous cooperative agents, and a mixture of scouting agents and cooperative agents. Each of the following figures shows the performance of the three types of societies under the same conditions. The parameter that is varied is the number of clusters in the world. In all cases, the sum of mineral samples in the clusters total 1800. Each of the simulations was repeated 5 times with different randomly chosen starting positions for the groups of agents. The same set of starting positions was used for each society simulation. Thus, in each figure, each data point is an average over 5 runs.

Figure 2 is a summary of the entire set of tests. It shows the percentage of mineral samples collected by each of the three architectures after the first 100 times steps. The parameter that is varied in this figure is the number of clusters in the environment, ranging from one cluster containing all 1800 mineral samples to 36 clusters each containing 50 mineral samples. The clusters are randomly distributed.

Of interest in this figure is the relative change in performance between the societies as the number of clusters increases. Starting with a single cluster, the society employing scout agents performs better than the homogeneous cooperative and homogeneous self-interested agent societies, this in spite of the fact that 20 of the 200 agents are scout agents and thus unable to collect mineral samples. As the number of clusters increases, the difference in performance of the three societies decreases.

This result suggests that the contribution of the scout agent with its enhanced mobility and field of vision more than makes up for its inability to collect mineral samples when considerable search is required, as is the case when there are few large clusters. However, as the number of randomly distributed clusters increases, the amount of search required decreases and the performance of the homogenous cooperative agent society gradually matches and eventually surpasses that of the heterogeneous society. In this setting the scout agent is less of an asset. If the

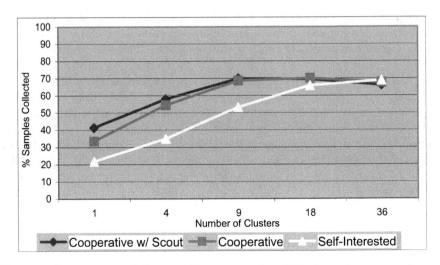

Fig. 2. Comparison of three architectures after 100 time steps according to number of sample clusters in a large-world environment

simulations are run long enough, the scout becomes a liability since it does not itself collect mineral samples.

Another observation that can be made is that the greater the number and distribution of clusters, the better the performance of the self-interested set of agents. This is not surprising, since self-interested agents are not penalized as heavily by their lack of cooperation when the mineral samples are distributed more uniformly and are thus easier to chance upon.

In Fig. 3, the evolution of sample collection for each society is displayed over a period of 300 time steps. In this figure, all simulations occur in the same large-world environment in which there is a single large cluster containing all 1800 mineral samples. The data points at time step 100 are in fact the same data points shown for 1 cluster in Fig. 2. Figure 3 shows in detail how the scouting society develops an initial performance advantage and how this advantage with respect to the homogeneous cooperative society is gradually lost over time as information is propagated between agents in the homogeneous cooperative society. The initial advantage that the scouting society enjoys is due to the rapidity with which the scouts are able to investigate their world. While agents in the homogeneous cooperative society are not able to search as rapidly or directly communicate over as great a distance as scout agents, their steady cooperation allows them to reach the performance level of the scouting society at the end of 300 time steps. This figure also shows that cooperative behavior has a decided advantage compared to a self-interested approach when considerable search is required to locate a single large cluster.

As the number of clusters is increased, the benefit provided by the scout agent's ability to rapidly investigate the world is diminished. Figure 4 shows

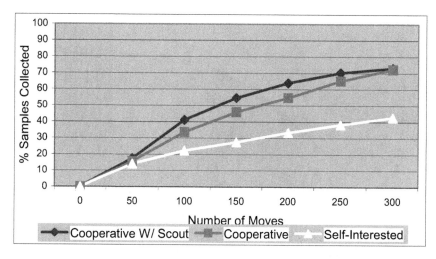

Fig. 3. Comparison of three agent architectures in a large-world environment containing a single large cluster of samples

the performance of the three agent societies in a large world environment where there are four randomly positioned clusters, each containing 450 mineral samples. Under these conditions, the scout agent society no longer has a performance edge over the homogeneous cooperative agent society. However, enough searching is required to find the clusters so that a cooperative approach significantly outperforms the non-cooperative approach of the self-interested agents. Another interesting observation is that for both cases of cooperative societies, the collection of mineral samples tapers off after the first 200 time steps. During the last 100 times steps of the simulation, very few additional samples are collected. We hypothesize that the agents have unevenly distributed themselves around the clusters, so that those agents that have not reached their carrying capacity are too far away from other clusters and most likely out of communication range to be able to locate any uncollected samples before the end of the simulation is reached.

Increasing the number of clusters even more reduces the benefit provided by cooperation. Figure 5 shows the performance of the three agent societies in a large world environment where there are nine randomly positioned clusters, each containing 200 mineral samples. Under these conditions, the scout agent society no longer has a performance edge over the homogeneous cooperative agent society. In fact, there are only 180 agents collecting samples in the scout society. As can be seen in this figure, after 100 times steps the homogeneous cooperative agent society with 200 agents collecting samples performs better.

More striking is the performance of the non-cooperating self-interested agent society. Its performance is now approaching that of the two cooperating agent societies. In simulations with even larger numbers of smaller clusters there is vir-

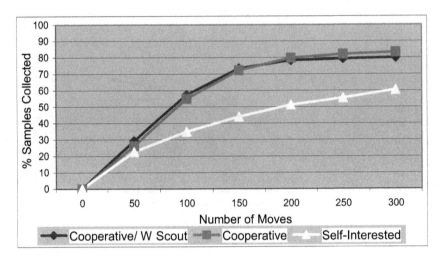

Fig. 4. Comparison of three agent architectures in a large-world environment containing four clusters

tually no difference between the performance of the self-interested agent society and the homogeneous cooperative agent society. In contrast, the performance of the scout agent society is slightly lower, because it contains 20 fewer collection agents.

5   Conclusions

The agents we construct *and the systems they implement, manage, and enact* must be trustworthy, ethical, parsimonious of resources, efficient, and *failing all else* rational. What we are investigating differs from current work in software agents in that:

- We are not researching new agent capabilities per se.
- We are not developing an agent-based system for a new application domain.
- We are investigating how agents can be the fundamental building blocks for the construction of general-purpose software systems, with the expected benefits of robustness and autonomy.
- We are characterizing agents in terms of mental abstractions, and multiple agents in terms of their interactions. These abstractions matter because anticipated applications go beyond. traditional metaphors and models in terms of their dynamism, openness, and autonomy.

The benefit of this architecture to complex missions such as future NASA planetary and deep space missions is fourfold: (1) it will support missions of much greater complexity than are possible under the current model of earth-based control, (2) it will reduce costs by minimizing the amount of earth-based

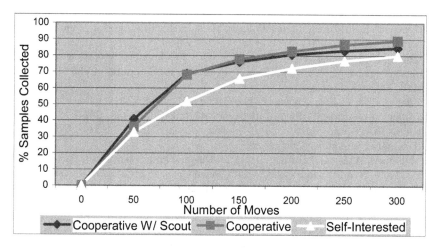

Fig. 5. Comparison of three agent architectures in a large-world environment containing nine clusters

support required for missions, (3) it will eliminate communication time lag as a significant factor in local task execution, providing the ability to react to and take advantage of serendipitous events, and (4) it will significantly enhance mission robustness. The development of the proposed architecture builds on developments in decision theory, agent societies, trusted systems, and ubiquitous computing.

Acknowledgements

This work was supported by the National Science Foundation under grant no. IIS-0083362 and by NASA under grant no. NAS5-98051.

References

[1] Asimov, I.: I, Robot. Gnome Books (1950) 204
[2] Asimov, I.: Foundation and Empire. Gnome Books (1952) 204
[3] Buhler, P. A. and Huhns, M. N.: Trust and Persistence. IEEE Internet Computing **5** (March/April 2001) 90–92
[4] Carnegie Mellon Center for the Advancement of Applied Ethics, http://www.lcl.cmu.edu/ CAAE/index.htm 203
[5] Castelfranchi, C.: Modeling Social Action for AI Agents. Artificial Intelligence **103** (1998) 157–182 202
[6] Castelfranchi, C., Dignum, F., Jonker, C. M., and Treur, J: Deliberate Normative Agents: Principles and Architecture. In: Proceedings of The Sixth International Workshop on Agent Theories, Architectures, and Languages (ATAL-99). Orlando, FL (July 1999) 202

[7] Cohen, P. R. and Levesque, H. J.: Persistence, Intention, and Commitment. In: Cohen, P. R., Morgan, J., and Pollack, M. E. (eds.): Intentions in Communication. MIT Press (1990) **202**

[8] Durfee, E. H., Lesser, V. R., and Corkill, D. D.: Coherent cooperation among communicating problem solvers. IEEE Transactions on Computers **C-36** (1987) 1275–1291 **202**

[9] Gasser, L.: Social conceptions of knowledge and action: DAI foundations and open systems semantics. Artificial Intelligence **47** (1991) 107–138 **202**

[10] Huhns, M. N. and Singh, M. P.: Cognitive Agents. IEEE Internet Computing **2** (November-December 1998) 87–89

[11] Mohamed, A. M. and Huhns, M. N.: Multiagent Benevolence as a Societal Norm. In: Conte, R. and Dellarocas, C. (eds.) Social Order in Multiagent Systems. Kluwer Academic Publishers, Boston, MA (2001) **202, 204**

[12] Muller, J. P., Pischel, M., and Thiel, M.: Modeling Reactive Behavior in Vertically Layered Agent Architectures. In M. J. Wooldridge and N. R. Jennings (eds.): Intelligent Agents, LNAI 890. Springer-Verlag, Berlin (1994) 261–276 **202**

[13] Rao, A. S. and Georgeff, M. P.: Modeling rational agents within a BDI-architecture. In: Proceedings of the International Conference on Principles of Knowledge Representation and Reasoning. (1991) 473–484 **202**

[14] Rose, J. R., Huhns, M. N., Sinha Roy, S., and Turkett Jr., W. H.: An Agent Architecture for Long-Term Robustness. In: Proceedings of the First Joint International Conference on Autonomous Agents and Multi-Agent Systems. ACM Press (2002) **207**

[15] Rose, J. R., Sengupta, A., Singh, S., and Valtorta, M.: Dynamic Decision Support for Command, Control, and Communication in the Context of Tactical Defense. ONR Grant No. N00014-97-1-0806

[16] Singh, M. P. and Huhns, M. N.: Social Abstractions for Information Agents. In: Klusch, M. (ed.) Intelligent Information Agents. Kluwer Academic Publishers, Boston, MA, (1999) **202**

[17] Sycara, K. and Zeng, D.: Coordination of multiple intelligent software agents. International Journal of Cooperative Information Systems **5** (1996) 181–212

[18] Tambe, M., Pynadath, D. V., and Chauvat, N.: Building Dynamic Agent Organizations in Cyberspace. IEEE Internet Computing **4** (March-April 2000) 65–73 **202**

[19] Vidal, J. M. and Durfee, E. H.: Building Agent Models in Economic Societies of Agents. In: AAAI-96 Workshop on Agent Modeling. Portland, OR (July 1996)

[20] Wooldridge, M. J. and Jennings, N. R.: Software Engineering with Agents: Pitfalls and Pratfalls. IEEE Internet Computing (May/June 1999)

Considering Hierarchical Hybrid Systems for Intelligent Animated Agents

Eric Aaron and Dimitris Metaxas

Department of Computer and Information Science
University Of Pennsylvania
200 South 33rd Street, Philadelphia, PA USA 19104-6389
{eaaron,dnm}@graphics.cis.upenn.edu

Abstract. We consider potential benefits of representing intelligent animated agents as hierarchical *hybrid dynamical systems* (i.e., systems with
both continuous and discrete dynamics). We begin by directly applying
hybrid systems theory to animation, using a general-purpose hybrid system specification tool to generate multi-agent animations. This application illustrates that a hybrid system architecture can provide a sys-
tematic, modular way to incorporate low-level behavior into a design for
higher-level behavioral modeling. We then apply the logical framework
of hybrid systems to animation, formally stating properties that may
not be readily expressed in other frameworks and mechanically checking
a collision-avoidance property for a simple race-like game.

1 Introduction

Autonomous animated agents may possess several kinds of dynamic intelligence
to facilitate reasonable, realistic navigation behavior. As a motivating example,
consider an animated actor navigating around obstacles in its virtual world. It
moves to its next target (goal) position, passing by many other entities, including
other actors and various kinds of obstacles (trash cans, flower beds, etc.). During
one particular segment of its navigation, this actor passes by a long row of
stationary obstacles. It starts out uncomfortable, maintaining a large distance
between itself and the obstacles. As time passes, it grows more comfortable and
changes to a different navigation system: It moves faster, gets closer to obstacles,
and generally becomes more aggressive. Throughout its course, it distinguishes
among different obstacles and among different actors around it. For instance,
upon nearing a distant target, it keeps a sizable distance between itself and an
obstacle, but it passes close to a friendly actor nearby.

Consider the diversity of dynamic intelligence demonstrated by the actor.
It autonomously reached its targets without colliding with obstacles, responding to moving obstacles in real time. It decided to change navigation behavior
in response to a dynamically changing quantity, its comfort. It distinguished
among entities around it, altering its course to reflect its subjective impressions. In this paper, we discuss general ideas for modeling this kind of diversely

W. Truszkowski, C. Rouff, M. Hinchey (Eds.): WRAC 2002, LNAI 2564, pp. 215–229, 2003.
© Springer-Verlag Berlin Heidelberg 2003

intelligent low-level navigation, and we present a specific, simple example navigation system that incorporates them. Our ideas extend the agent steering and crowd simulation approach of [11], retaining its reactive, scalable nature while augmenting its behavioral intelligence.

Our example navigation system is based in part on the observation that practical low-level navigation systems may be naturally modeled as *hybrid dynamical systems* (*hybrid systems*, for short), combinations of continuous and discrete dynamics. (We discuss hybrid systems in more detail in section 2.2.) For instance, consider the motivating example at the beginning of this section; the actor's position (and comfort level in its environment) may be described by continuous dynamics, and changes between different navigation strategies may be described by discrete dynamics. We implemented our navigation system as a hybrid system using the general-purpose hybrid system specification tool CHARON [5], concretely linking theoretical hybrid system models with practical navigation systems. In addition, we directly employed our CHARON implementation to generate animated worlds of targets, obstacles, and actors that demonstrate intelligent navigation.

Within the theoretical framework of hybrid systems, we also discuss another motivating application: reasoning about animations. Consider a fixed world of obstacles and targets, inhabited by one navigating actor. Given a particular set of initial parameter values for the actor, that animation system is fully determined; in such a fully determined system, an absence of agent-obstacle collisions might be verifiable by viewing one animation. Now consider the task of checking collision-avoidance for *all* the animation systems that could result from different initial sets of parameter values. This might not be possible to accomplish simply by viewing a small number of animations; in such cases, we might hope for formal, mechanical assistance.

In this paper, we discuss how logics for hybrid systems might be applied to animation systems, and we formalize some illustrative example properties. Although many properties of complex hybrid systems (such as the navigation system we implemented in CHARON) are theoretically undecidable, there are decidable cases, and we use the tool HYTECH [12] to mechanically check an example result about a simple race-like game.

2   Applying Hybrid System Theory to Multi-agent Animations

Systems with both continuous and discrete dynamics are not new in animation, but it is not always clear how these systems relate to well-understood hybrid system models. In contrast, we make a strong connection to existing hybrid system theory. We use the hybrid system tool CHARON [5] to implement multi-agent animation systems based upon the agent steering method presented in [11].

2.1   A Dynamical System for Agent Steering

There have been many approaches to guiding the behavior of autonomous agents. Logicist, artificial intelligence-based techniques have been used for cognitively empowered agents [14] and animated actors [10]; perception and dynamics-based techniques [7, 16, 20] are often more readily able to adapt to dynamic environments. Our particular approach to low-level navigation is based on the method in [11], a scalable, adaptive approach to modeling multiple autonomous agents in dynamic virtual environments. Like treatments of similar issues in behavioral robotics [13, 15], we consider only two-dimensional motion, although the mathematical foundations for three-dimensional navigation already exist [11].

Our animated worlds consist of three kinds of agents: *actors*, *targets* that represent actors' goals, and *obstacles* that actors attempt to avoid. There may be multiple actors, obstacles, and targets in an animation system. Further, obstacles and targets may be static and/or moving. These components provide a general conceptual palette that can be used to express a broad range of behaviors. For instance, an actor performing a multi-part task could be represented by its reaching a series of targets in sequence, each target corresponding to a component subtask.

At the mathematical core of our animated worlds are non-linear *attractor* and *repeller* functions that represent the targets and obstacles (respectively) in the system. Another non-linear system combines their weighted contributions in calculating an actor's angular velocity, dynamically adapting to real-time changes in the environment. Together, these non-linear systems generate natural-seeming motion, avoiding collisions and other undesirable behaviors. The agent heading angle ϕ is computed by a non-linear dynamical system of the form:

$$\dot{\phi} = f(\phi, \mathbf{env}) = |w_{tar}|f_{tar} + |w_{obs}|f_{obs} + n \qquad (1)$$

where f_{tar} and f_{obs} are the attractor and repeller functions for the system, and w_{tar} and w_{obs} are their respective weights on the agent. (n is a noise term, which helps avoid local minima in the system.)

The weights themselves are determined by computing the fixed points of:

$$\begin{cases} \dot{w}_{tar} = \alpha_1 w_{tar}(1 - w_{tar}^2) - \gamma_{12} w_{tar} w_{obs}^2 + n \\ \dot{w}_{obs} = \alpha_2 w_{obs}(1 - w_{obs}^2) - \gamma_{21} w_{obs} w_{tar}^2 + n \end{cases} \qquad (2)$$

where the α and γ parameters are designed to reflect conditions for the stability of the system. Many other parameters are also concealed in the terms presented above. For instance, a repeller function f_{obs} depends on parameters that determine how much influence obstacles have on an actor.

This is only an overview of one significant part of the agent steering system, but it gives a feel for the kind of mathematics involved. Further, it introduces the role parameters play in agent behavior, a notion to which we return frequently in the remainder of this paper.

2.2   Hybrid Systems and CHARON

Hybrid systems occur frequently and naturally in many contexts, and they are studied by both computer scientists and control theorists [1, 2]. Past domains of application for hybrid system models include descriptions of biological processes [4], air-traffic management systems [19], and manufacturing systems [18]. From a general, intuitive perspective, any system characterized by discrete transitions between modes of continuous control is a hybrid system.

There are several different formal models for hybrid systems. Net-based models such as Constraint Nets [22], for instance, have been acknowledged in literature on cognitive agents. We focus in particular on automata-theoretic models such as hybrid automata [6, 9]. As a brief, non-technical introduction to this perspective, we consider a hybrid automaton as having: a set of *discrete states* called *control modes*; a *continuous state space* (a subset of $\mathbb{R}^n$ for some n); and descriptions of system evolution, with constraints both on continuous evolution within a control mode and on discrete transitions between control modes. A state of the overall system is a pair (*control mode, continuous state*). Research and analysis of hybrid automata underlies practical tools such as CHARON [5] and the model checker HyTech [12]. For this paper, we use CHARON to implement animation systems and HyTech for verification.[1]

The architecture of a hybrid system in CHARON is expressed as *hierarchical agents*, a model conceptually similar to hierarchical hybrid automata. The key features of CHARON are:

Hierarchy. The building block for describing the system architecture is an *agent* that communicates with its environment via shared variables. The building block for describing flow of control inside an atomic agent is a *mode*. A mode is basically a hierarchical state machine, i.e., it may have submodes and transitions connecting them. CHARON allows *sharing* of modes so that the same mode definition can be instantiated in multiple contexts.

Discrete Updates. In CHARON, discrete updates are specified by *guarded actions* labeling transitions connecting the modes. Actions may call externally defined Java functions to perform complex data manipulations.

Continuous Updates. Some of the variables in CHARON can be declared *analog*, and they flow continuously during continuous updates that model passage of time. The evolution of analog variables can be constrained in three ways: *differential* constraints (e.g., by equations such as $\dot{x} = f(x, u)$), *algebraic* constraints (e.g., by equations such as $y = g(x, u)$), and *invariants* (e.g., $|x - y| \leq \varepsilon$) that limit the allowed durations of flows. Such constraints can be declared at different levels of the mode hierarchy.

We apply this agent-oriented architecture to model complex behavioral systems for intelligent actors.

---

[1] We used HyTech for verification because, as of this writing, the model checking facilities for CHARON are still under development.

3   A Hybrid System for Low-Level Navigation

We now present an example navigation system that demonstrates the kinds of intelligence underlying some low-level navigation. It substantially extends the system summarized in section 2.1, but it retains the desirable qualities discussed in [11], including the scalability required for multi-agent applications. Not coincidentally, we present our navigation system as a hybrid dynamical system. The agent-oriented hybrid system perspective both motivated and simplified our low-level navigation modeling. In particular, it enabled us to formally specify *navigation mode switching* in a rigorous, system-theoretic framework.

3.1   Selective Repeller Response

In typical low-level navigation examples generated by the framework in [11], the "aggressiveness" of an actor is held constant. (By "aggressiveness," [11] refers to the willingness of an actor to get close to repellers —obstacles and other actors— in its environment.) Thus, actors typically applied the same notion of "personal space" to other actors as to obstacles such as lamps, trash cans, etc. Further, the framework makes no distinction within classes. Every obstacle is treated the same as every other; actors could not recognize that some were less noxious than others (e.g., flower beds vs. trash cans). Similarly, with respect to other actors, an actor could not get closer to one (a friend) than another (a stranger). In our system, however, we extend the framework of [11] to allow an intelligent actor to respond *selectively* to the individual entities around it.

In each actor, there is a parameter d_0 in the framework of [11] that encodes aggressiveness: Raising/lowering d_0 will increase/decrease the effect of a repeller on that actor. As a constant, d_0 applies equally to all repellers. To enable selective repeller response, we instead implement d_0 as a function that returns a value for each repeller. Thus, each actor has its own relationships with every repeller in that world, enabling the selective responses described in the motivating example at the beginning of this paper. It also enables more complex relationships: The function itself could evolve over time, representing changes in interpersonal closeness in a virtual world as it applies to low-level navigation. For the example animations in section 4.2, however, our d_0 is a static lookup function.

3.2   Navigation Mode Switching

An intelligent actor might not rely on the same dynamical navigation system for its entire path. Recall, for instance, the motivating example at the beginning of this paper. An actor might alter its basic navigation behavior based on a variety of factors: increased comfort in its environment; awareness that it is among friends; simple recognition that it no longer requires complex obstacle avoidance to reach its goal. Following the framework in [11], each of these behaviors would be described by a different dynamical system, each essentially defining a *mode* of navigation, and an actor might engage in *navigation mode switching* as it follows its course, "changing its mind" about appropriate low-level behavior much as it would about high-level behavior (e.g., global path planning). We anticipate, in particular, that such mode changes would be real-time responses to real-time environmental changes. This observation motivates our utilizing a hybrid system framework for our navigation model; in it, we specify transition conditions independent of pre-determined spatio-temporal locations. If we restricted ourselves to transitions only at pre-determined points in space or time, we would be essentially abandoning the real-time dynamic nature of low-level navigation.

To enable the kind of real-time mode switching described in our motivating example, we introduce a variable *comfort* intended to represent how generally comfortable an actor feels in its current local environment. In our model, an actor's comfort varies dynamically in real time, just like its position. Therefore, we give a differential equation form to describe the evolution of an actor's comfort:

$$\dot{c} = k_m \, base_m + f(env). \tag{3}$$

In (3), c is the variable for comfort, and k_m and $base_m$ are real-valued parameters, both constant in a mode m but different in each mode. Parameter $base_m$ represents the base rate of change in that mode, the fundamental way the actor's comfort evolves. Parameter k_m is a scaling factor; for our demonstrations in section 4.2 and on the supplementary website [3], we use high scaling factors in some modes to induce faster mode changes. We further simplify equation (3) by making it such that $\dot{c}$ does not depend on c. No restriction on hybrid systems imposes this, however, and our general form can be readily extended beyond our simple (somewhat contrived) example.

An actor's comfort is also influenced by its environment, as represented in equation (3) by the function $f(env)$. Function f could be a well defined function on a thoughtfully designed set of arguments (world attributes, motivations, etc.). We are more interested in demonstrating the flexibility and generality of the framework than in positing a particular world model, however, so we implement $f(env)$ as a random number generator, bounded appropriately for our values of k_m and $base_m$.

In our model, an actor's behavior changes via navigation mode switching when its comfort reaches certain threshold levels. In particular, as an actor gets more comfortable in its environment, its velocity increases, it tends to become more aggressive (in the sense of section 3.1), and it changes the way its comfort evolves. Each of these new systems —marked by new velocity, new d_0 (either constant or function-valued d_0), and new parameters for the equation governing the evolution of c— is its own navigation mode; such navigation mode transitions in our model may depend on the trend of the actor's comfort (i.e., $\dot{c}$) as well as the comfort value itself. For instance, when deciding which mode of obstacle avoidant behavior to employ for a particular portion of a navigation, an actor takes a certain transition if its comfort level is very high *or* if comfort is moderately high but trending higher at that time (i.e., $\dot{c} > 0$). This exemplifies how the hybrid system perspective encourages a dynamically oriented approach to modeling some kinds of real-time decision making. Mode transition decisions may be made independent of time and space, dependent on both the zero'th-order value of comfort and its higher-order trends.

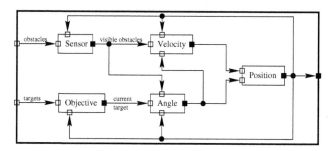

Fig. 1. The CHARON-agent-level architecture of an actor performing low-level navigation

3.3 System Architecture

The kind of navigation model featured in this paper is naturally described as a hybrid system: At its core are discrete transitions between continuous dynamical systems. Thus motivated, we implemented our example navigation system as a hierarchical hybrid system in CHARON.

Figure 1 shows the CHARON-agent architecture behind our model of a virtual actor performing low-level navigation. CHARON agents (as discussed in section 2.2) are represented as rectangles. Note the hierarchy: The navigating actor (i.e., the outermost agent) has five component sub-agents, including `Position` to determine its current position in a virtual world, `Sensor` to manage perception, `Objective` to determine its next target, and `Angle`, the dynamics of which we have described in this paper. Each of these CHARON sub-agents merits independent treatment; each embodies its own model of some aspect of navigation. For our implementation, we use a straightforward `Velocity` sub-agent, supplying a constant velocity that other sub-agents (e.g., `Angle`) can effectively change in real-time. Our underlying architecture, however, echoes the original presentation [11], allowing for a more complex treatment of velocity.

The navigation mode switching described in section 3.2 occurs in CHARON sub-agent `Angle`, in which each navigation mode is straightforwardly represented as a CHARON mode. (Section 2.2 discusses the roles of modes and agents in CHARON.) As an actor becomes more (or less) comfortable, it may switch navigation modes. Aggressiveness parameter d_0, velocity, and parameters of the dynamical system of evolution for comfort (see equation (3)) are then changed to create a new notion of appropriate proximity to others that reflects that actor's new comfort. A diagram of this straightforward transition system is available at the supplementary website [3].

We also include a mode-transition subsystem that emphasizes selective repeller response. When the actor reaches a certain point in its course, it enters this subsystem. The first navigation segment in this subsystem uses the standard, non-selective obstacle avoidance. After reaching a target, the actor then switches into one of two other possible modes: a simple, linear course (no ob-

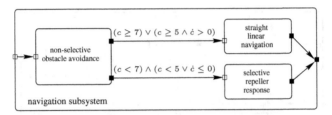

Fig. 2. A subsystem that emphasizes selective repeller response. This subsystem may be embedded in a larger navigation system (and altered, as needed). Note that transitions depend on both c (comfort) and $\dot{c}$

stacle avoidance); or a selective obstacle avoidance. A schematic diagram that shows transition conditions for this mode-switching subsystem is in Figure 2.

The particular system described in this section is merely a simple example, intended to straightforwardly illustrate the agent-oriented architecture supported by CHARON and our general ideas on low-level navigation. Hierarchical CHARON agents correspond neatly to actors and other world entities, as well as to computational sub-components of actors that merit independent treatment; CHARON modes correspond neatly to modes of behavior for these entities. By simultaneously integrating and distinguishing these conceptual levels, agent-oriented hybrid system models naturally represent abstractions that we consider when designing intelligent actors.

4   Applications and Experiments

4.1   Creating Animations from Hybrid System Models

Navigation systems may be implemented in CHARON using the key concepts noted in section 1. The agent metaphor is preserved: Navigating actors are implemented as CHARON agents (see section 3.3). Modes represent continuous behaviors; particular continuous dynamics (e.g., the non-linear system described in section 2.1) are represented as differential or algebraic constraints of a form such as `diff {d(angle) = AngleFunction(angle,...)}`. If constraints are necessary to limit the time in a particular mode, they are represented as invariants such as `inv {Cond && !Cond2 && distance(x,y)<=distance(x,z)}`. Guarded transitions between modes are presented in a straightforward `trans from Mode1 to Mode2 when Cond do Effect` syntax; when the guard `Cond` is true, the transition is enabled, and if it is taken, statement `Effect` is executed along with the system's jump from `Mode1` to `Mode2`. In this way, the underlying continuous mathematics and relations between modes of behavior are explicitly represented in a CHARON program. Further, the modularity of agent-oriented CHARON code makes it easy to change one aspect of a system while leaving others intact.

CHARON also generates numerical simulations of hybrid systems, which we exploited in creating animations from our formal system specifications. We simply simulated our navigation systems in CHARON, then used a small translation

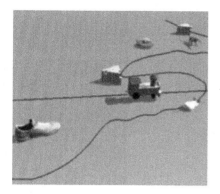

Fig. 3. An actor (white mouse, on right side of image), having already swerved around a stationary obstacle (sneaker), now reacting to avoid a moving obstacle (train)

Fig. 4. The actor (white mouse), having switched to simpler behavior. Its straight linear course takes it between two obstacles (a flying saucer and a dinosaur)

routine (like a Perl script) to format the output of those simulations so that a previously developed application (developed for research outside of the context of hybrid systems) could create graphical displays.

Figures in section 4.2 contain images from our animations. In our scenes and experiments, actors (white mice) navigate in a virtual world of targets (usually blocks of cheese), obstacles (usually toys one might find on the floor), and other actors. (CHARON-generated animations, including those from which these Figures were taken, may be seen at the supplementary website [3].)

4.2 Multi-agent Animations

Figures 3–6 show frames from animations that demonstrate our approach to intelligent low-level navigation. (Dark lines in those pictures indicate the paths of actors and moving obstacles.) An actor (white mouse), moving from the lower left to the upper right, begins a navigation with a comfort value of 0 and a uniformly applied d_0 value of 4. It starts out by moving around a series of obstacles (not shown here — see [3] for details), becoming more comfortable and more aggressive. The comfort and d_0 (aggression) values of the mouse are autonomously altered in accord with the navigation mode switching system in section 3.2; we, the designers of the animation, do not impose that those values be at any particular level at any particular place/time other than at the onset of the navigation.

Eventually, the white mouse arrives at a position where it begins a simple two-segment task: get the first/nearest block of cheese; then go get the more distant cheese. In the first segment (Figure 3), the actor avoids a static obstacle (sneaker) and a moving obstacle (train) on the way to the first target cheese. This is a straightforward application of obstacle avoidance without selective repeller

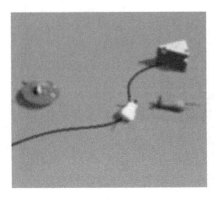

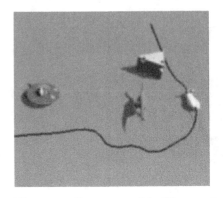

Fig. 5. Contrast with Figure 4: The actor (white mouse), having switched to selective repeller response. It passes close by the friendly-looking obstacle (toy mouse) on its right

Fig. 6. Contrast with Figure 4: The actor, maintaining the complex, obstacle-avoidant behavior. It goes around the unfriendly-looking dinosaur, taking a longer route to the target

response or navigation mode switching. The mouse applies a uniform d_0 value of 2.5 to both obstacles.

Our protagonist mouse need not engage in complex evasive behavior in the second segment. It could reach the second target simply by traveling in a straight line. Or, it might instead opt for selective repeller response, depending on its comfort level. In our experiment, we implement this by having the mouse enter the subsystem presented in Figure 2 when it reaches the first target. Then, because the mouse's comfort is 6.1 and trending higher (its derivative at the time is approximately 0.075), it opts for straight linear navigation, as displayed in Figure 4. As part of this navigation mode switch (see section 3.2), its d_0 value drops to 0 —it no longer even considers obstacles, it just moves straight— and its velocity rises from 0.3 to 0.5 units per simulated second.

If it were somewhat less comfortable in its environment, however, the actor might take a different course. For instance, consider a scenario with two major differences from the one just described: The mouse's comfort is only 4.1 when it makes a navigation mode switch; and there is a toy mouse as an obstacle in place of the dinosaur in Figure 4. Our white mouse protagonist might not be quite comfortable enough to decide to forgo complex obstacle avoidance, but it might be comfortable enough to recognize the toy mouse on its right as non-threatening (while the flying saucer on its left remains troubling). As a result, it would dynamically adjust its course to pass asymmetrically between the obstacles, as shown in Figure 5. We model this by giving our protagonist a d_0 value of 1.2 as applied to the flying saucer and a d_0 value of 0.6 as applied to the toy mouse. These changes permit the white mouse to autonomously determine its asymmetric course.

If it instead decided to maintain its complex obstacle avoidant behavior, treating all repellers the same, it would take a much longer path, going around both obstacles. This option represents a kind of control experiment, a continuation of the standard obstacle avoidance that guided it up until the first target; Figure 6 is a frame from the resulting animation, showing how much farther the white mouse goes if it does not consider navigation mode switching or selective repeller response. (See [3] for further discussion and other animations.)

5   Reasoning about Animation Systems

Properties of some animation systems (e.g., properties of all possible executions of a parameterized or non-deterministic system) may not be verifiable just by viewing a single animation. Even within a fully determined system, properties about relative speed or precise distance may be too difficult to judge by eye.

This touches upon a motivating observation behind our research: Well-known logics for hybrid systems are capable of expressing properties of animation systems. In addition, there are practical *model checkers* —tools that can mechanically verify some properties of simple hybrid systems— that we might apply to animation systems. These model checkers have significant limitations; many properties are theoretically undecidable, and as a practical matter, even decidable properties may only be feasibly checked in simple cases. Still, as we discuss in section 6, there are approaches that circumvent some undecidability barriers.

5.1   Modal Logic and Properties of Multi-agent Animations

There are many *modal* and *temporal* logics for hybrid systems, such as **CTL**, **LTL**, and the *μ-calculus*; [9] and [6] are good surveys of recent work on these logics. For readers unfamiliar with fundamental modal logic operators, we provide a brief review. In many ways, the treatment we consider here is similar to a framework presented in [21].

Modal logics are used to reason about *possibility* and *necessity* in *possible worlds*. For our application, a "world" is a state of a hybrid system and a "possible world" is a state reachable (under constraints on system evolution) from the current hybrid system state. A modal logic typically contains the standard propositional logic operators (negation, implication, etc.) along with various modal or temporal operators. For this paper, we introduce two common modal operators: the *possibility* operator $\Diamond P$ (intuitively, "It is possible that P"); and the *necessity* operator $\Box P$ (intuitively, "It is necessary that P"). As expected, they are duals: $\neg\Box\neg P \equiv \Diamond P$. In the context of a system execution, possibility and necessity also correspond to the intuitive readings of *eventually* and *always* (respectively). That is, $\Box P$ means that P is necessarily true of every state of the entire execution, always true; $\Diamond P$ means that P is not always false, i.e., eventually true. (From a rigorous logical standpoint, these explanations are overly simplistic, but they convey basic intuitions necessary for this paper.)

Logics for hybrid systems are powerfully expressive. In addition to having modal operators such as $\square$ and $\diamond$, they explicitly represent time, so we may specify that a condition be true at some particular time in an animation. We can also express properties of non-deterministic animation systems or parameterized classes of animations. We illustrate these points by presenting several example properties below. In each case, we formally express that the system execution E satisfies property P by writing $E \models P$, and we use the notation $loc(A)$ to refer to the location of an agent A. There are several ways to reason about parameterized or non-deterministic systems. In the logical formulas below, we do so by quantifying over all possible executions of a system.

- If the aggression parameter of actor a is set within the range $[2,4]$, actor a reaches target t:
  $(\forall E)E \models (aggression \in [2,4]) \Rightarrow \diamond(loc(a) = loc(t))$

- No matter what non-deterministic choices are made, at 5 seconds into the animation, agent a_2 is at least 100 units from agent a_1:
  $(\forall E)E \models \square((clock = 5) \Rightarrow distance(a_1, a_2) \geq 100)$

- No matter what non-deterministic choices are made, agent a_1 is at target t when agent a_2 is not, but agent a_2 eventually reaches target t:
  $(\forall E)E \models \diamond(loc(a_1) = loc(t) \wedge loc(a_2) \neq loc(t) \wedge \diamond(loc(a_2) = loc(t)))$

5.2 Verification

Despite significant undecidability barriers for general hybrid systems (including our hybrid system for low-level navigation), property verification is decidable in restricted cases [6]. Consider, for example, systems in which modes constrain every variable to constant velocity; changes require transitions between modes. Some animation systems can be specified in this restricted framework, and many properties are decidable for such systems.

To demonstrate this, we specified the rudiments of a race-like game in the model checker HYTECH [12] and mechanically checked collision-avoidance. Our animation system contains three agents, two racing actors and one obstacle, each moving at constant speed around a square, two-lane track. The rules of the race encode that each actor race on the inside lane whenever possible. Racers may move to the outside lane to pass slower agents, but they move promptly back when they are done passing.

Consider an infinite race, an endless execution of this animation system. Will the two racers ever collide? Although we thought we had specified collision-avoidant behavior, we were mistaken. HYTECH discovered a scenario in which a collision would occur: when the faster racer is changing lanes in front of the slower racer *at the corner of the track*, as represented in Figure 7. (Note that Figure 7 is not a frame from an actual animation. An animation and HYTECH output may be found at [3].)

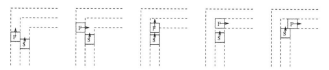

Fig. 7. A block diagram of unexpected collision behavior in a simple race game, as detected by HyTech. The faster racer (marked with "F") has passed the slower one (marked with "S"), but the slower one catches up on a corner

6 Conclusions

Animated actors require complex intelligence to successfully navigate in virtual worlds. Indeed, even when considering only low-level (local) navigation, actors must decide among different modes of behavior, distinguish among entities in the world around it, etc., and then incorporate all this information to create realistic paths that reach targets and avoid obstacles. For a low-level navigation strategy to be effective for a multi-agent system, it must account for all these kinds of intelligence in a fast, scalable manner.

Employing a hybrid systems framework, we extended the crowd simulation and agent steering system of [11] to accommodate many kinds of intelligence, including all those mentioned in the above paragraph. We presented our extensions in a simple example system, a hierarchical hybrid system for multi-agent steering that displays these kinds of intelligence; we directly used this formalized hybrid system model to generate multi-agent animations. Our example system also demonstrates how a hybrid system-oriented perspective can influence and simplify some reactive/behavioral modeling, naturally expressing and emphasizing the dynamic aspects of decision-making for navigation.

In the theoretical framework of hybrid systems, we also specified and reasoned about properties of animation systems. Although automatic verification of complex properties is infeasible in many cases, we did mechanically check a property about collisions in a race-like game animation. Furthermore, we need not abandon hope of verifying complex properties of complex systems: *Approximation* techniques for verification might apply to animation systems. For instance, if S is the set of states reachable by a system, and we cannot decide property P on S, we might instead overestimate S by a computationally simpler set $S' \supset S$ on which P is decidable. Then, if P holds on all states in S', we know P also holds on all states in S. Reasoning by approximation is an active area of research [8, 17] but has not yet been explored in the context of animation systems.

Artificial intelligence-based cognitive modeling [10] underscores a fundamental relationship between logic and animation: Our ability to reason about virtual worlds (and actors) is essential to our ability to create intelligent virtual agents. A hybrid systems approach to such reasoning could enable characters to reason directly about time, not just about endpoints of pre-determined discrete events. Heuristics could guide behavior on the basis of dynamics that many AI-based approaches cannot readily express. In addition, characters' cognitive and physical systems could be expressed in the same mathematical language. Animators could reason about cognitive states and physical systems using the same model checking methods. This opens the radical (and logically complex) possibility of truly *reflexive reasoning* — animated actors reasoning about their own cognitive states (using the same algorithms that their designers use).

Despite the relationship between hybrid system theory and animation systems, this natural interdisciplinary interface has not been well explored. Our current results suggest that hybrid systems can capture the interplay between continuous and discrete dynamics that naturally characterizes some intelligent behavior necessary for low-level agent navigation. We believe that further exploration will further extend our perspective on and vocabulary of multi-agent navigation and animation systems.

Acknowledgments

We thank: Harold Sun, Franjo Ivančić and Oleg Sokolsky for their substantial contributions; Siome Goldenstein for his advice and technical assistance; and Thao Dang, Jan Allbeck, and Norm Badler for helpful discussions. This research was supported in part by NSF grant NSF-SBR 8920230.

References

[1] *IEEE Transactions on Automatic Control, Special Issue on Hybrid Systems*, 43(4), April 1998. 218

[2] *Proceedings of the IEEE*, 88, July 2000. 218

[3] E. Aaron, H. Sun, F. Ivančić, and S. Goldenstein. CHARON-generated animations and other supplementary material. Available at http://www.cis.upenn.edu/~eaaron/WRAC.html. 220, 221, 223, 225, 226

[4] R. Alur, C. Belta, F. Ivančić, V. Kumar, M. Mintz, G. J. Pappas, H. Rubin, and J. Schug. Hybrid modeling and simulation of biomolecular networks. In *Hybrid Systems: Computation and Control*, volume 2034 of *Lecture Notes In Computer Science*. Springer Verlag, April 2001. 218

[5] R. Alur, R. Grosu, Y. Hur, V. Kumar, and I. Lee. Modular specification of hybrid systems in CHARON. In N. Lynch and B. H. Krogh, editors, *Hybrid Systems : Computation and Control*, volume 1790 of *Lecture Notes in Computer Science*. Springer Verlag, 2000. 216, 218

[6] R. Alur, T. Henzinger, G. Lafferriere, and G. Pappas. Discrete abstractions of hybrid systems. *Proceedings of the IEEE*, 88:971–984, July 2000. 218, 225, 226

[7] David Brogan, Ronald Metoyer, and Jessica Hodgins. Dynamically simulated characters in virtual environments. *IEEE Computer Graphics and Applications*, 18(5):59–69, Sep/Oct 1998. 217

[8] T. Dang and O. Maler. Reachability analysis via face lifting. In T. Henzinger and S. Sastry, editors, *Hybrid Systems : Computation and Control*, volume 1386 of *Lecture Notes in Computer Science*, pages 96–109. Springer Verlag, Berlin, 1998. 227

[9] J. Davoren and A. Nerode. Logics for hybrid systems. *Proceedings of the IEEE*, 88:985–1010, July 2000. 218, 225

[10] J. Funge. *AI for Games and Animation*. A K Peters, 1999. **217, 227**

[11] S. Goldenstein, M. Karavelas, D. Metaxas, L. Guibas, E. Aaron, and A. Goswami. Scalable nonlinear dynamical systems for agent steering and crowd simulation. *Computers And Graphics*, 25(6):983–998, 2001. **216, 217, 219, 221, 227**

[12] T. A. Henzinger, P.-H. Ho, and H. Wong-Toi. A user guide to HYTECH. In E. Brinksma, W. R. Cleaveland, K. G. Larsen, T. Margaria, and B. Steffen, editors, *TACAS: Tools and Algorithms for the Construction and Analysis of Systems*, volume 1019 of *Lecture Notes in Computer Science*. Springer-Verlag, 1995. **216, 218, 226**

[13] E. Large, H. Christensen, and R. Bajcsy. Scaling the dynamic approach to path planning and control: Competition among behavioral constraints. *International Journal of Robotics Research*, 18(1):37–58, 1999. **217**

[14] H. Levesque and F. Pirri, editors. *Logical Foundations for Cognitive Agents: Contributions in Honor of Ray Reiter*. Springer, 1999. **217**

[15] Maja J. Matarić. Integration of representation into goal-driven behaviour based robots. *IEEE Trans on Robotics & Automation*, 8(3):304–312, 1992. **217**

[16] H. Noser, O. Renault, D. Thalmann, and N. Thalmann. Navigation for digital actors based on synthetic vision, memory and learning. *Computer and Graphics*, 1995. **217**

[17] G. J. Pappas and S. Sastry. Towards continuous abstractions of dynamical and control systems. In P. Antsaklis, W. Kohn, A. Nerode, and S. Sastry, editors, *Hybrid Systems IV*, volume 1273 of *Lecture Notes in Computer Science*, pages 329–341. Springer Verlag, Berlin, Germany, 1997. **227**

[18] D. Pepyne and C. Cassandras. Hybrid systems in manufacturing. *Proceedings of the IEEE*, 88:1108–1123, July 2000. **218**

[19] C. Tomlin, G. J. Pappas, and S. Sastry. Conflict resolution for air traffic management : A study in muti-agent hybrid systems. *IEEE Transactions on Automatic Control*, 43(4):509–521, April 1998. **218**

[20] X. Tu and D. Terzopoulos. Artificial fishes: Physics, locomotion, perception, behavior. In *Proc. of SIGGRAPH '94*, pages 43–50, 1994. **217**

[21] M. Woolridge. *Reasoning About Rational Agents*. MIT Press, 2000. **225**

[22] Y. Zhang and A. Mackworth. Constraint nets: A semantic model for hybrid dynamic systems. *Theoretical Computer Science*, 138(1):211–239, 1995. **218**

Reasonable Machines:
Analogical Reasoning in Autonomous Agent Design

David C. Wyland

Reasonable Machines
15213 Bowden Ct., Morgan Hill, CA 95037 USA
dcwyland@ix.netcom.com

Abstract. This paper focuses on agents for open environments (AOE) and on the use of analogical reasoning (AR) in their design. The autonomous mobile robot is an example of an AOE. It operates in an open, dynamic environment, i.e. unpredictable but familiar. An AOE should be a reasonable machine: it should act as we would for the same environment, history and goals. A reasonable machine has responses that are mediated among its goals and actions in the current context. AR can be used to design reasonable machines that implement this mediation. An agent using AR reasons from known examples to define actions in the current context. This paper proposes a form of AR called Analog Logic and discusses its potential to achieve AOE design goals. AR provides philosophical grounding of the symbols used and a new approach for dealing with continuous symbol systems and agent communication.

1   Introduction

This paper focuses on agents for open environments (AOE) and on the use of analogical reasoning in their architecture and design. The autonomous mobile robot (AMR) is an example of an AOE. The AMR operates in an open, dynamic environment. Open, in this sense, means unpredictable but familiar. An AMR is never in exactly the same place or exactly the same state twice. Its position will not be the same, its goals will not be the same and it can encounter obstacles and perturbations at any time. However, it still must function to achieve its goals. Because they deal with open environments, AOE applications include exploration (planetary rovers), natural materials processing (food processing, agriculture), maintenance, security and human interaction. In the last case, simple human interaction itself is the open environment: unpredictable but familiar. This paper proposes that analogical reasoning as embodied in analog logic allows us to design what we want in such an autonomous agent.

W. Truszkowski, C. Rouff, M. Hinchey (Eds.): WRAC 2002, LNCS 2564, pp. 230-242, 2003.

1.1   Autonomous Agents: Some Definitions

An autonomous agent is a machine that must make decisions during its activities (run time) rather than before starting its activities (compile time). Autonomous agents can be classified in terms of their environment. An agent's environment can be classified in two ways: simple versus complex and closed versus open. Environmental complexity can be defined in terms of the agent's total number of internal, external and action states. External states are the number of unique states of all the external inputs. Internal states are the number of unique states of the agent's internal storage elements, and action states are the number of unique actions that the agent can take. The state spaces can be discrete or continuous. These states and their sequence determine the behavior of the agent. The size of the total state space defines the complexity of the agent's operating environment, both in space (external states), time (internal states) and activity (action states). Agents for simple environments, such as many software robots, have few states. See [1], [2] and [3] for discussions of agent design. See [4] and [5] for discussions of software agent design.

Simple agents can use simple planning, such as conventional programming and search techniques. As the state space of the agent increases, conventional deductive planning becomes exponentially more difficult. At this point, the designer begins to resort to heuristic methods and eventually heuristic planning in general. Planning based on analogy such as case based planning is an example of heuristic planning. Hammond in [6] describes case based planning as "planning by remembering." Bernard in [7] discusses a spacecraft application with pre-compiled contingency plans, effectively plans as "synthetic memories. "

Closed environments can be closed and passive or closed and active. In a closed, passive environment, all states are known and predictable in advance. The starting state and all state transitions are known in advance. Industrial robots such as painting and spot welding robots on automobile production lines are examples of machines that work in closed, passive environments. They execute pre programmed fixed action sequences with little or no feedback from their environment. These machines are not generally considered agents because they are not autonomous: they make no run time choices.

In a closed, active environment, all states are known but their sequence is not predictable in advance. The starting state is known in advance, but not all state transitions are known in advance. The agent must make choices at run time on actions to take depending on the context. Software robots, some industrial robots and most mobile robots fit this category. An industrial robot that picks parts from a moving belt must examine the orientation of the part and choose a grasp action plan for picking up the part. Mobile robots for closed environments know all the objects they may encounter, but they make choices about how to deal with the obstacles when they encounter them.

A spacecraft agent such as described in [7] is a good example of an agent in a closed, active environment. In this example, the spacecraft does pre-planned experiments using instruments and navigation elements that can fail. In addition to the nominal experiment plans, the spacecraft stores contingency plans for equipment failures. When a piece of equipment fails, the on-board planner invokes the appropriate contingency plan to compensate for the failure. Equipment failure in the spacecraft may not directly detectable. The on-board planner uses models of the equipment to detect failures. The models provide a generalized algorithmic method of detecting failure. They encode the failure mechanisms and the sensor readings they generate. The models provide a deductively generated heuristic for relating sensor readings to equipment failure detection.

In an open environment, all states are not known and not predictable in advance. The states themselves are only partially known in advance, and the state transitions are only partly predictable in advance. Open environments are inherently active: if the states are partially unknown, the results of the agent actions – and therefore the new state – cannot be predicted in advance. Outdoor mobile robots such as planetary rovers fit in this category. The terrain and obstacles are only generally known in advance, never exactly known.

Mobile robots in open environments are never in exactly the same place or exactly the same state twice. You can't return to exactly the same place because of natural limitations on measurement and positioning capability of the robot. "Near enough" is just that: you return to a similar place, not exactly the same place. This means that you have to deal with familiar places, not the same places. The same goes for the robot's state, which is the combination of all sense inputs and history. Your history may have changed because of learning, if nothing else. Also if you are not in exactly the same place, your sensors will not generate the same values, even if they are perfect, have no noise and there were no other changes in the environment. The rover also will never encounter the same object twice in the sense that, even if it re-encounters "the same" object, it will encounter it from a slightly different position the second time. Situations and objects are similar to but not the same as previous situations and objects.

We will consider agents for complex open environments (AOE). An AOE needs both autonomy and a method for dealing with incomplete knowledge at run time. Open environments need heuristic methods for dealing with incomplete knowledge. Complex environments also lead to heuristic methods as a tactic to deal with the combinational complexity of many states. The problem of combinational complexity is similar to incomplete information: the information may be there, but you cannot derive it due to the finite nature of compute resources.

1.2   What We Want: Reasonable Machines

What would we like in an AOE, beyond functionality? We would like it to act reasonably, to act as we would for the same environment, history and goals. A reasonable machine would have responses that are mediated among its goals and actions in the current context. For example, if we told an agent to get a cup of coffee, we do not want it to drop the tray of glasses it is carrying and immediately go get the coffee. This implies multiple, context dependent goals and priorities. It also implies autonomy: the agent must decide how and when to carry out its intended actions in order to mediate among its context dependent goals and priorities.

We also want a machine that can carry out commands in open environments. An open environment is unpredictable but familiar. How can an environment (or anything) be unpredictable but familiar? Faces are an example. When you meet someone new, he or she has an unpredictable but familiar face. It is unpredictable because you have never seen this particular face before; it is familiar because it has two eyes, a nose, a mouth, and so forth, like any other human face. The new face is familiar: it "looks like" many other faces you have seen. An open environment may have unpredictable but familiar features. You have never seen this exact rock before, this exact animal or person before, this box or obstacle before, but it is similar to other rocks, animals, persons, boxes and obstacles you have seen before. If an environment is unpredictable but familiar, you cannot pre-plan how you will respond to events and actions, but you can respond to the environment based on similar prior examples.

We want social agents that carry on conversations with us. If it is going to be a "gofer" (as in go get something for me) agent, we need to talk with it a lot. Not only to give it commands, but to give it the background of the commands. We also want to check on how it is doing and to instruct it in new behaviors. These conversations should be similar in form and content to conversations between human agents, for example a conversation between a human and a store clerk about an intended purchase. This does not mean discussing Eastern Philosophy or life in France; it means discussing the agent's goals, status, priorities, experiences, knowledge and capabilities. The reason for the conversations is to insure that the agent understands what we mean when we say something.

What can an agent talk about? Only what it has directly experienced, what it can experience or information about activities that it can relate to what it has or can experience. An agent can talk about its sensor values and abstractions (patterns) made from its sensor inputs. For example, it can tell whether it has something in front of it. It can also sense whether the object has a quality, such as being red. Further, it can have abstractions about something it senses infrequently, such as a specific person that it can uniquely identify. It can also have indirect abstractions about its actuators, as in what happens at sensor inputs when an actuator moves.

What would you want an agent to talk about? Examples include: 1) its current goals, its status in achieving them and new goals we would like it to pursue, 2) goal priorities and changes to them, 3) its current beliefs about the world, 4) its experiences and the relations between them, and 5) new behaviors to be directly learned and behaviors to be learned by example through stories. Although the list is extensive, each conversation is potentially simple and grounded in the experience of the robot. If the conversation is limited to topics that the robot can directly or vicariously experience, we can design a robot and conversational apparatus to do this.

Why not allow the agent to talk about things it cannot directly experience? Because we will wind up with a "parrot" agent that can respond convincingly to conversational cues, but has no understanding of the content of the conversation. A dictionary agent is an example. You could have an agent that would respond with dictionary text given a word as input. However, the agent would not "understand" the text it emitted. This is the symbol grounding problem, as discussed in [8] and [9]. The word is a symbol, but it is not related to the agent's ability to experience the thing the word refers to. This corresponds to cocktail party conversation by someone who has lengthy opinions on a book he or she has not read. The computer program Eliza does this. It uses a simple program to deceive the user into thinking that it understands its conversation with the user. Even though it is very convincing, it stands as an archetypical example of something that appears to the user to understand conversation but definitely does not.

What does "understand" mean, in agent terms? An agent understands a sentence and the words in it if it can relate them to its past experiences and actions, and make decisions based on this relationship. In story terms, this is equivalent to being able to paraphrase a story, to tell a new story that is equivalent to an existing story using different words, phrases and examples

2   Designing Reasonable Machines

Designing an AOE means designing a machine for an unknown and unpredictable environment. This is somewhat a contradiction in terms. Design is based on deductive reasoning. You select components for their known characteristics. These are the "axioms" of your "proof," i.e. your design. You combine these components to achieve the desired result in the same manner as constructing a proof. If you know how the components work, you can exactly predict how the design will work. If you do not have the component you need, you must create one. If you do not have the environment you need, you modify it until it meets your needs, or you model it as a new component and restart your proof. Sometimes the characteristics of the components or the environment are only partly known. In this case, you do testing during the design to complete your knowledge. You make the necessary adjustments before the design is done.

For an AOE, the characteristics of the components and the environment are never completely known, they change with time and we cannot modify the environment to suit the design. Therefore, we cannot design, in the sense outlined above. So how can we design one? The answer is that we design a machine that can work effectively with incomplete knowledge. It must do the best it can, since it cannot know how to do the best absolutely. Such a machine will never have (or at least never know that it has) the kind of complete knowledge we require for a design, even if it learns. If it ever does, it will mean that the environment is no longer open: it has become completely predictable. At this point it is no longer an AOE, as we have described it.

The AOE has to deal with incomplete information in an unpredictable environment, yet take effective action according to its goals. This is an important planning problem, as discussed in [10] who notes that plans fail more often from incomplete beliefs than false beliefs. How can an agent take effective action in a new situation? Answer: it will have to make a guess. And to be effective, it will have to make the best guess it can. It can make a good guess by comparing the current situation to similar situations it has previously encountered, then taking the action that worked best in those situations. Once the action has been taken and the results of that action have developed, the agent can record this as a new situation-action experience pair for use as a candidate in the next new situation.

This solves our small dilemma. Such a machine can be designed conventionally yet act reasonably. A simple analogy is a payroll program. The payroll program is rigorously designed, yet nothing in the design predicts what payroll checks will be printed next week.

3   Analogical Reasoning

An agent has to deal with an unpredictable environment and yet act in a reasonable manner. One way to do this is to have its current activities guided by past examples of activity given a similar environment. Since no combination of sensed environment, goals and history can be exactly the same as any previous combination, the agent will have to look for similarities between the current situation and prior situations. It then will mediate its actions between the actions corresponding to the previous situations.

This style of reasoning called analogical reasoning, which is reasoning by analogy to previously similar situations. Analogical reasoning assumes that what worked in the past will work in the future. Reasoning by analogy involves measuring the similarity between the current situation and past situations, and then taking the same action you took in past situations based on similarity. The action taken may be a blend of past actions weighted by similarity, or it may be a choice of the action associated with the most similar case.

Analogical reasoning depends on the measurement of similarity of the current state to remembered examples and on the blending (or choice of the best) of remembered actions based on similarity. The challenges in analogical reasoning are how similarity is measured, how the examples are remembered and how the actions associated with the examples are remembered and combined to create new action in the current situation.

To see how analogical reasoning works, let us compare it to deductive reasoning. Deductive reasoning is based on equality, while analogical reasoning is based on similarity. Both reasoning systems define and manipulate their symbols according to rules. The symbols in both systems "point" to things in some context, some part of the world. In deductive reasoning, symbols have a one of two possible values: true or not true. This value indicates whether the thing indicated by the symbol is equal or not equal to an ideal thing associated with the symbol. For example when counting stones, each stone is equal to all other stones and to an ideal stone for the purposes of counting. Otherwise, we could not count things.

In analogical reasoning, each symbol has one of many possible values indicating degree of similarity between the thing pointed to by the symbol and an ideal associated with the symbol. For example when comparing a dining room table to a small coffee table, the dining room table is more similar to an ideal example of a table than the coffee table is, and it would have a higher value for similarity to the ideal table as a result. Otherwise, we could not compare things.

To compare these two systems, consider Socrates and his mortality. In deductive reasoning, we state the following: 1) Socrates is a man, 2) all men are mortal and 3) therefore, Socrates is mortal. To put it more precisely: 1) Socrates meets the criteria of being a man, therefore Socrates is a man; 2) If x meets the criteria of being a man, x is mortal by assertion, and 3) Socrates meets the criteria of being a man, therefore Socrates is mortal. In step 2) we rely implicitly on the fact that x is either true or not true, and therefore the mortality of x is also asserted to be true if x is true.

An analogical reasoning version of Socrates mortality does not work well because man and mortal are true or false: there are no intermediate values. However, let's try Socrates' table, as follows: 1) Socrates' table is tall. 2) Tall tables have long legs. 3)

Therefore, Socrates' table has long legs. To put it more precisely: 1) Socrates' table has a measure of tallness. 2) To the degree that table x is tall, x has long legs. 3) Therefore, to the degree that Socrates' table is tall, Socrates' table has long legs.

Note that analogical reasoning, as described above, defines a continuous symbol system.

Analogical reasoning is becoming interesting as a tool for agent design. Pollock in [10] provides some justification for using analogical reasoning in planning. Hofstadter in [11] argues that pattern finding and corresponding analogy making is at the core of intelligence. In [12], analogical representation is recommended as an internal representation for reasoning.

Analogical reasoning has had successes in Case Based Reasoning (CBR) and fuzzy logic applications. CBR is reasoning by analogy, as discussed in [13] Each case in CBR is a remembered example of a situation-action plan that achieved (or failed to achieve) a goal. Cases are relatively large, complete plans. As a result, CBR is considered large grain (large, complex example) reasoning.

Fuzzy logic as used in almost all fuzzy logic control systems implements analogical reasoning as its control method. This is not generally recognized. However, the fuzzy logic control examples in [14] and [15] are most easily understood as examples of analogical reasoning.

Fuzzy logic has had successes in agent design, specifically autonomous mobile robots. The first and second place winners of the AAAI 93 autonomous mobile robot competition used fuzzy logic as the reactive layer that connects the sensors to the actuators and (digital) symbolic planners as supervisors. See [16] and [17].

Analogical reasoning can provide some significant benefits. Since analogical reasoning is heuristic and based on learned or taught examples, it avoids the frame problem. The frame problem, as reviewed in [18], is the problem of deductively predicting the future, an impossible task. The specific problem is to determine what changes and does not change one instant from now. Changes can occur because of actions an agent takes, or they may occur spontaneously as a result of outside forces. The problem is to predict the future so that a deductive reasoning system can plan for optimal action to achieve its goals. Analogical reasoning avoids the problem by making a basic assumption: what worked last time will work this time. This may not always be true, but it is the best we can do in an unpredictable world of chronically incomplete knowledge.

Analogical reasoning provides a new and potentially more effective way of dealing with words, language and conversation. Analogical reasoning can provide the basis for a continuous symbol system, and words represented in this system have degrees of meaning depending on context. This is compatible with current research on the mental concepts we use and the words that refer to these concepts, as discussed in [19] and [20]. By providing a more accurate understanding and representation of words and by grounding them in examples, analogical reasoning should be able to significantly improve and simplify communication between agents and humans.

3.1   Analog Logic

Analog logic implements analogical reasoning. It uses analogical inference to provide a formal bridge between similarity and implied action. Analog inference rules remember the relation between examples and their associated actions, and it combines the actions according to the relative value of their associated similarity values.

Analogical reasoning depends the measurement of the similarity of the current state to remembered examples and on the blending (or choice of the best) of remembered actions based on similarity. The challenges in analogical reasoning are how similarity is measured, how the examples are remembered and how the actions associated with the examples are remembered and combined to create new action in the current situation.

Analog logic uses the concept of measurement of qualities of things – such as temperature – to define similarity, and it uses the comparison of these measurements to relate similarities. The qualities of remembered examples are contained in measurement operators. These operators compare the current quality of a thing against an implied reference and return a relative similarity value between 0 and 100%.

Analog logic consists of symbols and inference operators. Symbols point to things in the world and represent abstract qualities of these things. Each symbol has a value between zero and one. This value indicates the degree to which a quality is present in the thing, from not at all present to fully present, for example the relative redness of a ball, from not at all red to maximally red. The value associated with the symbol is called a signal. In analog logic, this signal has a value between zero and one. In deductive, digital logic, this signal would have a value of either zero or one.

Signal values are defined as constants, generated by sensors or generated by inference. A sensor measures something in the outside world and returns a value that is a measurement of a quality of that thing, such as degree of redness of a ball. If the sensor's output does not directly indicate the desired quality, inference operators can be used to generate the desired quality value from the output of the sensor(s).

Inference maps one or more input quality values to an output quality value. Inference in analog logic is by assertion: for a given input value(s), the inference function asserts the output value. There are two types of inference operators: direct and indirect. Direct inference maps one or more inputs to a single output.

Indirect inference uses its inputs to map other inputs to a single output. In indirect inference, each inference input consists of two values: the control value and the recommended output value. For example in the choice operator, the control input with the maximum value selects the single recommended output value associated with that input. In the blend operator, the control inputs are used to perform a weighted average combination of the recommended values, weighted by their associated quality values.

Direct inference operators are called measurement operators (MO's). An MO is typically defined by identifying example points in the input space of the MO. These example points, or exemplars, define the output values for specific input values. Other values are derived by interpolation between the exemplars. For example, an MO indicating hot outside temperature might have exemplars at 70 degrees and 90 degrees. The resulting MO has a value of 0.0 at 70 degrees and below, rising to 1.0 at 90 degrees and above. This MO could convert a outside thermometer sensor output into the quality hot temperature of outside.

The examples that define an MO define the context of the measurement it performs. To define "red ball," we could use a red ball and a non-red ball as examples. Since the measurement operator is defined in reference to examples, its value is a measure of the similarity of the thing measured to those examples. It indicates the degree of similarity between the thing in the environment the symbol refers to and a perfect example of the quality. Zero means no similarity, and one means complete similarity.

MO's are often defined in sets by example points in the input space common to the set of MO's. Each example point, or exemplar, defines a separate MO. Each MO has a value of 1.0 at its exemplar point, declining to a value of 0.0 at adjacent exemplars and a value of 0.0 everywhere else. The result is a set of triangular MO's, with the peak of each triangle corresponding to its defining exemplar. For example, a set of MO's spanning outside temperature might have defining exemplars at (-20, 40, 65, 90, 120) degrees F corresponding to MO's of (maximum cold, cold, normal, hot, maximum hot). Such a set of MO's is useful in blend and choice inferences. As the temperature moves from −20 to + 120 degrees F, pairs of MO's become successively active, with one MO output value increasing to 1.0 as the other decreases to 0.0. When used with a blend operator, the blend operator output value moves smoothly from one recommended output value to the next. The combination of MO set definition by exemplars and its use with the blend operator results in analogical reasoning. The output from the blend operator is a weighted average of the recommend output values associated with the exemplar values that define the MO's.

The indirect inference operators, blend and choice, provide analogical inference as we have defined it. Analogical reasoning depends on the measurement of similarity of the current state to remembered examples and on the blending (or choice of the best) of remembered actions based on similarity. The blend operator performs a weighted average of recommended output values (the remembered actions), weighted by the relative values of the quality (similarity) input values. The choice operator selects the recommended output values (the remembered action), associated with the highest quality (similarity) input value.

3.2   Analog Logic and Language

Humans can define measurement operators by subjective testing. In MO definition by subjective testing, you give a candidate group of people a set of input values and ask them to specify the corresponding output values. The resulting values are statistically averaged to produce the values for the MO. For example, consider an MO that generates the quality of Hot Outside Temperature from a thermometer sensor reading. The candidate group might define Hot to have a value of 1.0 for 90 degrees F or above and a value of 0.0 for 70 degrees F or below, with values between 70 and 90 degrees by interpolation.

The subjective approach works. If the candidate group understands the quality being inferred, the group members return statistically similar values for the inferred values. [21] documents this somewhat surprising result. Perhaps this is not so surprising in retrospect. The qualities of analog logic correspond to words in ordinary language. To make decisions acceptable to a group of people based on whether a thing is hot or not, there must be a closely correlated agreement by each member of the group of what hot means in terms of temperature. This can allow a designer to directly define an MO by using knowledge held in common with the group of people concerned with the output of the MO. If all members agree closely on the MO inference values, anyone (including the designer) can define the MO. Group testing can then be used to verify the values, if necessary.

Humans can – and typically do – define MO's and other inferences so their output values correspond to commonly understood words, for example, hot temperature of outdoor air. This allows the human designer to understand and have proper expectations about the output value, and it allows philosophically grounded communication between the human and an agent. When the agent or the human uses the term "hot temperature of outdoor air," each knows what it means because each knows what it refers to.

3.3   Analog Logic and Fuzzy Logic

Analog logic is based on fuzzy logic as used in fuzzy logic control system design. (See [22], [23] and [14] for a discussion of fuzzy logic.) However since fuzzy logic is a general formalism for modeling degrees of truth including uncertainty and the ambiguity of language, it provides no specific guidance or conceptual grounding for the operations required in these control systems. If you study fuzzy logic for control applications, you find no formal method to justify the choice of inference (defuzzification) functions other than "these seem to work well and are popular." However, if you study fuzzy control application in [14] and [15], you will find fuzzy logic is used as a mathematical formalism for analogical reasoning, without being recognized as such.

In many of these fuzzy control designs, example points in the system input space define fuzzy membership functions, the fuzzifier operators. Each membership function has an output value indicating the degree to which the input is near its defining exemplar point relative to adjacent points. These membership function values are used for inference. Each membership function output is applied to an inference operator, the defuzzyfier operator. Associated with each membership function is a recommended output value that is supplied to the inference operator. The commonly used "center of moment" defuzzifier operator corresponds to the analog logic blend operator. It generates a weighted average of the recommended output values, weighted by the input values. The result of this operation is that the output of the defuzzifier is the blending of remembered actions (recommended output values) based on similarity (relative nearness to example points). Stripped of fuzzy logic terminology, this is equivalent to analogical inference.

Analog logic is a variant or subset of fuzzy logic that targets the domain of analogical reasoning, and analogical reasoning provides the conceptual grounding for its operations. Analog logic attributes its symbol values to measures of quality, rather than degrees of vagueness or ambiguity. The variables of fuzzy logic can measure many different things, including vagueness and ambiguity; however, this capability is not used in analog logic. Analog logic has no inherent vagueness. The membership functions of fuzzy logic become the measurement operators of analog logic. Measurement and other inference operators return specific values (crisp values in fuzzy terms) that indicate the degree to which a quality is present and that expresses the degree of similarity to remembered examples. Inference in analog logic is an asserted mapping from one quality measurement to a new quality measurement.

4   Summary

Autonomous agents such as planetary rovers work in open environments. Open environments are unpredictable but familiar. The challenge is to create agents that work effectively in these environments. We want agents that act as reasonable machines, to act as we would for the same environment, history and goals. This implies mediated responses, multiple context dependent goals and priority, and autonomy to carry out its goals. We also want the agent to be social, to carry on conversations about its experiences, its goals and its progress toward achieving its goals.

To design an agent for an open environment (AOE), we have to design a machine that works with limited knowledge in an unpredictable environment. Such a machine must make a guess about what to do next. By reasoning from experience, it tries to make the best guess it can. If it can learn the new experience, it may be able to make a better guess next time.

Reasoning from experience is analogical reasoning. Analogical reasoning makes one basic assumption: what worked before will work again. Analogical reasoning involves measuring the similarity between the current situation and past situations, and then taking the same action you took in past situations based on similarity. Analog logic implements analogical reasoning. It does this by creating a continuous symbol system with elements and operators that implement the analogical reasoning.

Analogical reasoning avoids the frame problem by assuming what worked before will work again. This may not always be true, but it is the best we can do in an unpredictable world of chronically incomplete knowledge. Also, by providing a more accurate understanding and representation of words and by grounding them in examples, analogical reasoning and analog logic should be able to significantly improve and simplify communication between agents and humans.

References

[1]   M. Wooldridge and N. R. Jennings, "Agent Theories, Architectures, and Languages: A Survey," Proc. {ECAI}-Workshop on Agent Theories, Architectures and Languages 1994, Springer-verlag 1995, ISBN 3-540-58855-8. url = "citeseer.nj.nec.com/wooldridge94agent.html"

[2]   Foundations of Rational Agency, ed. Rao and Wooldridge, Kluwer Academic Publishers 1999; ISBN: 0792356012

[3]   M. Wooldridge, Reasoning About Rational Agents, MIT Press 2000, ISBN 0-262-23213-8.

[4]   Richard Murch & Tony Johnson, Intelligent Software Agents, Prentice Hall 1999 ISBN 0-13-011021-3

[5]   Joseph Williams, Bots and Other Internet Beasties, Sams Publishing 1996 ISBN 1-57521-016-9

[6]   K. J. Hammond", "Case-Based Planning: A Framework for Planning from Experience", Cognitive Science, volume 14, pages 385--443, 1990", url = "citeseer.nj.nec.com/article/hammond90casebased.html"

[7]   D. Bernard and G. Dorais & C. Fry & E. Jr & B. Kanefsky & J. Kurien & W. Millar and N. Muscettola & P. Nayak & B. Pell and K. Rajan & N. Rouquette & B. Smith & B. Williams, " Design of the Remote Agent Experiment for Spacecraft Autonomy," Proceedings of the IEEE Aerospace Conference, Snowmass, CO: IEEE 1998 url = "citeseer.nj.nec.com/bernard98design.html"

[8]   Tom Ziemke, "Rethinking Grounding," Does Representation Need Reality?-Proceedings of the International Conference 'New Trends in Cognitive Science' (NTCS97) Perspectives from Cognitive Science, Neuroscience, Epistemology and Artificial Life, Austrian Society for Cognitive Science AsoCS technical Repore 97001, Vienna, Austria May 978.

[9]   Stevan Harnad, "Grounding Symbolic Capacity in Robotic Capacity," Building Situated Embodied Agents, ed. L. Steels & R. Brooks, Lawrence Erlbaum Assoc 1990.

[10] John Pollock, "Planning Agents," Foundations of Rational Agency, ed. Rao and Wooldridge, Kluwer Academic Publishers 1999; ISBN: 0792356012

[11] Douglas Hofstadter, Fluid Concepts and Creative Analogies, Basic Books 1995 ISBN 0-465-02475-0

[12] Luc Steels, "Exploiting Analogical Representations," Designing Autonomous Agents, ed. Pattie Maes, MIT Press 1990, ISBN 0-262-63135-0.

[13] Janet Kolodner, Case Based Reasoning, Morgan Kaufman Publishers 1993, ISBN 0-7923-9075-X.

[14] Constantin von Altrock, Fuzzy Logic & Neurofuzzy Applications Explained, Prentice-Hall 1995, ISBN 0-13-368465-2

[15] Earl Cox, The Fuzzy Systems Handbook, Acedemic Press, ISBN 0-12-194455-7.

[16] S. Goodridge, "A Fuzzy Behavior-Based Nervous System for an Autonomous Mobile Robot," Master's Thesis, North Carolina State University, 1994.

[17] Simon Parsons, Ola Pettersson, Alessandro Saffiotti, Michael Wooldridge, "Robots with the Best of Intentions", Artificial Intelligence Today, pages 329-338, Springer Verlag 1987; ISBN: 3540664289   url   =   "citeseer.nj.nec.com/196598.html"

[18] The Robot's Dilemma Revisited: The Frame Problem in Artificial Intelligence, ed. Kenneth M. Ford & Zenon W. Pylyshyn, Ablex Publishing Corporation 1996 ISBN 1-56750-143-5

[19] Ulrike Hann & Nick Chater, "Concepts and Similarity," Knowledge, Concepts and Categories, ed. K. Lamberts and D. Shanks, MIT Press 1997, ISBN 0-262-62118-5.

[20] Koen Lamberts, "Process Models of Categorization," Knowledge, Concepts and Categories, ed. K. Lamberts and D. Shanks, MIT Press 1997, ISBN 0-262-62118-5.

[21] Elenor Rosch, On the Internal Structure of Perceptual and Semantic Catego-
      ries,Cognitive Development and the Acquisition of Language, ed. Timothy
      Moore, Academic Press New York 1973.

[22] [Zadeh 96] Lofti Zadeh, Fuzzy Sets, Fuzzy Logic and Fuzzy Systems: Selected
      Papers by Lofti A. Zadeh, ed. George J. Klir & Bo Yuan. World Scientific
      1996, ISBN 9810224222.

[23] H. J. Zimmermann, Fuzzy Set Theory and its Applications, Kluwer Academic
      Press 1991, ISBN 0-7923-9075-X.

Seven Days in the Life of a Robotic Agent

Waiyian Chong[1], Mike O'Donovan-Anderson[2], Yoshi Okamoto[2,3], and
Don Perlis[1,2]

[1] Department of Computer Science, University of Maryland, College Park, MD 20742
[2] Institute for Advanced Computer Studies, University of Maryland
[3] Department of Linguistics, University of Maryland
{yuan,mikeoda,yoshi,perlis}@cs.umd.edu

Abstract. Bootstrapping is a widely employed technique in the process
of building highly complex systems such as microprocessors, language
compilers, and computer operating systems. It could play an even more
prominent role in the creation of computation systems capable of supporting intelligent agent behaviors because of the even higher level of
complexity. The prospect of a self-bootstrapping, self-improving intelligent system has motivated various fields of research in machine learning.
However, a robust, generalizable methodology of machine learning is yet
to be found; there are still a lot of learning behaviors that no existing
learning technique can adequately account for. We believe a uniform,
logic-based system such as active logic [1, 2], will be more successful in
the realization of this ideal. The overall architecture that we envision is
as follows: a central commonsense reasoner module attends to novel situations where the system does not already have expertise, and to its own
failures; it then reasons its way to solutions or repairs, and puts these
into action while at the same time causing "expert" modules to be either
created or retrained so as to more quickly enact those solutions on future
occasions. Thus what we propose is a kind of meld between declarative
and procedural techniques where the former has great expressive power
and flexibility (but is slow) and the latter is very fast but hard to adapt
to new situations. We will explore the possibilities of using reflection and
continual computation toward this end.

1 Introduction

A unifying theme of AI research is the design of an architecture for allowing an
intelligent agent to operate in a *common sense informatic situation* [3], where
the agent's perception (hence its knowledge about the world) is incomplete, uncertain and subjected to change; and the effect of its actions indeterministic and
unreliable. There are many reasons (e.g., scientific, philosophical, practical) to
study intelligent agent architecture; for our purposes, we will define our goal
as to improve the performance of the agent, where performance is in turn defined as resources (time, energy, etc) spent in completing given tasks. We are
interested in the question "What is the best strategy to build an agent which
can perform competently in a common sense informatic situation?" It is clear

W. Truszkowski, C. Rouff, M. Hinchey (Eds.): WRAC 2002, LNAI 2564, pp. 243–253, 2003.

that it will be impractical for the designer of the agent to anticipate everything it may encounter in such a situation; hence it is essential that some routes of self-improvement be provided for the agent if it is to attain reasonable level of autonomy. What should we provide to the architecture to open these routes?

For an agent to function competently in commonsense world, we can expect the underlying architecture to be highly complex. Careful attention should be paid to the designing process, as well as the designed artifact to ensure success. We identified the following requirements to guide our design: (i) In addition to fine-tuning of specialized modules the agent might have, more fundamental aspects of the architecture should be open to self-improvement. For example, an agent designed to interact with people may have a face recognition module; a learning algorithm to improve its face recognition accuracy is of course desirable, but it is not likely to be helpful for the agent to cope with unexpected changes in the world. (ii) Improvements need to be made reasonably efficiently. It's said that a roomful of monkeys typing away diligently at their keyboards will eventually produce the complete works of Shakespeare; in the same vein, we can imagine a genetic algorithm, given enough time and input, can evolve a sentient being, but the time it takes will likely be too long for us to withstand. (iii) Somewhat related to the previous two points, it is important to stress that the improvements made be transparent to us so that we can incrementally provide more detailed knowledge and guidance when necessary to speed up the improvements.

Toward building an intelligent agent, we can borrow a few lessons from builders of other sophisticated systems: in particular, the technique of bootstrapping is of relevance. Bootstrapping technique has been widely employed in the process of building highly complex systems such as microprocessors, language compilers, and computer operating systems. It could play an even more prominent role in the creation of computation systems capable of supporting intelligent agent behaviors, because of the even higher level of complexity. Typically in a bootstrapping process, a lower-level infrastructural system is first built "by hand"; the complete system is then built, within the system itself, utilizing the more powerful constructs provided by the infrastructure. Hence, it provides benefits in the ways of saving effort as well as managing complexity.

Ideally, as designers of the agent, we'd like to push as much work as possible to be automated and carried out by computer. There is no doubt that the study of specialized algorithms has been making great contributions to the realization of intelligent agency; however, we think that the study of bootstrapping behavior may be a more economical way to achieve that goal. Instead of designing the specialized modules ourselves, we should instead look for way to provide the infrastructure on which agents can discover and devise the modules themselves.

Once we accept bootstrapping as a reasonable way to proceed, a few natural questions arise: What constructs are needed in the infrastructure to support the bootstrapping of intelligence? How should they be combined? How should they operate? More generally, if we leave alone a robot agent in a reasonably rich environment for a long period of time, what will enable the robot to evolve itself into a more competitive agent? How do we provide a path for the agent to improve itself? We think an example will help us to answer the questions! In the next section, we will tell the story of Al the office robot, to show the importance and desirability of self-improving capability in an artificial agent. In light of the typical problems that a robot may encounter in the real world, the following two sections (Sec 3 and Sec 4) present a more detailed account of two key ideas: reflection and continual computation, which we think are essential to the success of the robot, and argue that the uniformity and expressiveness of a logic-based system can facilitate the implementation of complex agency. In section 5, we will give a brief introduction to Active Logic, the theoretical base of our implementation, and discuss why we think this approach is promising. It is nonetheless clear that there are still very many problems to solve before Al can be more than science fiction.

2   Seven Days in the Life of Al

Let us consider Al, a robot powered by active logic. Al is an "office robot", who roams the CS office building delivering documents, coffee, etc. Al was endowed at birth with the desire to make people happy. We will see how Al developed into an excellent office robot of great efficiency through its first week of work.

1st Day: Al was first given a tour of the building. Among other things, it was shown the power outlets scattered around the building so that it could recharge itself.

2nd Day: The morning went well: Al delivered everything on target. But during the afternoon Al ran into a problem: it found itself unable to move! The problem was soon diagnosed — it was simply a low battery. (Since thinking draws less energy than moving, Al could still think.) It turned out that although Al knew it needed power to operate and it could recharge itself to restore its battery, it had never occurred to Al that, "it would need to reach an outlet before the power went too low for it to move!" [1] The movement failure triggered Al to derive the above conclusion, but it was too late; Al was stuck, and could not deliver coffee on request. Caffeine deprived computer scientists are not happy human beings; Al had a bad day.

3rd Day: Al was bailed out of the predicament by its supervisor in the morning. Having learned its lesson, Al decided to find an outlet a few minutes before the battery got too low. Unfortunately for Al, optimal route planning for robot navigation is an NP-complete problem. When Al finally found an optimal path to the nearest power outlet, its battery level was well below what it needed to move, and Al was stuck again. Since there was nothing else it could do, Al decided to surf the web (through the wireless network!), and came upon an interesting article titled "Deadline-Coupled Real-time Planning" [4].

4th Day: After reading the paper, Al understood that planning takes time, and that it couldn't afford to find an optimal plan when its action is time critical.

---

[1] Counter to traditional supposition that all derivable formulas are already present in the system.

Al decided to quickly pick the outlet in sight when its battery was low. Unfortunately, the outlet happened to be too far away, and Al ran out of power again before reaching it. In fact, there was a closer outlet just around the corner; but since a non-optimal algorithm was used, Al missed it. Again, stuck with nothing else to do, Al kicked into the "meditation" mode where it called the Automated Discovery (AD) module to draw new conclusions based on the facts it accumulated these few days. Al made some interesting discoveries: upon inspecting the history of its observations and reasonings, Al found that there were only a few places it frequented; it could actually precompute the optimal routes from those places to the nearest outlets. Al spent all night computing those routes.

Meanwhile, Al also built a special-purpose (procedural) navigator module NM to navigate to those routes, so that (i) the navigation would be faster and (ii) it could spend more time attending to other matters such as sorting mail for delivery (this being a more error-prone task requiring commonsense analysis).

5th Day: This morning, Al's AD module derived an interesting theorem: "if the battery power level is above 97% of capacity when Al starts (and nothing bad happened along the way), it can reach an outlet before the power is exhausted." Al didn't get stuck that day. But people found Al to be not very responsive. Later, it was found that Al spent most of its time around the outlets recharging itself — since Al's power level dropped 3% for every 10 minutes, the theorem above led it to conclude that it needed to go to the outlet every 10 minutes.

It also turned out that two of the power outlets it used for recharging became inoperative and AL had to deliberately (reason its way to) override its navigator module NM, and retrain it to avoid those outlets.

6th Day: After Al's routine introspection before work, it was revealed that the knowledge base was populated with millions of theorems similar to the one it found the day before, but with the power level at 11%, 12%, ..., and so on. In fact, the theorem is true when the power level is above 10% of capacity. Luckily, there was a meta-rule in Al's knowledge base saying that "a theorem subsumed by another is less interesting;" thus all the theorems with parameter above 10% were discarded. Equipped with this newer, more accurate information, Al concluded that it could get away with recharging itself every 5 hours.

7th Day: That happened to be Sunday. Nobody was coming to the office. Al spent its day contemplating the meaning of life.

Analyzing the behavior of Al, we can see a few mechanisms at play: in addition to the basic deductive reasoning, goal directed behavior, etc., Al also demonstrates capabilities such as abductive reasoning (diagnoses of failures), explanation-based learning (compilation of navigation rules, derivation of recharging rules), reflection (examining and reasoning about its power reading, revision of recharging rule), and time-sensitivity (understanding that deliberations take time, people don't like waiting, etc). Of course, none of these is new in itself; however, the interactions among them has enabled Al to demonstrate remarkable flexibility and adaptivity in a ill-anticipated (by the designer of Al) and changing world. Below, we will elaborate on the reflective capability and the continual aspect of the agent's operations.

3   Reflection

A computational system is said to be reflective when it is itself part of its own domain (and in a causally connected way). More precisely, this implies that (i) the system has an internal representation of itself, and (ii) the system can engage in both "normal" computation about the external domain and "reflective" computation about itself [5]. Hence, reflection can provide a principled mechanism for the system to modify itself in a profound way.

We suggest that a useful strategy for a self-improving system is to use reflection in the service of self-training. Just as a human agent might deliberately practice a useful task, increasing her efficiency until (as we say) it can be done "unconsciously" or "automatically", without explicit reasoning, we think that once a reflective system identifies an algorithm or other method for solving a frequently encountered problem, it should be able to create procedural modules to implement the chosen strategy, so as to be able in the future to accomplish its task(s) more efficiently, without fully engaging its (slow and expensive) commonsense reasoning abilities.

Although reflection sounds attractive, it has largely been ignored by researchers of agent architecture, mainly because of the high computation complexity involved in doing reflective reasoning. However, we think the solution to the problem is not by avoiding reflection, but looking at the larger picture and considering the environment and extent in which an agent operates, and finding way to reap the benefits of reflection without being bogged down by its cost. We think the notion of continual computation is a promising venue for reflection to become useful.

4   Continual Computation

Any newcomer to the field of AI will soon find out that, almost without exception, all "interesting" problems are NP-hard. When a computer scientist is confronted with a hard problem, there are several options to deal with it. For example, one can simplify the problem by assuming it occurs only under certain conditions (which are not always realistic) and hoping bad cases don't happen frequently. One can also identify a simpler subproblem so that it can be solved algorithmically and automated, and leave the hard part for the human. Another option is for the scientist to study the problem carefully, derive some heuristics, and hope that they will be adequate most of the time. But none of these is quite satisfying: ideally, we would like the computer to do as much work for us as possible, and hopefully, be able to derive the heuristics by itself. A promising approach toward realizing this ideal is the notion of *continual computation* [6].

The main motivation behind continual computation is to exploit the *idle time* of a computation system. As exemplified by usage patterns of desktop computers, workstations, web-servers, etc. of today, most computer systems are under utilized: in typical employments of these systems, relatively long spans of inactivity are interrupted with bursts of computation intensive tasks, where the systems are taxed to their limits. How can we make use of the idle time to help improve performance during critical time?

Continual computation generalizes the definition of a *problem* to encompass the uncertain stream of challenges faced over time. One way to analyze this problem is to put it into the framework of probability and utility, or more generally, rational decision making:

> Policies for guiding the precomputation and caching of complete or partial solutions of potential future problems are targeted at enhancing the expected value of future behavior. The policies can be harnessed to allocate periods of time traditionally viewed as idle time between problems, as well as to consider the value of redirecting resources that might typically be allocated to solving a definite, current problem to the precomputation of responses to potential future challenges under uncertainty[7].

An implicit assumption of the utility-based work in continual computation is that the future is somehow predictable. But in many cases, this cannot be expected. For example, for long term planning, most statistics will probably lose their significance. Here is a place where logic-based systems with the capability to derive or discover theorems on its own (e.g., Lenat's AM system) can play a complementary role, similar to the way that mathematics plays a complementary role to engineering. Just as mathematicians usually do not rely on immediate reward to guide their research (yet discover theorems of utmost utility), AM can function in a way independent of the immediate utility of its work.

More precisely, if we adopt logic as our base for computation and look at problem solving as theorem proving [8], a system capable of discovering new theorems can become a very attractive model of a continual computation system. In such a system, every newly discovered theorem has the potential of simplifying the proof of future theorem; so in essence, theorems become our universal format for caching the results of precomputation and partial solutions to problems.

A simplistic embodiment of the model can just be a forward chaining system capable of combining facts in its database to produce new theorems using modus ponens, for instance. Such a system is not likely to be very useful, however, because it will spend most of its time deriving uninteresting theorems. So the success of this model of continual computation will hinge on whether we can find meaningful criteria for the "interestingness" of a theorem. In the classical AM [9, 10, 11], the system relies largely on human judgment determine interestingness. In a survey of several automated discovery programs, Colton and Bundy [12] identify several properties of concepts which seem to be relevant to their interestingness, such as novelty, surprisingness, understandability, existence of models and possibly true conjectures about them. Although these properties seem plausible, it is not obvious they are precise enough to be operational to guide automated discovery programs toward significant results.

5   Toward Implementation

Considering for a moment a few general requirements for a real-world agent like Al, it is obvious, first of all, that Al must perceive its environment. Further, if it is to reason about what he perceives, and use this reasoning to guide its actions, it must be capable of coming to have perceptually grounded empirical beliefs.[2] But the world is always changing, and if Al's beliefs are going to be useful, they would best reflect the world as it actually is — and that means that Al must be capable of forming new beliefs, and revising or getting rid of old beliefs, in response to real-time perceptual input from the world. Al's belief system, that is to say, must be appropriately reactive.

But it is clear that reactivity is not enough. For in any reasoning system, where new beliefs are constantly being derived from old ones, reactivity introduces a difficult problem: if a belief which is an antecedent condition in a sequence of reasoning itself changes, then the consequents of that sequence may be invalidated. Al must be able to recognize when this happens, and take appropriate steps to solve the problem. Thus, Al needs to be a perceiver, a believer, a reasoner, and a meta-reasoner, capable of reasoning not just *with* its beliefs, but *about* them. Further (and crucial to the possibility of boot-strapping), Al is concerned not just with meeting its various first-order goals (delivering coffee, recharging) in light of the changing environment in which it acts, but also in fulfilling second-order goals [13] — goals about what sort of agent to become — such as increased efficiency. Meta-reasoning in light of these second-order desires is a somewhat complicated and delicate task, for it can involve not just deciding how to do something, but deciding how to decide to do it, as when Al builds a special navigator module to compute paths to the various charging stations. Al, this is to say, must be both reactive and reflective, attending not just to the external world, but also to its own mind, finding ways to bring about its goals and desires in both spheres.

Al, therefore, must be able to recognize and react to changes in the environment, and to deal with the contradictions, irregularities, and invalidated conclusions that this will involve; further, in choosing when and how to act, it must be able to consider not just how best to achieve a given goal in light of the state of the world, but also which goals are the best to achieve, and which methods of achieving them are best given the sort of agent it wants to become.[3]

---

[2] For a simple example of why perceptions are not enough, consider that when Al needs to charge itself, it may not be able, at that moment, to perceive a charging station. In this case it will need to *remember* where (the nearest) one is; thus even this basic action requires both perception (that his battery is low) and belief (that there is a station around the corner).

[3] Interestingly, Aristotle's notion of character — roughly, a stable disposition for choosing which goals to achieve and which methods to employ in so doing — is more useful in understanding an agent like Al than are more modern notions of choice and agency, in which a radically free act of the will plays a larger role. For it is clear that the more decisions Al makes about what sort of agent to become — the more specialized modules and simple, reactive, procedural systems it builds for dealing with everyday,

Together, this suggests the need for extremely rich representations of AI's beliefs, goals, and desires, sufficient to support robust meta-reasoning. What is needed, then, for the reasoning engine of a real-world agent, is something reactive, flexible and expressive, a reasoning system in which beliefs can be added, changed, and removed in real-time without disrupting the reasoning process, and which can support introspection and meta-reasoning. Active Logic was designed, and is being continually developed, with these desiderata in mind.

As is detailed in, e.g., [18, 1, 19] active logic is one of a family of inference engines (step-logics) that explicitly reason in time, and incorporate a history of their reasoning as they run. Motivated in part by the thought that human reasoning takes place step-wise, in time—and that this feature supports human mental flexibility—Active Logic works by combining inference rules with a constantly evolving measure of time (a "Now") that can itself be referenced in those rules. As an example, from $Now(t)$—the time is now "t"—one infers $Now(t+1)$, for the fact of an inference implies that time (at least one 'time-step') has passed. All the inference rules in Active Logic work temporally in this way: at each time-step all possible one step inferences are made, and only propositions derived at time t are available for inferences at time $t+1$. There are special persistence rules so that every theorem α present at time t implies itself at time $t+1$; likewise there are special rules so that if the knowledge base contains both a theorem α and its negation $\neg\alpha$, these theorems and their consequences are "distrusted" so they are neither carried forward themselves nor used in further inference. These features, along with a quotation mechanism allowing theorems to refer to each other, give active logic the expressive and inferential power to monitor its own reasoning in a real-time fashion, as that very reasoning is going on, allowing it to watch for errors (such as mismatches between the environment and expectations), to note temporal aspects of actions or reasoning (an approaching deadline, or that progress is or is not occurring) which might dictate the adoption of a different goal or strategy, and to exert reasoned control over its past and upcoming inferential processes, including re-examination and alteration of beliefs and inferences. Active logic therefore supports flexible reasoning, and is well suited for complex and ever-changing real-world contexts like autonomous agency and human-computer dialog.

A simple example of active logic inference is shown, below.

$$i : Now(i), A, A \rightarrow B$$
$$i+1 : Now(i+1), A, A \rightarrow B, B$$

Here i and $i+1$ in the left margin indicate time steps, and the propositions to the right are (some of) the beliefs in the KB at those times. Among the latter

---

common situations — the more ossified its reactions to the world will become, and the more difficult it will be to change. Balancing the need for spontaneity against that for stability and efficiency is at the core of agency, both human and artificial. For more on the tensions of agency see, e.g. [14, 15]; for more on Aristotelian notions of character [16, 17].

are beliefs of the form $Now(t)$, i.e., the logic "knows" what time it is. This time-stratified knowledge representation and reasoning is crucial to many applications of active logics, from deadline-coupled planning [4], to time-sensitive inference in general [1], to contradiction-detection [20], to discourse pragmatics [21, 22] (allowing the introduction of temporal subtleties into certain formal treatments of presupposition such as [23]).

In the example above, at step $i + 1$, B has just been inferred from A and $A \to B$ at step i. Also illustrated is the fact that beliefs at one step need not be "inherited" to the next, e.g., $Now(i)$ is not inherited to step $i + 1$. This disinheritance feature can also be applied to other beliefs, and is important in dealing with contradictory beliefs. When contradictions are encountered, active logic can, first of all, disinherit the contradictands so they do not cause further untrustworthy beliefs, and second, retrace its history of inferences to examine what led to the contradiction, performing metareasoning concerning which of these warrants continued belief [20, 21]. (For certain domains in which the automated system is a helper or advice-taker, it can also simply pass along the contradictory situation to a human user and await advice.) Indeed, a primary aim of our research into active logics has been to explore the extent to which contradictions may be categorized and generic strategies found that successfully resolve particular contradiction types. The central point for now, however, is that our use of active logic is based on its expressive power, and its ability to support the kinds of metareasoning we appear to need for a fully situated agency.

In addition to providing support for the desiderata mentioned above — flexible, non-monotonic, real-time reasoning — active logic's time-sensitivity helped Al in other ways. For instance, the fact that Al recognized that its reasoning itself took time allowed it to realize that optimality is not necessarily desirable, especially when there is a deadline approaching. More fundamentally, the active logic treatment of time allowed Al to keep track of changes: that the battery level is X now does not imply that this is still true 5 hours later; active logic's $Now(i)$ predicate provides a natural and efficient way to deal with both reasoning *in* time, and also reasoning *about* time. Further, the history mechanism in active logic gave Al an opportunity to spot certain pattern in its past behavior, which helped it improve its future behavior (or, speaking more generally, the time-situatedness of Al's reasoning provides a natural framework to capture the future-orientation of agency, and the past-orientation required by learning).

Finally, because of the uniformity of a logic-based system, precomputation is seamlessly integrated into goal based problem solving through forward- and backward-chaining reasoning mechanisms. And the expressiveness of active logic made it possible to store the meta-rules about such things as interestingness of theorems, or the value and meaning of efficiency, which gave Al the basis for certain kinds of bootstrapping. These features allow for learning behavior without traditional learning mechanisms (explanation base learning, inductive learning, etc.) being explicitly programmed.

6   Conclusions

The so called *No Free Lunch Theorem* [24] states that "all algorithms that search for an extremum of a cost function perform exactly the same, when averaged over all possible cost functions." In other words, without domain specific structural assumptions of the problem, no algorithm can be expected to perform better on average than simple blind search. This result appears to be a cause for pessimism for researchers hoping to devise domain-independent methods to improve problem solving performance. But on the other hand, this theorem also provides compelling reason for embracing the notion of continual computation, which can be seen as a way to exploit domain dependent information in a domain independent way.

However, to take advantage of continual computation, we need to be able to express the concept of interestingness in a way sufficient to guide computation to profitable direction. Interestingness touches on the ultimate uncertainty: what to do next? Although utility theory has its place, we argued that there are aspects of interestingness not susceptible to utility based analysis. We believe that a forward and backward chaining capable logic system such as active logic, with its expressiveness, time sensitivity, and reflective ability to reason about theorems, proofs and derivations, is well-positioned to take advantage of the opportunity offered by continual computation, and can serve as a solid basis for the realization of intelligent agency.

References

[1] Elgot-Drapkin, J., Perlis, D.: Reasoning situated in time I: Basic concepts. Journal of Experimental and Theoretical Artificial Intelligence **2** (1990) 75–98 243, 250, 251

[2] Elgot-Drapkin, J., Kraus, S., Miller, M., Nirkhe, M., Perlis, D.: Active logics: A unified formal approach to episodic reasoning. Technical report, Computer Science Department, University of Maryland (1996) 243

[3] McCarthy, J.: Artificial intelligence, logic and formalizing common sense. In Thomason, R., ed.: Philosophical Logic and Artificial Intelligence. Klüver Academic (1989) 243

[4] Nirkhe, M., Kraus, S., Miller, M., Perlis, D.: How to (plan to) meet a deadline between *now* and *then*. Journal of logic computation **7** (1997) 109–156 245, 251

[5] Maes, P.: Issues in computational reflection. In Maes, D. N. P., ed.: Meta-Level Architectures and Reflection. Elsevier Science Publishers B. V. (North-Holland) (1988) 21–35 247

[6] Horvitz, E.: Models of continual computation. In: Proceedings of the 14th National Conference on Artificial Intelligence and 9th Innovative Applications of Artificial Intelligence Conference (AAAI-97/IAAI-97), Menlo Park, AAAI Press (1997) 286–293 247

[7] Horvitz, E.: Principles and applications of continual computation. Artificial Intelligence **126** (2001) 159–196 248

[8] Bibel, W.: Let's plan it deductively! In: IJCAI. (1997) 1549–1562 248

[9] Lenat, D. B. In: AM: Discovery in Mathematics as Heuristic Search. McGraw-Hill, New York, NY (1982) 1–225 248

[10] Lenat, D. B.: Theory Formation by Heuristic Search. Artificial Intelligence **21** (1983) 31–59 **248**

[11] Lenat, D. B., Brown, J. S.: Why AM and EURISKO appear to work. Artificial Intelligence **23** (1984) 269–294 **248**

[12] Colton, S., Bundy, A.: On the notion of interestingness in automated mathematical discovery. In: AISB Symposium on AI and Scientific Discovery. (1999) **248**

[13] Frankfurt, H.: The Importance of What We Care About. Cambridge University Press, Cambridge, UK (1988) **249**

[14] Bratman, M.: Faces of Intention. Cambridge University Press, Cambridge, UK (1999) **250**

[15] Bratman, M. E.: Intention, Plans, and Practical Reason. Harvard University Press (1987) **250**

[16] Aristotle: Nicomachean Ethics. N/A (350BC) **250**

[17] Broadie, S.: Ethics with Aristotle. Oxford University Press, Oxford, UK (1995) **250**

[18] Elgot-Drapkin, J., Kraus, S., Miller, M., Nirkhe, M., Perlis, D.: Active logics: A unified formal approach to episodic reasoning. Technical report, Computer Science Department, University of Maryland (1996) **250**

[19] Purang, K., Purushothaman, D., Traum, D., Andersen, C., Traum, D., Perlis, D.: Practical reasoning and plan execution with active logic. In: Proceedings of the IJCAI'99 Workshop on Practical Reasoning and Rationality. (1999) **250**

[20] Miller, M., Perlis, D.: Presentations and this and that: logic in action. In: Proceedings of the 15th Annual Conference of the Cognitive Science Society, Boulder, Colorado (1993) **251**

[21] Gurney, J., Perlis, D., Purang, K.: Interpreting presuppositions using active logic: From contexts to utterances. Computational Intelligence **13** (1997) 391–413 **251**

[22] Traum, D., Andersen, C., Chong, Y., Josyula, D., O'Donovan-Anderson, M., Okamoto, Y., Purang, K., Perlis, D.: Representations of dialogue state for domain and task independent meta-dialogue. Electronic Transactions on Artificial Intelligence (forthcoming) **251**

[23] Heim, I.: Presupposition projection and the semantics of attitude verbs. Journal of Semantics **9** (1992) 183–221 **251**

[24] Wolpert, D. H., Macready, W. G.: No free lunch theorems for optimization. IEEE Transactions on Evolutionary Computation **1** (1997) 67–82 **252**

Part V

Communication and Coordination

In Search of Simple and Responsible Agents

Henry Hexmoor and Gordon Beavers

Computer Science & Computer Engineering Department
Engineering Hall, Room 313, Fayetteville, AR 72701
{hexmoor,gordonb}@uark.edu

1   Introduction

An artificial agent is a computational entity (embodied or otherwise) that interacts with other agents and/or real-world entities. Being reactive is a standard property of agents. The agents considered here exhibit various degrees of sociability in the form of norms, roles, values, cooperation, motives, responsibilities, autonomies, and rights. Intentional agents have been modeled in multi-modal BDI logics, e.g. [8], with operators for belief, desire, and intention. This paper proposes the integration of social notions into BDI agent architectures to account for social decision-making. Although a large collection of notions is needed to explain the actions of complex social agents, this paper provides a somewhat simplified model of social agents built on a small set of agent properties (norms and values) and intentional notions (obligations). Since this model is a starting point for the investigation of social agents, it is expected that the model will be improved and expanded as the result of further research.

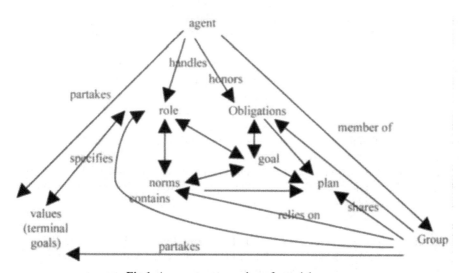

Fig.1. An agent as a member of a social group

W. Truszkowski, C. Rouff, M. Hinchey (Eds.): WRAC 2002, LNAI 2564, pp. 257-268, 2003.
© Springer-Verlag Berlin Heidelberg 2003

Figure 1 shows some of the influences among social agents, groups and social notions that a model should take into account. The figure has been simplified to emphasize the most salient features of sociality. The reality is much more complex and many of the relationships shown are part of ongoing research projects, however, our aim is to set the stage to discuss issues at a more abstract level.

As an example of the potential complexity that the model presented here avoids, values (or guiding principles) can have varying scope in terms of the set of agents to which they apply. Principles may guide the actions of individuals, groups, societies, or even be global guides to behavior. In this paper, in order to reduce the computational complexity of the model, principles will be taken to be constraints that are determined by roles, so that principles can be modeled with a filter on possible worlds[1]. These principles are terminal goals that any agent would be expected to observe when assuming the given role. Further developments might allow a group to set the principles to which its members will adhere with each agent helping to determine these principles, however, at this early stage in the development of social agents, principles will be determined off-line and will remain fixed. Values are things like "always cooperate with team members". When the group adopts a joint intention, the members of the group will negotiate a division of responsibilities, which determines the roles assumed by each agent. An individual role will normally be fulfilled in a standard way, that is, each role will imply a set of norms that the agent is expected to comply with in addition to the principles that it will observe. Norms and principles are at opposite ends of an abstract to concrete continuum of entities that generate obligations. Although there are complex relationships among roles, norms, and goals so that an agent might be expected to weigh the alternatives against one another in order to settle on a consistent set of intentions at any moment, only the simplest relationships will be treated in this model. The simplicity of the model will enable agents to use the relationships to predict the behavior of other agents.

Our legal system holds the owners of software agents responsible for the actions of those agents, therefore, agents capable of considering their responsibilities could offer some protection to the owner of the agent. Such software agents might be agents involved in electronic commerce, automated teller machines, proxy email agents, or robot assistants. Likewise in a command and control situation, a commander is responsible for the actions of the agents under his/her control and therefore would have greater confidence in responsible agents capable of considering the repercussions of their actions. The model proposed here allows agents to consider their individual responsibilities and thereby the model makes it possible for the agents to account for their actions. Having responsible agents will provide a safeguard to the owner of the agent as well as help the agent arbitrate practical actions and to recognize legal violations by other agents.

---

[1] Possible world semantics is a logical formalism for modal logic. See [Chellas, 1984]. Intuitively speaking, possible worlds capture the various ways the world might develop. Since the formalism in [Wooldridge 2000] assumes at least a KD axiomatization for each of B, D, and I, each of the sets of possible worlds representing B, D and I must be consistent. Since it is unreasonable to assume that an agent's set of desires is consistent we adopt a slightly different semantics from that found in Wooldridge.

Principles and norms guide the behavior of the agent through the generation of particular obligations. Responsibility is a general term covering principles, norms and the obligations that are generated by principles and norms. Responsible agents are true to their principles, obey the norms of behavior in specific situations, and take their obligations seriously. Varieties of responsibility include *responsibility to* concerning an agent's obligation to perform an action, *responsibility for* concerning an agent's obligation to see that a state of affairs obtains, *character responsibility* is the agent's obligation to behave in accordance with its principles, which are general and abstract, and its *norms* which are particular and concrete. The agent has an obligation to observe the norms that apply to a given situation. Whereas responsibilities tend to restrict the agent's choices, rights leave certain choices open and thus can be used to explore the limits of actions permitted to the agent. The relationships between rights and responsibilities regulate the agent's commitments.

2   VON-BDI Architecture

In this section we present an architecture for an individual agent. This architecture relates the interaction feedback loops we saw earlier in greater detail. Figure 2 shows the following feedback loops that are internal to an agent: belief, intention, attention, conversation, obligation and role. We call these feedback loops revision functions. In all, six feedback loops are shown as rounded comparator circle attached to each[2]. Desire does not have a revision function. This is partly because inconsistent desires are allowed and the set of desires changes less often. Desires are reassessed when intentions and beliefs change. Revision functions monitor prevailing conditions and maintain an agent's commitments by implementing revisions only when necessary. For example, the attention revision function has an agent maintain its attention on particular agents until the condition that justifies the attention no longer obtains. Planning, like desire determination, is a function, but not a "revision function". This is because intention revision is responsible for guiding planning when it becomes necessary [4]. In addition to the intentional notions of Belief, Desire, and Intention (BDI), Value, Obligation, and Norm (VON) are three notions that will prove useful in adding social properties to artificial agents. Taken together, they guide an agent's high-level behavior and help to provide a level of predictability, accountability, and responsibility. Values are understood as principles that govern the agent's behavior and which the agent will attempt to uphold as end-goals. Likewise, norms yield default behaviors that the agent is expected to observe whenever the agent finds itself in a situation to which the norm applies. We invoke a function that maps an agent a, a set of currently imposed values V, a set N of currently active norms, and a set of current Beliefs B to a set of obligations for the agent in that situation: $f: a \times V \times N \times B \rightarrow \{o1, \dots, on\}$.

---

[2] Figure 2 contains an abbreviated rendering of Feedback loops with the comparator circle gathering inputs. The feedback arc in each loop is not shown for brevity.

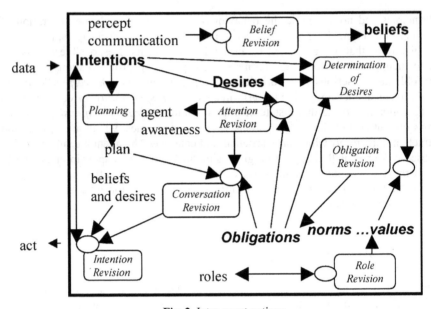

Fig. 2. Intra-agent notions

Figure 2 shows the salient relationships among VON-BDI concepts. These relationships are incorporated in an algorithm provided later. For instance the revision function for attention revision has obligations and intentions as inputs, and produces cues for the agent to be aware of certain other agents. Intentions are derived from the states of VON-BDI as determined by an intention revision function. In the model being developed all the elements of VON-BDI play a part in the determination of the revised set of desires, since it is reasonable to assume that current desires will influence future desires as will beliefs, intentions, values, obligations and norms. In this model obligations reflect the influence of principles and norms on the behavior of the agent. We see Values and Norms on a strong to weak continuum of tenets to uphold. Principles will be viewed as more general and abstract, e.g., "do no gratuitous harm" while norms are considered more specific and concrete, e.g., "when in area A and moving at a speed of one meter per second or faster make sure that there are no obstacles within a range of five meters". Norms are determined by roles and designate a range of behaviors that are consistent with the agent's having adopted a given role. When an agent accepts a role, the agent is expected to acquire the set of norms that are appropriate to the role and include them in the agent's set of beliefs. In natural agents some norms are characteristic behaviors that evolve over time in response to selective pressures while other norms are conventions selected through deliberation. Again, for simplicity in this early model, norms are to be determined off-line and thus are not alterable by the agents. The set of all obligations active at a given time may not be consistent; the intention determination function needs to select a consistent set of obligations to be honored. Since this is a computationally intensive task, we suggest a function running in the background continuously check for consistency of intentions and obligations. Norms and values differ in specificity. "When fulfilling the role of an ATM, always offer a receipt for each transaction" is a norm that can be rephrased as an obligation "ATMs ought to offer receipts for transactions" or as a fact "ATMs offer receipts for transactions". The specificity and concreteness of this standard suggest that it is a norm. In contrast "always cooperate with team members" is more general and abstract, in part because what constitutes cooperation requires interpretation. So "always cooperate with team members" is a principle. Obligations are implemented as modal operators, with distinct obligations having distinct operators. If agent A and agent B are both on the same team as agent C, then "agent C ought to cooperate with agent A" and "agent C ought to cooperate with agent B" are distinct obligations. Distinct obligations yield distinct modal operators in order to accommodate conflict of obligation without having the logical system degenerate into triviality.

Determining desires is as difficult as determining obligations. Wooldrige [8, page 32] suggests using an "option generating" function with inputs a set of beliefs and a set of intentions and output a set of desires. However, Wooldridge does not inform us about how this function goes about determining the resulting set of desires. In the model developed here all the elements of VON-BDI are assumed to play a part in the determination of the revised set of desires, since it is reasonable to assume that current desires will influence future desires as will beliefs, intentions, values, obligations and norms. Wooldridge requires that beliefs, desires and intentions all be consistent sets. Unlike intentions, which agents normally attempt to keep consistent, agents do not require their desires to be consistent and thus our model differs from Woolridge's by having distinct modal operators for distinct desires. Beyond that, social forces provide an influence on an individual agent's desires through obligations. This is shown as obligations feeding into the function that will determine the desires. We will continue to refer to this function as the option generator.

Imagine that an agent has a value to "protect oneself from danger" and also has the obligation to perform action α. Suppose that when the sensed data are right for executing α, the agent anticipates that it may come to harm from results of that action, so the value of protecting itself invokes another obligation, which is in conflict with the obligation to perform α. Agents that give more importance to their values are called *principled agents*. If the agent is principled, it may well give greater importance to protecting itself.

It is standard to require that beliefs, desires and intentions all be consistent sets. Unlike intentions, which agents normally attempt to keep consistent, agents do not require their desires to be consistent and thus our model differs from common BDI systems. Beyond that, social forces provide an influence on an individual agent's desires through obligations. Agents with plans might enter negotiation with other agents about obligations and roles. We discuss negotiation in a later section.

1.1   Algorithm

In this section we give a revision of the algorithm on page 32 in [8]. We introduce two flags whose values are determined concurrently with, but outside the algorithm. First $\alpha := \text{fn1}(O)$ which checks the current set of obligations for consistency. Next, $\beta := \text{sound}(\pi, I, B)$ checks the current plan for consistency with current beliefs and intentions. The functions that set these flags are envisioned to be running continuously in the background. When a flag is set that value is communicated to the process in the foreground, namely the algorithm below. For simplicity we assume that an agent's set of values and norms are completely determined by the role that the agent is currently fulfilling and thus V is immutable so long as the agent does not change roles. This algorithm extends that given in Wooldridge in two ways. First, we have introduced an obligation revision function (step 5) that updates the agent's obligations against its norms and values and in light of new percepts. Obligation revision considers the effects of the current beliefs on values and norms. Although we consider values and norms to be immutable in our agents (depending only on roles), their relevance to the current situation is in a constant state of flux.

Our second extension to Wooldridge's algorithm is to make the *options* function (step 7) account for the influences of obligations.

```
1. B = B₀;
2. I := I₀;
3. while true do
4.        get next percept ρ;
5.        O := orf(O,ρ);          // obligation revision, O is obligation
6.        B := brf(B, ρ);         // belief revision, B is beliefs
7.        A := af(I, O);          // attention revision, A is agent awareness
8.        R := rrf(C, r);         // role revision
9.        D := options(B, D, I, O);  // determination of desires, D is desires
10.       I := irf(B, D, I, O);   // intention revision, I is intentions
11.       π := plan(B, I);        // plan generation
12.       C := crf( π, O),        //conversation revision, C is conversational Context
13.       if α and β is true execute(π) else re-compute π
14. end while
```

Fig. 3. Deliberation algorithm

3   Interagent Sociality

Our purpose is to make preliminary suggestions for measures of social characteristics affecting the ability of artificial agents to collectively accomplish a task. The typical situation will have these agents working together to collectively accomplish tasks requiring the coordination of their actions with one another. The coordination can be more or less rigidly determined. If the agent group is highly structured, with well-defined roles that are to be filled in prescribed ways, then the coordination is highly orchestrated and rigid. On the other hand, if the agents in the group are allowed to develop their own structure in response to the environment in which they find themselves, coordination may take an unexpected turn. Since our space is limited, we cannot consider the spectrum of coordination, and thus make some assumptions to constrain the discussion. We consider only what Tuomula [6] calls "plan-based cooperative joint action". This is the simplest of his cooperation types that is explicit and agreement-based between agents who share a plan.

In an earlier work [1], we have argued that in order for an agent to be a member of a team, the agent must recognize itself as a team member and have the intention to cooperate with other team members in the achievement of the common goal.

Tuomela [6] gives the following necessary and sufficient conditions for agents a and b "intentionally acting together" in performing X:

1) X is a collective action type, viz., an "achievement-whole" divided into a's and b 's parts;
2) a and b each intend to perform X together and act in accordance with this intention;
3) a and b each believe that the other will do its part in the performance of X; and
4) a 's and b 's intentions in 2) are in part because of the beliefs in 3).

We leave open the question whether or not the participating agents have come to an agreement about how the goal is to be achieved. It is possible that a powerful manager has imposed intentions and the corresponding roles. This leaves the agents no room for dissent. Agreements also need not be negotiated in the case that a plan has been adopted where the plan specifies actions for each of the team members.

Agents that work together must reciprocate in order to reach equilibrium levels of sociality [7]. This means agents must adjust their own social attitudes in order to experience a sense of fair exchange. In game theory, agent actions that are equilibrium inducing are called *policies*. We borrow this notion from game theory to refer to an agent's mental attitude about social relationships. Here we will briefly outline a few of the attitudes about relationships that help establish equilibrium. For each social attitude, such as, autonomy we will introduce notations that help us refer to a quantity of (or degree of) that attitude. Since our statements apply to all social notions, instead of repeating, we will label the social attitude as v, which is a member of the set of social notions N = {Autonomy, Control, Power, Obligation, Dependence}. There are many works that discuss these social attitudes and have influenced us such as [2]. In this section we state a number of useful definitions and conditions.

Notation:
The maximum amount of v the agent allows itself to tolerate is denoted by v_{max}.
The minimum amount of v the agent allows itself to experience is denoted by v_{min}.
The amount of v the agent actually experiencing is denoted by $v_{experiences}$.
The amount of v the agent wishes to exert is denoted by v_{exerts}.
The actual amount of v the agent achieves is denoted by $v_{accomplishes}$.

Definition 1: Internal Normality
When the amount of social attitude an agent a experiences is between a maximum and a minimum level, the agent's social attitude in general has normal internal condition.

$$v_{min} <= v_{experiences} <= v_{max}$$

The normality condition specifies that an agent may tolerate sociality within its acceptable range and this is perhaps part of the agent's inherent personality. However, when this is violated the agent experiences frustration.

Definition 2: Internal Frustration
If the internal normality condition does not hold, the agent experiences internal frustration.

A frustrated agent may consider announcing its frustration or act it out by changes in a related social notion to rectify the frustration. We will give examples of this later in this section. But first, let's introduce more relationships.

Definition 3: Exchange Normality
When the amount of social attitude an agent b exerts on agent a ($v_{exerts-ba}$) compliments the amount agent b experiences from agent a ($v_{experiences-ab}$), agent a is said in general to have normal exchange condition.

$$v_{experiences-ab} + v_{exerts-ba} = 1$$

Definition 4: Exchange Frustration
If the exchange normality condition (as in definition 3) does not hold, i.e., $v_{experiences-ab} + v_{exerts-ba} = x$, the agent experiences exchange frustration by the amount of $|1-x|$

The amount of exchange frustration for the experiencing agent varies in proportion to discrepancy between exertion and experience.

From above definitions, four combinations are possible combining internal normalcy and frustration and exchange normalcy and frustration. Internal-normalcy-exchange-frustration is clearly an interaction issue. Whereas, internal-frustration-exchange-normalcy is discomfort that the agent must deal with, perhaps by negotiation with the agent who is exerting the influence. Internal-frustration-exchange-frustration is doubly complex since not only is the interaction faulty, but also the agent is experiencing an internal discomfort. Perhaps a parallel attempt can be made to remedy the discrepancies.

Definition 5: External Normality
When the amount of a social attitude exerted by an agent a is between a maximum and a minimum level, the agent's social attitude in general has external normal condition.

$$v_{min} <= v_{exerts} < = v_{max}$$

This normality condition specifies that an agent may exert sociality within its comfort range and this is perhaps part of the agent's inherent personality. However, when this is violated the agent experiences frustration.

Definition 6: External Frustration
If the internal normality condition does not hold, the agent experiences external frustration.

A frustrated agent may consider changing its role or rank in the group.

Definition 7: Efficacy Normality
When the amount of a social attitude exerted by an agent a equals the amount of that attitude accomplished by a, the agent a is said to have efficacy normality.

$$v_{accomplishes-ab} = v_{exerts-ab}$$

The exerting agent will be satisfied if it manages to produce the effect of its attitude in intended agent.

Definition 8: Efficacy Frustration condition
If the efficacy condition does not hold, the agent experiences frustration.

The amount of exchange frustration for the exerting agent varies in proportion to the discrepancy between exertion and experience.

From the last four definitions, four combinations are possible combining external normalcy and frustration and efficiency normalcy and frustration. External-normalcy-efficiency-frustration is clearly an interaction issue. Whereas, external-frustration-efficiency-normalcy is discomfort that the agent must deal with, perhaps by negotiation with the group so it returns to its comfort range. External-frustration-efficiency-frustration is doubly complex since not only the interaction is faulty, the agent is experiencing an external discomfort. Perhaps a parallel attempt can be made to remedy both discrepancies.

So far we have been discussing limits and quantities of an agent's attitude when dealing with a single social attitude. Next, we turn to interactions among agents involving multiple social attitudes. We will sketch how the relationship between two agents involving one type of social attitude leads to indirect levels in another social attitude.

Control and autonomy are related. When agents consent to a balance of control between them, their balance of autonomy is complimentary to their control. I.e., control affects autonomy in the sense that as control is imposed on an agent, that agent's autonomy decreases. Autonomy does not affect control. There may not be a control relationship between an agent that has greater autonomy and another with lower autonomy. Over a common set of choices, the autonomy of the agent who has agreed to be controlled is lower than the agent who is controlling choices. Exerting control is representative of the degree to which power is asserted. There is a direct relationship between experiencing control and the amount of power that an agent feels imposed. "Actual control" is the amount to which an agent concedes to power asserted. If social power is disputed, control is not established but a sense of defiance exists. Naturally, the degree of autonomy is affected by control to the extent the agent allows or resists control. The relationship between autonomy and power is complimentary.

"Trust" is an ambiguous term, and furthermore, trust and control can interact in various and complex ways. See Castelfranchi and Falcone for a discussion [3]. For simplicity we consider only "strict trust" which takes trust and control as opposite and complementary notions in the sense that the exercise of control represents a lack of trust, and likewise, if agent a has a high degree of trust in agent b, then agent a will refrain from attempting to control agent b. That is, if agent a trusts that agent b will successfully accomplish a task without interference or assistance, then agent a will not attempt to control agent b, however, to the extent that agent a lacks trust in agent b's ability or intention, agent a will attempt to guide or control agent b.

Consider a simplistic view of the relationship between obligation and dependence. To motivate the relationship consider an example of automobile rental where a clerk agent a and a customer (renter) agent b interact. a must first determine the reliability of b in being a good customer and in a typical case b will present its valid driver's license to a. a then establishes trust in b based on this evidence. Trust is the catalyst for a contract between a and b. As the contract is signed, four simultaneous things will happen. b will have an *obligation* to a about the terms of the contract and a will come to *depend* on b to follow through with the terms of the contract. a will have an *obligation* to rent a vehicle to b and b will *depend* on having this car from a.

Let's turn to a simplistic view of a relationship between obligation and delegation with the above automobile-renting example. If an agent c is delegated by a to find a vehicle to give to b and c agrees, c will have a kind of obligation to a. This obligation may not be a legal, but rather a kind of moral one that should be further formulated. A caveat is that a's trust in b must be high enough before a decides to delegate the task to c.

When two agents enter a consenting delegation, the delegee may experience diminished autonomy. However, the delegating agent may also experience a lower level of autonomy. If two agents share a choice set and a delegation action gives permission over a part of the choice set to delegee, both delegee and delegator agents agree to lower their freedom over the shared choice set, thereby, lowering their autonomy.

Tuomela gives an immediate connection between control and "dependence", with control is as an inverse of dependence" [6, page 212]. If an agent a has control over another agent b, b depends on a. In a game theoretic sense, for a shared choice set, if a has freedom of strategy and by its choices forces b into a strategy, a has control over b and b depends on a. Tuomela goes further and says that social control is connected to social power. If an agent a has control over another agent b, a has power over b, and vice versa [6]. Changes in either Power or Control influence the other proportionately.

When there is a control relationship between two agents, the controlling agents may experience social permission to delegate a task to the controlling agent. The controlled agent may feel a deontic pressure to be receptive to delegated tasks.

Ideally, agents should not be frustrated. However, when frustrated they may either try to remedy it directly or to seek other social attitudes for indirect relief. Consider an agent who is frustrated by its inability to control another agent, a lack of effective control. The agent may choose to act out by an expression of dissatisfaction with control or other attempts to rectify the situation directly. Here we point out the complimentary relationships with control. Such a frustrated agent might act out by causing imbalances in autonomy. An agent who is frustrated by obligation, may not choose to act out by expression of dissatisfied dependence or attempts to rectify the situation directly, but instead act out by changing its obligations.

4   Toward Guarantees

Let's summarize the structure we have sketched, Figure 4. The agent internally reasons about its values and norms and that leads to its adoption of obligations. That type of consideration influences the agent's social relationships in various ways. We choose to focus on one particular influence illustrated in Figure 2, obligations (i.e., a kind of responsibility). Obligations affect an agent's dependence as well as autonomy.   We have argued that autonomy depends upon ability and social permissions [1]. The bottom half of Figure 4 shows the relationships we discussed in the previous section.

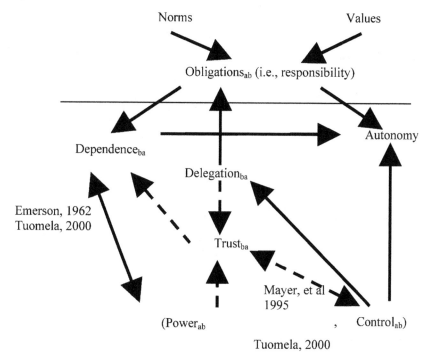

Fig. 4. Exploring relationships for guarantees

We envision four possible approaches that can be used for building predictable behavior. Each approach focuses on adjusting a different social attitude in Figure 4. The first method is to adjust control. Consider a sphere of social control between two agents in which one agent sets goals and monitors the other agent. We stipulate for agents that control can be designed to be at various levels, e.g., master-slave, supervisory, recommender levels. This is much more complex in humans. The tighter we set the control the more we can rely on the subordinate agent's behavior. The controlling agent is responsible for the behavior of the other agent. A second approach is to adjust the power level. If two agents have a differential power relationship, they can affect one another's behavior. Command and control authority relationships are one example of establishing power relationships. By setting agent **a** in charge of agent **b**, **a** directly controls the actions of **b**.

A third method of adjustment is with setting specific obligations (i.e., responsibilities) for the agent. An agent might be given specific obligations about certain tasks to perform on behalf of a chosen agent (or the human user in case the agent interacts with a human) and that affects its autonomy and control with respect to the agent (or the user). Value and norm adjustment is a fourth method we are proposing. Although this is the least direct method of controlling behavior, it can be used to design an agent who will uphold certain general principles.

We believe we have set up the foundation for delineating relationships among social attitudes. Much more work remains. The links among social attitudes are naturally defeasible since the agent might find it necessary to violate them.

5   Conclusion

Agents must maintain complex relationships of social attitudes. The resulting web of relationships provides cohesive forces in the group. We outlined basic relations among social attitudes and pointed out a research direction that can be used to develop mechanisms to adjust individual attitudes. We have shown how that can be used in developing methods that will guarantee individual behavior and system performance.

Acknowledgements

This work is supported by AFOSR grant F49620-00-1-0302.

References

[1]   G. Beavers and H. Hexmoor, 2001. Teams of Agents, In Proceedings of the *IEEE Systems, Man, and Cybernetics Conference.*

[2]   C. Castelfranchi, M. Miceli, A. Cesta, 1992. Dependence relations among autonomous agents. In Proceedings of *MAAMAW'92*, Elsevier Science Publishers B. V., Amsterdam, pages 215-227, 1992.

[3]   Castelfranchi and R. Falcone 2002. Tuning the Agent Autonomy: the relationships between Trust and Control, In Autonomy, Control, and Delegation workshop in AAAI 2002, Edmonton.

[4]   N. Lacey, H. Hexmoor, and G. Beavers, 2002. Planning at the Intention Level, In Proceedings of the 15th International FLAIRS Conference (FLAIRS-2002), Pensacola, Florida.

[5]   R.C. Mayer J.H. Davis, F.D. Schoorman, 1995. An integrative model of organizational trust, Academy of Management Review, Vol.20, N°3, pp. 709-734.

[6]   R. Tuomela, 2000. Cooperation: A Philosophical Study, Philosophical Studies Series, Kluwer Academic Publishers.

[7]   W. Walsh and M. Wellman. Efficiency and Equilibrium in Task Allocation Economies with Hierarchical Dependencies, In The International Joint Conferences on Artificial Intelligence Workshop on *Agent-Mediated Electronic Commerce*, August 1999.

[8]   M. Wooldridge, 2000. *Reasoning about Rational Agents,* The MIT Press.

Exploiting Reusable Knowledge to Enhance Multi-agents Capabilities: Explorations with Data Model and Glossary Repositories

Gary Berg-Cross

Knowledge Strategies Division, SLAG, Inc.
Potomac, Maryland 20854, USA
Gbergcross@yahoo.com

Abstract. The main goal of this paper is to explore knowledge reuse in the rapidly evolving area of multi-agent ontology as agents deal with less structured information. There are now numerous examples of "intelligent & knowledgeable agents" within a broadly heterogeneous body of R&D underway to provide standard electronic services and multi-agent solutions. Direction of ontological work is broadly divided by two complementary philosophies - the "semantic web" approach [1] which argues for letting a "hundred ontologies bloom", and traditional E-Commerce approaches that attempt terminological standards. With proper ontologizing mediating agents may be able use local repositories for concept and terminological "Views" of knowledge and make it available for structured activities such as found in E-Commerce. Data model and glossary knowledge sources are analyzed for useful content.

1   Introduction

This paper considers the possibility of supporting information needs of multi-agent systems in an evolutionary fashion through the use of intermediate agents that bridge to standard terminologies and concepts. In the future such mediating agents would be designed to spend time mining pre-existing repositories of conceptual models and domain glossary information to extract useful "Views" of knowledge for distributed communities such as proposed for a semantic web applications [1] and as E-Commerce agents.

The breakdown of the paper is as follows. Section 2 describes some basics of multi-agent approaches in E-Commerce with an emphasis on mediating agents. Section 3 walks through examples of information for different ontology sources and identifies various types of information possible from unstructured information in glossaries and more the structured information found in conceptual data models. Through a takes a light ontological engineering approach to illustrate knowledge reuse from conceptual data models and glossaries presented as complementary

W. Truszkowski, C. Rouff, M. Hinchey (Eds.): WRAC 2002, LNAI 2564, pp. 269-288, 2003.
© Springer-Verlag Berlin Heidelberg 2003

sources. Section 4 describes the communication aspects and necessary capabilities of mediators and discusses mediating agent dialog reusing intermediate forms of structured and less structured domain knowledge to enable agent knowledge reuse. An enriched concept of agent dialog is described. Section 5 concludes the paper by discussing next steps and scenario for future semantic web application.

2   Multi-agent Systems in E-commerce

Historically, software agents provide an abstract view of computational system tasks to allow cooperative work across inter-operating networks. The recognized range of agents types is large, diverse and growing with ongoing research about collaborative agents, interface agents, data collection and information /internet agents, which if taken together as a set makes possible a diverse system of heterogeneous agents. Such multi-agent systems (MAS) are usually defined as a set of agents that interact with each other, and possibly with the environment, to solve particular problems in a coordinated manner. MASes feature the system-level aspects of agents and emphasizes the organization or society of agents over individual agents. As previously noted, agents are usually distinguished by their functional functions, e.g. InfoBots for information retrieval and integration, mobile agents etc. However, for MASes we can imagine a set of heterogeneously functional agents cooperating on a larger task. For example, information retrieval, information integration and human communication agents may all be involved in supporting analysis if they can share and understanding of the problem domain and have a common vocabulary to coordinate activities and share information. An "infrastructure" to hold activities is the Reusable Task Structure-based Intelligent Network Agents called RETSINA [2]. RETSINA has three types of agents: interface agents, which interact with the user taking user specifications and delivering results of queries, task agents that help solve problems by developing queries for other agents, and information agents with access to collections of data and information. Like most of the MAS work, RETSINA is centered around relatively short-term transactional activities. The present work considers what knowledge collection and communications issues would be faced by an agent whose task it is to gather new data and integrate it with other agents' knowledge over longer periods of time. Such knowledge would be of potential use by a diverse set of e-commerce agents that use different, local knowledge bases. However, a different type of agent is needed for this because the volume of knowledge is large (megabytes to kilobytes), there may be many different types of data also, and the task lifetime is potentially hours or days rather than seconds [3].

Motivations for information and search agent research such as RETSINA has increased with the explosion of information on the internet and these often involve multi-agent applications since solving distributed information problems are inherently distributed and too large for a single centralized agent. However, it is recognized [4] that to be successful such systems should allow for interconnecting and interoperating multiple "legacy" systems whose individual agents may have been independently designed and employ differing data/ knowledge bases that need to be converged in support of the common task. One major research area concerns how agent language might be used to coordinate joint work with differing knowledge. When different knowledge bases are used to store knowledge provided by multiple sources, we are faced with the problem of integrating multiple knowledge bases [5]. Data and knowledge engineers have worked extensively on this task, so we now understand the process well enough to allow the design of research agents for such tasks.

2.1   Intelligent Agents in Electronic Commerce

One emerging research area investigate knowledge reuse by agents is in the Internet sales and electronic commerce (E-Commerce or just EC) area. This is a major subset of research building on the on the World Wide Web and agent technology to enable problem-solving methods. EC encompasses several functions including: the acquiring and storing of information, finding, filtering and securing it etc. Early work noted a need for intelligent agent technology and while progress has been made, most current electronic markets provide limited services, such as, communication supports between buyers and sellers, DB agents to increase the selections, & market information to help estimation of reasonable transaction prices. Among the recognized challenges is a need for mechanisms to support agent advertising, finding, fusing, using, presenting, managing, and updating agent services and information. Early efforts to address such capabilities include Mediator architectural concept of agents [6] to exploit encoded knowledge in order to create services for higher level of applications as well as work at CMU on "middle agents" [7]. Such architectures use several types of middle agents to support the flow of information in electronic commerce. For example, [7] uses the RETSINA architecture specialized to assist a chain of activities necessary to locate & connect an ultimate information source with an originating information requester. RETSINA illustrates a MAS approach employing 3 coordinated agents that together provide a middle agent function – matchmakers, blackboards and brokers. Matchmakers act as directory or "yellow" page agents to process request ads; while blackboard agents collect requests, and broker process them. The Matchmaker agent acts as an information agent to make connections between agents that request services & agents that provide services and allows original task-oriented agents to find each other by "registering" each agent's capabilities. An agent's registration information is stored as an ``ad,'' which provides a short description of the agent, a sample query, input and output parameter declarations, and other constraints. When the Matchmaker agent receives a query from a user or another software agent, it searches its DB for a registered agent that can fulfill the incoming request. The Matchmaker thus serves as a liaison between agents that requests services and agents that can fulfill requests for services (implying an agreed upon ontology for services).

Implementations have found that the lack of expressive "ad" standards limits covering the diversity of all products needed for EC applications. Despite the growing need for agents to support both customers and suppliers full automation of electronic commerce (EC) is not feasible due to lack of standards for product ontologies, messages and negotiation protocol between agents and brokering [8]. This line of research has constructed some cooperative multi-supplier EC ontologies to be used as open infrastructure for the EC agents. Groups of agents represent users, organizations and services and these agents engage in conversations as patterns of messages, to negotiate, exchange information, and so on. A complete system might employ a community of role-based agents, serving as customer, search, catalog, manufacturer, dealer, delivery and banker agents. Each interacts and negotiates with each other and each agent has a knowledge base, a reasoning engine, and a communication capability. As part of this, intelligent agent systems:

- Perform translations (semantic mappings) between content languages
- Exchange agents communications to negotiate contract terms and conditions
- Provide business registries support to enable interoperation
- Provide agent-based execution environments for bidding and buying co-operatives.

The common very high-level language among and between such agents includes some now standard ideas such as sender/initiators that "ask", "tell", "accept" and "counter". In addition to these communication types there must be a common terminology for the domain.[1] In an EC sale or auction message exchanges might concerns "price" for a "product" and circumstantial information about product size, packaging etc. This type of information is typically found in on-line product databases. This raises the one topic of the paper: knowledge reuse of online resources. Such reuse and dual use could be a big factor in expanding MAS application as well as making it more productive. To make this reuse effective, however, mediator agents need to go beyond simple data mapping function and negotiation between agents.

2.2   Knowledge Problems in Support of Electronic Commerce

Reuse has long been a problem in agent ontologies because content semantics may be so tightly integrated with agent design that they seem restricted to an enumeration lists i.e. a list of sentences in the content language, which represent the ontology.[2] However, in a MAS, the union of agent ontology is not like a data dictionary and can not rely on simple enumeration of terms comprising the application domain. There is an integration need that has to consider other agent terms especially where many terms have a fuzzy boundary that will affect communication. Where traditional DB aiding of agents ignore communication and assume well -formed agent data requirements, the scope of middle agents supporting EC is broader. When content language is used to combine terms for an agent ontology into likely, agent-meaningful sentences, these may expand substantially beyond agent committed ontology. Using a larger, pre-established repository of terms and concepts may be a useful way for agents to expand their vocabulary. Groups of agents may each point to such DDs/ repositories of terms as places for reaching a common vocabulary.

It is now widely recognized that Ontologies may play a major role in supporting information exchange processes in areas of EC, by providing a shared and common understanding of a domain that can be communicated between people and application systems [9]. Constructing formal agent ontologies is a program of ongoing research and like earlier knowledge base development is not yet an engineered science.

---

[1] The RosettaNet'ssupply chain initiative is an ongoing consortium attempt to map XML-based B2B using a set of supply-chain collaboration guidelines that are simpler than what is discussed here, but relevant.

[2] Increasingly intelligent systems are built a degree of knowledge modularity and with more concern about a formal ontological structure. For example, task knowledge (T) is separated from domain knowledge (D) for easier reuse & a T-D binding is specified. This does not overcome the problem being considered here.

Ontologies range in abstraction, from very general terms forming the foundation for knowledge representation in all domains e.g., space, time, parts, and subparts are terms that apply to all domains[3], to terms that are restricted to specific knowledge domains. malfunction applies to engineering or Bio domains; while transistor applies to electronics. Current EC agents tend to use very specific product attributes for purchase/delivery. Some EC integration is eased by standardization such as the use of UN Standard Products and Services Codes (UNSPSC). In addition to UNSPSC's Commodity ID Code (CID) that uniquely identifies its commodities, companies may base EC on a variety of XML-based infrastructure approaches to interoperable electronic business information. This includes Commerce One's XML Common Business Library (xCBL), CommerceNet, UN/CEFACT and OASIS, XCBL etc.

Despite a move towards some terminological standardization, the problems of data integration across different systems in an EC community are increasing, as more business is put online. Problems include varying data/knowledge sources include differences in representation, data attributes and vocabulary. For example, one provider may maintain a structured product DB while another provider use text to describe product features. The schema integration and data integration problems for structured data are well known in the federated DBs and heterogeneous systems literature. The challenge is to offer matching services across both structured and unstructured collections of data. Even within a common representation, one business /content provider may use a local product schema that enhances an existing standard by including secondary attributes such as "color" or "weight". Heterogeneity may also be due to naming conflicts in product schemas; the use "colour". Synonyms like "product, goods and merchandise" are another conflict. This problem has been known within the field of heterogeneous DBs for some time, but is compounded in EC when integrating data distributed across the web for several reasons as discussed by [10].

1. EC agents and systems are in communication with foreign sources where there may be limited or no real knowledge of the "local" schema due to proprietary sources protection as trade secretes. In such a case agents may need background knowledge to make reasonable inferences. Generic ontologies may be helpful in part but lack orientation to a business domain to handle some issues.
2. The large number of local schemas & the rapid response needed makes it unlikely than agent-human dialog can be used to handle integration. Even training of agent KBs might be too time consuming. Thus an automated or at least semi-automated solution seems required. This may require a mediating agent that learns over time and holds some beliefs as more or less founded than others.
3. Local DB schemas change rapidly changing due to product changes such as product update or internal data changes.

In contrast to this DB orientation, the Semantic Web (SW) approach of [1]) has a much simpler approach. The intent is to globalization "Knowledge Representation" in the same way that the Web initially generalized Hypertext. While SW's intent is to link "structured collections of information" it wants to do this in a machine

---

[3] For example the Upper Cyc® Ontology from Cycorp with 3,000 of the most general human concepts/terms capturing a consensus of reality.

processable way so that agent systems would be able to participate and help in web-based activities. SW structuring relies on the eXtensible Markup Language (XML) and the Resource Description Framework (RDF). XML lets us create new tags—hidden labels such as <product code> that annotate Web pages. The semantics of SW is simply metadata about XML expressed by RDF. This metadata is encoded as sets of triples, written using XML tags, where each triple is similar to the subject, verb and object of an elementary sentence. The RDF model is like an ERA model except that it open to multiple interpretations since relationships are not rigid definitions. Instead they are "identified" by a Uniform Resource Indicator (URI). The implication is that anyone on the web can make a relationship to a topic. Similarly, the attributes of an object are not defined at class definition. Instead SW would technically allow anyone to provide a view via a URI. This means that a relationship between two objects is defined apart from any other information about the two objects. The effort recognizes that decentralized knowledge will link inconsistent things. E.g. one person may define a "product" as merchandise for sale, while another definition stresses the manufactured nature of an industrial product and its features (size, color, function), still another assumes that products are grown and not manufactured. As part of a sales view definition one may use a URI to connect to marketing and ad information, while the manufacturing view may point to a URI listing standard functions.

Taken as a whole SW argues that we "let a hundred ontologies bloom" focusing on heterogeneous universality using linked content to varied ontologies, with some metadata and location constraints. The SW belief is that a community/subculture starting small has a conceptual coherence that allows innovate knowledge growth. The decentralized path throws away consistency, but this does not mean that we can't move towards merged agreement in steps. My experience is that there are some communities without formal ontologies that have some coherent views around conceptual models and/or glossaries that can be leveraged as a starting. Two directions of research of research are discussed to elaborate and explore this hypothesis: exploring the knowledge structuring issues for reuse of pre-existing intermediary knowledge & enhanced agent communication to support integrated activities.

3   Agent Ontology Issues: Reuse & Merging of Data Model and Glossary Knowledge

It is recognized that reusing existing ontologies in Ontology Servers such as Ontolingua Server [11] and Ontosaurus [12], is vital to building robust EC systems. Two additional digital knowledge sources are proposed that may be mined by agents to provide intermediation help – data models and domain glossaries. While recognized as ontologies, use of data models, applications conceptual models or glossaries are not often found in the ontology literature. One reason is that these are analytic tools built for human processing and cannot be queried directly like a DB.

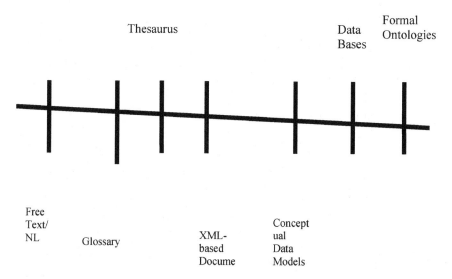

Fig. 1. Ontology continuum

Hence an additional level of mediation is necessary for their use. Each fits into an intermediate position between highly structured and focused knowledge sources like DB schemas and the broad, unstructured sources of documents that a simple XML path takes.

An intuitive ordering of the structure of some ontological information sources is depicted in Figure 1. Formal ontologies are the most structured and can be taxonomically or axiomatically based. Structure typically includes atomic formulae/ predicate relations used to express factual assertions along with rules. Databases lack much of the scope of this formality, but are well structured as are the related concept of conceptual data models (CDMs). Data models are structured, although with a different focus than data schema. Formalisms exist for CDMs, for example, the Object-Role Model (ORM), but the range of expression and the informality of specification is typically wider than for DBs, depending on the carefulness of the modeler. In between in an evolutionary group of semi-structured XML documents with that structure defined relative to an external DTD or schema. A thesaurus organizes terms in a structured may, and has some standard semantic relations to categorize information (broader, narrower). Finally, glossaries (also called vocabularies) add to a thesaurus a textual body of informally structured definitions. Glossaries have no explicit formal structural or semantic requirements, but the content usually has some form of implied conceptual categories, usually hierarchical and may include examples of categories and instances as well as distinguishing attributes, and like thesauri, synonyms and related terms.

It seems worthwhile to consider the advantages of exploiting both CDMs and glossaries, since they are not often mined[4] and could be complementary - CDMs providing explicit concepts and Glossaries providing concepts more implicitly with terminology being explicit. It would be useful to link such repositories and identify some issues to successfully employ these resources using mediators.

3.1   Conceptual Data Model Knowledge

A well-developed conceptual data model (CDM) aims at identifying unique meanings, rather than surface forms and terminology. A CDM is constructed through analysis and representation of the entities that an enterprise/organization must understand. CDMs serve an architectural blueprint for database and application development and is often available locally as a resource for enterprises. Unlike high-level ontologies, CDM knowledge should map tightly with a developing organization's data systems and contain knowledge relevant to the specification of the business components. Finally, they are metadata for DBs and thus can easily provide rudimentary meaning for a SW.

CDMs include scope and fit information, class inclusive taxonomies, commonly known as is-a hierarchies. CDMs usually are organized around subject areas, a structure not carried through in a visible way in DB implementation. Subject areas represent a conceptual grouping of information. Thus, a Sales CDM might include subject areas of customer, sales, product catalog, advertising, marketing territory, and market analysis. At a high level the CDM provides important constraint relationships between these upper concepts and main entities such as identifying that, "Each Salesman may have one or more Marketing Territories and Sales are made in a Marketing Territory."

Within a subject like Sales we typically find sub-type entity information such as commercial customers and business customers. There is a close relationship between entity attributes in a CDM and data column information in a DB schema, except that the CDM attributes are usually named with full terms, rather than abbreviated.

One common problem with heterogeneous data is that different entities will share the same name. One reason for this is that they are named within an assumed context. CDMs allow us to see this hierarchy and make use of it post-hoc for distinguishing between concepts. For example "Account" is a subject area and an entity within an Accounting CDM and at the same time a subject area and an entity within a Purchasing CDM. However, they have different definition, attributes and relations. An example of an Accounting concept of Account is as follows, "A business document used to record/retain monetary information associated with business transactions", while the purchasing concept of Account is "an organizational unit capable of making purchases and funding the payment of those purchases".

It is relatively easy to see how such information expressible in RDF and derived from simple categorizing rules to produce unique Views for the concepts of Purchasing account and Accounting account by combination. Categorical information

---

[4] However, he Workflow Mangement Coalition (WfMC) compiled a glossary to serve as a common framework for workflow vendors calling it communication ontology (see www.aiim.org/wfmc/maintrame.htm).

in the definitions includes relations to other major model concepts or subjects. So in Accounting, "Account" is a type of document, a business document, and is associated with business transactions. In Purchasing "Accounts" are associated with payment[5].

The nature of such information and its fit with traditional agent ontology information is illustrated by looking at published enterprise data models such as [13] as a source of ideas for the data model/schema concepts. This is a broad work that illustrates likely content for a range of DB schemas, all of which might be aimed at describing a business, its processes and resources.

What we seek to illustrate is that conceptual data models provide a basis of ready-made ontological grounding for agents dealing with data to support EC as well as linking to other information through the use of the same information as metadata in an RFD sense. Two very preliminary examples illustrate how we might expand typical mediator ontologies and customize it for a particular organization or enriching it within a focus – product type and organizational relations.

3.1.1 Product Model & Organization Examples

Agents differ as to their representation formalisms, but at a minimum information must be extensively articulated and represent a view of disjoint classes. The experience of ontology engineers suggests that extensive knowledge is needed to resolve mismatching problems, such as we described for "product". Typically ontologies need rules to partition information into type hierarchies meaningfully and provide constraints. Such rules are used to determine whether a new class has to be added to any partitions under the existing parent class. These are usually based on attribute differences between the concepts. For example, consider an ontology that contains a partition under the class "product" where it is relatively easy to distinguish between the disjoint classes "manufactured-product " and "farm-product ". An addition of a new sub-type of product, say "genetically engineered product" raises partition challenges. "Genetically engineered product" may be classified as a direct sub-class of "farm", but it may not be disjoint from the other sub-classes of product.

Conceptual models such as developed for data warehouse efforts offer some flexible structure that may be helpful to an open approach like the SW, where a community can provide an open source to its semantics that can be linked as part of a SW or for EC agents. We illustrate the extensive knowledge derivable in just a small portion of CDMs. For example, CDMs note that a local or departmental DB schema may show that a PRODUCT is of one and only one PRODUCT TYPE, but from the point of view of a company data warehouse, a PRODUCT may be of one or more PRODUCT TYPES [14]. This captures a simple truth about genetically engineered products – it is more than one type. Within our concept of operation an information-gathering mediator may attempt to match a seeker with a provider for product types. For this example a conceptual model is an appropriate source for such integration [6] and serves as a form of vertical integration within the Product topic.

---

[5] "Payment" in turn might be defined as the exchange of monetary considerations for previously delivered goods or services – a level general enough to be close to enterprise-level Ontological concepts.

[6] One may want to use a conceptual model to extend an existing agent ontology, but this must be approached carefully, because there are organizational issues of optimization that may require human judgment and generally ontology reorganization and maintenance is approached with care.

Another illustration concerns the confusion between the roles of people and organizations. The "Party" concept is generalization of the Person or Organization concept. While widely used in conceptual modeling it is less often used in physical schemas. Person and Organization are both sub-typed into a Party entity because there is common information related to both people and organizations such as their address, phone number, or e-mail address. A Person and an Organization are each types of Parties and Parties are related to each other in that they may serve similar roles. Both people and organizations may be buyers, sellers, as well as members or parties to a contract. Parties may be broken into various categories (i.e., industry codes, minority classifications) using a party definition. This may be local categories as well as general so navigation/inference using this relationship can provide linkage to appropriate, remote information over the web. For example, managers (person/employee type) have a different relation to a Department sub-type of Organization than do administrative assistants. Such role types are often key identifiers in data warehousing efforts and can be reused to provide simple semantics to remote agents and appropriate relations for web-based resources using RDF.

A CDM mediator interacting with a local DB could use such a concept to identify super-type entities and particular classification information. Two parties are linked through party relationship. This may be a customer relationship linking 2 organizations. The relationship may be between a person and an organization--for example, an employee of a supply company. Finally, the relationship may be between two people. An example of this is the relationship between a purchasing agent and their preferred supplier. The party relationship type defines the possible types of relationships and allows appropriate linking. Typical instances of party relationship type are "employer/employee," "parent/subsidiary," and "customer/ customer representative." The party type role defines the two parts of the relationship. For example, one role of the relationship may be "employer" and the other role for that same relationship may be "employee." By allowing information to be associated with the party or the party relationship, a community view can avoid misunderstanding, such as not allowing for several sales representatives to have distinct relationships and status with the same party.

A second illustration area is within the employment, location & networks of resources area. Having information integrators that have detailed models of "employment" and human resources makes them potentially very useful. Such an agent may view knowledge that an Employee is a sub-type of Person as part of its existing ontology. Current agent traders are too focused to include this information and the actual relation of an Employee with an Organization structurally. Data models provide the detailed information to correctly access instances.

3.2   Glossary Knowledge

Glossaries represent a considerable range of stored knowledge that is weakly structured. There are 3 reasons to attempt to mine them. First, they represent important repositories of vocabulary/terminological information such of which is not captured in DB models. Second, they may be useful within XML thrusts to take unstructured information and add more structure. Thus, in the future there will exist glossary XML schemas that can be mined by agent crawlers using some rules to acquire knowledge about the XML schema defined part of a Glossary entry -

synonyms, related terms and term hierarchies found in glossary. Third, they are complementary to the information that we have seen in CDMs and also in some ontologies. An example of the type of knowledge available is shown by this except from a glossary defining adjectives and verbs used in HR [14].

ACCOUNTABLE   -   adjective
The state of being liable to be called to account; answerable for an action or decision and for the consequence for that action or decision. An accountability is the measured effect of the job end results.

ACTS   -   verb
Does or performs something; plays the part of; carries out an action; operates or functions in a specific way; serves or functions as a substitute for someone or something;; brings about; produces as an effect; discharges or performs the office or duties of; serves in the capacity of; acts as or for. For example, the Executive Vice President may act as President in the latter's absence in order to provide continuity of top management in the daily overall operations of an organization.

3.2.1 Glossary Examples

Examples of glossary information come from expanded view of EC to include a Sales Person, Team and organization orientation as information in the "acts" glossary item above suggests. Many of the EC entities are indeed concepts organized in an enterprise ontology such as [15] which includes a range of concepts around marketing and sales. Within Marketing the following terms are defined in that ontology: Sale, Potential Sale, For Sale, Sale Offer, Vendor, Actual Customer etc. These concepts are also found in glossaries. I illustrate this in the glossary entries below which are partially marked with related terms indicated by underlining, to stand for hyperlinks that could be used by an agent to build a net of related terms. This is an approach used by internet sites such as Yahoo!'s financial glossary. Thus Account links us to a Customer concept a representative term not found in the Enterprise Ontology [15]:

Account: A customer, usually an institution or another organization, that purchases a company's products or services.

Glossaries are typically broader than CDM definition such as the following where formal relations are explicit:

"Sale" Instance-Of:
Class, Primitive, Relation, Set, Thing ;Subclass-Of: Eo-Entity, Individual, Individual-Thing, Thing[15]

We can the contrast this tightly structured listing with the more expansive glossary-like discussion of Sales interrelating items, some of which we identify by underlining in the definitions below.

Sale, which have is an agreement between two Legal-Entities for the exchange of a Product for a Sale-Price. Normally the Product is a good or service and the Sale-Price is monetary, however other possibilities are included. The Legal-Entities play the (usually distinct) Roles of Vendor and Customer.

A Sale can have been agreed in the past, and a future <u>Potential-Sale</u> can be envisaged, whether or not the actual Product can be identified, or even exists.

These two approaches are somewhat complementary in that the ontology entry is clear about hierarchy, while the glossary-like entry connects sales to several other major concepts like Customer and Price that are part of the inference slots of the formal entry. By following connections we can see the implied conceptual structure. Thus Customer is also a glossary entry – " The people and companies a business sells to. A generalization of <u>People</u> and <u>Organizations</u> who are <u>using</u> <u>products</u> and <u>services</u>. Also known as a purchaser or a buyer." While it does not connect to a legal entity idea this does give us alternate names that an information gathering agent may include in its ontology.

3.2.2 Mining Glossary Knowledge

How could glossary information be mined and gathered to augment DB schema? One way is via rule-based machine-aided /automatic indexing (MAI). MIA agents find major topics in texts, map them to an internal DB or controlled vocabulary, and apply indexing terms automatically. They may also extract important names, disambiguate words, and identify new terminology for indexers to add to the system [16]. For example, "use merchandise" as an indexing term whenever a document is about "product". Typically MAI offers candidate terms to indexers for their approval, while automated indexing applies these terms with no human intervention. Beyond classification, many simple rules could be developed in future to help extract useful ontological information, especially as glossary XML DTDs and RDFs are developed. For example, extraction rules may use - if "include" near a term take Phrase as sub-type. This rule and others is illustrated in the next section, which gives a surface flavor to some of the terms in rule that an information mediator may need to employ.

3.2.3 Examples of Glossary Knowledge

We get a further idea of content differences between glossary and CDM based information from the following example taken from the same sources as before.

In a glossary a Market is described as "all Sales and Potential Sales within a scope of interest. The Market may include Sales by <u>Competitors</u>. The Market may be decomposed into Market Segments in many ways in many levels of detail. This can be done by any properties of the Product, Vendor, Customer, Sale-Price or of anything else associated with a Sale. " See Market Analysis.

There is clear structured information embedded here. Sales types are noted (Potential Sales), but also the" includes" rule derives "Sales by Competitors" as a type of "Market". Another candidate rule used the "decomposed" term in the 3rd sentence to come up with sub-type idea "Market Segment" which is complex. A list of Market Segment properties is offered, but some additional rule for "segment" is needed to make this inference. The entry for "Market segmentation" provides guidance that this is sub-typing:

Market segmentation. The process of dividing a total market into sub-groups of consumers who exhibit differing sensitivities to one or more marketing mix variables.

Glossaries may contain "see also links" and one for "market analysis" is given in the above example. An entry for market analysis is:

Market Analysis may involve understanding of Features of Products, Needs of Customers, and Images of Brands, Products, or Vendors. May support Promotions.

This begins to provide a convergence between the concepts if "property" and "feature" are known as synonyms.

Each entry provides some convergence, but it also leads elsewhere in the network in the spirit of a Semantic Web. In the above case it points to promotions.

Promotions are Activities whose Purposes relate to the Image in a Market.

Consider, by contrast to this entry a CDM-based and more structured definition of Promotion where some additional hierarchy is covered using specific semantics of relationships.

```
PROMOTION,
( a part of : SALES)
(a part of: TECHNIQUE) )
 ( role : ( WORK ),
(( (actor : SALES MANAGER )
(locus : FIRM ) ),
( (actor : SALES PERSON )
(locus : DEPARTMENT ) ),
( (actor : CUSTOMER )
(locus : SALES REGION ) ))
```

Clearly there is a complementary set of information in these. Potential uses include identifying some critical players in the Marketing and Promotion area.   Integrating these in a formal way is a major ontological engineering challenge, but it is a useful linkage guide and a mediator may leverage XML forms of glossary and use an NLP approach like [17] where knowledge is extracted from an on-line encyclopedic corpus stored and defined by an XML DTD. The general application underlying this work is a question-answering system on proper nouns within an encyclopedic reference.

A final example area is offered to show a mapping of glossary content into a conceptual graph form, which in turn is mappable into an RDF. We start with the entry for Account.

"A customer, usually an institution or another organization, that purchases a company's products or services."

This maps to a conceptual graph form:

```
Account: Customer -
        ( prototype ) ->[institution, organization]
    [State: [Customer] -> (Agent) ->        [purchase ] ->      [product/service]
        ( poss) -> [institution]]
```

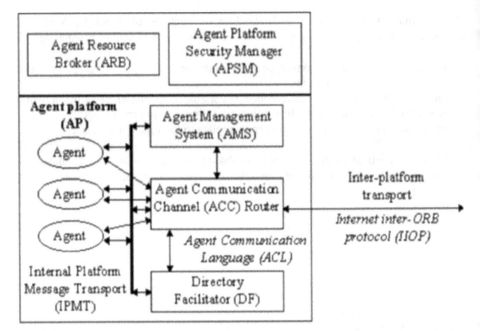

Fig. 2. Simplified FIPA standard with ACL

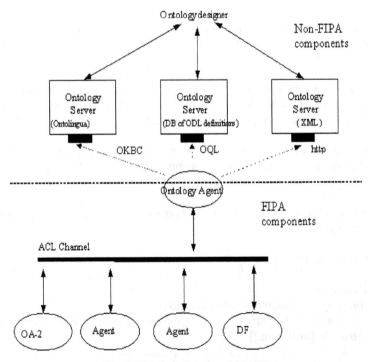

Fig. 3. Ontology Servers within FIPA

As part of a semantic web evolution it is possible to make glossaries an XML document by defining a DTD for a glossary. whose schema would specifies an ordering for the following XML elements: definition, synonyms, super-type and sub-type, attributes, related terms.

4   Mediating Agent Capabilities and Dialog

Multi-agent systems require agent communication for coordination and knowledge sharing. Little of this has been defined for the Semantic Web, but some ideas can be built on existing MAS and EC work to allow agent discussion of diverse information found on such a web. To support communication with a wide set of agents many MASes can build around general standards such as technologies based on FIPA (Foundation for Intelligent Physical Agents). Agent communication   [17] is accomplished through the use of three components shown in Figure 2, but we will focus on the FIPA Agent Communication Language (ACL), content language, and ontology - which is now a common approach for agent systems. The standard includes yellow pages functionality via a Directory Facilitator (DF). Registration in a given DF defines a domain (agent community).

FIPA agent communication language is based on speech acts and has a formal semantics that also includes several predefined protocols (e.g., contract-net negotiation and auction protocols), and the concept of registered generic and application-specific protocols. Basic FIPA vocabulary includes senders and receivers implementing messages of "reply-with", "in-reply-to" and "reply-by as a foundation for communication.   A "recruiting" protocol includes a sub-vocabulary for interactions between a sender-initiator and a target agent. Message types include "agree", "not-understood" and "refuse (with a reason")[7]. Ontologies play a notable part in ACL semantics and include a reference model to help structure of particular domain such as EC. Ontologies help provide at least the concepts for domain vocabularies. For example the set of relationships and properties that hold for the domain entities denoted by a domain vocabulary. Figure 3 shows agent ontology services within the FIPA reference model. Examples of existing ontology servers include Ontolingua, XML/RDF ontology servers, ODL databases ontologies servers. As shown in the figure, access to the services provided by these ontologies servers are based on various APIs such as the OKBC interface, the ODL interface or HTTP.

In EC a major part of agent communication concerns matching seekers and providers and we can use this to provide a launching point for improved communication. The coordination process allowing consumers, seeking products and services providing product specifications can be informed about the product by as a process called matchmaking.   Successful matchmaking may put seekers in contact with providers whose products and service match the specifications. Providers may "adverstize" and also seek consumers in a similar fashion. An assumption often made for a matchmaking task is that a consumer specifications (usually formed as a query) will differ from the representation of the provider's products and services. In such cases a more complex, iterative communication is driven in part by the degree of

---

[7] Some systems use "decline" as synonymous element.

"similarity" found in matchmaking. For example, as the seeker's product is sought, the seeking system may construct an ideal match and then resort to approximate similarity methods to find the good matches, those that are close to the ideal match. This approach is used in the Tsimmis project [18], where the mediating agents are translators that perform query and result set conversions between the native source

Ontology Servers within FIPA. and a common format understood by other agents. For queries, this can mean conversion to a specific query language, invocation of a keyword search mechanism or some other conversion. Typical implementations include mappings between multiple standard controlled vocabularies if multiple vocabularies are standardized in the domain(s) of interest. The CoABS Grid middleware [19] might be used to support such agent coordination by registering agents and advertising their capabilities.

As previously noted we cannot assume a globally understood query language or data exchange format and just have translation mediators which know how to map from one data type to another and from one query language to another. Within a FIPA archtiecture Knowledge Query Manipulation Language (KQML) is a simple means for matching sender/receiver intentions (i.e. the sender intends for the receiver to store the content, forward it on, validate it, etc), based on the speech act precondition that the sender holds certain beliefs about the mental state of an "addressee". This provides a basis for an individual sender communicating with one other agent which may be a mediator. However, in the complex case where several possible mediators that may be used we need some mechanism to hold multipart and evolving conversation within a group of mediators. But, as noted in [17], FIPA communication acts provides no well defined semantics for group communication, especailly in broadcast situations as in EC where senders may have no direct knowledge of what receivers to handle the local data problems noted in the previous section communication could be expanded to include group, topic-focused discourse. Such functionaloity can be implemented in a Coordination Language like COOL [20] that relies on speech act based communication, but integrates it in a structured conversation framework to capture the coordination mechanisms mediators use when working together. Work at the university of Toronto has used this language to represent coordination mechanisms for the supply chain of manufacturing enterprises modeled as intelligent agents.

One way to think of such extended diaglogs is as schema or topic-based. Topic-based discourse differs from query-based speech in that memory of discourse topics are cached in memory and used to aid integration. Conversational topic schemas such as designed by [21] can be used to define conversational interactions over time and behavior at a topic level. Conversational topics are defined as a 3-tuples of Topic id, Agents, and Arguments. In turn conversations are 5-tuples involving these Agents in exchange about Topics and their Internal state is noted along with an Message acts performed on Exchanges and Arcs record the relation between Acts and States. An example offered by Fuhua et al [22] represents conversations to reach agreement about a product order using order date, price and delivery location.

Such discourse falls somewhere between the basic query-driven type and full natural language processing, which seems more than necessary to handle data integration applications. However, it has the spirit of the Semantic Web initiative [1] where web agent comprehension is founded on a key word understanding together with an indefinitely large and unstructured set of links governed by metadata build around the subject, verb, object relation. Such capabilites have also been working themselvs into information retrieval tools and systems built around WordNet and automatic indexers . How far we can go with this is uncertain since large web expansion is taking place without enforcing knowledge consistency, but modifications in mediator agents to support local consistency could be as simple as a dialog memory service to hold 5-tuples conversations and lower-level conversational acts as a part of a goal oriented scheme for mediation. This intermedation becomes more valuable in combination with additional knowledge sources in the spirit of linking inconsistent sources in order to offer some possible understand local data. Selfridge and Feurzeig [23] discuss purpose-driven agent systems implemented as hierarchies of adaptive control structures built from a basic set of elementary adaptive modules (EAMs). This functionality may be useful in helping mediators adapt to misunderstandings between agents and mediators.

A simple way to do this is to define an XML-based language for communicating in the particular problem area. For example, using an agent-oriented VCR buyer's bidding language -simplified in the example, a seller advertises an offer to all potential buyer agents, of which Agent2 is one:

```
<bidding version="1.2" sender="agent1seller"
receiver="Agent2]l-potential-buyers">
 <offer startingprice="250" currency="USD"
expire="10/23/01 5pm EST"/>
 <item code="33475" units=12> Sony 340</item>
</bidding>
```

My Agent2 would then respond to bid on three books:
```
<bidding version="1.2" sender="gary"
receiver="seller">
<bid    price="260"   currency="USD"
expire="10/24/01 2pm PST"/>
 <item code="33475" units=1/>
</bidding>
```

5   Conclusions

Taken as a whole corporate glossaries and extended models may provide a bridge from a rudimentary Semantic Web to help EC agents to bid on such things as a "combined package" or in post processing include delivery in the contract. Post processing of an order is another potentially very important for EC and the integration of such things via mediators is highly desirable. Current EC systems have directory services and naming for agents. Despite our best intentions, such agents will not be designed with the same ontology or the same degree of world and situated knowledge and thus have communication issues. It seems likely that to include fixed resources and views from CDMs and local glossaries to facilitate EC agent cooperation.

A direct solution is to introduce mediators for the situation that are agent discourse experts, who help facilitate the communication.

While this is a barest start a preliminary look suggests that CDMs and Glossaries might provide a rich source of information for an agent enhanced Semantic Web and related EC thrusts. Like the Semantic Web thrust we envision a small community of user trying this and in this process useful steps will include work in many areas including:

- Drafting a robust schema for Glossaries to help simplify processing
- Constructing extraction rules for CDMs and Glossaries
- Defining and assembling a core infrastructure necessary to demonstrate the feasibility of an operational set of information gathering mediator functions
- Further specifying the agent communication to handle a larger set of examples

Corporate Glossaries and extended models may provide a bridge for an agent to bid on a combined package or in post processing include delivery in the contract. Some aspects of such automation seem challenging, but ongoing efforts using RDF may make them tractable.

The following scenario lays out how these might operate in the domains that we have already described. The simplest concept of operation might be a EC seeker request that broadcasts requirements using a FIPA-based speech act. This request would be acted on by one or more matchmaking mediators. In situations where the usual matchmaking process has trouble, the matchmaker seeks auxiliary information via information gathering mediators to help understand the request or local schema. One class of mediators might specialize in CDMs and another in glossaries. Essentially, the Matcher can dialog with the CMD mediator to see if it can help disambiguate local knowledge. The mediator's use of a conceptual model is analogous to a design operation where the CDM mediator expands a Mediator's ontology and vocabulary either for general reasons or because there is a specific target DB in mind. While this is the immediate service use of a CDM agent its overall concept of operations includes a long-term information gathering operation focused on assimilating semantic information from data model. Most of its time would be spent gathering information, organizing it and testing it against known schema perhaps accessing a physical schema to learn instance knowledge such as, which employee handles VCR product shipping. As previously noted, a variety of enhanced agent capabilities will make this possible. See [24] for a discussion of steps towards a practical infrastructure of the BDI (Belief Desire Intention) approach form building rational, cooperative agency into a system of agents. For quality assurance some periodic reports and interaction with human ontologists would be required and being able to discuss this at the Belief and Intention level may be necessary.

The agent-oriented alternative is to give all components a very similar, simple interface, but to allow the messages to have a much more complex structure. These messages can easily be changed and extended dynamically as the system evolves.

References

[1]   Berners-Lee, Tim: Future of the Web, http://www.w3.org/2000/Talks/0516-sweb-tbl/

[2]   Sycara, K. , Decker, K. , Pannu, A. , Williamson M. and Zeng, D.: "Distributed Intelligent Agents", IEEE Expert, 11(6):36--46, December 1996

[3]   Kauffman, Robert J. , March, Salvatore T. and Wood , Charles Agent Sophistication: Mapping Out Design Aspects For Data-Collecting Agents, Ninth Workshop On Information Technologies And Systems, 1999

[4]   Zhang , Qin : Software agents, MS submitted to Department of Computer Science, The University of Western Ontario, August, 2000

[5]   Subrahmanian, V.S.: ACM Transactions on Database Systems, 19, 2, pps 291--331, 1994

[6]   Wiederhold, G. "Mediators in the Architecture of Future Information Systems" In: IEEE Computer, pgs. 38-49 March 1992

[7]   Decker, K., Sycara, K. and Williamson, M. Middle-Agents for the Internet. In: Proceedings of the International Joint Conferences on Artificial Intelligence (IJCAI-97), January, 1997

[8]   Lee, J.G. , Kang, J. Y. & Lee., E. S. "ICOMA: An open infrastructure for agent based intelligent Electronic Commerce on the Internet ", In Proceedings of the International Conference on Parallel and Distributed Systems (CPADS). IEEE Comp Soc., pp 648-655, 1997

[9]   Fensel. D. Ontologies: Silver Bullet for Knowledge Management and Electronic Commerce. Springer-Verlag, Jan./Feb.2001

[10] Yan, G.-H. , Ng, W.-K. , and Lim, E.-P. "Incremental Maintenance of Product Schema in EC: A Synonym-Based Approach," Proc. Second Int'l Conf. Information, Communications & Signal Processing (ICICS), 1999

[11] Farquhar, A., Fikes, R., Rice, J. The Ontolingua Server: A Tool for Collaborative Ontology Construction. Proceedings of KAW96. Banff, Canada,1996.

[12] Swartout, B., Patil, R. , Knight K. and Russ, T. Towards Distributed Use of Large-Scale Ontologies. Spring Symposium Series on Ontological Engineering. Stanford University, CA. 1997, Pages: 138-148

[13] Hay, David Data Model Patterns, Dorsett Publishing, 1999

[14] Brown University HR GLOSSARY OF TERMS, http://www.brown.edu/ Administration/Human_Resources/hrweb/ compensation/glossary.htm, 2001

[15] Barbuceanu, Mihai and Fox, Mark S. Capturing and modeling coordination knowledge in multi-agent systems. International Journal on Cooperative Information Systems, 5(2 & 3):275--314, 1996

[16] Liddy, E.D., Paik, W. & Woelfel, J. Use of subject field codes from a machine-readable dictionary for automatic classification of documents. Proceedings of 3rd ASIS Classification Research Workshop. (1992)

[17] FIPA 1998. FIPA 97 specification – Part 2: Agent Communication Language – version 2.0, October 1998

[18]   Chawathe, S., Garcia-Molina H., Hammer, J, Ireland, K. Papakonstantinou, Y., Ullman, J. and Widom J., The TSIMMIS Project: Integration of Heterogeneous Information Sources". In Proceedings of IPSJ Conference, pp. 7-18, Tokyo, Japan, October 1994

[19]   Martha Kahn and   Cynthia Della Torre Cicalese   The CoABS Grid, This volume

[20]   Barbuceanu, M. and Fox, M.S. : *COOL: A Language for Describing Coordination in Multiagent Systems*, First International Conference on Multiagent Systems, San Francisco, 12-14 june 1995

[21]   Kumar, Huber, McGee, Cohen, & Levesque: "Semantics of Agent Communication Languages for Group Interaction," in The Seventeenth National Conference on Artificial Intelligence (AAAI 2000), AAIT Press/The MIT Press, pp. 42-47, Austin, Texas, July 30-August 3, 2000

[22]   22. Lin, Fuhua, Norrie, Douglas, Shen, Weiming, Kremer, Rob: A Schema-Based Approach to Specifying Conversation Policies. 193-204, Issues in Agent Communication, 2000

[23]   Selfridge, Oliver and Feurzeig, Wallace: Toward Purpose-Driven Adaptive Agent Systems, This Volume

[24]   Marian Nodine   Communication and Coordination Support for Mobile, Transient and Distributed Agent Applications

Communication and Coordination Support for Mobile, Transient and Distributed Agent Applications

Marian Nodine

Telcordia Technologies
106 E. 6th St.
Austin, TX 78701, USA
(512) 478-8923
nodine@research.telcordia.com

Abstract. Agent-based applications are executed as sets of complex *tasks*, each of which is defined or planned as a set of cooperative *roles* to be executed by a dynamic set of autonomous processes, called *agents*. The composition of the agent-based system may be *dynamic*, in that agents can enter and leave the system at will. The agents may also be *unstable*, due to unstable hardware, processes, and communication channels. Agents in such a system need to be able to bring to bear their intelligence and autonomy on the problem of maintaining application stability. This means that the agent services / roles must be designed defensively, anticipating and avoiding failures inherent when other agents leave the system. Some defense mechanisms include the ability to design roles that are mobile, transient and/or distributed across several agents. Such mechanisms should be supported generically by the underlying agent infrastructure. In this paper, we discuss specific features agent infrastructures can implement to facilitate implementation of these defensive roles.

1   Motivation

Many current agent-based systems operate under the false assumption that they are running on a firm foundation – their underlying hardware, communications, and software components and services are robust and free from failure. Thus, for instance, large information agent systems often are developed based on the assumption of a collection of agents, each operating on a 24x7 basis, each with its own task within an information process.

In reality, the foundations that agent systems run on may be quite a bit more treacherous. For instance, the dynamic and autonomous nature of agents indicates that an agent should be allowed to enter and leave the system over time, at its own recognizance, and possibly without warning. Other agents may become available for use at will. The agents themselves may be fronting services that are not robust; and the

W. Truszkowski, C. Rouff, M. Hinchey (Eds.): WRAC 2002, LNAI 2564, pp. 289–302, 2003.
© Springer-Verlag Berlin Heidelberg 2003

early demise of the service due to programming errors or congestion may bring down the agent itself. Hardware or communication errors may also occur – either killing or disconnecting the agent. Furthermore, an agent that is mobile may be diverted from its itinerary, or be partitioned from the remainder of the agent system. Finally, active sabotage may cause agents to misbehave within the society, and not fulfill their obligations.

In a system that is designed to run on a firm foundation, if one of the agents fails, the information process halts, sometimes in an unknown state. This disrupts the application itself, and possibly forces the (expensive) recomputation of partial results. Recovery may require manual intervention on the part of the system administrator.

The solution to this issue is to develop methodologies for agent application design that involve defensive operation. This intention follows along the same lines as, say, database transaction management and replicated fault-tolerant applications. However, an agent community can take a more flexible approach where the agents themselves bring their intelligence and autonomy to bear onto the problem of survival through failures. There are many different types of survival that an agent-based system can strive for, including:

Individual Survival. The agent's goal is to continue to operate in the face of operational hindrances and failures.

Application Survival. The agents supporting the application collectively have the goal to ensure that the application will continue to operate in the face of agent failure.

Population Survival. The agent community itself takes responsibility for ensuring that it has a sufficient and adequately diverse population of agents to maintain its application support capabilities even in the face of agent failures.

In this paper, we consider the problem of building survivable agent-based applications on unstable, limited, and/or intermittently available hardware and platforms – in other words, the issue of application survival. Application survival has the potential to support long-running applications in a more robust manner than individual survival. We examine three different strategies – mobility, transience and distribution – that agents in a community can use to enhance their application survival. These approaches are especially useful in any situation where the lifetime of the application is expected to exceed the lifetimes of the individual agents that comprise the application.

Our paper focuses on the impact of mobility, transience, and distribution on the underlying support for the agent-based application itself – how agents are assigned to roles, how they converse, and how they maintain their state information. We do not address issues of how to design mobile, transient and/or distributed roles; many of these are discussed in other areas of the literature such as distributed and parallel programming. We do, however, look at the underlying aspects of communication and coordination that should be supported by an agent platform in which roles may have these properties, independent of the specifics of the implementation of the role. This includes both generic functionality that these applications can utilize, and new generic agent types such as messenger agents. While some of these features are supported within current agent frameworks (e.g., location services) many of the generic services and conversational requirements are in the research phase.

2   Approach

Agent-based applications are executed as sets of complex *tasks*, each of which is defined or planned as a set of cooperative *roles* to be executed by a dynamic set of autonomous processes, called *agents*. If an agent application is meant to be robust, survivable and extensible, the assignment of roles to agents must be flexible. For instance, a role may be executed on more than one agent, or it may not always be assigned to an agent. If a role is particularly long-lived, it may be appropriate to design the role so that another agent can resume it if the current agent either fails or relinquishes the role (*transience*). This notion can be extended to the extreme of starting up an agent each time the role receives a message or notification, with the sole intention that the agent process that one message. Similarly, if a role requires a lot of intensive processing and/or the hardware is limited, it might be desirable to spread the role across multiple agents (*distribution*). Note that the set of agents the role is distributed over is expected to vary over time. Lastly, if communication is a bottleneck, or is unreliable, then an agent may benefit from being able to move around from one location to another, staying close to the other agents and applications with which it is interacting (*mobility*).

Currently, many intelligent agent systems implement (heterogeneous) agents that rely exclusively on stationary, monolithic, persistent roles, and therefore are rigid and do not adapt well to failure or change. Another popular type of agent-based system is the peer-to-peer type, which at any point in time is comprised of an ad-hoc collection of homogeneous transient agents. The latter is more robust, partly due to the transience of the peer agents and the peer-to-peer application style. The monolithic agent systems can take a lesson from the peer-to-peer world by relaxing the assumption that agents will always complete their long-running subtasks, and that roles may need to be taken up by multiple agent in order to complete successfully. To this end, we define an *activity* as the execution of a role by a specific agent. At any time, any number (0-n) of activities may be executing a role.

For example, let us assume that a task has a mobile, distributed role that travels around a group of sensors, forwarding their collected information to a central repository. This role may be implemented by having a group of mobile agents partition the group of sensors among themselves so that each sensor is visited by exactly one mobile agent. Each agent currently visiting a group of sensors then has one (mobile) activity of that role. If one of the agents leaves the system before returning the information, another agent must pick up that activity in order for the role to complete.

The methodologies used for assignment of agents to activities, communication and coordination among the activities executing a given task, and the need to maintain some observable state of the task depend highly on the properties of its roles. However, roles with similar properties have similar requirements. Therefore, it is appropriate to consider providing support for transient, mobile and/or distributed roles generically within the agent platform. The support requirements may include such functionality as:

- A location service to track addresses and online/offline status of agents and activities.
- A matchmaker to match (partial) roles to agents by capability.
- A mailbox or messenger agent to deliver messages when a role is offline.
- A public, group or private locker to store role and conversation state information when a role goes offline or state information needs to be shared among activities.
- The ability to suspend and resume conversations between roles.
- The support of intra-role conversations among the activities filling a given role.
- In the following sections, we discuss in more detail how the agent platform can view its agents and the tasks they execute, the requirements that role mobility, transience and distribution place on the agents, and the support that can be provided within the agent platform.

3   Terminology

3.1   Tasks, Roles and Activities

In an agent-based system, a task is executed by multiple cooperating agents. The types of tasks that an agent system can execute are called *abstract tasks*[1], and are composed of a set of *abstract subtasks* that communicate among themselves using an *extended conversation*. The abstract subtasks form a hierarchy within the abstract task. They may be fixed, or they may be plannable. Each task has a span of time over which it executes (its *time*) and a portion of the services, knowledge and information that it accesses during its execution (its *space*). At a given time, a task is accessing a specific subset of its space.

A *role* is an abstract subtask that has been partially instantiated with input parameters based on a user request. Different roles may be initiated and terminated as a task progresses; thus a role occupies a subset of its task's time. Furthermore, each role accesses a subset of the services, knowledge and information (space) accessed by its task. In other words, the task's space-time is naturally the union of the space-time of all of its roles.

Within the agent system, different agents have different capabilities, and every role in the system (hopefully) corresponds to one or more agents' capabilities. An agent takes on a role when there is a need for the role to execute, one of the agents' capabilities matches that role, and there is no other agent currently executing that role in the given space-time. We call the instantiation of a role on an agent an *activity*. Each activity is identified by the tuple <*task, role, agent*>, where *task* is the identifier of the task that has the role, *role* is the identifier of the role within the task, and *agent* is the identifier of the agent that is assigned the role (see Figure 1).

---

[1] Jennings *et.al* [6] use the terms *complex service* and *task* to represent our notions of *complex task* and *subtask*, respectively.

A role may be in any one of three states at any point in its life: *unassigned, offline,* or *online*. An unassigned role currently has no activities. An offline role only has activities on agents that are currently offline. An online role has one or more roles assigned to agents that are online.

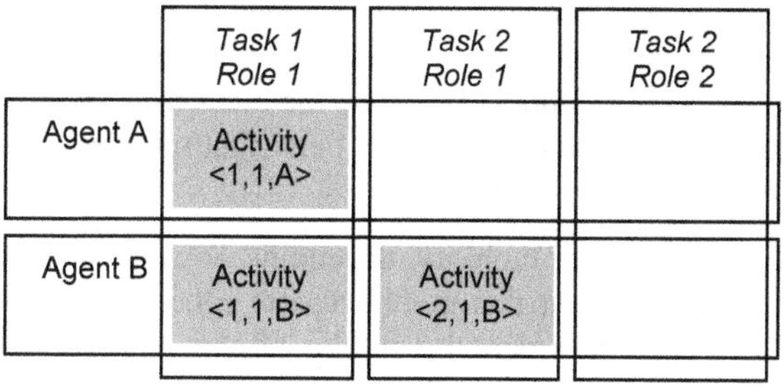

	Task 1 Role 1	Task 2 Role 1	Task 2 Role 2
Agent A	Activity <1,1,A>		
Agent B	Activity <1,1,B>	Activity <2,1,B>	

Fig. 1. Relationships between agents, roles and activities

3.2   Properties of Roles

A role may execute on different agents in different areas of space-time, as a set of activities. A *distributed* role has multiple activities running at a given time, and the activities must agree on how to partition the space-time of the role. A *transient* role may or may not have an activity running at any given time. A *mobile* activity may be in different places at different times, or be unavailable because it is in transit. In this section we will discuss these properties and their use in applications.

Transience. *Transience* is characterized by the relationship between the lifetime of the role and the expected lifetime of its activities. If the same agent is expected to take on the whole role for its whole lifetime (as a single activity), then we call the activity *persistent* with respect to the role. If, however, different agents can execute the role at different times (as different activities), then each activity is *transient*.

An example where persistent roles are used is in agents that incorporate independently-developed services such as COTS or legacy services. These services are typically monolithic and large, and have no "hooks" that help them to function in an agent-based world. Typically also agents that implement directory or other "mandatory" services in the agent-based system must at least provide an illusion of persistence.

Transient roles are useful when the role itself only executes intermittently or periodically. In this situation, it makes sense to start up the agents on an "as-needed" basis. Another situation where transience is useful is when the underlying machines that the agents are running on are less stable than the application is expected to be, and the roles themselves do not need to be running all the time. In this situation, the application can "checkpoint" itself periodically, saving any relevant internal state. The application must also have the ability to restart from the checkpoint. This allows a set of transient activities to give an illusion of a persistent role. We have found this type of approach to be useful, for instance, in applications that process (buffered) streams of input information, e.g. document classifiers.

Mobility. *Mobility* is characterized by the stability of the location of the activity(-ies) that are assigned to the role. Using the terminology of [15], let us define the *place* of an activity as the location at which (one of) its agent(s) executes – machine, internet address, etc. If the agent stays in the same place for the entire time that it participates in the role, then the activity is *stationary*. If, on the other hand, it moves from place to place as it executes the role, then it is *mobile*. Persistent mobile agents may be offline for short periods of time when they move.

There are different aspects of mobility, depending on what state the agent must be in when it moves. Note, however that mobile agents either carry their state internally or store some of their state in a private location. If an agent stores its state in some more public location, completely shuts down, and restarts completely at a new location, then it is more properly viewed as being transient.

Mobility is appropriate for roles that are on networks of devices that can disconnect periodically, as the agent can move from device to device as connections become available. It is also useful for roles that filter through large amounts of data local to different places, but carry a small state. However, because mobile roles are susceptible to corruption by any place in which it resides, as well as carrying the normal security risks, they may not be appropriate for certain classes of application.

Distribution. *Distribution* has to do with whether or not there can be concurrent activities in the role. A *monolithic* role has only one activity filling the role at any given time; i.e., the activities are sequential. A *distributed* role may have multiple concurrent activities; furthermore, the set of activities filling the role may change over time. The principal effect of distribution on the design of a role in an agent system is that the role must implement some means of partitioning its space-time among concurrent activities so that they do not interfere with each other's work. Thus, distribution is appropriate for agents that provide large, easily-partitionable services such as filtering and indexing partitionable sets of data.

3.3   Combinations

Note that the properties of mobility, transience and distribution are conceptually orthogonal; thus, any particular role can have any combination of the three. These combinations include:

Stationary-Persistent. A single, specific activity fills a role for the role's lifetime, and that activity remains at the same place with the same identifier throughout its lifetime.

Mobile-Persistent. A single, specific activity fills a role for the role's lifetime. However, that agent may move around to different places, and may be offline temporarily while moving. It does, however, maintain the same activity identifier.

Stationary-Transient. Different activities may fill a role at different times, though at most one activity may be filling that role at any given time. Any activity that fills the role will be located at the same place, but the activities will be expected to have different identifiers and to externalize their state.

Mobile-Transient. Different activities may fill a role at different times, though at most one agent may be filling that role at any given time. A given activity that fills the role may be located at different places at different times.

Stationary-Persistent-Distributed. Multiple activities may fill the role at the same time, and these agents remain at their respective places throughout the lifetime of the role. This model is appropriate for agents that encapsulate large, distributed services or services that are easily partitioned.

Mobile-Persistent-Distributed. Multiple activities may fill the role at the same time, and these agents may move around to different places. An activity may be offline temporarily while moving.

Stationary-Transient-Distributed. Different activities may fill a role at different times, and multiple activities may be filling that role at any given time. Activities that fill the role may be accessible via some predefined set or system of places (e.g., sitting at the same port on different machines).

Mobile-Transient-Distributed. Different activities may fill a role at different times, and multiple activities may fill that role at any given time. Activities that fill the role may change places. They are not accessible explicitly at any common place, but require some explicit methodology for routing messages to them.

4   Communication

The methodologies used for communication among the activities executing a given task depend highly on the properties (transience, mobility, distribution) of the activities involved in the particular dialog. As agent technologies have matured, patterns and policies relating to agent conversations have been developed and expanded. However, when a system supports transient, distributed or mobile roles, the agent infrastructure required to support conversations between roles requires more complex abilities, such as the ability to hold a *side conversation* related to the conversation, while the conversation is in process. An example of a side conversation is one that saves the state of the conversation before the activity involved in the conversation moves or terminates. The side conversation interrupts the conversation, and also must be able to reference the original conversation that it concerns. See [11] for methodologies for implementing and enforcing side conversations.

Mailboxes and Messengers. If a role is filled by a mobile or transient activity, there will be periods of time when the role is offline. Other roles that are conversing with such a role may find themselves in a position where the receiver of their messages is temporarily unavailable. There are several ways the agent infrastructure can support message delivery in this situation, two of which are *mailboxes* and *messengers*. A mailbox is a relatively stable storage area where messages to a given role or activity may be placed. The receiving role or activity will pick up the messages at a later time.

A messenger is a special agent that moves around the network carrying messages and looking for their receivers. When a messenger locates a receiver that it is looking for, it then can forward the message to that receiver. Messengers are particularly useful in ad-hoc agent-based systems.

Group/Role Message Delivery. If a role is distributed across multiple activities, then a message to that role from another role may not necessarily be able to target which activity should be the actual receiver of the message. Messages sent to that role must be somehow filtered and distributed to the correct activities, based on some application-specific criteria, or there is a risk that work will be duplicated or lost. While the process of deciding to which activity to deliver a message is mostly an application-specific problem, the agent infrastructure may need to support the addressing and delivery of messages to *all* activities filling a role, so that the activities can filter the messages themselves.

A related situation occurs with transient agents, which may be started as work is available. In this case, in order to deliver to the role, the message delivery service must ensure that a new agent is started to fill the role, then deliver the message to the new agent.

Intra-role Conversations. Multiple activities filling a transient or distributed role may need to communicate among themselves to correctly partition the role at any given time and to share other relevant state information. In this case, each activity in the role is conversing at two levels. The first level of conversation is at the role level, where the role is interacting with other roles about the overall task. At this level, the messages are effectively addressed and delivered to roles. This is the type of conversation normally referred to within the ACL literature.

The second level of communication is at the level of the activity, where an activity within a role is interacting with other activities in the same role about how they are coordinating the execution of the role. At the activity level, messages are addressed and delivered to specific activities. Activity-level conversations may be implemented as side conversations to the role conversations.

Message exchange at the role and activity levels place different requirements on the messaging support within the agent infrastructure, and need to be considered separately. This is due both to the group nature of role-level message exchange (as opposed to the individual nature of activity-level message exchange), and to the side-conversation nature of the activity-level conversations.

Conversation Suspension, Resumption, Externalization. Agents communicate by exchanging messages within extended contexts in a meaningful way. A group of related messages (within the same context) is called a *conversation*. In addition to being able to deliver messages from role to role, the conversations between roles must also maintain their context and state across activities. For example, if a role is sending a sequence of messages to a transient role, then different messages in the sequence may be delivered to different activities filling that transient role. As the order that the messages are received may matter, it is important that the activities in the receiving role be able to coordinate enough to ascertain the conversation context; therefore an external conversation state must be accessible to all such activities.

On a related note, these conversations also may need to be maintained with mobile agents. A receiving role that is mobile may need to retain the right to suspend the conversation while it moves. While the conversation is suspended, all messages must be held. When the mobile agent reaches its new place, it can then resume where it left off, processing any messages that were held in the interim. In an agent system with mobile agents, such suspension and resumption best occurs within the agent messaging system.

These communication abilities are summarized in Table 1.

5   State Maintenance and Coordination

We have already alluded to the need for storing information about roles, in the context of storing the role's conversation state for transient applications, and in the context of storing messages when a single receiving activity is not apparent because the role is distributed and/or transient.

Obviously, each activity can store state and receive messages actively for as long as it is in existence, without using a repository. However, any agent-based system that can implement roles that are distributed, transient or mobile also has need for temporary storage locations scoped to various levels (roles, tasks, public). Gamma *et. al* [5] allude this as the *memento pattern*. These repositories can be either stationary (requiring the activities that fill the role to go to the storage location to get things out) or mobile (requiring the storage location to go to the activity so the activity can get things out). Regardless, the storage locations must be accessible at all times. If the repository role itself is not persistent, then an illusion of persistence may be maintained by providing a comprehensive data storage location and starting up one-shot repository agents each time the information is queried.

Lockers. *Lockers* are used for individual roles or conversations, and in some cases, activities as well [1]. If a role is transient, then each activity can save its state in the locker before it terminates and/or at specific checkpoints. Ensuing activities can then pick up the execution of the role from the state they retrieve from the locker. For a given role, the state may include the conversation states of each of the conversations the role is involved in, as well as the coordination state that must be preserved between activities for a smooth transfer of control.

Lockers can also be used for data- or state- driven coordination among activities that share a distributed role. This approach is useful, for instance, in applications that generically process large amounts of information that can be easily segmented, such as taking snapshots of segments of the World Wide Web or generically filtering large document repositories for specific features. The state information in the locker changes as the different activities process segments of the data.

One other use of lockers is with mobile activities that may need to shed some of their code or data before moving to a new location. For instance, a mobile activity may store away sensitive data when it is not convinced of the security of the place it is moving to. Also, a mobile activity may shed code or data if the connection to the place it is moving to is weak or slow, and not all of the code or data is needed at the destination.

Task Repositories. Storage that should be accessible to the task as a whole may be stored in a task-level repository. One example of this is the virtual blackboards in [14], where intermediate results from some of the roles in the task are externalized for later access and processing. This situation is especially useful when a task contains a role that is long-running and/or generates bulky results, and multiple other roles access those same results.

Table 1. Impact of Agent Properties on Communication

Property	Communication Features
Mobile agent(s) fill role.	1. Ability to suspend conversations and resume at a different address. 2. Ability to temporarily hold message traffic for later delivery.
Transient agent(s) fill role.	3. Ability to externalize conversation state so that it can be picked up later by another agent. 4. Ability to send a message to a receiver that is not available. 5. Ability to start a receiving agent before transmitting the message.
Role distributed across multiple agents.	6. Ability to have a group of agents as receiver and/or to determine to which agents to transmit a message based on message-dependent criteria. 7. Ability for agents that share a role to be able to converse among themselves as to how to partition the role.

Public Message Boards. The most public approach involves posting notices and information in a public area such as a bulletin board or tuple space, e.g., as in [12]. Activities that read the bulletin board may either remove the notices or leave them on, depending on the application semantics.

Table 2 summarizes the approaches to coordination and some ways to apply them to mobile, transient and distributed roles.

Table 2. Impact of Agent Properties on Coordination Approaches

Property	Coordination Approach
Mobile agent(s) fill role.	1. Ability to shed code and state into a locker for later retrieval, especially when moving to an insecure place. 2. Ability to use task repositories to share state and data with other agents filling other roles in the task.
Transient agent(s) fill role.	3. Ability to save state in a locker for access by later activities filling the role. 4. Ability to use task repositories to share state and data with other agents filling other roles in the task.

Role distributed across multiple agents.	5. Ability to use role lockers to coordinate how the role is being distributed among the different active agents filling the role. Ability to share common state information. 6. Ability to use public message boards to enable the location of other agents that may be able to help fill this role. 7. Ability to use task repositories to share state and data with other agents filling other roles in the task.

Table 3. Impact of Agent Properties on Agent Location

Property	Agent Location Approach
Mobile agent(s) fill role	1. Minimal impact on code and data size. 2. Ability to advertise location and capabilities to a facilitator. 3. Ability to browse a facilitator looking for activities to do. 4. Ability to use agent-based matching when facilitation-based matchmaking becomes difficult or impossible due to communication limitations.
Transient agent(s) fill role.	5. Ability to use an agent factory to manufacture transient agents as needed. 6. Ability to do simple agent-based matching within the transient activity to locate other activities to communicate with.
Role distributed across multiple agents.	7. Ability to advertise location and capabilities to a facilitator. 8. Ability to use a facilitator to aid in searching for other agents over which the role can be distributed. 9. Ability to do detailed and more sophisticated semantic matching problems, especially when determining how to distribute the role across the agents that are executing it.

6   Matching and Location

As a task is executed, new roles become instantiated as the need for them becomes apparent. Roles must then be *matched* to agents that can fill them, in accordance with shared properties and semantics. The role to be filled propounds its needs (to some level of detail) in the form of a query ("Help Wanted"). The matching process then compares this query to agent advertisements describing their offered capabilities ("For Sale") until one or more matches are found.

Different agent systems publicize information on their capabilities to varying depths, from interfaces [2] to ontology-based descriptions [9] to logical descriptions [13]. The depth of information that is advertised needs to be adequate to correctly distinguish the agent that provides the best match to the requested role. In an agent system where the available agents fall into fairly homogeneous classes in terms of their capabilities, less information needs to be publicized for bad matches to be avoided. However, if the agents in the system are very heterogeneous in their services offered, then more detailed semantics must be published in order to avoid bad matches.

The matching process can either match a query to an existing agent, or locate an agent factory or proto-agent that can be used to start a new agent that will fill the role. Additionally, matching can take place in the agent placing the query, the advertising agent, or a third-party facilitator.

Facilitation. Facilitator agents specialize in matching queries to advertisements. In one alternative, the facilitator agents keep a repository of advertisements, and receive queries. Each facilitator agent iterates through the set of stored advertisements to locate matches with the query. In the other alternative, the facilitator agents keep a repository of queries, and receive advertisements. Each facilitator iterates through the set of stored queries to locate matches with the advertisement. Third-party facilitators are useful in very heterogeneous communities, where advertisements may be very detailed and matching complex. Since facilitators typically tend to be persistent or at least to maintain an illusion of persistence, they require some level of stability in both their connectivity and in the underlying system on which they run.

Agent-Based Matching. Agent-based matching may be used in agent systems where the agents are transient, or where the matching itself is fairly simple. In this approach, agents keep their own advertisements, and possibly also attempt to acquire advertisements of close neighbors. When an agent requires a new role / activity to be started, it sends queries to its neighbors (possibly looking in its own repository first to see if it already knows a suitable neighbor). When an agent receives a query, it checks to see whether or not it can provide the service itself by matching the query to its own capability advertisement. If there is a match, the agent returns its own location and criteria to the agent that sent the query. This neighbor propagation continues up to some maximum number of hops.

Agent Factories. Earlier we stated that matching could either be geared towards locating an existing agent, or alternatively towards locating an agent factory that can start an agent that has the capacity to take up the role. Agent factories may be implemented in a similar manner to a matchmaker, in that they may contain advertisements of the capabilities of the types of agents they can start. A factory, when it receives a request to match a particular capability, can use a matching process to locate an agent type that has a matching capability, and then start an agent of that type at an appropriate location. The factory will then return the location of the new agent.

Table 3 summarizes the different methods for agent location and their applicability in mobile, transient and distributed roles.

7   Related Work

This paper extends work published in [10] and [14] on conversational issues with designing robust agent interactions. Agent communication languages are addressed in both the KQML [8] and FIPA [3] standards. The notion of conversations is codified in FIPA as a set of interaction protocols [4]. These protocols do not yet handle many of the side issues described here.

The application of software engineering techniques to agent-based systems is not new. Design patterns that originated in the object-oriented world [5] are often applicable to agents. Kendall *et.al* [7] and Lange *et.al* [1] have published studies of design techniques for agent-based systems.

8   Conclusions

The assumption of stability in an agent-based system, both with respect to the agents themselves and with respect to the supporting software and communications services, is not appropriate in the situation where the expected lifespan of the agents exceeds the expected lifespan of the applications they are participating in. Failure can come from many causes – communication failure, software faults or congestion, routine maintenance, autonomous decisions to stop participating, or even active sabotage. Because of this, agent applications should be designed to be robust in the face of failures and shutdowns. This is especially true for 24x7 agent applications, as well as applications operating in ad-hoc environments.

One approach to robustness is to bring the intelligence of the agents to bear to the problem of survival; allowing the agent to do such things as move when it discovers its operational environment is not stable, or only become active during brief intervals when there is work to do. In this paper, we have studied the support of robust applications by endowing agent applications with defensive properties such as transience, mobility and distribution, and the facilities that are required to support them. *Transience* is the ability of a role to be executed sporadically, by different agents at different times, as different activities. *Mobility* is the ability of a single activity, executing a given role, to move from place to place as it executes. *Distribution* is the ability for multiple concurrent activities, in different agents, to partition the execution of a given role.

At any given time, a particular role in a conversation can be taken by zero, one, or more than one activity, each running on different agents. This affects the *conversations* among roles, because messages are not necessarily sent from an active sending process to an active receiving process. Alternative forms of message delivery must instead be developed. This also affects the *state maintenance* of roles, as the state cannot necessarily be maintained within the context of a single active process. Thirdly, it affects *the instantiation of roles* on agents, as such aspects as where and when a role is instantiated on an agent as a new activity may be affected by the availability and lifetime of the agents.

Communication and coordination within agent-based systems becomes complicated when the agents are neither stationary, nor reliably accessible, and when roles may be partitioned across multiple agents. Agent frameworks that support such agents and roles must provide added internal services to ensure the correct execution of their tasks.

References

[1]   Yariv Aridor and Danny B. Lange, "Agent Design Patterns: Elements of Agent Application Design", in *Proc. Int'l Conference on Autonomous Agents*, 1998, pp. 108-115.

[2]   OMG and X/Open, The Common Object Request Broker: Architecture and Specification, Revision 1.1, John Wiley and Sons, 1992.

[3]   The Foundation for Intelligent Physical Agents, 2001. http://www.sfipa.org.

[4]   IPA Interaction Protocol Library Specification, FIPA, 2000. http://www.fipa.org/specs/fipa0025.

[5]   E. R. Gamma, R. Helm, R. Johnson and J. Vlissides, Design Patterns: Elements of Object-Oriented Software, Addison-Wesley, 1994.

[6]   N. R. Jennings, P. Faratin, T. J. Norman, P. O'Brien and B. Odgers, "Autonomous Agents for Business Process Management", *Int'l Journal of Applied Artificial Intelligence* 14(2):145-189, 2000.

[7]   Elizabeth A. Kendall, P. V. Murali Krishna, Chirag V. Pathak and C. B. Suresh, "Patterns of Intelligent and Mobile Agents", in *Proc. Int'l Conference on Autonomous Agents*, 1998, pp. 108-115.

[8]   Y. Labrou and T. Finin, "A Proposal for a New KQML Specification", 1997. http://www.cs.umbc.edu/kqml/kqmlspec.ps.

[9]   Marian Nodine, William Bohrer, Anne H.H. Ngu and Anthony Cassandra, "Scalable Semantic Brokering over Dynamic Heterogeneous Data Sources in InfoSleuth", *IEEE Transactions on Data and Knowledge Engineering*. (to appear).

[10]   Marian Nodine, Damith Chandrasekara and Amy Unruh, "Task Coordination Paradigms for Information Agents", *in Proc. Int'l Workshop on Agent Theories, Architectures and Languages*, 2000.

[11]   Marian Nodine and Amy Unruh, "Constructing Robust Conversation Policies in Dynamic Agent Communities", in *Issues in Agent Communication*, Frank Dignum and Markb Greaves, Ed., Springer-Verlag, New York, 2000 (Lecture Notes in Artificial Intelligence, v. 1916).

[12]   Matt Storey and Gordon Blair, "Resource Configuration in Ad Hoc Networks: The MARE Approach", in *Proc. IEEE Workshop on Mobile Computing Systems and Applications*, 2000.

[13]   Katia Sycara, Jianguo Lu, Matthias Klusch and Seth Widoff, "Matchmaking Among Heterogeneous Agents on the Internet", in Proc. AAAI Spring Symposium on Intelligent Agents in Cyberspace, 1999.

[14]   Amy Unruh and Marian Nodine, "Industrial-Strength Conversations", in *Proc. Workshop on Agent Languages and Conversation Policies*, 2000.

[15]   James E. White, "Mobile Agents", in *Software Agents*, chapter 19, J. Bradshaw, ed., MIT Press, 1997.

Where Should Complexity Go? Cooperation in Complex Agents with Minimal Communication

Joanna J. Bryson

Department of Computer Science, University of Bath
Bath BA2 7AY, United Kingdom
J.J.Bryson@bath.ac.uk

Abstract. The 'Radical Agent Concept' in this chapter is that communication between agents in a MAS should be the simplest part of the system. When extensive real-time coordination between modules is required, then those modules should probably be considered elements of a single modular agent rather than as agents themselves. The advantage of this distinction is that system developers can then leverage standard software-engineering practices and more centralized coordination mechanisms to reduce the over-all complexity of the system. In this chapter I provide arguments for this point and also examples, both from nature and from my own research in building modular agents.

1 Introduction

Animal intelligence is complex, but the semantic content of animal communication tends to be simple. In contrast, artificial agents tend to be relatively simple, yet a great proportion of the current agent research deals with communication and negotiation between agents in Multi-Agent Systems (MAS) e.g. [34, 48].

In this chapter, I question the wisdom of this approach. I have been concerned for some time that the MAS coordination community is overlooking fifteen years of research in action selection for individual modular agents (IMA). I am taking the opportunity of the Workshop on Radical Agent Concepts to air work in progress on a fairly basic question: what parts of an AI system should be decomposed into agents, what parts should be decomposed into modules in a single agent, and what the difference between these might be. I will propose that the main difference is whether the interactions between modules is really best modeled as communication, or more standard software conventions such as method calls or pipes.

I begin with a discussion of agents which are clearly individuated: mammals. I then consider the problems that action-selection in IMA address, and how these relate to coordination techniques in MAS. I then give an example of a MAS agent where all the agents are IMA, and show how increasing the coordination between agents can be done with very minimalist signal communication, embedding the complexity in the IMA instead. The IMA in this system are built with an AI

W. Truszkowski, C. Rouff, M. Hinchey (Eds.): WRAC 2002, LNAI 2564, pp. 303–319, 2003.

methodology based on object-oriented design, and can thus exploit standard software engineering for debugging. Finally, I summarize my claims.

2   Societies without Language

We have many animal models of social agents capable of complex behavior, both individually and systematically, while communicating only by signal, not by language [24, 25]. A signal is bound to a single meaning, while a language implies arbitrary links between symbols and semantics, as well as other powerful mechanisms such as compositionality and grammar. Despite extensive research, to date only humans have been shown to have languages, yet even humans communicate a great deal through signaling.

Many such signals, when expressed by humans, are generally accepted to be without intention. For example, facial expression is generally (though not always) unintentional, and some signals, such as blushing are nearly impossible to control. Other signals we often consider deliberate, such as physical threats or bowing. However, these actions may also be often automatic — reflexive responses tuned by social conditioning, exhibited in response to emotionally salient stimuli [3].

Although their communication is simple, the intelligence and behaviors of animals are incredibly complicated, particularly when compared to artificial agents. Animals manage enormous numbers of sensors and actuators, and pursue many conflicting goals that require intricate behavior in unpredictable environments. Why in nature is the complexity of individual agent behavior consistently higher than that of inter-agent communication? What are the circumstances that might lead to the evolution of such an arrangement?

3   Motivations from Nature for Simple Communication

Although the underlying causes of evolutionary trends can seldom be proved deductively, they are still open to the scientific method. For example, if we find any hypotheses of interest, we can test their predictive power in the performance of artificial agents. The following are four hypotheses for explaining why non-human animal communication seems to occur at a very high, abstract level of signaling, rather than at a potentially more informative level of detail and complexity such as languages provide.

The Environment Demands Attention. Attentional constraints are a fact of animal intelligence [17] — for whatever reason, animals simply can't attend to very many things simultaneously. Infrequently-occurring combinations of semantically meaningful percepts take time and resources to process [29], and such time and resources are often required for conventional perception and action [42]. Thus signals need to be sufficiently easy to recognize and sufficiently persistent so that other multi-tasking agents have a good opportunity to observe them.

Detailed Direction Requires Significant Two-way Information Exchange. The purpose of communication is to influence the action of another agent. But at what level should this influence take place? It would be very difficult for one agent to give another detailed directions (such as precise path plans of foot placement) in a complex dynamic environment. Each agent is itself best situated for detailed observation of its opportunities, dangers, and requirements, and has the most experience for guiding its own actions and learning their probable outcomes. For example, each individual deer in a herd will have different jumping ranges and current energy levels. Thus if one agent wanted to micro-manage the behavior of another, it would require communicating current models *to* the directing agent, as well as transmitting rapid and detailed instructions *from* it. As stated in the previous point, such transmission is difficult to accommodate in nature.

Perception is Unreliable. This means signals must be very distinct, which in turn provides interdependent limits on how many different signals can exist, and how long processing or generating them might take. (Human language has required a large number of evolutionary innovations in both generation and perception [41, 20].)

Conspecifics Share a Great Deal of Intelligence. This fact does not limit how detailed communication *can* be, rather it limits how detailed it *needs* to be. Species tend to largely share both perceptual abilities and behavior patterns. Further, a species' innate behavior repertoire is likely to include behaviors that benefit other individuals, such as their offspring or kin. Consequently, in many common situations there would be no need for one agent's detailed management of another. It could be sufficient to communicate only a high-level goal or even simply an emotion in order to trigger appropriate behavior in a conspecific.

Either individually or taken in combination, these hypotheses could explain why communication in animals is generally limited to the high level, such as directing attention to goals, rather than managing a goal's completion in detail. Humans offer the only possible counter-example to this argument, yet even between humans, the true efficacy of communication is often overestimated. Even with our exceptionally complex speech production apparatus [20] and high-speed perceptual-event processing [41], complex, structured language is not used much in urgent or simply time-critical situations. For example, during a sporting event, utterances are generally limited in length and highly ritualized.

Humans must hold enormous systems of shared beliefs in order to communicate new ideas verbally [18], yet even between close, collaborating colleagues or carefully trained working crews misunderstandings frequently occur [47]. On the other hand, very effective real-time task coordination can be generated with very simple, even non-linguistic utterances [1]. Language is used primarily in social contexts [30], where it can alter or update another person's knowledge (and therefore behavioral repertoire) during times of relative calm.

4   Communication vs. Control

The extent to which the previous four observations about animal communication apply to an artificial MAS will vary from system to system. A few agent systems are biomimetic for the sake of being biomimetic — that is, to serve as models of animals. The emphasis of this chapter is more general. Here I am focusing on the extent to which limited communication is desirable from a purely engineering perspective.

There is no longer any debate that it makes good engineering sense to break a large, complex program or system into smaller, simpler elements which communicate only in a limited way through a well-defined interface. This is widely accepted in conventional software engineering [40, 4, 15] as well as in artificial intelligence [37, 32, 7].

The question I am asking is about the role of communication in control. This can also be seen as the question of agent decomposition: what entities need to be agents? I have previously spent some time addressing the question of *behavior* / module decomposition within modular (behavior-based) agents [6, 14, 10]. I took the answers from standard software engineering and object-oriented design. First, modular decomposition takes place around variable state. A module's core is one or a few related pieces of variable state with specialized representations to support learning correct values as efficiently and reliably as possible. A module consists of that state, any sensing required to create that state, and whatever actions are dependent on it.

The 'radical concept' I am proposing in this chapter is that, to the extent possible, the complexity of an intelligent system belongs *within* agents, where it can be designed, addressed and debugged exploiting the advances of more-or-less conventional software engineering. What this implies about agent decomposition is that a module of a system should be an agent precisely when the hypotheses in Section 3 hold—when communication is costly and needs to be minimized.

In order for this claim to be true, coordination (also known as action selection or behavior arbitration) within modular agents must be easier than coordination within MAS. The next two sections examine the extent to which this is true.

5   Coordination in Individual Modular Agents (IMA)

Historically, there have been two dominant strategies for action selection in autonomous agents. The first is *constructive* (search-based) *planning* e.g. [39, 38]. The second is simply hard-coding the relationship or prioritization between modules e.g. [5, 23]. This latter strategy is sometimes referred to as *reactive planning*, because it replaces planning in a conventional agent with a system that reacts reflexively given the current context. In the last decade, a large amount of research has focused on combining these two strategies e.g. [27, 33, 22, 31] by having constructive planning create the structures underlying reactive planning when there is time available to do so.

One strategy that has been almost universally adopted, at least within robotics and virtual reality, is the modular (often called behavior-based) approach [32, 43]. Behavior-based AI originally decomposed all of the agent's intelligence into semi-autonomous modules which coupled motor control (or more generally, action) to whatever sensing was required by that action. The system also provided for minimalist, decentralized arbitration confined to connections between modules' input and output streams [5]. Subsequent research has generally favored more centralized and programmatic arbitration but nevertheless continues to emphasize the importance of modularity in simplifying the design and coordination tasks [26, 32, 7]. I will refer to such agents incorporating modularity as Individual Modular Agents (IMA) to contrast with Multi-Agent Systems (MAS).

In contrast to the hybrid of constructive and reactive planning, relatively little work has been done to control autonomous agents via techniques anything like those employed in the coordination of multi-agent systems. One exception is the Agent Network Architecture (ANA) [35], which uses a system of spreading activation between modules. The activation sources are modules linked to perception and to goals. All modules in the system are interconnected for passing activation; the connections are weighted to reflect relevance. The first module that passes a particular threshold activation is allowed to operate the agent. This mechanism is somewhat akin to MAS auction-style coordination. However, it still relies on significant engineering for both the weights (though these are sometimes learned) and the modular decomposition. Further, the Maes architecture is generally considered impractical for large-scale systems due to difficulties maintaining behavioral coherence [46].

A few other autonomous agent architectures also use MAS coordination strategies. For example, Humphrys [28] uses voting, and Luis Correia and A. Steiger-Gargão [16] use chains of pair-wise negotiation. Overall, however, I am unaware of any such architecture other than ANA that has a wider user base than its developers[1]. Lack of current use does not *necessarily* imply that these architectures or strategies are not potentially useful, but it does increase the probability that they are being out-competed for some good reason.

6   Could MAS Coordination Be Useful for IMA?

The concept presented in Section 4 claimed that a module should only be treated as an agent if constraints on communicating information between that and other modules are animal-like – that is, if perception is slow and noisy so signaling takes a long time relative to the action-selection cycle of the agent. If this is true, then it implies that there is no reason to use MAS coordination within a single agent.

---

[1] Another exception might be systems like the Open Agent Architecture [36] or Retsina [45], which are to some extent agent architectures, but I do not include them here since they are fully-fledged MAS.

In other words, I have no difficulty understanding when MAS technology is used on the World-Wide Web or across physically distributed problem solvers. But this paper is more concerned with the fact that MAS coordination technology is increasingly being applied into areas that have traditionally seen the application of other sorts of modularity, such as robotics [44] or shop-floor planning and scheduling [2]. In this context, it seems worthwhile to consider whether the arbitration schemes developed for IMA may be more efficient than coordination schemes developed for MAS. Or in other words, does it ever make sense to use MAS strategies to coordinate IMA?

At least two conditions have to hold in order for MAS coordination strategies to be useful for IMA.

1. The coordination process (voting, negotiation, bartering or such) must conclude quickly enough that its outcome (e.g. the action selected) can be expressed in the time-window when it is needed. Time has been a considerable problem for constructive planning, and underlies the wide-spread acceptance of reactive planning as at least one element (if not *the only* element) of on-line autonomous agent action selection. Unless a MAS coordination strategy can guarantee a good solution in a short, fixed length of time, it cannot be used for time-critical action selection.
2. The engineering process is shorter for developing the MAS coordination system than for specifying a reactive (hard-coded) plan for doing the same thing. Unlike the previous point, this is a pragmatic argument rather than a logical necessity—one could choose the slower development strategy, but it would be a waste.

For an IMA with heterogeneous modules, it seems likely that the cost of programming MAS coordination will be at least of the same order as that of encoding prioritizations for reactive planning. This is because each heterogeneous module must be described in a set of parameters meaningful to each other module. This presumably amounts to roughly the same amount of work that is necessary for reactive planning as specifying priorities per context. Given that this prioritization must take place anyway, the aforementioned timing advantages of reactive planning give it the edge.

The above points do not necessarily imply that MAS coordination can never be useful for IMA, but they do provide criteria for characterizing an IMA for which MAS coordination would be useful:

1. Part of the agent's remit must include some processes which do not require response times so quick that they violate the first point above. The prevalence of agent architectures that still include constructive planners as one of their elements is an indication this condition holds for some agents see further [22].
2. The agent must contain a sufficient number of homogeneous modules that the second point above does not apply.

It is the second of these conditions that almost never holds in current IMA. Most modular decomposition strategies focus on functional or behavioral criteria.

Even where behaviors are largely homogeneous, the slight difference between them is critical to action selection. For example the modules controlling each leg of a six-legged robot operate identically, but at different times (e.g. during the gait) or in different contexts (e.g. left vs. right turns).

This is also not to say that MAS coordination can't be useful for MAS. In many cases, individual MAS agents may be homogeneous from a software perspective, and differ only in terms of the hardware on which they are running or the users they represent. In this case, it may be that establishing prioritization can be done through existing standards (e.g. using money), while communication might be too slow for conventional IMA control. In this case, the arguments in Section 3 would to come into play.

7   Example: Where Complexity Goes in a MAS of IMA

I will now illustrate the approach I am advocating — placing complexity within modular agents in order to simplify communication — with a simulation which does happen to be biomimetic. The system is a pilot study on a simulation being built to explore a hypothesis about social organization across species of non-human primates. Again, although this example is biomimetic, I believe the engineering approach taken may make sense for more standard, industrial modular intelligent systems.

The research shown here derives from the work of de Waal [19] on the evolution of specifically social behaviors such as those used in conflict resolution. In particular, this research is intended as part of the thesis work of Flack, who is seeking to understand the interaction between the number of conflict resolution behaviors expressed by a species and the social structure of its colonies [11]. Flack's research explores a hypothesized trade-off between egalitarian social models and complex conflict-resolution behaviors. This research has relevance to issues such as behavioral specialization within communities and time spent monitoring other agents.

7.1   Approach: Behavior Oriented Design

The IMA in this simulation were developed under Behavior Oriented Design (BOD) [14]. BOD modules are called behaviors [5, as in]. BOD uses hierarchical reactive plans for action selection / behavior arbitration. Behaviors are encoded in any standard object-oriented language; the reactive plan representation is more specialized, though also relatively standard [13]. The interface between plans and behaviors is an encoding of plan primitives in terms of methods on the objects which encode the behaviors.

As mentioned earlier, BOD takes inspiration from Object-Oriented Design [40, 15] in that variable state serves as a starting point for determining modular decomposition. Further, BOD provides a set of heuristics for simplifying an agent by shifting the specification of intelligent control between its basic representations, the behavior modules and the reactive plans. Details of BOD are available elsewhere [14, 9]. To understand the argument relating to the theme of this paper it is sufficient to see the increase in complexity and/or number of behaviors (where complexity is determined both by the amount of state contained and the amount of program code, as roughly indicated by the number of primitives / methods supported), and the size of the reactive plans.

7.2   Simulation Results—Impact of Increased Communication

The simulation concerns simple agents with two conflicting drives. One is social: the desire to groom. The other is individual: the desire to wander in relative isolation—a stand-in for slightly more complex behavior such as foraging. Each drive is placated when the agent engages for a while in activities consummatory to that drive (grooming or wandering). If the agent has no active desires, it rests in place. The agents also have a desire to avoid bumping into each other which is constant—it invokes avoidance behavior whenever another agent blocks its path.

The results shown in Figure 2 are for 16 rectangular agents co-inhabiting a walled, rectangular enclosure 140 times larger than each agent. For each condition shown in the figure the simulation was run until 11,000 behavior transitions had been recorded, or approximately 690 per agent. By 'behavior transition' I mean changing from one expressed behavior (e.g. sitting) to another (e.g. approaching a grooming partner.)

The results show the amount of time spent engaged in three activities: grooming, attempting to groom, and avoiding jostling. Grooming is a consummatory (fulfilling) action for the grooming drive—the agents would prefer (are driven) to engage in it 14 percent of their time. Attempting to groom covers a range of behavior including approaching another agent and aligning with their body in a way to facilitate grooming. These behaviors are not in themselves rewarding, but are motivated by the grooming drive. Similarly, avoiding jostling is not exactly consummatory, it simply facilitates other, more useful behavior. Thus the optimal time use for any individual agent would show the grooming bar at 14 percent and the other two at zero. Of course, this ideal cannot be realized, but the simulations examine how it can be approached.

The difference between the three experimental conditions is essentially one of communication. In the first condition, the agents are completely unaware of each other's actions other than their locations. In the second and third, the grooming agent transmits to the groomee its role as a target for grooming, and the groomee holds still. In the second condition, this happens only when the groomer is actively grooming the agent. In this case, the communication is analogous to *feeling the action* of grooming. In the third condition, this transmission takes place during the groomee's approach. Here the communication is analogous to *seeing or hearing the intent* to groom from a distance.

It is interesting that the communication behavior in condition 3 does not significantly reduce the time the groomer spends approaching the agent over condition 2, but it does have significant impact on how much time the agents have to dedicate to their more primal drives, as witness the decrease in grooming time. Thus if the simulated agents were a valid model of some animal species,

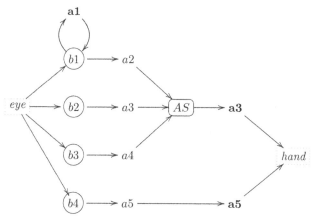

Fig. 1. The architecture of a BOD agent. *Behaviors* ($b_1 \ldots$) generate *actions* ($a_1 \ldots$) based on their own perception (derived from *sensing*, the eye icon, and their internal variable state). Actions which affect state external to their behavior (*expressed actions*, the hand icon), may be subject to arbitration by *action selection* (AS) if they are mutually exclusive (e.g. sitting and walking). In this diagram, three actions 1, 3 and 5 are taking place concurrently, while 2 and 4 have been inhibited by action selection

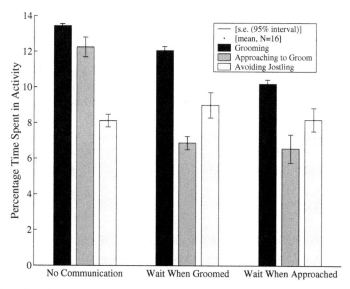

Fig. 2. Results showing the impact of adding simple communication to facilitate social grooming. In the first condition there is no communication, in the second recipients are informed of (and tolerate) active grooming, in the third they these behaviors apply also during the approach to groom

these results would indicate a selective pressure for the behavior patterns in condition 2, but not for those in condition 3.

7.3   Complexity in the IMA Supporting Simple Communication

At what engineering cost was the cooperation shown in Figure 2 achieved? First, consider the design of the original agents in condition 1 (Figure 3). The behaviors are simplified, but the reactive-plan is precisely represented. The plan determines the agent's priorities, but both their assessment and their achievement are carried out by the behaviors. Items on the left of the plan are more abstract; solid vertical lines indicate sub-plans. Higher items on a sub-plan have higher priority. Parenthetical expressions are perceptual preconditions. Boxes surround primitive actions.

The farthest left sub-plan is the root of the plan hierarchy, referred to as the *drive collection* (D). Other sub-plans are called *competences* (C). The program cycle of the action-selection module has two phases. During the first phase, the highest priority drive which is currently triggered by its preconditions passes action attention to whichever of its children was most recently active. In the second phase, the child performs the next pending step in its own execution. The first phase provides for alertness or reactivity, the second for persistence within a particular plan. When a sub-plan terminates, attention is returned to the root of that particular drive. For full details of the plan representation (including quantitative experimental evaluation) see Bryson [8].

The exact mechanisms of BOD are not significant to the point of this chapter; they are drawn here partly to show the sorts of coordination developed in the IMA community — this system is similar to many other hybrid architectures (see Section 5 above) — but more to illustrate an implementation of very simple communication in an IMA MAS. Contrast Figure 3 with Figure 4. The additions are in italics. Communication is handled by the new action *notify*, which signals the target of the groomer to set its *groomed-when* variable to the current time. This allows a new perceptual primitive, *being-groomed?* to tolerate the grooming (that is, to hold still.) Notice that *notify* has been added into an action sequence with 'groom'. The only change in condition 3 (not shown) is that notify is added into the 'align' and 'approach' boxes as well.

8   Summary

This chapter has argued that the agent-decomposition problem should be considered continuous with the behavior-decomposition problem. Sometimes a module within an intelligent system should be an agent, and sometimes it should just be part of an agent. I have suggested that the heuristic for determining which condition holds has to do with communication: it is better to embed complexity within a single agent than within the communication process for two reasons: because communication is unreliable and because existing AI and software engineering techniques can reduce the complexity of within-agent coordination.

	Navigate	Groom	Explore
state	x, y, size, name focus-of-attn	drive-level partner	drive-level direction-of-interest
actions	approach wait, align untangle	groom choose-partner partner-chosen?	choose-new-location lose-target, explore want-novel-loc?

(a) Behaviors

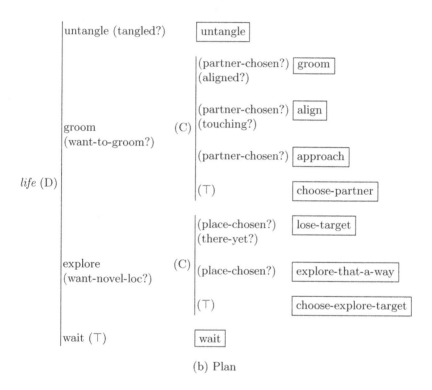

(b) Plan

Fig. 3. Behaviors and action-selection plans for IMA in condition 1

In Section 3 I motivated my claim by using natural intelligence as an example; I then illustrated it by modeling a natural system. I now close by returning to the hypothetical reasons why mammals communicate so simply in order to answer to the question: When is a module an agent?

The Environment Demands Attention. If communication cannot take place in time, then MAS and communication are not an option. This constraint clearly doesn't apply to agents which are situated in entirely stable, predictable environments with no real time constraints. However, do such

	Navigate	Groom	Explore
state	x, y, size, name focus-of-attn	drive-level, partner *groomed-when, being-groomed?*	drive-level direction-of-interest
actions	approach wait, align untangle	groom, choose-partner partner-chosen? *tolerate, notify*	choose-new-location lose-target, explore want-novel-loc?

(a) Behaviors

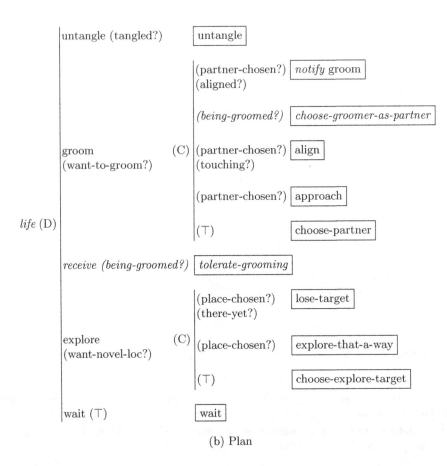

(b) Plan

Fig. 4. Behaviors and action-selection plans for IMA in condition 2

agents exist and, if so, do they need to communicate? Communication indicates mutual interdependence, and therefore some form of time constraint. A program that can compute a solution quickly enough that time doesn't matter and return its result reliably doesn't need to be anything as complicated as an agent — it could be a subroutine.

Detailed Direction Requires Significant Two-Way Information Exchange. This might not hold for an artificial entity — it might know exactly what another entity needs to know, and be able to feed that information directly. In this case, again, there is no reason for these entities to be agents. They could use pipes instead of KQML.

Perception (Communication) is Unreliable. This is obviously more true of satellite arrays than modules on the same CPU, but in general it is solved in MAS by protocols. That is, communication reliability issues have been replaced by increasing costs in time of transmission and in the complexity of designing two-way exchanges[2]. However, although modules in IMA may run in parallel, their action selection is often sequential. Consequently, if timing or reliability in communication *are* issues, MAS coordination strategies may be better than IMA ones.

Conspecifics Share a Great Deal of Intelligence. Section 6 argued that only within homogeneous agents does it make sense to coordinate through negotiation, because between heterogeneous agents the amount of work creating a common negotiation framework might as well be put into creating a reactive-plan framework instead. When agents do share a great deal of common code, very sparse, simple communication should be possible.

These are obviously broad generalizations and claims. These issues should probably be studied more formally, and the procedures for agent / behavior module decomposition tested and refined. Further, their may be hybrid cases when *parts* of a MAS may want to be *temporarily* unified in an IMA-like structures. Gajos [21] describes a system that does this within an intelligent environment — IMA-like coordination is used to coordinate care for both individual users and individual rooms. Bryson et al. [12] propose a similar solution, where an individual user agent's action-selection may temporarily absorb as a module agent-like services discovered on the Web.

Nevertheless, my conclusion is that the agent abstraction makes the most sense when transmitting information between components of a system takes some time. In that case, communication should be kept as simple as possible. Where modularity can help simplify the system further, it is generally best coordinated as an IMA, not a MAS.

---

[2] A significant but frequently-overlooked contribution of the Subsumption Architecture [5] was the specification that messages are sent with no hand-shaking and no guarantee of reception. Consequently, no single packet could be crucial, but rather the entire communication stream could be viewed as homologous with continuous sensor information. Section 7 uses this model.

Acknowledgments

Jessica Flack, Will Lowe and Lynn Andrea Stein contributed to the research in this chapter. Will Lowe, Krzysztof Gajos and Marc Hauser helped refine earlier drafts.

This work was begun in the MIT AI Laboratory and moved to Franklin W. Olin College of Engineering. At both locations is was conducted under the sponsorship of the Defense Advanced Research Projects Agency (DARPA) and Air Force Research Laboratory, Air Force Material Command, USAF, under agreement number F30602-01-2-0512[3]. The work in this chapter was completed at Harvard University in the Primate Cognitive Neurosicence Laboratory where it was sponsored by National Science Foundation (NSF) grant EIA-0132707.

References

[1] Philip E. Agre and David Chapman. What are plans for? In Pattie Maes, editor, *Designing Autonomous Agents: Theory and Practice from Biology to Engineering and Back*, pages 3-15. MIT Press, Cambridge, MA, 1990. 305

[2] Sivaram Balasubramanian and Douglas H. Norrie. A multi-agent architecture for concurrent design, process planning, routing and scheduling. *International Journal of Concurrent Engineering: Research and Applications*, 4(1):7-16, March 1996. Special Issue on the Application of Multi-Agent Systems to Concurrent Engineering, (eds. Brown, Lander and Petrie). 308

[3] John A. Bargh, Peter M. Gollwitzer, Annette Lee-Chai, Kimberly Bamdollar, and Roman Trtschel. The automated will: Nonconscious activation and pursuit of behavioral goals. *The Journal of Personality and Social Psychology*, 81(6):101427, Dec 2001. 304

[4] Frederick P. Brooks, Jr. *The Mythical Man-month: Essays on Software Engineering*. Addison-Wesley Publishing Company, Reading, MA, 20th anniversary edition edition, 1995. 306

[5] Rodney A. Brooks. A robust layered control system for a mobile robot. *IEEE Journal of Robotics and Automation*, RA-2:14-23, April 1986. 306, 307, 309, 315

[6] Joanna J. Bryson. The reactive accompanist: Adaptation and behavior decomposition in a music system. In Luc Steels, editor, *The Biology and Technology of Intelligent Autonomous Agents*. Springer-Verlag, 1995. 306

[7] Joanna J. Bryson. Cross-paradigm analysis of autonomous agent architecture. *Journal of Experimental and Theoretical Artificial Intelligence*, 12(2):165-190, 2000. 306, 307

[8] Joanna J. Bryson. Hierarchy and sequence vs. full parallelism in reactive action selection architectures. In *From Animals to Animats 6 (SABOO)*, pages 147-156, Cambridge, MA, 2000. MIT Press. 312

---

[3] The views and conclusions contained herein are those of the author and should not be interpreted as necessarily representing the official policies or endorsements, either expressed or implied, of DARPA, the Air Force Research Laboratory, or the U.S. Government. The U.S. Government is authorized to reproduce and distribute reprints for Governmental purposes notwithstanding any copyright annotation thereon.

[9] Joanna J. Bryson. *Intelligence by Design: Principles of Modularity and Coordination for Engineering Complex Adaptive Agents.* PhD thesis, MIT, Department of EECS, Cambridge, MA, June 2001. AI Technical Report 2001-003. 310

[10] Joanna J. Bryson. Modularity and specialized learning: Reexamining behavior-based artificial intelligence. In Martin V. Butz, Pierre Gerard, and Olivier Sigaud, editors, *Adaptive Behavior in Anticipatory Learning Systems,* Edinburgh, August 2002. Springer. *forthcoming.* 306

[11] Joanna J. Bryson and Jessica C. Flack. Action selection for an artificial life model of social behavior in non-human primates. In Charlotte Hemelrijk, editor, *Proceedings of the International Workshop on Self-Organization and Evolution of Social Behaviour,* Monte Verita, Switzerland, September 2002. *forthcoming.* 309

[12] Joanna J. Bryson, David Martin, Sheila I. McIlraith, and Lynn Andrea Stein. Agent-based composite services in daml-s: The behavior-oriented design of an intelligent semantic web. In Ning Zhong, Jiming Liu, and Yiyu Yao, editors, *Web Intelligence.* Springer, 2002. *forthcoming.* 315

[13] Joanna J. Bryson and Lynn Andrea Stein. Architectures and idioms: Making progress in agent design. In C. Castelfranchi and Y. Lesperance, editors, *The Seventh International Workshop on Agent Theories, Architectures, and Languages (ATAL2000).* Springer, 2001. 309

[14] Joanna J. Bryson and Lynn Andrea Stein. Modularity and design in reactive intelligence. In *Proceedings of the 17th International Joint Conference on Artificial Intelligence,* pages 1115-1120, Seattle, August 2001. Morgan Kaufmann. 306, 309, 310

[15] Peter Coad, David North, and Mark Mayfield. *Object Models: Strategies, Patterns and Applications.* Prentice Hall, 2nd edition, 1997. 306, 309

[16] Luis Correia and A. Steiger-Gargão. A useful autonomous vehicle with a hierarchical behavior control. In F. Moran, A. Moreno, J. J. Merelo, and P. Chacon, editors, *Advances in Artificial Life (Third European Conference on Artificial Life),* pages 625-639, Berlin, 1995. Springer. 307

[17] Nelson Cowan. The magical number 4 in short-term memory: A reconsideration of mental storage capacity. *Brain and Behavioral Sciences,* 24(1):87-114, 2001. 304

[18] D. Davidson. *Inquiries into Truth and Interpretation.* Clarendon Press, Oxford, 1985. 305

[19] Frans B. M. de Waal. Primates-a natural heritage of conflict resolution. *Science,* 289:586-590, 2000. 309

[20] W. Tecumseh Fitch. The evolution of speech: A comparative review. *Trends in Cognitive Sciences,* 4(7):258-267, 2000. 305

[21] Krzysztof Gajos. Rascal - a resource manager for multi agent systems in smart spaces. In *Proceedings of CEEMAS 2001,* 2001. 315

[22] Erann Gat. Three-layer architectures. In David Kortenkamp, R. Peter Bonasso, and Robin Murphy, editors, *Artificial Intelligence and Mobile Robots: Case Studies of Successful Robot Systems,* **pages 195-210. MIT Press, Cambridge, MA, 1998.** 306, 308

[23] M. P. Georgeff and A. L. Lansky. Reactive reasoning and planning. In *Proceedings of the Sixth National Conference on Artificial Intelligence (AAAI-87),* **pages 677682, Seattle, WA, 1987.** 306

[24] Alexander H. Harcourt. Coalitions and alliances: Are primates more complex than non-primates? In Alexander H. Harcourt and Frans B. M. de Waal, editors, *Coalitions and Alliances in Humans and Other Animals,* **chapter 16, pages 445472.** Oxford, 1992. 304

[25] Marc D. Hauser. *The Evolution of Communication.* **MIT Press, Cambridge, MA, 1996.** 304

[26] Henry Hexmoor, Ian Horswill, and David Kortenkamp. Special issue: Software architectures for hardware agents. *Journal of Experimental & Theoretical Artificial Intelligence,* 9(2/3), 1997. 307

[27] Henry H. Hexmoor. *Representing and Learning Routine Activities.* **PhD thesis, State University of New York at Buffalo, December 1995.** 306

[28] Mark Humphrys. *Action Selection methods using Reinforcement Learning.* **PhD thesis, University of Cambridge, June 1997.** 307

[29] Daniel Jurafsky and James H. Martin. *Speech and Language Processing: An Introduction to Natural Language Processing, Computational Linguistics, and Speech Recognition.* **Prentice Hall, Englewood Cliffs, New Jersey, 2000. ISBN 0130950696.** 304

[30] Chris Knight, Michael Studdert-Kennedy, and James R. Hurford, editors. *The Evolutionary Emergence of Language: Social function and the origins of linguistic form.* **Cambridge University Press, 2000.** 305

[31] Kurt Konolige and Karen Myers. The Saphira architecture for autonomous mobile robots. In David Kortenkamp, R. Peter Bonasso, and Robin Murphy, editors, *Artificial Intelligence and Mobile Robots: Case Studies of Successful Robot Systems,* **chapter 9, pages 211-242. MIT Press, Cambridge, MA, 1998.** 306

[32] David Kortenkamp, R. Peter Bonasso, and Robin Murphy, editors. *Artificial Intelligence and Mobile Robots: Case Studies of Successful Robot Systems.* **MIT Press, Cambridge, MA, 1998.** 306, 307

[33] John E. Laird and Paul S. Rosenbloom. The evolution of the Soar cognitive architecture. In D. M. Steier and T. M. Mitchell, editors, *Mind Matters.* **Erlbaum, 1996.** 306

[34] Victor R. Lesser. Reflections on the Nature of Multi-Agent Coordination and Its Implications for an Agent Architecture. *Journal of Autonomous Agents and MultiAgent Systems,* **1(1):89-111, 1998.** 303

[35] Pattie Maes. The agent network architecture (ANA). *SIGART Bulletin,* **2(4):115120,1991.** 307

[36] David L. Martin, Adam J. Cheyer, and Douglas B. Moran. The Open Agent Architecture: A framework for building distributed software systems. *Applied Artificial Intelligence,* **13(1-2):91-128, 1999.** 307

[37] Marvin Minsky. *The Society of Mind.* Simon and Schuster Inc., New York, NY, 1985. 306

[38] Hans P. Moravec. The Stanford Cart and the CMU Rover. In I. J. Cox and G. T. Wilfong, editors, *Autonomous Robot Vehicles,* pages 407-419. Springer, 1990. 306

[39] Nils J. Nilsson. Shakey the robot. Technical note 323, SRI International, Menlo Park, California, April 1984. 306

[40] David Lorge Pamas, Paul C. Clements, and David M. Weiss. The modular structure of complex systems. *IEEE Transactions on Software Engineering,* SE-11(3): 259-266, March 1985. 306, 309

[41] E. Pöppel. Temporal mechanisms in perception. *International Review of Neurobiology,* 37:185-202, 1994. 305

[42] Ronald A. Rensink. The dynamic representation of scenes. *Visual Cognition,* 7: 17-42,2000. 304

[43] Phoebe Sengers. Do the thing right: An architecture for action expression. In Katia P Sycara and Michael Wooldridge, editors, *Proceedings of the Second International Conference on Autonomous Agents,* pages 24-31. ACM Press, 1998. **307**

[44] Carles Sierra, Ramon López de Màntaras, and Dídac Busquets. Multiagent bidding mechanisms for robot qualitative navigation. In C. Castelfranchi and Y. Lesperance, editors, *The Seventh International Workshop on Agent Theories, Architectures, and Languages (ATAL2000).* Springer, 2001. **308**

[45] Katia Sycara, Keith Decker, Anandeep Pannu, Mike Williamson, and Dajun Zeng. Distributed intelligent agents. *IEEE Expert,* pages 36-45, December 1996. **307**

[46] Toby Tyrrell. *Computational Mechanisms for Action Selection.* PhD thesis, University of Edinburgh, 1993. Centre for Cognitive Science. **307**

[47] Mary J. Waller. The timing of adaptive group responses to nonroutine events. *Academy of Management Journal,* 42:127-137, 1999. **305**

[48] Gerhard Weiß, editor. *Multiagent Systems: A Modern Approach to Distributed Artificial Intelligence.* MIT Press, Cambridge, MA, 1999. **303**

Ontology Negotiation:
How Agents Can Really Get to Know Each Other

Sidney C. Bailin[1] and Walt Truszkowski[2]

[1] Knowledge Evolution, Inc.
1215 17th Street, NW, Suite 101, Washington, DC 20036, USA
sbailin@kevol.com
[2] NASA/Goddard Space Flight Center
Advanced Automation Technology Branch, Greenbelt, MD 20771, USA
walt.truszkowski@gsfc.nasa.gov

1   Introduction

The past several years have witnessed a proliferation of information sources on the world-wide-web, and of information agents with widely varying specialties. The unmanageability of massive amounts of information is becoming apparent and is having an impact on professions that rely on distributed archived information.

Ontology negotiation is becoming increasingly recognized as a crucial element of scalable agent technology. This is because agents, by their very nature, are supposed to operate with a fair amount of autonomy and independence from their end-users. Part of this independence is the ability to enlist other agents for help in performing a task (such as locating information on the web). The agents enlisted for help may be "owned" by a different end-user or organization (such as a document archive), and there is no guarantee that they will use the same terminology or understand the same concepts (objects, operators, theorems, rules) as the recruiting agent.

For NASA, the need for ontology negotiation arises at the boundaries between scientific disciplines. For example: modeling the effects of global warming might involve knowledge about imaging, climate analysis, ecology, demographics, industrial economics, and biology. The need for ontology negotiation also arises at the boundaries between scientific programs. For example, a Principal Investigator may want to use information from a previous mission to complement downloads from the instruments currently deployed.

1.1   Summary of Achievements

We have developed an ontology negotiation protocol (ONP) and a framework for implementing agents that use the protocol. We have created a test-bed in which a user agent and agents representing two large earth science archives cooperate to improve information retrieval performance. Specifically, the test-bed can handle queries that match documents in either or both archives but are not formulated in terms of either archive's taxonomy. The translation knowledge involved in satisfying the query is then added to the archives' ontologies, thereby improving future performance. For

W. Truszkowski, C. Rouff, M. Hinchey (Eds.): WRAC 2002, LNAI 2564, pp. 320–334, 2003.

these experiments we have used NASA's Global Change Master Directory and NOAA's Wind and Sea Index.

The absence of an explicit ontology in these (and most existing) archives presents an obvious challenge to the work. We have addressed it in the short term by deriving lightweight ontologies from the classification pages provided by each archive's web interface. In order to support the ONP, an ontology must provide more than a topic classification; it must provide answers to certain questions concerning synonyms and relations between topics. We have articulated these questions in the form of an application program interface (API) that an ontology must implement in order to support the ONP. For the purpose of experimentation, we developed simple forms of these functions for both the NASA and the NOAA archives.

In the longer term, we expect that web-based knowledge management techniques (involving XML, RDF, topic maps, or similar ideas) will gain widespread currency. This will enable automated agents to obtain ontology information from scientific archives through something resembling our current API.

2   Metaphors for Ontology Negotiation

In order to describe an ontology negotiation process, we have developed a couple of metaphors that suggest the kinds of dialogue that might occur. The first is that of a cocktail party; the second concerns information seeking in an office environment.

2.1   Agents in Hollywood: The Cocktail Party Metaphor

Consider a party attended by a multitude of agents, some of whom are strangers to each other. Imagine that two agents introduce themselves to each other and embark on a conversation. A frequent springboard for such conversations is the question, "What do you do?" In response, each agent would describe its job to the other. Depending on the level of mutual interest and the effectiveness of the communication, the conversation could progress to various levels of understanding.

At the most superficial level, each agent can answer the other, and the other agent, treating the exchange as a simple ritual of courtesy, might take no notice. It is conceivable that even such formalities might have a role in a world populated by agents. They could, for example, reassure an agent that it is moving among friendly peers.

A deeper level of communication would occur if each agent really tried to understand what the other agent does. A still deeper level would ensue if one of the participants intended to make practical use of that information. These distinctions can be expressed in terms of the progress of the conversation, with the deeper levels occurring only as the dialogue progresses:

Stage 1: Talking Distinct Languages. Since we assume that the agents are *strange* to each other, they may not even have the concepts necessary to understand what the other one does. Suppose agent A_1 has described its job to agent A_2 in terms that A_2 does not understand.

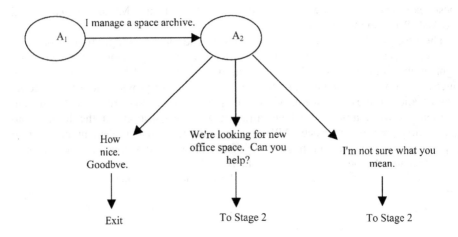

Fig. 1. An agent may respond to a misunderstood utterance in several ways

Three outcomes are possible, as illustrated in Figure 1:

- A_2 does not understand, and does not care. The conversation ends at this point.
- A_2 thinks it understands, although it does not. In this case, the process moves to the next stage, in which A_1 tries to clarify.
- A_2 does not understand, but wants to. The conversation proceeds to the next stage.

Stage 2: Guess and Confirm or Clarify. In the next stage, A_2 makes a guess as to what A_1 meant. This involves A_2 reformulating A_1's description in terms that A_2 understands. Three outcomes are again possible, as illustrated in Figure 2:

- A_1 understands A_2's reformulation, and confirms that it is correct.
- A_1 understands A_2's reformulation, but it is not correct. A_1 offers another description, trying to avoid the terms that A_2 evidently did not understand correctly.
- A_1 does not understand A_2's reformulation. The process may recursively enter the first stage again. This time, it is A_2's reformulation of A_1's description that requires clarification.

Stage 3: Take Note of the Other Agent's Self-Description. If the conversation has arrived at this stage, then A_2 thinks he understands A_1's self-description. This perception may or may not be correct (note the first possible outcome of Stage 1), but there is not necessarily any immediate need to test it. A_2 may then make a note of A_1's self-description for possible future reference. In the cocktail party metaphor, this is the point at which the agents ask for each other's card. Since further cooperation is deferred until a later conversation, there is no need for the agents to try to reconcile or merge their respective ontologies at this point.

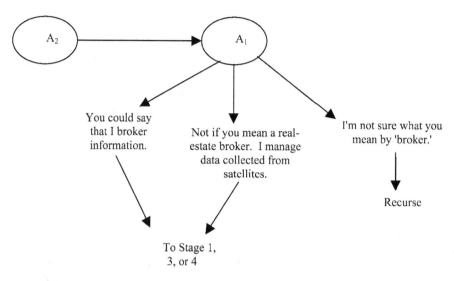

Fig. 2. Clarification of a misunderstood utterance may move the dialogue forward or lead to further misunderstanding

Stage 4: Dialogue to Deepen Mutual Understanding. If the desire for future cooperation is strong, the agents might expend more effort ensuring that they understand each other correctly. This would prevent them from embarking down a blind alley in the future, e.g., if there really were no opportunity for cooperation. A_2 will then try to make full semantic sense of A_1's self-description. This entails placing A_1's self-description within A_2's ontology. If A_1's self-description involves concepts that are new to A_2, then A_2's ontology must now expand. This is likely to involve a back-and-forth conversation between the agents. With each interchange, the agents may gain more confidence that they understand each other. In terms of the cocktail party metaphor, A_2 might ask A_1 a question such as,

> If we were tasked with XYZ and needed an ABC to do PQR, we would call on someone like you?

A_1 might respond,

> You *could* call on me in that situation, but a more appropriate use of my expertise would be to provide a UVW within XYZ.

This stage manifests the exploratory nature of ontology negotiation. It shows why there will always remain some doubt about the shared understanding of any particular concept. A continuing dialogue, however, can move the players asymptotically towards an acceptable level of mutual understanding.

Stage 5: Engage the Other Agent in a Task. Some time after the party is over, A_1 and A_3, having been introduced to each other by A_2, may want to contact each other. In our space mission scenario, if A_1 and A_3 are the respective agents for two mission archive agents, then A_1 may contact A_3 to help in satisfying the scientist's information request.

2.2   Back at the Office: The Information Retrieval Task

We now consider how the process might unfold when one agent tries to enlist the help of another in performing an information retrieval task. As a model of how the process might go, consider what happens in a purely human information access situation when the parties involved do not speak the same specialized language. The following series of steps illustrates a growing realization among the parties that there is a conceptual disconnect that must be resolved:

Stage 1: Respond to Query with Minimal Effort. The agent whose help is requested tries to acquit himself of his obligation with as little effort as possible. He returns information that matches the query at a superficial level, but is not really what the requester wanted. This is a common phenomenon in human organizations. Under time and resource pressure, the person whose help is being sought—the *server*—will try to minimize the work required to satisfy the request.

The server may quickly match terms in the request to a known category in his own conceptual organization. He will return whatever is found in that category, instead of trying to understand the requester' needs, goals, constraints, and any other context of the request. This is the state of practice in database systems, as well.

Stage 2: Express Dissatisfaction with Initial Response. In a database query setting, the user who has received an inadequate response typically tries to reformulate the query. She could relax certain constraints and add others. Choosing a different set of terms is often a matter of guesswork. The requester can try to explain why the initial response was unsatisfactory:

> This is not what I wanted. What I need is X, whereas what you gave me is Y.

With a better understanding of what the requester wants, the server can try again. The server may or may not request further clarification. If not, the requester's needs may still not be adequately understood, and the process will repeat itself.

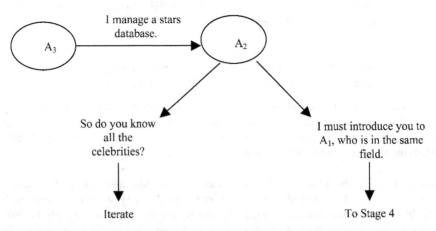

Fig. 3. A general understanding may suffice to identify another agent as a potential contact

Stage 3: Enlist Additional Help. The improved understanding that the server now has may lead it to contact another server. If the second server returns any information to the original server, the original server will package it together with his own data, perhaps filtered according to the requester's previous expression of dissatisfaction.

Stage 4: Negotiate Ontologies to Construct Integrated Story. The first and second servers must now negotiate to construct an integrated response to the query. They may discover that their ontologies are quite different, despite their use of many of the same terms. They may discover, in particular, that there are differences in the conceptual structures used to organize their respective data.

Stage 5: Evolve Ontologies. A successful negotiation between the two servers results in a shared understanding of concepts that were previously not held in common, or were understood differently. One way to do this is to explore the compositional history of a concept being negotiated. If the concept itself is not understood (or not understood properly) by the other agent, an agent can try to define the concept in more basic terms, which stand a better chance of being shared. This process can be iterated until the agents find fine-grained concepts in common. The second agent can then use the common concepts in one of the following ways:

- Add the new concept to its ontology
- Find the term in its ontology that represents the same, or a similar, concept
- Respond with a different understanding of the same term

The third case represents the greatest potential for ontology evolution. If the two understandings of the same term are similar but not identical, then the agents have different interpretations of the world, and not just different foci of attention.

3   Overview of the Protocol

Our goal is to specify and implement a robust method of ontology negotiation that allows web-based information agents to resolve semantic mismatches in real time without human intervention. The resulting software provides "strange" agents with a means of arriving at a common language in which to converse. "Common language" refers not just to syntax, but also to the *meaning* of terms exchanged by the agents. The meaning of a term can be represented by an ontology in any of several forms: e.g., as facts pertaining to the term, as rules governing the use of the term, or as structural information relating the term to other terms (e.g., the "is-a" relation).

Between information agents, the "terms exchanged" consist primarily of the *query content* and *document descriptors* for the query results. Both of these can be viewed as keywords describing the document that is either desired (query) or found (results). Our research to date indicates that there are three processes involved in this type of negotiation:

- *Clarifying* the meaning of keywords
- *Explaining* the relevance of the query results

- *Evolving* an agent's ontology on the basis of clarification and relevance explanation

In addition, agents need to be able to locate other agents capable of performing specific search, fusion, or filtering tasks. Other researchers have extensively explored the mechanisms for discovering an agent with specific capabilities and engaging it in a task. Their research, however, has tended to ignore the problems of semantic mismatch: When an agent announces that it has (or needs) a particular capability, will other agents necessarily understand the terms in which the capability is described? The question suggests that semantic clarification, and therefore ontology negotiation, should play a role in the negotiation of capabilities and assignments, as much as in the satisfaction of information requests.

3.1   Objects of the Protocol

The ONP is based on a small set of object types and operations on those objects. The available object types are presented in Table 1; some of them warrant explanation. *Queries* are requests to locate documents and/or URLs that are relevant to a set of descriptors (keywords). *Declination* expresses an agent's unwillingness to respond to a query (for reasons of capacity or capability), while *rejection* is an agent's expression of dissatisfaction with the current results of a query.

Confirmation of interpretation is an agent A's validation of an agent B's tentative understanding of a previous message from A. *Clarification* is the means by which an agent makes explicit the meaning of a previous message it sent.

An agent receives the results of a query as a set of URLs and document descriptors. It uses the descriptors (keywords) to *evaluate* the relevance of the results to the query. If it cannot see why a particular URL is relevant to the query, it can ask the agent that returned the results for an *explanation of relevance*. The structure of such an explanation is discussed in Section 4.3; here we just note that the explanation may include facts that are true in the server agent's ontology. When the querying agent receives an explanation of relevance, but it cannot derive a particular fact used in the explanation, it can request the server agent for an *explanation of fact*.

3.2   States and Transitions of the Protocol

States of the straw-man protocol correspond to performance of one or another operation on a particular type of object. The available operations are shown in Table 2.

Obviously not every combination of an operation and object represents a meaningful state. Table 3 presents the states of the ONP, using the abbreviations listed in Tables 1 and 2. For example, an agent can *wait* for a *capability statement* (if it has requested one) but it cannot *wait* for a *declination*. Similarly, an agent can *receive* a *declination* from another agent, but it cannot *receive* an *ontology*.

The behavior of agents participating in the protocol is determined by transitions between the possible states. Since there are 46 states defined in the straw-man protocol, the transitions are selected from the 46 x 46 element matrix of state pairs.

The range of possible transitions presents a challenge in implementing the protocol—especially to implement it in a maintainable fashion. We have addressed this problem through a tool that provides a high-level table-based means of specifying the states and transitions.

Table 1. Objects of the Ontology Negotiation Protocol

Object Type	Abbreviation	Object Type	Abbreviation
Query	Que	Confirmation of Interpretation	Cfi
Query Results	Qre	Clarification	Cla
Acknowledgement	Ack	Explanation of Relevance	Exr
Rejection	Rej	Explanation of Fact	Exf
Declination	Dcl	Ontology	Ont
Capabilities Statement	Cap		

Table 2. Operations of the Ontology Negotiation Protocol

Operation	Abbreviation	Operation	Abbreviation
Wait for	Wtg	Return	Ret
Request	Req	Interpret	Int
Receive Request for	Rrf	Interpret Request for	Irf
Receive	Rcd	Evaluate	Evl
Process	Pro	Evolve	Evo
Forward	Fwd		

Table 3. States of the ontology negotiation protocol

	Que	Qre	Ack	Rej	Dcl	Cap	Cfi	Cla	Exr	Exf	Ont
Wtg	x	x	x			x	x	x	x	x	
Req						x	x	x	x	x	
Rrf						x	x	x	x	x	
Rcd	x	x	x	x	x	x	x	x	x	x	
Pro	x										
Fwd	x										
Ret		x	x	x	x	x	x	x	x	x	
Int	x	x				x					
Irf						x					
Evl		x				x					
Evo											x

4   Ontology Negotiation Process

The state machine structure determines the shape of ontology negotiations. It does not determine how an agent decides whether to ask for clarification, or how an agent chooses to clarify a previous message. This is the heart of the ontology negotiation process. The fundamental tasks are interpretation, clarification, relevance evaluation, and ontology evolution

4.1   Interpretation

Interpretation is the process of determining whether a message just received is properly understood. In the test-bed, messages are sequences of keywords, and the recipient agent tries to interpret each keyword in turn. First, the agent checks its own ontology to see whether the keyword occurs there. If not, the agent queries the lexical database WordNet [1] to find synonyms of the keyword. Then it checks the ontology for any of these synonyms. If a synonym is located in the ontology, it represents an interpretation of the keyword. Since WordNet may identify distinct meanings for the keyword (homonyms), each synonym is only a possible interpretation, which must be confirmed by the source of the message. The recipient agent therefore requests a *confirmation of interpretation* from the source agent.

4.2   Clarification

If an agent is not able to interpret some of the keywords of a message it has received, it can decide to proceed anyway (if enough other keywords are understood), or it can request a *clarification* from the source of the message. Given the richness of its database, it would be tempting to invoke WordNet as the primary means of clarifying a keyword. This would be pointless, however, since the recipient agent has already gone to WordNet during the interpretation process. Instead, the message source draws on the following methods of clarification:

- Locating synonyms in the source agent's ontology
- Providing a complete set of specializations (keyword as the union of its subclasses) from the source's ontology
- Providing a weak generalization from the source's ontology
- Providing a definition in formal logic—in particular, defining the keyword as the conjunction of other keywords

The interfaces to these clarification methods are formulated abstractly in the ontology API. It is up to the ontology to decide how to implement them.

4.3   Relevance Analysis

Relevance analysis is the process of evaluating the results of a query against the query itself. In our approach the query is specified via keywords, and the results are documents or URLs that are also described by keywords. So the problem reduces to evaluating how well these sets of keywords match. The evaluation is performed for each URL that is returned. The current implementation computes a relevance measure for each result by accumulating *evidence of relevance* from the result document's keywords. Each keyword of the URL is examined in turn; if evidence of the keyword's relevance to the query can be found, the relevance measure is incremented.

Relevance analysis therefore reduces to the following question: given the set of *query* keywords, and a particular *result* keyword (of one of the returned URLs), what would constitute evidence that the result keyword is relevant to the query? If the result keyword *is* a query keyword, then clearly it is relevant. However, it is desirable to have other criteria since we are assuming an environment where there may not be a single controlling ontology. In the ontology API, the following tests are provided for determining whether keyword A and keyword B are relevant to each other:

- A is a specialization of B
- A and B have a common close generalization ("close" means not too far up the generalization tree)
- A and B have similar meanings (as decided by the ontology)
- A implies B
- The ranges of A and B intersect (i.e., A and B are compatible properties)
- A and B are connected by a series of facts that pair-wise have at least one predicate in common

The precise statement of the last criterion is rather involved; there are several variations, all of which contribute different degrees of relevance.

While the accumulation of relevance over terms is standard practice for general-purpose search engines, recourse to an ontology for semantic tests of the above-listed criteria is not. Discipline-specific engines may well resort to such criteria, and to the extent that they do, our inclusion of the criteria in the API is justified by example. In order to maintain flexibility with different levels of semantic support, the API allows an ontology to implement only a subset of the relevance criteria. In our current test-bed we have implemented only the specialization and connectedness tests.

4.4   Ontology Evolution

The negotiation process culminates in one or both agents modifying their ontology to introduce a new concept, a new distinction, or simply a new term for an existing concept. As in the case of explaining relevance, the algorithms and/or rules for modifying the ontology will depend on the ontology's representation and the tools used to maintain it. The API specifies only the kinds of updates that may be performed.

5   Example

The protocol attempts to capture these ideas just described. In a typical NASA scenario, a scientist enters a query to determine whether there is any research on cyclical interactions between global warming and industrial demographics, i.e., whether the geographic effects of warming impact economies in ways that might, in turn, impact climate change. Such an example has abundant potential for multidisciplinary input and consequent ontology mismatches. The user agent broadcasts a Request for Capability Statement to determine which agents (representing which archives) might be helpful in satisfying the scientist's request. Some of the archives consult WordNet to find familiar terminology that is synonymous with the terminology of the Capability Statements. They then send a Request for Confirmation of Interpretation to the user agent. If it is not able to interpret some terms in the Capability Statement at all, an archive agent can issue a Request for Clarification.

In response to a Request for Confirmation of Interpretation, the user agent may send a Confirmation or, if the interpretation was inaccurate, a Clarification. The process continues until the archive agent decides it has enough information to respond with a Capability Statement.

Now it is the user agent's turn to interpret and, if necessary, request confirmation of interpretation or clarification of the Capability Statement. The same sub-protocol that just occurred at the archive agent's initiative may now occur in reverse. Eventually the user agent will choose one or more archives to receive the query itself. If an archive's agent decides that it lacks the ability to respond to the query, it may decline. Alternatively, it may try to get other archives to respond. In that case, it forwards the query using the same protocol as the user agent has used (and is using) on behalf of the scientist.

When an archive returns search results to the user agent, another interpretation process ensues. First the user agent tries to interpret the keywords of the document descriptors in the result set. If there is a problem understanding the descriptors, another interpret-clarify-confirm cycle starts. When the user agent has decided it understands the search result descriptors enough to evaluate their relevance to the scientist's query, it begins the relevance evaluation.

The user agent then looks for evidence that each document is relevant to the query. The user agent consults the scientist's ontology to determine the relationships between the document keywords and the query terms. If a document achieves a relevance score greater than a certain threshold, it is accepted and its descriptor is cached for display to the scientist. If not, the user agent sends a Request for Explanation of Relevance to the archive that located the document.

When an archive's agent receives a Request for Explanation of Relevance, it goes through the same evidence collection process as the user agent did, but with the archive's ontology rather than the scientist's. It then returns the accumulated evidence to the user agent.

The user agent analyzes the Explanation of Relevance to determine three things: first, whether the explanation is credible; second, whether the explanation improves the relevance score of the document; third, if the score has improved, why the user agent was not able to accumulate this evidence itself, using the scientist's ontology.

The credibility of an explanation may depend on facts that the archive's agent accepts as true but the user agent does not (yet). For example, a fact might assert the close interdependency of two phenomena. If the user agent does not recognize the fact as a fact, it may send a Request for Explanation of Fact to the archive's agent. The archive's agent responds with an Explanation of Fact—in effect, an inference trail that summarizes how the fact came to be established in the archive's ontology. If no such record can be retrieved or inferred, the archive's agent can return an empty explanation.

GCMD Agent
Requesting Confirmation of Interpretation

Message I sent to User:

ask-all

:content ReqCfi [onto02.CapabilityRequest, [0] ['global warming' industry]
[onto02.Interpretation, ['global warming' industry, [Meaning Not Yet Confirmed]
[commercial enterprise] [manufacture] [manufacturing] [business enterprise]
[business] [diligence] [industriousness] [determination] [purpose]]]]

:reply-with GCMD993869700570
:sender GCMD
:receiver User

Fig. 4. Any agent can initiate an interpretation/clarification dialogue. In this case, the agent represents NASA's Global Change Master Directory (GCMD)

The Explanation of Fact may or may not be acceptable to the user agent. If it is acceptable, the relevance evaluation process continues with the added information obtained from the archive's agent. In addition, the user agent may decide to incorporate the relevance and fact explanations into the scientist's ontology, thus alleviating the need to go through this process again for similar search results.

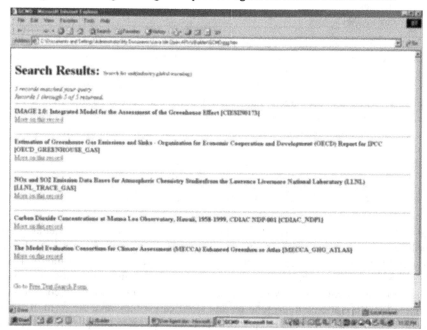

Fig. 5. Search results are returned in the form of a set of document descriptors. The raw results have not yet been evaluated by the user agent, and are not actually displayed to the user until they have been

---

User Agent
Requesting Explanation of Relevance

Message I sent to GCMD:

ask-all

:**content** ReqExr [onto02.QueryResult, [0] [POLICY] [] [PRECIPITATION] []
[ECOSYSTEMS]   []   [onto02.QueryResult.explanationOfRelevance]
[onto02.RelevanceExplanation,   [Relevance   Components,
[onto02.RelevanceComponent, ['global warming' industry] [INDUSTRY AND
ENERGY] [CONNECTED]] [onto02.RelevanceComponent, ['global warming'
industry] [INDUSTRIAL PRODUCTION] [CONNECTED]]] [Explanation of
Connected Terms]] [POLICY AND INSTITUTIONS] [] [BIOSPHERE] []
[INDUSTRY AND ENERGY] [] [INDUSTRIAL PRODUCTION] []
[ALGORITHM] [] [PREFERENCES; AND BEHAVIOR] [] [HUMAN
ATTITUDES;] [] [onto02.QueryResult.documentRef] [IMAGE 2.0: Integrated
Model for the Assessment of the Greenhouse Effect (CIESIN0173)]
[TEMPERATURE] [] [EOSDIS] [] [ATMOSPHERE] [] [LAND USE] []
[CLIMATE CHANGE] [] [MODEL] [] [GREENHOUSE GASES] [] [ENERGY]
[] [LAND AND FRESHWATER RESOURCES] []]

:**reply-with** User993870735909
:**sender** User
:**receiver** GCMD

Fig. 6. Several relevance criteria are used to map the document descriptors back to the query terms. If the mapping does not yield a high enough relevance score, the querying agent may request help from the server (archive) agent

Finally, when the user agent has filtered out those search results that it deems insufficiently relevant to the query, it presents the remaining results to the scientist. The scientist can then examine the results, access the documents directly through the source archive, or refine the search as with a conventional search engine.

6   Discussion: Ontology Conflict and Negotiation

The system employs the WordNet lexical database [1] as a source of extending each ontology's concept repertoire. However, the heart of the process lies in the exchanges between agents when WordNet by itself does not allow the agents to interpret each other's concepts. The exchanges, structured by the rules of the ONP, allow each agent to ask for clarification of previous messages and for confirmation or correction of attempted interpretations. Interpretation and clarification may take the form of simple substitution of synonyms, but the protocol provides for more complex forms such as formal logical definitions, operational descriptions (i.e., rules governing the use of concepts), and approximations to a concept's meaning.

At the same time, we have drawn a boundary between these exchanges and the way in which an agent modifies its ontology. The boundary takes the form of an application program interface (API) that specifies several ways of querying and evolving an ontology, but leaves the implementation of the operations unspecified. The semantics of the evolution operations are specified only insofar as they are reversed directions of the clarification and interpretation methods. For example, the operation addSlightGeneralization reverses the getSlightGeneralization. The semantics of the interpretation and clarification methods, also part of the ontology API, are to some extent specified by the rules of the ONP. There are logical barriers to completely specifying the semantics of these operations since that would be tantamount to defining truth, which cannot be done formally [2].

The notion of defining an API to an ontology deserves some explanation. Usually an ontology is considered as a relatively passive entity. Ontology authoring frameworks provide inference and computations to support the construction of an ontology and to perform queries against it, but the ontology itself is usually distinguished from this set of functions. In our work we are exploring the possibility of ongoing evolution of an ontology under the control of an autonomous agent. In the long-term vision, agents rather than humans are the primary authors and users of an evolving ontology, even if they start from a human-authored one. To support this, the ontology must reside within a framework that allows agents not only to query but also to modify the ontology. The API we have defined may be viewed as a minimal set of requirements for such a framework. Our belief that it is minimal is based on the kinds of functionality typically provided to the user by today's ontology authoring systems.

Our contribution is therefore not in a novel way of resolving ontology conflicts, which is an issue being addressed by work in ontology construction [3,4,5,6], semantics for world-wide-web searches [7,8,9], and mediation in information retrieval [10]. The ONP is, rather, a set of rules for cooperatively attacking the problem when it arises during agent communication. Consider what happens when two people try to negotiate an ontology conflict. They try to elicit from each other information that allows each of them to understand the other's utterances. It is ultimately up to each person to decide what to do with the new information, e.g., to assimilate a new concept, to place it in relation to previously known concepts, to create a distinction not previously acknowledged, etc. The ONP is an attempt to automate the inter-agent dialogue. It neither replaces the necessary methods for modifying an ontology, nor is it subsumed by those methods.

As a protocol for agent communication, the ONP is related to standards such as the Knowledge Query Markup Language [11] and the Federation for Intelligent Physical Agents (FIPA) Agent Communication Language [12]. The ONP is built on top of KQML, and could easily be adapted to FIPA ACL. In addition, while this is not currently the case, the Knowledge Interchange Format [13] could be used to represent the logical descriptions that are exchanged within these messages.

7   Conclusion

We have described a novel approach to attacking the proliferation of information agent ontologies. We have created a software implementation framework that facilitates continued experimentation as well as the development of agents representing other scientific archives. We have layered the reasoning process so that an ontology need only support a well-defined API in order to operate within the framework. We have demonstrated the utility of the approach in a test-bed that includes ontology proxies for NASA's Global Change Master Directory and NOAA's Wind and Sea index.

References

[1]   Fellbaum, C. WordNet: An Electronic Lexical Database. MIT Press, 1998.

[2]   Tarski, A. On Undecidable Statements in Enlarged Systems of Logic and the Concept of Truth. Journal of Symbolic Logic, Vol. 4, 1939. Pages 105-112.

[3]   Clark, P. and Porter, B. Building Concept Representations from Reusable Components. AAAI 97, pages 369 - 376.

[4]   Cybenko, G. and Jiang, G. Matching Conflicts: Functional Validation of Agents. Agent Conflicts: Papers from the 1999 AAAI Workshop. Technical Report WS-99-08, AAAI Press, Menlo Park, CA, 1999. Pages 14 - 19.

[5]   McCallum, A., Nigam, K., Rennie, J., and Seymore, K. Building Domain-Specific Search Engines with Machine Learning Techniques. Intelligent Agents in Cyberspace: Papers from the 1999 AAAI Symposium, March 22 - 24, Stanford, CA. Technical Report SS-99-03, AAAI Press, Menlo Park, CA, 1999. Pages 28 – 39.

[6]   Takeda, H., Iwata, M., Sawada, A., and Nishida, T. An Ontology-based Cooperative Environment for Real-world Agents. Second International Conference on Multi-Agent Systems (ICMAS 96). AAAI Press, 1996. Pages 353 - 360.

[7]   Decker, S., Brickley, D., Saarela, J., and Angele, J. A Query and Inference Service for RDF. QL'98: The Query Languages Workshop, Boston, MA 1998. Available at: http://www.w3.org/TandS/QL/QL98/pp/queryservice.html.

[8]   Guarino N., Masolo C., and Vetere G., OntoSeek: Content-Based Access to the Web, IEEE Intelligent Systems 14(3), May/June 1999, pages 70-80.

[9]   Heflin, J., Hendler, J., Luke, S. Coping with Changing Ontologies in a Distributed Environment. *Ontology management, Papers from the AAAI Workshop*, Technical Report WS-99-13, American Association for Artificial Intelligence (AAAI) Press, 1999.

[10]   Wiederhold, G. Mediators in the architecture of future information systems, IEEE Computer 25, 1992.

[11]   Finin, T., Labrou, Y., Mayfield, J. KQML as an Agent Communication Language , in *Software Agents*, ed. J. Bradshaw, MIT Press, Cambridge, Available at http://www.cs.umbc.edu/kqml/papers. 1997.

[12]   FIPA Agent Communications Language, FIPA 97 Specification, Version 2. Available at: http://fipa.org/repository/index.html. October, 1998.

[13]   KIF. Knowledge Interchange Format: Draft Proposed American National Standard, NCITS.T2/90-004. Available at:
       http://logic.stanford.edu/kif/dpans.html . 1998.

An Extended Bayesian Belief Network Model of Multi-agent Systems for Supply Chain Management

Ye Chen and Yun Peng

Department of Computer Science and Electrical Engineering
University of Maryland Baltimore County, Baltimore, MD 21250, USA
{yechen,ypeng}@cs.umbc.edu

Abstract. In this paper, we describe our on-going research on uncertainty analysis in Multi-agent Systems for Supply Chain Management (MASCM). In a MASCM, an agent consists of automation processes within a legal entity in the specific supply chain network. It conducts supply chain planning, execution and cooperation on behalf of its owner. Each day these agents have to process a large volume of data from different sources with mixed signals not to be anticipated in advance. Thus, one challenge every agent has to face in this volatile environment is to quickly identify the impact of unexpected events, and take proper adjustments in both local procedures and related cross-boundary interactions. To facilitate the study of uncertainty in the complex system of MASCM, we model agent system behaviors by abstracting its significant operational aspects as observation, propagation and update of uncertainty ifnromation. The resulting theoretical model, called an extended Bayesian Belief Network (eBBN), may serve as the basis for developing an uncertainty management component for a large-scale electronic supply chain system. We also briefly describe ways this model can be used to solve different supply chain tasks and some simulation results that demonstrate the power of this model in improving the system performance.

1 Introduction

A Multi-agent System for Supply Chain Management (MASCM) comprises of a number of software agents (or agents for short in this paper) that sell and buy products (goods or services) on behalf of their owners. In a MASCM, the essential business activities of individual agents can be defined as an *Order Fulfillment Process* (OFP), which is the effort for an agent to satisfy the requests triggered by its customers' orders. At the system level, the supply chain management is the combination of all agents' activities ignited by one end order from the system's end customer. When an end order arrives, a Virtual Supply Chain (VSC), consisting of agents at different tiers in the chain, may emerge through multiple interconnected OFPs. The ultimate goal of the system management is to form VSCs that can successfully complete this

W. Truszkowski, C. Rouff, M. Hinchey (Eds.): WRAC 2002, LNAI 2564, pp. 335-346, 2003.
© Springer-Verlag Berlin Heidelberg 2003

end order, and the system's performance can be measured by the rate that all end orders are completed.

In the real life the formation of VSCs is affected by many unexpected factors within the system. They can be physical failures such as electricity outages, virus attacks, strikes, and so on. In addition, agents may change their trading partners following the owners' instructions, reflecting the change of the market. Uncertainty brought by these unexpected events may have negative impact on the system performance, e.g. prolong the time of VSC formation or breaking down an already formed VSC [1]. To protect their common interest of attracting more customers from such negative impacts, agents in a MASCM are often willing to cooperate with each other by sharing uncertainty information and analysis.

Bayesian Belief Network (BBN) has been established as a powerful and theoretically well-founded framework for representing and reasoning with ucnertainty. BBN initially arose from an attempt to incorporate the probability theory into expert systems, and has an origin and long history in decision analysis [2]. Nowadays, BBN model has been used in the fields such as diagnosis, reinforce learning, speech recognition, tracking, data compression, etc. One of the best-known examples of BBN applications is a decision-theoretic reformulation of the Quick Medical Reference (QMR) model [3] for internal medicine. Other practical applications include real time decision under uncertain situations [4], human-computer interaction analysis [5], deep-space exploration and knowledge acquisition [6], and the popular productive software Microsoft Office, to mention just a few.

In this paper, we present our research effort to develop a theoretical model, by extending the conventional BBN formulation, that formalizes agents' interactions in an uncertain environment. The model can be directly implemented as a separate component for MASCM system uncertainty management, and may also serve as the platform to analyze the relationship between uncertainty and various measures of system performance.

The rest of this paper is organized as follows. Section 2 gives a description of agent behaviors in OFPs and a general discussion on eBBN approach to modeling agent interactions; Section 3 introduces a simplified type of MASCM, called $MASCM_1$; Section 4 presents two eBBN models for the formation and evolution of VSCs in a $MASCM_1$. Finally, Section 5 concludes the paper with a brief discussion on how this model can be used to solve some important supply chain management tasks together with some simulation experiment results, and suggestions for further research. Due to the page limitation, proofs for theorems and lemmas are omitted.

2   Modeling Agent Behaviors

Suuply chain activities an agent is involved in can be abstracted as an order fulfillment process (OFP) [9], which can be logically divided into the following steps.

Order Generation. Based on the commitment that is made to its customer's order or set by its human owner, the agent selects suppliers for the products needed to fulfill this commitment, generates orders and chooses negotiation strategies for each of the selected suppliers. The agent may generate more than one order in order to fulfill a given commitment.

Negotiation. The agent sends orders to the selected suppliers and negotiates with them. An agent can negotiate simultaneously with different suppliers. However, we assume in this paper that at any time, the agent only negotiates with one supplier. That is, the default negotiation protocol between two agents is bilateral. At the end of this stage, through negotiation, a mutual commitment between two agents may be reached.

Commitment Processing. The agent processes the outstanding commitment it made to its customer, handles the unexpected events, and exchanges information with its supplier and customers about the status of the commitment. At the end of this stage, an order an agent receives (e.g., the commitment its made to its customer) may or may not be eventually fulfilled. When one of the agent's suppliers aborts the commitment and there is no alternative supplier to provide the same product, it has to cancel the commitment to its customer. The consequence of commitment cancellation also causes the agent to cancel all orders to other direct suppliers involved in this particular transaction, provided these orders have not yet been eventually solved. The order cancellation may propagate both upstream and downstream. However, when all direct suppliers of an agent fulfill their commitments, that is, deliver all the products the agent needs, an OFP initialized by this agent is considered completed.

The OFP triggered by an end order will propagate through OFPs of its suppliers, and suppliers' suppliers, etc. and a virtual supply chain (VSC) consisting of all agents involved is dynamically formed. In OFPs, agents interact with each other in order to reach mutual agreement and when they indeed reach one, agents will keep contacting the other parties until their agreed commitments are fulfilled. In other words, the commitment plays a central role in agent interactions. Therefore, the probability that a commitment will be fulfilled successfully or unsuccessfully can be used to measure the uncertainty of an agent's behaviors in the process. Accordingly, the system performance in an uncertain environment can be described as the likelihood of commitments held by the end customer agents being successfully fulfilled.

Also note that in a particular OFP, as described above, the customer agent initiates the process, but the supplier agents determine the progress of the process. From this perspective, the supply-demand relationship between an agent and its direct suppliers can be viewed as a causal one where the failure of fulfilling commitments by one's suppliers may cause its commitment to its downstream customers to fail. Therefore, the failure probability of commitments held by a pair of supply and customer agents are causally linked. More specifically, in a VSC, commitments held by individual agents and the supply-demand relationships between them form a casual network. This observation allows us to use BBN as a framework to formalize agents' interaction in the uncertain environment as the following.

- Model commitment failure probabilities as agents' beliefs.
- Model direct supply-demand relationships between pairs of agents as directed causal links (from the direct supplier to the customer).
- Model information sharing between agents as belief propagation.

However, the conventional BBN framework is inadequate in modeling MASCM agent interactions for at least the following reasons. First, causal links in conventional BBNs are static (unless learning or adaptation is involved) while the supply-demand relationships among MASCM agents may change over time. Although each agent in the system has in its inventory a certain level of safety stock of products it needs, such safety stock can only smooth out the uncertain fluctuation of supplies to an extent. Significant change of current suppliers' commitments may cause an agent to terminate its current orders to one supplier and switch to another one for the same product. Therefore, the causal network of commitments is not static but dynamically created and updated with the evolution of a VSC. Secondly, conventional BBN can only represent observations but not actions [???]. However, agents' actions such as the decisions to cancel a commitment or to switch suppliers, as well as other strategic actions, are the important uncertain sources that impact the failure probabilities of commitments of other agents. These impacts can be propagated through agents in the whole VSC through interconnected OFPs and, thus, have to be modeled within the framework. In the following sections, we introduce extended Bayesian Belief Network (eBBN) models for a simply type of MASCM that can represent the dynamic casual structure and actions according to VSC evolution.

3   MASCM₁

In this section we define a simple type of MASCM, called $MASCM_1$. We first introduce the notations used, then state the assumptions that define $MASCM_1$.

3.1   Symbols

We use symbol A_i to denote an agent. Accordingly, the MASCM is defined as a set of agents $S = \{A_1, A_2, \ldots A_n\}$. The set of all products provided by all agents in a MASCM is denoted as $G = \{g_1, g_2, \ldots g_m\}$. The final product that sells to the end customers is denoted as g_F, and usually is the first element in G, i.e., $g_1 = g_F$. We use notation $G(A_i)$ to denote the products agent A_i provides to its direct customers. We use symbols A_i^s, A_i^c to denote the sets of A_i's direct suppliers and customers, respectively in a VSC; and $|A_i^s|$ and $|A_i^c|$ their cardinalities. Symbol $A_i \cdot A_j$ is used to denote that agent A_i and its direct supplier agent A_j are currently engaged in some business activities such as negotiation and exchange of commitment information.

3.2   Assumptions

Our work in this paper is based on a simplified MASCM system, $MASCM_1$, which is defined by the following assumptions.

- **Assumption 1.** There is only one end customer agent in the system, denoted as $A_1 \in S$. In other words, $A_1^c = \phi$ since its customer is not an agent but an entity outside the MASCM.

- **Assumption 2.** Each agent, except agent A_1, has exactly one customer in a VSC. That is, $\forall A_i \in S$, if $i \neq 1$, then $|A_i^c| = 1$.
- **Assumption 3.** Each agent makes or holds no more than one commitment to its customer agent at a given time.
- **Assumption 4.** No agent will order the same product from two or more different suppliers at the same time. That is, at any given time, if $\exists A_i \cdot A_j$ and $\exists A_i \cdot A_k$, and $G(A_j) = G(A_k)$, then $j = k$.
- **Assumption 5.** $\forall A_i \in S$, its commitment made to its customer has certain probability to fail when any of its demand for certain product to its suppliers is not satisfied. However, if all these demands are satisfied, the commitment will be fulfilled successfully, unless its owner decides to cancel it.
- **Assumption 6.** Different OFPs triggered by A_i are independent of each other.

Assumptions 1 and 2 simplify the system architecture, and Assumptions 3 and 4 simplify the agent interaction transactions. Assumption 5 says any failure from an agent A_i's direct supplier may cause its own commitment to fail. When all commitments (if there are any) by its direct suppliers have been fulfilled, the commitment that an agent made to its own customer agent is considered as successful accomplished. Assumption 6 regulates that OFPs between two agents, agent A_i and one of its direct supplier agent A_j, are not created or affected by other on-going or finished OFPs initiated of A_i's other suppliers. Assumptions 5 and 6 are similar to "Accountability" and "Exception Independence" assumptions made for Noisy-Or networks, a type of special BBN. A MASCM that follows above assumptions (Assumptions 1 - 6) is a system of $MASCM_1$.

4   eBBN Models for $MASCM_1$

In this section we show how to use and extend BBN framework to model $\textbf{\textit{MASCM}}_1$ agent interactions in an uncertain environment. Two models, $\textbf{\textit{eBBN}}_0$ and $\textbf{\textit{eBBN}}_1$, will be presented.

Fig. 1. A direct link between two CFVs

4.1 $eBBN_0$: Modeling a Formed VSC

A formed VSC in a $MASCM_1$ consists of agents connected by OFPs, all the way to the upper most tiers of suppliers, triggered by one end order. If all commitments made by the agents in the VSC are successfully fulfilled, the order of the end customer will be accomplished. A formed VSC is thus represents an possible solution to an end order. The likelihood of the end order been accomplished is affected by the likelihood of commitments made by other agents to fail. Since a formed VSC is static, it can be modeled by a standard BBN without involving actions. This leads to our first model $eBBN_0$ as follows.

Definition 1. Commitment Failure Variable (CFV) x_i is a binary random variable. Each CFV x_i is associated with an agent A_i in a formed VSC, representing the current belief of the status of the commitment made by agent A_i to its customer. $x_i = 1$ means the commitment fails; $x_i = 0$ means the commitment is successfully accomplished.

The CFVs are represented as nodes in the belief network, connected by direct causal links. Specifically, for any pair of agents A_j and A_i in a formed VSC and $A_j \in A_i^s$, there is a directed link $< x_j, x_i >$ from x_j to x_i, as illustrated in the following figure, indicating that x_j (failure of commitment of A_j to A_i) is a direct cause of x_i (failure of commitment of A_i to its customer).

Definition 2. For a given formed VCS, define $eBBN_0 = (V_0, E_0)$, where $V_0 = \{x_i \mid x_i \in VSC\}$ and $E_0 = \{< x_j, x_i > \mid A_i \cdot A_j \in VSC\}$.
Model $eBBN_0$ has two important properties.

Theorem 1. Model $eBBN_0$ is a tree.

Theorem 1 comes directly from Assumptions 1 – 4 and Definition 2. To represent the underlying causal mechanism, as suggested in [7, 8], we use a random variable c_{ji} to denote the causal connection from x_j to x_i. If $c_{ji} = 1$, then $x_j = 1$ indeed causes $x_i = 1$. Otherwise, $x_j = 1$ does not affect $x_i = 1$. Then, we have the following Lemma, which comes directly from Assumptions 5 and 6..

Theorem 2. The model $eBBN_0$ is a Noisy-Or network.

Theorems 1 and 2 show agent interaction in a formed VSC can be formalized as a Noisy-Or network. Therefore, agents can share and analyze uncertain information through the well-established rules for this type of belief networks. For example, at any given time, an agent can estimate the failure probability of the current commitment it holds based on the failure probabilities of its direct suppliers using the following equation [7,8],

$$P(x_i = 1) = 1 - \prod_{x_j \in \pi_i} (1 - e_{ji} P(x_j = 1)) \tag{1}$$

where e_{ji} is the causal strength of link $<x_j, x_i>$, π_i is the set of parents of x_i (i.e., direct suppliers of A_i). Moreover, since $eBBN_0$ has a tree structure, belief propagation in $eBBN_0$ can be computed in time polynomial to the network size $|VSC|$ [7].

$eBBN_0$ captures causal relations in a static VSC. However, in the uncertain environment, VSC hardly remain static. Cancellation of a commitment by an agent (either due to failures of its suppliers or other reasons) may cause the agent's customer to seek another, alternative supplier. In other words, the structure of a VSC in a $MASCM_1$ may undergo changes over time, moving from one formed VSC to another, until a final solution VSC is realized or the end order fails eventually. To model the dynamic change of VSC in a $MASCM_1$, we introduce the model of $eBBN_1$ in the following subsection.

4.2 $eBBN_1$: Modeling an Evolving VSC

After an end order arrives at the system until it is eventually resolved, a VSC keeps evolving as agents adjust their behaviors, e.g. canceling orders to one supplier and switching to another one, according to its accumulated uncertain information. To model the evolution of VSC, two types of nodes/variables are introduced and added into $eBBN_0$. The resulting model is called $eBBN_1$.

4.2.1   Definition of $eBBN_1$

To model the dynamic change of the VSC, we need to represent the selection of a particular supplier for a given product an agent needs at a given time, as well as the change of the selection as the VSC evolves. We also need to ensure that, when all selections are made at a time, the model should works like $eBBN_0$ because all selected agents form a VSC. This is achieved by the introducing into $eBBN_0$ the following two types of new variables, l_{ji} and y_{ji}.

Definition 3. l_{ji} is a binary random variable associated with an agent A_i and one of its supplier A_j. If $l_{ji} = 1$, then $A_i \cdot A_j$ is in A_i's OFP (i.e., A_j is selected as one of A_i's supplier), if $l_{ji} = 0$, then agent A_j is not currently involved in agent A_i's OFP.

Variable l_{ji} represents an observable consequence of agent A_i's decisions for selecting or switching negotiation partners (suppliers). According to Assumption5, each agent in a $MASCM_1$ can only chooses one direct supplier for certain product it needs at a time. This lead to the following lemma.

Lemma 1. At any given time, if $l_{ji} = 1$ and $l_{ki} = 1$, $A_j, A_k \in A_i^S, G(A_j) = G(A_k)$,, then $j = k$.

The commitment failure variable x_j becomes a direct cause of x_i only when A_j is selected as a direct supplier of A_i (i.e., $l_{ji} = 1$). Otherwise, they are causally unrelated. This is captured by another type of node y_{ji}.

Definition 4. The binary random variable y_{ji} has two parents l_{ji}, and x_j; and one child x_i, with the following conditional probability distribution

$$P(y_{ji} = x_j \mid l_{ji} = 1, x_j) = P(y_{ji} = x_j \mid l_{ji} = 1) = 1;$$
$$P(y_{ji} = 0 \mid l_{ji} = 0, x_j) = P(y_{ji} = 0 \mid l_{ji} = 0) = 1.$$

The node y_{ji} serves as a "gate" between two CFV x_j and x_i, and is controlled by variable l_{ji}. When the gate is open (when $l_{ji} = 1$), node y_{ji} serves as the proxy node of x_j and passes its influence to x_i, causing x_i to update its belief. When the gate is closed (when $l_{ji} = 0$), y_{ji} becomes zero regardless the value of x_j, implying that x_j does not influence x_i (i.e., A_j is not part of the current VSC). With these variables and the links $< x_j, y_{ji} >$, $< y_{ji}, x_i >$, and $< l_{ji}, y_{ji} >$ among them, we can formally define $eBBN_1$.

Definition 5. For a given $MASCM_1$, define $eBBN_1 = (V_1, E_1)$, where

$$V_1 = \{x_i, l_{ji}, y_{ji} \mid A_i, A_j \in S, A_j \in A_i^S\} \text{ and}$$
$$E_1 = \{< x_j, y_{ji} >, < y_{ji}, x_i >, < l_{ji}, y_{ji} > \mid A_i, A_j \in S, A_j \in A_i^S\}.$$

The following figure shows a portion of an $eBBN_1$

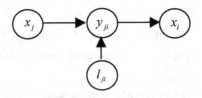

Fig. 2. Nodes and links related in $eBBN_1$

4.2.2 Properties of $eBBN_1$

We have the following theorem about the structure of $eBBN_1$, based on Theorem 1 and Definition 5.

Theorem 3. Mode of $eBBN_1$ is a tree.

Similar to model of $eBBN_0$, $eBBN_1$ formalize agents' interactions in an evolving VSC as the probability distributions of individual CFV change. But unlike $eBBN_0$, this model can represent dynamically changing causal structures with evolving VSC and extends the representation capability of conventional BBN. Accordingly, agents can use the following theorem to estimate the impact of outside uncertain factors on the commitment it holds.

Theorem 4. $P(x_i = 1) = \prod_{\substack{l_{ji}=1 \\ x_j \in \pi_i}} (1 - e_{ji} P(x_j = 1)), A_i, A_j \in S, A_j \in A_i^s$.

Theorem 4 can be proved using Theorems 2 and 3, Lemma 1, Definitions 4 and 5, and Eq. (1) in Subsection 4.1. The apparent similarity of Theorem 4 and Eq. (1) is due to the fact that all agents in $MASCM_1$ paired with $l_{ji} = 1$ form a VSC which can be modeled by . Therefore, The belief updates in $eBBN_1$ can be carried our in a way similar to $eBBN_0$, provided the values of l_{ji} are properly determined.

5   Experiment

Limited computer simulations have been conducted to validate our theoretical models and to see if the system performance can be improved when some of these algorithms are used. In this section, we briefly discuss the simulation and experiment result.

The implemented MASCM consists of eight different agents. They sit at three different tiers. At Tier 0, there is only one end customer agent. At Tier 1, there are three agents. They are suppliers of the end customer agents. At Tier 2, there are four agents. Agents have known their direct customer and suppliers at system design time. When there is an end order arrives, the inter-connected OFPs will be triggered and an evolving VSC emerges. Each agent has similar architectures to complete an OFP with three processes inside, a supplier selection procedure, a customer relationship management process, and a local order fulfillment decision process. The system satisfied all of the assumptions we listed in Section 4, thus it can be modeled by an $eBBN_1$.

We intend to compare different information cooperation schemas in an uncertain environment based on the model of $eBBN_1$. The uncertain environment here is measured by the rate of unexpected events that occurring in the agents at Tier 2 during the time period between an end order's arrival and its disappearance. The unexpected events represent the uncontrollable factors from inside or outside of MASCM that are observed by agents. These events change the possibility of the on-going OFP that the agent is currently processing. Use the term of $eBBN_1$, these changes update the failure probability distribution of variable of x_i

Two cooperation schemas in the experiment represent the most likely long-term cooperation strategies in terms of supply chain management. The first one is that agent will notify others whenever there are some observed changes that might cause the OFP not to be finished according to the original negotiated contracts; in the second schema, an agent notifies the others when an OFP has been finalized, that is, either is successfully accomplished or aborted in the half way. We called these two schemas as S1 and S2 respectively.

In the experiment we compare two schemas by counting the ratio of the number of successful accomplished orders to total incoming orders given certain amounts of unexpected events occurs during one end order life cycle. The ratio is defined as the system performance. The experiment shows without considering other factors, the overall system performance, which is measured by the rate or the percentage of all end orders that can be successfully fulfilled by the formed VSCs, is heavily affected by the number of unexpected events occurring in the system. The higher frequency of unexpected event occurs, the lower system performance is. However, our result also shows if agents interactions follow S1, and when algorithms discussed above are used in agent decision procedures, system performance can keep at a relatively stable level even when the number of total uncertain events increases. The following figure shows the comparison of system performance when agent interactions follow S1 and S2 as the number of unexpected events in the system increases with 1000 end orders. Additional experiments show that this trend continues when the number of end orders increased to 3000.

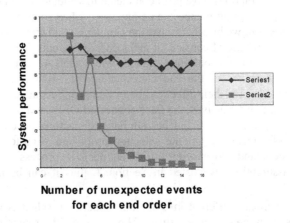

Fig. 3. System performance comparison in computer simulation

6   Conclusions

In the previous sections, we have discussed how to formalize agent interactions in a formed and evolving VSC in a $MASCM_1$ using conventional and extended BBN frameworks, $eBBN_0$ and $eBBN_1$, respectively. Model $eBBN_0$ establishes the theoretical basis to study agent interactions in an OFP. Model $eBBN_1$ further extends the representation capabilities of conventional BBN to describe the dynamically updating supply-demand relationship when interactions are exposed in an uncertain environment. These models can be used to help solving various supply chain management tasks, and several algorithms have been developed. They include algorithms for individual agents to compute beliefs of their commitments based on beliefs of commitments from their direct suppliers, to select prospective suppliers (either initially or when a previously selected supplier fails) during VSC evolution, to cancel an existing commitment based on the expected utility function, and algorithms to identify the most critical link (the agent in a VSC whose commitment has the highest failure probability) and the most fragile link (the agent in a VSC who is most responsible when the end order fails).

Work reported in this paper represents the first step of our effort toward a comprehensive solution to the uncertain management in supply chain. One obvious limitation of this work is with the assumptions made $MASCM_1$ and $eBBN_1$. Future work is needed to relax these restrictions so that more realistic situations can be modeled. This include allowing each agent to received multiple orders from more than one direct customers at the same time, and each type of product to supplied by more than one suppliers in a VSC. These may be achieved by extending our models from Noisy-Or like networks to more general ones with more complex conditional probability distributions. Also, one of the important uncertainty source, agents' strategic actions based on its internal decision process, are not included in the representation. How to incorporate these actions into our uncertainty models, and what information sharing rules and algorithms are needed for that purpose is another direction of further investigation.

Acknowledgement

The authors would like to thank Rakesh Mohan, Reed Letsinger, and Tim Finin for their valuable contributions to this research.

References

[1]   H. L. Lee, V. Padmanabhan, and S. Whang, "The Bullwhip Effect in Supply Chains," *Sloan Management Reviews*, Spring, pp. 46-49, 1997.

[2]   R. E. Neapolitan, Probabilistic Reasoning in Expert System: theory and algorithms, John Willey & Sons, Inc, 1989.

[3]   K. P. Murphy, "A Brief Introduction to Graphical Models and Bayesian Networks," *http://www.cs.berkeley.edu/~murphyk/Bayes/bayes.html.*

[4]   E. Horvitz, "Thinking Ahead: Continual Computation Policies for Allocating Offline and Real-Time Resources," in *Proceedings of the Sixteenth International Joint Conference on Artificial Intelligence, IJCAI '99*, pp. 1280-1286, 1999.

[5]   E. Horvitz, J. Breese, D. Heckerman, D. Hovel, and K. Rommelse, "The Lumiere Project: Bayesian User Modeling for Inferring the Goals and Needs of Software Users," in *Proceedings of the Fourteenth Conference on Uncertainty in Artificial Intelligence*, pp. 1068-1069, July 1998.

[6]   J. Stutz, W. Taylor, and P. Cheeseman, "AutoClass C: General Information," http://ic-www.arc.nasa.gov/ic/projects/bayes-group/autoclass/autoclass-cprogram.html#AutoClass C.

[7]   J. Pearl, Probabilistic Reasoning in Intelligent Systems: Networks of Plausible Inference, Morgan Kauffman, CA, 1988.

[8]   Y. Peng, and J. Reggia, *Abductive Inference Model for Diagnostic Problem Solving*, Springer-Verlag, New York, 1990.

[9]   T. J. Strader, F. Lin, and M. J. Shaw, "Simulation of Order Fulfillment in - Divergent Assembly Supply Chains," *Journal of Artificial Societies and Social Simulation*, Vol. 1, No. 2, pp. 36-37, 1998.

Agent Communication in DAML World*

Youyong Zou, Tim Finin, Yun Peng, Anupam Joshi, and Scott Cost

Computer Science and Electrical Engineering
University of Maryland Baltimore County, USA
{yzou1,finin,peng,joshi,cost}@cs.umbc.edu

Abstract. Darpa Agent Markup Language (DAML) [7] is the newest effort for Semantic Web [5]. It can be used to create ontologies and markup information resource like web pages. The information resource can be read by human and understood by agent programs. We believed DAML could be used to markup agent communication content and promote knowledge sharing and exchanging between agents. This paper also suggested an alternative model to connect web and agent together. We defined the necessary ontologies for agent communication in DAML language and described the agent communication scenario occurred in the ITTalks Project.

Keywords: Agent Communication Language, Ontology, Semantic Web, Software Agents, DAML

1 Introduction

Semantic Web activities from W3C and other groups like On-To-Knowledge, Darpa, defined specifications and technologies to support knowledge sharing across applications. DAML is the joint effort from US DAML group and Europe Semantic Web Technologies, supported by US Darpa. DAML Language is based on RDF, RDF Schema and benefit from SHOE [10] and OIL [11]. The goal is to markup and embed ontology into the massive web pages so that they are not only viewable by humans, also understandable by programs.

Agent Communication Language (ACL) provides agents with a means of exchanging information and knowledge. Knowledge Query and Manipulation Language (KQML) and the Foundation for Intelligent and Physical Agents (FIPA) ACL are two most widely used ACLs. The work described in this paper was based on FIPA ACL. The FIPA ACL [2, 3] specification consists a set of message types and the description of their effects to the sender and receiver agents. It can be used build high-level interaction protocols, such as contract net and auctions.

---

* This work was supported in part by the Defense Advanced Research Projects Agency under contract F30602-00-2-0 591 AO K528 as part of the DAML program (http://daml.org/). Submitted to the First GSFC/JPL Workshop on Radical Agent Concepts

W. Truszkowski, C. Rouff, M. Hinchey (Eds.): WRAC 2002, LNAI 2564, pp. 347–354, 2003.
© Springer-Verlag Berlin Heidelberg 2003

FIPA ACL RDF Content Language [1] and Agent toolkit Jade [8] defined ontologies for ACL message content and modeled ACL message in RDF language. As the data model intended for describing metadata, RDF is not strong enough to represent the rich forms of content. Research works in [6] suggested building an Abstract Ontology Representation(AOR) for agent language (include FIPA-SL, FIPA-KIF and FIPA-ACL) using DAML language, and used the AOR to support multilingual agents. The using of SL and KIF improved the opinion of semantic. However, it is difficulty to efficiently processed and conveyed multiple languages. Also, SL and KIF did not fit well with context of XML-based web. This paper suggested using DAML to encode ACL message. We defined the ontology of objects, propositions and actions in DAML language. Agents communicated with each other by exchanging DAML-encoded documents. Compared with RDF and XML, DAML can express richer meaning and support knowledge sharing among agents using different ontologies. Compared with SL and KIF, DAML's style is more readable and easier for agent programs to parse and understand.

The next section revealed the model of agents working in semantic web. Section 3 introduced the agent communication scenario in ITTalks† project. The design of encoding ACL in DAML language was presented in Section 4. Section 5 concluded our work and pointed out future works.

2   Agent that Speaks for Web Pages

The semantic web [5] is a vision in which web pages are augmented with information and data that expressed in a way that facilitates its understanding by machines. The current human-centered web is mostly encoded in HTML, which mainly focuses on how text and images are rendered for human viewing. Over the past few years we have seen a rapid increase in the use of XML, which is intended primarily for machine processing, as an alternative encoding. The machine that processed XML documents could be the end consumers of the information or could transform the information into a form appropriate for human understanding (e.g., HTML, graphics, synthesized speech). As a representation language, XML provided essentially a mechanism to declare and use simple data structures and thus leaved much to be desired as a language of expressing complex knowledge. The enhancements to basic XML, such as XML Scheme, addressed some of the shortcomings, but still did not result in an adequate language for representing and reasoning about the kind of knowledge essential to realizing the semantic web vision. RDF (Resource Description Framework) and RDFS (RDF Schema) attempted to address these deficiencies by building on the top of XML. They provided representation frameworks that were roughly the equivalent to semantic networks in the case of RDF and very simple frame languages in the case of RDFS. However, RDFS was still quite limited as a knowledge representation language, lacking support for variables, general quantification, rules.

DAML is the attempt to build on XML, RDF and RDFS and produces a language that is well suited for building the semantic web. The goal of the DAML program [7],

---

† http://www.ittalks.org

which began in August 2000, is to develop a universal semantic web markup language that is sufficiently rich to support intelligent agents and other applications. DAML can dramatically improve traditional ad hoc information retrieval because its semantic improves the quality of retrieval results. Also, DAML allows the intelligent agents to retrieve and manipulate the information on the semantic web.

The exact role of agent and its relationship to the knowledge encoded in documents on the semantic web is one part of the semantic web vision that has not yet been fully articulated. Most works to date had followed one of two models described below, each of which had serious shortcomings. The semantic web assumed that information and knowledge were encoded in a semantic rich web language (e.g., DAML, OIL and RDF) and made available in the form of web pages. The information may ultimately reside in databases, knowledge bases, but it must be accessible in the form of documents partially or completely marked up in a semantic web language.

Agents using semantic information used two models. The active model used by SHOE[10] system assumed that one knowledge acquiring agent existed which was responsible for searching the web for possible semantic marked web pages of interest. All found pages were processed and knowledge inside was loaded into the SHOE system's knowledge base (KB). Subsequently, the KB could answer other agent's questions about the information on the pages. The passive model was that the agent with inference ability located the related pages of interest at runtime whenever a question arose. The desired knowledge was extracted from marked pages, loaded into inference engine. Hence the question was answered by inference engine.

The two models both suggested that one agent in the system carried all the responsibility of finding and understanding the massive semantic information of the entire web. The website may defined and used its own ontologies that agent had no prior knowledge. The rules and policies used inside the website may be complex and closed to outside agents for security reason.

We were pursuing an alternative distributed model in which the web page marked up in semantic web language would appointed an existing agent as service agent. Any question related to the page could be answered by this agent. The web site supporting this model would provider both web based content for human and agent based services for other agents.

The benefits of the distributed model included:

- Distributed agent environment fit massive web environment. There is no centralized agent that has to search all web pages and understand every ontology;
- The best agent to ask question was always present. This model didn't depend on web service discovery or agent services search.
- Ontologies and rules were stored in local and accessed only by local agent. We could define personalized ontologies and rules. It would help resolving the problem of security and trust.

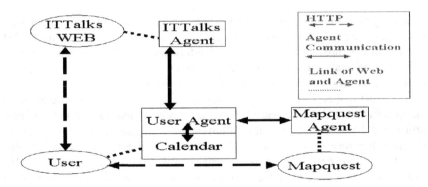

Fig. 1. ITTalks Scenario

3   Agent Communication Scenario

This section talked about the agent communication scenario occurred in the ITTalks project (http://www.ITTalks.org). ITTalks was designed by UMBC as part of the DAML Project. It provided users with numerous details about the IT events, including location, speaker, hosting organization, and topic. Unlike other event web sites, ITTalks employed DAML for knowledge base representation, reasoning, and agent communication. The use of DAML enabled more sophisticated functions that would otherwise be unavailable. For example, a simple representation scheme might be able to provide the user with talks based on interest, time and location. When both ITTalks and the user agreed on a common ontologies, the ITTalks web portal was able to perform further filtering based on sophisticated inference. In addition to enhancing knowledge representation and reasoning, DAML is used for all communication, including agent messages and queries. Moreover, ITTalks offered the capability for each user to use his/her personal agent to communicate with ITTalks on his/her behalf and provided a higher level of service

Consider the following scenario (Figure 1) which include three agents.

User Jim already registered with ITTalks, and has left instructions with the system to be notified of the occurrence of certain types of talks. The editor of ITTalks added a new IT talk into ITTalks web site. Based on information in Jim's preferences, ITTalks agent thought Jim would be interested in this talk and decided to notify Jim's User Agent.

First task of the ITTalks agent is to find Jim's user agent. This was done by searching Jim's DAML-encoded personal profile, which was submitted when Jim registered at ITTalks. ITTalks agent sended out the new talk announce to Jim's User Agent and asked whether he would join or not. The announce was encoded in DAML language. The query ACL message was delivered to the user agent using agent-based messaging system. Upon receiving the message, Jim's User Agent parsed the DAML content and loaded into an inference engine. User Agent consulted with Jim's Calendar agent to determine his availability, and contacted the MapQuest agent to find out the driving distance from Jim's predicted location at the time of the talk. There could be more sophisticated interactions. For example, Calendar agent and User agents may decide to alter Jim's calendar to resolve the schedule conflict, contact the other individual's User agent for advisory. After all, the User Agent made decision and sent the notification message back to the ITTalks agent indicating whether Jim plan to attend. The ITTalks agent made the appropriate adjustments to event attendant at the ITTalks site.

4   Approach

To accomplish the ITTalks scenario, the DAML ontology for agent communication was needed. Physically, the FIPA ACL message consists of three layers: Content, ACL and Agent Message Transport.

4.1   DAML Encoded ACL Message Content

FIPA ACL were designed to use multiple content languages [3]. This had generally been seen as a good design choice in that it provided agents with the flexibility to choose a content language best suited to its domain of discourse, so long as it is one that is mutually understood by its conversational partners. FIPA defined a mechanism by which one can offer a particular content language to the FIPA community for inclusion in the FIPA Content Language Library (CLL) [3]. Inclusion in the library means that certain minimum requirements were met and that there was a specification document for the canonical version of the language to which implementers could refer.

We designed the preliminary version of a specification of DAML ontology as a FIPA compliant content language. To be fully general and support all of the FIPA communicative acts, our ACL DAML Content Language included:

Objects: RDF Content Language [1] assumed that both an ACL object and an RDF resource were defined as descriptions of a certain identifiable entity. RDF resource identifiers and references could be used as ACL object identifiers and references. Same idea could be used in RDF-based DAML. Here, we used resource as ACL object.

Propositions: statements expressing that some sentences is true or false

Actions: express an activity that carried out by an object. It included three properties: the act identifies the operative part of the action; the actor identifies the entity that performs the act; the argument identifies the entity that used by the actor to perform the act.

Rule and Query: For the rule, the if statement included Prem part and Conc part. For the query, the statement included question part and result part.

4.2   DAML Encoded ACL

ACL described the conversation part of the ACL. In the ontology for FIPA ACL, we treated performative as DAML Class and treated attribute-value pairs as property of the performative Class. Following is a example of inform message. It included agent identifier of sender and receiver, ontology used and content language.

```
<acldaml: inform>
     <acldaml: sender>
     <fipa:agent-identifier>
               <fipa:name>sender@bar.com</fipa :name>
               <fipa:addresses>

               <fipa:url>http://bar.com/acc</fipa:url>
               </fipa:addresses>
               </fipa:agent-identifier>
     </acldaml: sender>
     <acldaml: receiver> .......</acldaml: receiver>
          <acldaml: language value =  FIPA-DAML />
          <acldaml:content-length value =  12 />
     <acldaml:ontology value =ITTalks />
     </acldaml:inform >
```

4.3   DAML Encoded Agent Message Transport

The ontology of Agent Message Transport defined Message Transport Envelope.
FIPA supported HTTP, IIOP, WAP as transport protocol. Following was an example
of message using HTTP protocol. It included the agent identifier of sender and
receiver, ACL representation language and information about already received
message.

```
<fipa :envelope>
<amt:params index="1">
  <amt:to>
   <fipa:agent-identifier>
   <fipa:name>user@foo.com</fipa :name>
   <fipa:addresses>
      <fipa:url>http://foo.com/user </fipa:url>
   </fipa:addresses>
   </fipa:agent-identifier>
  </amt:to>
  <amt:from> ....... </amt:from>
<amt:acl-representation>fipa.acl.daml</amt:acl-representation>
<amt:payload-encoding>US-ASCII</amt:payload-encoding>
  <amt:received >
     <amt:received-by value="http://foo.com/user" />
     <amt:received-id value="123456789" />
  </amt:received>
  </amp:params>
</fipa:envelope>
```

4.4   Parsing of DAML Message

Figure 2 showed how the DAML file parsing was done in our system. We used XSB system [9] as the inference engine and defined XSB rules for RDF, RDF Schema and DAML. The agents could submit DAML file, which would be parsed into triples and asserted into XSB inference engine. The facts in the XSB can also be retracted when expired. The XSB system supported query of the facts through a frame based language defined in our system. The user agent could own more complex rules. The XSB Engine determined the agent's behavior based on default rules and user agent's own rules.

5   Conclusion

This paper talked about the agent communication scenario utilizing DAML language, defined ACL message in DAML Language and implemented the reasoning engine for the purpose of parsing DAML messages. To define Agent Message Transport ontology using DAML language and support popular FIPA platforms are one of the future works. The popular FIPA platforms like Jade and FIPA-OS support HTTP, IIOP, WAP as message transport protocol. SOAP and Message Queue may become transport protocol for future agent systems. In this paper, we defined simple rule and query using DAML language. In the future, we will consider enrich this part by using new development like ruleML [4], DQL. Ontology sharing and resolving semantic differences between heterogeneous agents could also be another future work. Forcing all agents to use a common vocabulary defined in one or more shared ontology is an oversimplified solution especially when these agents are designed and deployed independently of each other.

There is no doubt DAML, as the name "Agent Markup Language" suggested, will be an important actor in the agent world.

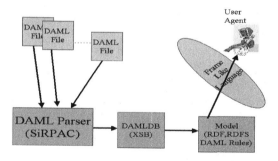

Fig. 2. DAML file parsing

References

[1]   FIPA Report XC00011B: FIPA RDF Content language, Foundation for Intelligent Physical Agents (2001).

[2]   FIPA Report XC00008D: FIPA SL content language, Foundation for Intelligent Physical Agents (2001).

[3]   FIPA Report XC00009A: FIPA CCL Content Language, Foundation for Intelligent Physical Agents (2001).

[4]   Harold Boley, Said Tabet, and Gerd Wagner: Design Rationale of RuleML: A Markup Language for Semantic Web Rules, Proc. SWWS 01, Stanford, (2001).

[5]   Tim Berners-Lee, James Hendler and Ora Lassila: The Semantic Web, Scientific American, May (2001).

[6]   Steven Willmott, Ion Constantinescu, Monique Calisti, Multilingual Agents: Ontology, Language and Abstractions, OAS (2001).

[7]   Dan Connolly, Frank van Harmelen, Ian Horrocks, Deborah L. McGuinness, Lynn Andrea Stein: DAML+OIL Reference Description, W3C Note (2001).

[8]   Fabio Bellifemine, Agostino Poggi, Giovanni Rimassa : JADE – A FIPA-compliant agent framework, in Proceedings of PAAM'99, London, April (1999), 97-108.

[9]   Kostantinos Sagonas , et. al. XSB as an efficient deductive database engine, In ACM Conference on Management of Data (SIGMOD) (1994).

[10]   Heflin, J. and Hendler, J. Searching the Web with SHOE. In Artificial Intelligence for Web Search. Papers from the AAAI Workshop. AAAI Press, (2000). 35-40.

[11]   D. Fensel et al.: OIL in a nutshell In: Knowledge Acquisition, Modeling, and Management, Proceedings of the European Knowledge Acquisition Conference (2000).

Semantic Resolution for E-commerce

Yun Peng[1], Youyong Zou[1], Xiaocheng Luan[1], Nenad Ivezic[2], Michael Gruninger[2], and Albert Jones[2]

[1] Department of Computer Science and Electrical Engineering
University of Maryland Baltimore County (UMBC)
Baltimore, MD 21250, USA
{ypeng,yzou1,xluan1@cs.umbc.edu}
[2] National Institute of Standards and Technology (NIST)
100 Bureau Drive, Gaithersburg, MD 20899, USA
{nivezic,gruning,ajones}@nist.gov

Abstract. We describe a research project on resolving semantic differences for multi-agent systems (MAS) in electronic commerce. The approach can be characterized as follows: (1) agents in a MAS may have their own specific ontologies defined on top of a shared base ontology; (2) concepts in these ontologies are represented as frame-like structures based on DAML+OIL language; (3) the semantic differences between agents are resolved at runtime through inter-agent communication; and (4) the resolution is viewed as an abductive inference process, and thus necessarily involves approximation reasoning.

1   Introduction

Understanding the meaning of messages exchanged between software agents has long been recognized as a key challenge to interoperable multi-agent systems (MAS). Forcing all agents to use a common vocabulary defined in shared ontologies is an oversimplified solution when agents are designed independently. This is the case for agent applications in E-commerce which (1) is a huge, ***open*** marketplace accommodating many companies capable of entering and leaving the market freely; (2) involves ***dynamic*** partnerships which are formed and dissolved easily and frequently; and (3) contains ***heterogeneous*** representations of agents for different enterprises [4]. It is, therefore, impractical to restrict all agents to use the same vocabulary or to require the availability of inter-ontology translation services prior to the deployment of the agent systems. Semantic differences between individual agents in the system should be allowed and be resolved when they arise during agent interaction. These points are captured by the following assumptions, which are similar to those made in [1, 20]:

1.   Interacting agents share one or more base ontologies;
2.   Agents use different ontologies defined on top of the base ontology; and
3.   Runtime, semantic resolution is unavoidable.

W. Truszkowski, C. Rouff, M. Hinchey (Eds.): WRAC 2002, LNAI 2564, pp. 355–366, 2003.
© Springer-Verlag Berlin Heidelberg 2003

Assumption 1 is reasonable because it is hard to imagine heterogeneous agents built in a total vacuum – at least some shared vocabulary and understanding of that vocabulary should be assumed. The base ontology can be viewed as an ontology for a community, it defines general terms shared by members of that community, and should be relatively stable (any change must be based on a community-wide consensus). It can be defined either in some agreed-upon ontology specification languages (e.g., Ontolingua [7] or DAML+OIL) or in some other forms (e.g., WordNet, a natural language-based taxonomy, as in work in [1]). Assumption 2 allows each agent to develop its own specialized vocabulary, reflecting its particular needs or perspectives. Usually, the agent-specific ontologies are changed more frequently than the base ontology. Since these ontologies are defined on top of the base ontologies, they are also called *differentiated ontologies* in the literature [20].

Research work on ontology engineering attempts, in part, to provide semantics for information exchanged over the Internet [5, 6, 12]. The most noticeable, recent development in this direction is the *Semantic Web* effort jointly launched by W3C [2, 16], the DARPA Agent Markup Language Project [5], and EU's Information Society Technologies Program (IST) [12]. One result from this effort is the set of DAML+OIL specifications, a language for ontology definition, manipulation, and reasoning [5]. Although the technologies developed in this effort are aimed at making Web pages understandable by programs, they may serve, we believe, as a basis for resolving semantic differences between heterogeneous agents. However, additional methodology and mechanisms need to be developed if semantic resolution is to be done at runtime through agent interaction. This is the primary objective of our project, which is performed jointly by The Laboratory for Advanced Information Technology at UMBC and the Manufacturing Systems Integration Division at NIST.

The rest of this paper is organized as follows. Section 2 further motivates our approach for semantic resolution with a simple E-commerce scenario of buying and selling computers over the internet; Section 3 describes how the base and agent-specific ontologies are defined using DAML+OIL language; Section 4 defines the two basic operations needed for our semantic resolution approach; Section 5 presents an agent communication protocol; and Section 6 outlines several approximate algorithms for semantic mapping. Section 7 concludes the paper with directions of future research.

2   A Simple E-commerce Scenario

Consider the following simple, E-commerce scenario of **RFQ** (Request For Quote) involving two agents: the buyer A1 representing a whosaler of computers and the seller A2 representing a computer manufacturer. Both A1 and A2 share a common ontology ONT-0, which gives semantics of some basic terms that describe business transactions such as RFQ and generic names for computer systems and components such as notebooks, CPU, and memory. Each of the two agents has its own specialized ontology. ONT-1 defines semantics of products to order for A1, organized to meet the intended usage of its customers. ONT-2 defines items in the product catalog for A2, based on technical specifications of manufactured computer systems.

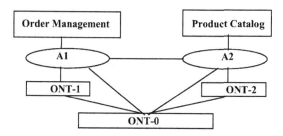

Fig. 1. A simple RFQ scenario involving two agents

Suppose A1 sends an RFQ to A2 for a number of "PC_for_Gamers", a term defined in ONT-1. Before A2 can determine a quote, it needs to understand what A1 means by this term and if a semantically similar term is in its catalog as defined in ONT-2. We use phrase "*Semantic Resolution*" for the process of identifying the meaning of terms defined in different ontologies and, if possible, matching these terms semantically.

3   Ontology Design and Representation

The bulk of the base ontology ONT-0 is devoted to define the common terms for computer systems and their components. Here we adopt part of the classification of UNSPSC (*Universal Standard Products and Services Classification Code* by United Nations Development Program and Dun & Bradstreet) [19], and organize these terms as a taxonomy. For example, "notebook-computers" is defined as a subclass of "computers", which is in turn defined a subclass of "Hardware", etc. Common terms used in RFQ such as price, weight, size, date, are also defined in ONT-0.

Agent specific ontologies ONT-1 and ONT-2 define terms that reflect different views of A1 and A2, respectively, of computer systems. As a computer retailer, A1 names their computer systems according to different usage of these computers by its customer, e.g., "PC for Gamers", PC for Family", "PC for Students", etc. On the other hand, A2, as a computer manufacturer, organizes its catalog of products according to their technical and configuration specifications, e.g., "Entry Level", Professional Level", "Portable", etc. ONT-1 and ONT-2 organize their respective terms into taxonomies. In addition, each term is also given a set of properties. Therefore, each term is defined by the set of its superclasses in the taxonomy and its properties. Also note that, these two agent specific ontologies are defined on top of the base ontology ONT-0, this can be seen in the example in Figure 2 where the term "PC for Gamers" in ONT-1 is defined in part by terms from ONT-0.

Although some researchers have used full first-order logic for ontology representation (see Ontolingua [7]), the current trend has been to use description logics (DL) of different flavors [5, 6, 17 - 20]. DAML+OIL can be seen as a combination of DL and web standards such as RDF, RDF Schema [10], and XML. One of its useful features is the use of namespaces to reference individual ontologies. We use ns0, ns1, and ns2 as namespaces for the three ontologies ONT-0, ONT-1, and ONT-2 in the above E-commerce scenario.

The following is an example of an XML-encoded DAML+OIL definition of a class of "PC_for_Gamers" in ONT-1. Symbols starting with "#" are terms defined in the home ontology ONT-1, whose namespace ns1 is omitted, and prefix symbols "daml" and "rdfs" denote namespaces for DAML and RDF Schema specification, their URIs (e.g., xmlns:daml = http://www.daml.org/2001/03/daml+oil#) are given as part of XML Schema at the beginning of the ontology definition.

In essence, this definition says that the concept of "PC_for_Gamers" is a sub-class of "Computers-to-order" in ONT-1 and sub-class of "Workstations, desktop-computers" defined in ONT-0, with "good video card", "good sound card", and "fast CPU", the meanings of these terms are also defined in ONT-1, the home ontology and ONT-0, the base ontology.

```
<daml:Class rdf:ID="PC_for_Gamers ">
    <rdfs:subClassOf rdf:resource="#Computers-to-order"/>
    <rdfs:subClassOf rdf:resource="
        ns0: Workstations, desktop-computers "/>
    <rdfs:subClassOf>
        <daml:Restriction>
            <daml:onProperty rdf:resource="ns0:hasVideoCard"/>
                <daml:hasValue rdf:resource="#GoodVideoCard "/>
                </daml:Restriction>
    </rdfs:subClassOf>
        <rdfs:subClassOf>
        <daml:Restriction>
            <daml:onProperty rdf:resource="ns0:hasSoundcard"/>
            <daml:hasValue rdf:resource="#GoodSoundcard"/>
        </daml:Restriction>
    </rdfs:subClassOf>
        <rdfs:subClassOf>
        <daml:Restriction>
            <daml:onProperty rdf:resource="ns0:hasCPU"/>
            <daml:hasValue rdf:resource="#FastCPU "/>
        </daml:Restriction>
    </rdfs:subClassOf>
    </daml:Class>
```

Fig. 2. An example ONT-1 class defined in DAML-OIL

4   Operations for Semantic Resolution

Our approach to semantic resolution is motivated by the way humans resolve their semantic differences. When two people engage in a conversation and one does not understand a term mentioned by the other, the listener would *ask* the other to clarify or explain the meaning of the term. The other person would try to answer it by define the term in terms she thinks the listener would understand. If the answer is not understood, more questions may follow. This process may continue until the term in question is completely understood (either the term is mapped to one the listener is familiar with or a new term with clear semantics is learned) or the listener gives it up. The listener can understand a foreign term because the two people share the meanings of some common terms, which we attempt to model by the base ontology in our approach. The process of achieving semantic resolution here involves two basic operations, *Semantic Querying*, which gradually reveals the definition of the foreign term in the terms of the base ontology, and *Semantic Mapping,* in which the definition of the foreign term is mapped to a term in the listener's ontology. Each of these two operaions has its own research issues. We briefly describe each in the following subsections, and address technical issues involved in the subsequent sections.

Semantic Querying. Following the example in the simple E-commerce scenario, since A2 only understands ONT-0 and ONT-2, it does not understand the term such as ns1:*PC_for_Gamers* in the RFQ from A1 defined in ONT-1. Similar to a conversation of two strangers, A2 would ask what A1 means by this term via some agent communication language. We call this process of obtaining the description of a term from a different ontology *Semantic Querying*, and the two agent-specific ontologies ONT-1 and ONT-2 in our example are called the *source* and *target* ontologies. The description of a source term includes both slot name and filler name of each slot in its definition in the source ontology. In our example, the first semantic query to A1 gives A2 the following information (with proper namespace designations).

ns1:PC_for_Gamers
List of primitive super-classes
- ns1: Computers-to-order
- ns0:Workstations, desktop-computers

List of properties
- ns0:HasGraphics_card = ns1:GoodGraphicCard
- ns0:HasSound_card = ns1:GoodSoundCard
- ns0:HasCPU= ns1:FastCPU
- ns0:Memory=ns1:BigMemory

Additional queries on ns1 terms in the above description gives

ns1:PC_for_Gamers
List of primitive super-classes
- ns1: Computers-to-order
- ns0:Workstations, desktop-computers
- ns0:Computers

List of properties
- ns0:HasGraphics_card = (ns0:size >= 1000)
- ns0:HasSound_card = (ns0:size >= 24)
- ns0:HasCPU = (ns0:size >= 1000)
- ns0:Memory = (ns0:size >= 256).

This can be viewed as an extended normal form of the given ONT-1 concept with respect to ONT-0[1].

Semantic Mapping. The extended normal form of ns1:PC_for_Gamers from the semantic querying step provides much information to A2. However, for A2 to truly understand this concept, it needs to *map* or *re-classify* this description into one or more concepts defined in its own ontology ONT-2. This is accomplished by the *Semantic Mapping* step. Note that due to the structural differences, concepts from different ontologies are likely to match each other only partially.

Semantic resolution is thus similar to abductive reasoning process, semantic querying corresponding to evidence collection, and semantic mapping to hypothesis generation. All partially matched target concepts are considered candidate or hypothesized maps of the source concept, each of which can explain the source concept to different degrees based on the base ontology. If the best candidate is satisfactory, then a quote is generated by A2 and sent to A1. Otherwise, additional steps of inter-agent interactions may be taken. For example, if the best candidate, although unsatisfactory, is sufficiently better than all others, then its description is sent back to A1 for confirmation. If the first few leading candidates have similar level of satisfaction, then questions that discriminate some candidates over others will be sent to A1. The details of the algorithms are described in Section 6.

5   Communication Protocol for Semantic Resolution

To support agent communication for both semantic querying and semantic mapping, we need to have (1) an agent communication language (ACL) to encode messages, (2) a content language to encode the content of a message, and (3) a communication protocol that specifies how these messages can be used for meaningful conversations. For reasons including clearly defined semantics and standardization support, we have selected FIPA ACL [9] as the ACL for our project. We choose DAML+OIL as the content language because it is also the language for ontology specification. The most relevant work to date on developing agent communication protocols for semantic resolution between different ontologies can be found in [1]. Their Ontology Negotiation Protocol is an extension of KQML [8] with additional performatives, such as *Request Clarification, Clarification, Interpretation, Confirmation*, etc.

Our *Semantic Resolution Protocol* combines our earlier work [4] and the work in [1]. The design follows FIPA Interaction Protocol convention, which requires the definitions of (1) the acts involved in interaction processes, (2) the roles played by the actors in interaction processes, and (3) the phase transitions of the interaction process. There are two players in our protocol (it may be easily extended to involving multiple players), the buyer (A1) and the seller (A2). The buyer plays the role of *the initiator* while the seller is the *participant*. Performatives used in the protocol represent the

---

[1]   In description logics, a normal (or canonical) form of a concept C consists of two lists: a list of all of C's primitive super-classes and a list of all of C's properties, including those inherited from its super-classes. These two lists are called P list and R list in this paper.

communicative acts intended by the players. The following FIPA performatives are selected for the protocol.

- **Call-for-Proposal:** (CFP): the action of calling for proposals to perform a given action. This is used by buyer to ask the seller to propose a quote for a RFQ.
- **Propose:** the action of submitting a proposal to perform a certain action, given certain preconditions. This is used to turn a proposed quote.
- **Accept-Proposal:** the action of accepting a previously submitted proposal to perform an action.
- **Reject-Proposal:** the action of rejecting a submitted proposal to perform an action
- **Terminate:** the action to finish the interaction process.
- **Inform:** the action of informing that certain propositions are believed true.
- **Not-Understood:** the action of informing the other party that its message was not understood. This is used by the seller to request the buyer to send the description of a term it does not understand in the previous message.
- **Query-if:** The action of asking another agent whether or not a given proposition is true. This is used by the seller in semantic mapping to ask the buyer to confirm if a candidate concept is an acceptable match for the given source concept.
- **Confirm:** the action of confirming that given propositions are believed to be true. This is used by the buyer to confirm a target concept received in the incoming "query-if" message from the seller.
- **Disconfirm:** the action of informing that given propositions are believed false

The first 5 performatives are for RFQ; the rest are for semantic querying and mapping. (See [9] for a detailed description of these performatives.) The phase transitions in the protocol are given in the message-flow diagram in Figure 3.

6   Algorithms for Semantic Mapping

The objective of semantic resolution is to find a concept in the target ontology whose description best matches the description of a given concept defined in the source ontology. Because agent-specific ontologies often have different structures and use different concept names, concept matching is seldom exact. Partial matches, which can occur even if a single ontology is involved, become more prevalent when different agent-specific ontologies are involved. Consequently, the simple techniques used in DL for partial matches (e.g., most general subsumees and most specific subsumer) are no longer adequate. Approximate reasoning that at least gives a ranking for all partially matched target concepts is required. Commonly used approximate reasoning techniques include *rough set theory* [18], fuzzy *set theory* [15], and *probabilistic classification* [13, 15]. In many applications, these more formal approaches may not work, either because the assumptions made for them cannot be met or the information needed is not available. Heuristic approximation becomes necessary [18].

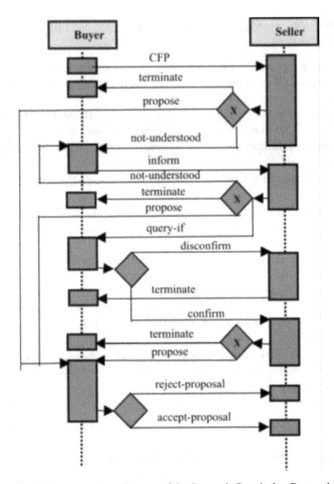

Fig. 3. State transition diagram of the Semantic Resolution Protocol

In this section, we focus on heuristic methods for approximating partial matches. The main algorithm *subsumption(A, B, theta)* is an extension of the structural comparison for subsumption operation in DL. It returns a numeric score, theta, in [0, 1] that quantifies the degree that concept A subsumes concept B. In DL, A subsumes B if and only if every object in A is also an object in B. A structural comparison approach [3, 11] works with normal forms of concepts, which include a list of all primitive super-classes *S* and a list of all properties *P* for a concept, and requires that (1) *Sa* is a subset of *Sb*, and (2) constraints on *Pb* is compatible with (i.e., is at least as strict as) that of *Pa*. These requirements cannot be established logically if the normal forms of A and B involve terms from different ontologies. This can be seen by comparing the extended normal form of ns1:PC_for_Gamers in Section 4 obtained via semantic querying operation and the extended normal form for ns2:Professional_Use_Desktop given below. Besides ns0 terms, these two normal forms contain ns1 and ns2 terms from ONT-1 and ONT-2, respectively.

ns2:Professional_Use_Desktop

List of primitive super-classes

- ns2:Desktop
- ns0:Workstations, desktop-computers
- ns2:Copmuter_Systems
- ns0:Computers

List of properties

- ProductName = "xxx4"
- ProductNumber = "yyy4"
- ns0:HasSound_card = (ns0:size = 24)
- ns0:HasCPU = (ns0:size = 1800)
- ns0:Memory = (ns0:size = 512)
- ns0:Price = (ns0:size = 2300)
- ns2:HasColorMonitor = subproperty(ns0: HasMonitor ns0:size = 19)

One may suggest that we ignore all of these ns1 and ns2 terms and conduct the subsumption operation based solely on those ns0 terms. However, doing so would overlook the important information on the structural differences. Moreover, it is generally believed that if two concepts are far apart in structure, they are less likely to match each other, even if they agree well on terms of the base ontology. In what follows we describe the methods to compute a measure to compare two concepts' P and R lists and the method to combine them into a single score.

Comparing the Superclass Lists Sa and Sb. The objective of this comparison is to obtain a measure for the degree that Sa is a subset of Sb. First, we check if any member Sa_i in Sa is logically inconsistent with any member Sb_j in Sb, e.g., if (**and** Sa_i Sb_j) is unsatisfiable. One type of inconsistency would be that Sa_i and Sb_j are disjoint. For example, as defined in ONTO_0, "ns0:Notebook-computers", "ns0:Workstations, desktop-computers", and "ns0:Servers" are disjoint with each other. If inconsistency is detected, then A cannot subsume B. Otherwise, we proceed to compute a heuristic measure of the degree that Sa is a subset of Sb (e.g., the degree that A subsumes B in terms of their respective super classes).

$$inclusion\_measure(Sa, Sb) = \begin{cases} -1 & \textit{if Sa and Sb are inconsistent} \\ |Sa \cap Sb| / |Sa| & \textit{otherwise} \end{cases}$$

If this measure is –1, then the entire matching process stops (no comparison of properties will be performed), and returns –1, meaning that A cannot subsume B.

This measure is 1 when Sa is a subset of Sb, 0 if none of the members of Sa is also a member of Sb. One benefit of this heuristic rule is that is can be viewed as the conditional probability $Pr(x$ in $Sb \mid x$ in $Sa)$ when members of Sa and Sb are treated as sample points from the same space. This allows us to generalize the measure with more sophisticated probabilistic computation when the interdependency of these members are known.

Applying this rule to our example of ns1:PC_for_Gamers and ns2:Professional_Use_Desktop, we have the inclusion measure of 2/3 because 2 of the 3 members in superclass list of the former are members of superclass list of the latter.

Comparing the Property Lists *Pa* and *Pb*. This comparison is done in two steps.

Step 1: Identify all matching pairs between *Pa_i* in *Pa* and *Pb_j* in *Pb*. *Pa_i* matches *Pb_j* if 1) they have the identical property name, including the name space, or 2) *Pb_j* is a sub-property of *Pa_i* or vise versa. For any *Pa_i* in *Pa* that does not pair with any member of *Pb*, then a measure of –1 is given for that *Pa_i*.

Step 2: Compute compatibility measure for each matching pair Pa_i in Pa and Pb_j in Pb. If their constraints (i.e., cardinalities and value ranges) are incompatible (i.e., the logical expressions of their constraints are not satisfiable simultaneously). If incompatibility is detected, a measure of –1 is given to that Pa_i. Otherwise (i.e., they are compatible), use some heuristic rule to compute a (positive) measure for that pair. This is summarized by the following rule.

$$compatibility = \begin{cases} -1 & \textit{if Pa\_i does not havea a match in Pb} \\ -1 & \textit{if range\_i} \cap \textit{range\_j} = \varnothing \\ 1 & \textit{if range\_j} \subseteq \textit{range\_i} \\ \alpha_{ij} & \textit{otherwise} \end{cases}$$

where α_{ij} is the overlapping ratio between *range_i* and *range_j*, which can be computed by additional rules that handle different types of value ranges such as close intervals, open intervals, and intervals involving infinities.

Applying this rule to our example, we have one –1 measure (for GraphicCard) and three 1 measures (for all other proerties).

Combining Comparison Results. When inclusion_measure retunes a positive value, then this value and all measures of property comparisons (some may be positive and some may be negative) are combined to generate an overall score. Here we use rules similar to those given for certainty factors in MYCIN. First, each measure is given a weight w_i, reflecting the importance that property is for establishing subsumption relation for concept A. Recall that each measure is for one property (plus one more for superclass) of A. Therefore, there are total of |Pa| + 1 weights. When such weights are not provided by the designer of the ontology of A, we use 1/(|Pa| + 1) as the default weight for each of them. Then the combination takes the following steps

Step 1: Combine all positive measures as $C1 = 1 - \Pi_i(1 - w_i \cdot measure_i)$, and combine all negative measures as $C2 = \Pi_i(1 + w_j \cdot measure_j) - 1$.

Step 2: Combine C1 and C2 as $C = (C1 + C2)/(1 - \min\{|C1|, |C2|\})$.

Step 3: Finally, normalize C by the weights as $CN = C/(1 - \Pi_i(1 - w_i))$, where, i is over all |Pa| + 1 weights. CN is then returned as *theta*, the final score of A subsuming B. The rationale for normalization is that when all measure are +1 then CN = 1, and when all measures are –1 then CN = –1.

Applying this rule to our example, we have five measures (2/3, -1, 1, 1, 1), each with a weight 1/5. This yields C1 = 0.55626, C2 = -0.2, C = 0.4457, and the overall score CN = 0.6629.

Search for the Plausible Subsumees. The semantic resolution seeks a most plausible target concept B that either approximately subsumes or is subsumed by A, as measured by the heuristic score theta. Finding the most plausible subsumee can be done by a depth-first search plus backtracking or more efficiently by a best-first style search of the target ontology graph. Candidate target concepts are normalized when they are generated during the search.

7   Conclusions

The work presented in this paper represents the first step of our ongoing effort toward a comprehensive solution to the problem of semantic resolution. Many issues, both practical and theoretical, remain to be addressed. To answer some of them, we will continue our project along the following directions. First, we plan to build a prototype agent system based on the approach outlined in this paper. This system will be used as a testbed to validate the methods we develop and to test emerging tools and approaches. It can also serve as a bridge connecting the research community and the industry by incorporating ontologies of real-world enterprises engaged in E-commerce activities. Second, we plan to develop a more formal treatment for approximating semantic mapping with partially matched concepts. One approach is to incorporate probability theory, in particular the Bayesian belief network [13, 14], into the ontology class hierarchies. Finally, we plan to extend the semantic resolution process to become a cycle of *hypothesize-and-test*, as with most abductive, evidential reasoning systems. Instead of separating semantic querying and mapping as two steps, they will be interwoven together so that additional evidence will be collected only when it is needed, and the hypothesized mappings are refined and discriminated against each other with each new evidence until the solution is gradually emerged [14].

8   Disclaimer

Certain commercial software products are identified in this paper. These products were used only for demonstrations purposes. This use does not imply approval or endorsement by NIST, nor does it imply that these products are necessarily the best available for the purpose.

References

[1]   Bailin, S.C. and Truszkowski,W., Ontology Negotiation between agents supporting intelligent information management, *Workshop on Ontologies in Agent Systems,* 2001.

[2]   Berners-Lee, T. What the Semantic Web can represent, http://www.w3.org/DesignIssues/RDFnot.html, 1998.

[3]   Borgida, A., *et al.* CLASSIC: A Structural Data Model for Objects. In *Proc of ACM SIGMOD Intern'l Conference on Management of Data,* Portland, OR, June 1989, 59-67.

[4]   Chen, Y., *et al.* A Negotiation-Based Multi-agent System for Supply Chain Management. In *Proc. of The International Conference on Autonomous Agents,* Seattle, May, 1999.

[5]   DAML home page, http://www.daml.org/.

[6]   Decker, S. et al, Knowledge representation on the Web. Proceedings of the 2000 International Workshop on Description Logics.

[7]   Farquhar, A., Fikes, R., and Rice, J. The Ontolingua server: a tool for collaborative ontology construction. *Intl. J. Of Human-Computer Studies* **46**(6):707-727, 1997.

[8]   Finin, T., Labrou, Y., and Mayfield, J. KQML as an Agent Communication Language, in Jeff Bradshaw (ed.), *Software Agents,* MIT Press, Cambridge, MA, 1997.

[9]   FIPA (The Foundation of Intelligent Physical Agents) home page, http://www.fipa.org.

[10]   Lassila, O. and Swick, R. Resource Description Framework (RDF) Model and Syntax Specification, http://www.w3.org/TR/1999/REC-rdf-syntax-19990222/, Feb, 1999.

[11]   MacGregor, R.M. The Evolving Technology of Classification-based Knowledge Representation Systems. In *Principles of Semantic Networks: Explorations in the Representation of Knowledge,* J. Sowa (ed.), Morgan Kaufmann, 1991.

[12]   OIL (Ontology Inference Layer) home page, http://www.ontoknowledge.org/oil/.

[13]   Pearl, J. Probabilistic Reasoning in Intelligent Systems: Networks of Plausible Inference, Morgan Kaufman, San Mateo, CA, 1988.

[14]   Peng Y and Reggia J: Abductive Inference Models for Diagnostic Problem Solving, Springer-Verlag, New York, NY,1990.

[15]   Russell, S. and Norvig, P. *Artificial Intelligence, A Modern Approach.* Prentice Hall, Englewood Cliffs, NJ, 1995.

[16]   Semantic Web home page, http://www.w3.org/2001/sw/.

[17]   Stuckenschmidt, H., Using OIL for semantic information Integration. *Proceedings of the ECAI workshop on Ontologies and PSMs 2000.*

[18]   Stuckenschmidt,, H. and Visser. U., Semantic translation based on approximate re-classification. *Proceedings of the Workshop "Semantic Approximation, Granularity and Vagueness, KR'00.*

[19]   UNSPSC, home page, http://www.unspsc.org.

[20]   Weinstein, P. and Birmingham, W.P., Comparing concepts in differentiated ontologies. Proceedings of the 12th Workshop on Knowledge Acquisition, Modeling and Management (KAW'99).

An Approach to Knowledge Exchange and Sharing between Agents

Jan Smid[1], Marek Obitko[2], and Walt Truszkowski[3]

[1] Department of Computer Science
Morgan State University
Baltimore, USA
jsmid@jewel.morgan.edu
[2] Department of Cybernetics
Czech Technical University
Karlovo náměstí 13, Prague, Czech Republic
obitko@labe.felk.cvut.cz
[3] NASA/GSFC 588
Greenbelt, MD 20771, USA
Walt.Truzskowski@gsfc.nasa.gov

Abstract. In this paper, we are interested in studying the communication of knowledge between abstract systems (agents). Finite state machines (FSM) are used both as the formalism of knowledge and communication. Some machines acquire procedural knowledge by evolving strategies using a protocol that communicates FSM fragments with other agents. The communication protocol is in the form of a dialogue automaton. The selected formalism can fully describe both the procedural knowledge in simple abstract systems and the dialogue between agents. Therefore we conclude that the FSM formalism is appropriate for describing a class of abstract game playing agents.

1 Introduction

Not all agents are equal. Some "know" more than others and are capable of more procedural actions. Others are looking for pieces of knowledge to enhance their own capabilities. This paper discusses the possible dynamics of exchanging or sharing bits of knowledge between agents.

The purpose of this paper is to demonstrate the exchange of procedural knowledge between agents in a community of agents via an example of formalized knowledge and communication. Exchange between agents requires communication between agents. The mechanism for inter-agent communication [8] together with basic negotiation principles [5] is well described theoretically. There are also some practical recommendations regarding communication between agents [2]. In this paper, we build on these frameworks and describe a process for exchanging procedural knowledge using a restricted formal representation.

Let us suppose that an agent A_i has specific knowledge K_i of how to perform a task in a domain D_i . This knowledge may have been acquired by agent A_i

W. Truszkowski, C. Rouff, M. Hinchey (Eds.): WRAC 2002, LNAI 2564, pp. 367–376, 2003.

through some learning process. Another agent, A_j, also desires this knowledge, but might not be capable to acquire this knowledge through its own learning process. A more direct approach to obtaining this knowledge is to attain it directly from an agent A_i.

There are two possibilities for exchanging desired knowledge between agents. Firstly, the two agents may communicate with each other directly and negotiate the exchange of the desired knowledge. To do so, the two communicating agents A_i and A_j must be able to establish which information to exchange and how to update their knowledge. The agents must share an ontology in order to communicate within the domain where knowledge exchange will occur. However, if they have differing ontologies, the agents must proceed through ontology negotiation in order to resolve differences. As a second possibility for information exchange, a mediator agent can be used to overcome an ontology barrier. Such an agent must have access to the ontologies of both agents and be able to translate messages from one agent to the other.

The mediator agent can be more than just a translator of inter-agent messages. It can also serve in a proactive knowledge management mode where it can collect and process transient pieces of knowledge and share the results with both knowledge-transfer agents. This mediation approach enables agents A_i and A_j to be more focused on their individual responsibilities and avoid wasting time with processing that can be done by a specialized agent. The mediator agent must be capable of determining the pieces of knowledge best suited for updating in the knowledge bases of both agents. This mediator agent will recommend to both agents the specific knowledge they should modify either during or at the end of the dialogue. This specialized mediator agent approach is similar to the idea of an ontology agent as discussed in [3]. In this paper, examples of both approaches are briefly described.

2 Formalization of Procedural Knowledge: Resource Protection Game

For the purposes of this paper we have chosen formalization of a procedural knowledge in a form of a finite-state machine (FSM). This approach is inspired by the Resource Protection Game introduced in [7]. This game is originally a twoplayer game on a toroidal board of squares. Each square corresponds to a resource, and the two players (the "defender" and "adversary") compete for squares on the board. If the board is of size $N \times N$, then the defender will start at square $(1, 1)$ and the adversary will start at square (N, N). The remaining squares are initially unoccupied. Since the board grid represents real networks, such as power grids or communication networks, and in the real world networks may be highly interconnected and will have few geophysical boundaries, our board is toroidal (has no edges). Each player can only perceive limited information, namely, the status of the north, south, east, and west squares neighboring the current position of the player. The diagonal squares cannot be seen. The status of each neighboring square will be one of the following: unoccupied, occupied by that player, or occupied by the opponent. Each time step the players alternate taking an action, which consists of moving to a neighboring resource to control/protect that resource. A player can move to an unoccupied square or back to a square that it has previously occupied, but not to a square occupied by the opponent. A game ends when all squares are occupied or time runs out. The agent with the most resources at the end of the game wins.

The procedural knowledge of agents, i.e. how to behave in order to protect as many resources as possible, is represented via FSM with perceived input and a few states. We have adapted this approach for its relative simplicity. While the procedural knowledge can be obviously represented in more complicated ways, the FSM seems to be a good formalization for our purposes.

In this paper, we assume that agents have already acquired their own knowledge to some degree through some mechanism such as learning FSMs using genetic algorithms (GAs) [7] and that the knowledge is represented in a FSM format. We are interested in the manner by which parts of knowledge can be exchanged or shared between agents.

For two agents to transfer or share new knowledge with each other through the mediator, they must be able to differentiate between their respective knowledge bases. Based on this differentiation, they will be able to formulate requests that might enhance their own knowledge bases. Essentially the agents will be looking for isomorphism between their respective FSMs. Isomorphic or near-isomorphic pieces represent common knowledge. Dissimilar portions of the FSM representations may be shared to improve agent's knowledge. Here, we focus on the mechanism and manner in which the agents enter into a dialogue and how each FSM is subsequently changed. In previous experiments conducted by Spears and Gordon [7], only one cell was communicated and we propose to communicate more than one cell in a row of a FSM.

3   Formalization of a Dialogue: Dialogue Automata

Once we have defined the knowledge that may be exchanged via communication, the next important question arises—how to represent the dialogue. One powerful alternative is to use automaton formalism.

The communication of procedural knowledge can be represented by dialogue automata. The dialogue automaton defined by Kopecek [4] provides platform for both representation and for negotiating procedural knowledge. This type of mathematical description allows us to introduce the concept of agent personality and agent emotions, see for example workshop in Sonthohen on user adaptivty [1]. These attributes are probably unavoidable when we start analyzing agent behavior in complex situations.

Dialogue automata (DA) generalize the notion of FSM (Mealy-type automata). We use this concept as a simple model of the participant agent's dialogue. States of the DA correspond to the agent's internal states and input and output symbols correspond to the dialogue utterances. Transition functions represent the pattern of the agent behavior. The formal definition of the DA can be stated as follows.

Let U, T, V be nonempty sets and let f be a mapping of the set $U \times T$ into V. Then the ordered quadruple

$$S = (U, T, V, f)$$

is said to be an information system (see [6]). The elements of U are called objects, the elements of T attributes, and the elements of V values of attributes. Let

$$\mathbf{S} = (S, A_S, V_S, f_S) \quad \text{and} \quad \mathbf{X} = (X, A_X, V_X, f_X)$$

be information systems. We will assume that the sets of attributes f_S and f_X are finite. Dialogue automaton is an ordered quadruple

$$\mathbf{A} = (S, X, \lambda, \delta)$$

where

$$\delta : S \times X \to S \quad \text{and} \quad \lambda : S \times X \to X$$

are transition function and output function, respectively. Sets S and X are the sets of states and dialogue utterances, respectively. Being in the state $a \in A$, the automaton detects the actual input symbol (dialogue utterance of the other participant of the dialogue), changes its state according to the function δ and outputs a dialogue utterance according to the function λ.

4   Symbolic Example

As an example of agent communication, we present a dialogue system structure. The dialogue system consists of a set of states, a set of utterances, and transition functions. In this very simple example, states are represented as 4-tuples where attributes and their values are defined as follows:

State Attributes SA
$SA = \{SA1$ — an agent estimate of the solution distance,
$\qquad SA2$ — an agent estimate of the possible solution improvement,
$\qquad SA3$ — resource level,
$\qquad SA4$ — confidence level that other agent can provide useful information,
$\qquad SA5$ — level of cooperativeness$\}$

For example, the state $SA1$ expresses an agent *estimate* of distance of his procedural knowledge to the optimal solution. The value of state $SA2$ expresses an agent's beliefs about the extent to which it is possible to improve his knowledge encoded in FSM. Both of these measures are based on results of games that were played to evaluate the quality of each agent's knowledge. The values of state attributes can have the following values.

State Attribute Values SAV
$SAV(SA1) = \{SAV11$ - small, $SAV12$ - medium, $SAV13$ - high$\}$
$SAV(SA2) = \{SAV21$ - small, $SAV22$ - medium, $SAV23$ - high$\}$
$SAV(SA3) = \{SAV31$ - small, $SAV32$ - medium, $SAV33$ - high$\}$
$SAV(SA4) = \{SAV41$ - small, $SAV42$ - medium, $SAV43$ - high$\}$
$SAV(SA5) = \{SAV51$ - small, $SAV52$ - medium, $SAV53$ - high$\}$

The transition function between values of state attributes describes agent behavior in response to his actual state and utterance that he receives from other agent. As a result of a transition, an agent also produces an utterance as a response to another agent.

Utterances X
A set of utterances X consists of several types of sentences. We can categorize utterances that we will illustrate later in three groups: handshaking, requests, answers.

As in the case of state attributes, utterances have also attributes. These attributes give an additional quality to utterances since they can describe an agent's mood and expectations of dialog results. For example, the first attribute $XA1$ expresses an agent's estimate of the information-transfer cost from an external source/agent. The second attribute estimates the cost of acquiring information by internal means, in other words by learning the material with no help from other agents. The attribute values and actual utterances provide an agent with a decision-making basis used to choose with whom the agent will prefer to communicate. Note that the attributes of utterances are influenced by attributes of states of the agent's dialogue automaton — namely by $SA4$ and $SA5$.

Dialogue Utterance Attributes XA
$XA = \{XA1$ — information cost via communication with other agents,
        $XA2$ — information cost via processing within the agent$\}$

Dialogue Utterance Attribute Values XAV
$XAV(XA1) = \{XAV11$ - low, $XAV12$ - medium, $XAV13$ - high$\}$
$XAV(XA2) = \{XAV21$ - low, $XAV22$ - medium, $XAV23$ - high$\}$

In this simplified example, we assume that each utterance has one of the two attributes and each attribute has three intensity values (low, medium and high). Given the configuration introduced above we may describe the transition functions δ and λ. We will illustrate only one sample transition from the whole dialogue automaton.

Transition Function $\delta : S \times X \rightarrow S$
$\delta : ((SAV1 = $ large, $SAV2 = $ large, $SAV3 = $ small, $SAV4 = $ medium,
        $SAV5 = $ low), $(X = $ request, $XA1 = $ high, $XA2 = $ low))
        $\rightarrow$
        $(SAV1 = $ large, $SAV2 = $ large, $SAV3 = $ small, $SAV4 = $ medium,
        $SAV5 = $ medium)

Transition Function $\lambda : S \times X \to X$
$\lambda : ((SAV1 = \text{large}, SAV2 = \text{large}, SAV3 = \text{small}, SAV4 = \text{medium},$
$\quad SAV5 = \text{low}), (X = \text{request}, XA1 = \text{high}, XA2 = \text{low}))$
$\qquad \to$
$\quad (X = \text{confirmation (i.e. will communicate)}, XA1 = \text{high}, XA2 = \text{low})$

Under the given example of the transition function the value of the fourth component changed from "low" to "medium", which means that the agent is more open to communication with other agents. The change is due to the utterance request with attributes expressing belief that the communication will be very helpful ($XA1 = \text{high}$). The change also caused the resulting utterance— confirmation of continuing communication.

This particular transition can be interpreted as the increase of the level of cooperativeness induced by the environment and the utterance attribute values. The environment did not change. This particular transition can be initially built-in or learned from the data later. Informal samples of utterances are presented below. The tables of transition functions will be extensive in real-world situations and we will provide additional illustrative examples rather than a complete formal description. The strength of the FSM description is that the formal learning theory can be used to solved various tasks. The dialogue automaton outlined above is used for initiating a dialogue between two agents. Each agent knows its own state (the estimate of the solution distance, the resource level and the confidence level) and estimates the state of the opponent/collaborator. Based on this information, the agent is able to decide whether to initiate a dialogue or not. For example, agent $A2$ might be in a self-oriented mood because it is close to a solution and does not want to help agent $A1$. Consequently agent $A2$ refuses the communication. A dialogue can go on as follows:

$Agent\ 1$ — $SA1 = SAV11$ (small)
$Agent\ 2$ — $SA1 = SAV13$ (high)

$Agent\ 1 \to Agent\ 2$: help me
$Agent\ 2 \to Agent\ 1$: I can't (because I am close to the solution and I don't
$\qquad$ want to communicate now — the level of cooperativeness
$\qquad ASV5$ is low).

The dialogue automaton described above describes fragments of an initial communication between agents. In the next section, we assume that the dialogue has already begun (i.e. both agents acknowledged that they want to exchange information) and we further describe the dialogue.

5   Dialogue

The dialogue can go on between two or more parties. One of the dialogue's participants can be a mediator. The mediator might have more skills or resources than participating agents. We can differentiate the following two cases:

1. No mediator — in this type of exchange compatible agents communicate pieces of their knowledge. A possible type of this exchange may be "blind" exchange of information (GA-like information exchange) because the agents do not posses skills or resources for more general communication strategies.
2. A powerful mediator is available — the informed exchange of information can take place. For example the mediator may request parts of knowledge (FSMs) from both agents and based on some heuristics decides which information will be exchanged and recommends this exchange to both agents.

Next, we will present more fragments of the dialogue process.

5.1   Dialogue Using the Mediator

Initiating the Dialogue There are two possibilities — either an agent knows which agent he wants to exchange knowledge with or the mediator is responsible for finding appropriate knowledge. In the second case, a mediator may randomly ask agents until one is willing to enter the dialogue and knowledge exchange with the requesting agent.

$A1 \rightarrow M$: I would like to improve my procedural knowledge.

1. using any agent's FSM $\rightarrow M$ looks for some agent (suppose it finds $A2$), then responds to $A1$
2. using particular agent's FSM, e.g. $A2 \rightarrow M$ asks $A2$, then responds to $A1$

$M \rightarrow A2$: Do you want to share your knowledge with A1?
$A2 \rightarrow M$: Yes.
$M \rightarrow A1$: Acknowledge from A2.

Gathering Information by Mediator The mediator asks both agents for information

$M \rightarrow A1$: please send me your whole FSM[1]
$M \rightarrow A2$: please send me your whole FSM
$A1 \rightarrow M$: here it is: ... (FSM of A1)
$A2 \rightarrow M$: here it is: ... (FSM of A2)

The mediator now finds that out of five states the three states are equivalent and two states are different for the agents (see the figure 1). The mediator recommends to exchange the state (a row in FSM) in the next step.

---

[1] This is the simplest example of sending whole FSM — a more intelligent mediator may request only parts of FSMs to prevent communication overhead.

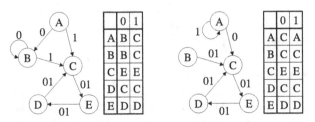

Fig. 1. Example of two different FSM's. The FSM's have the same output for the some of the inputs, however there are situations where outputs are not the same (e.g. different responses to input 0 from states A). This is because the states C, D, E are equivalent states, however the states A, B are not equivalent

Distributing Knowledge by Mediator The mediator distributes the knowledge

$M \rightarrow A1$: You may try to replace your $x - th$ row with ... (differing from $A2$)
$M \rightarrow A2$: You may try to replace your $x - th$ row with ... (differing from $A1$)

Both agents may evaluate whether to use the suggested knowledge using the same automaton as described above for starting the dialogue.

$A1 \rightarrow M$: Ok, I will try it.
$A2 \rightarrow M$: Ok, I will try to replace just some elements.

The decision of acceptance of course does not have to be communicated as in the above example. A feedback can provide useful information to mediator in case of agents with substantial computational resources.

Finishing Dialogue Mediator finishes the dialogue.

$M \rightarrow A1$: I have no more recommendations for you.
$M \rightarrow A2$: I have no more recommendations for you.
$A2 \rightarrow M$: Thanks.
$A1 \rightarrow M$: Thanks.

5.2   Dialogue without a Mediator

Initiating the Dialogue This is straightforward in this case.

$A1 \rightarrow A2$: Let's share our knowledge.
$A2 \rightarrow A1$: Ok.

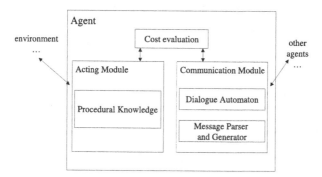

Fig. 2. Agent architecture with added communication and cost evaluation module

Information Exchange Both agents look for elements of FSM to exchange. The exchange of entries can be based on random GA-like exchange.

$A1 \rightarrow A2$: Give me the second row of your FSM.
$A2 \rightarrow A1$: Ok, here it is: ...
(the agent $A1$ accepts it and replaces his own second row if it evaluates this to be useful — and the dialogue may continue here until both agents are satisfied)

Finishing Dialogue This is again straightforward here.

$A1 \rightarrow A2$: Thanks, bye.
$A2 \rightarrow A1$: Thanks, bye.

6   Agent Architecture

We have presented possible structure of dialogue between agents sharing their procedural (or other) knowledge. From our previous description it follows that an agent should consist of these components (see figure 2):

1. procedural knowledge module—formalized by FSM
2. communication module—formalized by dialogue automaton
3. cost evaluation module—work versus communication cost evaluation

Procedural knowledge expresses the necessary steps for achieving desired goals. Simple yet useful formalization adapted from Spears and Gordon [7] is made via FSM. The original paper assumes the evolution of procedural knowledge by GAs. We add new components to this existing concept, namely a communication module and a cost evaluation module.

The communication module is formally described by dialogue automaton (DA). Alternatively we propose FIPA compliant format for expressing DA-based communication. We used FSM procedural knowledge formalism in this proposal, however, there is no need to limit to this kind of formalism.

The cost evaluation module is important to an agent that must be able to determine autonomously whether to work or communicate (i.e. to find the balance between work and communication). To enable this capability, we add a simple reasoning module that determines next action of agent.

7   Conclusion

The FSM's formalism can be used for solving planning problems. For example, a group of agents (robots, spacecrafts) is assigned a task that needs to be solved using only limited resources within the group. The task is to find a dialogue that is optimal in terms of associated cost. The goal was to represent the evolution as a communication procedure and to determine the cost of each operation and communication procedure. For example, for a small agent it may be an expensive problem to perform technical analysis of its own knowledge that may be represented by a FSM. Alternatively a transmission of its own FSM to a more powerful mediator agent can be more cost effective. The FSM representation allows us to use mathematical methods developed already in the respective fields. In particular a FSM can be found to represent a set of dialogues and this representations can be processed further using principled methods. The FSM and its generalizations for dialogues between agents provides a useful platform for modeling communication processes for certain classes of agents.

References

[1] *UM2001 Workshop on "Attitudes, Personality and Emotions in User Adapted Interaction.* Sonthofen 2001. `http://aos2.uniba.it:8080/ws-um01.html` 369
[2] FIPA. ACL Specification. 1997. `http://www.fipa.org/specs/fipa00003` 367
[3] FIPA. Ontology Service Specification. 1998.
    `http://www.fipa.org/specs/fipa00006/` 368
[4] I. Kopecek. Personality and Emotions - Finite State Modelling by Dialogue Automata. *UM2001 Workshop on "Attitudes, Personality and Emotions in User-Adapted Interaction"*, Sonthofen, 2001 369
[5] H. Jurgen Muller, Negotiation Principles in G. M. P. O'Hare and N. R. Jennings: *Foundations of Distributed Artificial Intelligence.* A Wiley-Interscience publication, 1996 367
[6] Pawlak, Z. "Information Systems, Theoretical Foundations". *Information Systems* 6 (1981), pp. 205-218, 1981 370
[7] William M. Spears and Diana F. Gordon. Evolving Finite-State Machine Strategies for Protecting Resources. *Proceedings of ISMIS'00*, 2000 368, 369, 375
[8] Eric Werner. Logical Foundations of Distributed Artificial Intelligence, in G. M. P. O'Hare and N. R. Jennings: *Foundations of Distributed Artificial Intelligence.* A Wiley-Interscience publication, 1996 367

Learning Communication for Multi-agent Systems

C. Lee Giles[1,2] and Kam-Chuen Jim[2]

[1] School of Information Sciences & Technology and Computer Science and
Engineering
The Pennsylvania State University
University Park, PA 16801 USA
giles@ist.psu.edu
[2] NEC Labs
4 Independence Way, Princeton, NJ 08540 USA
kamjim@research.nj.nec.com

Abstract. We analyze a general model of multi-agent communication in which all agents communicate simultaneously to a message board. A genetic algorithm is used to learn multi-agent languages for the predator agents in a version of the predator-prey problem. The resulting evolved behavior of the communicating multi-agent system is equivalent to that of a Mealy machine whose states are determined by the evolved language. We also constructed non-learning predators whose capture behavior was designed to take advantage of prey behavior known a priori. Simulations show that introducing noise to the decision process of the hard-coded predators allow them to significantly ourperform all previously published work on similar preys. Furthermore, the evolved communicating predators were able to perform significantly better than the hard-coded predators, which indicates that the system was able to learn superior communicating strategies not readily available to the human designer.

1 Introduction

Allowing agents to communicate and to learn what to communicate can significantly improve the flexibility and adaptiveness of a multi-agent system. This paper studies an ideal case where each agent has access to a small set of local information and through experience learns to communicate only the additional information that is important. While many researchers have shown the emergence of beneficial communication in multi-agent systems, very few have looked into how communication affects the behavior or representational power of the multi-agent system. This paper shows the relationship between the communication behavior of a multi-agent system and the finite state machine that completely describes this behavior. With this knowledge we demonstrate how evolved communication increases the performance of a multi-agent system.

W. Truszkowski, C. Rouff, M. Hinchey (Eds.): WRAC 2002, LNAI 2564, pp. 377–390, 2003.

1.1 Previous Work

Previous work has shown that beneficial communication can emerge in a multi-agent system. [1] show that agents can evolve to communicate altruistically in a track world even when doing so provides no immediate benefit to the individual. [2] use genetic algorithms to evolve finite state machines that cooperate by communicating in a simple abstract world. [3] study the emergence of conventions in multi-agent systems as a function of various hard-coded strategy update functions, including update functions where agents communicate to exchange memories of observed strategies by other agents. [4] show that vocabulary can evolve through the principle of self-organization. A set of agents create their own vocabulary in a random manner, yet self-organization occurs because the agents must conform to a common vocabulary in order to cooperate. [5] allow agents to communicate real-valued signals through continuous communication channels and evolved agents that communicate the presence of food in a food trail-following task. [6] showed that communication significantly improves performance of robot agents on tasks with little environmental communication, and that more complex communication strategies provide little or no benefit over low-level communication.

While many researchers have shown the emergence of beneficial communication, very few have analyzed the nature of the communication and how communication affects the behavior or representational power of the multi-agent system. [7] developed a "Recursive Modeling Method" to represent an agent's state of knowledge about the world and the other agents in the world. Furthermore, Gmytrasiewicz, Durfee, and Rosenchein used this framework to compute the expected utility of various speech acts by looking at the transformation the speech act induces on the agents' state of knowledge. [8] show that with certain assumptions, communication can be treated as an n-person game, and the optimal encoding of content by messages is obtained as an equilibrium maximizing the sum of the receiver's and speaker's expected utilities. More recently, we have shown that communication increases the representational power of multi-agent systems, and derived a method for estimating the language size for any multi-agent problem ([9], [10]).

2 Predator Prey Problem

The predator-prey pursuit problem is used in this paper because it is a general and well-studied multi-agent problem that still has not been solved, and it is a simplied version of problems seen in numerous applications such as warfare scenarios and computer games. The predator-prey pursuit problem was introduced by [11] and comprised four predator agents whose goal is to capture a prey agent by surrounding it on four sides in a grid-world. [12] used genetic programming to evolve predator strategies and showed that a linear prey (pick a random direction and continue in that direction for the rest of the trial) was impossible to capture reliably in their experiments because the linear prey avoids locality of movement. [13] studied a version of the predator prey problem in which the predators were allowed to move diagonally as well as orthogonally and the prey moved randomly. [14] used reinforcement learning and showed that cooperating predators that share sensations and learned policies amongst each other significantly outperforms non-cooperating predators. [15] study a simple non-communicating predator strategy in which predators move to the closest capture position, and show that this strategy is not very successful because predators can block each other by trying to move to the same capture position. Stephens and Merx also present another strategy in which 3 predators transmit all their sensory information to one central predator agent who decides where all predators should move. This central single-agent strategy succeeds for 30 test cases, but perhaps the success rate would be much lower if the agents were to move simultaneously instead of taking turns.

We use an implementation which is probably more difficult for the predators than in all previous work:

1. In our configuration, all agents are allowed to move in only four orthogonal directions. The predators cannot take shortcuts by moving diagonally to the prey, as they do in [13].
2. All agents have the same speed. The predators do not move faster than the prey, nor do they move more often than the prey, as they do in [12].
3. All agents move simultaneously. Because the agents do not take turns moving (e.g. [15]) there is some uncertainty in anticipating the result of each move. In addition, moving the agents concurrently introduces many potential conflicts, e.g. two or more agents may try to move to the same square.
4. The predators cannot see each other and do not know each other's location. If this information is essential then the predators will have to evolve a language that can represent such information.

The world is a two dimensional torus discretized into a 30x30 grid. If an agent runs off the left edge of the grid it would reappear on the right edge of the grid, and a similar behavior would be observed vertically. No two agents are allowed to occupy the same cell at the same time, and agents cannot move through each other. If two or more agents try to move to the same square they are blocked and remain in their current positions. At the beginning of each scenario the agents are randomly placed on different squares. Each scenario continues until either the prey is captured, or until 5000 time steps have occurred without a capture.

Two prey strategies are used in the simulations. The Random Prey chooses it's next action at each time step from the set N, S, E, W using a uniform random distribution. The Linear Prey picks a random direction at the beginning of a trial and continues in that direction for the duration of the scenario. It has been shown that the Linear Prey can be a difficult prey to capture [12, 4] because it does not stay localized in an area. In our simulations this is an even more difficult prey to capture because the prey and predators move at the same speed.

3   Non-communicating Predators

The first set of experiments in this section is done using predators with human-designed strategies, while the second set is done using evolved predators.

3.1   Hard-Coded Predators

The Follower agent moves in the direction that minimizes its Manhattan distance to the prey's current location. Ties are broken randomly. [13] used a similar greedy heuristic for a version of the predator prey problem where the agents take turns moving. [12] modified the algorithm to work in the predator prey problem with simultaneous moves. Both of these previous approaches are deterministic and thus suffer from deadlock.

The Herder agent is similar to the Follower agent but takes advantage of coordination at the initiation of each trial. At the beginning of each trial, each agent is assigned a role of either N, S, E, or W Herder. Their task is to move to the respective cell adjacent to the prey in their assigned direction, in effect herding the prey from four sides in an attempt to capture it. The Herder agent uses the same Manhattan distance heuristic as the Follower agent.

The HerderCounter agents attempt to herd the prey like the Herder agents, but takes advantage of *state information* by counting the number of times the prey has moved in the same direction. This count is used as an offset to predict the prey's future position, which is computed by projecting the prey in the direction of its previous move a number of steps equivalent to the count. The predators attempt to herd the prey using this predicted position. The count has a ceiling of 10, and when the prey changes direction the count is reset to zero. Since the agents all move at the same speed, it is impossible for the predators to catch up to a Linear prey once it is directly behind it. This modification was designed using knowledge of the Linear prey, and allows the predators to catch up to the prey by shortcutting to the prey's predicted position. We expect this modification to improve performance only against the Linear prey.

Deadlock occurs frequently when the predators and prey have deterministic strategies. For all three predator strategies in this section we vary the amount of noise that is introduced into the strategies in order to help prevent deadlock. In this paper, these agents will be named by appending the amount of noise to the name of it's strategy. For example, "Follower-10%" is a Follower agent which, for each move, has a 10% chance of choosing a random action.

Performance of Hard-Coded Predators Each predator strategy was tested on the Random and Linear preys. 10, 000 runs were performed on each predator-prey pairing. Each run terminates when either the prey is captured, or after 50, 000 cycles have elapsed, whichever occurs first. The results can be summarized by the following observations:

- *The Linear prey is more difficult to capture than the Random prey.* See Figure 1.

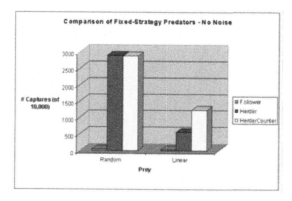

Fig. 1. Performance of Fixed-Strategy Predators on the Random and Linear Preys

- *Noise Significantly Improves Performance.* See Figures 2 and 3. In many cases, the predators cannot capture without noise. Using more noise can actually reduce the capture time, and unlike previous work which report results as percentage of captures this paper reports the average capture time because we observe 100 percent capture rate.
- *Coordination Can Improve Performance.* Herder and HerderCounter make use of implicit communication by coordinating their roles at the initiation of each run, and they both outperform the Follower strategy.
- *State Information Can Improve Performance.* HerderCounter agents use the count state information to offset the desired capture position. Figure 3 shows that of the three predator strategies in this section, the HerderCounter performs the best on the Linear prey. As expected, the HerderCounter strategy shows no significant improvement over the Herder strategy when attempting to capture the Random prey (see Figure 2). This shows that proper state information can be very important, but determining what state information is useful can be very problem specific.
- *Our noisy predators perform better than all previously published work to our knowledge.* A previous work whose experimental setup is most similar to our work is perhaps [12], although their setup makes the predators' job easier because they are allowed to move more frequently than the prey. Haynes and Sen and other previous work [13] on similar preys report results as a percentage of trials that lead to capture, whereas the results reported here show 100% capture rate.

3.2   Evolved Predators

This section describes how a genetic algorithm is used to evolve predator strategies, and compares the performance of these strategies with the fixed-strategy

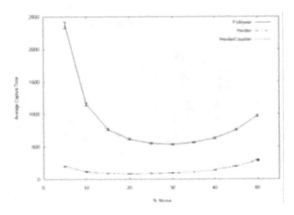

Fig. 2. Performance of Fixed-Strategy Noisy Predators on Random Prey. Error bars show 95% confidence intervals obtained by running 10000 simulations on each point

predators of the previous section. Each individual in the GA population represents a predator strategy that is used by all 4 homogenous predators in each scenario.

Encoding Predator Strategies The sensory information available to the predators comprise only the range and bearing of the prey. The range is measured in terms of the Manhattan distance. Both the range and bearing are discretized into $N_{range} = 8$ and $N_{bearing} = 8$ sectors. The predators can detect when the prey is 0, 1, 2, and 3+ cells away, measured in terms of the Manhattan distance. Ranges of 3 or more cells away are lumped under the same sector. The bearing of the prey from the predator is discretized into 8 equal sectors similar to the slices of a pizza pie. The 4 available actions are the moves $\{N, S, E, W\}$.

The behavior of each evolved predator is represented by a binary chromosome string. The number of binary bits required to represent the 4 actions are $b_{actions} = 2$. The total length c of the GA chromosome is given by the following equation:

$$c = N_{range} N_{bearing} b_{actions}$$
$$= 128$$

Evaluating Fitness The fitness of each evolved strategy is determined by testing it on 100 randomly generated scenarios. Each scenario specifies unique starting locations for the predator and prey agents. The maximum number of cycles per scenario is 5000, after which the scenario times out and the predators are considered to have failed. Since the initial population is randomly generated, it is very unlikely that the first few generations will be able to capture the

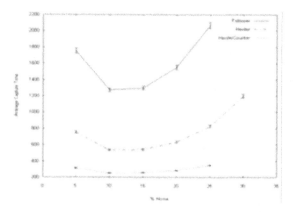

Fig. 3. Performance of Fixed-Strategy Noisy Predators on the Linear Prey. Error bars show 95% confidence intervals obtained by running 10000 simulations on each point

prey. We attempt to speed up the evolution of fit strategies by rewarding those strategies that at least stay near the prey and are able to block the prey's path. The fitness f_i of individual i is computed at the end of each generation as follows, where $N_{\max} = 5000$ is the maximum number of cycles per scenario, $T = 100$ is the total number of scenarios for each individual, and n_c is the number of captures:

- If $n_c = 0$, $f_i = \frac{0.4}{d_{avg}+0.6\frac{n_b}{N_{\max}T}}$ where d_{avg} is the average distance of the all 4 predators from the prey during the scenarios, and n_b is the cummulative # of cycles where the prey's movement was blocked by an adjacent predator during T scenarios. The fitness of non-capture strategies can never be greater than 1.
- If $0 < n_c < T$, $f_i = n_c$.
- If $n_c = T$, $f_i = T + \frac{10000T}{\sum\limits_{j=0}^{T} t_j}$, where t_j is the number of cycles required to capture the prey at scenario j.

GA Setup The following parameters of the GA algorithm were found experimentally to be most effective. The population size of each generation is fixed at 100 individuals. The mutation rate is set at 0.01. We use 2-point crossover with a crossover probability of 0.4. The idea behind multi-point crossover is that parts of the chromosome that contribute to the fit behavior of an individual may not be in adjacent substrings. Also, the disruptive nature of multi-point crossover may result in a more robust search by encouraging exploration of the search space rather than early convergence to highly fit individuals. For a discussion of 2-point crossover and generalized multi-point crossover schemes see [16]. A Tournament selection scheme [17] with a tournament size $Tour$ of 5 is used to select the parents at each generation. In Tournament selection, *Tour* individuals are chosen randomly from the population and the best individual from this group is selected as a parent. This is repeated until enough parents have been chosen to produce the required number of offsprings for the next generation. The larger the tournament size, the greater the selection pressure, which is the probability of the best individual being selected compared to the average probability of selection of all individuals.

The following pseudocode describes the methodology:

1. Repeat the following for 10 trials on selected prey:
   (a) Randomly generate a population of 100 individuals.
   (b) Repeat the following until the predators show no improvement after 200 generations:
       i. Simulate each predator strategy on 100 scenarios and evaluate its fitness based on the performance on those scenarios.
       ii. Select 100 individuals from the current population using Tournament selection, pair them up, and create a new population by using 2-point crossover with mutation.
   (c) The best strategy found over all generations is used as the solution of this trial. The fitness of this strategy is then recomputed by testing on 1000 new randomly generated scenarios.
2. The strategy that performed best over all 10 trials is used as the solution to this prey.

Performance of GA Predators The results of the best GA predators evolved for each prey are shown in Figure 4. Also shown in the figure are results of the fixed predator strategies at their optimal noise levels, which were obtained by taking the best average capture times found for each predator in Figures 2 and 3. The GA predator strategy is denoted as *GaPredator(0)*, where *(0)* indicates that there is no communication.

The performance of GaPredator(0) against the Random prey is comparable to the performance of the Herder and HerderCounter predators (though taking on average 30 cycles longer to capture), and significantly better than the performance of the Follower predators. However, none of the evolved predators were able to reliably capture the Linear prey. In the next Section we explore whether or not allowing the predators to evolve communication would improve their performance against the Linear prey.

4   Communication

All predator agents communicate simultaneously to a *message board* (Figure 5). At every iteration, each predator speaks a string of symbols which is stored on the message board. Each agent then reads all the strings communicated by all the predators and determines the next move and what to say next. Strings are restricted to have equal length l. We vary the length l of the strings and study the effect on performance.

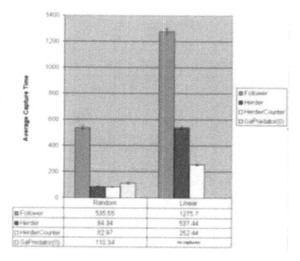

Fig. 4. Performance of best non-communicating predator strategies. Error bars show 95% confidence intervals

4.1   Communicating Agents as One FSM

This type of communication may be represented as shown in Figure 5, where $\{A_m\}$ is the set of homogenous predator agents, $\{O_m\}$ are the actions of the predators, and $\{I_{mn}\}$ is the set of environmental inputs, where n is the number of inputs and m is the number of communicating agents. The message board can be interpreted as a set of *state nodes*.

The entire set of agents can be viewed as one finite state machine (FSM) with the set of possible states specified by the state nodes $\{S_{ml}\}$. The whole multi-agent system is equivalent to a finite state automaton with output, otherwise known as a finite state transducer. One type of finite state transducer is the Mealy finite state machine, in which the output depends on both the state of the machine and its inputs. A Mealy machine can be characterized by a quintuple $M = (\Sigma, Q, Z, \delta, \lambda)$, where Σ is a finite non-empty set of input symbols, Q is a finite non-empty set of states, Z is a finite non-empty set of output symbols, δ is a "next-state" function which maps $Q \times \Sigma \rightarrow Q$, and λ is an output function which maps $Q \times \Sigma \rightarrow Z$.

It is easy to show that the multi-agent system is a Mealy machine by describing the multi-agent system in terms of the quintuple M. The input set Σ is obtained from the set $\{I_{00}I_{01}...I_{0n}I_{10}I_{11}...I_{mn}\}$ of all possible concatenated sensor readings for the predator agents (for all possible values of I). The states Q are represented by concatenation of all symbols in the message board. Since the communication strings comprise binary symbols $\{0,1\}$, the maximum number of states N_{states} in the Mealy machine is therefore determined by the number of communicating agents m and by the length l of the communication strings: $N_{states} = 2^{lm}$. The output set Z is obtained from the

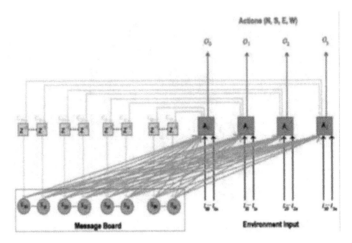

Fig. 5. Multi-agent Communication as a single Finite State Machine

set $\{O_{00}O_{01}..O_{0p}O_{10}O_{11}...O_{mp}\}$ of all possible concatenated actions for all the communicating agents, where p is the number of bits required to encode the possible actions for each agent (for all possible values of O). In the general case where the actions do not have to be encoded as binary bits, the output set is simply the set $\{O_0O_1...O_m\}$ of all possible concatenated actions for the m communicating agents. The next state function δ and output function λ are determined by the agents' action and communication strategies. The strategies themselves may be FSMs or something with even more representational power, in such a case the multi-agent FSM is a hierarchical FSM.

4.2   States and Partially Observable Environments

From Figure 5 it is clear that communication allows the agents to use state information. This state information is contributed by all communicating agents and represents the state of the multi-agent system. Although each individual agent may maintain its own state information, such information will be limited by the available sensors of the agent. Communication allows agents to "tell" each other environmental information that may have been observable only to a subset of the agents. Obviously, communication will be of little use in this respect in the limit when the same set of environmental information is observable to all agents. It is rare for all agents to have access to the same amount of information. This is due to the fact that an individual agent will usually have its own internal state that is not observable by other agents. If an agent's internal state helps determine its behavior, communication may be instrumental in allowing the agents to converge on an optimal plan of action.

4.3   Experimental Setup

A genetic algorithm is used to evolve predators that communicate. This section describes sets of experiments with strings of varying length l. As the length l increases, the number of strings that are available for communicative acts increases exponentially.

Encoding Predator Strategies   The sensory information available to the predators include the range and bearing of the prey as discussed in Section 3.2. In addition, the predator agents have access to the contents of the message board. Since each agent speaks a string of length l at each time step, the number of symbols on the message board is ml, where m is the number of predator agents.

The behavior of each predator is represented by a binary string. The number of binary bits required to represent the 4 movements are $b_{moves} = 2$. In addition, each agent speaks a string of length l at each iteration. Thus, the total number of action bits is

$$b_{actions} = b_{moves} + l \qquad (1)$$

The range and bearing are discretized to $N_{range} = 8$ and $N_{bearing} = 8$ sectors. In addition, since there are ml binary symbols on the message board, the message board can have $N_{messages} = 2^{ml}$ possible messages. The total number of states that can be sensed by a predator is $N_{states} = N_{range}N_{bearing}N_{messages}$ This provides the following equation for the chromosome length c_{ml} of a GA predator:

$$c_{ml} = b_{actions}N_{states}$$
$$c_{ml} = N_{range}N_{bearing}(2 + l)2^{ml} \qquad (2)$$

so the chromosome length increases exponentially with communication string length and number of agents.

Growing GA Predators - Coarse to Fine Search   To improve efficiency, it would be useful to *grow* the predators. Growing means taking a population of predators that have already evolved a language from a set of possible strings, and evolving them further after increasing the set of possible strings they are allowed to communicate. This re-uses the knowledge acquired by predators that were limited to a smaller language. This is effectively a coarse-to-fine search. By starting with a smaller set of possible strings (and therefore smaller search space) the agents are forced to evolve a minimalistic language to communicate the most important state information. As we increase the search space by increasing the number of possible strings, the agents can refine the language and communicate other useful, but possibly less critical, information.

When a population of GA predators with chromosome length c_{ml} is grown to a length of $c_{m(l+1)}$, each new chromosome is encoded such that the behavior of the new predator is initially identical to that of the chromosome it was grown from. The portions of the larger chromosome that are new are not visited initially

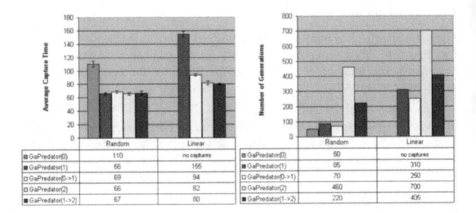

	GaPredator	Random	Linear
▨	GaPredator(0)	110	no captures
■	GaPredator(1)	66	155
▢	GaPredator(0->1)	69	94
▢	GaPredator(2)	66	82
■	GaPredator(1->2)	67	80

	GaPredator	Random	Linear
▨	GaPredator(0)	50	no captures
■	GaPredator(1)	85	310
▢	GaPredator(0->1)	70	250
▢	GaPredator(2)	460	700
■	GaPredator(1->2)	220	405

Fig. 6. Best capture times and the corresponding number of evolutionary generations required to evolve the communicating predators against the Random and Linear preys, at communication string lengths 0, 1, and 2. Error bars on the capture times show 95% confidence intervals using the Student's t distribution, obtained by running 1000 simulations at each point

because the predator is making exactly the same decisions as before and will therefore see the same set of sensory states. As the evolutionary process begins, new sensory states will be visited and the agent will evolve accordingly.

The population size of the grown $c_{m(l+1)}$ predators is always twice the population size of the c_{ml} predators they were grown from. Half of the population of $c_{m(l+1)}$ predators are grown from the c_{ml} predators, the other half are generated randomly. In this manner the population of grown predators do not have to rely solely on mutation for introducing new genetic material to the genes that were copied from the c_{ml} predators. They can obtain new genetic material through crossover with the randomly generated individuals.

Setup In the sections that follow, the GA predators are labelled as GaPredator(l), where l is the length of the communication strings. $l = 0$ means the predators are not communicating, and is identical to the GaPredator discussed in Section 3.2. Grown predators are labelled as GaPredator($l_0 \rightarrow l_1$), where l_0 is the communication string length before the agent is grown, and l_1 is the length it was grown to. Five predator populations GaPredator(0), GaPredator(1), GaPredator(2), GaPredator(0 $\rightarrow$ 1), and GaPredator(1 $\rightarrow$ 2) are matched against the Random and Linear preys. Each matchup is performed similarly to the set-up described in Section 3.2, except that each predator population is evolved until there is no further improvement in 200 generations. The initial GaPredator(0 $\rightarrow$ 1) population that is matched up against the Linear prey is grown from the GaPredator(0) population with the best average fitness against the Linear prey.

4.4   Results

Figure 6 shows the best average capture times, and the number of evolutionary generations that were required to achieve those capture times. The number of generations reported for the grown predators are recursively cumulative with the number of generations needed to evolve them before they were grown. Below is a summary of the results:

- Communication improves capture performance.
- As the length of the communication string increases, the capture time decreases. However, the best performance of GaPredator(1) against the Random prey is comparable to the best performance of GaPredator(2) and GaPredator($1 \rightarrow 2$), which indicates that a communication string of length 1 is sufficient against the Random prey.
- The evolutionary generations required increases with the length of the communication string.
- The performance of grown predators is comparable to that of the equivalent non-grown predators but requires significantly less evolution time.
- The evolved communicating predators perform better than all previously published work to our knowledge, and better than the noisy, hard-coded predators presented in the previous Section.

5   Conclusions

Introducing noise to the decision process of our human-designed predator strategies allows the predators to overcome deadlock and thus outperform predator strategies both programmed and learned in all previously published work. Furthermore, a genetic algorithm can evolve communicating predators that outperform all (noisy) human-designed predator strategies reported in this paper.

A multi-agent system in which all the agents communicate simultaneously is equivalent to a Mealy machine whose states are determined by the concatenation of the strings in the agents' communication language. The simulations show that increasing the language size, and thus increasing the number of possible states in the equivalent Mealy machine, can significantly improve the performance of the predators.

References

[1] Ackley, D.H., Littman, M.L.: Altruism in the evolution of communication. In Brooks, R.A., Maes, P., eds.: Artificial Life IV: Proceedings of the International Workshop on the Synthesis and Simulation of Living Systems, MIT Press (1994) 40–49 378

[2] MacLennan, B.J., Burghardt, G.M.: Synthetic ethology and the evolution of cooperative communication. Adaptive Behavior 2 (1993) 161–188 378

[3] Walker, A., Wooldridge, M.: Understanding the emergence of conventions in multi-agent systems. In Lesser, V., Gasser, L., eds.: Proceedings of the First International Conference on Multi-Agent Systems, Menlo Park, CA, AAAI Press (1995) 384–389 378

[4] Steels, L.: Self-organizing vocabularies. In Langton, C., ed.: Proceedings of Alife V, Nara, Japan (1996) 378, 379

[5] Saunders, G.M., Pollack, J.B.: The evolution of communication schemes over continuous channels. In Maes, P., Mataric, M., Meyer, J., Pollack, J., eds.: From Animals to Animats 4: Proceedings of the 4th International Conference on Simulation of Adaptive Behavior, MIT Press (1996) 580–589 378

[6] Balch, T., Arkin, R.C.: Communication in reactive multiagent robotic systems. Autonomous Robots 1 (1994) 27–52 378

[7] Gmytrasiewicz, P.J., Durfee, E.H., Rosenschein, J.: Toward rational communicative behavior. In: AAAI Fall Symposium on Embodied Language, AAAI Press (1995) 378

[8] Hasida, K., Nagao, K., Miyata, T.: A game-theoretic account of collaboration in communication. In Lesser, V., ed.: Proceedings of the First International Conference on Multi–Agent Systems (ICMAS), San Francisco, CA, MIT Press (1995) 140–147 378

[9] Jim, K., Giles, C.L.: Talking helps: Evolving communicating agents for the predator-prey pursuit problem. Artificial Life 6(3) (2000) 237–254 378

[10] Jim, K., Giles, C.L.: How communication can improve the performance of multi-agent systems. In: 5th International Conference on Autonomous Agents. (2001) 378

[11] Benda, M., Jagannathan, V., Dodhiawalla, R.: On optimal cooperation of knowledge sources. Technical Report BCS-G2010-28, Boeing AI Center, Boeing Computer Services, Bellevue, WA (1985) 378

[12] Haynes, T., Sen, S.: Evolving behavioral strategies in predators and prey. In Wei, G., Sen, S., eds.: Adaptation and Learning in Multiagent Systems. Springer Verlag, Berlin (1996) 113–126 378, 379, 380, 381

[13] Korf, R.E.: A simple solution to pursuit games. In: Working Papers of the 11th International Workshop on Distributed Artificial Intelligence, Glen Arbor, Michigan (1992) 183–194 378, 379, 380, 381

[14] Tan, M.: Multi-agent reinforcement learning: Independent vs. cooperative agents. In: Proc. of 10th ICML. (1993) 330–337 379

[15] Stephens, L.M., Merx, M.B.: The effect of agent control strategy on the performance of a dai pursuit problem. In: Proceedings of the 10th International Workshop on DAI, Bandera, Texas (1990) 379

[16] Jong, K.A.D., Spears, W.M.: A formal analysis of the role of multi-point crossover in genetic algorithms. Annals of Mathematics and Artificial Intelligence Journal 5 (1992) 1–26 383

[17] Goldberg, D., Deb, K.: A comparative analysis of selection schemes used in genetic algorithms. In Rawlins, G., ed.: Foundations of Genetic Algorithms. Morgan Kaufmann Publishers, San Mateo, CA (1991) 69–93 383

Part VI

Innovative Applications

Biological Analogs and Emergent Intelligence for Control of Stratospheric Balloon Constellations

Matthew Kuperus Heun[1], R. Stephen Schlaifer[1], Kim Aaron[1], Alexey Pankine[1], Kerry Nock[1], Naomi Erich Leonard[2], Edward Belbruno[3], and Pradeep Bhatta[2]

[1] Global Aerospace Corporation, 711 W. Woodbury Road, Suite H, Altadena, CA, 91001-5327, USA
{matthew.k.heun, r.stephen.schlaifer, kim.m.aaron, alexey.a.pankine, kerry.t.nock}@gaerospace.com
http://www.gaerospace.com
[2] Mechanical and Aerospace Engineering, Princeton University, Princeton, NJ, 08544
{naomi, pradeep}@princeton.edu
http://www.princeton.edu/~mae/MAE.html
[3] Program in Applied and Computational Mathematics, Princeton University, Princeton, NJ, 08544
belbruno@Math.Princeton.edu
http://www.pacm.princeton.edu/

Abstract. Global Aerospace Corporation is developing a revolutionary concept for a global constellation and network of hundreds of stratospheric superpressure balloons. Global Aerospace Corporation and Princeton University are studying methods of controlling the geometry of these stratospheric balloon constellations using concepts related to and inspiration derived from biological group behavior such as schooling, flocking, and herding. The method of artificial potentials determines control settings for trajectory control systems in the steady flow regions. Weak Stability Boundary theory is used to (a) determine the interfaces between smooth flow and areas where chaotic conditions exist and (b) calculate control settings in regions of chaotic flow.

1 Introduction

Global Aerospace Corporation (GAC) is studying, under NASA Institute for Advanced Concepts (NIAC) funding, a new generation of low-cost stratospheric platforms, called *StratoSat™ platforms*, based on advances in NASA's Ultra Long Duration Balloon (ULDB) technology currently under development. StratoSat™ networks and constellations can address issues of high interest to the Earth science community including global change, especially tropical circulation and radiation balance; global and polar ozone; hurricane forecasting and tracking; global circulation; and global ocean productivity [1, 2]. Regional and global constellations of stratospheric superpressure balloons can measure stratospheric gases, collect data on atmospheric circulation, observe the Earth's surface, and detect and monitor weather

W. Truszkowski, C. Rouff, M. Hinchey (Eds.): WRAC 2002, LNAI 2564, pp. 393-407, 2003.

and environmental hazards. The following figure shows an example StratoSat™ platform and a network of 100 stratospheric balloons distributed evenly around the globe.

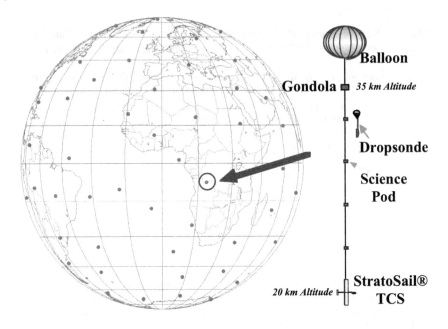

Fig. 1. Example global constellation of 100 stratospheric balloons

Low-cost StratoSat™ platform constellations could provide good diurnal coverage of the entire globe or specific regions, improve resolution and/or signal-to-noise ratios of measurements due to their low altitude observations, enable new observational techniques because of their low speed, provide frequent to continuous measurements of geographic locations, measure horizontal gradients in addition to vertical profiles, and operate for an extended duration of 3-10 years. StratoSat™ platforms can provide a cost effective method for science and satellite validation, verification, and calibration.

StratoSat™ platform constellations operating at a 35-km altitude and for 3 to 10-years in duration could augment and complement satellite measurements and possibly replace satellites for making some environmental measurements. The keys to this new concept are (a) affordable, long-duration balloon systems, (b) balloon trajectory control capability, and (c) a global communications infrastructure. GAC will summarize the development of technology for these very long-duration and guided stratospheric balloons that enable affordable global and regional constellations of formation-flying, stratospheric platforms.

2   Constellation Trajectory Control Capability

The following figure illustrates one concept for a balloon trajectory control system. The StratoSail® TCS consists of a wing on end connected to a rudder and a counterweight all located on a boom and suspended from a tether up to 15 km below the balloon to take advantage of the variation in wind velocity with altitude [3, 4]. The wing generates a horizontal lift force that can be directed over a wide range of angles. This force, transmitted to the balloon by the tether, alters the balloon's path. The TCS is scaleable over a very wide range of sizes. The magnitude of the trajectory control capability depends on the relative sizes of the balloon and the wing, coupled with the ratio of air densities and the magnitude of the wind velocity difference between the two altitudes.

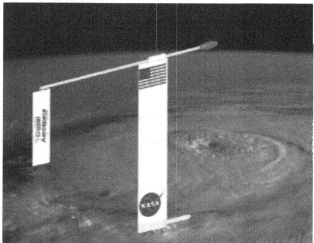

Fig. 2. StratoSail® trajectory control system

Such an approach to balloon trajectory control:
- offers increased balloon operations flexibility and cost reduction,
- permits balloon to remain at fixed altitude,
- avoids overflight of uncooperative countries,
- increases number of potential landing sites,
- enables balloon to travel over desired locations,
- passively exploits natural wind conditions,
- does not require consumables,
- avoids payload disturbances caused by propulsive trajectory control methods,
- requires very little electrical power,
- operates day and night,
- offers a wide range of control directions regardless of wind conditions, and
- can be made of lightweight materials.

A StratoSail® TCS provides a sideways (lateral) lift force and has a backward drag force. These forces are applied at the wing. The following figure illustrates the model of the lift and drag forces used to simulate the performance of the StratoSail® TCS.

The drag force is essentially constant and in the same direction as the relative wind at the wing. The lateral force can be directed to the left or right of the relative wind at the wing. And, the lateral forces vary in magnitude as a function of the angle of attack of the wing.

The StratoSail® TCS is an example of a bounded and underactuated control system. A bounded control system is one in which control inputs have bounded magnitude; in this case the bound is less than typical external forces (winds). An underactuated control system is one in which control forces cannot be applied in all desired directions. The StratoSail® TCS is both bounded (because it cannot fight the winds to maintain station) and underactuated (because it provides control forces over about 90° of the full circle).

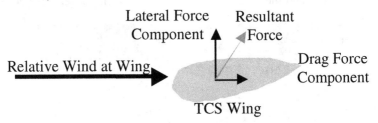

Fig. 3. Lateral (lift) and drag force components on StratoSail® TCS

3   Weak Stability Boundary Theory

Weak Stability Boundary (WSB) theory is a way to predict where sensitive (or chaotic) motion will occur as an object is moving under the influence of various forces. It will also analytically approximate the regions of sensitive motion. These regions are termed weak stability boundaries. The sensitive nature of the motion can be exploited to minimize trajectory control requirements, depending on the application. This theory was originally developed in 1986 for the application to the motion of spacecraft [5]. It was used to salvage the Japanese spacecraft Hiten and enabled it to reach the Moon on October 2, 1991. This was the first operational proof of WSB theory [6, 7].

An important result of this work is analysis that shows that WSB theory can be applied to control the motion of balloons in the stratosphere. By modeling stratospheric vortices as Newtonian potentials, WSB regions can potentially be identified near these vortices. Balloons moving near these locations will move in a sensitive manner which can be exploited to minimize control effort for maintaining the nominal path of the balloon and to also change its path.

An example WSB surface and an illustration of how it is used is shown in the three-dimensional plot in the following figure.

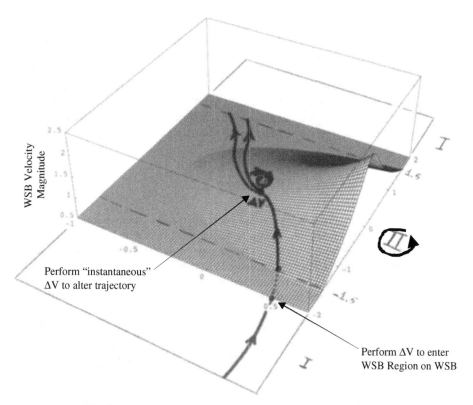

Fig. 4. Example use of WSB theory to alter balloon trajectories

In this example, there is a pair of cyclones, one modeled as a source and one as a sink. In the plot the xy-plane corresponds to the physical plane where x is a local coordinate for latitude and y a local coordinate for longitude. The z-axis represents the energy associated with the surface. This energy is a measure of the velocity a balloon can have at a given value of x and y while being on the WSB surface. The higher the surface, the greater the range of velocities the balloon can have at a given point (x; y). This means that there is a larger range of possible velocity values to choose from in order to be on the boundary, giving more flexibility in the control of the balloon's motion. The control is achieved by applying small maneuvers to achieve large changes in the trajectory. In the following figure, the balloon trajectory is seen to start in Region I at x=.5, y=-4. It moves with no delta-V until it gets to the threshold of Region II at the position x=.5, y=-2. There a delta-V is applied so that the velocity at this point corresponds to one in which the balloon will be able to enter Region II and be approximately at the WSB. After this point the balloon moves with no delta-V across Region II and remains on the WSB. Moving on the WSB implies that its motion should be sensitive to small maneuvers (delta-V's). This fact is demonstrated when the balloon is approximately at the middle of the WSB region at the position x=-.2, y=0. This point is slightly below one of the cyclones (the one that is modeled as a source) which has its origin at x=0, y=0. Here, a small maneuver is performed. For comparison, in the case in which no maneuver is performed, the trajectory freely moves on the path to the right. When the maneuver is performed, the path to the left is shown. Since 1 unit in the xy-plane corresponds to 5,000 km, a significant deviation is obtained, as is shown. The maneuvered trajectory is the path of a balloon which is given a delta-V of –5 m/s tangential to its path in the WSB region. This causes a shift of 2000 km in 12 days. It would require a higher control effort to cause this amount of shift were the control effort applied elsewhere along the trajectory of the balloon. It is expected that applying delta-V's at more places or continuously along the trajectory would cause a much greater shift.

4   Artificial Potential (AP) Theory

Biologists who study animal aggregations such as swarms, flocks, schools, and herds have observed the remarkable group-level characteristics that are exhibited as "emergent" properties from individual-level behaviors [8, 9]. These include the ability to make very fast and efficient coordinated maneuvers [10], the ability to quickly process data, and a significantly improved decision making ability (as compared to individuals) [11]. The following figure illustrates these natural behaviors with a pod of dolphins.

Fig. 5. Example biological group: a pod of dolphins

The use of artificial potentials to generate control laws that emulate schooling behavior is inspired by the observations and models of the biologists. Groups in nature make use of a distributed control architecture whereby individuals respond to their sensed environment but are constrained by the behavior of their neighbors. Biologists suggest that the following elements are basic to maintaining a group structure: (1) attraction to distant neighbors up to a maximum distance, (2) repulsion from neighbors that are too close and (3) alignment or velocity matching with neighbors [9]. In our control synthesis framework, these local traffic rules are encoded by means of (local) artificial potentials that define interaction forces between neighboring vehicles. Each of these potentials is a function of the relative distance between a pair of neighbors [12]. Using such a method, the control forces drive the vehicles to the minimum of the total potential. Artificial potentials can also be defined as a function of relative orientation in order to produce control laws to align neighboring vehicles [13].

In robotics, artificial potentials have been used extensively to produce feedback control laws [11, 14, 15, 16] that avoid stationary obstacles as well as obstacles in motion [17] and have been used in motion planning [18, 19]. Potential shaping has also been used successfully for stabilization of mechanical systems [20, 21, 22, 23, 24]. Progress has been made in using artificial potentials in group tasks such as in addressing the problem of autonomous robot assembly [25] and the coordination of a constellation of spacecraft [26]. In the artificial intelligence and computer animation industries, heuristic traffic rules are imposed of a similar sort in order to yield life-like coordinated behaviors [27]. In recent work, the artificial potentials framework has been considered to enable vehicle groups to efficiently climb gradients in a spatial distribution [28].

5   Constellation Geometry Management with Artificial Potentials

5.1   Method of Artificial Potentials

We have successfully utilized artificial potentials to control constellations of hundreds of stratospheric balloons for simulated constellations. This is the first known application of AP theory for bounded and underactuated control systems (StratoSail® TCSs) in the presence of a non-uniform external flow field (stratospheric winds).

We assume that science data is to be collected by remote observation of the surface of the earth. Emission angles greater than 2° are acceptable, so the "footprint" for one balloon includes all points on the globe that can view the balloon with 2° elevation angle or higher. For this application, it is desired to have uniform coverage over the entire region of interest. The StratoSail® TCS, being a bounded control system, does not provide station-keeping capabilities, so we choose to utilize enough balloons to cover the latitude band in which the desired region lies. For the case of uniform coverage in the Northern Hemisphere (+15° latitude to the pole), 383 balloons are sufficient.

The following figure shows an example constellation of balloons for this application. Note that balloon locations are shown as red dots, the coverage zone for each balloon is shown as a yellow circle, and overlapping coverage regions are shown in green.

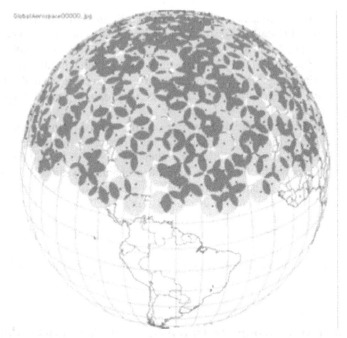

Fig. 6. Northern hemisphere constellation of 383 stratospheric balloons

For these simulations, we used the artificial potential (AP) theory to set the desired magnitude and direction of the forces applied by the trajectory control system. The artificial potential is given by the following equation:

$$
V_{ij} = \begin{cases} \left[k \left(\ln(r_{ij}) + \left(\dfrac{d_0}{r_{ij}} \right) \right) \right] & 0 < r_{ij} < d_1 \\[4mm] \left[k \left(\ln(d_1) + \left(\dfrac{d_0}{d_1} \right) \right) \right] & r_{ij} \ge d_1 \end{cases}, \tag{1}
$$

where

V_{ij}	=	artificial potential between balloons i and j,
k	=	$2.0 \times 10^6 \, \text{m}^2/\text{s}$,
d_0	=	$4.8 \times 10^6 \, \text{m}$,
d_1	=	$9.6 \times 10^6 \, \text{m}$, and
r_{ij}	=	vector from the ith balloon to the jth balloon.

The velocity influence of the jth balloon on the ith balloon is given by:

$$
\mathbf{u}_{ij} = \begin{cases} -\nabla V_{ij} & 0 < r < d_1 \\ 0 & r_{ij} \ge d_1 \end{cases}, \tag{2}
$$

where

∇V_{ij} = the gradient of V along the direction from i to j.

For each balloon, the desired total velocity is given by:

$$\mathbf{u}_i = \mathbf{u}_{wind,i} + \sum_{j=1, j \neq i}^{j=n} \mathbf{u}_{ij} \quad , \tag{3}$$

where

$\mathbf{u}_{wind,i}$ = wind vector at balloon i and

n = total number of balloons in the network.

In cases where the desired velocity vector is not achievable by the TCS, we choose to preserve the lateral component (as shown in **Fig. 3**) of the desired velocity vector (up to the maximum lateral magnitude).

5.2   Results

Simulation Process. We simulated a 383-balloon constellation covering the area from +15° latitude to the north pole. The start of the simulation is at 2000-06-01T00:00:00. Historical wind conditions for the period of the simulation were supplied by the United Kingdom Meteorological Office (UKMO). The integration time step for the simulation is 1 hour, and the TCS control directions are reset at each time step. The balloons float at 35 km ± 1 km. The altitudes of the balloons are randomized in that range at that beginning of the simulation. The balloons remain at their initial altitude throughout the simulation. The simulation ran for more than 1 year.

Without the use of trajectory control, the balloons tend to cluster together in low-pressure regions. Fig. 7 illustrates this clustering behavior with a smaller network of balloons (from +15° to +55° latitude) operating without trajectory control within the latitude band. (The initial condition is an evenly-distributed network.) Undesirable voids and clusters appear in the network after 76 days of the simulation.

However, with the artificial potential trajectory control algorithm operating, near-uniform coverage is obtained as shown in Fig. 8, 277 days into the simulation. As a whole, the constellation of balloons acts in a manner analogous to biological groups (flocks of birds, for example). By using simple control laws for individuals in the network, we see emergent group behavior (intelligence) that is more interesting and important for science data collection than the behavior of each individual.

Coverage Ratio Statistics. To evaluate the quality of coverage provided by such a network, we selected 100 random sites in the United States and plotted the ratio of the number of sites that are covered by at least one balloon to the total number of sites as a function of time. The following figure shows that excellent coverage is afforded throughout the year. Note that the period from 210 to 240 days from launch includes significant activity of the polar vortex. The vortex is bifurcated and offset from the north pole. Despite the challenging conditions presented by the non-uniform external flow field, the coverage ratio remains high.

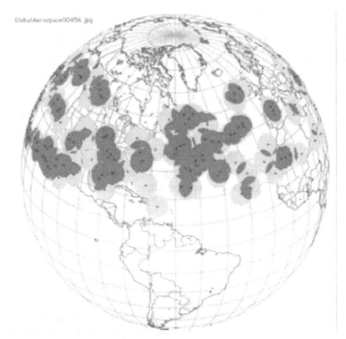

Fig. 7. Constellation without trajectory control

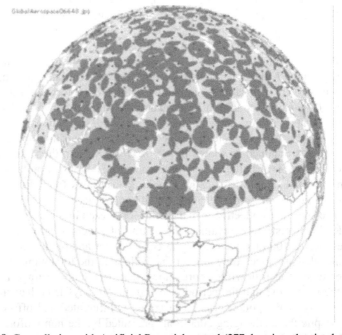

Fig. 8. Constellation with Artificial Potential control (277 days into the simulations)

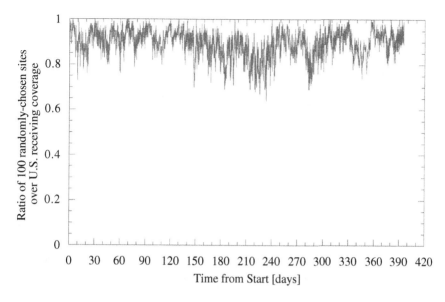

Fig. 9. Coverage ratio as a function of time (controlled constellation)

Outage and Recovery Duration Distributions and Percentiles. Another way to evaluate the quality of coverage is to examine the distribution of outage durations at the 100 US sites. An outage is defined as a period of time during which a site on the ground cannot emit to any balloon in the constellation at greater than 2° elevation angle. The outage duration is the length of time that the outage persists. We see from Fig. 10 that a plurality of the outages experienced in the simulation have durations equivalent to the time step of the integration (1 hour) in the simulation. Thus, we conclude that outages are expected to be 1 hour or less in duration.

One can also determine the distribution of recovery durations. A recovery is defined as the return of emission at greater than 2° elevation angle after an outage. The duration of the recovery is the length of time that the recovered condition persists. Fig. 11 shows that the most frequent recovery duration time is 13 hours (780 minutes) and indicates that there will be sufficient opportunities for data transmission upon recovery. Furthermore, the distribution has a significantly large tail toward longer recovery times.

6   Next Steps

There are several future directions for this research. First, we want to integrate the AP and WSB theories into a unified framework so that we can utilize all available trajectory control options near meteorological features such as vortices. It will be important to develop algorithms to recognize these meteorological features in the atmospheric data. We can further use that information in prescribing desirable control actions to achieve constellation geometry objectives.

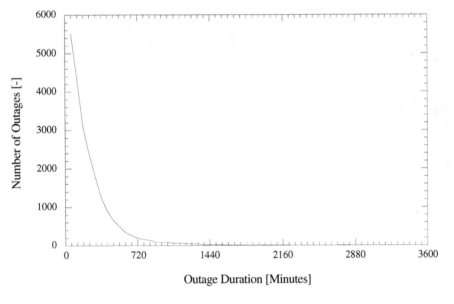

Fig. 10. Outage duration distribution (controlled constellation)

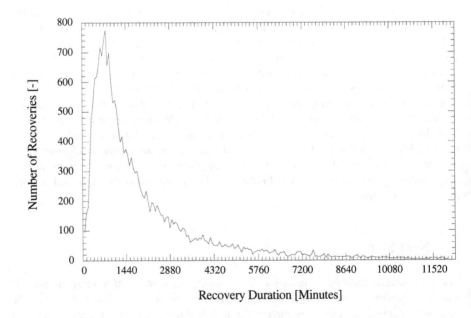

Fig. 11. Recovery duration distribution (controlled constellation)

When features such as vortices or jets are identified, modified control laws can be applied in a coordinate system local to the meteorological feature. The primary benefit to these developments will be reduction of the number of balloons required for the constellation. Finally, we are interested in adaptive constellations that organize resources in the constellation for specific science objectives, for example, intensive observation periods over regions of high sensitivity for meteorological forecasts. Such adaptive constellations could make use of "virtual" members of a constellation that attract balloons to a desired area or repel balloons from other regions. Another possibility is using the schooling approach for gradient climbing as discussed earlier.

7   Other Potential Applications

There are other potential applications for the work presented here. For example, the control actions of small or micro satellites in an orbital constellation could be determined by the Artificial Potential and Weak Stability Boundary theories. Such systems are often discussed for Earth and planetary science applications. Another example application is adaptive ocean sampling using underwater ocean vehicles that carry science instruments and utilize buoyancy changes and mass redistribution to generate sideways trajectory control forces. Such systems meet the definition of bounded and underactuated control systems. Furthermore, these underwater systems operate in the presence of non-uniform external flow fields (ocean currents). Schools of these systems could benefit from the algorithms discussed here.

8   Conclusion

We studied options and theories for the control of a constellation of stratospheric balloons. We found that behavior analogous to that of natural biological groups (flocks of birds and schools of fish) can be obtained for vehicles with bounded and underactuated control systems in the presence of non-uniform external flow fields. We successfully demonstrated for the first time the use of Artificial Potential theory for this application.

References

1.   K. T. Nock, M. K. Heun, and K. M. Aaron. Global Stratospheric Balloon Constellations. Paper PSB1-0014 presented at COSPAR 2000, Warsaw, Poland, July 2000.
2.   K. T. Nock, M. K. Heun, and K. M. Aaron. Global Constellations of Stratospheric Satellites. Paper presented at *15th ESA Symposium on European Rocket and Balloon Programmes and Related Research*, May 2001.
3.   K. M. Aaron, M. K. Heun, and K. T. Nock. Balloon Trajectory Control. Paper number AIAA-99-3865 presented at AIAA Balloon Technology Conference, June 1999.
4.   K. M. Aaron, K. T. Nock, and M. K. Heun. A Method for Balloon Trajectory Control. Paper PSB1-0012 presented at COSPAR 2000, Warsaw, Poland, July 2000.

5. E. A. Belbruno. Lunar capture orbits, a method of constructing earth-moon trajectories and the lunargas mission. In *AIAA Paper n.87-1054, AIAA/DGLR/JSASS* Inter. Elec. Propl. Conf., May 1987.
6. E. A. Belbruno and J. Miller. Sun-perturbed earth-to-moon transfers with ballistic capture. *Journal of Guidance, Control, and Dynamics*, pages 770–775, August 1993.
7. A. Frank. Gravity's rim: Riding chaos to the moon. *Discover*, pages 74–79, September 1994.
8. J. K. Parrish and W. H. Hammer, editors. *Animal Groups in Three Dimensions*, page 378. Cambridge University Press, 1997.
9. A. Okubo. Dynamical aspects of animal grouping: swarms, schools, flocks. *Advances in Biophysics*, pages 1–94, 1985.
10. J. K. Parrish and L. Edelstein-Keshet. From individuals to emergent properties: Complexity, pattern, evolutionary trade-offs in animal aggregation. In *Science*, pages 99–101,April 2 1999.
11. O. Khatib. *Commande dynamique dans l'espace opérational des robots manipulateurs en présence d'obstacles*. PhD thesis, ENSAE, France, 1980.
12. N. E. Leonard and E. Fiorelli, Virtual leaders, artificial potentials, and coordinated control of groups, *Proc. IEEE Conference on Decision and Control*, 2001.
13. T. R. Smith, H. Hanssmann and N. E. Leonard, Orientation control of multiple underwater vehicles, *Proc. IEEE Conference on Decision and Control*, 2001.
14. O. Khatib. Real time obstacle avoidance for manipulators and mobile robots. *Int. J. Robotics Research*, pages 90–99, 1986.
15. P. Khosla and R. Volpe. Superquadric artificial potentials for obstacle avoidance. In *Proc. IEEE International Conference on Robotics and Automation*, pages 1778–1784, April 1988.
16. E. Rimon and D. E. Koditschek. Exact robot navigation using artificial potential functions. *IEEE Transactions on Robotics and Automation*, pages 501–518, 1992.
17. W. S. Newman and N. Hogan. High speed robot control and obstacle avoidance using dynamic potential functions. In *Proc. IEEE Int. Conf. Robotics and Automation*, pages 14–24, 1987.
18. J. Barraquand, B. Langlois, and J. C. Latombe. Robot motion planning with many degrees of freedom and dynamic constraint. In *Proc. 5th Int. Symp. Robotics Research*, pages 74–83, August 1989.
19. C. W. Warren. Global path planning using artificial potential fields. In *Proc. IEEE Int. Conf. Robotics and Automation*, pages 316–321, May 1989.
20. A. J. van der Schaft. Stabilization of Hamiltonian systems. *Nonlinear Analysis, Theory, Methods and Applications*, pages 1021–1035, 1986.
21. R. A. Ortega, A. Loria, R. Kelly, and L. Praly. On passivity-based output feedback global stabilization of Euler-Lagrange systems. *Int. J. Robust and Nonlinear Control*, pages 313–325, 1995.
22. N. E. Leonard. Stabilization of underwater vehicle dynamics with symmetry-breaking potentials. *Systems and Control Letters*, pages 35–42, 1997.
23. A. M. Bloch, D. E. Chang, N. E. Leonard, and J. E. Marsden, Controlled Lagrangians and the stabilization of mechanical systems II: Potential shaping, *IEEE Transactions on Automatic Control*, 2001, in press.
24. F. Bullo. Stabilization of relative equilibria for underactuated systems on riemannian manifolds. *Automatica*, 2000.
25. D. E. Koditschek. An approach to autonomous robot assembly. *Robotica*, pages 137–155, 1994.
26. C. R. McInnes. Potential function methods for autonomous spacecraft guidance and control. *Advances in the Astronautical Sciences*, pages 2093–2109, 1996.

27. Craig W. Reynolds. Flocks, herds, and schools: a distributed behavioral model. *Computer Graphics*, 21(4):25–34, 1987.
28. R. Bachmayer and N. E. Leonard, Experimental test-bed for multiple vehicle control, navigation and communication, *Proc. 12th Int. Symposium on Unmanned Untethered Submersible Technology*, 2001.

Cooperative Agents and the Search for Extraterrestrial Life

Mark L. Lupisella[1,2]

[1] NASA Goddard Space Flight Center
Code 584, Greenbelt Road, Greenbelt MD, 20771, USA
mark.l.lupisella@nasa.gov
[2] University of Maryland, USA
College Park, Department of Biology

Abstract. The primary purpose of this paper is to suggest how a cooperative agents exploratory approach could be useful in searching for extraterrestrial life. Certain features of cooperative agent approaches such as distribution of varied functions in space and time, and increased reliability and robustness through redundancy, map well to the requirements of searching for extraterrestrial life. This paper will outline the advantages of cooperative agent approaches and, more specifically, scenarios and architectures that might be used to leverage a cooperative agents approach to enable the effective and efficient search for extraterrestrial life.

1   Introduction

If tenuous abodes of life are hiding in remote extraterrestrial environmental niches, and if we want to assess the biological status of a given locale, region, or entire planet before sending humans to the locale in question (e.g. perhaps because of safety or contamination concerns), then we face the challenge of robotically exploring a large area efficiently and in enough detail to have confidence in our assessment of the biological status of the area in question. On our present schedule of roughly two missions per opportunity, we will likely need a different exploratory approach than singular stationary or mobile landers and sample return, because there appear to be fundamental limitations to those mission profiles that would limit our ability to obtain the many samples we will likely need if we want to have confidence in assessing the biological status of a region, locale or entire planet. Singular rover missions can potentially accommodate sampling over a fairly large area, but are still limited by sample size and range (e.g. "single cache" missions) [1], and can be a single point of failure. More importantly, such mission profiles often have a limited number of detection capabilities because of various engineering constraints, and hence are unlikely to meet the demanding requirements of searching for, detecting, and confirming the presence of what may be a very different form of life. Sample return has the advantage of allowing sophisticated analysis of the sample when it is returned

W. Truszkowski, C. Rouff, M. Hinchey (Eds.): WRAC 2002, LNAI 2564, pp. 408–416, 2003.

to earth, but it is very expensive and, more importantly, has severe limitations associated with only being able to bring back a limited number of samples, whose integrity could be compromised by the return process.

Given the premises stated above, it appears at least two fundamental challenges have to be met simultaneously: (1) covering a large space efficiently, and (2) performing a wide variety of detection/experiment strategies and functions in order to (a) address the difficult challenge of not knowing exactly what we're looking for by being prepared to detect any number of different kinds of life from what may be a large possibility space, and to (b) increase confidence that life has been found by bringing to bear a sophisticated suite of detection and experimental payloads on any specific location.

A cooperative agents approach lends itself to this kind of problem because cooperation among the combined capabilities of a variety of simple, single function agents can give rise to fairly complex task execution such as the search, detection, and confirmation of extraterrestrial life. More generally, a cooperative agent approach has the additional advantages of (1) increased reliability and robustness through redundancy, (2) decreased task completion time through parallelism, (3) decreased cost through simpler individual robot design (e.g. simpler algorithms, and (4) a division of labor approach for task execution which is useful at many levels.

A cooperative agents approach can be considered a subset of the broader domain of Multi-Agent Systems (MAS) for which there has been increasing interest [2,3] and which can be viewed as a broad emerging scientific discipline, instead of solely an engineering discipline [4,5]. As noted by Chainbi in this volume [6],conceptions of MAS can vary corresponding to particular trends in research and can be logically grouped into *individual* conceptions and *mass* conceptions. Individual conceptions focus on the formal representations or "intentional stance" of individuals only, and mass conceptions focus on inter-agent interactions and roles within a larger organization. Indeed, as stressed by Chainbi, cooperation is a key concept of MAS and is consistent with a mass conception of MAS. The approaches outlined in this paper fit primarily within the mass conception of MAS, although there are also individual conception aspects associated with the simpler architectures.

This paper will explore two general cooperative agent architectures for exploration that have the potential to address the above noted challenges and facilitate efficient and thorough life-detecting exploration of a large space, namely, (1) a flat architecture, or "shot-gun" approach, and (2) a hierarchical architecture, or cooperative "family" approach.

There have been a number of efforts to explore the use of multi-agent systems, or cooperative robots, in the context of space exploration [7], particularly for surface activities having to do with site preparation [8], surface science exploration [9], and planetary robotic outposts [10,11,12]. This paper attempts to analyze the use of cooperative agents in the context of the surface science application of searching for, detecting, and confirming the existence of extraterrestrial life—a task, as noted above, that is, in principle, uniquely suited for a cooperative agents approach.

It should be noted that while there has been some debate about how to define an agent, and while it appears generally accepted that an agent can be thought of as a sophisticated kind of robot, this paper assumes a working characterization that any robot with a reasonable degree of autonomy can be considered an agent. Assessing what constitutes a "reasonable degree of autonomy" is not necessarily trivial and is clearly important for understanding agency within this working characterization, but it is not of critical importance for the purposes of this paper. Indeed, "robot" and "agent" will be used interchangeably throughout this paper.

2   A Cooperative Agents "Shot-Gun" Approach

A flat architecture such as a cooperative agents "shot-gun" approach [13] can address the key challenges by distributing a large variety of simple detection functions across many mobile agents who respond to each other's detections/experiments in a fairly straightforward way. For example, successful detection by any agent could be communicated to other agents with different functionality, which could then go to that specific location and perform their function, perhaps in a pre-determined order by function, or by a process involving relative distances, or a combination of both. Tens to hundreds or more small robots, each with a singular life-detection capability such as detection of water, organic molecules, nucleic acids, amino acids and associated chirality, or such as metabolism measurement experiments, epiflourescence microscopy, molecular sequencing, culturing, sub-surface boring payloads, and imaging capabilities, could cover much area with either a random walk approach or something more controlled. Communicating results to the rest of the "swarm" could allow for an efficient response by nearby members of the swarm which could then focus on the particular location in question with their own detection and experimental capabilities.

   In general, this approach can been seen as a kind of biologically inspired exploration methodology, perhaps as a form of "swarm intelligence" [14]. Again, the benefit of this kind of approach is that large areas can be covered with diverse detection and experimental techniques which increase the chance of detecting life, and obtaining comprehensive data in an efficient manner during just one mission opportunity.

2.1   Shot-Gun Mission Scenarios

As a specific example of a mission scenario, tens to hundreds or more "nanorovers/nanobots" (kg or less) could be deployed from either near surface platform(s) like a balloon (e.g. via small parachutes), or from lander(s) directly to the surface, e.g. via Pathfinder-type missions, or via higher precision landing technique if required.

Direct Surface Deploy Scenario. For a direct surface deployment from a lander, 40 nanobots with the following functional distribution listed below, could be randomly released from the lander to execute their detection tasks in fixed time intervals so each agent would be making a detection randomly in space but on fixed time intervals. 10 robots (perhaps 2 of each kind) might stay stationary on board for subsequent deploy as needed, and perhaps as back-up.

- 10 water detectors
- 10 organics detectors (e.g. mini GC-MS)
- 10 metabolism experiments
- 10 microscopic imagers, and
- 10 diggers/drillers

Random Walk. A random walk approach might be the simplest approach and would enable the following exploratory characteristics:

- Navigation: Random walk/search for all 40, first robot drops beacon when there is a positive detection
- Sampling: Sampling at fixed time intervals
- Decision making: All swarm on first detection, first to arrive performs function on or near beacon, the rest follow and only perform function once they are close enough to the beacon.
- Location knowledge: No knowledge of location is necessarily required if the beacon can be used to control navigation to the beacon. For example, the strength and/or direction of the beacon detection could be the only navigation information required to navigate to the beacon.

Random Walk in Teams. A team approach would be a slightly more controlled scenario that has the advantage of not monopolizing the entire swarm after the first positive detection is communicated to the rest of the swarm. 4 teams of 10 robots could be released at 90° angles from each other at the first deploy location. This would allow all team members to be relatively close to each other for a limited period of time making swarming to any location within the quadrant easier.   In this kind of team approach, the robots don't necessarily need to know their location or function because the whole team could swarm to any location of interest and the closest and/or soonest to arrive gets there first performs its function.

Random Walk Plus Decision Making. More complicated decision making, such as determining which agent(s) should go next to the site of interest, could be driven by proximity only, function only, or a combination of both.

For proximity only, only the closest agents would respond. This implies location knowledge which could be distributed among the entire swarm. That is, each agent would have a map and knowledge of its location and the location of all other agents. Individual robots could transmit and poll at small time intervals to maintain location knowledge. Or a lander station could coordinate the sharing of knowledge and/or direct individual robots based on its own spatial knowledge.

If the decision regarding what agent is to respond next is driven primarily by function only, then agents would respond (go to the site of interest) in a pre-determined order of their function. This would require at least a simple algorithm dictating the relative order of detections/experiments to be performed. A disadvantage of this approach is that the robot that might be needed next at any given location might be relatively far away and would have to traverse that distance and execute its function before other robots could, hence losing time waiting for subsequent robots to get to the site. To counter this, there might be a process by which subsequent robots would begin navigating to the site but would not go directly to the site, but instead stop short so that the agent needed next could perform its function first. This would prevent losing time from subsequently needed robots having to wait serially before moving close to the location of interest. However, the success of any given function could, and perhaps should, dictate whether a subsequent function is needed, in which case, if many other robots had made their way to the site without being called directly by the robot that should precede them, part of the swarm could end up using time and resources to get to a location where they are not required.

This function-based decision making approach could fit well with the team approach since any two robots with serial functionality could be sufficiently close in space because the team had been released in a particular direction, namely, into a quadrant of the broader area as noted above. This approach wouldn't monopolize the rest of the team because the rest of the team robots with other functions would be close enough to respond relatively quickly, allowing the rest of the team to continue sampling while others are responding and performing as dictated by the pre-determined order of functions algorithm.

By using a combination of proximity and function for decision-making we might achieve more efficient task execution since only the nearest of the next desired function would respond by going to the site in question. This would allow all of the rest of the team, or the entire swarm depending on the approach used, to continue their sampling and not use their resources to traverse to a location they might not be needed. If the numbers of agents involved were high enough, we might call two or more of the nearest next functions to the site for redundancy, while still having enough agents with that function to maintain that same active sampling/detection function elsewhere in the space.

3   A Cooperative Agents "Family" Approach

A second form of a cooperative agents approach might be characterized as cooperative family agents approach where a larger parent rover carries smaller rovers with additional specialized functionality to be deployed as required by the higher level analysis of the more mobile larger parent rover. A hierarchical architecture like this could be scaled to be very large or very small.

The primary advantages of a hierarchical, or "family", approach is that specialized functions can be selectively deployed in real-time by the parent rover which would have a greater range of mobility and which would act as a central coordinating agent as well as an infrastructural support system for power recharging of the smaller robots and for more sophisticated forms of navigation, drilling, and communication.

A mission scenario might involve a large mobile parent rover that could release smaller teams of robots as it encounters interesting areas. The smaller robot teams could either perform random exploration as in the shot-gun approach, or more controlled exploration whereby the parent rover acts as a centralized coordinator for the smaller agents, directing activities in some cases (e.g. being larger will enable a better survey of the terrain) and calling the smaller agents "home" to the parent vehicle for sample transfer and/or storage, transport to another area, or recharging.

To realize the advantages of this approach, the parent rover should be able to negotiate unforeseen difficult terrain, as well as cover fairly large distances quickly. Walking can enable navigation of difficult terrain, but is slow. Wheels enable faster transport, but have difficulty with extreme terrain. A walking rover with lockable well-gripping wheels as feet could provide the advantages of both walking and rolling.

As a interesting related aside, cooperating agents could self-assemble if larger vehicles and more sophisticated vehicles are required, allowing launch costs and perhaps certain kinds of mission risks to be reduced by delivering pieces separately. Smaller robots could also perform a limited kind of self-assembly to perform more complex tasks depending on the task required, for example, if a particular sample has to be passed from one detector/experiment to the next, especially without exposure to the ambient environment, perhaps due to sample handling constraints.

3.1   A Cooperative Family Architecture Example

A single or several large rovers capable of carrying tens (perhaps 40-50 as in the flat "shot-gun" architecture example above) that can deploy either selective functionality or a team with distributed functionality when an area of interest is located, will enable the ability to traverse long distances over challenging terrain and still satisfy the requirement of needing much functionality to search for and confirm the presence of life. The movements of any given robot or team could be coordinated by the larger parent rover which will likely have a better overview of the terrain. Any given team may also have a team leader which could coordinate smaller scale movements of the team members, so as to mitigate navigation conflicts such as collisions, facilitating a more controlled pattern of coverage, within the coordinating control constraints of the parent rover.

3.2   A Cooperative Family Scenario

The parent rover, containing five teams of ten agents with distributed functionality, detects off-color terrain in the distance near the edge of what appears to be a dangerous drop-off. The parent rover reaches the area of interest and because of the potential danger presented by the terrain, releases either one or a few robots with limited range and certain functions that may be pre-determined reflecting the order of successful life-detection criteria. The parent rover, before deployment, communicates navigation constraints to the agents about to be deployed regarding the dangerous drop-off in the terrain. If one of those agents is a water detector and water is successfully detected, that agent would drop a beacon and signal the parent rover which might then deploy a cooperative team with a full compliment of functionality, all with the same navigation constraints to avoid the terrain drop-off, but perhaps also with a designated team leader that will coordinate the smaller scale movements as dictated by smaller scale terrain constraints and/or resolve navigation conflicts between agents.

4   Deployment Scenario Comparison

For a direct deploy from a lander, the range of coverage could be one to tens of square kilometers. The density of coverage would be relatively high providing virtually complete coverage of an area without needing more stored robots for subsequent deployment to a specific location. A disadvantage of a lander deployment is that high precision landing will likely be required since the range of coverage of the robots is relatively small since the robots themselves will likely be small. Different modes of traversing the terrain could help address range limitations, for example, a combined walking, rolling, and perhaps even hopping capability for each robot. However, this would not likely be cost-effective because building many individual robots with that kind of sophisticated mobility would require substantial development, manufacturing, and testing resources.

For near surface deployment from an aerial platform the range of coverage could be 1 km^2 to tens or hundreds of km^2, or possibly global coverage depending on the aerial platform. Balloons, for example, could provide global coverage. The density of the distribution of robots and hence the density of coverage would be relatively low in the absence of precise landing technologies for each robot. The primary advantage of an aerial form of deployment would be a wide range of coverage and the ability to selectively deploy in space and time. A disadvantage would be the requirement to store a full complement of functionality on the aerial platform and be able to deploy a group of robots with relatively high precision.

For an orbit deployment capability the range of coverage would be global, although the density of coverage would be low, even with many hundreds of agents or more. An advantage would be the ability to reach and sample the widest variety of diverse areas across the planet and selectively deploy in space and time as needed in real-time. As with an aerial deployment, a disadvantage would be the requirement to store robots in an orbital platform that can precisely deliver subsequent detection agents to a previous detection location.

5   Knowledge Sharing, Autonomy, and Mission Robustness

Knowledge sharing between agents is clearly important for complex cooperative task execution [15]. The architectures and scenarios suggested here will require varying degrees of knowledge sharing which will likely need to be hard-coded into the agents prior to mission execution in order to bound the behavior space within known constraints that will engender confidence for mission safety (e.g. strategies for collision avoidance [16]) and mission success. In the challenging unknown and distant environments of other planets, too much autonomy could result in complete failure and loss of systems either because of compromised safety of individual agents or collections of agents, or because agents make bad decisions with irreversible consequences.

These mission robustness concerns are being addressed by researchers, many in this volume [17,18,19, 20], and it will be critical for mission managers to have confidence regarding these challenges before launching what will likely be a challenging mission profile.

It is worth noting that while the approaches outlined in this paper are intended primarily to be used in the absence of humans, these approaches could also be applicable for use during a human mission. This would likely affect the mission robustness requirements and degrees of autonomy for the cooperative agents systems used to search for extraterrestrial life.

References

[1]   Huntsberger, T.: Autonomous Multirover System for Complex Planetary Retrieval Operations. In Schenker, P. and McKee, G. (eds.) Proc. Sensor Fusion and Decentralized Control in Autonomous Robotic Systems, SPIE Vol 3209, (1997) 220-229

[2]   Mataric, M.: Issues and Aproaches in the Design of Collective Autonomous Agents. Robotics and Autonomous Systems, 16 (1995)

[3]   Cao, Y., Fukunaga, A., Kahng, A. Cooperative Mobile Robotics: Antecedents and Directions. Autonomous Robots, 4 (1997) 1-23

[4]   Kaminka, G: On the Monitoring Selectivity Problem. In: Truszkowski, W., Rouff, C., Hinchey, M.G. (eds): Radical Agents Concepts. Lecture Notes in Artificial Intelligence, Vol. 2564. Springer-Verlag, Berlin Heidelberg New York (2003) (this volume)

[5]   Malone, T., Crowston, K.: Toward an Interdisciplinary Theory of Coordination. Technical Report CCS TR#120   SS WP# 3294-91-MSA, Massachusetts Institute of Technology, (1991)

[6]   Chainbi, W.: Communication and Organization Concepts for an Agent. In: Truszkowski, W., Rouff, C., Hinchey, M.G. (eds): Radical Agents Concepts. Lecture Notes in Artificial Intelligence, Vol. 2564. Springer-Verlag, Berlin Heidelberg New York (2003) (this volume)

[7]   Huntsberger, T., Rodriguez, G., Schenker, P.: Robotics Challenges for Robotic and Human Mars Exploration. Proceedings of Robotics, Alburquerque (2000) 84-90

[8]   Parker, L., Guo, Y., Jung, D.: Cooperative Robot Teams Applied to the Site Preparation Task. http://citeseer.nj.nec.com/455532.html

[9]   Estlin, T. et al: An Integrated System for Multi-Rover Scientific Exploration. 16th National Conference on Artificial Intelligence (AAAI-99), Orlando (1999) 541-548

[10] Pirjanian, P.: CAMPOUT: A Control Architecture for Multi-robot Planetary Outposts. Proc. SPIE Symposium on Sensor Fusion and Decentralized Control in Robotic Systems III, vol 4196, Boston (2000)

[11] Huntsberger, T., Pirjanian, P., Schenker, P.: Robotic Outposts as Precursors to a Manned Mars Habitat. Proc. Space Technology and Applications International Forum (STAIF-2001), Albuquerque (2001)

[12] Hunstberger, T. et al.: Behavior-Based Control Systems for Planetary Autonomous Robot Outposts. Proc. Aerospace 2000, Albuquerque (2000)

[13] Lupisella M.: "Life" Looking for Life, Jet Propulsion Laboratory Biomorphic Explorer Workshop presentation (1998)

[14] Bonabeau E., Dorigo M., Theraulaz G.: Swarm intelligence: from natural to artificial systems. New York: Oxford University Press (1999)

[15] Smid, J., Obitko, M., Truszkowski, W.: An Approach to Knowledge Exchange and Sharing Between Agents. In: Truszkowski, W., Rouff, C., Hinchey, M.G. (eds): Radical Agents Concepts. Lecture Notes in Artificial Intelligence, Vol. 2564. Springer-Verlag, Berlin Heidelberg New York (2003) (this volume)

[16] Aaron, E., Metaxas, D.: Considering Hierarchical Hybrid Systems for Intelligent Animated Agents. In: Truszkowski, W., Rouff, C., Hinchey, M.G. (eds): Radical Agents Concepts. Lecture Notes in Artificial Intelligence, Vol. 2564. Springer-Verlag, Berlin Heidelberg New York (2003) (this volume)

[17] Wan, A.: Requirements on Swarm Behavior in Autonomous Adaptive Agents. In: Truszkowski, W., Rouff, C., Hinchey, M.G. (eds): Radical Agents Concepts. Lecture Notes in Artificial Intelligence, Vol. 2564. Springer-Verlag, Berlin Heidelberg New York (2003) (this volume)

[18] Wan, A., Braspenning, P., and Vreeswijk, G.: Limits to Ground Control in Autonomous Spacecraft. Telematics and Informatics, 12 (1996) 247-259

[19] Purang, K.: Agents Should Know How to Say "Oops!". In: Truszkowski, W., Rouff, C., Hinchey, M.G. (eds): Radical Agents Concepts. Lecture Notes in Artificial Intelligence, Vol. 2564. Springer-Verlag, Berlin Heidelberg New York (2003) (this volume)

[20] Rose, J., Huhns, M.: An Agent Architecture for Comprehensive Mission Robustness. In: Truszkowski, W., Rouff, C., Hinchey, M.G. (eds): Radical Agents Concepts. Lecture Notes in Artificial Intelligence, Vol. 2564. Springer-Verlag, Berlin Heidelberg New York (2003) (this volume)

Agents Making Sense of the Semantic Web*

Lalana Kagal, Filip Perich, Harry Chen, Sovrin Tolia, Youyong Zou,
Tim Finin, Anupam Joshi, Yun Peng, R. Scott Cost, and Charles Nicholas

Laboratory for Advanced Information Technology
University of Maryland Baltimore County
1000 Hilltop Circle, Baltimore, MD 21250, USA
{lkagal1,fperic1,hchen4,stolia1,yzou1}@csee.umbc.edu
{finin,joshi,peng,cost,nicholas}@csee.umbc.edu

Abstract. Effective use of the vast quantity of available information and
services on the Internet will require multi-agent systems to be tightly
integrated with existing web infrastructure. This however will be impossible unless the information on the web is presented in a semantic
language, such as the DARPA Agent Markup Language (DAML), which
is one aim of the "Semantic Web". As part of our exploration of Semantic Web technology, and DAML in particular, we have constructed
ITTALKS, a web-based system for automatic and intelligent notification
of information technology talks. In this paper, we describe the ITTALKS
system, and discuss the numerous ways in which the use of Semantic Web
concepts and DAML extend its ability to provide an intelligent online
service to both the human community and, more interestingly, the agents
assisting them.

1 Introduction

With the vast quantity of information already available on the Internet, it is only
beneficial for multi-agent systems to be integrated with the web and be able to
act upon and converse about web objects. However, in order to allow intelligent agents to retrieve and manipulate pertinent information, there is a need
for presenting the web in a machine-readable style. This requires marking up
the web information with a semantic language, such as DARPA Agent Markup
Language (DAML) [18]. Moreover, if our goal is to have agents acting upon and
conversing about web objects, they will also have to take advantage of existing
infrastructure whenever possible (e.g., message sending, security, authentication,
directory services, and application service frameworks). Since the key goal of the
DAML program is to develop a Semantic Web markup language that provides
sufficient rules for ontology development [12] and that is sufficiently rich to support intelligent agents and other applications [14, 24], we believe that DAML
will be central to the realization of the agent-web integration.

---

* This work was supported in part by the Defense Advanced Research Projects
Agency under contract F30602-00-2-0 591 AO K528 as part of the DAML program
(http://www.daml.org/).

W. Truszkowski, C. Rouff, M. Hinchey (Eds.): WRAC 2002, LNAI 2564, pp. 417–433, 2003.
© Springer-Verlag Berlin Heidelberg 2003

In support of this claim, we have constructed a real, fielded application, ITTALKS, which supports user and agent interaction in the domain of talk discovery. It provides a web-driven infrastructure for agent interaction. In addition, ITTALKS serves as a platform for designing and prototyping the software components required to enable developers to create intelligent software agents capable of understanding and processing information and knowledge encoded in DAML and other semantically rich markup languages. To date, we have focused on developing the support and infrastructure required for intelligent agents to integrate into an environment of web browsers, servers, application server platforms, and underlying technologies (e.g., Java, Jini, PKI).

On the surface, ITTALKS is a web portal offering access to information about talks, seminars and colloquia related to information technology (IT). It is organized around domains, which typically represent event hosting organizations such as universities, research laboratories or professional groups. ITTALKS utilizes DAML for its knowledge base representation, reasoning, and agent communication. DAML is used to markup all the information and to provide additional reasoning capabilities otherwise unavailable. With information denoted in a semantically machine-understandable format, the computer can deduce additional information, a task which is difficult in a traditional database system. For example, if both ITTALKS and the user agree on a common semantics, the ITTALKS web portal can provide not only the talks that correspond to the user's profile in terms of interest, time, and location constraints, but can further filter the IT events based on information about the user's personal schedule, inferred location at the time of the talk, distance and current traffic patterns, etc. ITTALKS can also dynamically update the user's profile with incremental learning of the user's usage patterns.

ITTALKS demonstrates the power of markup languages such as DAML for the Semantic Web, drawing on its ability to represent ontologies, agent content languages and its ability to improve the functionality of agents on the web. We have developed DAML-encoded ontologies for describing event, temporal, spatial, personal, and conversational information, which enable us to represent all required knowledge in a DAML-encoded format. Moreover, these ontologies enable us to execute a computer understandable conversation. Furthermore, any web page presented on the ITTALKS web sites contains the necessary information for an agent to retrieve the DAML-encoded description of this page as well as the contact information of a responsible agent in order to provide more effective conversation. ITTALKS thus provides each agent with the capability to retrieve and manipulate any ITTALKS-related information via a web site interface or through a direct agent-to-agent conversation. Hence, by combining the features of currently existing web applications with the DAML-based knowledge and reasoning capabilities, ITTALKS presents a true Semantic Web application supporting various levels of agent interactions.

2   Background

The Semantic Web [3] is a vision in which web pages are augmented with information and data that is expressed in a way that facilitates its understanding my machines. The current human-centered web is still largely encoded in HTML, which focuses largely on how text and images would be rendered for human viewing. Over the past few years we have seen a rapid increase in he use of XML as an alternative encoding, one that is intended primarily for machine processing. The machine which process XML documents can be the end consumers of the information or they can be used to transform the information into a form appropriate for human understanding (e.g., as HTML, graphics, synthesized speech, etc.) As a representation language, XML provides essentially a mechanism to declare and use simple data structures and thus leave much to be desired as a language in which to express complex knowledge. Recent enhancements to basic XML, such as XML Scheme, address some of the shortcomings, but still do not result in an adequate language for representing and reasoning about the kind of knowledge essential to realizing the Semantic Web vision [13, 15].

RDF (Resource Description Framework) and RDFS (RDF Schema) attempt to address these deficiencies by building on top of XML. They provide representation frameworks that are roughly the equivalent to semantic networks in the case of RDF and very simple frame languages in the case of RDFS. However, RDFS is still quite limited as a knowledge representation language, lacking support for variables, general quantification, rules, etc. DAML is one attempt to build on XML, RDF and RDFS and produce a language that is well suited for building the Semantic Web.

The goal of the DAML program, which officially began in August 2000, is to develop a universal Semantic Web markup language that is sufficiently rich to support intelligent agents and other applications. DAML can dramatically improve traditional ad hoc information retrieval because its semantics will improve the quality of retrieval results. Also, it will allow the intelligent agents of tomorrow to retrieve and manipulate the information on the semantic web.

3   ITTALKS

As part of UMBC's role in the DAML Program, we have developed ITTALKS; a web portal that offers access to information about talks, seminars, colloquia, and other information technology (IT) related events. ITTALKS provides users with numerous details describing the IT events, including location, speaker, hosting organization, and talk topic. More importantly, ITTALKS also provides agents with the ability to retrieve and manipulate information stored in the ITTALKS knowledge base.

Unlike other web services, ITTALKS employs DAML for knowledge base representation, reasoning, and agent communication. The use of DAML to represent information in its knowledge base, in conjunction with its use for interchangeable type ontologies as described in Section 5.6, enables more sophisticated reasoning than would otherwise be available. For example, a simpler representation

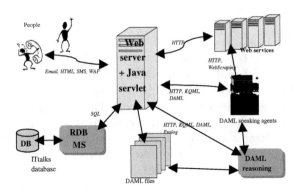

Fig. 1. The architecture for ITTALKS is built around a web server backed by a relational database. Interfaces are provided to human users, software agents and web services

scheme might be able to provide the user with talks based on interest, time and location. When both ITTALKS and the user agree on a common semantics, the ITTALKS web portal will be able to perform further filtering, based on more sophisticated inference. In addition to enhancing knowledge representation and reasoning, DAML is used for all communication, including simple messages and queries, using the ITTALKS defined ontology. Moreover, ITTALKS offers the capability for each user to use his/her personal agent to communicate with ITTALKS on his/her behalf and provide a higher level of service.

3.1   Users

ITTALKS can be used anonymously, or, more effectively, with personalized user accounts. Users have the option to register with ITTALKS either by entering information manually via web forms, or by providing the location (URL) of a universally accessible DAMLized personal profile, which includes information such as the users location, his/her interests and contact details, as well as a schedule. Subsequently, this information is used to provide each user with a personalized view of the site, displaying only talks that match the user's interests and/or schedule.

Since DAML is not yet in widespread use, ITTALKS provides a tool for creating a DAML personal profile. Currently, the tool constructs a profile containing only items used by the ITTALKS system. However, we believe that the profile, in one form or another, will ultimately provide a unique and universal point for obtaining personal information about the user, not just for ITTALKS, but for all information needs, and will include any sort of information the user would like to share. In the future, all services that require personal information about the user should access the same user profile, eliminating the need for the user to repeatedly enter the same information for a multitude of services. We believe that the new standard for XML Signature and Encryption under development may provide a mechanism by which users can have some control over access to parts of their profile.

3.2 Domains

To support our vision of a universal resource for the international IT research community, ITTALKS is organized around domains, which typically represent event hosting organization such as universities, research laboratories or professional groups. Each domain is represented by a separate web site and is independently maintained by a moderator who can, among other things, define the scope of the domain and delegate to other registered users the ability to edit talk entries. For example, the Stanford University may choose to include talks on `stanford.ittalks.org` domain that are hosted on its campus only. On the other hand, another domain, `sri.ittalks.org`, might be configured to include not only talks about Semantic Web topics that are held at SRI, but also those at Stanford, as well as any talks within 15 mile range of the SRI facility in Palo Alto.

3.3 Access

The ITTALKS system is accessible either to users directly via the web portal, or to agents acting on their behalf through the use of Jade [11, 2]. The web portal allows a user to browse desired information in a variety of formats, to provide the highest degree of interoperability. It permits a user to retrieve information in DAML, standard HTML format, which includes a short DAML annotation for DAML-enabled web crawlers, or WML format, which supports WAP enabled phones. The ITTALKS web portal also has the ability to generate RDF Site Summary (RSS) files for certain queries. These RSS files can then be used for various external purposes, such as displaying upcoming talks on a departmental web site for some particular university or domain. To provide access for agent based services, ITTALKS employs a surogate agent described below that provides talk-related services to personal agents.

3.4 Agents

In order to extend the capabilities of the system, we have defined a number of agents that support the operation of ITTALKS. Some can be seen as supporting services (such as external information services), while others we assume will exist in the general environment in the future.

ITTALKS Agent. The ITTALKS agent is a front-end for the ITTALKS system. It interacts with ITTALKS through the same web-based interface as human users, but communicates via an ACL with other agents on the web, extending the system's accessibility. At present, the agent does not support any advanced functionality, but acts primarily as a gateway for agent access.

User Agents. One longtime goal of agent research is that users will be represented online by agents that can service queries and filter information for them. While ITTALKS does not require that such agents exist, we recognize the added power that could be gained by the use of such agents. Therefore, ITTALKS supports interaction with User Agents as well as their human counterparts. The User Agent that we have developed understands DAML, supports sophisticated reasoning, and communicates via a standard agent communication language. Reasoning is accomplished with the use of the XSB, a logic programming and deductive database system for Unix and Windows developed at SUNY Stony Brook.

Calendar Agent. Although a user agent may contain the necessary knowledge about its user's schedule, we believe that it will benefit from assigning the calendar-based facts and preferences to a separate agent - the calendar agent. This enables the user agent not only to consult the user calendar, but also to use the same protocol to consult other calendar agents that may represent other users or groups the user belongs to. In addition, the calendar agent may only represent abstraction to already existing infrastructure, such as Microsoft Outlook or other desktop/server applications. Finally, the calendar agent may also be used to represent a room, and thus allow for re-use of the same principles of participation scheduling as well as event scheduling.

Classifier Agent. ITTALKS uses a Classifier (or recommender) Agent that is invoked when a user is entering a new talk. Based on the talk's abstract, the Classifier returns ACM Classification Hierarchy Classification numbers along with a rank, in descending order. Using a local table of classification numbers and names, ITTALKS suggests to the user ten possible topics.

MapQuest Agent. The MapQuest Agent is a wrapper agent that allows ITTALKS to make use of external services. It interacts directly with agents (e.g. the ITTALKS agent, User Agents), and accepts requests for information such as the distance between two known locations. It then phrases an appropriate request to the MapQuest system [21], parses the results, and generates an appropriate response. Note that this agent could be generically named a Distance Agent, and make use of any external service (or combination of several, as needed).

3.5   Ontologies

The ITTALKS system is based on a set of ontologies[1] that are used to describe talks and the things associated with them, e.g., people, places, topics and interests, schedules, etc. Figure 2 shows some of the dependencies that exist among these ontologies. The ontologies are used in the representation and processing

---

[1] http://daml.umbc.edu/ontologies

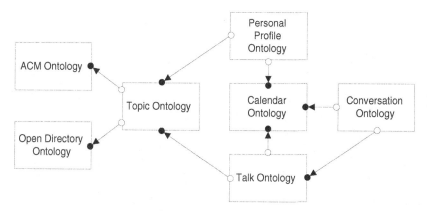

Fig. 2. The relationships among the various ontologies used by the ITTALKS system

of DAML descriptions and also as "conceptual schemata" against which the database and various software APIs are built.

We have developed a general ontology for describing the topics of arbitrary talks and papers. Using this, we have implemented an ontology to describe IT related talks based on the ACM's Computer Classification System. In addition, we currently are developing a DAML ontology for IT talks based on a portion of the Open Directory, and are considering additional classification ontologies. Figure 3 sketches some of the major classes and properties in these ontologies. These topic ontologies are used to describe talks as well as the users' interests throughout the system. This includes an automated talk classification, for which we have obtained a training collection for the ACM CCS and are also generating an Open Directory training collection to develop the necessary components. In addition, the DAML ontologies will give a user the ability to add additional assertions in DAML to further characterize their interests. Lastly, we are also in the process of developing a component that can map topics in one ontology into topics in another, by taking advantage of the fact that nodes in each ontology have an associated collection of text as well as DAML information.

3.6   Data Entry

Currently ITTALKS requires that information about talks be manually entered via a web form interface, or be available in a DAML description available at a given URL. Although we have made this process as simple as possible (e.g., by supporting automatic form completion using information from the knowledge base and the user's DAML profile) it is still a time consuming process. Therefore, we are developing a focused web spider to collect talk announcements from open sources on the web. This spider will identify key information items using a text extraction system, and will automatically add information to the ITTALKS

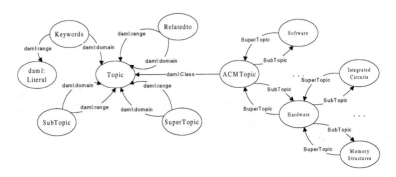

Fig. 3. The Ontologies used by IITALKS are relatively simple, such as the topics ontology used to describe talk topics and user interests

knowledge base. We are working with the Lockheed-Martin research group on the above task, and will use their AeroText information extraction system [1].

3.7   Architecture

The current implementation of ITTALKS uses a relational database, in combination with a web server, to provide user access to the system. To enable agents to access the system, the ITTALKS provides an interface for agent-based communication.

Database. The main software packages that are used in the ITTALKS system are the MySQL relational database software and a combination of Apache and Tomcat as the web portal servers. The contents of the ITTALKS knowledge base are stored in a database whose schema is closely mapped to our ontologies describing events, people, topics and locations. We have chosen MySQL because of its known reliability, and because we required software with a license that allows us to make the ITTALKS package available to additional academic and commercial institutions.

Web Server. As stated above, for our web, we have chosen a combination of Apache and Tomcat. This enables us to present the IT talk descriptions to the user using Java servlets and JSP files, which dynamically generate requested information in DAML, XML, HTML, RSS, and WML formats. The current ITTALKS implementation can provide information suitable for viewing on either a standard, computer-based or a WAP-enabled cellular phone.

Extensions. In addition, we are currently employing the Jackal agent communication infrastructure developed at UMBC and the Lockheed-Martin's AeroText information extraction system in order to facilitate ITTALKS-user agent interaction and the automated text extraction, respectively. We are in the process of modifying Jackal to provide support for FIPA ACL interoperability. Also, we are considering the possible replacement of MySQL with native XML database software such as dbXML.

4   Scenarios

We describe here a couple of typical interactions that illustrate some of the features of ITTALKS. The first involves direct use by a human user, and the second, advanced features provided through the use of agents.

4.1   Human Interaction

In this first scenario, a user, Jim, learns from his colleagues about the existence of the ITTALKS web portal as a source of IT related events in his area; Jim is affiliated with Stanford University.

Jim directs his browser to the www.ittalks.org main page. Seeing a link to stanford.ittalks.org (a Stanford ITTALKS domain), he selects it, and is presented with a new page listing upcoming talks that are scheduled at Stanford, SRI and other locations within a 15-mile radius (the default distance for the Stanford domain).

Jim browses the web site, viewing announcements for various talks matching his interests and preferred locations (as provided in his explicit search queries). He is impressed that he can see the talk information not only in HTML, but also in DAML, RSS and WML formats. Finding a talk of potential interest to a colleague, Jim takes advantage of the invitation feature, which allows him to send an invitational e-mail to any of his friends for any of the listed talks. Finally, using the personalize link on the bottom of the page, Jim creates his own ittalks.org main page, by providing the URL of his DAML-encoded profile. This customized page, listing talks based on his preferences, will be Jim's entrance to the ITTALKS site whenever her returns.

4.2   Agent Interaction

This scenario assumes that user Jim has already registered with ITTALKS, and has left instructions with the system to be notified of the occurrence of certain types of talks.

In the course of operation, ITTALKS discovers that there is an upcoming talk that may interest Jim, and of which Jim has not been notified. Based on information in Jim's preferences, which have been obtained from his online, DAML-encoded profile, from information entered directly, and from Jim's interaction with ITTALKS web site interface, ITTALKS opts to notify Jim's User Agent directly. This is done via ITTALKS own agent, which forwards the message using an ACL.

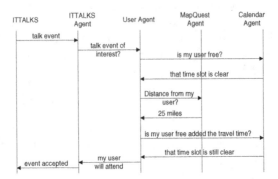

Fig. 4. Interactions between the various agents described in the ITTALKS/Agent scenario

Upon receiving this information, Jim's User agent needs to know more; it consults with Jim's Calendar agent to determine his availability, and with the MapQuest agent to find the distance from Jim's predicted location at the time of the talk. Some more sophisticated interactions might take place at this time; for example, the Calendar and User agents may decide to alter Jim's schedule, and request more information about the speaker and the event by contacting other agents or web sites, such as CiteSeer-based agent [4, 22, 5], to obtain more information necessary to make a decision. Finally, after making this decision, the User Agent will send a notification back to the ITTALKS agent indicating that Jim will/will not plan to attend. The ITTALKS agent will make the appropriate adjustments at the ITTALKS site, and provide further interaction based on Jim's User agent decision.

In a more complex interaction scheme, Jim may be employed by a research group, which possesses a limited funding and is therefore enforcing a policy that allows only one researcher at a time to attend a particular IT event. As a result, the User agent cannot decide on Jim's participation until it successfully interacts with other agents representing Jim's employer and colleagues. Therefore, the decision whether anyone from the research group could attend the IT event and the further election of the group representative requires an interaction of agent virtual community.

From a slightly different perspective, the User agent will also benefit from participating in virtual communities thanks to recommendations it obtains from other User agents. One User agent may recommend an IT event given its owner's experiences from attending a past talk of the same speaker. Another User agent may decide to share comparisons of two competing times and locations for an identical IT event. Yet another User agent may simply share its owner's intensions on attending a particular IT event. Thus, each member of the virtual community can profit from these and many other positive and negative recommendations, and reflect these social filtering methods in its own decisions.

Finally, in a 'Smart Office' scenario [17, 6], the ITTALKS agent may also be directly contacting an agent representing the location where a given IT event will be held. This 'room' agent may then use varying service discovery techniques [7, 25] to locate a projector presented in the room and inform it to pre-download the powerpoint presentation before the speaker arrival. Moreover, the 'room' agent may also try to contact additional agents in the IT event vicinity to decrease possible noise level from other rooms and to verify that a 'hallway' agent has requested enough refreshments during the IT event.

5   Benefits of DAML

We believe that ITTALKS benefits significantly from its use of a semantic markup language such as DAML. DAML is used to specify ontologies that we use extensively in our system. It is also used for personal profiles, and as an agent content language. Without DAML, specifying schedules, interests and assertions about topics would be very difficult. In ITTALKS, a user can specify that according to the user a couple of topics are equivalent or related or dissimilar, etc. This will allow ITTALKS to tailor the searching of talks to the users needs. As an agent content language, DAML provides more flexible semantics than KIF or other content languages that currently provide syntax only. The ultimate benefit of using DAML then lies in the ability of ITTALKS to independently interact with any DAML-capable agent without the need of a human supervision. Consequently, all these benefits, which are described in further details below, enable more efficient interaction between the system and its users, let them be humans or software agents.

5.1   Interoperability Standard

As an interoperability layer, DAML allows the content of ITTALKS to be easily shared with other applications and agents. For example, a Centaurus room manager agent [17] could watch ITTALKS for events happening in a room for which it is responsible in order to enable better scheduling. DAML also acts as an interoperability standard allowing other sites to make their talks available for inclusion in ITTALKS by publishing announcements marked up in our ontology.

5.2   Agent Communication Language

DAML and ACLs can be successfully integrated. DAML documents will be the objects of discourse for agents that will create, access, modify, enrich and manage DAML documents as a way to disseminate and share knowledge. Agents will need to communicate with one another not only to exchange DAML documents but also to exchange *informational attitudes* about DAML documents. Using an Agent Communication Languages (ACL) agents can "talk" about DAML documents. Integrating ACL work and concepts with a universe of DAML content is our first goal. Using DAML as an agent content language will add more meaning to the message.

5.3   Distributed Trust and Belief

Agents face a difficult problem of knowing what information sources (e.g. documents, web pages, agents) to believe and trust in an open, distributed and dynamic world, and how to integrate and fuse potentially contradictory information. DAML can be used to support *distributed trust and reputation management* [16, 19, 20]. This will form the basis of a logic for *distributed belief transfer* that will enable more sophisticated, semantically-driven rule-based techniques for information integration and fusion.

We are making use of DAML's expressiveness and employing it to describe security policies, credentials and trust relationships, which form the basis of trust management. These policies contain more semantic meaning, allowing different policies to be integrated and conflicts to be resolved relatively easily. Also, it will be possible for other applications to interpret the agent's credentials, e.g. authorization certificates, correctly, making these credentials universal.

Similarly, describing beliefs and associating levels of trust with these beliefs is more straightforward and the deduction of belief is uniform by different applications and services.

5.4   Data Entry Support

ITTALKS supports intelligent form filling, making it easier for users to enter and edit information in their profiles, and also to enter and edit talk announcements and other basic information. In addition, we provide automatic form filling when an editor tries to enter information about an entity (e.g. a talk, person, room) that already present in the knowledge base.

Entering Talks. In order to make ITTALKS successful, as we need to make it as easy as possible new talk descriptions to be entered into the system. We are addressing this problem using three complimentary approaches: an enhanced web interface, accepting marked up announcements, and automated text extraction. DAML plays a key role in the first two and is the target representation for the third.

Enhancing the Web Interface. We have used several techniques to enhance the web form interface for entering talk announcements. One of the simplest and most effective is to recognize then some of the information being entered about an object such as a person, a room or an organization has already been entered into the ITTALKS system and to "pre-fill" the remaining parts of the form from our stored information. For example, most talks at an organization are given in a small number of rooms. Once the complete information about a particular room (e.g., room number, building, address, seating capacity, longitude and latitude, A/V equipment, networking connection, etc.) has been entered for one talk, it need not be entered again.

Although the current implementation of this does not directly use DAML, its use can support a more generalized version of a web form-filling assistant. The approach depends on two ideas: (i) tagging web form widgets with DAML descriptions of what they represent and (ii) capturing dependencies among data items in DAML and (iii) compiling these dependencies into an appropriate execution form (e.g., JavaScript procedures) that can drive the web form interface.

In addition, we plan to investigate the possibility of a multi-modal support, where user can enter new information via standard keyboard input as well as through voice recognition means. Here, we understand that when presenting the user with a new form, the user will be allowed to use her own voice to enter data in each field. Then upon submittion of voice-filled form, ITTALKS will try to infer the meaning of the recorded sound, obtain additional information based on the knowledge and rules stored in ITTALKS system, and present back the user with a text-prefilled form for verification purposes. This enhancement will then allow ITTALKS to provide talk entry support for devices with limited keyboard functionality, such as PDAs or cellular phones.

Text Classification. For ITTALKS to filter talk announcements on topic matches, we need to know the appropriate topics for each talk. Initially, we required that users manually select appropriate topic categories from a web interface to the ACM CCS hierarchy. This turns out to be a daunting task requiring the user to navigate in a hierarchy of nearly 300 topics, many of which about whose meaning he will not be sure. Some users will face a similar problem in trying to select topics to characterize their own interests. Ultimately we would like to use more that one topic hierarchy to classify both talk topics and user interests (e.g., ACM CCS and Open Directory nodes), which makes the problem even more difficult for our users.

To address this problem, we have built an automatic text classifier that can suggest terms in a hierarchy that are appropriate for classifying a talk based on its title and abstract. The classifier package used was from the Bag Of Words (BOW) toolkit [23] by Andrew McCallum at CMU. This library provides support for a wide variety of text classification and retrieval algorithms. We used the Naive Bayes algorithm, which is widely used in the classification literature, fairly effective, and quick to learn the 285 classes in our test collection. We plan to use the same classification agent to suggest interest terms for users based on the text found by searching their web pages.

Accepting Marked Up Announcements. One of the simplest ways to enter new talk announcements is to provide them as a document that is already marked up. The current ITTALKS interface allows one to enter a URL for a talk announcement that is assumed to be marked up in ontologies that ITTALKS understands. Currently, these are just the "native" ontologies that we have built for this application. In general, if some talk announcements were available with semantic markup using other ontologies, it might be possible to provide rules and transformation that could map or partially map the information into the

ITTALKS ontologies. We expect that, as the Semantic Web develops, it will be more and more likely that talk announcements with some meaningful mark up will be found on the web.

Automated Information Extraction from Text. We would like to be able to process talk announcements in plain text or HTML and automatically identify and extract the key information required by ITTALKS. This would allow us to fill the ITTALKS database with information obtained from announcements delivered via email lists or found on the web. The problem of recognizing and extracting information from talk announcements has been studied before [10, 9] mostly in the context of using it as a machine learning application. We are developing a information extraction use the Aerotext [1, 8] system that can identify and extract the information found in a typical talk announcement and use this to automatically produce a version marked up in DAML which can then be entered in the ITTALKS database.

5.5   User Profiles

We use personal profiles to help ITTALKS meet the requirements of individual users. A profile is a widely accessible source of information about the user, marked DAML, to which other services and individuals can refer. In the future, such a profile may be used by all web-based services that the user wants to access. The profile will ultimately provide a unique and universal point for obtaining personal information about the user for all services, preventing the need for duplication and potential inconsistencies. This profile can be easily shared, and with the use of DAML, will allow more expressive content for schedules, preferences and interests. The notion of a personal profile and a user agent are closely linked; a user might have one or the other, or both. The profile would likely express much of the information that might be encoded in a user agent's knowledge base. Conversely, an agent would likely be able to answer queries about information contained in a profile.

5.6   Modularity

With the use of DAML, we can define several ontologies for topics and switch between them with ease. Furthermore, to restrict the retrieval results, a user can perform the search with respect to a certain set of ontologies, such as the ACM or Open Directory Classification.

5.7   Application Scalability Support

As ITTALKS becomes the central repository of IT related information for various research institutes the ITTALKS knowledge base will be distributed among numerous, and possibly apriori-unknown, locations in order to provide a higher scalability and reliability support. Yet, it will be imperative that users and agents not be required to interact with all locations in order to find or manipulate the desired information. Instead, we envision that each user agent will interact with only one ITTALKS agent, which in turn will be able to efficiently locate and manage the distributed ITTALKS information. For this, we believe that a system of DAML-enabled agents can act as an intermediate between the distributed databases.

6   Future Directions

Since most users do not currently have personal agents, we have been developing one that can be used with this system. It is our goal, however, that ITTALKS be able to interact with external agents of any type. The agent we are developing reasons about the user's interests, schedules, assertions and uses the MapQuest agent to figure out if a user will be able to attend an interesting talk on a certain date.

We are developing a framework to use DAML in distributed trust and belief. DAML expressions on a web page that encodes a statement or other speech act by an agent are signed to provide authentication and integrity. We are working on an ontology to describe permissions, obligations and policies in DAML and allow agents to make statements about and delegate them.

In order to make the process of data entry more efficient, we are developing a focused web spider, which will collect talk announcements from source on the web and to identify the key information in these announcements using a text extraction system. The spider will add all found and relevant information to the ITTALKS knowledge base.

7   Conclusion

Effective use of the vast quantity of information now available on the web necessitates semantic markup such as DAML. With the use of such a tool, we can enable the automated or machine-facilitated gathering and processing of much information that is currently 'lost' to us. ITTALKS, our system for automatic and intelligent notification of Information Technology talks, demonstrates the value of DAML in a variety of ways. DAML is used throughout the ITTALKS system, from basic knowledge representation, to inter-agent communication.

References

[1] AeroText. site: http://mds.external.lmco.com/products_services/aero/.   424, 430
[2] Fabio Bellifemine, Agostino Poggi, and Giovanni Rimassa. Developing multi agent systems with a fipa-compliant agent framework. *Software - Practice and Experience*, 3, 2001. 421
[3] Tim Berners-Lee, James Hendler, and Ora Lassila. The semantic web. *Scientific American*, May 2001. 419

[4] Kurt D. Bollacker, Steve Lawrence, and C. Lee Giles. *Citeseer: An autonomous web agent for automatic retrieval and identification of interesting publications.* Proceedings of the Second International Conference on Autonomous Agents (Agents '98). ACM Press, Minneapolis, 1998. 426

[5] Sergey Brin and Lawrence Page. *The Anatomy of a Large-Scale Hypertextual Web Search Engine.* Proceedings of the 7th International World Wide Web Conference. April 1998. 426

[6] Andrej Cedilnik, Lalana Kagal, Filip Perich, Jeffrey Undercoffer, and Anupam Joshi. A secure infrastructure for service discovery and access in pervasive computing. *Technical report, TR-CS-01-12, CSEE, University of Maryland Baltimore County, 2001.* 427

[7] Dipanjan Chakraborty, Filip Perich, Sasikanth Avancha, and Anupam Joshi. Dreggie: Semantic service discovery for m-commerce applications. *Workshop on Reliable and Secure Applications in Mobile Environment, 20th Symposiom on Reliable Distributed Systems,* October 2001. 427

[8] Lois C. Childs. Aerotext - a customizable information extraction system. unpublished technical report, Lockheed Martin, 2001. 430

[9] Fabio Ciravegna. Learning to tag for information extraction from text. *ECAI Workshop on Machine Learning for Information Extraction,* August 2000. workshop held in conjunction with ECAI2000, Berline. 430

[10] T. Elliassi-Rad and J.Shavlik. Instructable and adaptive web-agents that learn to retrieve and extract information. *Department of Computer Sciences, University of Wisconsin, Machine Learning Research Group Working Pap,* 2000. 430

[11] FIPA. Fipa 97 specification part 2: Agent communication language. *Technical report, FIPA - Foundation for Intelligent Physical Agents,* October 1997. 421

[12] N. Guarino. *Formal Ontology in Information Systems,* chapter Formal ontology and information systems. IOS Press, 1998. 417

[13] Jeff Heflin, James Hendler, and Sean Luke. Shoe: A prototype language for the semantic web. *Linkping Electronic Articles in Computer and Information Science, ISSN 1401-9841,* 6, 2001. 419

[14] James Hendler. Agents and the semantic web. *IEEE Intelligent Systems,* 16(2):30–37, March/April 2001. 417

[15] James Hendler and Deborah McGuinness. The darpa agent markup language. *IEEE Intelligent Systems,* 15(6):72–73, November/December 2000. 419

[16] Lalana Kagal, Harry Chen, Scott Cost, Timothy Finin, and Yun Peng. An infrastructure for distributed trust management. *Autonomous Agents Workshop on Norms and Institutions in Multiagent Systems, AA'01, Montreal, Canada,* May 2001. 428

[17] Lalana Kagal, Vlad Korolev, Harry Chen, Anupam Joshi, and Timothy Finin. A framework for intelligent services in a mobile environment. *Proceedings of the International Workshop on Smart Appliances and Wearable Computing (IW-SAWC),* April 2001. 427

[18] DARPA Agent Markup Language. site: http://www.daml.org/. 417

[19] Ninghui Li, Joan Feigenbaum, and Benjamin Grosof. A logic-based knowledge representation for authorization with delegation (extended abstract). *Proc. 12th IEEE Computer Security Foundations Workshop, Mordano, Italy,* June 1999. IBM Research Report RC 21492. 428

[20] Ninghui Li and BBenjamin Grosof. A practically implementable and tractable delegation logic. *IEEE Symposium on Security and Privacy,* May 2000. 428

[21] MapQuest. site: http://www.mapquest.com/. 422

[22] James Mayfield, Paul McNamee, and Christine Piatko. The jhu/apl haircut system at trec-8. *The Eighth Text Retrieval Conference (TREC-8)*, pages 445–452, November 1999. **426**

[23] McCallum and Andrew Kachites.   Bow: A toolkit for statistical language modeling, text retrieval, classification and clustering, 1996.   site: http://www.cs.cmu.edu/ mccallum/bow. **429**

[24] Sheila A. McIlraith, Tran Cao Son, and Honglei Zeng. Semantic web services. *IEEE Intelligent Systems*, 16(2), March/April 2001. **417**

[25] Olga Ratsimor, Vladimir Korolev, Anupam Joshi, and Timothy Finin. Agents2go: An infrastructure for location-dependent service discovery in the mobile electronic commerce environment. *ACM Mobile Commerce Workshop*, July 2001. **427**

Generic Agent Architecture for Embedded Intelligent Systems

Charles-Antoine Brunet, Jean de Lafontaine, and Gérard Lachiver

Université de Sherbrooke, Quebec, Canada
charles-antoine.brunet@usherbrooke.ca
jean.delafontaine@usherbrooke.ca
gerard.lachiver@Usherbrooke.ca

Abstract. This paper takes a different point of view at agent architectures, an agent tool design one. From this point of view, a generic agent architecture for embedded real-time systems is designed. More precisely, this paper identifies three levels of genericity in agent architectures. From these levels, a generic agent architecture named CIPE is designed and presented. CIPE promotes reusability, maintainability and portability, thus helping to reduce system footprint and system readiness time. Then, a generic agent development environment named GEMAS is presented; its foundation of GEMAS rests on the CIPE architecture. Applications realised with CIPE and GEMAS are also presented. The paper concludes with a discussion on the concepts and realisations and their implications.

1 Introduction

Agent and multiagent systems are often used for modelling and implementing complex systems ; they are a convenient and useful abstraction for this type of systems. When opting for an agent approach, a designer is faced with the existence of many agent architectures and related agent technologies. Such diversity is desirable, but it may make it difficult to identify and select the appropriate technologies for a given agent. Moreover, good development tools, small footprint, portability and reuse are desirable for intelligent embedded real-time systems in general and to reduce system readiness time. Liberty of choice is also important when designing a system. For example, the liberty to choose the most appropriate paradigm for each agent, paradigms such as BDI, fuzzy logic and artificial neural networks.

The word paradigm is used in this paper in the same way it is used when discussing about the *object-oriented paradigm*; it is used to refer to an organisation principle. Typically, paradigms for agent architectures are inspired by theories, abstract concepts and new ideas. Paradigms are born from the materialisation of these inspirations. For example (see [21]), the BDI architecture has its roots in the theory of practical reasoning developed by the philosopher Bratman [5].

This paper takes a different point of view at agent architectures, an agent tool design one. From this point of view and given a set of paradigms, how can we bring about a generic agent architecture? One that can support many paradigms

W. Truszkowski, C. Rouff, M. Hinchey (Eds.): WRAC 2002, LNAI 2564, pp. 434–443, 2003.

Table 1. Levels of genericity in agent architectures

Name	Level of genericity
γ_1	task
γ_2	knowledge representation
γ_3	paradigm
γ	all of the above

and their related technologies. The primary benefits sought for are the reusability and maintainability of architectural components, including paradigms. On the other hand, for the agent developers, the primary benefits sought for are the reusability and portability of developments and small footprint.

As will be shown in the next sections, this inverted point of view (agent architectures are not usually designed from a tool design point of view) coupled with software engineering techniques generates other benefits such as the definition of low-level agent APIs, the promotion and enforcement of standards, and the downsizing of system footprint (or agent footprint) by reuse of common components. These benefits reduce the time of system development and of system readiness. They are also in line with the requirements of real-time embedded intelligent systems, which have a relatively small footprint and often have heterogeneous hardware and software platforms.

The next section, section 2, presents three levels of genericity that are present and needed in generic agent architectures. A generic agent architecture, named CIPE, supporting all three levels is presented in section 3. Section 4 introduces GEMAS, a generic environment for multiagent systems based on CIPE. Section 5 presents the implementation and experimentations done with CIPE and GEMAS. Section 6 discusses and concludes on the exposed concepts, realisations and significance of the work presented in this paper.

2   Levels of Genericity in Agent Architectures

Existing agent architectures (AAs) differ from one another in many ways. The level of genericity of each one can be categorised into three levels as shown in table 1.

Task Genericity. (named γ_1) Contemporary AAs support at least one type of genericity, task genericity. They are γ_1 compliant. This type of genericity is generally implicit and rightfully taken for granted by developers. A γ_1 compliant AA is independent of task specifics and can be programmed to do any type of task. γ_1 compliance promotes the reuse of user developments and of the reuse of the AA throughout a system and across projects. Examples of existing γ_1 compliant architectures are in JADE [2], JAM [14] and ZEUS [17].

Knowledge Representation Genericity. (named γ_2) The capacity to select or construct the appropriate knowledge representation is important; it impacts on overall performance [18]. Different problems may have different representation needs and an appropriate knowledge representation has to be selected. Hybrid agent architectures, where reactive and deliberative components are integrated, exhibit certain form of γ_2 compliance [18]. Examples of hybrid AAs are TouringMachines [11], INTERRAP [15] and 3T [3].

Paradigm Genericity. (named γ_3) Paradigm genericity is the ability of an AA to support different paradigms. Agent paradigms can be known organisation principles, such as BDI [6], or custom tailored for specific needs. They can also be based on AI's paradigms, such as fuzzy logic or artificial neural networks, or simply be object-oriented. If the AA is independent of paradigm specifics then it is γ_3 compliant. A paradigm (user defined or standardised) can be added to the set of already supported ones. γ_3 compliance enables developers to choose the most appropriate paradigm for a given agent, the one that best fits the task at hand.

If the AA is compliant to all levels of genericity (γ compliant), then it can offer a collection of paradigms and their related technologies. An agent developer can then select the most appropriate one for an agent. Moreover, since the AA is γ_3 compliant, the developer can use any knowledge representation and program the agent to do any task. This flexibility can be advantageously offered in a unique integrated agent development environment. As will be shown in the next sections, a γ compliant AA is the underlying conceptual basis to reach the main goal posed in the introduction: to devise a generic AA.

3   The CIPE Architecture

The previous section introduced three levels of genericity. From these, an AA named CIPE is designed and is now presented.

3.1   The Architecture of CIPE

CIPE is composed of four levels: communication, interface, paradigm and exploitation, hence the name CIPE. A component diagram [4] of CIPE is shown in figure 1. CIPE is a variation of an AA named GAM introduced in [8] and detailed in [7]. Here is a description of each level of CIPE.

Communication Level. The communication level (CL) provides the BasicCommunication API as shown in figure 1. This level implements the basic functionalities to interact with the environment in general and to establish communication links with local or remote entities. The CL ensures the correct

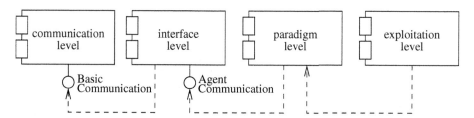

Fig. 1. Component diagram of the CIPE architecture

transmission of messages between entities and has no comprehension or knowledge about their meaning. The CL provides a standardised API of its functionalities to the interface level. As shown in figure 1, only the next higher level (the interface level) interacts with the CL.

Interface Level. The interface level (IL) provides the `AgentCommunication` API as shown in figure 1. The IL has two main purposes. The first is to provide an API to the next higher level (the paradigm level) for agent communications. For example, provide an API to an agent communication language (ACL) such as KQML [12] or FIPA-ACL [13]. It can also provide APIs for social behaviours, such as a negotiation strategy like the Contract Net Protocol [10]. Its second purpose is to provide an API to the functionalities offered by the CL and to provide communication managing functionalities, like multiple message lists that are multi-thread safe.

Paradigm Level. The paradigm level (PL) implements the paradigm on which the agent is based. For example, if a developer needs a BDI based agent, the PL would be composed of BDI's deliberation process and its related representations [22]. Another example would be a simple logic agent that is based on the Prolog language [9], the PL would be then composed of Prolog's inference engine and its associated functionalities.

If a paradigm has no standardised agent communication functionalities, then they must be added. These functionalities, corresponding to those offered by IL's API, are made available to the programmer at the exploitation level. All communication functionalities offered by a paradigm are built using IL's API and made available to the exploitation level in the appropriate formalism.

Exploitation Level. It is at this level that agent developers do their programming. The abilities and the knowledge of the agent are specified at this level. The exploitation level (EL) specifies PL's exploitation. Once a PL is chosen, the EL is the only part that is application dependent. For example, continuing with the simple logic (Prolog) agent, the EL would be composed of facts and rules in the Prolog language. The communications are made in Prolog using the communication API offered by the PL.

3.2   Discussion

CIPE is a low-level AA as opposed to high-level AAs such as deliberative or reactive ones. Low-level AAs are used to build high-level ones. In the case of CIPE, a high-level architecture is a specialisation of the PL. For example, a reactive architecture can be realised by implementing and instantiating an appropriate PL. Implementation of known AAs is achieved through the implementation of a PL.

With the CIPE architecture, perceptions (inputs) received by the agent go up the *pipeline*, from the CL, to the IL, then to the PL and eventually to the EL where user code can process it. Inversely, generated actions are passed down the *pipeline* from the PL down to the CL. This is true for all AAs, since they can all be perceived as specialisation of the black box model [15]. This emphasises the fact, as mentioned in the introduction, that paradigms are organisation principles, organisation specified by the PL in the case of CIPE.

Globally, CIPE is a two pass vertical architecture [16]. Locally, with a specific PL instantiated, an agent developer may not perceive it as such. The agent developer has an EL point of view of the AA. For example, if the PL specifies a reactive architecture, then the agent developer perceives the AA as a horizontal one. The PL is the deciding factor on EL's (users') vision of the type of AA.

Each component of CIPE interacts only with the adjacent ones through a standardised API, as shown in figure 1. The exception is the EL; its API to the PL is dependent on the effective paradigm instantiated. This enforced modularity promotes reusability and maintainability of the architecture itself.

CIPE promotes the standardisation of internal agent APIs; they are the keys of the architecture. CIPE requires standardised APIs for low-level (`Basic-Communication`) and mid-level (`AgentCommunication`) communication functionalities. This standardisation has the benefit of permitting the seamless integration of user defined and implemented paradigms to CIPE's standard ones. CIPE also promotes conformity to the standards that are implemented by the APIs. The conformity of communications (incoming or outgoing) can be checked at all levels, since they must pass through the CL, the IL and the PL. They can be rejected or corrected, if they do not conform to expected standards.

The γ_1 and γ_2 levels of genericity are encapsulated in the PL and possibly in the EL, depending on the paradigm. The γ_3 level is encapsulated in the PL. The γ_3 compliance is well supported by the component approach use in CIPE; the paradigms are standard pieces of the architecture and are interchangeable.

CIPE supports many paradigms and promotes their reuse and the reuse of all its other components. CIPE is a modular, component-based AA that is maintainable and extendable. Moreover, agent communication functionalities situated in the CL and the IL are reused for all paradigms: generic, reusable and standardised low and mid-level agent APIs can be defined. All PLs use the same communication API (`AgentCommunication`) and are independent of hardware and software platforms. This level of standardisation means that paradigms are portable, reusable and can be standardised and be reused throughout projects. Since all user code is based on the underlying paradigms, the user developments are platform independent, portable and reusable. Also, the reuse of all levels of the CIPE helps in reducing system footprint.

From these conceptual observations, the main goal and the anticipated benefits stated in the introduction are reachable in principle. Section 6, the conclusion, will discuss if they are effectively met.

4   The GEMAS Agent Development Environment

The flexibility and adaptability provided by CIPE makes it a good candidate as the building block for a generic agent development environment (GADE). CIPE provides standardised heterogeneous agents and agent related technologies. A GADE can manipulate the components of CIPE like pieces of a puzzle to satisfy the requirements of the agent developers. These requirements may vary on aspects such as communications, paradigms, agent platforms and social abilities. All aspects of CIPE are components and sub-components that can be added or removed by the GADE building tools according to user specifications.

The core of a GADE named GEMAS (Generic Environment for MultiAgent Systems) is composed of an implementation of CIPE, a set of PLs, an online trace collector/viewer and a global time stamp generator for trace ordering [20]. A more complete environment would add graphic building tools to specify the requirement of agents and specialised tools for each paradigm.

From a practical point of view, when an application is deployed, runtime instantiation of the agent's components must be done in an orderly fashion. In the case of CIPE, the instantiation order is from the lower levels to the upper ones. Low-level communications at the CL must be instantiated so that the higher ones at the IL can use them. The IL must be instantiated before the PL so that the PL can use communication functionalities offered by the IL. The PL must be instantiated before the EL so that its exploitation by the EL can be done. The instantiation order can be informally expressed in anthropomorphic terms:

1. Instantiation of the body, the CL and IL components.
   This level of instantiation is called an abstract agent, see figure 2(a). An abstract agent has a body, but cannot live (be instantiated) because it has some vital parts missing: an actual brain and some knowledge to go with it.
2. Instantiation of the brain, the PL component.
   The second level of instantiation is called a specialised agent, see figure 2(b). It is specialised in the sense that it adds a specific paradigm to the abstract agent; it gives the agent a brain. The specialised agent can live (be instantiated), but it can't perform any tasks because it has an empty brain.
3. Instantiation of the brain's knowledge, the EL component.
   The third level of instantiation is called a functional agent or simply an agent, see figure 2(c). The functional agent has all levels of CIPE instantiated and

performs whatever tasks it has been designed to do. The functional agent has a body, a brain and some knowledge to use them. He is a complete being.

The effect of runtime considerations on CIPE is the addition of a new API, the `Paradigm` API as shown in figure 2(b). The `Paradigm` API gives to the abstract agent some basic control over the instantiated PL, like starting and stopping its execution.

5   Implementation and Applications

The core of GEMAS has been implemented: its CIPE architecture, its debugging tools and its three types of agents (abstract, specialised and functional). They were all realised in JAVA [1]. The CIPE architecture was realised level after level, from bottom to top.

To test CIPE's γ compliance, five PLs where implemented: logic (Prolog), fuzzy logic, artificial neural networks, genetic algorithms and object-oriented (JAVA). These PLs where selected for two main reasons. First, their implementations are well known and their development times are relatively short. Second, a proof of concept of an actual γ compliant AA was needed before plunging into the implementation of more complex paradigms such as BDI. Test applications were implemented for unit testing of the PLs: simple heterogeneous multiagent systems (MAS) where implemented with each paradigm.

A software simulator for an autonomous highway vehicle was then built with GEMAS, see [7] for more details. The simulator is composed of the pilot model, the vehicle dynamics and the user interface. The simulator is composed of agents that are heterogeneous in their tasks and in their paradigms:

– use of logic (Prolog) to find the shortest route to destination and for dynamic adaptation of driving to environmental conditions

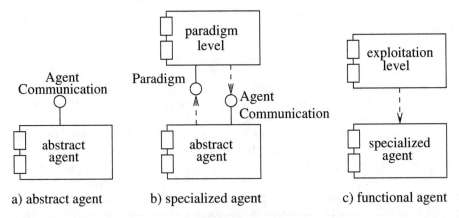

Fig. 2. Levels of instantiation of agents in GEMAS

- use of fuzzy logic for proximity detection and collision avoidance
- use of object-oriented language (JAVA) for vehicle dynamics, path selection on the road and the user interface

The implementation of GEMAS, its CIPE architecture and the autonomous highway vehicle simulator was a *proof of concept* effort that lead to conclusive results on all aspects. The true real-time performance of the CIPE architecture will be evaluated in another project, a real-time simulator for autonomous landing of spacecrafts.

This second research project is currently under way in our research group at the Université de Sherbrooke. The simulator consists of a *lander* and a real *planetary surface*. The *lander* is composed of a robotic cart for translation and a gimballed pointing mechanism for rotation to allow three-dimensional simulated landings over the *planetary surface*. The *lander*, equipped with surface and inertial sensors, processes on-board the measurements of the latter to allow study of autonomous and intelligent landing techniques using terrain recognition and hazard avoidance.

The *lander* software architecture of the on-board systems is a heterogeneous multiagent system. Each agent will be based on a C++ [19] implementation of the CIPE architecture and resides on an embedded platform with real-time capabilities. Each agent performs a different set of tasks and uses the paradigm that is best suited for it. The tasks vary from CPU intensive image processing to intelligent higher level tasks for autonomous and safe landing.

The development of the landing simulator will also bring about the realisation of more tools for GEMAS, especially tools for the dynamic management of deployment, monitoring and configuration of a real-time multiagent system.

6   Conclusion

The design of a generic agent architecture for embedded real-time systems that supports many paradigms was the main goal of this paper. This goal has been reached and takes form in the CIPE agent architecture.

The underlying principle of the CIPE architecture is its three degrees of liberty, which are presented as three levels of genericity: task, knowledge representation and paradigm. CIPE supports all three levels of genericity; it is γ compliant.

The CIPE architecture is composed of four levels: communication, interface, paradigm and exploitation. CIPE is the foundation on which is built a generic agent development environment named GEMAS.

CIPE and GEMAS were used to implement a simulator for autonomous highway vehicles. The system is composed of agents that are heterogeneous in their tasks, knowledge representation and paradigm, making full use of the capabilities of CIPE and its γ compliance. The implementation of CIPE, GEMAS and the simulator shows that γ compliant agent architectures and their development tools are a reality. They can generate benefits for tool designers and their users. Even if the current implementations have some shortcomings, the results obtained validate CIPE's underlying conceptual basis.

The benefits anticipated were the reusability and maintainability of common architectural components and paradigms of the agent architecture and the promotion of reusability and portability of user developments. The implementations show that these benefits were met, the communication, interface and paradigm levels of CIPE were reused by different agents and on different platforms. The reuse of the lower levels throughout the system helped reduce the overall system footprint. User code at the exploitation level of CIPE was effectively reused and was portable. Currently under way is another project, a simulator for autonomous and intelligent landing of spacecrafts. This distributed real-time and embedded system corroborates the results at a conceptual level and will show the true real-time value of the CIPE architecture.

Agent architectures that are γ compliant have an impact on agent design. One example, with the CIPE architecture, is that nothing prevents an agent to dynamically change its paradigm and exploitation levels. An agent could autonomously change its paradigm dynamically, from artificial neural networks to BDI for example, if it thinks it is advantageous in a given situation. This could lead to agents that adapt more advantageously to their environment. The mechanisms for the management of such behaviour still need to be investigated.

γ compliant agent architectures also have an impact on tool designers and their users. If standardised and globally accepted agent APIs at the communication, interface and paradigm levels of CIPE can be established, then user developments will be reusable and portable across different agent development environments and platforms. These same development environments will let users choose from a set of agent architectures and agent technologies that best fits the task at hand to the benefit of better agent systems.

References

[1] K. Arnold, J. Gosling, and D. Holmes. *The Java Programming Language.* Addison-Wesley, 3 edition, 2000. **440**

[2] F. Bellifemine and A. Poggi. JADE - a FIPA-compliant agent framework. In *PAAM'99: Proceedings of the Fourth International Conference on the Practical Applications of Intelligent Agents and Multi-Agents,* pages 97–108. Practical Application Company, 1999. **435**

[3] R. P. Bonasso, D. Kortenkamp, D. P. Miller, and M. Slack. Experiences with an architecture for intelligent, reactive agents. In M. Wooldridge, J.-P. Müller, and M. Tambe, editors, *Intelligent Agents II – Agent Theories, Architectures, and Languages – Proceedings of IJCAI'95-ATAL Workshop,* volume 1037 of *LNAI,* pages 187–202. Springer-Verlag, 1996. **436**

[4] G. Booch, J. Rumbaugh, and I. Jacobson. *The Unified Modeling Language User Guide.* Addison-Wesley, 1999. **436**

[5] M. E. Bratman. *Intentions, Plans, and Practical Reason.* Harvard University Press, 1987. **434**

[6] M. E. Bratman, D. J. Israel, and M. E. Pollack. Plans and resource-bounded practical reasoning. *Computational Intelligence,* 4:349–355, 1988. **436**

[7] C.-A. Brunet. *GEMAS: un environnement générique de développement de systèmes multiagents hétérogènes*. PhD thesis, Université de Sherbrooke, Sherbrooke, Québec, Canada, 2001. 436, 440

[8] C.-A. Brunet, R. Gonzalez-Rubio, and M. Tétreault. A multi-agent architecture for a driver model for autonomous road vehicle. In *Proceedings of the Canadian Conference on Electrical and Computer Engineering*, pages 772–775, September 1995. 436

[9] W. F. Clocksin and C. S. Mellish. *Programming in Prolog*. Springer-Verlag, 4 edition, 1994. 437

[10] R. Davis and R. G. Smith. Negotiation as a metaphor for distributed problem solving. *Artificial Intelligence*, 20(1):63–109, 1983. 437

[11] I. A. Ferguson. On the role of BDI modeling for integrated control and coordinated behavior in autonomous agents. *Applied Artificial Intelligence*, 9(4):421–47, 1995. 436

[12] T. Finin, Y. Labrou, and J. Mayfield. KQML as an agent communication language. In J. M. Bradshaw, editor, *Software Agents*, chapter 14, pages 291–316. MIT Press, 1997. 437

[13] FIPA. FIPA ACL (Agent Communication Language) message structure specification. Specification XC00061, Foundation for Intelligent Physical Agents, 2000. http://www.fipa.org/specs/fipa00061. 437

[14] M. J. Huber. JAM: A BDI-theoric mobile agent architecture. In O. Etzoni, J.-P. Muller, and J. F. Bradshaw, editors, *Agents'99: Proceedings of the Third International Conference on Autonomous Agents*, pages 236–243, 1999. 435

[15] J.-P. Müller. *The Design of Intelligent Agents : A Layered Approach*, volume 1177 of *Lecture Notes in Artificial Intelligence*. Springer-Verlag, 1996. 436, 438

[16] J.-P. Müller, M. Pischel, and M. Thiel. Modelling reactive behavior in vertically layered agent architectures. In M. J. Wooldridge and N. R. Jennings, editors, *Intelligent Agents – Proceedings of ECAI-94 Workshop on Agent Theories, Architectures, and Languages*, volume 890 of *LNAI*, pages 261–276. Springer-Verlag, 1995. 438

[17] H. Nwana, D. Ndumu, L. Lee, and J. Collis. ZEUS: A tool-kit for building distributed multi-agent systems. *Applied Artificial Intelligence*, 13(1):129–186, 1999. 435

[18] J. F. Sowa. *Knowledge Representation: Logical, Philosophical and Computational Foundations*. Brooks Cole, 2000. 436

[19] B. Stroustrup. *The C++ Programming Language*. Addison-Wesley, 3 edition, 1997. 441

[20] M. H. Van Liedekerke and N. M. Avouris. Debugging multi-agent systems. *Information and Software Technology*, 37(2):103–12, 1995. 439

[21] M. Wooldridge. Intelligent agents. In G. Weiss, editor, *Multiagent Systems: a Modern Approach to Distributed Artificial Intelligence*, chapter 1, pages 27–77. The MIT Press, 1999. 434

[22] M. Wooldridge. *Reasoning About Rational Agents*. The MIT Press, 2000. 437

Part VII

Poster Presentations

Agents with Several Bodies

Eric Sanchis

Laboratoire Gestion et Cognition, IUT Ponsan – Université Paul Sabatier
115, route de Narbonne, 31077 - TOULOUSE – Cedex, France
`sanchis@iut-rodez.fr`
Tel: +33 5 65.77.10.80, Fax: +33 5 65.77.10.81

Abstract. The aim of this short paper is to present a new agent architecture called the *systemion model*. Its purpose is to allow the construction of agents (called *systemions*) able to execute several different tasks in their life. This architecture relies on
- a classification of properties associated to the agents in two separate groups : *qualities* and *attributes*
- a clear distinction between the task the agent must do and the agent characteristics which are independent from this task.

Keywords: agent architecture, qualities, attributes, pluritask agent

1 Why a New Agent Architecture?

A *common software agent* is designed and implemented to fulfill one specific task : the body of an agent integrates all which is necessary for the execution of the application. This architecture presents several drawbacks:

- the agent is designed as a monolithic unit (even though implemented in a modular fashion)
- It is difficult to compare qualitatively two agents having the same properties (i.e. two autonomous agents) but executing different applications
- the agent is designed and implemented to fulfill only one application: the agent is monotask.

A *systemion* (*systemic daemon*) is designed and implemented to distinguish *executing vectors* and *tasks*. The systemion body is divided into two parts :

- the properties specific to the task are implemented in a *functional subsystem*
- the properties which are independent of the current task are implemented in a *behavioral subsystem*.

2 Qualities and Attributes

Many works since the 1990's have been done to define precisely what an agent would be. Different definitions of an agent exist (Jennings [1], Franklin [2], Huhns [3]).

W. Truszkowski, C. Rouff, M. Hinchey (Eds.): WRAC 2002, LNAI 2564, pp. 447-450, 2003.

These definitions are both different and similar because the agents share some common properties.

Most proposed definitions enumerate **properties** that an agent should possess (*autonomy, mobility, intelligence, perception, replication, temporal continuity, sociability, proactivity* and many others) and/or classify agents along several application types (*intelligent user interfaces, mobile agents,* etc.).

We claim that these properties are very different in their nature and should be divided into two categories: **qualities** and **attributes**.

Autonomy, intelligence, sociability are qualities. Generally, a quality is not well defined. That means that no definition is universally accepted. Qualities are measurable by degrees or levels. For instance, it is only possible to define levels of autonomy or degrees of intelligence of an agent. A quality cannot be simplified to simple components and a single definition of autonomy or intelligence doesn't exist. Nevertheless, different **models** of a **quality** exist: Varela's autonomy model, Castelfranchi's autonomy model [4], autonomy with regard to an attribute [5]. These observations could be made for the other qualities (i.e. *intelligence*).

It is easier to characterize an attribute. Broadly speaking an attribute is a mechanism : *mobility, perception, replication, continuous execution* are well known mechanisms. An agent includes or not an attribute, i.e. an agent is designed as a mobile entity or a static one, an agent integrates or not a replication function and an agent always contains a perception component.

Contrary to qualities an attribute has a definition accepted by the majority of experts.

3   A Mobile Systemion Executing Several Tasks

The systemion architecture is divided into two layers (Fig. 1.) :

- the *functional subsystem* implements what is relative to the achievement of the task (or function) temporarily assigned to the agent. This task can change during the systemion life-cycle and constitutes the most flexible part of the systemion. Application complexity (including cooperation, coordination and communication interactions) is embedded into the task abstraction. To be able to integrate in its functional subsystem the first task or to change current function, a systemion incorporates into its behavioral subsystem, the evolution attribute

- the *behavioral subsystem* implements the qualities and the attributes that personalize the agent behavior. In the application described below three attributes are used : **mobility, perception** and **evolution**.

  - *mobility* : the agent is able to migrate from host to host.
  - *perception* : the agent perceives hosts, repositories and tasks.
  - *evolution* : the agent is able to carry out the task Ta at time t, then to execute the task Tb at time $t+1$. This attribute allows the systemion to suppress and/or add a task in its functional subsystem.

We can now describe how a systemion is able to have "several bodies" in its life. The application description is as follow (Fig. 2.) : when a systemion arrives on host A it executes its own task (T_0) and then executes one or more other tasks (T_1 and T_2). Task T_2 "asks" the systemion to migrate to host B. The systemion carries T_2 on host B (task T_2 is moved to host B and is deleted on host A). T_2 and T_3 are executed on host B and the systemion migrates with T_3 on another system.

4   Conclusion

Common software agents are designed to implement a specific application : these agents are *monotask* agents.

The two layered architecture of a systemion clearly distinguishes an *executing vector* (a systemion with an empty functional subsystem) an the *task* to be executed. This separation allows a systemion to be *pluritask*.

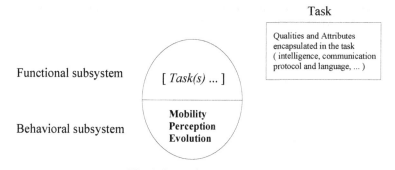

Fig. 1. Systemion architecture

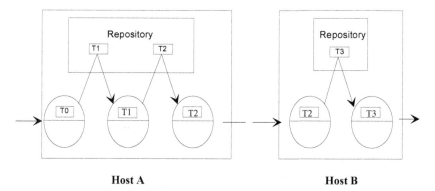

Fig. 2. A systemion with several bodies

References

[1]   Jennings, N., Wooldridge, M., "Applications of Intelligent Agents", in "Agent Technology: Foundations, Applications, and Markets" (Edited by N.R. Jennings and M. Wooldridge), Springer Computer Science, 1998.

[2]   Franklin, S., Graesser, A. "Is it an Agent, or just a Program ?: A Taxonomy for Autonomous Agents", in "Intelligent Agents III – Proceedings of the Third International Workshop on Agent Theories, Architectures and Languages (ATAL 96), (Edited by Müller J. P., Wooldridge M. and Jennings N.), Lecture Notes in Artificial Intelligence, 1193, Springer Verlag, 1996.

[3]   Huhns, M. N., Singh, M. P., "The agent test", IEEE internet computing, September-October 1997.

[4]   Castelfranchi, C., "Guarantees for autonomy in cognitive agent architecture", in M. Wooldridge ans N.R. Jennings (eds), Intelligent Agents: Theories, Architectures and Languages, LNAI 890, , Springer Verlag, 1995.

[5]   Sanchis, E., "Modular Autonomy for Simple Agents", Third International Conference on Autonomous Agents, Workshop on Autonomy Control Software, May 1-5 1999, Seattle (Washington).

Automatic Code Writing Agent

John Thomas Riley

NASA Goddard Space Flight Center
Code 740.3, Greenbelt, Maryland 20771 USA
john.t.riley@nasa.gov
+1 301 386 0712

1   Code Writing Agents

The idea of an agent that writes your computer code for you at first seems like nonsense, but you can now buy off-the-shelf software to write code. Clearly the critical information must be provided in some way other than typing in the code by hand. The question is whether changing to a new way of providing information is valuable enough to warrant the difficulty of the transition. For critical applications, such as space flight and medicine, the answer to this question turns on whether the new agents can reduce risk while efficiently producing quality code.

Current code writing agents move the problem to the realm of graphic representation. Instead of typing words, the programmer manipulates images. Software is now available off-the-shelf to convert formal graphics into Java code [1]. The design is developed in the Unified Modeling Language (UML), which can use up to nine different types of drawings with standard formats. With the press of a key the software converts these drawings into Java.

The question is, can we use UML as an effective means of writing aerospace code? Can we develop an effective subset of the UML drawings that allow us to capture the program information, present the information for effective review, and then press a button to direct an agent who magically writes the code? The surprising answer looks like a yes.

2   Risk Control

Inherent project risk is controlled in aerospace work by establishing an overall design then flowing that information down into documents with very precise specifications in each area of technical specialty. One detailed specification is then used as the basis for writing the code.

The code must be tested to prove that it does all that is specified, only what is specified, and that it does it without error. This testing is very difficult when the code is written lines of text. Tests are developed based on the documents, not the code itself. The checking is extremely labor intensive and often leaves only a single person being knowledgeable about many lines of the actual code. This is unacceptably risky.

W. Truszkowski, C. Rouff, M. Hinchey (Eds.): WRAC 2002, LNAI 2564, pp. 451-452, 2003.
© Springer-Verlag Berlin Heidelberg 2003

The new agent will be of great value to us if we can develop a subset of the UML graphics that will capture the specification from detailed design documents and make the information available for efficient review. Reviewing graphics is far easier than reviewing text. The agent then must dependably convert the checked graphics to code by a proven process. This approach looks promising.

3   Flow

Flow is a common state of being for humans in which the mind is clearly focused on the task at hand and distractions are cut off. Most software is produced under Flow, as is most fiction and graphic arts. Flow is very enjoyable and produces a great volume of work. It does not, however, guarantee quality. Quality can be achieved under Flow if the writer has the necessary training and experience, and if the work environment supports quality. The level of complexity of the task must also be above boring but below stressful. Software writers love this state of being and insist on using it even if they do not always know its name.

It is certainly possible to Flow a software writing task either as text or as graphics, but different parts of the brain are used in each case. People who have learned to produce text code under Flow are at first uneasy with graphic code writing and resist the change.

Flowing graphics tends to cut off the language centers of the brain just as it cuts off mental clocks and anxiety centers. It is difficult to Flow in graphics and at the same time explain what you are doing in language. After a section is complete, however, the process of explaining the work in language is surprisingly enjoyable, indeed, almost compulsive. Mechanical design has been done this way for a great many years.

4   Conclusion

Agents that convert formal graphic information into text code are currently available. They show real promise in reducing risk for critical applications, but substantial work is needed to apply them to this purpose. Programmers can learn to produce code under Flow with the new procedures and efficiently produce quality code in a low-stress environment. Review of graphically presented software can be efficient and effective.

References

[1]   TogetherSoft, Together Control Center, http://www.togethersoft.com/ Internet
[2]   The author's related works may be found at:
       http://www.charm.net/~jriley/gagarin/project.html Internet

The Agentcities Initiative:
Connecting Agents Across the World

Jonathan Dale[1], Bernard Burg[2], and Steven Willmott[3]

[1] Fujitsu Laboratories of America
Network Agents Research Group, 595 Lawrence Expressway, California 94085, USA
jonathan.dale@fla.fujitsu.com
[2] Hewlett-Packard Laboratories
1501 Page Mill Road, MS 1137, Palo Alto, California 94304, USA
bernard.burg@hp.com
[3] Ecole Polytechnique Fédérale de Lausanne
Artificial Intelligence Laboratory, Lausanne CH-1015, Switzerland
steve.willmott@epfl.ch

Abstract. This paper describes the aims, goals and current status of Agentcities, a worldwide initiative to create a test bed for the large-scale deployment of agents and services.

1   Introduction

Agents are an important paradigm and abstraction when considering and designing large-scale, distributed systems that have a need to interact and cooperate. However, most agent-based systems have been constructed as closed systems to test or prove a particular aspect of the interaction and cooperation amongst a well-defined set of agents. We introduce Agentcities [4], a global initiative to create a worldwide network of agents that is:

- *Heterogeneous*: To support communication and coordination between diverse agent systems owned by many different organisations, allowing them to access each other's services.
- *Open*: To enable any agent developer to deploy their own agents which may then interact with those of others.
- *Permanently available*: To create a continuously evolving, feature-rich online environment for agent research and development and for business service deployment.
- *Global*: To connect agents that are deployed on systems across the globe and to make such a network accessible from anywhere in the world.

Furthermore, Agentcities is based on the principles of:

- *Consensual standards*: Communication and interaction in the network will be based on the publicly available standards, such as those developed by the Foun-

W. Truszkowski, C. Rouff, M. Hinchey (Eds.): WRAC 2002, LNAI 2564, pp. 453–457, 2003.

dation for Intelligent Physical Agents (FIPA) [5], and the W3C [6] *Semantic Web* effort. and   European Union/DARPA funded research projects On-toKnowledge, OntoWeb, DAML and others are developing Web-friendly ontology frameworks that will affect way agents experience the environment, as well as infrastructure services such as Web Services and electronic business frameworks such as ebXML and RosettaNet.

- *Open source*: Although commercial technologies are not discouraged, Agentcities will promote freely accessible open source implementations to ensure free and open access to the Agentcities Network.
- *Open access*: Any organisation or individual can set up their own node in the network to host their own agents and services, provide access to them and access those deployed by others.
- *Shared resources*: As researchers access agent-based services in the Network, such as directory, naming, ontology and application services, they are encouraged to add their own services to extend the utility and diversity of the services available to the community.

2   The Agentcities Initiative

The nodes in the Agentcities Network (see Figure 1) are agent platforms that are running on one or more machines and are hosted by an organisation or individual. Agents running on a particular Agentcity are able to connect to other publicly available cities and can communicate directly with their agents. Applications involving agents on multiple different cities can be created through the flexible use of inter-agent communication models and semantic frameworks, shared ontologies, content languages and interaction protocols that support it. This model consists of the following levels:

- *Network level*: Platforms in the Agentcities Network interoperate and exchange basic communications at the communication and infrastructure level.
- *Service composition level*: In July 2002, the first services will appeared in the Network and provide an open test bed where anybody can observe services at work, run services, and/or add new services into this network. This level is able to host business components including their service and behaviour descriptions.
- *Semantic interoperability level*: In the longer term, Agentcities will become a test bed for system-system communications in an open environment that is capable to dynamically host business components without requiring human intervention to set perform service discovery and invocation.

In early February, 2003, the Agentcities Network contained over 60 registered platforms, which are based on heterogeneous technologies using agent platforms from 8 different providers, and reached the five continents.

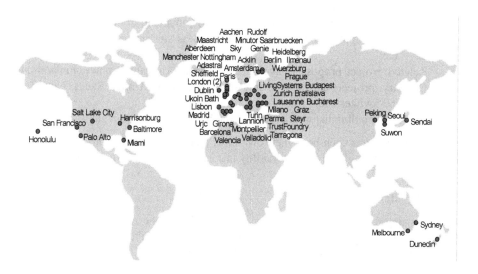

Fig. 1. Agentcity platforms around the world which were registered in the Agentcities Network as at February, 2003

2.1   Application Domains

Developing a platform in the Network to model services that are available in a town or city (hence the name Agentcities) simply provides a convenient domain focus to begin tackling the problems of semantics, ontologies and dynamic service composition in manageable proportions. Several Work Groups have been formed in the Agentcities Task Force (ACTF) [3] which address different aspects of the large-scale deployment of agent technology, such as: business service infrastructures; ontologies and semantics; network architecture; Web Services; communication; wireless access and applications; human-agent interaction; coordination technologies; service description and composition; self-organizing applications; travel, tourism and entertainment services; medical and healthcare services; manufacturing and supply chain integration; security services; service coordination for emergency response; ELearning.

2.2   Agentcities-Related Projects

At the time of writing, there are the following Agentcities activities that are being planned or are in existence:

- Two projects Agentcities.RTD [1] and Agentcities.NET [2] funded by the European Commission's 5th Framework IST program. Agentcities.RTD investigates technologies, finds solutions and builds basic agents and service infrastructures for a core set of 14 platforms in a traditional European project closed consortium. The Agentcities.NET project is a take-up measure aiming to spread the Agentcities Network and to encourage platform, agent and service deployment. This project is an open consortium to which anybody can subscribe, and it distributes grants to assist with platform deployment, organizes a competition for the best application deployment, as well as student exchange, information days, etc.

- Related project proposals have been funded in Australia, France, Finland and Hungary, projects are planned in Canada, Japan, the United States, New Zealand and Switzerland.
- An active mailing list with over 150 members from over 80 organisations.

Although projects each have their own aims and goals, they are unified in the objective of creating a global interoperability infrastructure based on common standards.

2.3   Agentcities Task Force

With so many projects in development, the formation of the ACTF to act as an open forum for the global coordination of various Agentcities related efforts is currently under discussion. The ACTF will have the following roles:

- *Coordination*: To facilitate coordination between different projects and activities which contribute to and use the Agentcities Network.
- *Network support*: To encourage and support joint resources such as directories, ontology repositories, etc.
- *Promotion, dissemination and liaison*: To raise awareness of work being carried out in the Network and to effectively contribute to existing standards bodies and encourage increased interest, participation and development.

The ACTF will need to act as a coordinating body between different Agentcities projects, and will also have to liaise with relevant standard bodies where the Agentcities community might bring valuable experimental feedback on agent platforms, content representation, ontologies, content manipulation, agent communication and interaction protocols. At the time of writing, the ACTF is still being formed and a consultation process is underway.[1]

3   Conclusions

We believe that the Agentcities initiative will have a significant impact on the global deployment of agents and services, and will provide a useful resource for the development of the next generation of networked systems. However, Agentcities much of the future hard work will be involved in developing ontologies, using semantic frameworks and content languages before heterogeneous agents can successfully communicate. Therefore, the role of the Agentcities initiative is to stimulate this activity and to encourage researchers to think in an open context and to envisage their systems in a worldwide environment. The process of connecting an increasing number of diverse agent systems will teach us much about which details matter when it comes

---

[1] For more information visit http://www.agentcities.org/

to creating true interoperability, not just at the syntactic layer, but also at the semantic layer.

References

[1]   Agentcities.RTD: Test Bed for a Worldwide Agent Network-Research and Deployment. European Union Project Number IST-2000-28385 (2000). http://www.agentcities.org/EURTD/

[2]   Agentcities.NET: Test bed for a Worldwide Agent Network-Take Up Measure: Trial/Test Bed. European Union Project Number IST-2000-28386 (2000). http://www.agentcities.org/EUNET/

[3]   Willmott, S., Dale, J., Burg, B., Charlton, P. and O'Brien, P., Agentcities Task Force Proposal. http://www.agentcities.org/

[4]   Willmott, S., Dale, J. and Burg, B., Agentcities: A Worldwide Open Agent Network. In: Agentlink Newsletter, 8, (2001) 13-15. http://www.agentlink.org/newsletter/8/AL-8.pdf

[5]   The Foundation for Intelligent Physical Agents (FIPA). http://www.fipa.org/

[6]   W3C World Wide Web. http://www.w3c.org/

Use of Ontology for Virtual Humans

Majdi Mukhar

Eleanor Roosevelt High School
Research Practicum and Internship Program
spyman83@yahoo.com

NASA was given a direct mandate by Congress to support American education. Under this mandate, NASA has established internships for students to utilize high technologies such as those developed at NASA.

One such technology, the creation of Virtual Humans, is currently being researched by leading corporations like Microsoft and at major universities like the Massachusetts Institute of Technology. Soon NASA may be able to use this technology to encourage students to pursue careers in science and research. The next generation of students may very well be the Americans who explore space or even land a human on Mars. Virtual Humans can help give these students a clear image of themselves succeeding in these ventures.

Virtual Humans may prove to be extremely handy and may increase human productivity in space, but they must first be tested for two key characteristics: real-life practicality, and user-friendliness. The paper is the result of a research project under Eleanor Roosevelt High School's Research Practicum and internship program at NASA Goddard Space Flight Center. The research explored the use of ontology and the interaction between high school students and Virtual Humans.

Virtual Humans can interact with human beings in their everyday lives. Virtual Humans can be a child's playmate, a student's homework guide, a personal assistant, or a scientific tool. Virtual Humans will be able to do more than the average human can do. For example, Virtual Humans will be sent into regions of space that real humans can not handle. Regardless of what Virtual Humans are used for, they can only increase human productivity. The human-computer interface must be one the human loves. Humans love other humans though, so a computer screen with a Virtual Human that looks, sounds, acts, and thinks like a real person will be quite successful. It is a difficult challenge, however, to make a Virtual Human that can understand and communicate with a real human. A Virtual Human will have to be able to formulate correct grammar, understand variations in human grammar, and recognize differences in tone. Tone can often be misleading, especially in cases of sarcasm. Virtual Humans must over come these obstacles in order to further students' interest in careers as well as increase human productivity in general. Virtual Humans will be highly valuable, so even major corporations are working hard at developing this new technology. To date, a completely successful Virtual Human has not been created.

In order to create a successful Virtual Human, a programmer must know and understand ontological concepts of how the mind works in order to duplicate it. After a study of human ontology, public domain software was modified so that its

W. Truszkowski, C. Rouff, M. Hinchey (Eds.): WRAC 2002, LNAI 2564, pp. 458–459, 2003.

vocabulary lists for two Virtual Humans support the ontology studied. People would interact with the Virtual Humans through a simple java chat applet while their satisfaction level was observed. The people's conversations with the Virtual Humans, along with their comments and opinions were used to test the program and modify it adequately. Tests with real people, most of whom were high school students, found glitches in the program responses. The conversations were saved for analysis and surveys were voluntarily filled out to refine the program. The programmer fixed the problems and released a new version for testing. The cycle was repeated until the Virtual Humans showed improvement and project time frame ended.

People's time length varied when testing the Virtual Humans. Most people believed the Virtual Humans were sentient; however, there are some people who believed the Virtual Humans were just a computer program and strongly resisted working with them. High school students showed a high level of interest in conversing with the Virtual Humans using the computer interface, but many were displeased with the lack of responsiveness shown by the program. Still, most of the students spent substantial amounts of time interacting with the Virtual Humans.

This preliminary testing showed that students will accept a Virtual Human computer interface if it is sufficiently responsive. The test subjects agreed that Virtual Humans have high potential for commercial development and filled out surveys in which they rated how well the Virtual Humans appealed to their emotions.

Although Virtual Humans are an interesting technological concept, people are not fond of them for real life application yet. Virtual Humans have a tendency to repeat themselves and are unable to answer questions that real humans ask. People have a tendency to be lazy and use incorrect grammar, which often confuses the Virtual Humans. However, when a Virtual Human stated it was confused, people thought the Virtual Humans were ignorant and oftentimes, people would blame their own faults on the Virtual Humans. Despite the errors, people still liked the Virtual Humans. Further research will be required since the current public domain software is not adequate. Nevertheless, these studies showed that humans would be willing to cooperate with artificial beings provided that the responsiveness of the Virtual Humans increases.

The first explorers of Mars could very well be Virtual Humans who will be able to interact with people. Like the moon landing, Virtual Humans may give people a better perception of what mankind can accomplish.

Person Perception for Social Agents: Research on Outfitting Social Agents with a Facial Trait Perception System

Sheryl Brahnam

Computer Information Systems
Southwest Missouri State University, Springfield, Missouri 65804, USA
shb757f@smsu.edu

Abstract. It is no secret that people are predisposed to form impressions of a person's character, intentions, abilities, and social status based on nothing more than that person's physical appearance. Although these impressions are often discounted, they serve a number of important social functions, including informing physical self-presentations. This article outlines some of the advantages that a facial trait perception system would offer social agents and presents a review of my research in modeling the trait impressions of the face using Principal Component Analysis (PCA).

1 Introduction

A number of researchers have begun to investigate the cultural aspects of faces for embodied agents. One area that has received considerable attention concerns facial expressiveness, especially as it enhances the believability of the agent. The face is a complex communication system, however, where transitory signals, such as emotional displays, facial posturing, and other behaviors, modulate a morphology that is also pregnant with meaning. Although recently several studies and position papers have noted that the facial appearance of embodied agents plays a significant role in human-computer interaction, no researcher to date has suggested that an observer's trait impressions be modeled to provide embodied agents with a means of perceiving the physical appearance of the face in terms of the social impressions they create. A major benefit in providing embodied agents with such a model is that it would furnish the agents with a rudimentary social awareness sufficient enough to allow them 1) to participate more intelligently in social encounters and 2) to create and alter their own facial forms to better suit various social situations and tasks. This paper summarizes some applications of a person perception system for embodied agents as well as my research in modeling the trait impressions of the face using PCA.

W. Truszkowski, C. Rouff, M. Hinchey (Eds.): WRAC 2002, LNAI 2564, pp. 460-462, 2003.
© Springer-Verlag Berlin Heidelberg 2003

2   Modeling the Trait Impressions of the Face

Currently, I am investigating modeling the trait impressions of the face using PCA. Thus far, I have explored training PCAs to match the human classification of faces into binary trait classes (e.g., high dominance/low dominance) and synthesizing faces with a high probability of eliciting specific trait impressions from within the PCA trait space.

In order to train PCA to classify faces according to their trait impressions, a training set of faces had to be obtained. For this purpose, a large number of faces were randomly generated using a limited dataset of facial features found in the popular composite software program *FACES* by Interquest and Micro-Intel [1]. The trait impressions of each face were then determined by having human subjects classify the faces along the eight trait dimensions of adjustment, dominance, facial maturity, masculinity, sociality, warmth, trustworthiness, and degree of certainty regarding gender. Once the stimulus faces were rated for each face, they were averaged and ranked from low to high along one bipolar trait descriptor within each trait dimension. Subsets of faces clearly representative of high and low rankings were used to form two class sets (high and low) for each trait dimension. These trait class sets were then used to train and test a separate PCA for each trait dimension. In every case, the PCA classification of faces matched human classification of faces significantly better than chance [2]. Work is now underway to improve the classification rate by using face classification approaches based on Fisher's linear discriminants.

In addition to face classification, I have tentatively explored face synthesis from within several trait spaces by projecting faces rated either high or low in a trait dimension onto a PCA trained with faces rated at the opposite end of the scale, and then reconstructing the image. This results in the generation of novel faces. One hundred faces were synthesized in this fashion and judged by human subjects. In all but one case, the synthesized faces were judged at the same end of the trait scale (high or low) as the faces used to train the PCA that generated them [2]. The results of this investigation suggest that PCA or similar neural network classification techniques might provide embodied agents with the means of designing their own culturally meaningful embodiment.

3   Some Applications of a Trait Impression Perception System

Human observers are continuously caught up in the physical appearances of others, and people are equally preoccupied with managing their own appearances. If embodied agents could *perceive* the social aspects of faces in ways that mimic human observers, then these *virtual observers* could also respond with a degree of convincing social realism to the physical presentations of others. Moreover, embodied agents that are able to see themselves as human observers see them could learn to adjust their facial forms to suit the nature of their roles and their dealings with specific types of individuals. Discussed in this section are some of the benefits the ability to read and to make faces would offer embodied agents.

Reading and Responding to Facial Presentations. A model of the trait impressions of face would provide agents with a more perceptive basis for dealing with users. Human observers orient themselves in their dealings with others by making use of the information that people bodily advertise about themselves. If agents were endowed with a perception system capable of perceiving the cultural aspects of faces, this information could be used by the agents in understanding the intentions of people and in formulating plans of interaction. For example, rather than predefine an initial set of interaction tactics and practices for an agent, the cultural information visible in the user's face or physical appearance might serve the agent as a basis for formulating an initial interaction strategy that could then be adjusted as further information about the user is obtained.

Automating Socially Intelligent Embodiment. A number of studies in the person perception literature show that people rely on facial impressions when trying to make sense of ambiguous statements or actions. It is reasonable to expect that people will likewise make use of the facial appearance of embodied agents when an agent's actions are confusing due to limitations in the agent's ability to interact socially. An agent's face will either clarify its actions and intentions or further complicate them. As anyone needing directions in an unfamiliar city knows, some people look more approachable then others. Thus, for example, if an agent is given the task of assisting others, it could advertise its function by generating a face people would automatically be willing to approach. Just as people learn to control the impressions their faces make, so agents could learn to prepare social masks that are suited to their tasks [3].

References

[1]   Freierman, S.: Constructing a Real-Life Mr. Potato Head. Faces: The Ultimate Composite Picture. The New York Times (February 17, 2000) 6

[2]   Brahnam, S.: Modeling Physical Personalities for Embodied Agents by Modeling Trait Impressions of the Face: A Neural Network Analysis. Ph.D. Thesis, The Graduate Center of the City University of New York, www.sherylbrahnam.com (2002)

[3]   Brahnam, S.: Agents as Artists: Automating Socially Intelligent Embodiment. Proceedings of the First International Workshop on the Philosophy and Design of Socially Adept Technologies, in conjunction with CHI 2002, Minneapolis, MN (2002) 15-18

Adapting Agent Infrastructure
for Models of Human Agency

Robert E. Wray

Soar Technology, Inc.
3600 Green Road Suite 600, Ann Arbor, MI USA 48105
wray@soartech.com
http://www.soartech.com/

Many agent systems seek to emulate human behavior. Using human behavior as a model for agent design can be useful for three reasons. 1) In some domains emulating human behavior may be a requirement. Examples include simulation and training, virtual actors and pedagogues, and computer game opponents. 2) Human knowledge about performance of a task can often be readily transferred to an agent that uses human-like representations. The value of such transfer is apparent for tasks that humans perform. However, it may also be valuable for humans designing other agent systems. 3) Human-like behavior provides natural modes of interaction with human users, improving usability.

Agents modeled on human behavior using the Soar architecture [4] have been developed for complex, highly interactive, real-time domains such as agent pilots for military air missions in real-time distributed simulation environments [2] and intelligent adversaries in interactive computer games [3], among many others. The functional design of Soar is based on cognitive science principles such as long-term associative memory, declarative short-term memory, and goal-driven processing. Although Soar has been used for cognitive science research, achieving human-like behavior usually does not require a detailed cognitive model but rather an understanding and encoding of the human knowledge used for a task.

Research Questions

Although Soar provides a substrate on which agents with human-like behavior can be readily created, it is not currently compatible with common agent infrastructures. The following surveys some of the issues we are exploring to better enable our human behavior models to capitalize on agent infrastructure.

Agent Communication: Soar agents communicate; however, the communication methods typically are domain-dependent or based on human language. For instance, in TacAir-Soar, simulated human communication was initially implemented as part of the agent pilot's task knowledge. Recently, we have undertaken a re-design the communications infrastructure for TacAir-Soar, basing our methodology on research in agent communications languages such as KQML and the FIPA ACL. Our goal is to provide a general, scalable, customizable, and maintainable messaging infrastructure. The new communications supports not

W. Truszkowski, C. Rouff, M. Hinchey (Eds.): WRAC 2002, LNAI 2564, pp. 463–465, 2003.

just simulated radio messages, but indicators and warnings for agent operators, new (simulated) on-board communication devices, and distributed messaging to registered applications [5].

Agent Knowledge Resources: No one has yet attempted to integrate factual, largely declarative, knowledge bases (e.g., WordNet [1]) with a procedural system such as Soar. Such knowledge could potentially speed agent development and improve robustness. Accessing knowledge bases is a more than an engineering problem. It requires both an translation interlingua and possibly new architectural mechanisms for the representation of declarative knowledge.

Agent Learning: Although the Soar architecture provides a learning component that has demonstrated a wide variety of deductive and inductive learning, learning has been largely unused in agent domains. Having recently resolved some technical difficulties for learning in agent domains [7, 6], learning will be more frequently applied in our agents. However, important questions remain. What is the role of learning for expert-level agents? Can expert-level agents develop from limited initial knowledge but powerful learning? How can learning be incorporated into a system with behavior validation and verification requirements?

Evaluation of Agent Systems: How do we evaluate agent systems modeled on humans? Obviously, cognitive science provides an approach, but one that is often overly constrained when high-fidelity replication of human performance is not desired. In general, we have used domain experts to evaluate human-like agent systems, which provides good anecdotal feedback. However, we need a testing regime and evaluation methodology that can provide both qualitative and quantitative measures of success.

The goals outlined above are not specific to building human-like agents: in general, agents should communicate more generally, interact with external knowledge bases, learn, be evaluated more rigorously. Thus, while we explore issues in creating agents with human-like behavior, we also hope to contribute general results towards the goals of understanding agents and applying them to real-world problems.

References

[1] C. Fellbaum, editor. *WordNet: An Electronic Lexical Database.* MIT Press, Cambridge, MA, 1998. **464**

[2] R. M. Jones, J. E. Laird, P. E. Neilsen, K. J. Coulter, P. Kenny, and F. V. Koss. Automated intelligent pilots for combat flight simulation. *AI Magazine*, pages 27–41, Spring 1999. **463**

[3] J. E. Laird and M. van Lent. Human-level AI's killer application: Interactive computer games. *AI Magazine*, 22(2):15–25, 2001. **463**

[4] A. Newell. *Unified Theories of Cognition*. Harvard University Press, 1990. **463**

[5] R. E. Wray, J. C. Beisaw, R. M. Jones, F. V. Koss, P. E. Nielsen, and G. E. Taylor. General, maintainable, extensible communications for computer generated forces. In *Proceedings of the Eleventh Conference on Computer Generated Forces and Behavioral Representation*, Orlando, Florida, May 2002. Institute for Simulation and Training. **464**

[6] R. E. Wray and R. M. Jones. Resolving contentions between initial and learned knowledge. In *Proceedings of the 2001 International Conference on Artificial Intelligence*, Las Vegas, NV, June 2001. **464**

[7] R. E. Wray, J. Laird, and R. M. Jones. Compilation of non-contemporaneous constraints. In *Proceedings of the Thirteenth National Conference on Artificial Intelligence*, pages 771–778, Portland, Oregon, August 1996. **464**

Part VIII

Panel Reports

Evolution of Agent Architectures

Henry Hexmoor

Computer Science & Computer Engineering Department
Engineering Hall, Room 313, Fayetteville, AR 72701
hexmoor@uark.edu

Agent architectures provide the blueprints for the design and development of individual agents. The purpose of agent architecture is to define modes and modules of agent's interaction in the world as well as connections among internal components of an agent. An agent can be understood in terms of its architectural description of its perceptual, deliberation, and acting capabilities. Architectures have been used to describe robot control software [Musliner, Durfee, and Shin, 1993]. Such architectures emphasized rapid processing of early perception and low-level actuation capabilities. Brooks' subsumption architecture has been an influential guide for fast and reactive robotic actions [Brook 1986]. Although subsumption was good for real-time processing needed in robotics, it never became useful for agents. This is partly because being reactive is a standard property of agents. Pro-active architectures such as logic-based, utility-based, or belief-desire-intention (BDI) have been more popular in agent architectures [Wooldridge, 2000]. Intentional agents are modeled in multi-modal BDI logics. Each architecture has its strengths and weaknesses that make it suitable for particular roles or particular types of problems. Instead of comparing and contrasting architectures, here we give a partial list of collective properties for pro-active architectures: logical correctness, ability to initiate a new course of action, ability to form and manipulate explicit intentions, ability to reason based on nontrivial models of the world, ability to adapt, ability to learn, ability to interact with emotions, and ability to react when there is not enough time to complete reasoning. In nontrivial monolithic systems, proactive architectures addressed many issues including: world modeling, modularity of cognitive functions (such as planning and learning), affect, and uncertainty management. For agent-based systems, reasoning about autonomy is a specific area of concern. Finally, nontrivial agents who have to account for other agents and be social must address many issues. A partial list is: coordination, cooperation, teamwork, and other relationships and social attitudes such as autonomy, veracity, awareness, benevolence, rationality, roles, obligations.

More complex agents must exhibit self-awareness, self-modifying behavior, dealing with time-constraints, and nontrivial social actions. Once an agent faces time and resource limits, it becomes important for the agent to incorporate into its architecture the ability to model its own capabilities and limitations, along with modeling the external environment. Principled adaptation techniques are needed to improve performance based on experience. These adaptation methods are also needed to improve self-modifications to satisfy human users. Verification and validation of performance within guaranteed time-critical boundaries are needed in mission critical applications. Agents operating under uncertain conditions need to formulate policies

W. Truszkowski, C. Rouff, M. Hinchey (Eds.): WRAC 2002, LNAI 2564, pp. 469-470, 2003.
© Springer-Verlag Berlin Heidelberg 2003

to do the best they can in response to the uncertain unfolding of their environment. Resource-limited and time-constrained agents need to balance responsiveness with farsightedness. Functionally independent plug and play design of agent architectures will be useful to install or remove components that allow favorable behaviors that are predictable in large time scales. Self-modifying agents need to make changes that are justifiable and still ensure sufficient predictability in behaviors upon which operators depend. Rapid reasoning is required about resource allocation to competing demands as well as preserving missions and goals in which they are deployed.

Agents are being deployed in ever more common as well as complex places to take over dirty, dull, and dangerous tasks. This requires agents to be aware of the operating context of their environment and to work sociably and responsibly with humans in the environment. Agents need to automatically acquire user preferences to form valid probabilistic projections about future courses of events and the desirability of each of them to the human whose interests are being represented. Much progress has been made along many of these fronts, but much remains yet to be done. In particular, further work should be strongly encouraged in developing agents that are capable within the constraints of dynamic and uncertain application domains.

Acknowledgement

This work is supported by AFOSR grant F49620-00-1-0302.

References

[1]   R. Brooks, 1986. *A Robust Layered Control Systems for a Mobile Robot.* IEEE Journal of Robotics and Automation, RA 2-1:14-23.
[2]   D. Musliner, E. Durfee, and K. Shin, 1993. *CIRCA: A Cooperative Intelligent Real-Time Control Architecture.* IEEE Transactions on Systems, Man, and Cybernetics.
[3]   M. Wooldridge, 2000. *Reasoning about Rational Agents,* The MIT Press.

Panel Discussion on Ontologies

Sidney C. Bailin[1], Gary Berg-Cross[2], and Tim Finin[3]

[1] Knowledge Evolution, Inc., 1215 17th Street, NW, Suite 101
Washington, DC 20036, USA
sbailin@kevol.com
[2] Knowledge Strategies Div., SLAG Inc.
13 Atwell Ct., Potomac, MD 20854
Gary.Berg-Cross@tma.osd.mil
[3] Computer Science and Electrical Engineering
University of Maryland, Baltimore County
Baltimore, MD, 21250, USA
finin@umbc.edu

A discussion on the topic of ontologies in agent-based systems had Drs. Sidney Bailin, Gary Berg-Cross, and Tim Finin as panel members. Bailin, who chaired the session, led off with a series of questions for consideration:

1. Can we properly speak of *an ontology* (an artifact, as opposed to just *ontology* as a field of study)? Can we properly speak of multiple ontologies?
2. Is an ontology different from a dictionary? A taxonomy? A class hierarchy? A domain model?
3. Will the semantic web be an ontology?
4. Are ontologies needed now more than ever?

Bailin answered his first question by noting that his Microsoft Word grammar checker continually objects to the phrase *an ontology* as well as to the plural *ontologies*. Nevertheless, he finds it impossible to do without these constructions given current conventions. He noted that ontologies have characteristics in common with dictionaries, taxonomies, class hierarchies, and domain models, and that the term is sometimes used synonymously with one or another of these alternates. It tends to connote things that the alternates do not imply, however. Ontologies typically have more structure than dictionaries, e.g., in their arrangement of concepts into an *is-a* hierarchy (that is, into a taxonomy). They may have more precise semantics than taxonomies, e.g., by identifying attributes associated with a given concept, and possibly rules governing the values that the attributes assume. They are, in this respect, similar to class hierarchies, but they tend to be used at the problem-domain level while classes are often viewed as solution domain (i.e., design or implementation) constructs. In this respect they are like domain models; but a domain model may contain, in addition, a variety of other kinds of information. One participant pointed out that a domain model may *use* an ontology.

Bailin suggested that the semantic web can be viewed as a distributed collection of multiple, overlapping, possibly complementary but possibly also partially conflicting ontologies. He suggested that ontologies are useful, though not necessarily more useful now than in the past. But he noted that there are hazards in relying too much on

W. Truszkowski, C. Rouff, M. Hinchey (Eds.): WRAC 2002, LNAI 2564, pp. 471-473, 2003.
© Springer-Verlag Berlin Heidelberg 2003

ontologies since they encourage us to reify our experience. In the process, though we gain computability, we may lose a lot of richness.

Finin began his presentation by describing a spectrum of knowledge representations ranging from the highly informal to the highly formal, noting that the term *ontology* usually refers to structures on the formal side of the spectrum. He then proceeded to cast the role of ontologies in the context of a changing paradigm of agent communications. He observed that much work in multi-agent systems (MASs) is based on a communication paradigm developed *circa* 1990 (including such languages as KQML and FIPA ACL), and that this approach has not, overall, left the laboratory. During the same period, however, the World Wide Web (WWW) has changed the world. Does this suggest that we should try something different?

Drilling down into what that difference might be, Finin suggested that the older agent communications paradigm had its roots in client-server architectures, messaging systems, and object-oriented technology., The semantic web, on the other hand, assumes a somewhat different *publish/subscribe* paradigm that will require some changes to agent communication languages and the software that uses them. Finin described the role of agents in this context as two-fold, consisting of searching for and *discovering* relevant content on the web (the subscribe side), and *representing* content (the publish side). Ontologies play a key role in this process since they are the vehicle for expressing properties of web content that agents can understand and process—for example, to decide whether or not a given web page is relevant to the agent's current task.

Finin concluded his presentation by noting that there is much about the new paradigm that we do not yet understand. Much experimentation is needed. In the process, we should set our short-term goals modestly, and gradually move from the simple to the complex. Thus, returning to the question of ontologies vs. dictionaries etc., he argued that we might start with ontologies that are little more than vocabularies, move towards more complex forms, and eventually reach highly formal representations such as theories in first-order logic. In the meantime, we should allow many ontologies to bloom, and reject the idea of *the* ontology for a domain X. His concluding thought was that "the evolution of powerful machine readable ontologies will occur of multiple human generations; incremental benefits will more than pay for the effort."

Berg-Cross opened his presentation with a Venn diagram showing the intersection of the ontology concept with philosophy, psychology, linguistics and information science. He suggested that we focus on the intersection of this to avoid too broad a philosophical discussion. Thus we avoid some issues on whether evolution has produced a natural common sense, human ontology. His opinion was that it is pragmatic to speak of ontologies built for a particular purpose and also took the position of Deb McGuiness at Stanford that we can arrange things like dictionaries, glossaries, taxonomies and semantic models in a continuum from informal to formal (see Dr. Berg-Cross's paper in this volume for a diagram and discussion of this). He listed a set of alternatives definitions of *ontology*, starting with Tom Gruber's pithy "specification of a conceptualization." A more expansive description relies on the notions of:

- Primitives (fundamental concepts to be included in an ontology)

- Distinctions (important differences that should be modeled)
- Categories and hierarchy

Yet another approach to defining *ontology* is through its purpose, which is to enable knowledge sharing and reuse. Berg-Cross agreed with the previous presenters that, in use, ontologies typically have more semantics than plain taxonomies. He also drew a distinction between ontologies and definitions in formal logic, suggesting that formal definitions merely add terminology, while ontologies can genuinely add knowledge to the world by introducing concepts that are not fully defined but are rather constrained in their usage. According to J. Sowa, ontologies are distinguished from logic in that subtypes can be defined by prototypes (or exemplars) rather than by axioms. This is often useful in knowledge base building, a major area of ontology use. As for lexicons, they may include an ontology as their means of describing word senses, but they also are terminological and typically contain information about the syntax, spelling, pronunciation, and usage of words—areas outside of typical ontology uses, but part of natural language applications.

Berg-Cross went on to describe a primary use of ontologies, which is to mediate and map between multiple systems. Examples include various levels of business ontologies:

- The enterprise level
- Derived ontologies (inventory, product requirements, etc.)
- Foundational ontologies (describing such things as spatial entities and relationships)

In addition to the focus levels of these ontologies, he discussed format and formality levels similar to those found within data modeling. We often start with such data models, say to support a data warehouse, with a foundational, conceptual model. From there we make a logical model, which is more constrained, as an intermediate form. This is typically used as an organization for a physical model that will be implemented as a relational database. Ontologies also move from a general form to one where we may implement them as knowledge bases or databases. He then discussed the issue of mapping and alignment between ontologies, stressing the potential need to introduce new specializations or generalizations in one or both ontologies in order to achieve such alignment. The presentation ended with a discussion of the essential role of ontologies in e-commerce, stressing the current role of XML as a vehicle for starting the very kind of transition that we had heard advocated by Finin, from present-day MASs to a web-based framework.

Author Index

Lecture Notes in Artificial Intelligence (LNAI)

Lecture Notes in Computer Science